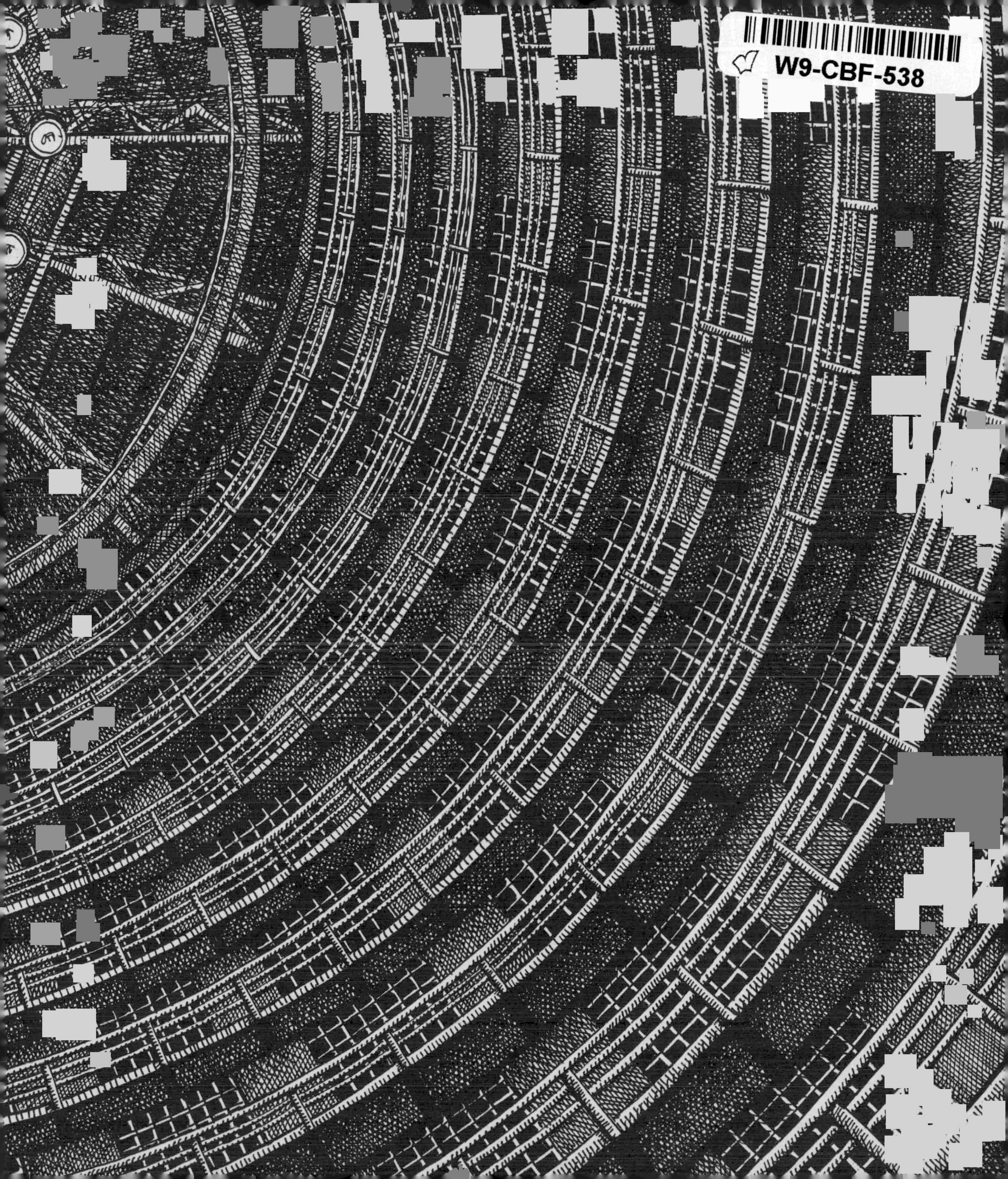

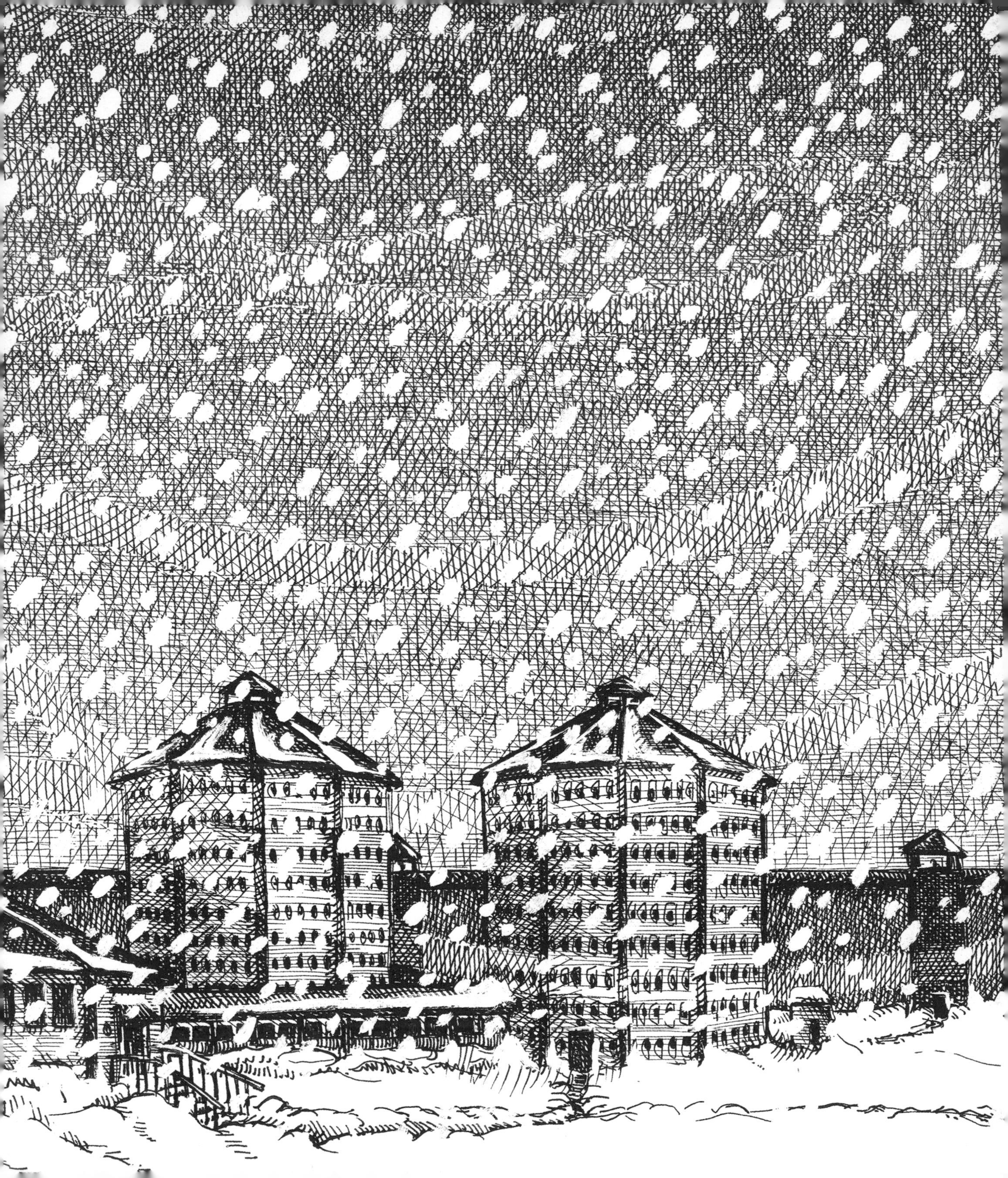

THE HUNTING ACCIDENT

A TRUE STORY OF CRIME AND POETRY

DAVID L. CARLSON
LANDIS BLAIR

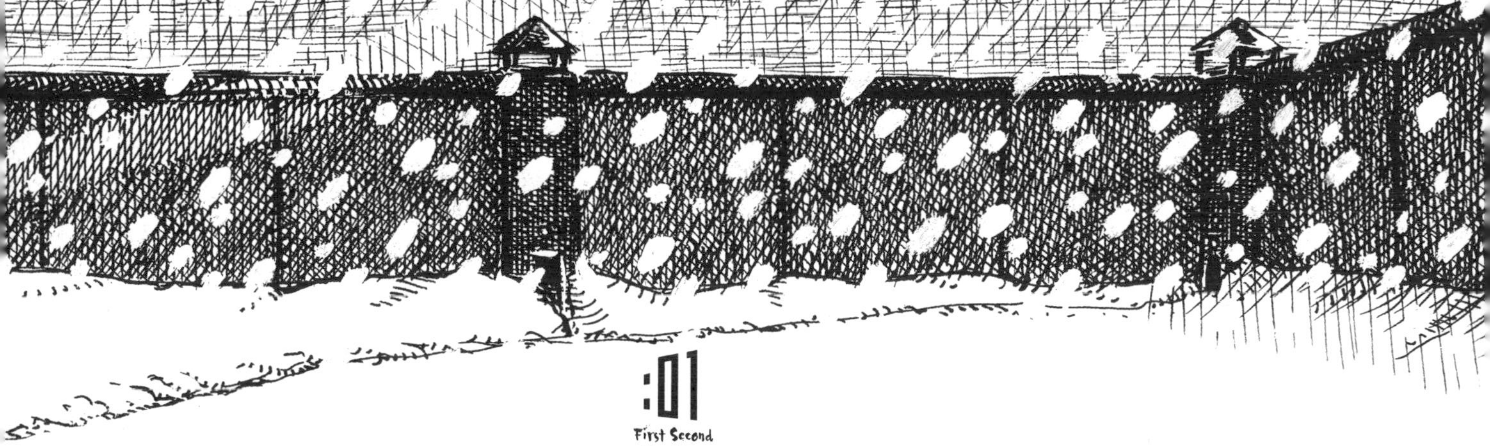

:01
First Second
New York

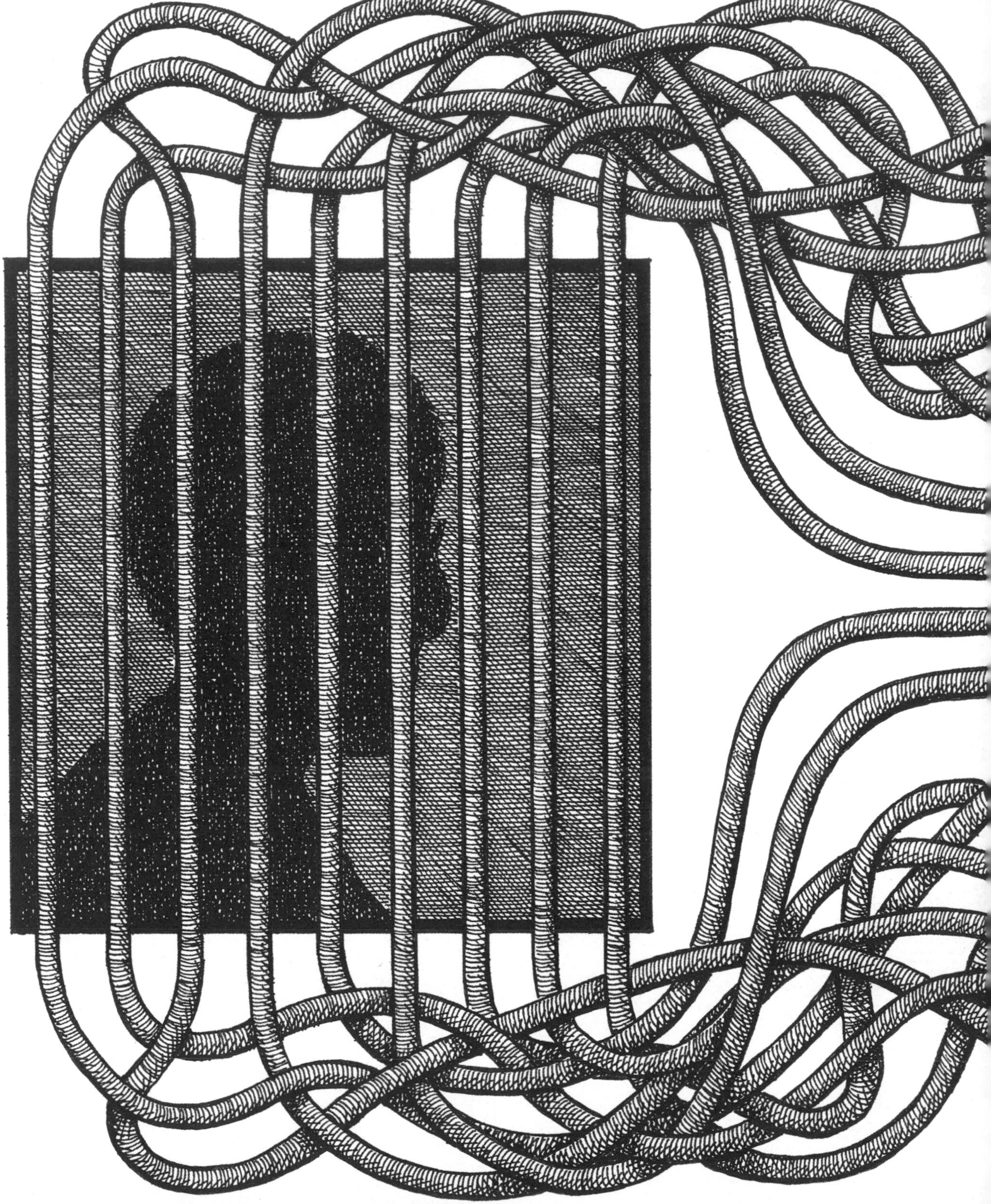

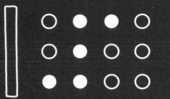

THE HUNTING
ACCIDENT

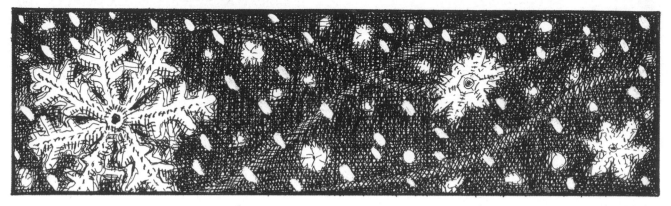

CHICAGO, 1959

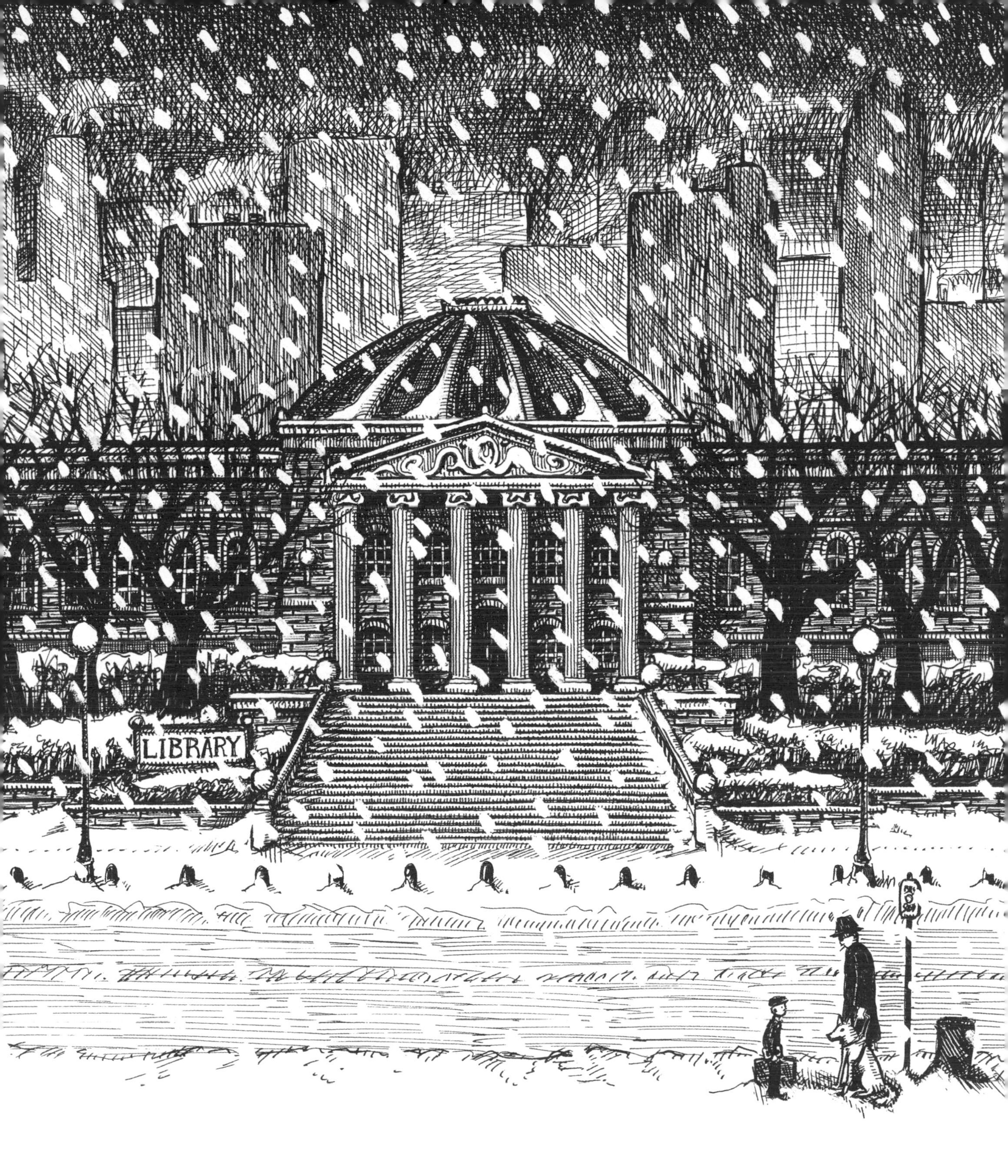
LIBRARY

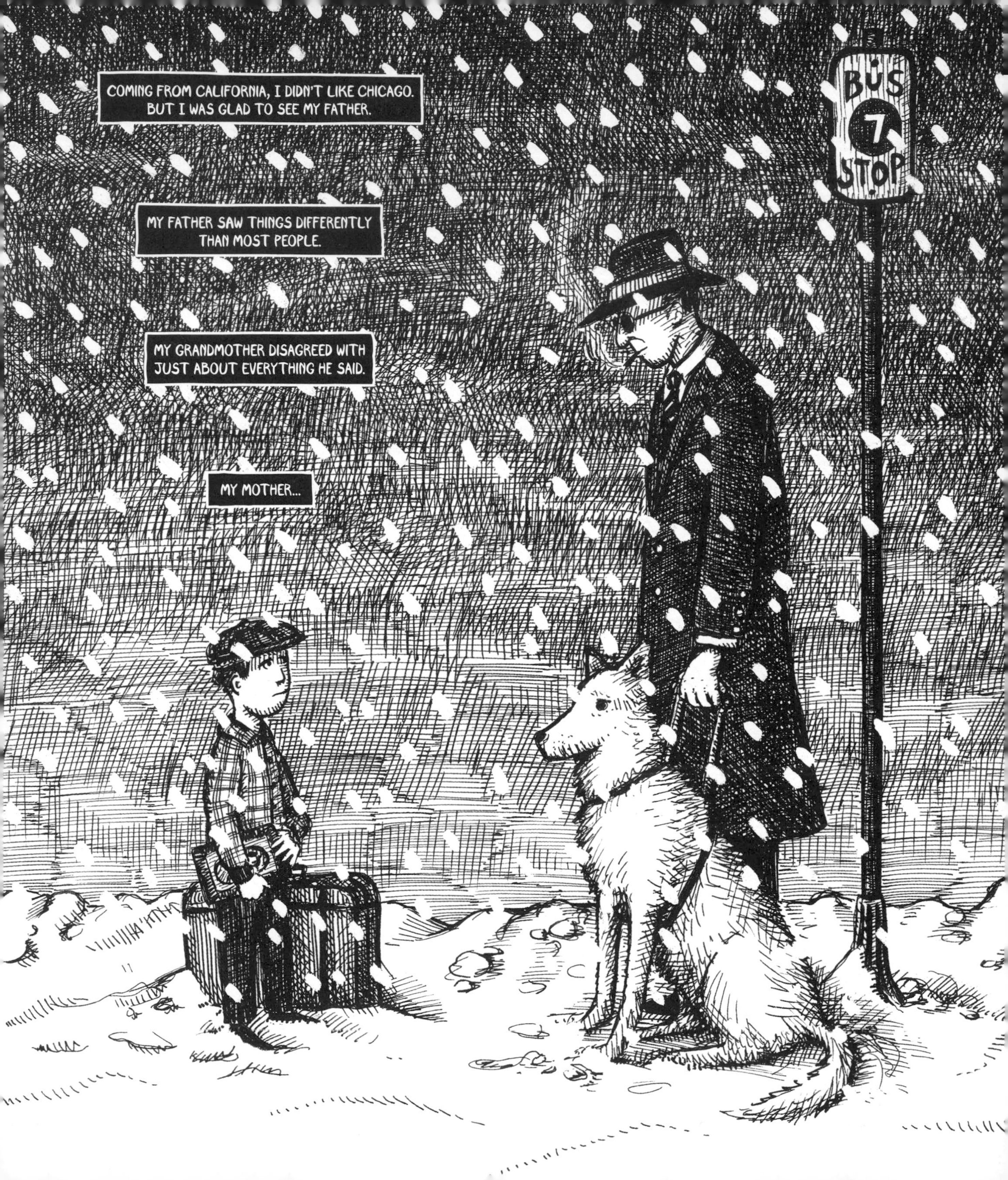
COMING FROM CALIFORNIA, I DIDN'T LIKE CHICAGO. BUT I WAS GLAD TO SEE MY FATHER.
MY FATHER SAW THINGS DIFFERENTLY THAN MOST PEOPLE.
MY GRANDMOTHER DISAGREED WITH JUST ABOUT EVERYTHING HE SAID.
MY MOTHER...
BUS 7 STOP

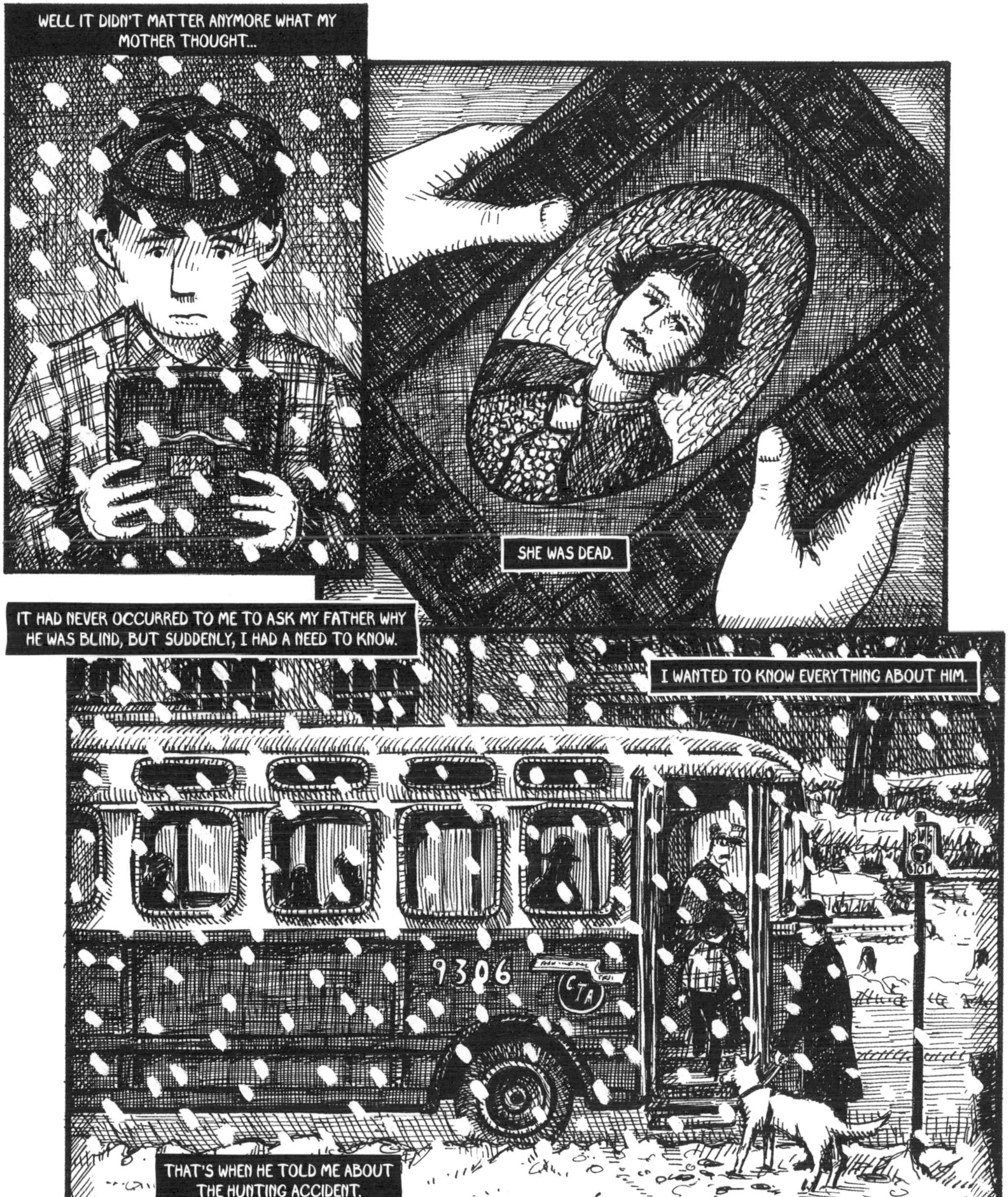
WELL IT DIDN'T MATTER ANYMORE WHAT MY MOTHER THOUGHT...
SHE WAS DEAD.
IT HAD NEVER OCCURRED TO ME TO ASK MY FATHER WHY HE WAS BLIND, BUT SUDDENLY, I HAD A NEED TO KNOW.
I WANTED TO KNOW EVERYTHING ABOUT HIM.
9306
CTA
THAT'S WHEN HE TOLD ME ABOUT THE HUNTING ACCIDENT.

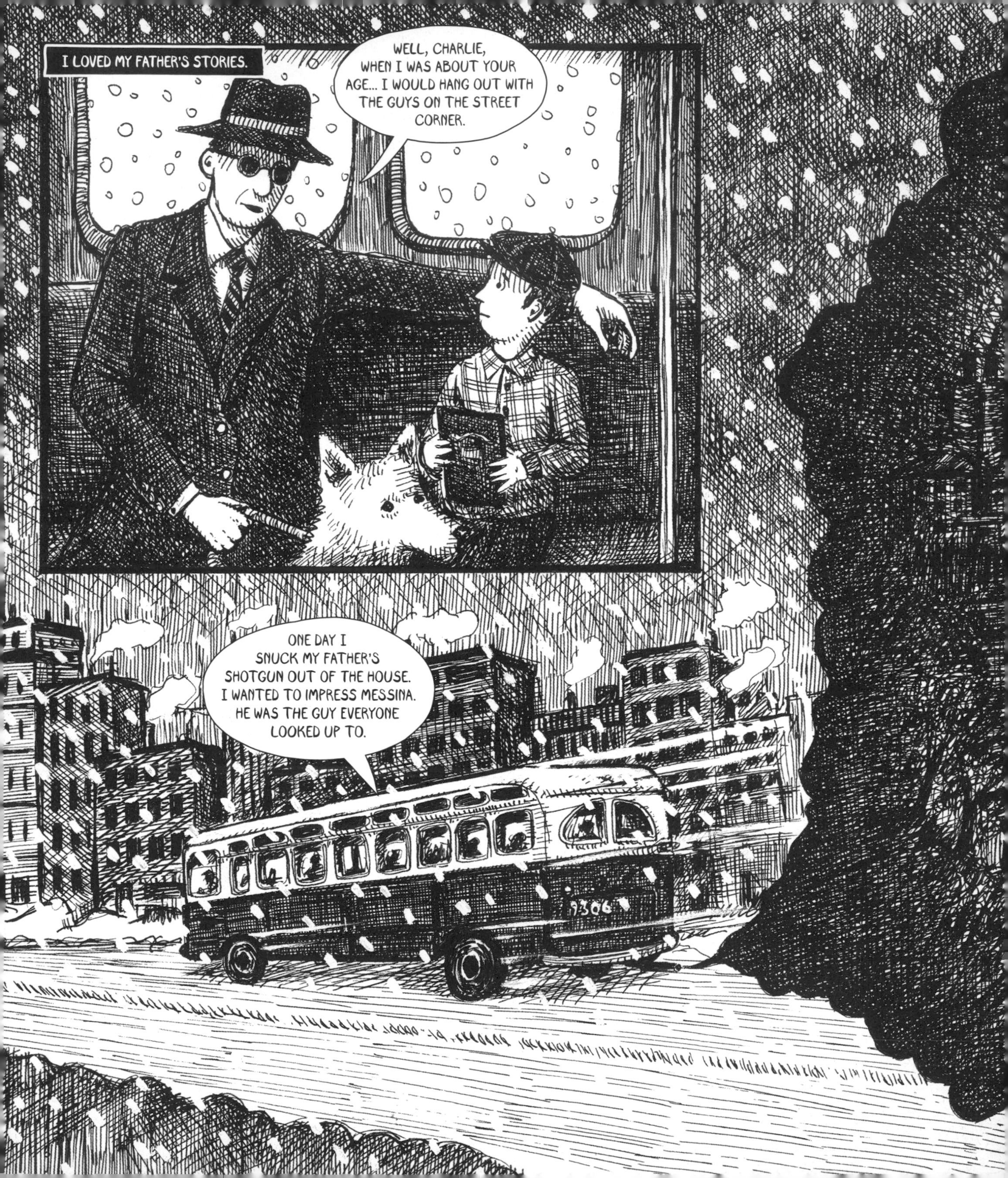
I LOVED MY FATHER'S STORIES.
WELL, CHARLIE, WHEN I WAS ABOUT YOUR AGE... I WOULD HANG OUT WITH THE GUYS ON THE STREET CORNER.
ONE DAY I SNUCK MY FATHER'S SHOTGUN OUT OF THE HOUSE. I WANTED TO IMPRESS MESSINA. HE WAS THE GUY EVERYONE LOOKED UP TO.
9306

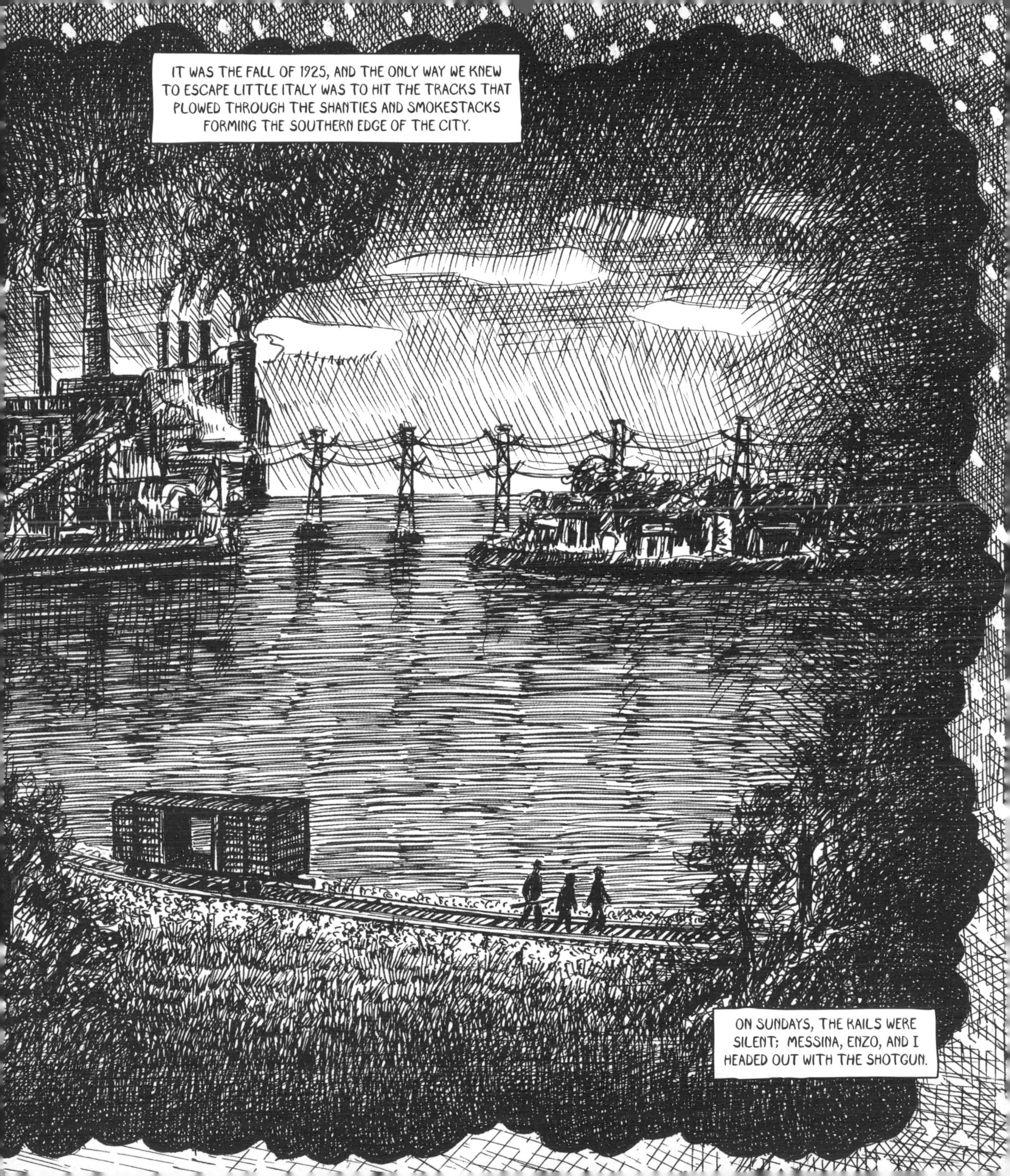
IT WAS THE FALL OF 1925, AND THE ONLY WAY WE KNEW TO ESCAPE LITTLE ITALY WAS TO HIT THE TRACKS THAT PLOWED THROUGH THE SHANTIES AND SMOKESTACKS FORMING THE SOUTHERN EDGE OF THE CITY.
ON SUNDAYS, THE RAILS WERE SILENT; MESSINA, ENZO, AND I HEADED OUT WITH THE SHOTGUN.

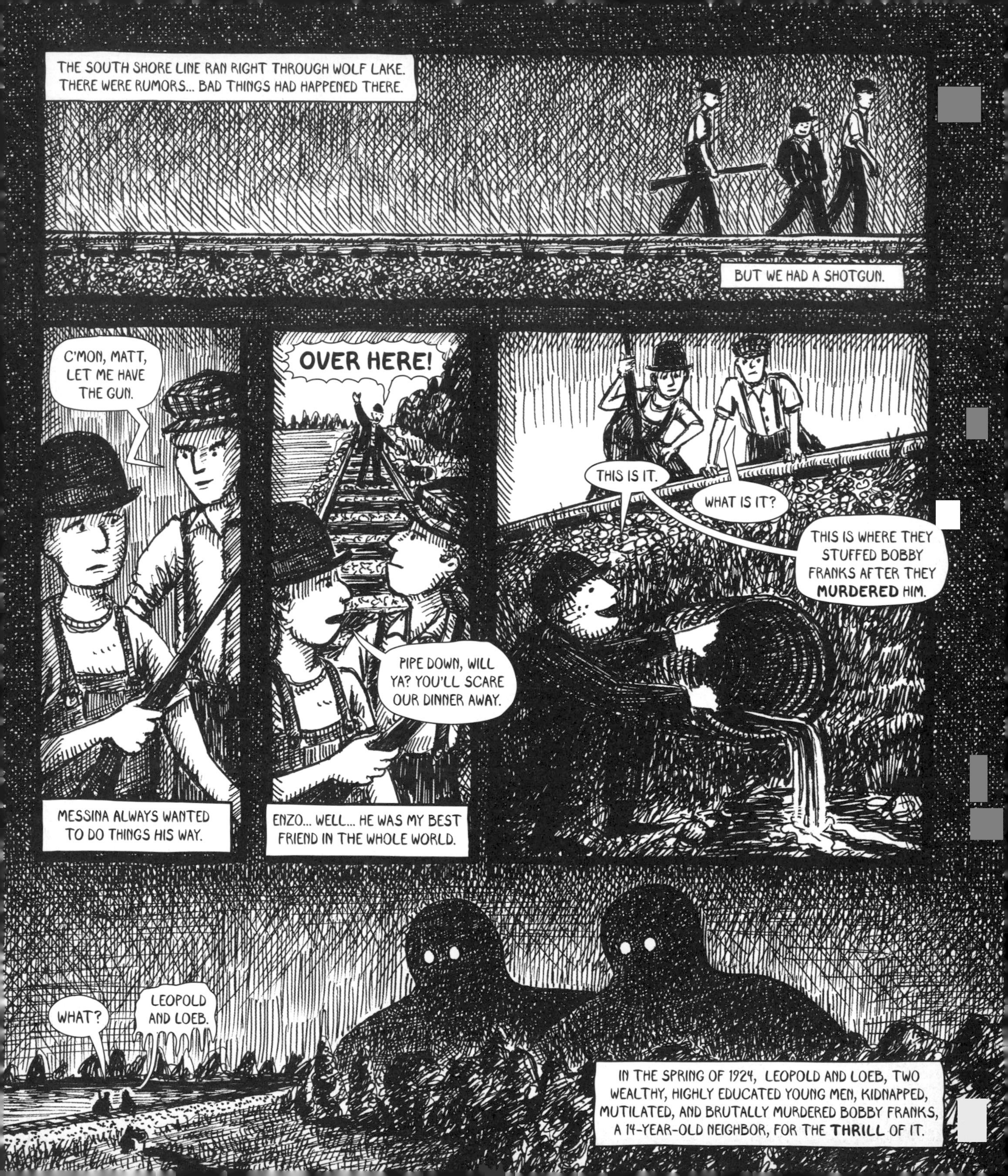

THE SOUTH SHORE LINE RAN RIGHT THROUGH WOLF LAKE. THERE WERE RUMORS... BAD THINGS HAD HAPPENED THERE.
BUT WE HAD A SHOTGUN.
C'MON, MATT, LET ME HAVE THE GUN.
MESSINA ALWAYS WANTED TO DO THINGS HIS WAY.
OVER HERE!
PIPE DOWN, WILL YA? YOU'LL SCARE OUR DINNER AWAY.
ENZO... WELL... HE WAS MY BEST FRIEND IN THE WHOLE WORLD.
THIS IS IT.
WHAT IS IT?
THIS IS WHERE THEY STUFFED BOBBY FRANKS AFTER THEY **MURDERED** HIM.
WHAT?
LEOPOLD AND LOEB.
IN THE SPRING OF 1924, LEOPOLD AND LOEB, TWO WEALTHY, HIGHLY EDUCATED YOUNG MEN, KIDNAPPED, MUTILATED, AND BRUTALLY MURDERED BOBBY FRANKS, A 14-YEAR-OLD NEIGHBOR, FOR THE **THRILL** OF IT.

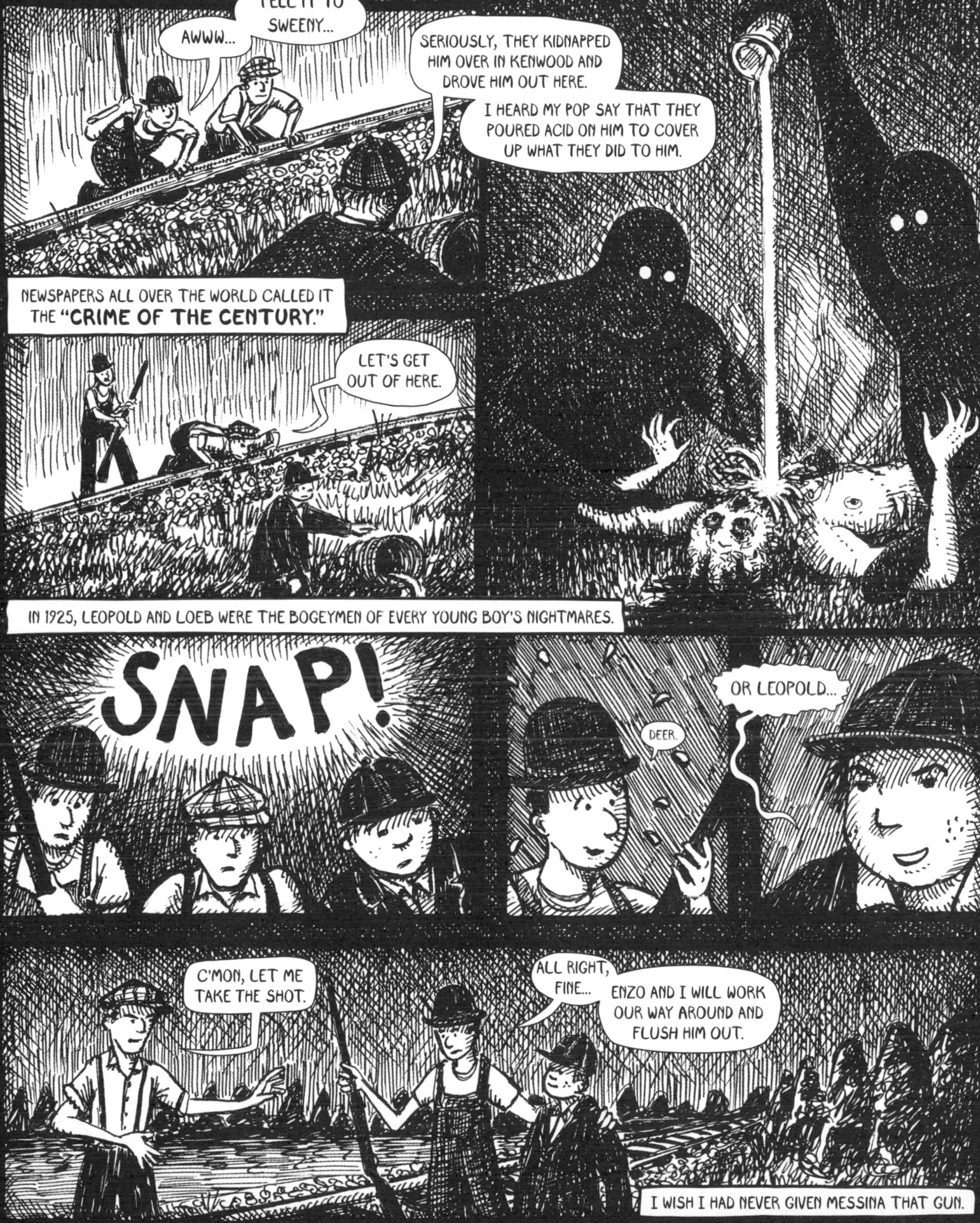
AWWW...
TELL IT TO SWEENY...
SERIOUSLY, THEY KIDNAPPED HIM OVER IN KENWOOD AND DROVE HIM OUT HERE.
I HEARD MY POP SAY THAT THEY POURED ACID ON HIM TO COVER UP WHAT THEY DID TO HIM.
NEWSPAPERS ALL OVER THE WORLD CALLED IT THE "CRIME OF THE CENTURY."
LET'S GET OUT OF HERE.
IN 1925, LEOPOLD AND LOEB WERE THE BOGEYMEN OF EVERY YOUNG BOY'S NIGHTMARES.
SNAP!
DEER.
OR LEOPOLD...
C'MON, LET ME TAKE THE SHOT.
ALL RIGHT, FINE...
ENZO AND I WILL WORK OUR WAY AROUND AND FLUSH HIM OUT.
I WISH I HAD NEVER GIVEN MESSINA THAT GUN.

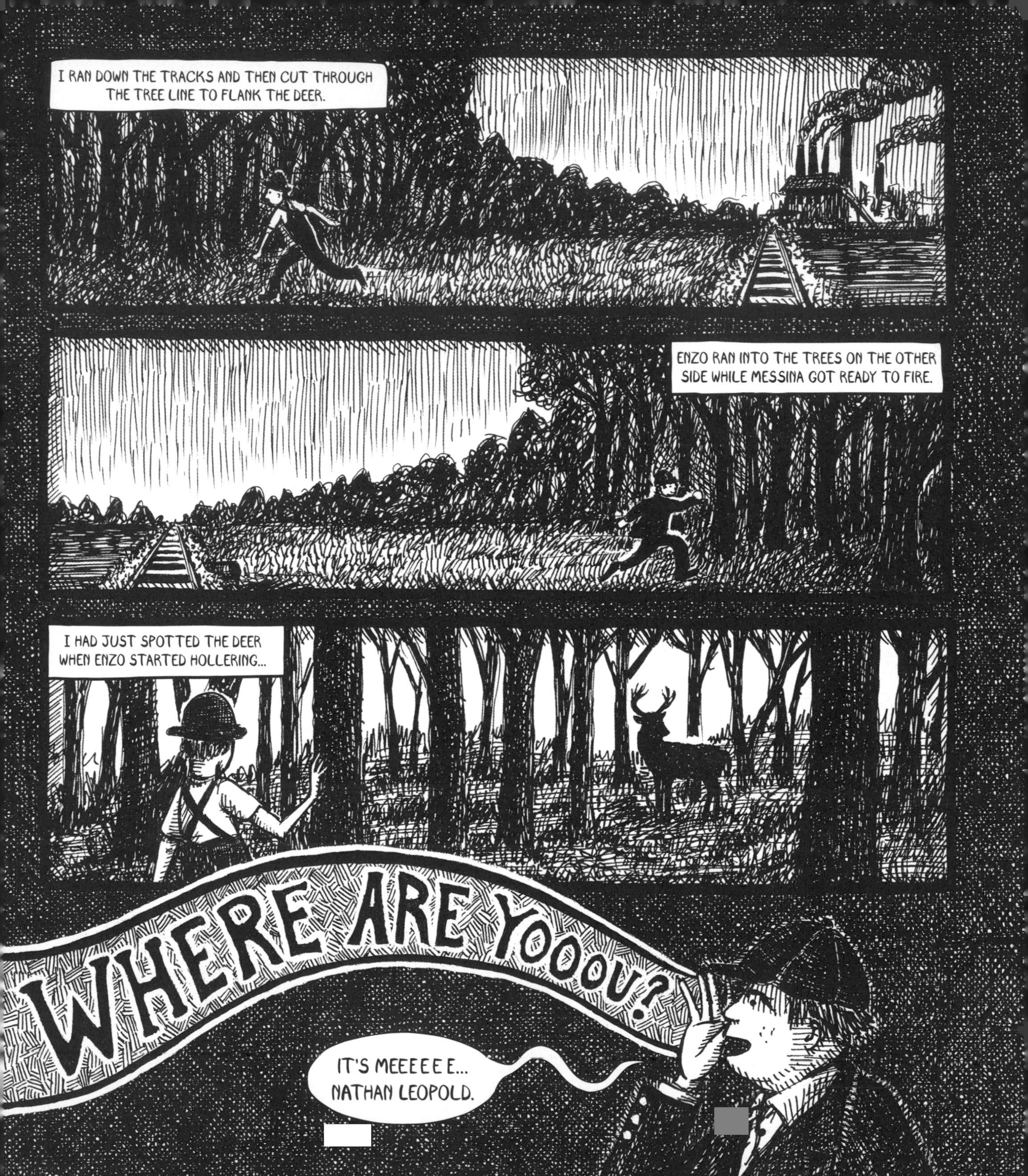
I RAN DOWN THE TRACKS AND THEN CUT THROUGH THE TREE LINE TO FLANK THE DEER.
ENZO RAN INTO THE TREES ON THE OTHER SIDE WHILE MESSINA GOT READY TO FIRE.
I HAD JUST SPOTTED THE DEER WHEN ENZO STARTED HOLLERING...
WHERE ARE YOOOU?
IT'S MEEEEEE... NATHAN LEOPOLD.

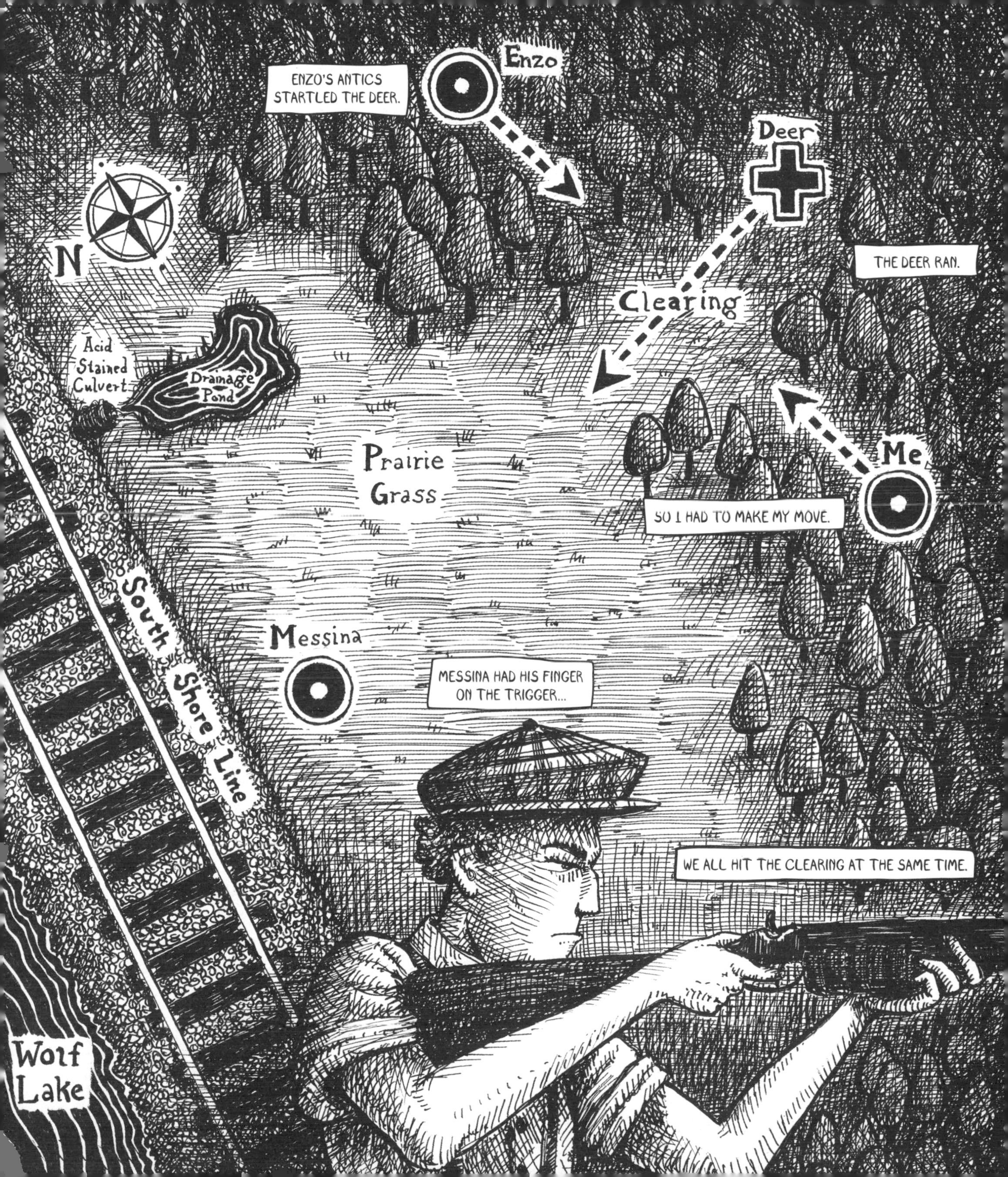
ENZO'S ANTICS STARTLED THE DEER.
Enzo
Deer
N
THE DEER RAN.
Clearing
Acid Stained Culvert
Drainage Pond
Prairie Grass
Me
SO I HAD TO MAKE MY MOVE.
Messina
MESSINA HAD HIS FINGER ON THE TRIGGER...
South Shore Line
WE ALL HIT THE CLEARING AT THE SAME TIME.
Wolf Lake

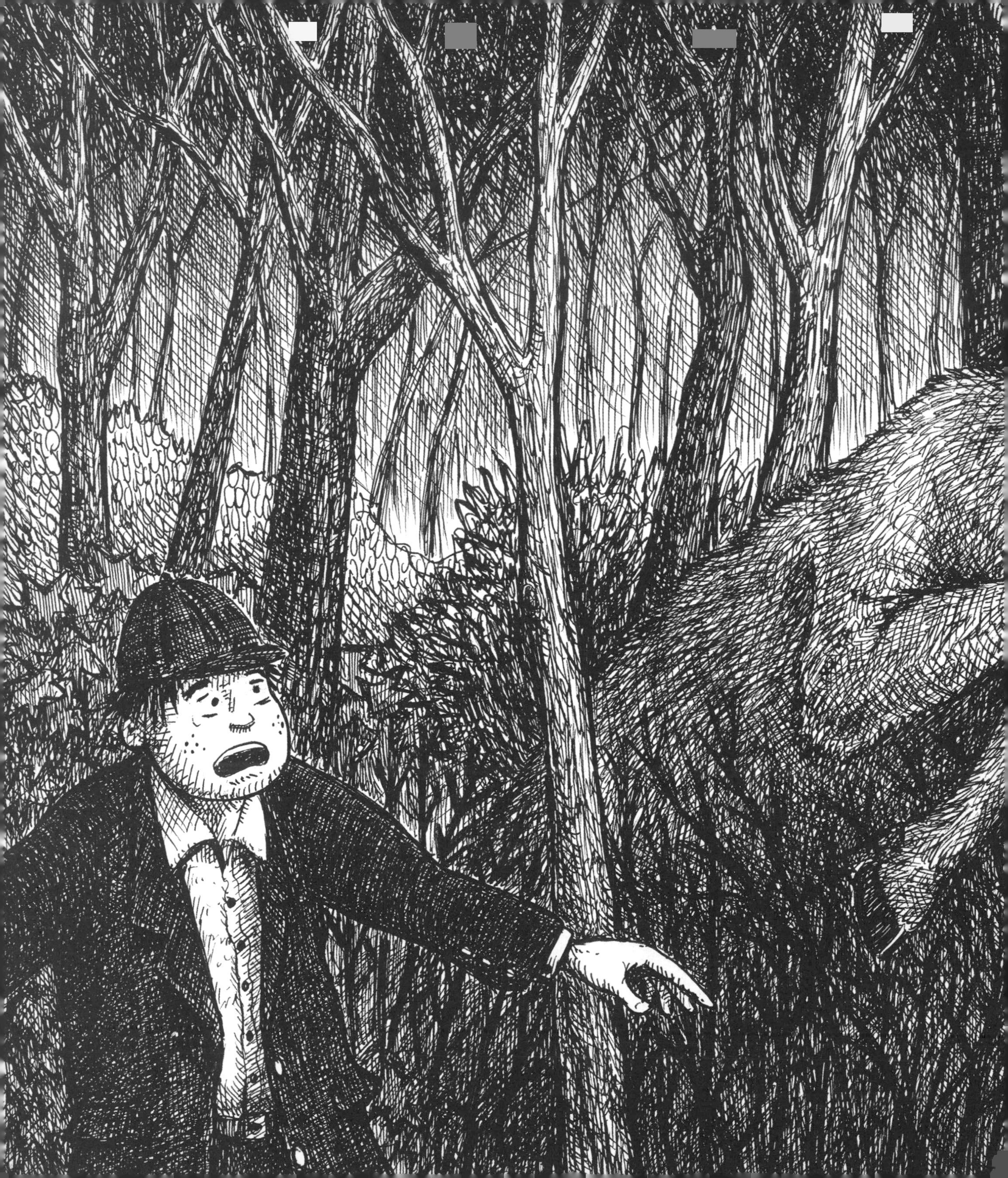

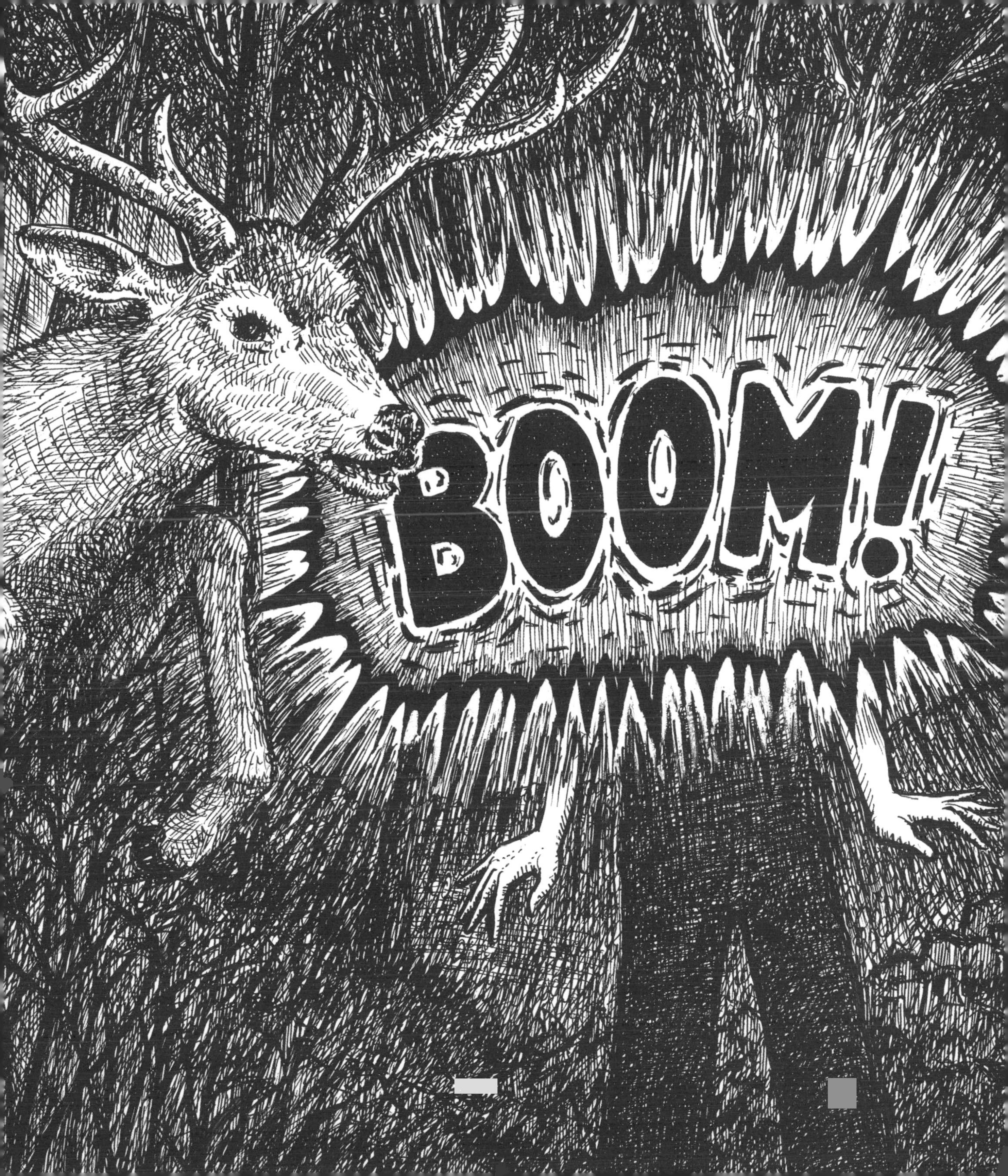
BOOM!

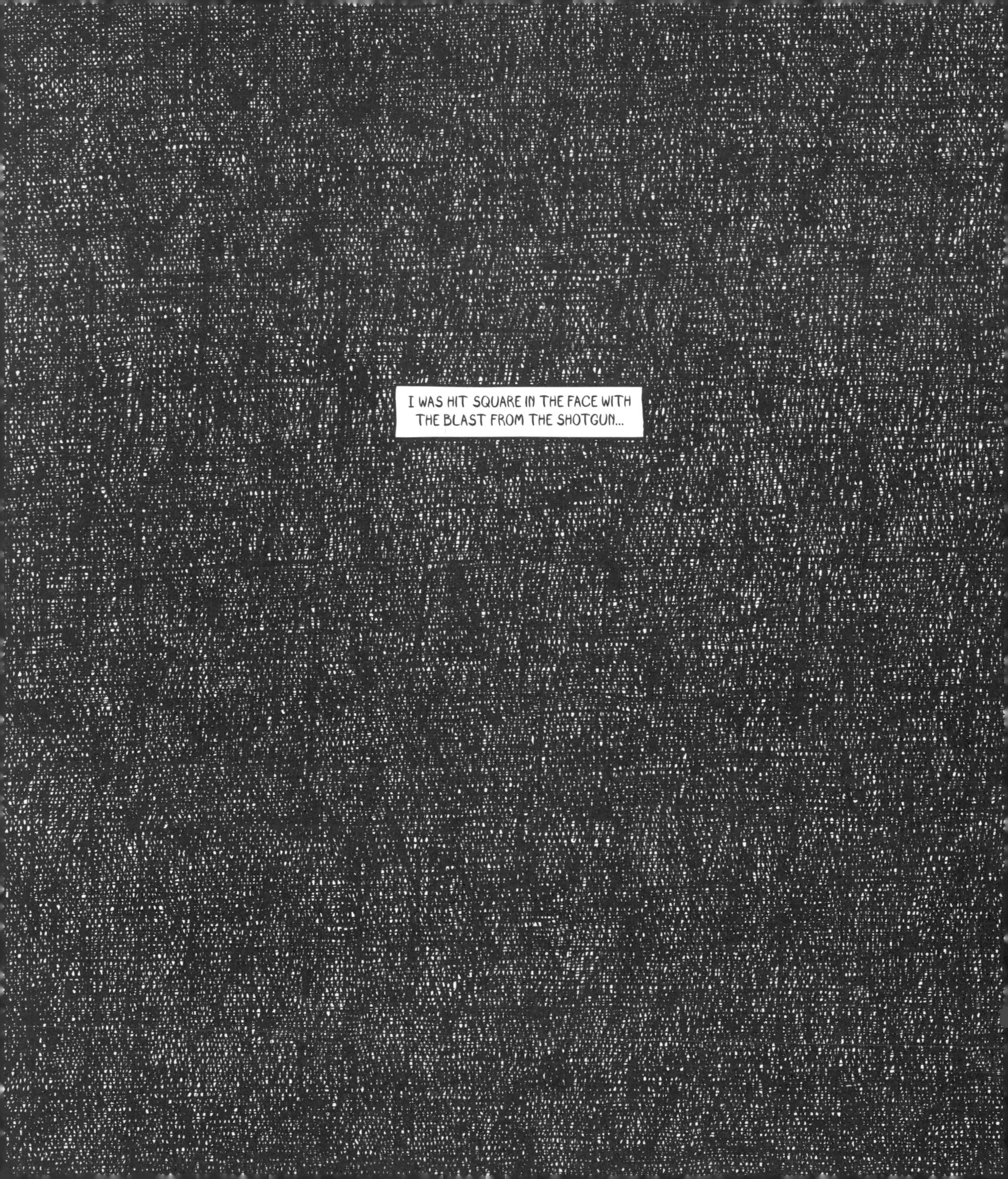
I WAS HIT SQUARE IN THE FACE WITH THE BLAST FROM THE SHOTGUN...

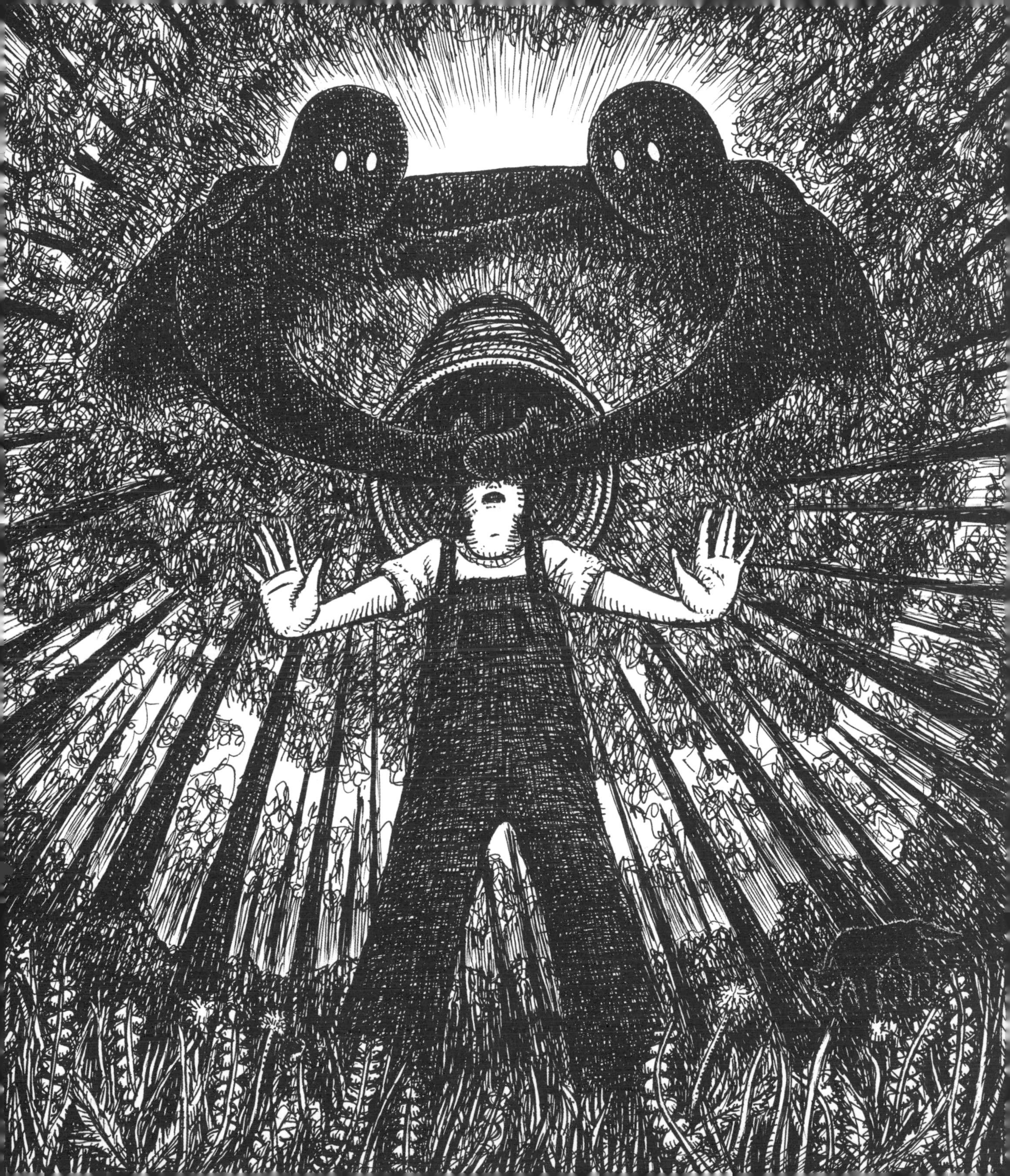

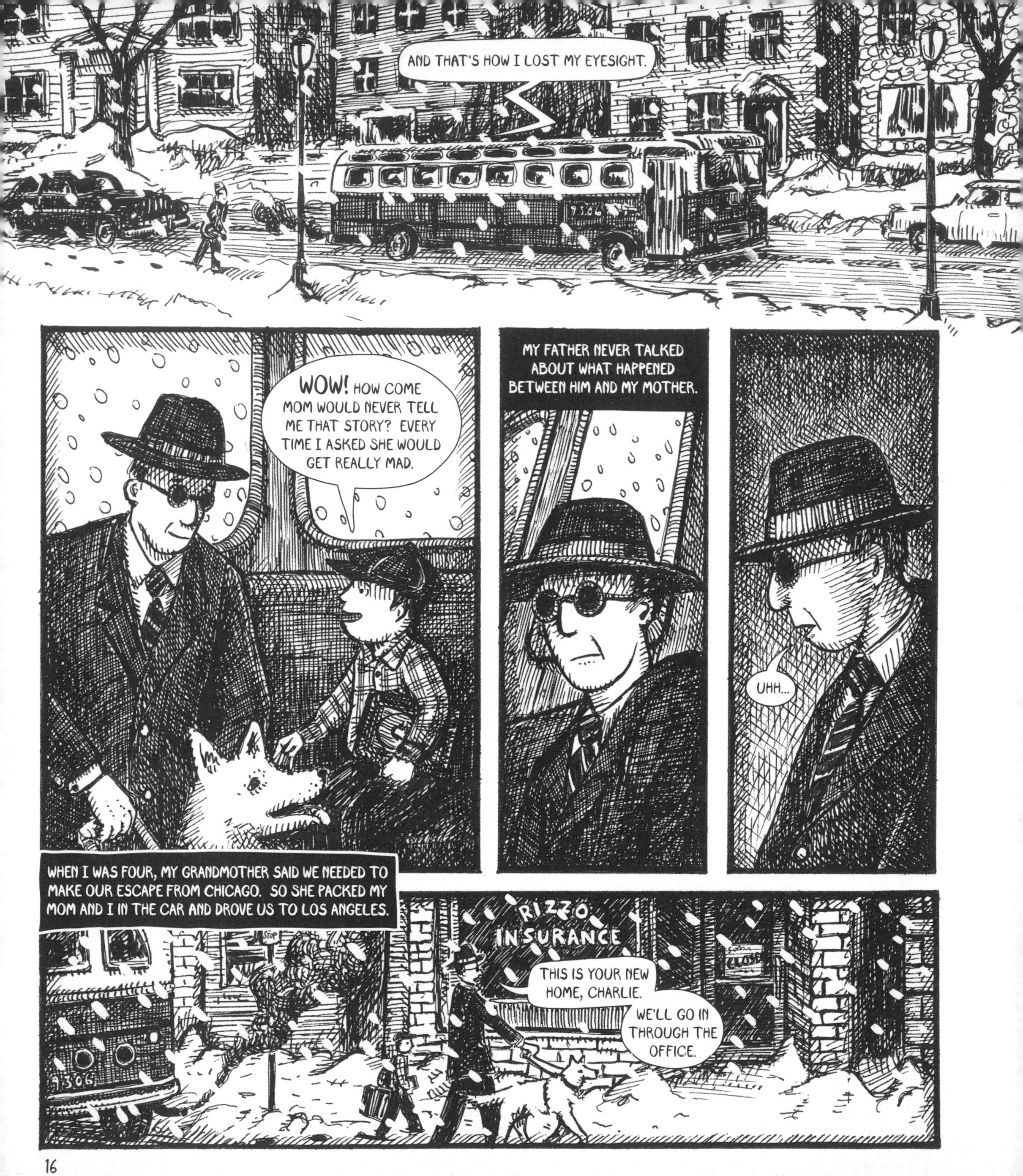
AND THAT'S HOW I LOST MY EYESIGHT.
WOW! HOW COME MOM WOULD NEVER TELL ME THAT STORY? EVERY TIME I ASKED SHE WOULD GET REALLY MAD.
MY FATHER NEVER TALKED ABOUT WHAT HAPPENED BETWEEN HIM AND MY MOTHER.
UHH...
WHEN I WAS FOUR, MY GRANDMOTHER SAID WE NEEDED TO MAKE OUR ESCAPE FROM CHICAGO. SO SHE PACKED MY MOM AND I IN THE CAR AND DROVE US TO LOS ANGELES.
RIZZO INSURANCE
THIS IS YOUR NEW HOME, CHARLIE.
WE'LL GO IN THROUGH THE OFFICE.

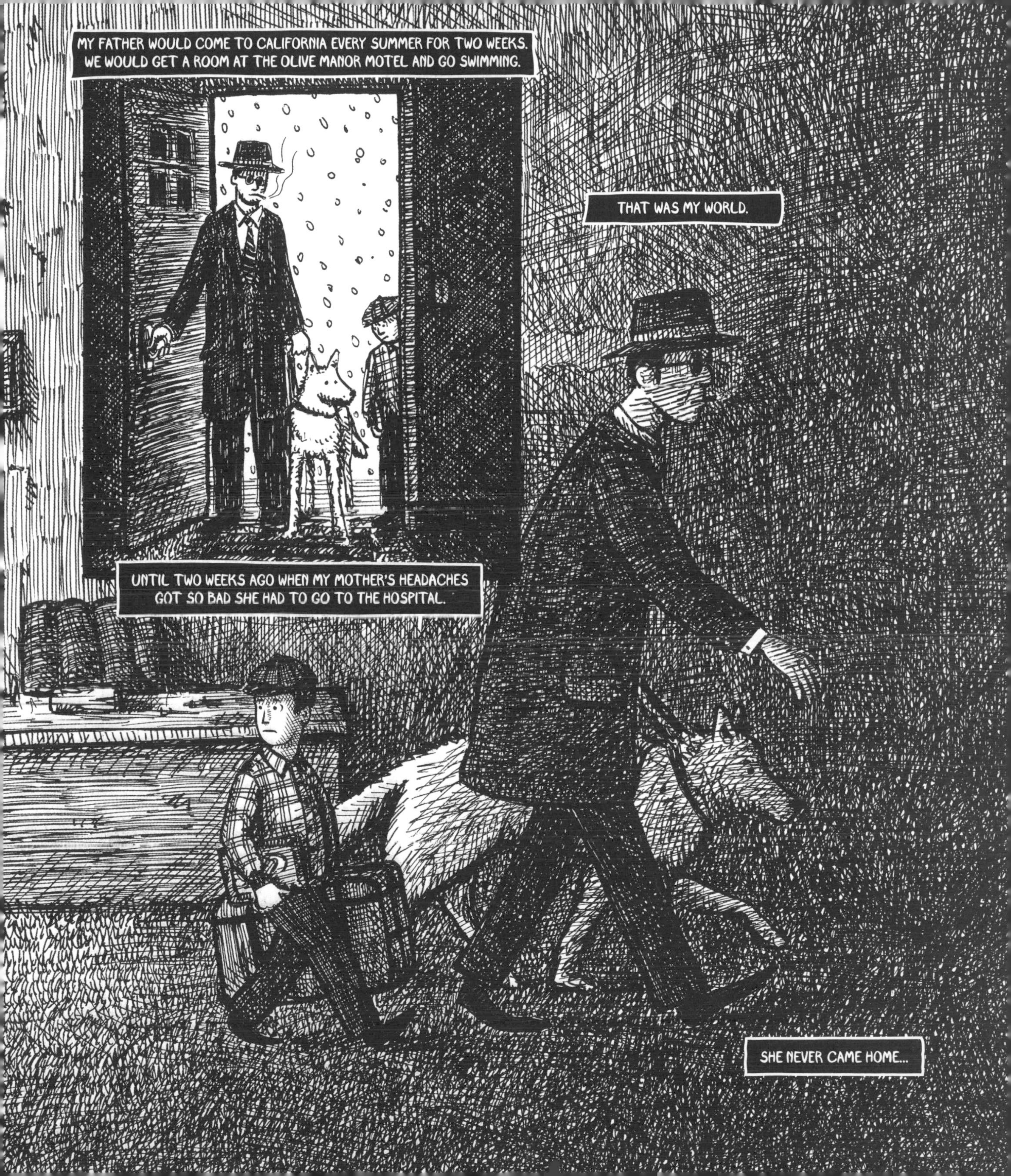
MY FATHER WOULD COME TO CALIFORNIA EVERY SUMMER FOR TWO WEEKS. WE WOULD GET A ROOM AT THE OLIVE MANOR MOTEL AND GO SWIMMING.
THAT WAS MY WORLD.
UNTIL TWO WEEKS AGO WHEN MY MOTHER'S HEADACHES GOT SO BAD SHE HAD TO GO TO THE HOSPITAL.
SHE NEVER CAME HOME...

MY FATHER'S WORLD WAS VERY DIFFERENT.
DAD?
FLIP
SORRY. BACK HERE.
FOR ONE THING, HE NEVER TURNED THE LIGHTS ON.

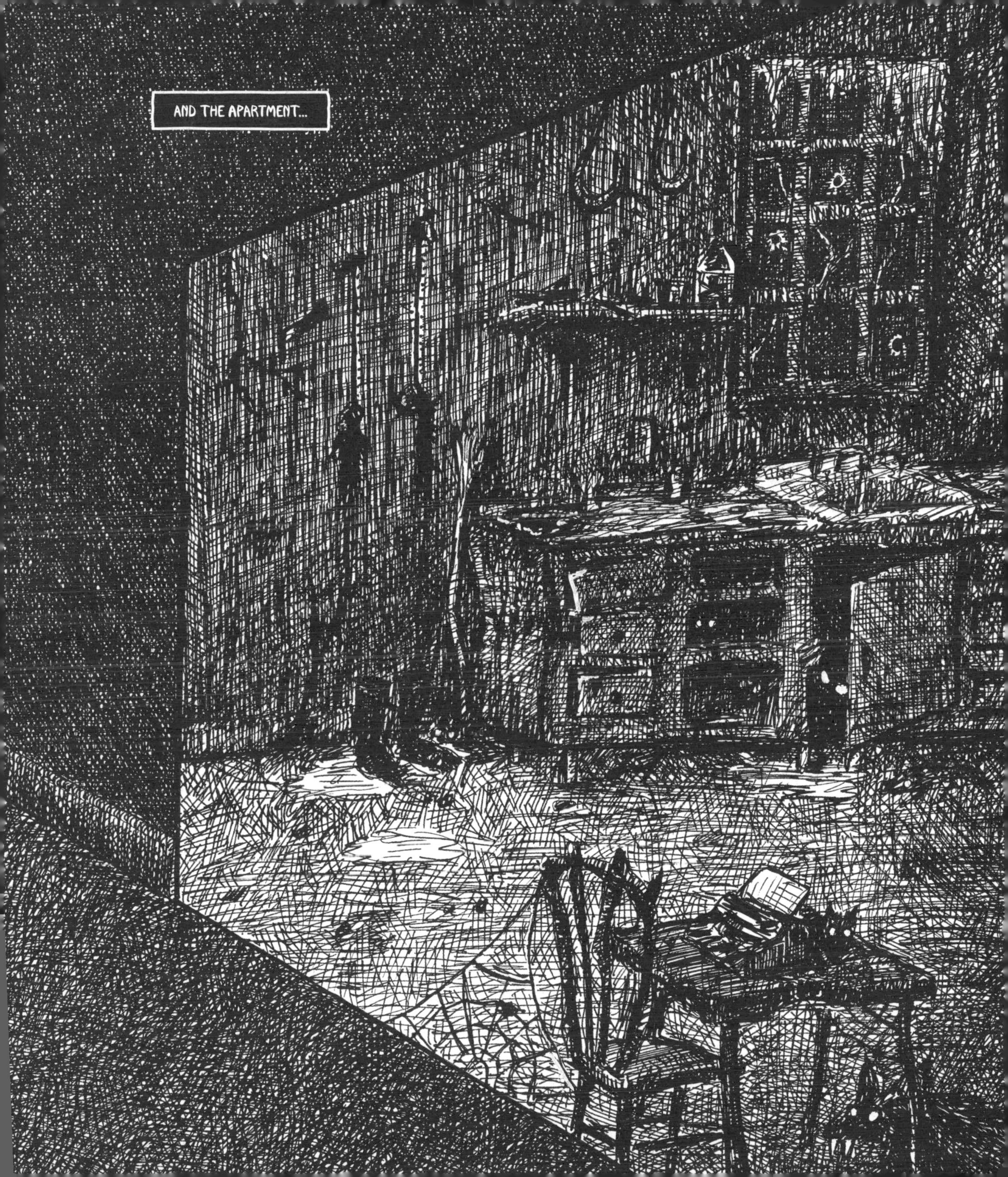
AND THE APARTMENT...

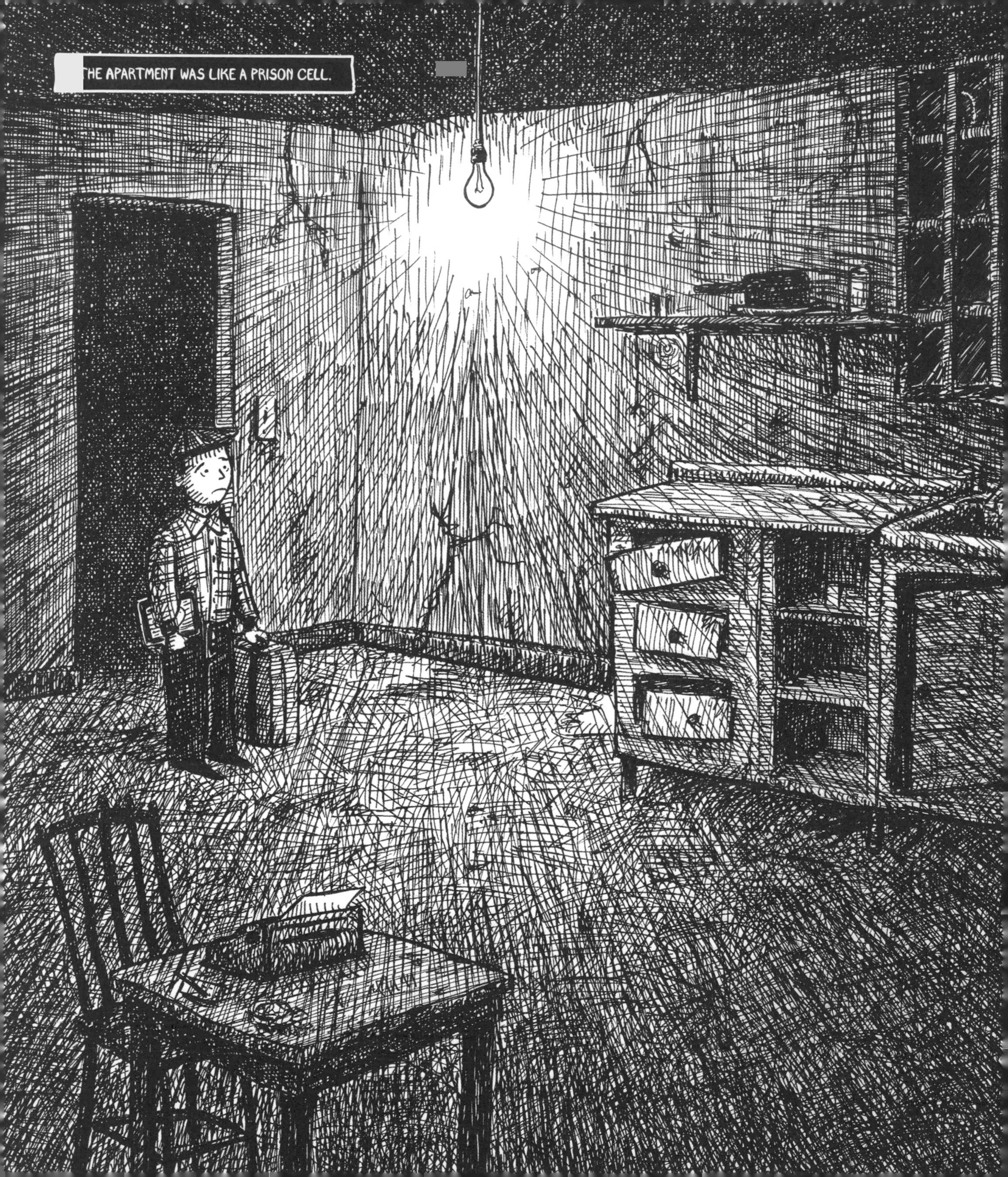
THE APARTMENT WAS LIKE A PRISON CELL.

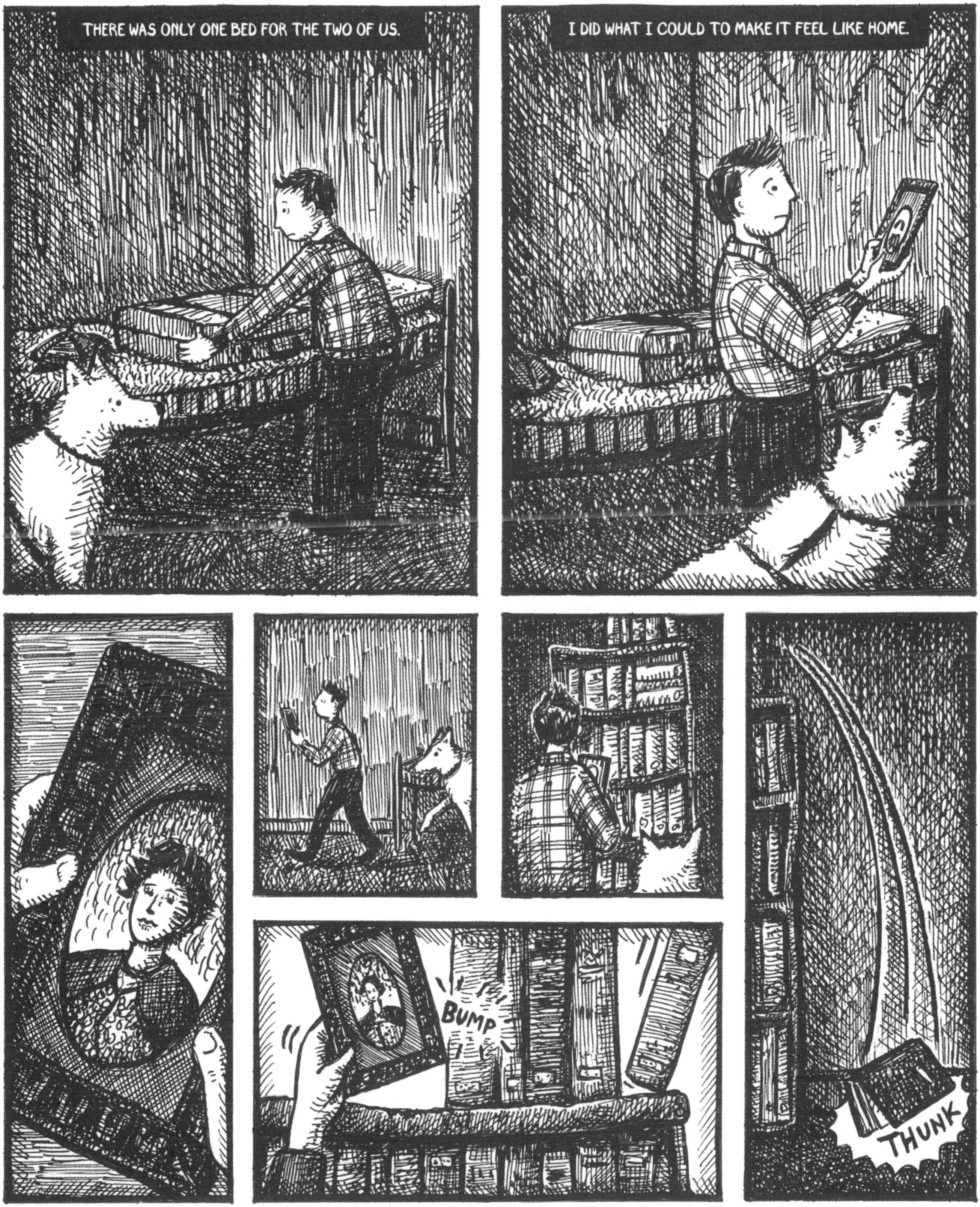
THERE WAS ONLY ONE BED FOR THE TWO OF US.
I DID WHAT I COULD TO MAKE IT FEEL LIKE HOME.
BUMP
THUNK

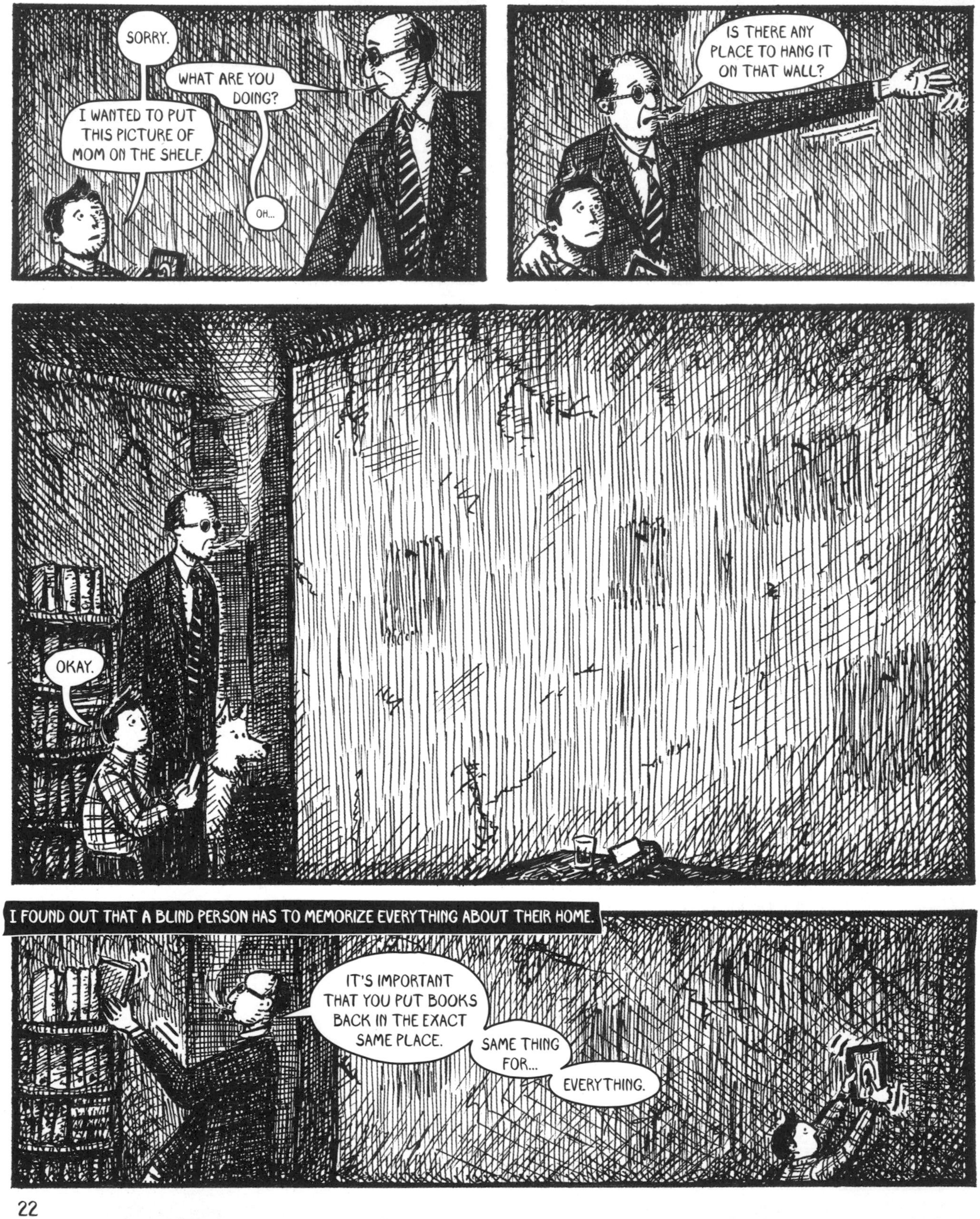
SORRY.
I WANTED TO PUT THIS PICTURE OF MOM ON THE SHELF.
WHAT ARE YOU DOING?
OH...
IS THERE ANY PLACE TO HANG IT ON THAT WALL?
OKAY.
I FOUND OUT THAT A BLIND PERSON HAS TO MEMORIZE EVERYTHING ABOUT THEIR HOME.
IT'S IMPORTANT THAT YOU PUT BOOKS BACK IN THE EXACT SAME PLACE.
SAME THING FOR...
EVERYTHING.

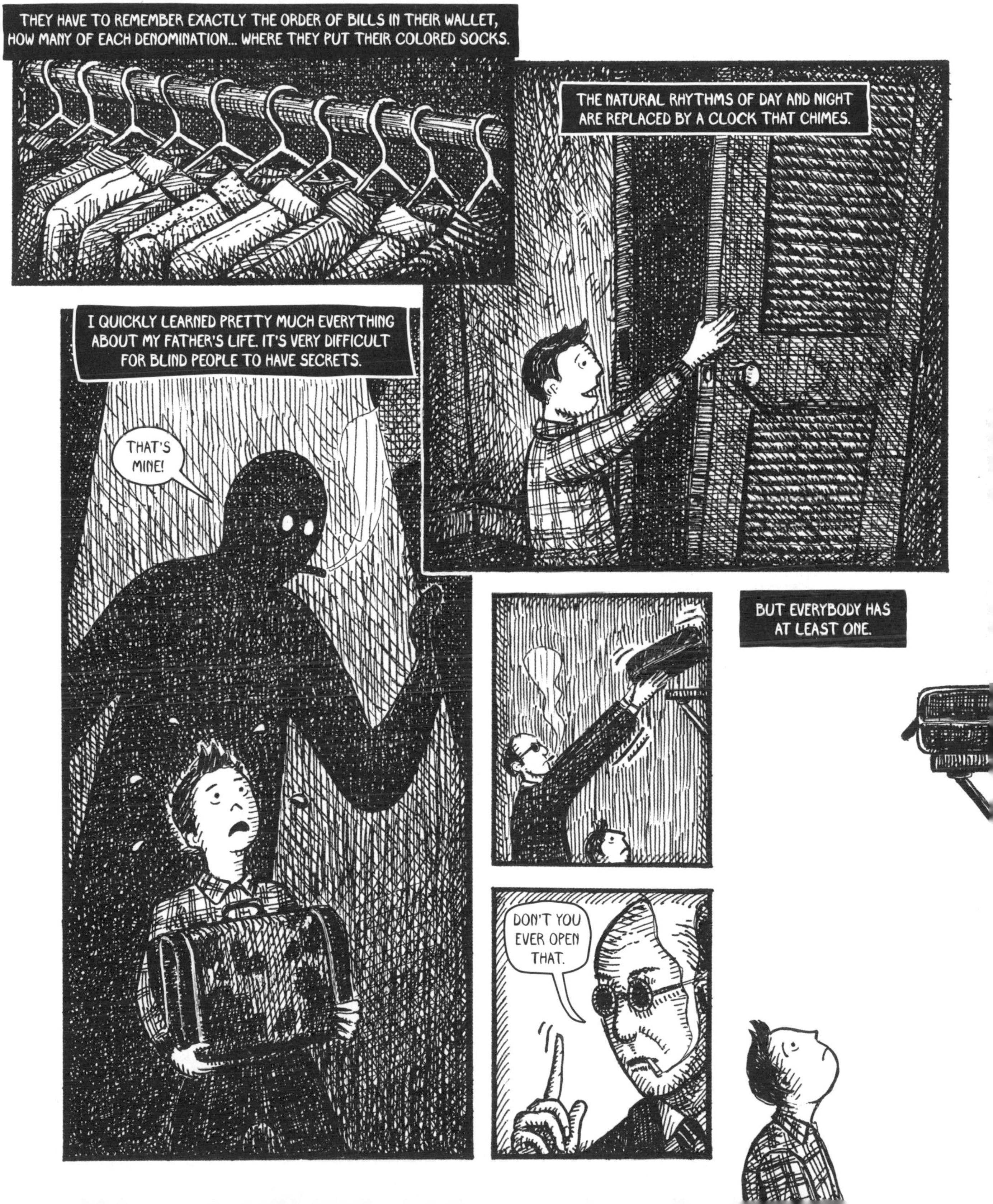
THEY HAVE TO REMEMBER EXACTLY THE ORDER OF BILLS IN THEIR WALLET, HOW MANY OF EACH DENOMINATION... WHERE THEY PUT THEIR COLORED SOCKS.
THE NATURAL RHYTHMS OF DAY AND NIGHT ARE REPLACED BY A CLOCK THAT CHIMES.
I QUICKLY LEARNED PRETTY MUCH EVERYTHING ABOUT MY FATHER'S LIFE. IT'S VERY DIFFICULT FOR BLIND PEOPLE TO HAVE SECRETS.
THAT'S MINE!
BUT EVERYBODY HAS AT LEAST ONE.
DON'T YOU EVER OPEN THAT.

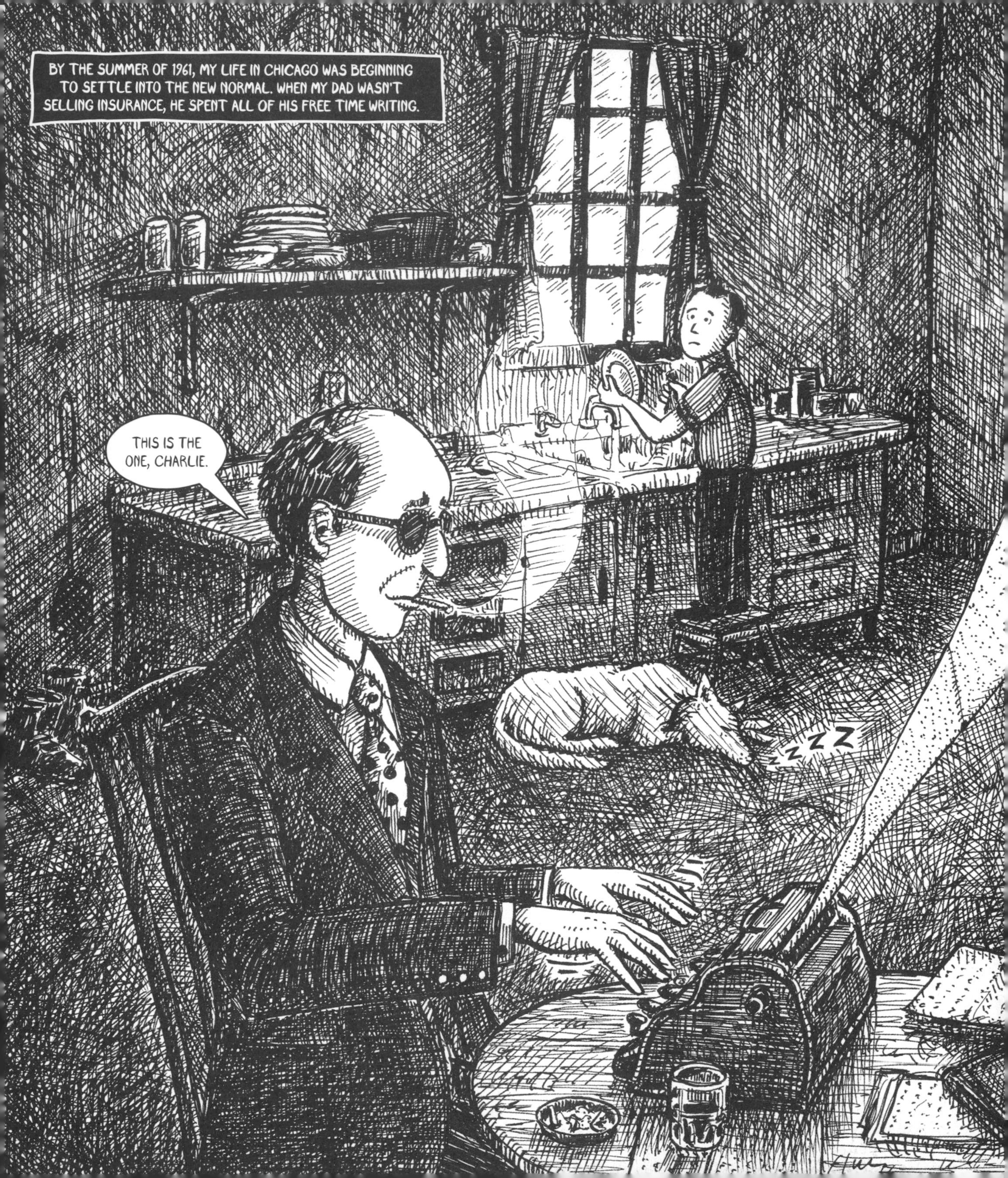
BY THE SUMMER OF 1961, MY LIFE IN CHICAGO WAS BEGINNING TO SETTLE INTO THE NEW NORMAL. WHEN MY DAD WASN'T SELLING INSURANCE, HE SPENT ALL OF HIS FREE TIME WRITING.
THIS IS THE ONE, CHARLIE.
ZZZZ

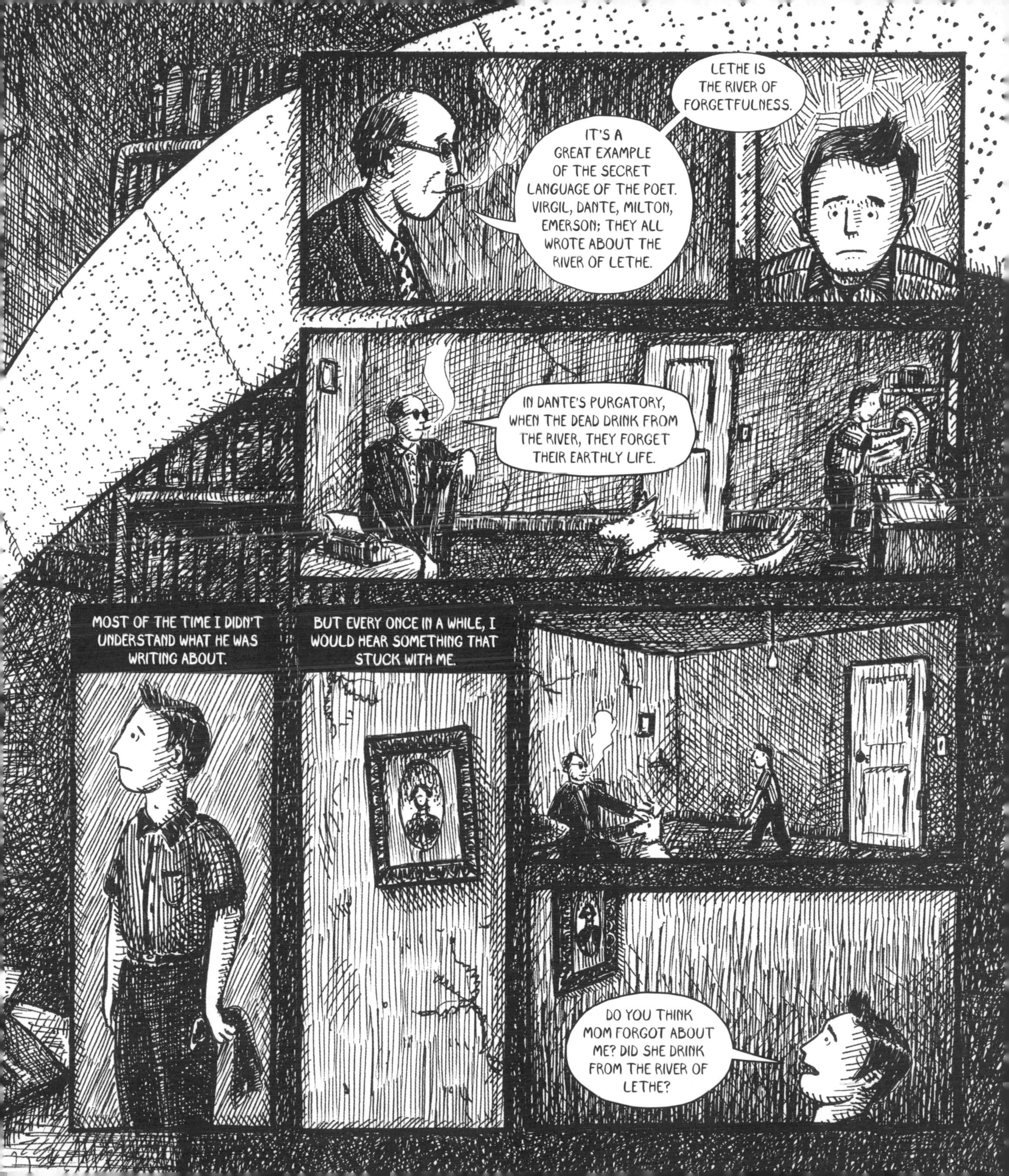
LETHE IS THE RIVER OF FORGETFULNESS.
IT'S A GREAT EXAMPLE OF THE SECRET LANGUAGE OF THE POET. VIRGIL, DANTE, MILTON, EMERSON; THEY ALL WROTE ABOUT THE RIVER OF LETHE.
IN DANTE'S PURGATORY, WHEN THE DEAD DRINK FROM THE RIVER, THEY FORGET THEIR EARTHLY LIFE.
MOST OF THE TIME I DIDN'T UNDERSTAND WHAT HE WAS WRITING ABOUT.
BUT EVERY ONCE IN A WHILE, I WOULD HEAR SOMETHING THAT STUCK WITH ME.
DO YOU THINK MOM FORGOT ABOUT ME? DID SHE DRINK FROM THE RIVER OF LETHE?

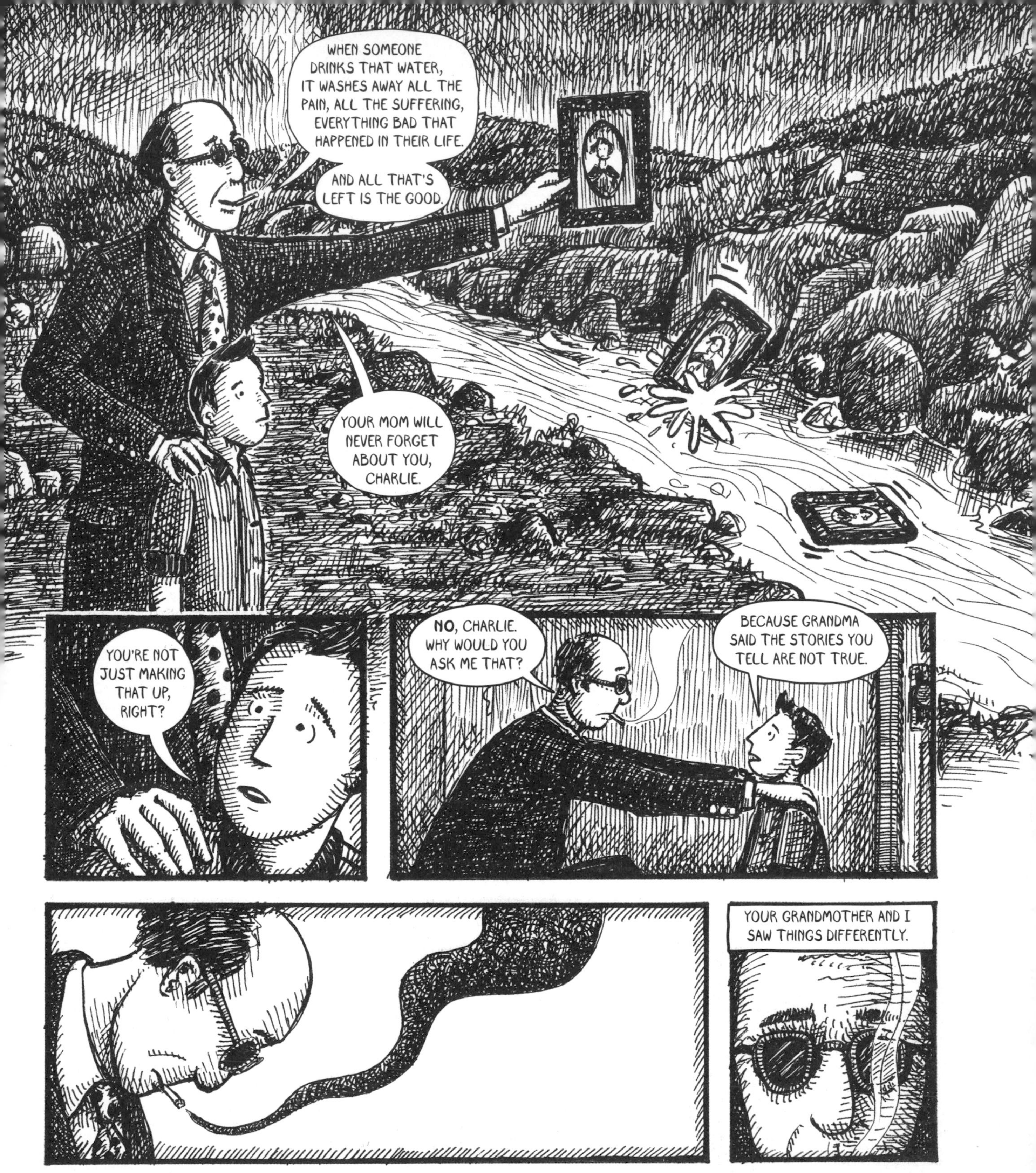
WHEN SOMEONE DRINKS THAT WATER, IT WASHES AWAY ALL THE PAIN, ALL THE SUFFERING, EVERYTHING BAD THAT HAPPENED IN THEIR LIFE.
AND ALL THAT'S LEFT IS THE GOOD.
YOUR MOM WILL NEVER FORGET ABOUT YOU, CHARLIE.
YOU'RE NOT JUST MAKING THAT UP, RIGHT?
NO, CHARLIE. WHY WOULD YOU ASK ME THAT?
BECAUSE GRANDMA SAID THE STORIES YOU TELL ARE NOT TRUE.
YOUR GRANDMOTHER AND I SAW THINGS DIFFERENTLY.

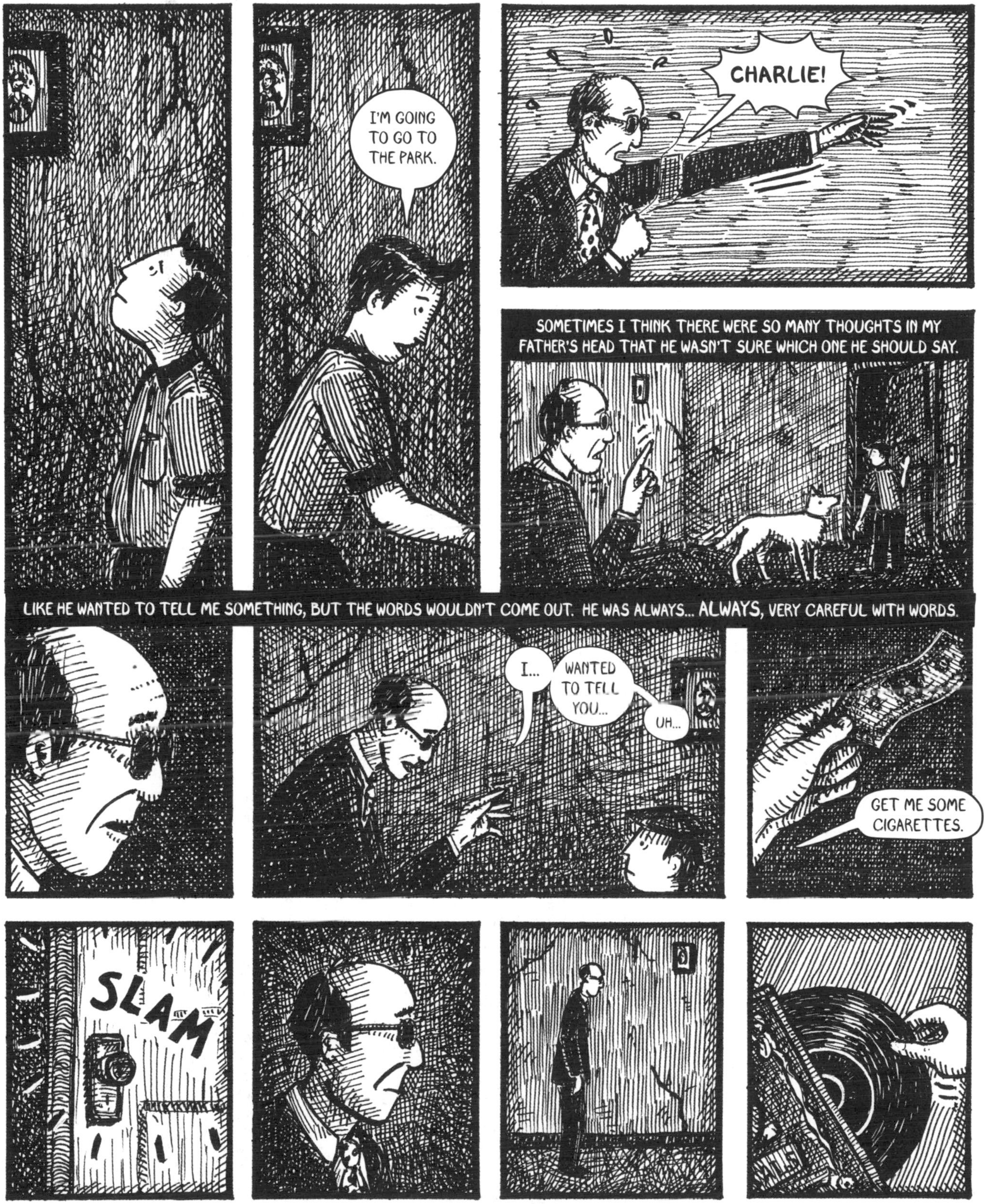
I'M GOING TO GO TO THE PARK.
CHARLIE!
SOMETIMES I THINK THERE WERE SO MANY THOUGHTS IN MY FATHER'S HEAD THAT HE WASN'T SURE WHICH ONE HE SHOULD SAY.
LIKE HE WANTED TO TELL ME SOMETHING, BUT THE WORDS WOULDN'T COME OUT. HE WAS ALWAYS... ALWAYS, VERY CAREFUL WITH WORDS.
I...
WANTED TO TELL YOU...
UH...
GET ME SOME CIGARETTES.
SLAM

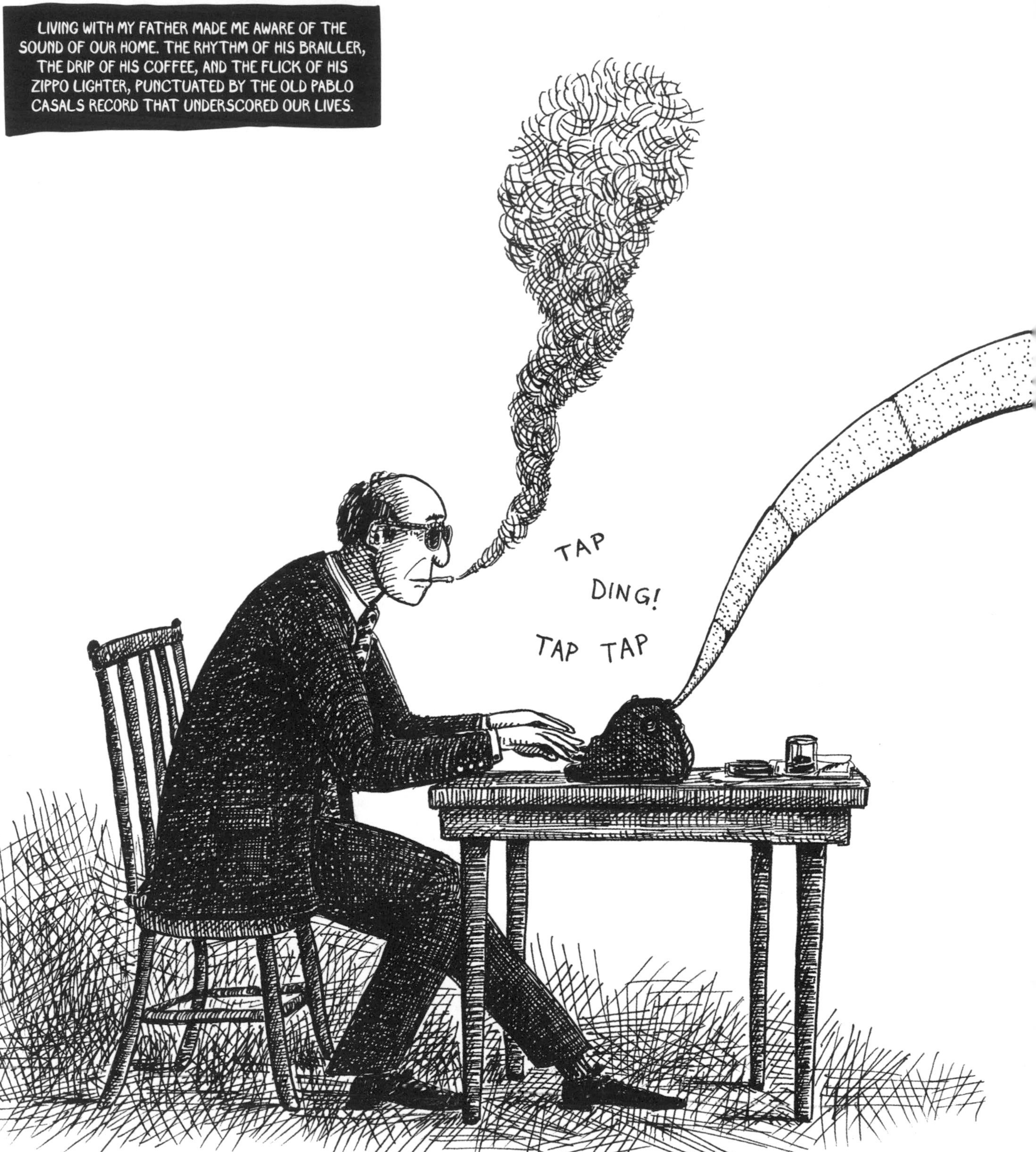
LIVING WITH MY FATHER MADE ME AWARE OF THE SOUND OF OUR HOME. THE RHYTHM OF HIS BRAILLER, THE DRIP OF HIS COFFEE, AND THE FLICK OF HIS ZIPPO LIGHTER, PUNCTUATED BY THE OLD PABLO CASALS RECORD THAT UNDERSCORED OUR LIVES.
TAP
DING!
TAP TAP

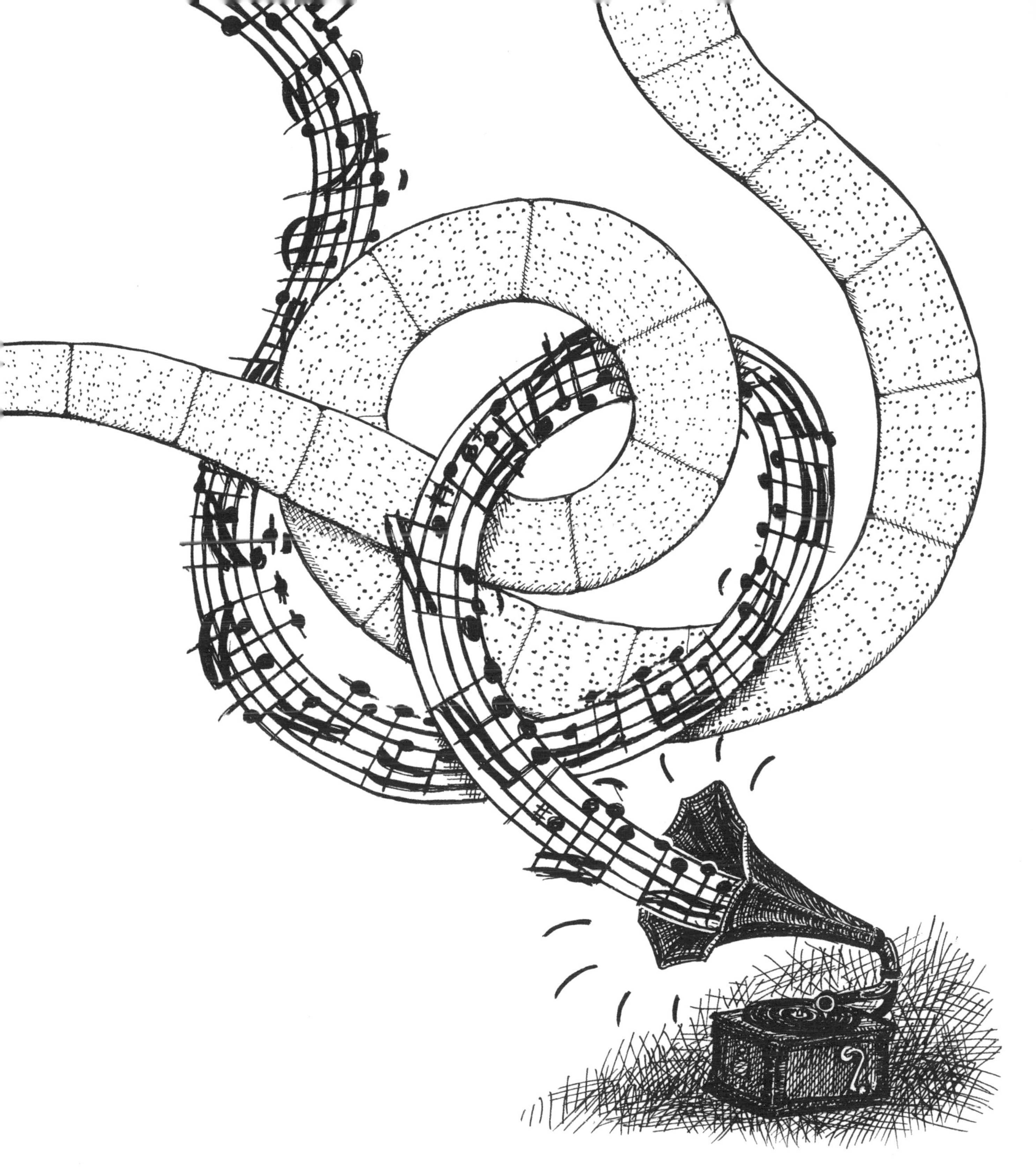

II

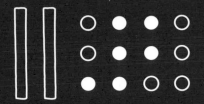

LITTLE ITALY

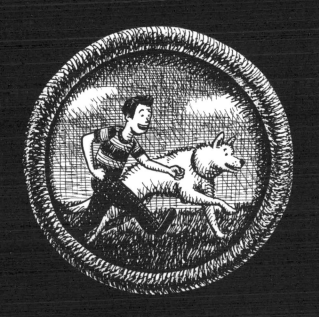

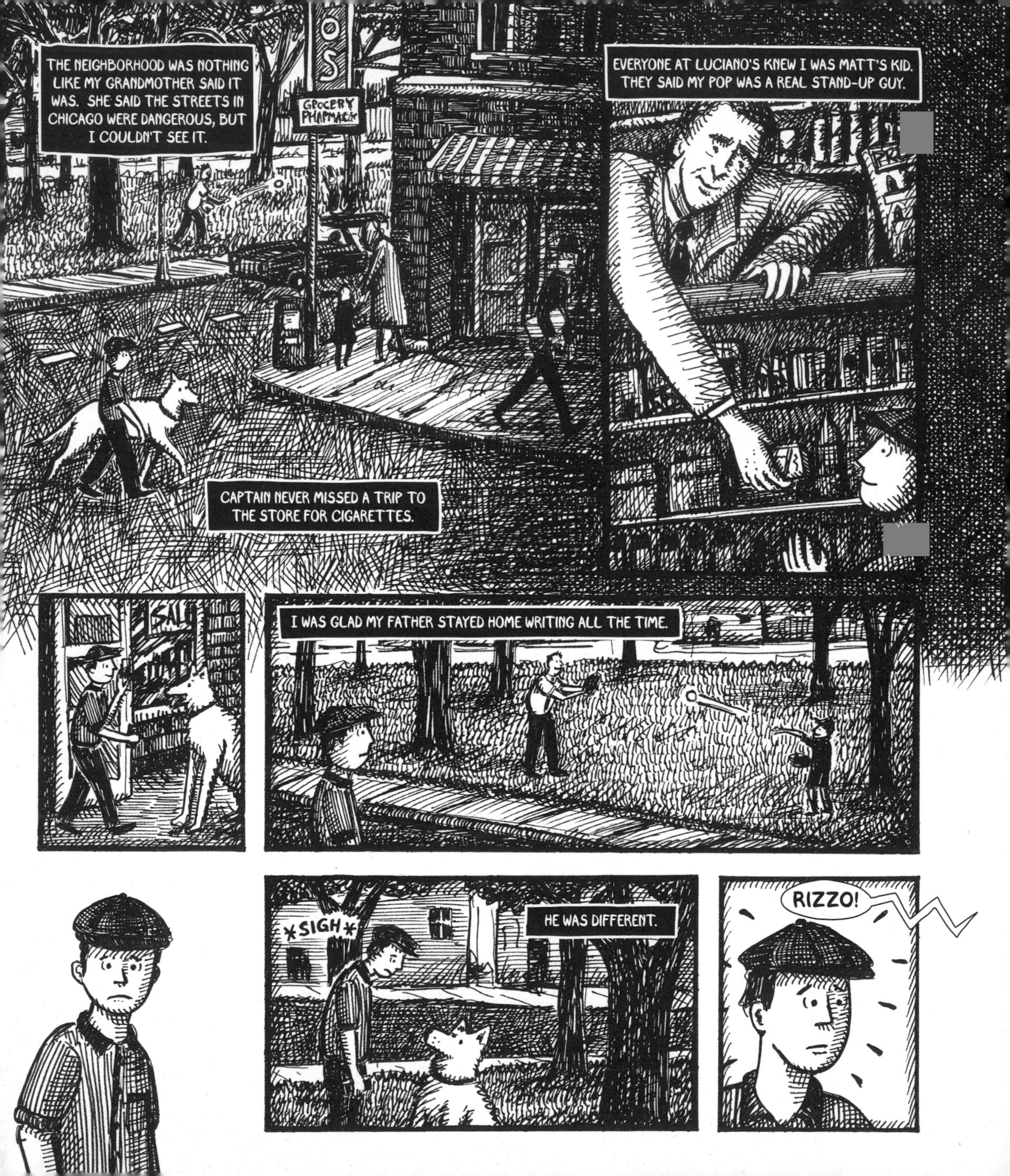
THE NEIGHBORHOOD WAS NOTHING LIKE MY GRANDMOTHER SAID IT WAS. SHE SAID THE STREETS IN CHICAGO WERE DANGEROUS, BUT I COULDN'T SEE IT.
GROCERY
CAPTAIN NEVER MISSED A TRIP TO THE STORE FOR CIGARETTES.
EVERYONE AT LUCIANO'S KNEW I WAS MATT'S KID. THEY SAID MY POP WAS A REAL STAND-UP GUY.
I WAS GLAD MY FATHER STAYED HOME WRITING ALL THE TIME.
SIGH
HE WAS DIFFERENT.
RIZZO!

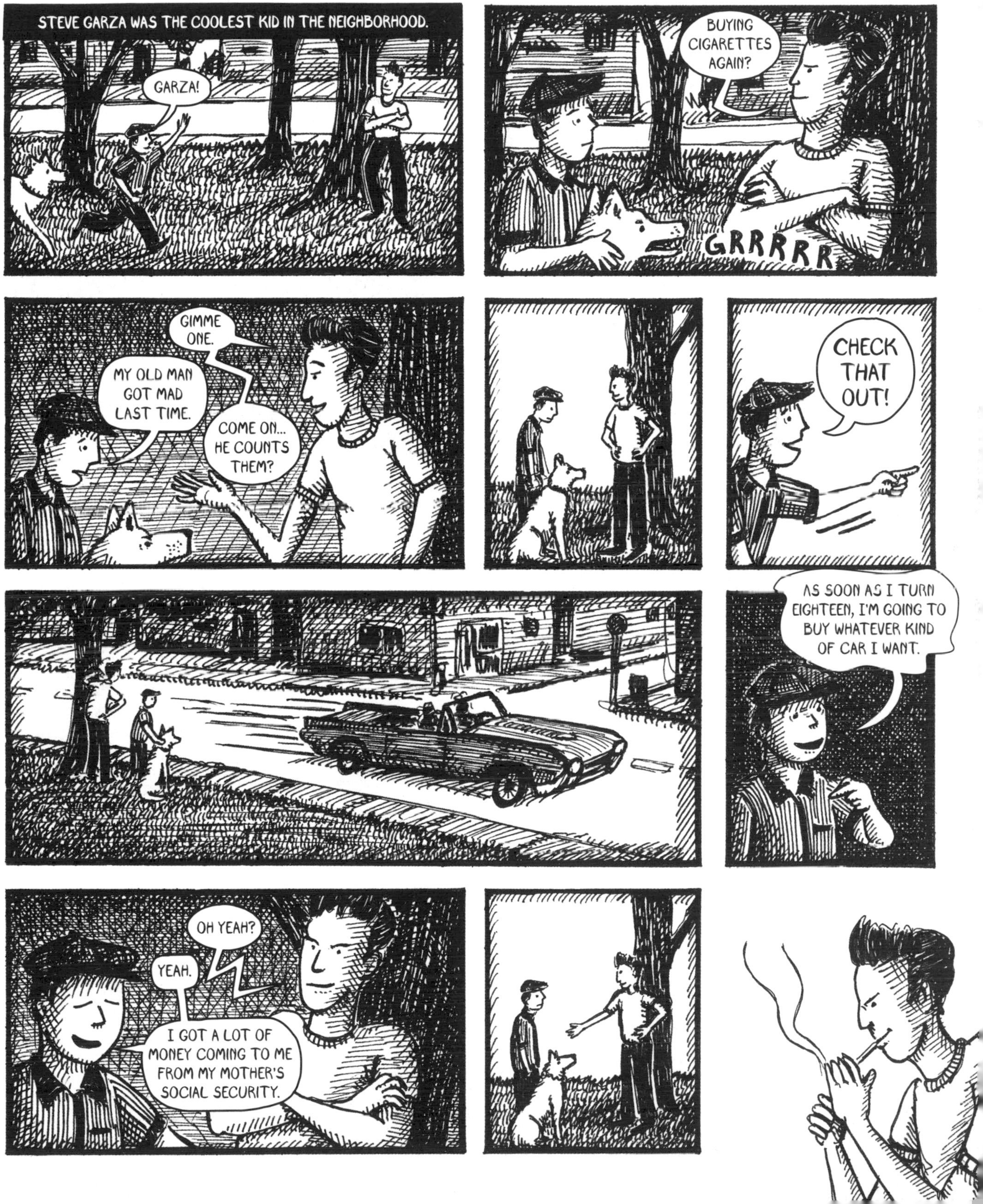
STEVE GARZA WAS THE COOLEST KID IN THE NEIGHBORHOOD.
GARZA!
BUYING CIGARETTES AGAIN?
GRRRRR
GIMME ONE.
MY OLD MAN GOT MAD LAST TIME.
COME ON... HE COUNTS THEM?
CHECK THAT OUT!
AS SOON AS I TURN EIGHTEEN, I'M GOING TO BUY WHATEVER KIND OF CAR I WANT.
OH YEAH?
YEAH.
I GOT A LOT OF MONEY COMING TO ME FROM MY MOTHER'S SOCIAL SECURITY.

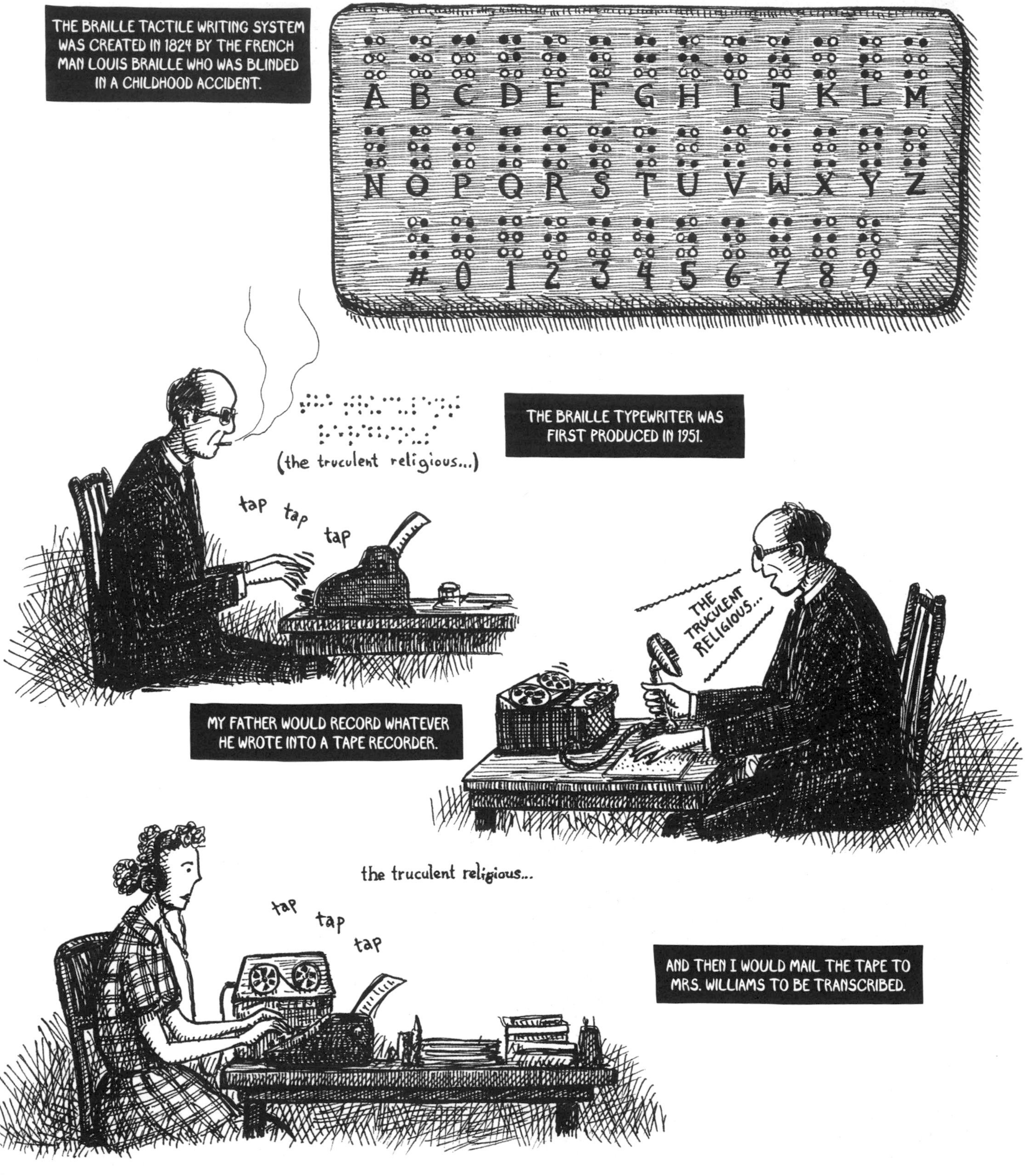
THE BRAILLE TACTILE WRITING SYSTEM WAS CREATED IN 1824 BY THE FRENCH MAN LOUIS BRAILLE WHO WAS BLINDED IN A CHILDHOOD ACCIDENT.
A B C D E F G H I J K L M
N O P Q R S T U V W X Y Z
0 1 2 3 4 5 6 7 8 9
THE BRAILLE TYPEWRITER WAS FIRST PRODUCED IN 1951.
(the truculent religious...)
tap tap tap
THE TRUCULENT RELIGIOUS...
MY FATHER WOULD RECORD WHATEVER HE WROTE INTO A TAPE RECORDER.
the truculent religious...
tap tap tap
AND THEN I WOULD MAIL THE TAPE TO MRS. WILLIAMS TO BE TRANSCRIBED.

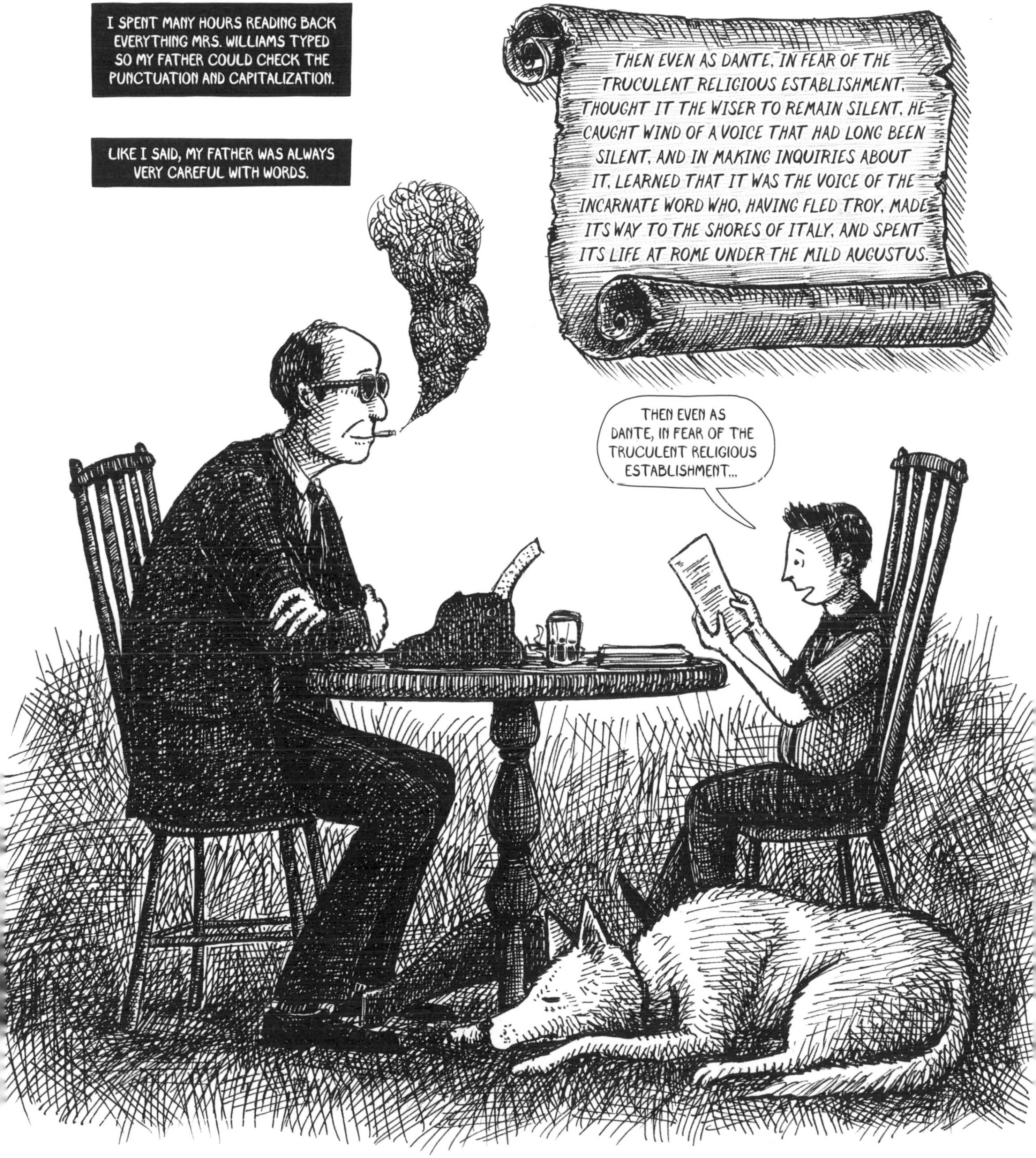
I SPENT MANY HOURS READING BACK EVERYTHING MRS. WILLIAMS TYPED SO MY FATHER COULD CHECK THE PUNCTUATION AND CAPITALIZATION.
LIKE I SAID, MY FATHER WAS ALWAYS VERY CAREFUL WITH WORDS.
THEN EVEN AS DANTE, IN FEAR OF THE TRUCULENT RELIGIOUS ESTABLISHMENT, THOUGHT IT THE WISER TO REMAIN SILENT, HE CAUGHT WIND OF A VOICE THAT HAD LONG BEEN SILENT, AND IN MAKING INQUIRIES ABOUT IT, LEARNED THAT IT WAS THE VOICE OF THE INCARNATE WORD WHO, HAVING FLED TROY, MADE ITS WAY TO THE SHORES OF ITALY, AND SPENT ITS LIFE AT ROME UNDER THE MILD AUGUSTUS.
THEN EVEN AS DANTE, IN FEAR OF THE TRUCULENT RELIGIOUS ESTABLISHMENT...

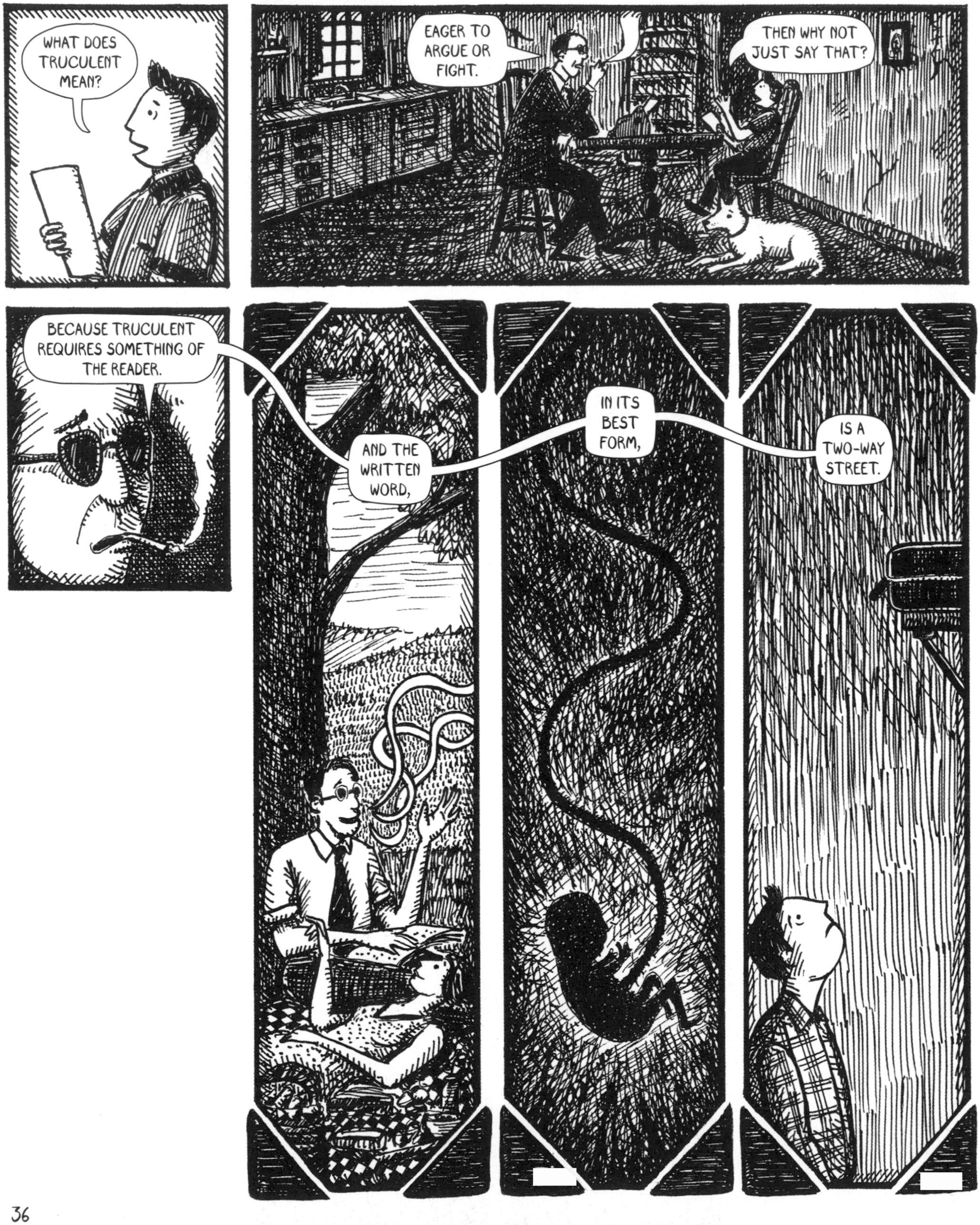
WHAT DOES TRUCULENT MEAN?
EAGER TO ARGUE OR FIGHT.
THEN WHY NOT JUST SAY THAT?
BECAUSE TRUCULENT REQUIRES SOMETHING OF THE READER.
AND THE WRITTEN WORD,
IN ITS BEST FORM,
IS A TWO-WAY STREET.

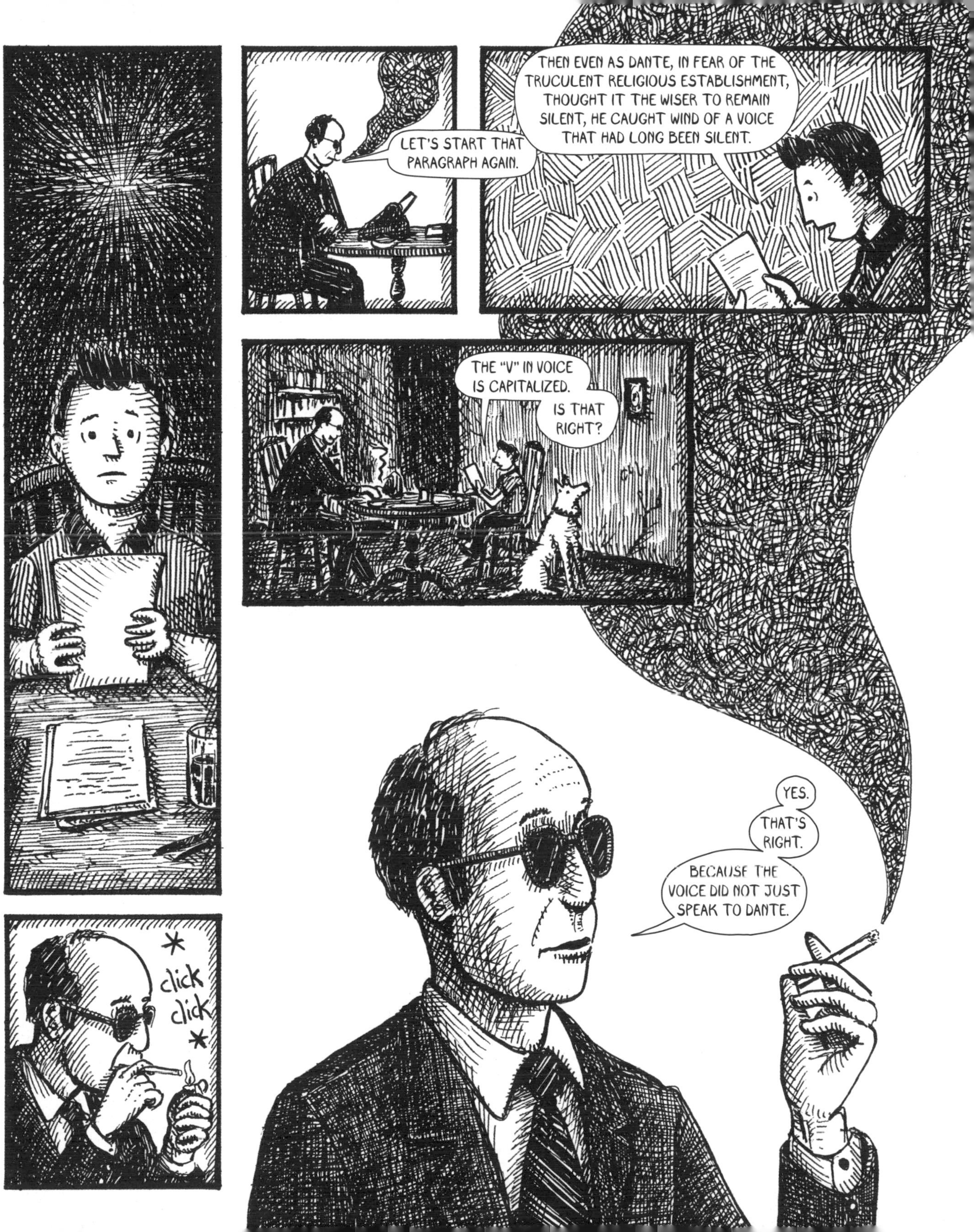
LET'S START THAT PARAGRAPH AGAIN.
THEN EVEN AS DANTE, IN FEAR OF THE TRUCULENT RELIGIOUS ESTABLISHMENT, THOUGHT IT THE WISER TO REMAIN SILENT, HE CAUGHT WIND OF A VOICE THAT HAD LONG BEEN SILENT.
THE "V" IN VOICE IS CAPITALIZED.
IS THAT RIGHT?
* click click *
YES.
THAT'S RIGHT.
BECAUSE THE VOICE DID NOT JUST SPEAK TO DANTE.

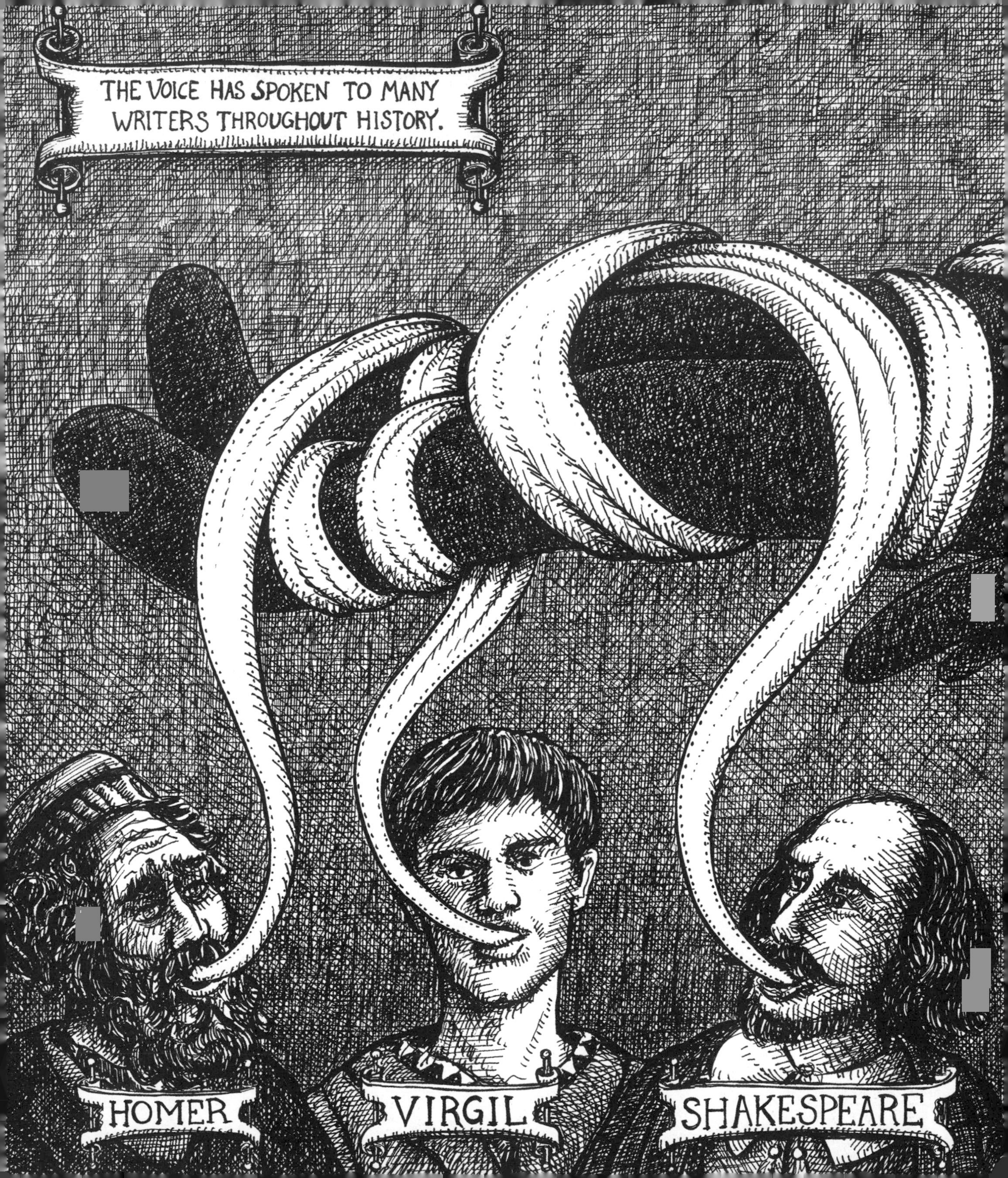
THE VOICE HAS SPOKEN TO MANY WRITERS THROUGHOUT HISTORY.
HOMER
VIRGIL
SHAKESPEARE

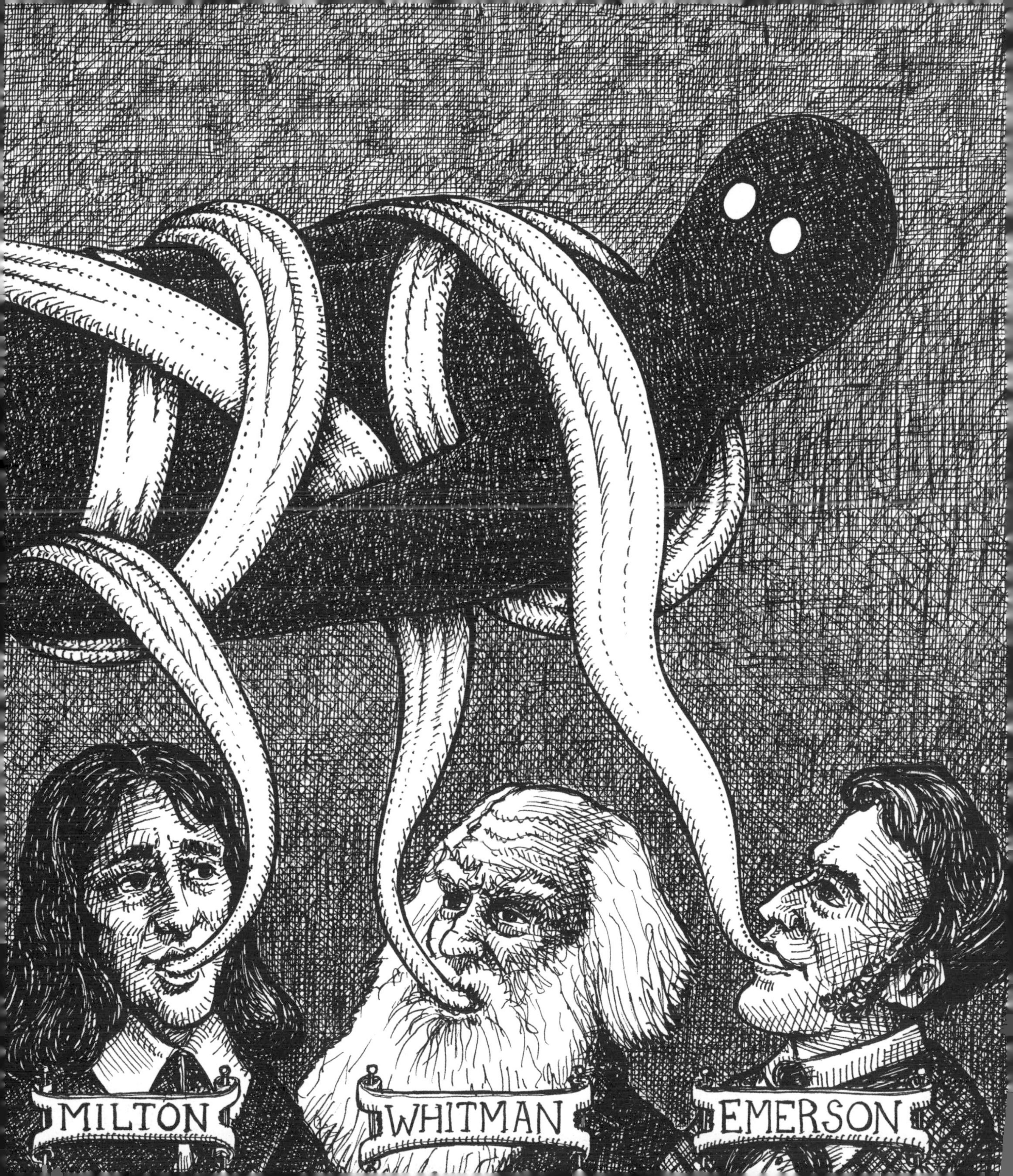
MILTON
WHITMAN
EMERSON

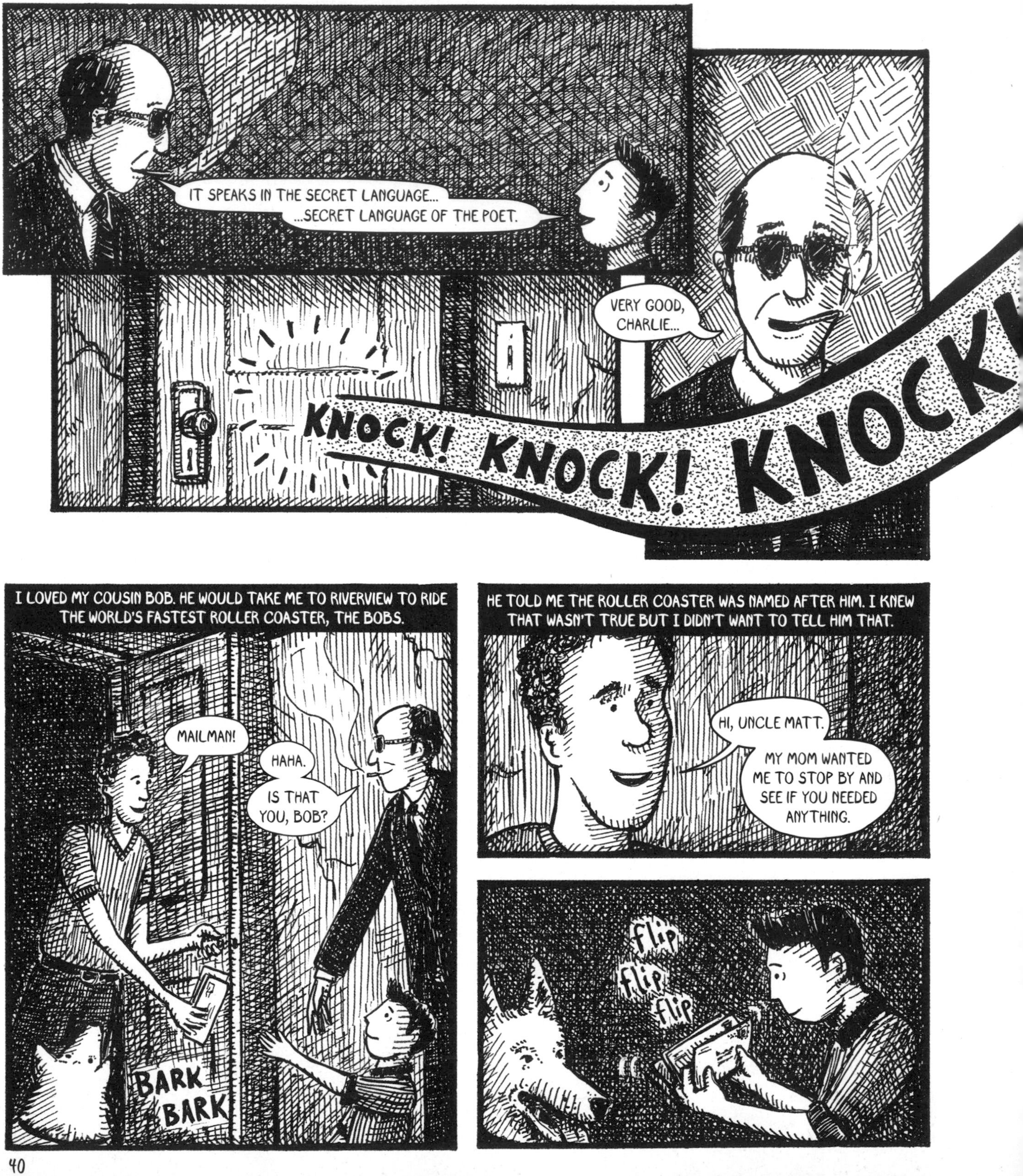
IT SPEAKS IN THE SECRET LANGUAGE...
...SECRET LANGUAGE OF THE POET.
VERY GOOD, CHARLIE...
KNOCK! KNOCK! KNOCK!
I LOVED MY COUSIN BOB. HE WOULD TAKE ME TO RIVERVIEW TO RIDE THE WORLD'S FASTEST ROLLER COASTER, THE BOBS.
MAILMAN!
HAHA.
IS THAT YOU, BOB?
BARK BARK
HE TOLD ME THE ROLLER COASTER WAS NAMED AFTER HIM. I KNEW THAT WASN'T TRUE BUT I DIDN'T WANT TO TELL HIM THAT.
HI, UNCLE MATT.
MY MOM WANTED ME TO STOP BY AND SEE IF YOU NEEDED ANYTHING.
flip flip flip

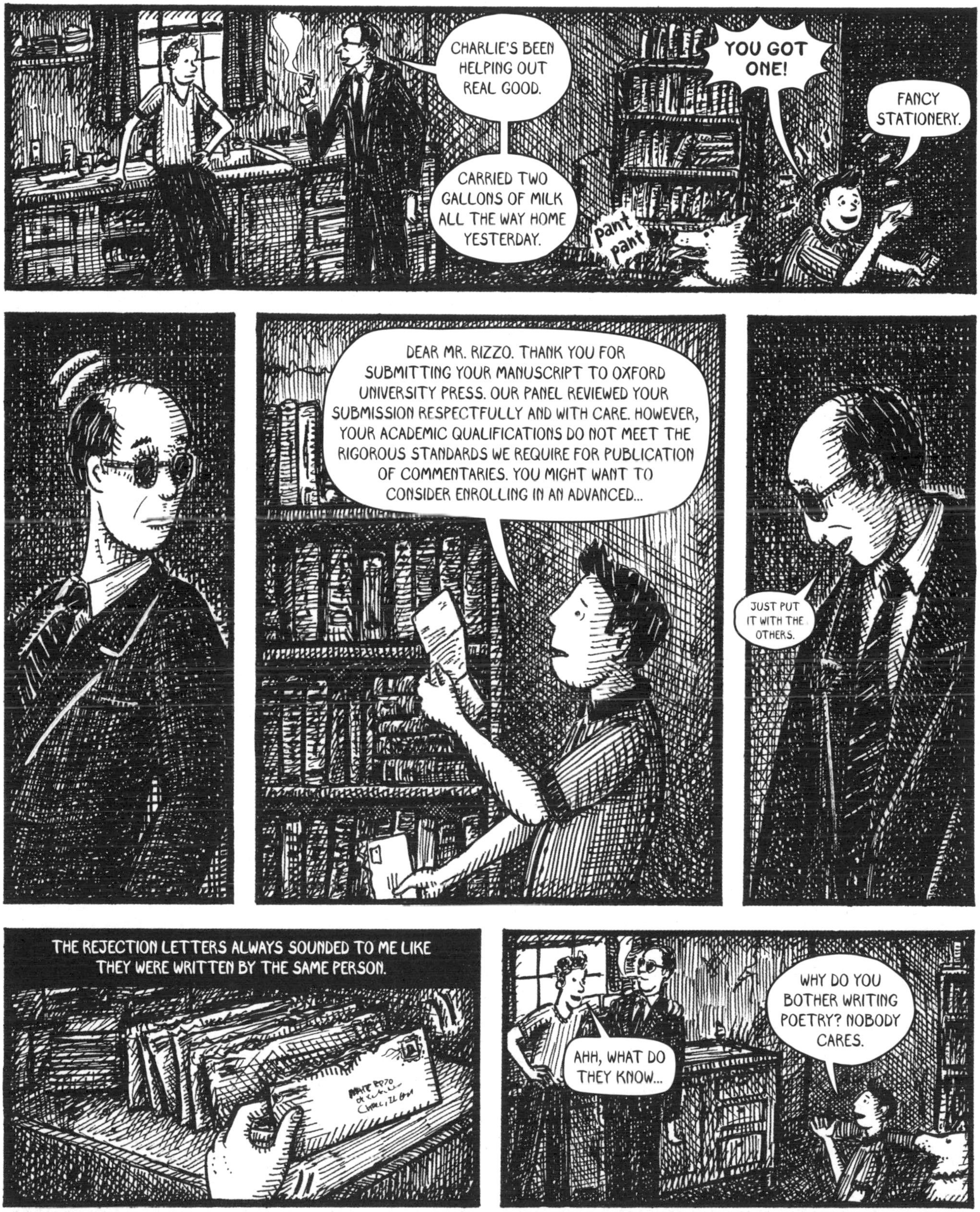
CHARLIE'S BEEN HELPING OUT REAL GOOD.
CARRIED TWO GALLONS OF MILK ALL THE WAY HOME YESTERDAY.
pant pant
YOU GOT ONE!
FANCY STATIONERY.
DEAR MR. RIZZO. THANK YOU FOR SUBMITTING YOUR MANUSCRIPT TO OXFORD UNIVERSITY PRESS. OUR PANEL REVIEWED YOUR SUBMISSION RESPECTFULLY AND WITH CARE. HOWEVER, YOUR ACADEMIC QUALIFICATIONS DO NOT MEET THE RIGOROUS STANDARDS WE REQUIRE FOR PUBLICATION OF COMMENTARIES. YOU MIGHT WANT TO CONSIDER ENROLLING IN AN ADVANCED...
JUST PUT IT WITH THE OTHERS.
THE REJECTION LETTERS ALWAYS SOUNDED TO ME LIKE THEY WERE WRITTEN BY THE SAME PERSON.
WHY DO YOU BOTHER WRITING POETRY? NOBODY CARES.
AHH, WHAT DO THEY KNOW...

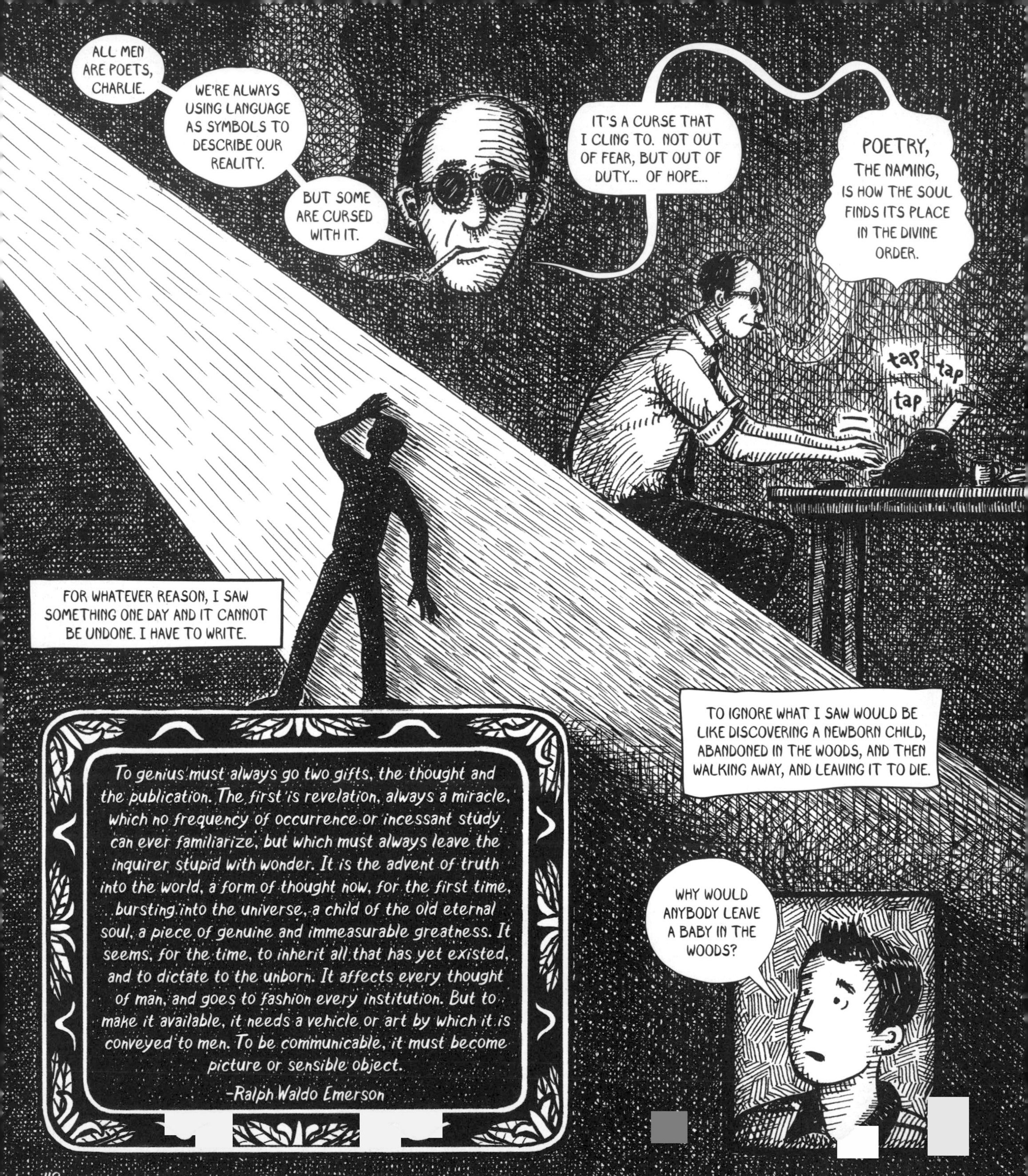
ALL MEN ARE POETS, CHARLIE.
WE'RE ALWAYS USING LANGUAGE AS SYMBOLS TO DESCRIBE OUR REALITY.
BUT SOME ARE CURSED WITH IT.
IT'S A CURSE THAT I CLING TO. NOT OUT OF FEAR, BUT OUT OF DUTY... OF HOPE...
POETRY, THE NAMING, IS HOW THE SOUL FINDS ITS PLACE IN THE DIVINE ORDER.
tap tap tap
FOR WHATEVER REASON, I SAW SOMETHING ONE DAY AND IT CANNOT BE UNDONE. I HAVE TO WRITE.
TO IGNORE WHAT I SAW WOULD BE LIKE DISCOVERING A NEWBORN CHILD, ABANDONED IN THE WOODS, AND THEN WALKING AWAY, AND LEAVING IT TO DIE.
To genius must always go two gifts, the thought and the publication. The first is revelation, always a miracle, which no frequency of occurrence or incessant study can ever familiarize, but which must always leave the inquirer stupid with wonder. It is the advent of truth into the world, a form of thought now, for the first time, bursting into the universe, a child of the old eternal soul, a piece of genuine and immeasurable greatness. It seems, for the time, to inherit all that has yet existed, and to dictate to the unborn. It affects every thought of man, and goes to fashion every institution. But to make it available, it needs a vehicle or art by which it is conveyed to men. To be communicable, it must become picture or sensible object.
–Ralph Waldo Emerson
WHY WOULD ANYBODY LEAVE A BABY IN THE WOODS?

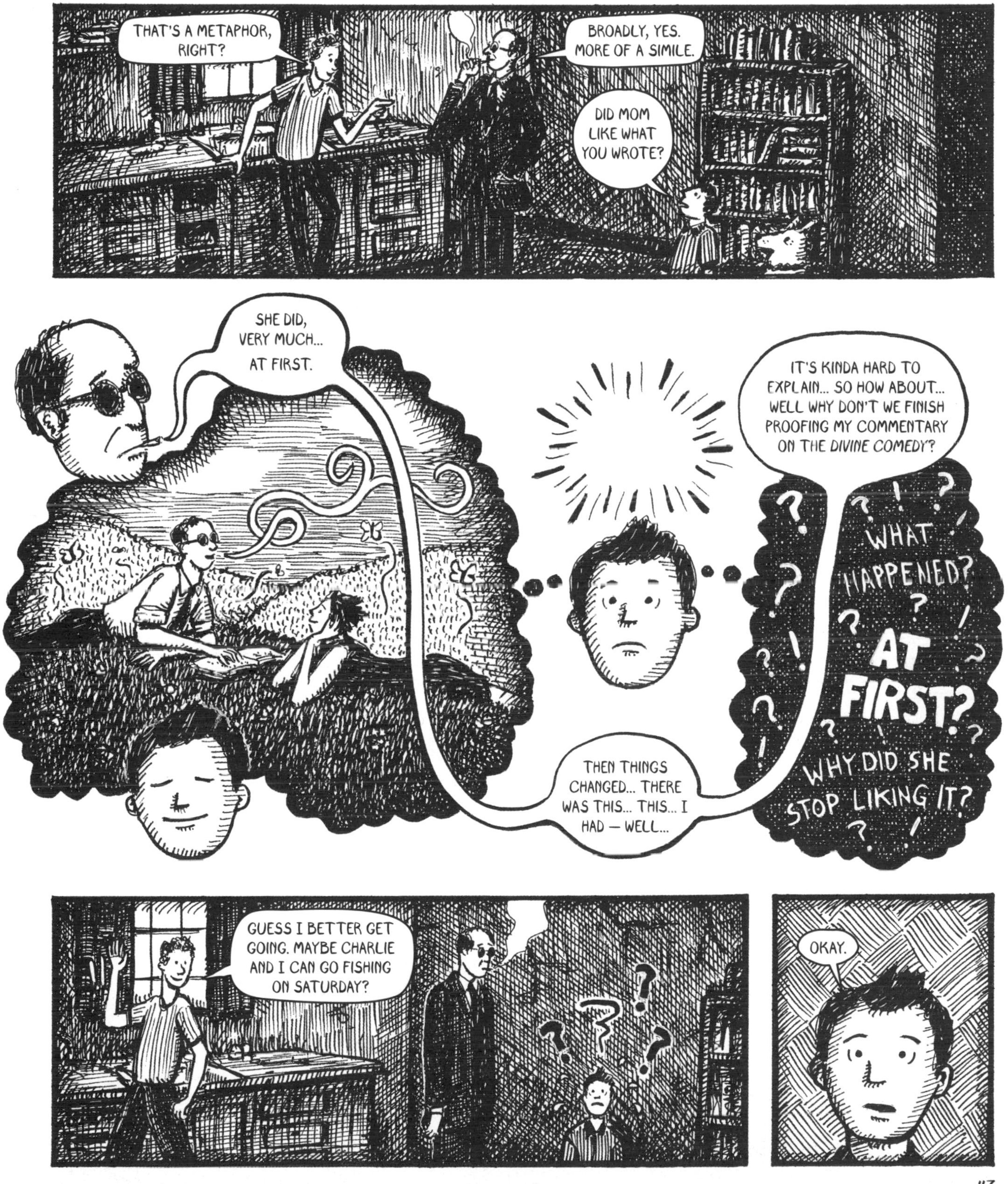

THAT'S A METAPHOR, RIGHT?
BROADLY, YES. MORE OF A SIMILE.
DID MOM LIKE WHAT YOU WROTE?
SHE DID, VERY MUCH... AT FIRST.
IT'S KINDA HARD TO EXPLAIN... SO HOW ABOUT... WELL WHY DON'T WE FINISH PROOFING MY COMMENTARY ON THE *DIVINE COMEDY*?
THEN THINGS CHANGED... THERE WAS THIS... THIS... I HAD — WELL...
WHAT HAPPENED? AT FIRST? WHY DID SHE STOP LIKING IT?
GUESS I BETTER GET GOING. MAYBE CHARLIE AND I CAN GO FISHING ON SATURDAY?
OKAY.

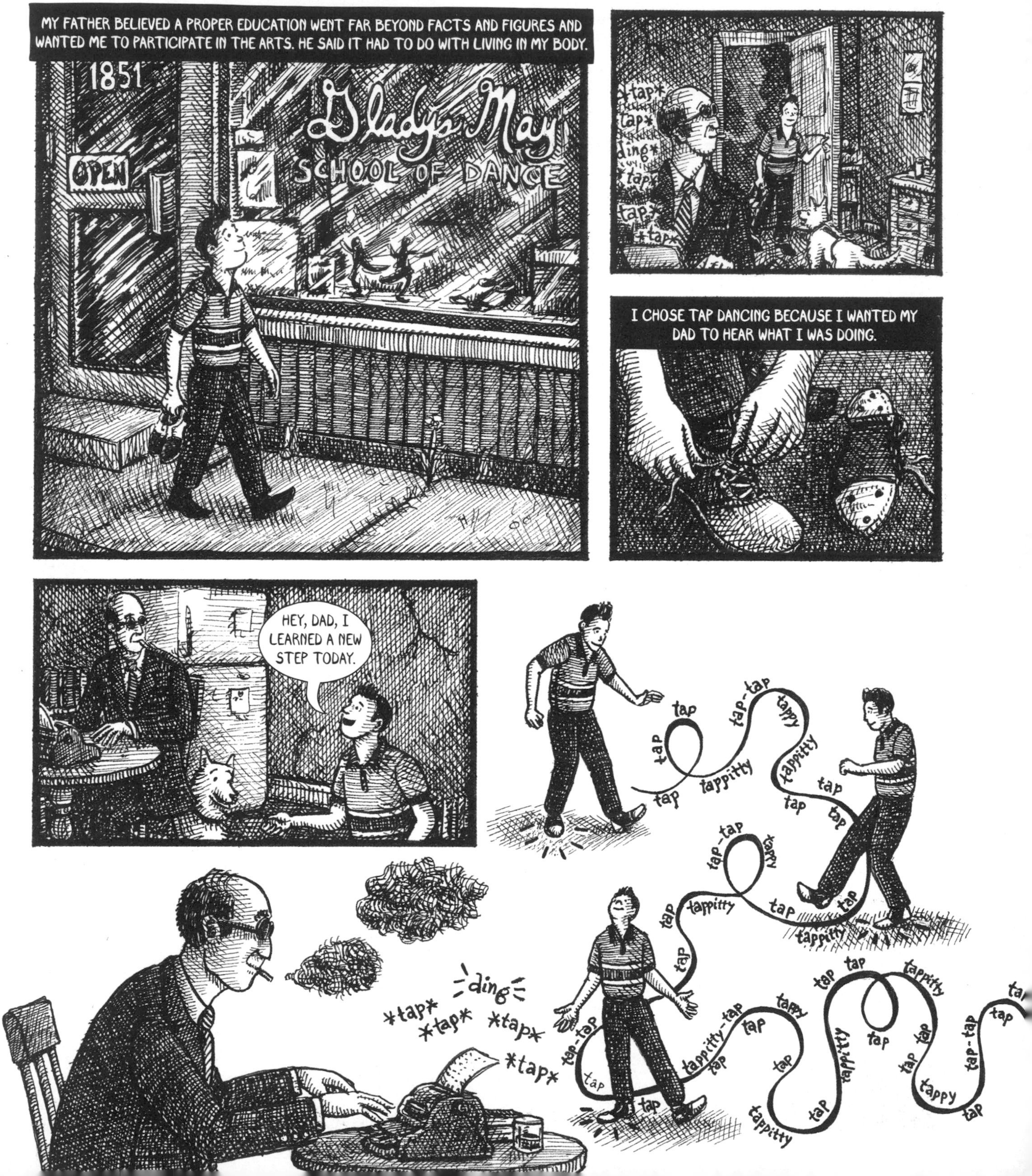
MY FATHER BELIEVED A PROPER EDUCATION WENT FAR BEYOND FACTS AND FIGURES AND WANTED ME TO PARTICIPATE IN THE ARTS. HE SAID IT HAD TO DO WITH LIVING IN MY BODY.
1851
OPEN
Gladys May
SCHOOL OF DANCE
tap
tap*
ding*
tap
tap*
tap
I CHOSE TAP DANCING BECAUSE I WANTED MY DAD TO HEAR WHAT I WAS DOING.
HEY, DAD, I LEARNED A NEW STEP TODAY.
tap
tap
tap
tappitty
tap-tap
tappy
tappitty
tap
tap
tap
tap-tap
tappy
tap
tappitty
tap
tap
tappitty
ding
tap
tap
tap
tap
tap-tap
tap
tap
tappitty-tap
tap
tappy
tap
tappitty
tap
tappitty
tap
tap
tappitty
tap
tap
tap
tappy
tap-tap
tap
tap

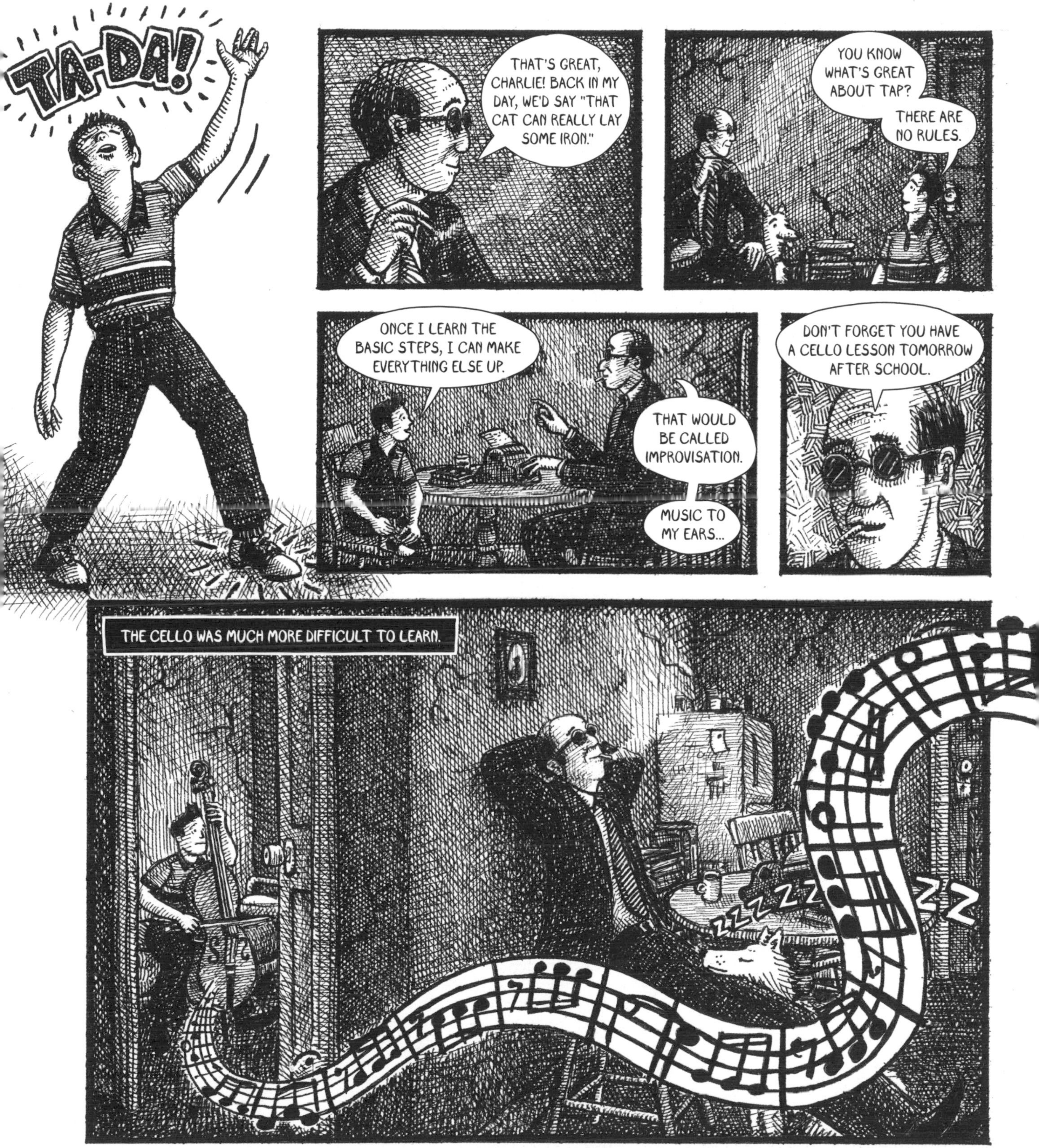
TA-DA!
THAT'S GREAT, CHARLIE! BACK IN MY DAY, WE'D SAY "THAT CAT CAN REALLY LAY SOME IRON."
YOU KNOW WHAT'S GREAT ABOUT TAP?
THERE ARE NO RULES.
ONCE I LEARN THE BASIC STEPS, I CAN MAKE EVERYTHING ELSE UP.
THAT WOULD BE CALLED IMPROVISATION.
MUSIC TO MY EARS...
DON'T FORGET YOU HAVE A CELLO LESSON TOMORROW AFTER SCHOOL.
THE CELLO WAS MUCH MORE DIFFICULT TO LEARN.
ZZZZZZ ZZ

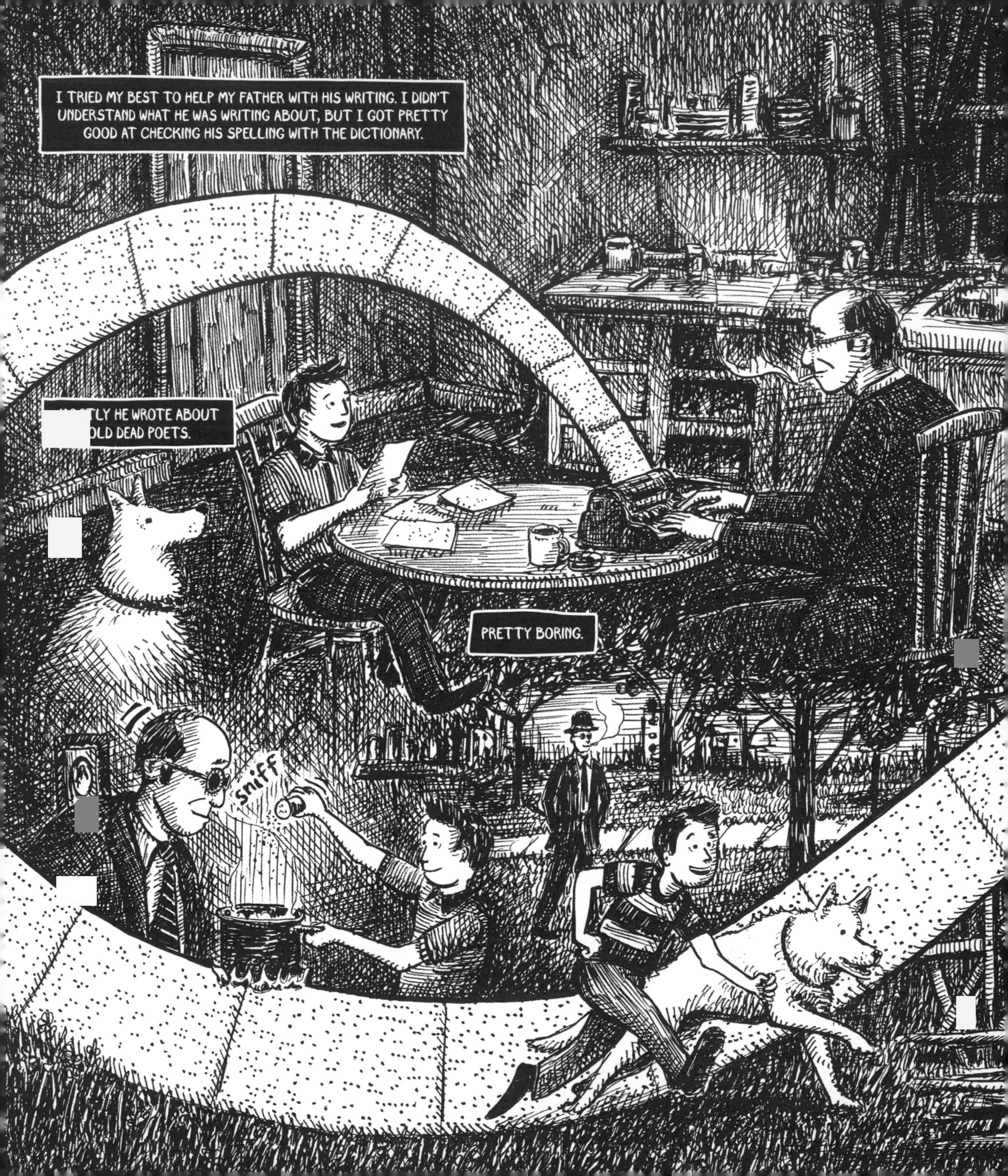
I TRIED MY BEST TO HELP MY FATHER WITH HIS WRITING. I DIDN'T UNDERSTAND WHAT HE WAS WRITING ABOUT, BUT I GOT PRETTY GOOD AT CHECKING HIS SPELLING WITH THE DICTIONARY.
TLY HE WROTE ABOUT OLD DEAD POETS.
PRETTY BORING.
Sniff

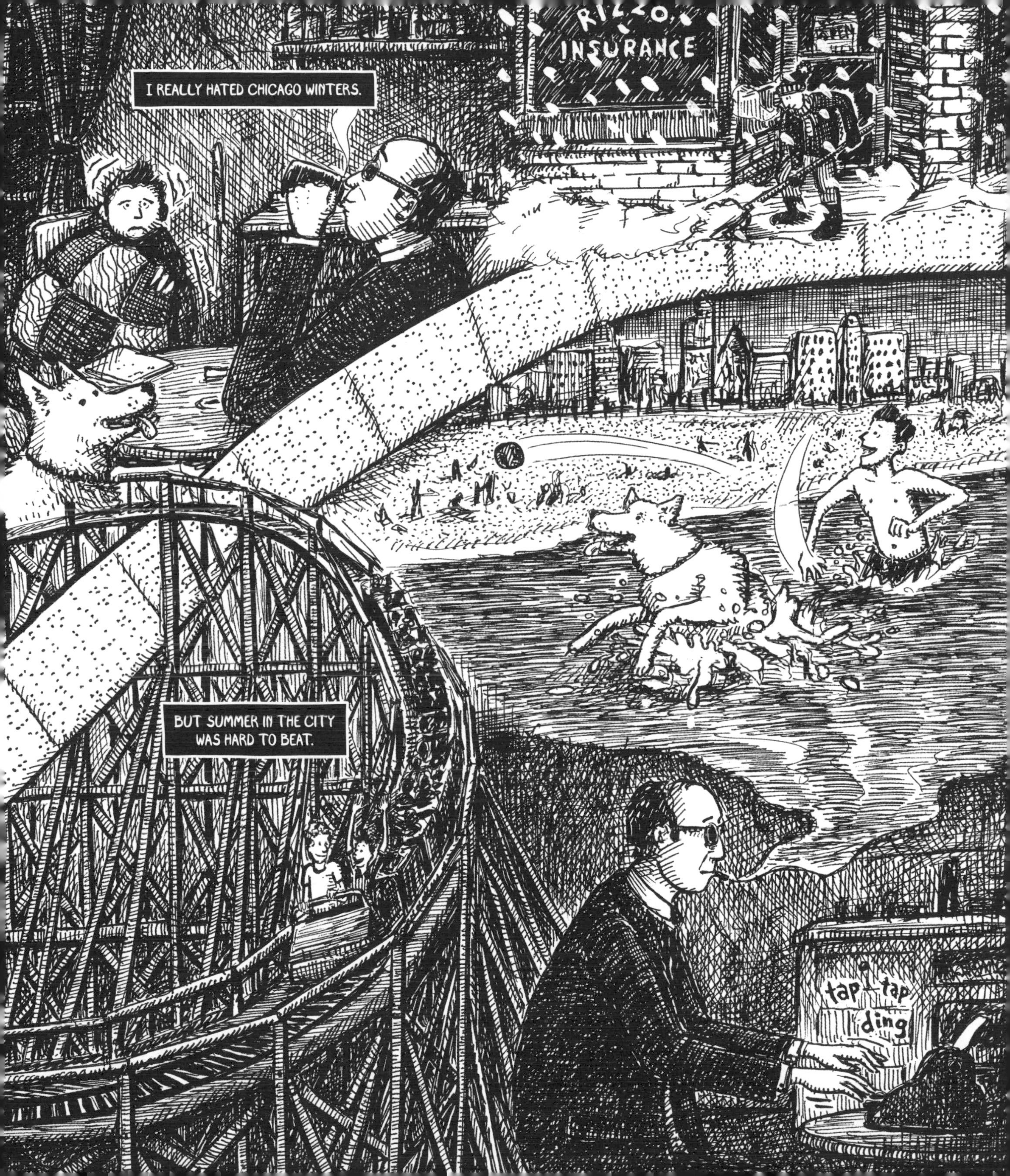
RIZZO
INSURANCE
I REALLY HATED CHICAGO WINTERS.
BUT SUMMER IN THE CITY WAS HARD TO BEAT.
tap tap
ding

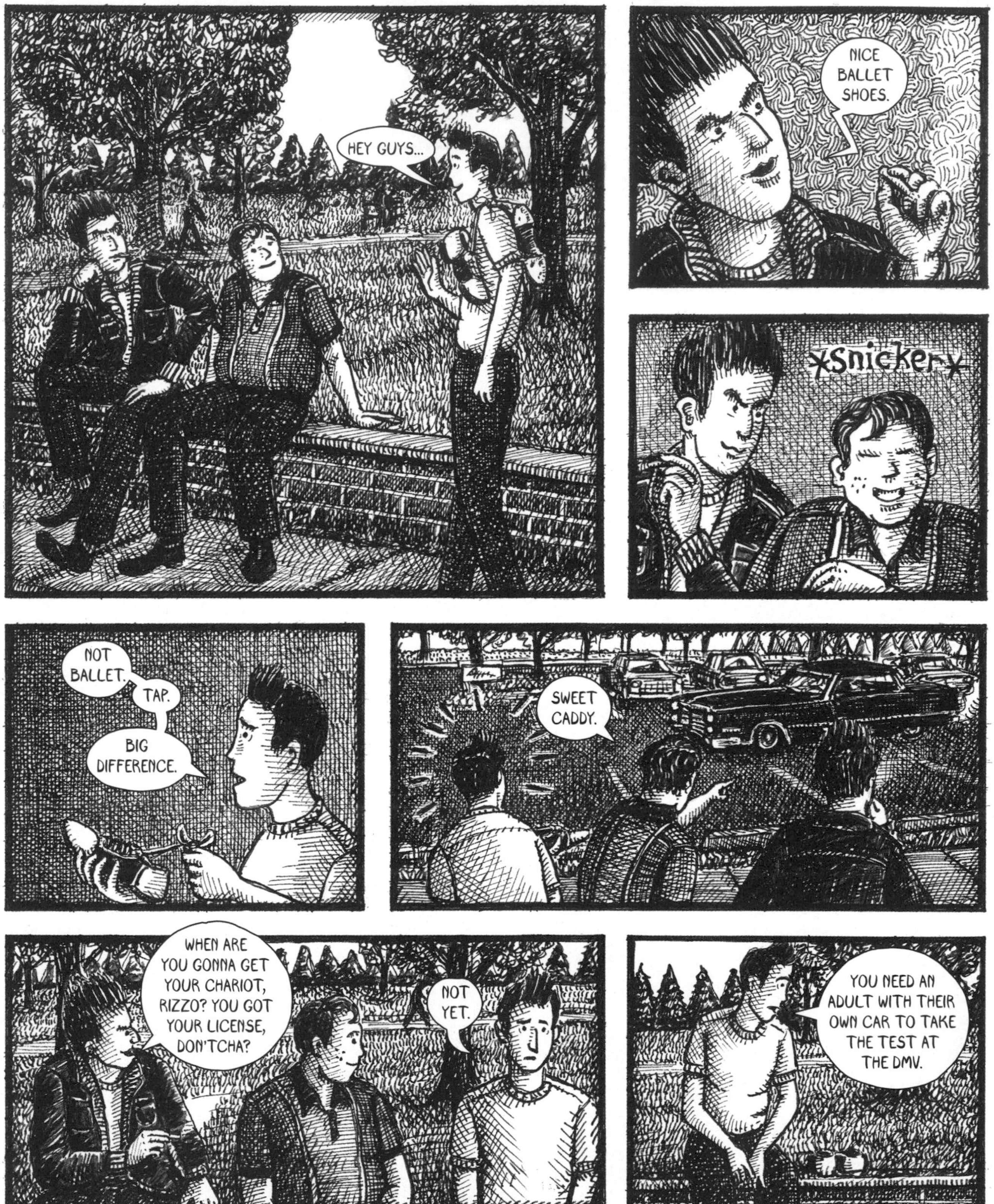
HEY GUYS...
NICE BALLET SHOES.
Snicker
NOT BALLET.
TAP.
BIG DIFFERENCE.
SWEET CADDY.
WHEN ARE YOU GONNA GET YOUR CHARIOT, RIZZO? YOU GOT YOUR LICENSE, DON'TCHA?
NOT YET.
YOU NEED AN ADULT WITH THEIR OWN CAR TO TAKE THE TEST AT THE DMV.

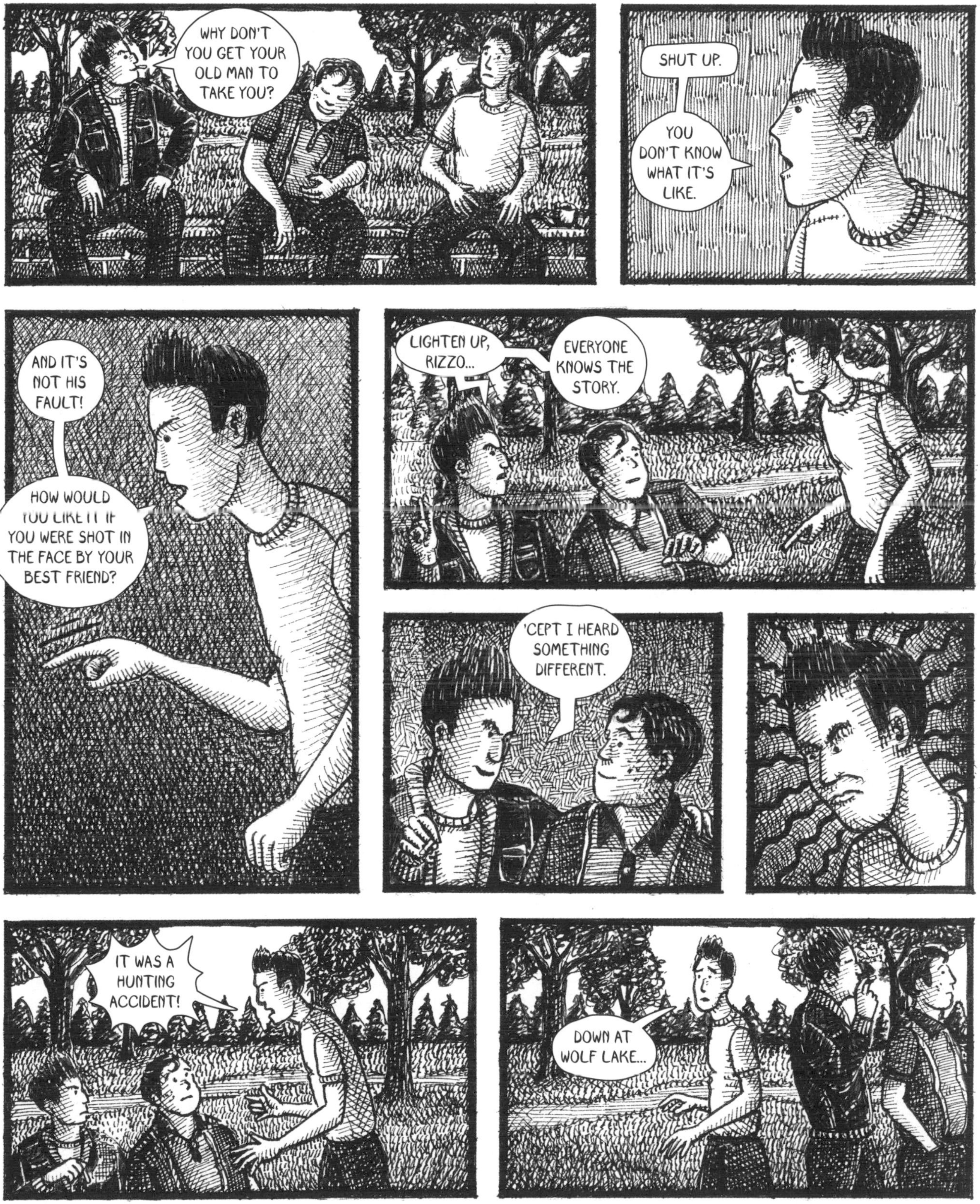
WHY DON'T YOU GET YOUR OLD MAN TO TAKE YOU?
SHUT UP.
YOU DON'T KNOW WHAT IT'S LIKE.
AND IT'S NOT HIS FAULT!
HOW WOULD YOU LIKE IT IF YOU WERE SHOT IN THE FACE BY YOUR BEST FRIEND?
LIGHTEN UP, RIZZO...
EVERYONE KNOWS THE STORY.
'CEPT I HEARD SOMETHING DIFFERENT.
IT WAS A HUNTING ACCIDENT!
DOWN AT WOLF LAKE...

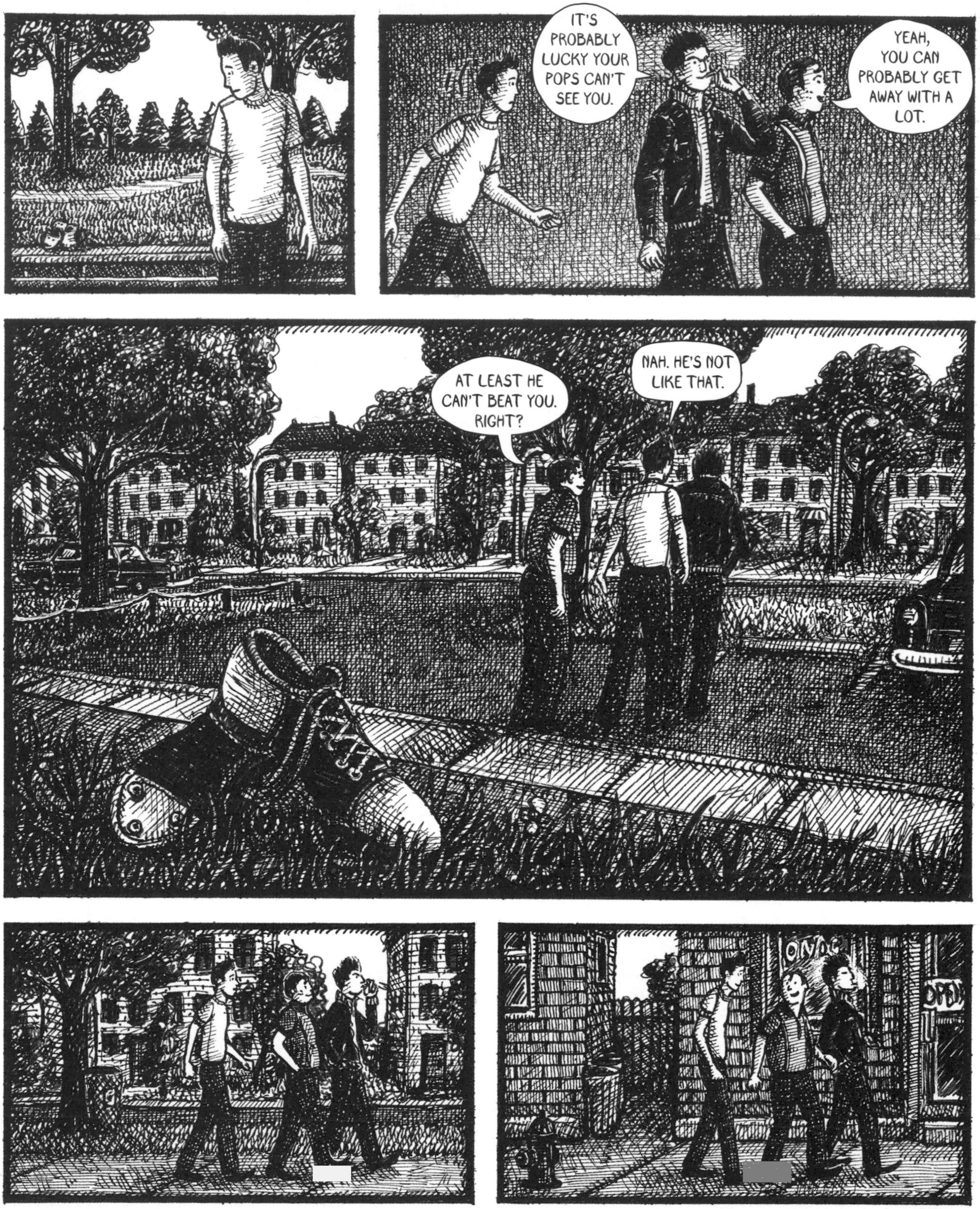
IT'S PROBABLY LUCKY YOUR POPS CAN'T SEE YOU.
YEAH, YOU CAN PROBABLY GET AWAY WITH A LOT.
AT LEAST HE CAN'T BEAT YOU. RIGHT?
NAH. HE'S NOT LIKE THAT.
OPEN

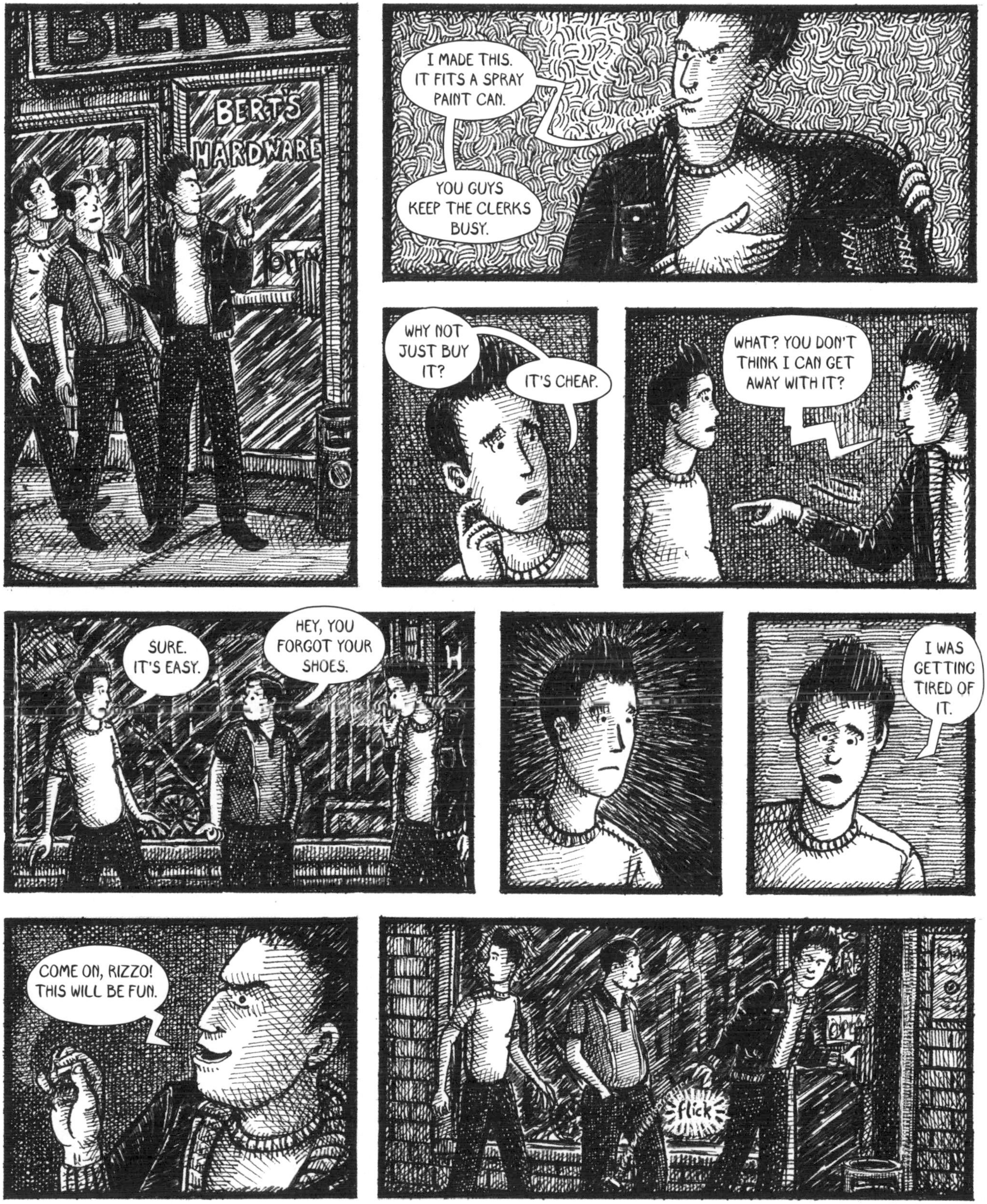
BERT'S
HARDWARE
OPEN
I MADE THIS. IT FITS A SPRAY PAINT CAN.
YOU GUYS KEEP THE CLERKS BUSY.
WHY NOT JUST BUY IT?
IT'S CHEAP.
WHAT? YOU DON'T THINK I CAN GET AWAY WITH IT?
SURE. IT'S EASY.
HEY, YOU FORGOT YOUR SHOES.
I WAS GETTING TIRED OF IT.
COME ON, RIZZO! THIS WILL BE FUN.
flick

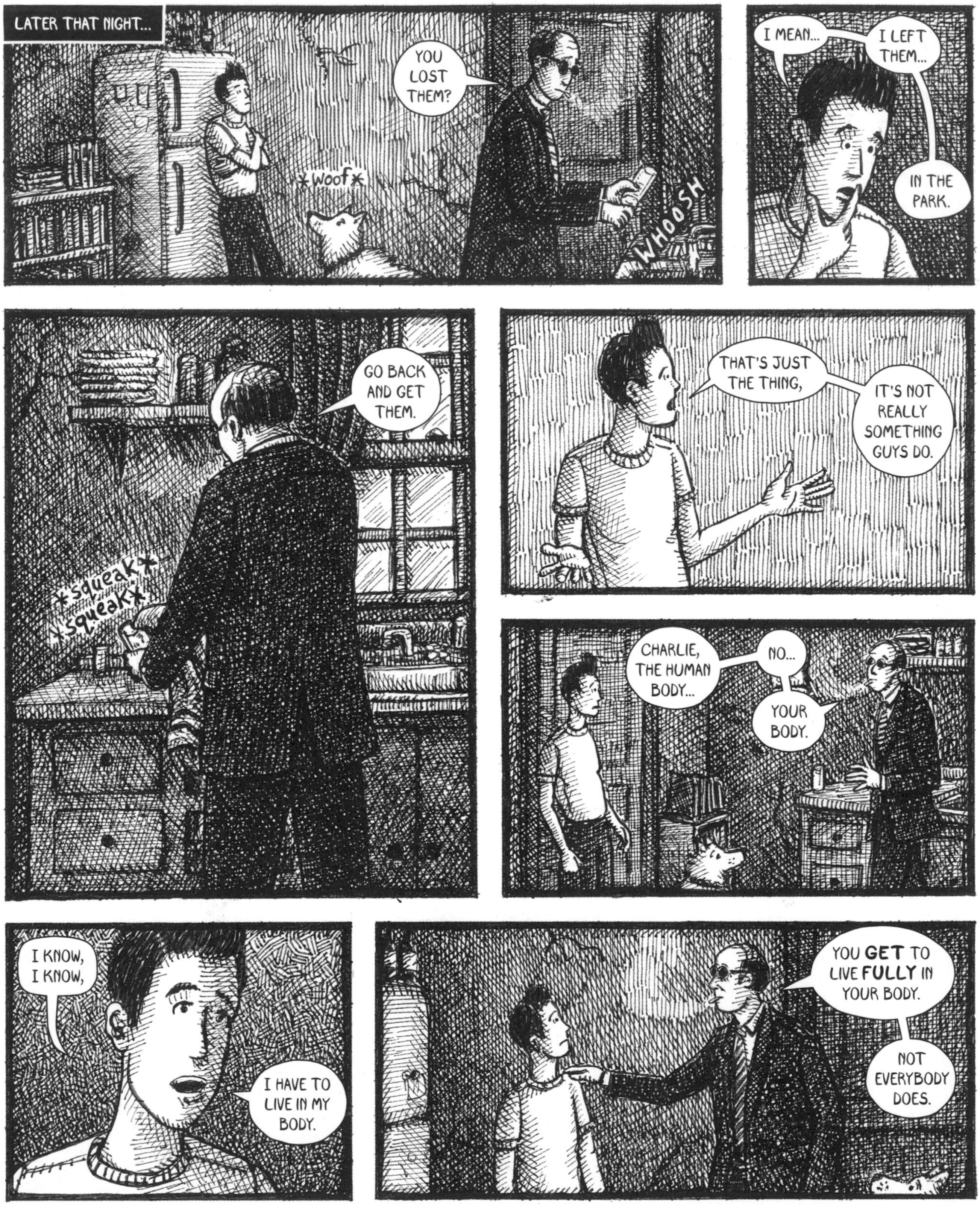

LATER THAT NIGHT...
YOU LOST THEM?
woof
WHOOSH
I MEAN...
I LEFT THEM...
IN THE PARK.
GO BACK AND GET THEM.
squeak
squeak
THAT'S JUST THE THING,
IT'S NOT REALLY SOMETHING GUYS DO.
CHARLIE, THE HUMAN BODY...
NO...
YOUR BODY.
I KNOW, I KNOW,
I HAVE TO LIVE IN MY BODY.
YOU **GET** TO LIVE **FULLY** IN YOUR BODY.
NOT EVERYBODY DOES.

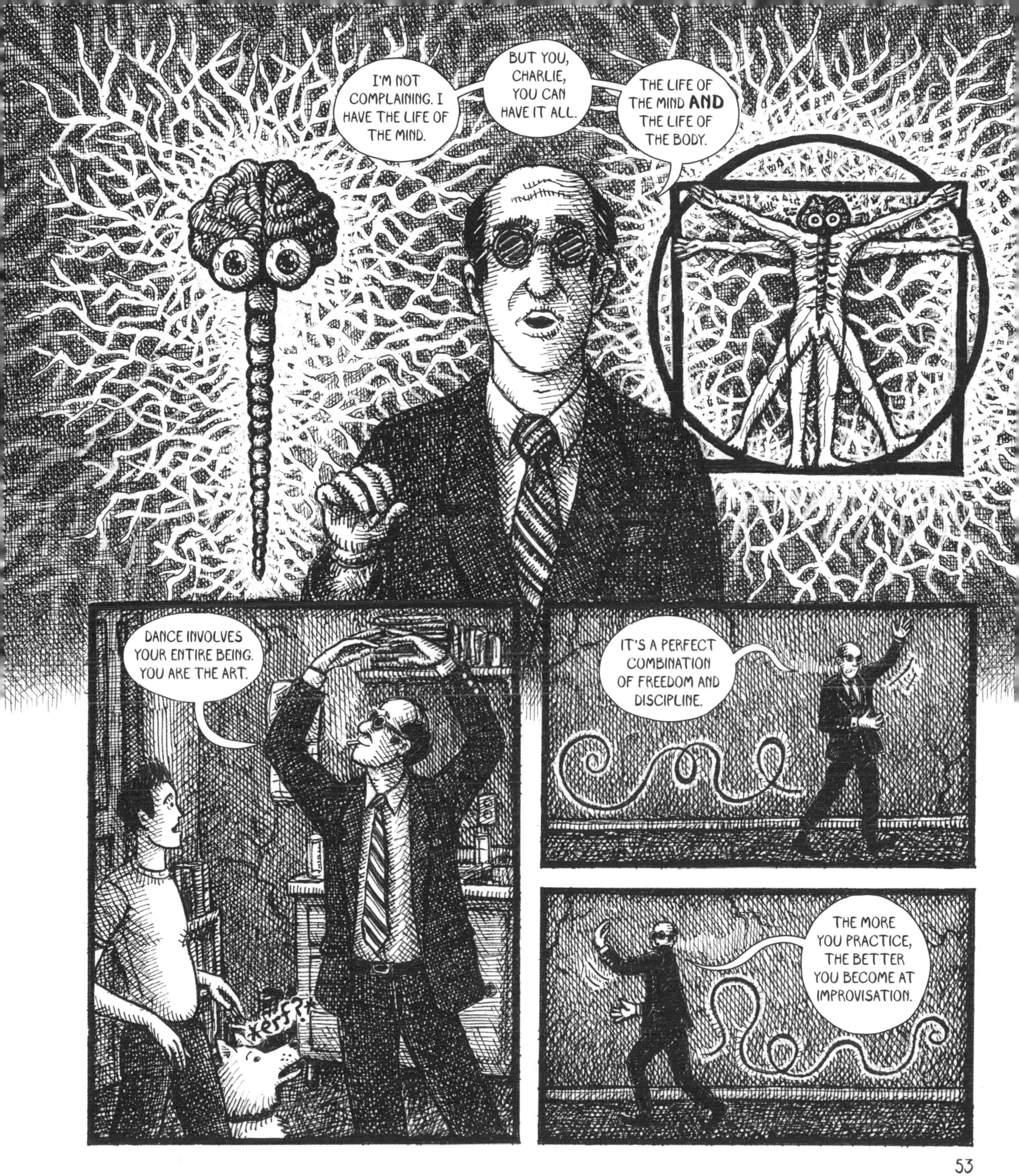
I'M NOT COMPLAINING. I HAVE THE LIFE OF THE MIND.
BUT YOU, CHARLIE, YOU CAN HAVE IT ALL.
THE LIFE OF THE MIND **AND** THE LIFE OF THE BODY.
DANCE INVOLVES YOUR ENTIRE BEING. YOU ARE THE ART.
erf?
IT'S A PERFECT COMBINATION OF FREEDOM AND DISCIPLINE.
THE MORE YOU PRACTICE, THE BETTER YOU BECOME AT IMPROVISATION.

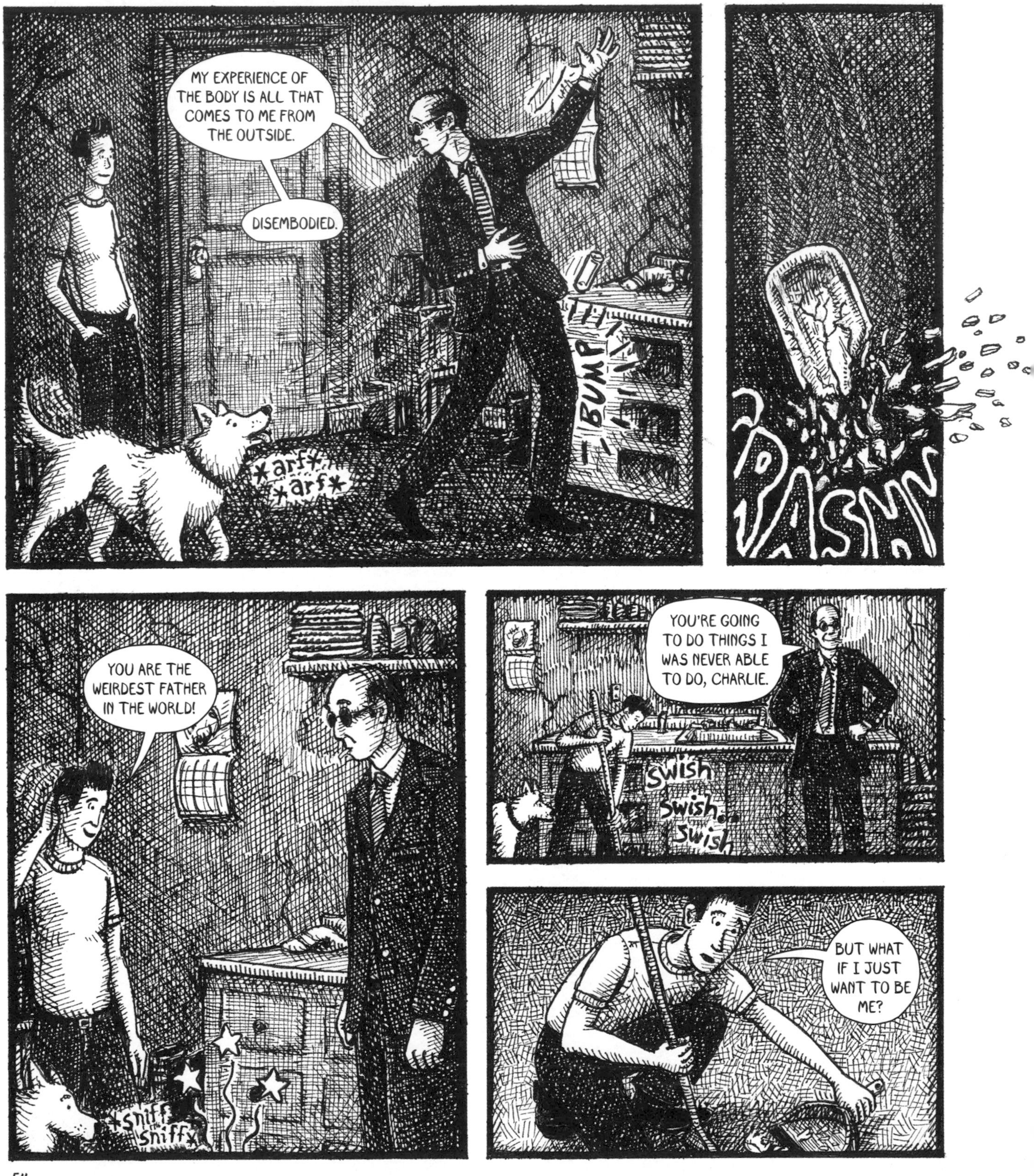

MY EXPERIENCE OF THE BODY IS ALL THAT COMES TO ME FROM THE OUTSIDE.
DISEMBODIED.
BUMP
arf *arf*
YOU ARE THE WEIRDEST FATHER IN THE WORLD!
sniff sniff
YOU'RE GOING TO DO THINGS I WAS NEVER ABLE TO DO, CHARLIE.
swish swish... swish
BUT WHAT IF I JUST WANT TO BE ME?

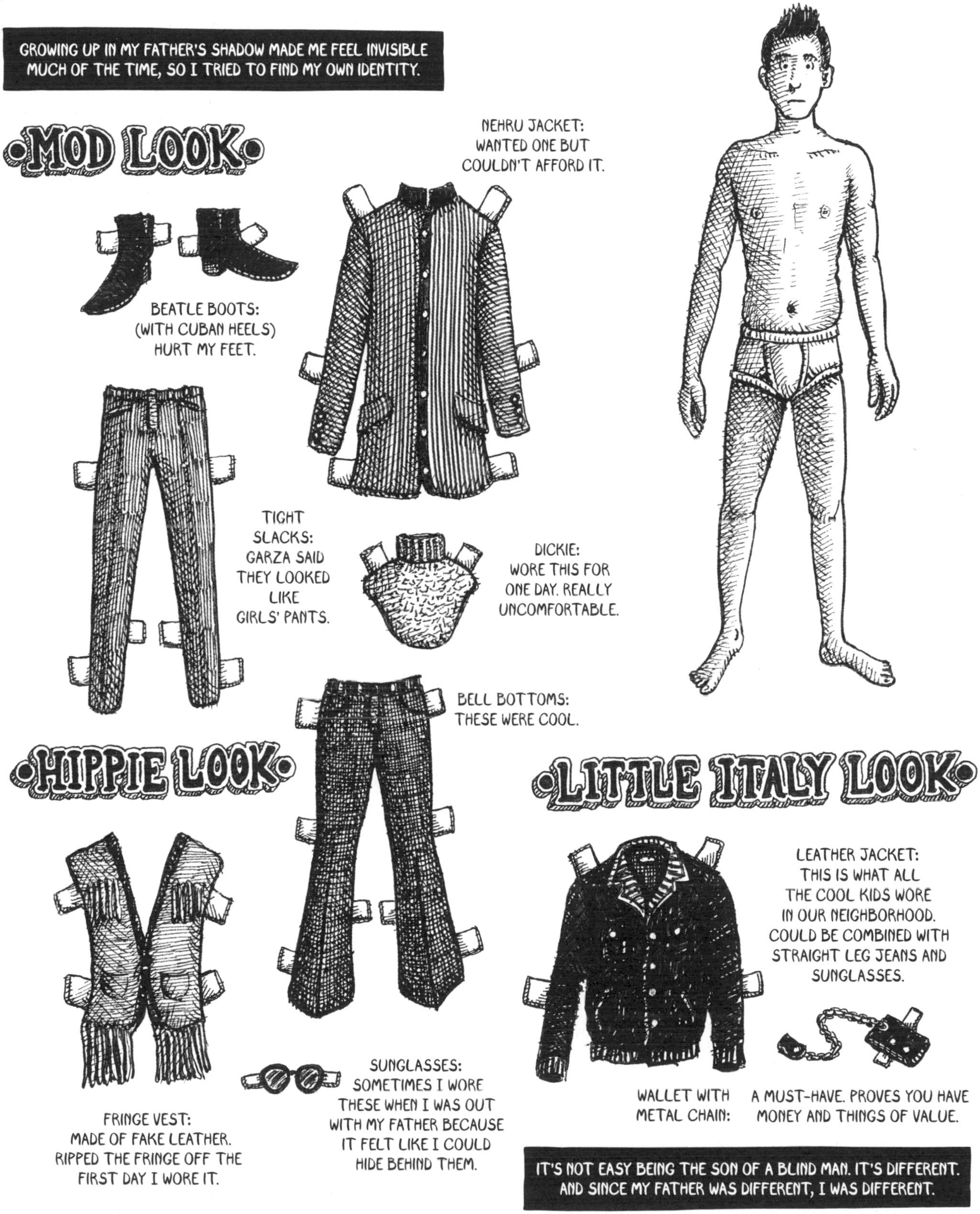
GROWING UP IN MY FATHER'S SHADOW MADE ME FEEL INVISIBLE MUCH OF THE TIME, SO I TRIED TO FIND MY OWN IDENTITY.
MOD LOOK
NEHRU JACKET: WANTED ONE BUT COULDN'T AFFORD IT.
BEATLE BOOTS: (WITH CUBAN HEELS) HURT MY FEET.
TIGHT SLACKS: GARZA SAID THEY LOOKED LIKE GIRLS' PANTS.
DICKIE: WORE THIS FOR ONE DAY. REALLY UNCOMFORTABLE.
BELL BOTTOMS: THESE WERE COOL.
HIPPIE LOOK
FRINGE VEST: MADE OF FAKE LEATHER. RIPPED THE FRINGE OFF THE FIRST DAY I WORE IT.
SUNGLASSES: SOMETIMES I WORE THESE WHEN I WAS OUT WITH MY FATHER BECAUSE IT FELT LIKE I COULD HIDE BEHIND THEM.
LITTLE ITALY LOOK
LEATHER JACKET: THIS IS WHAT ALL THE COOL KIDS WORE IN OUR NEIGHBORHOOD. COULD BE COMBINED WITH STRAIGHT LEG JEANS AND SUNGLASSES.
WALLET WITH METAL CHAIN: A MUST-HAVE. PROVES YOU HAVE MONEY AND THINGS OF VALUE.
IT'S NOT EASY BEING THE SON OF A BLIND MAN. IT'S DIFFERENT. AND SINCE MY FATHER WAS DIFFERENT, I WAS DIFFERENT.

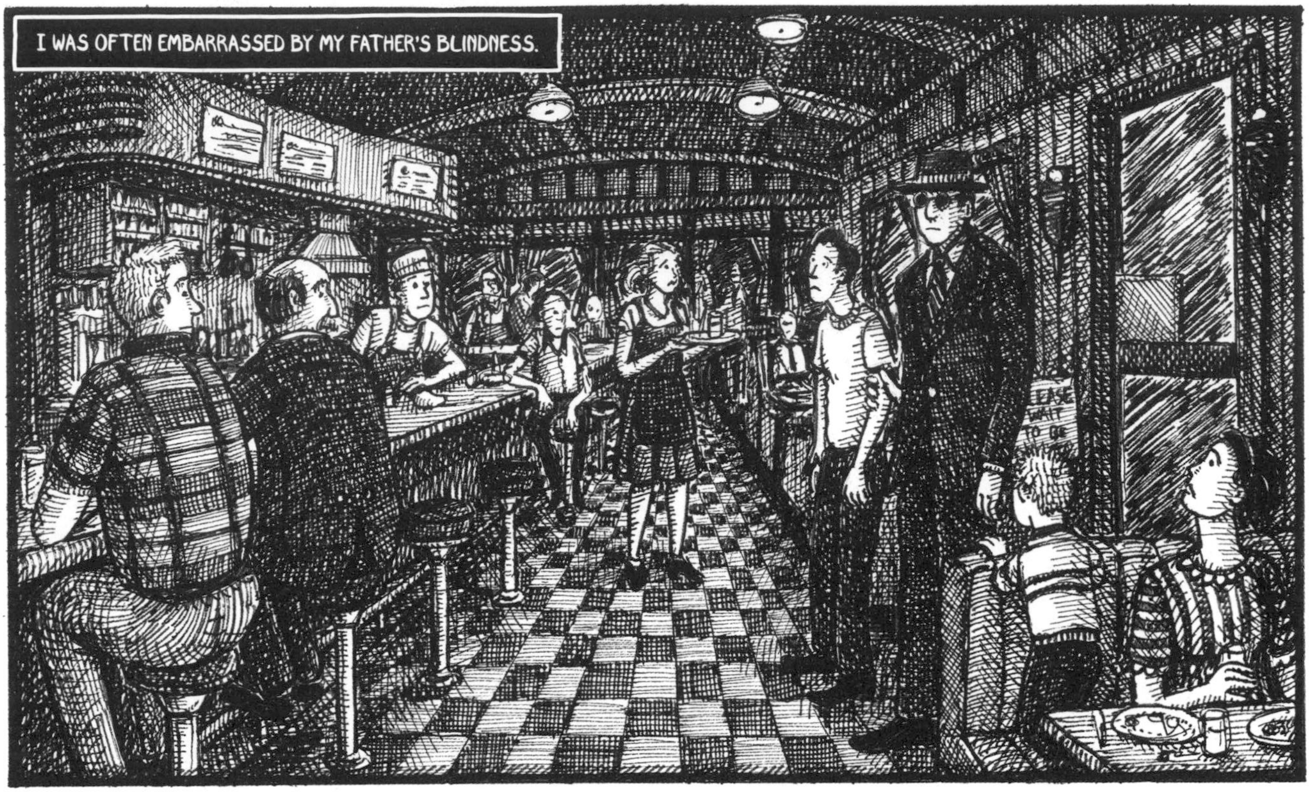
I WAS OFTEN EMBARRASSED BY MY FATHER'S BLINDNESS.

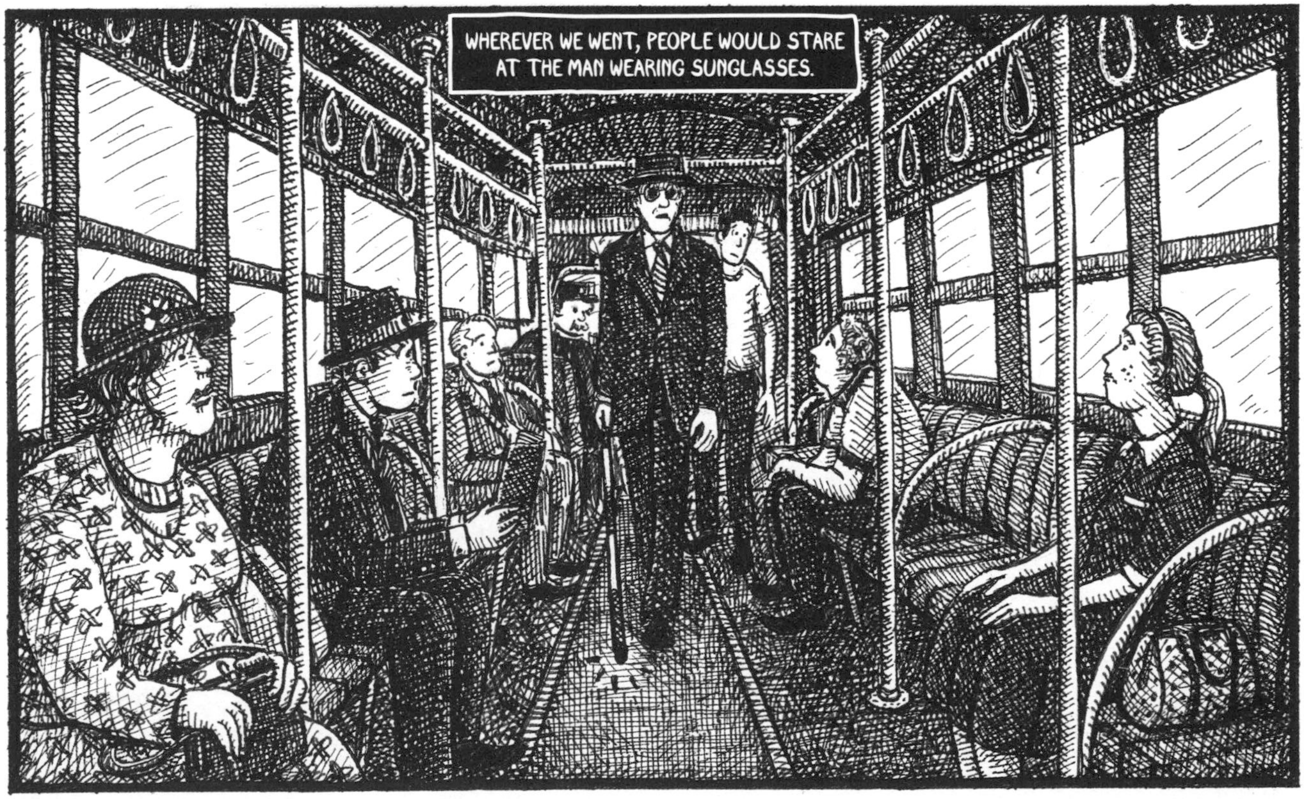
WHEREVER WE WENT, PEOPLE WOULD STARE AT THE MAN WEARING SUNGLASSES.

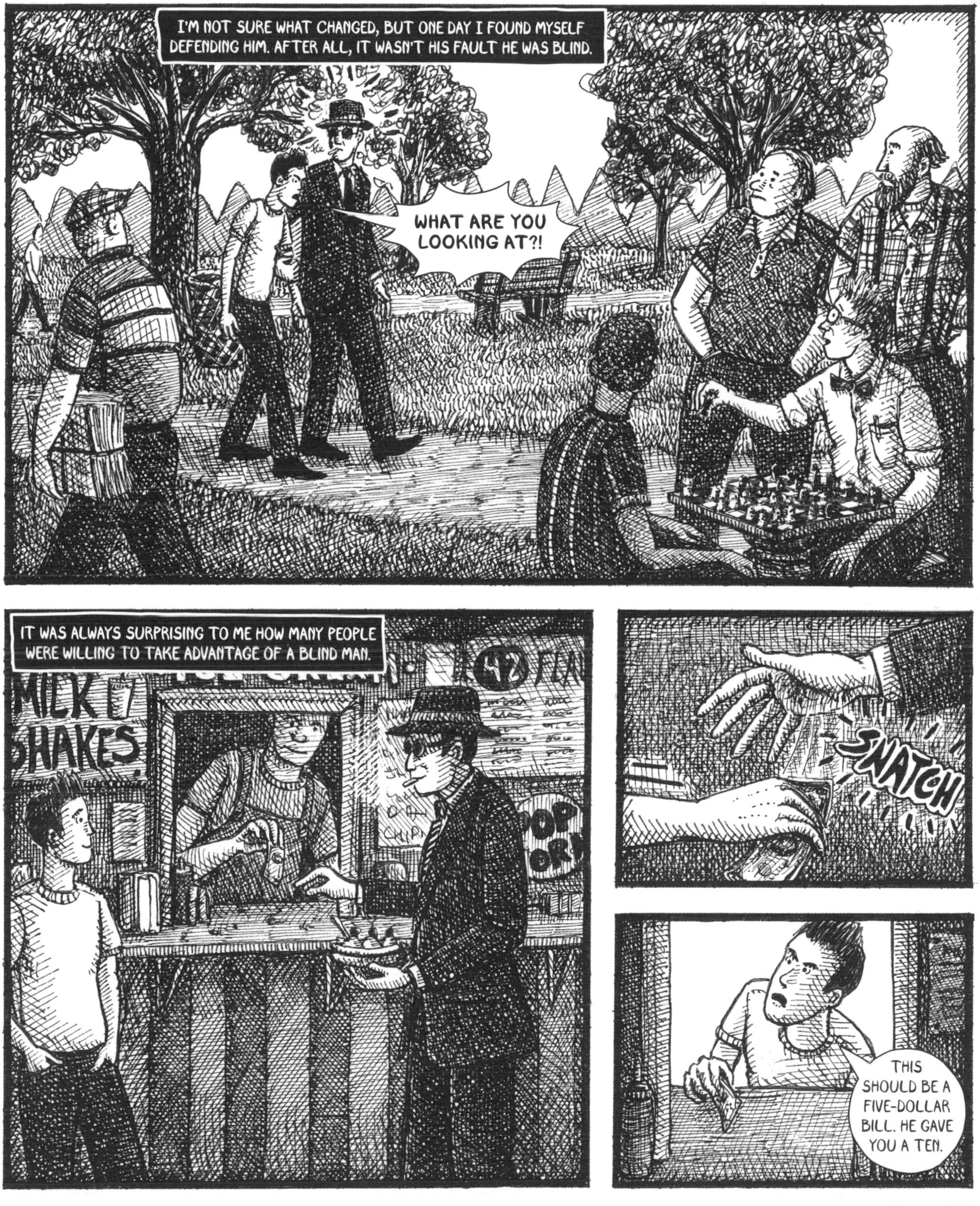
I'M NOT SURE WHAT CHANGED, BUT ONE DAY I FOUND MYSELF DEFENDING HIM. AFTER ALL, IT WASN'T HIS FAULT HE WAS BLIND.
WHAT ARE YOU LOOKING AT?!
IT WAS ALWAYS SURPRISING TO ME HOW MANY PEOPLE WERE WILLING TO TAKE ADVANTAGE OF A BLIND MAN.
MILK SHAKES
SNATCH
THIS SHOULD BE A FIVE-DOLLAR BILL. HE GAVE YOU A TEN.

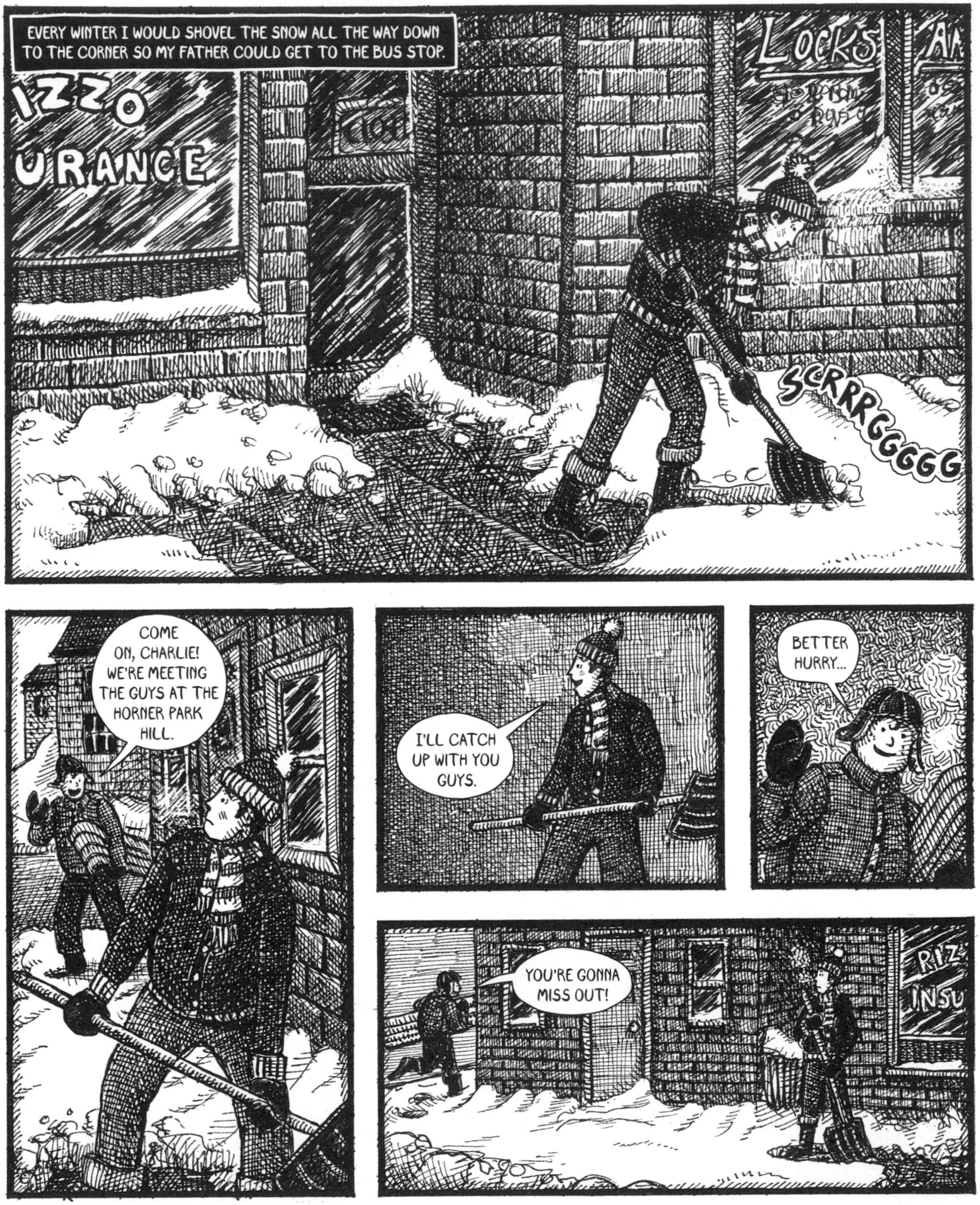
EVERY WINTER I WOULD SHOVEL THE SNOW ALL THE WAY DOWN TO THE CORNER SO MY FATHER COULD GET TO THE BUS STOP.
IZZO
URANCE
LOCKS
SCRRRGGGGGG
COME ON, CHARLIE! WE'RE MEETING THE GUYS AT THE HORNER PARK HILL.
I'LL CATCH UP WITH YOU GUYS.
BETTER HURRY...
YOU'RE GONNA MISS OUT!
RIZ
INSU

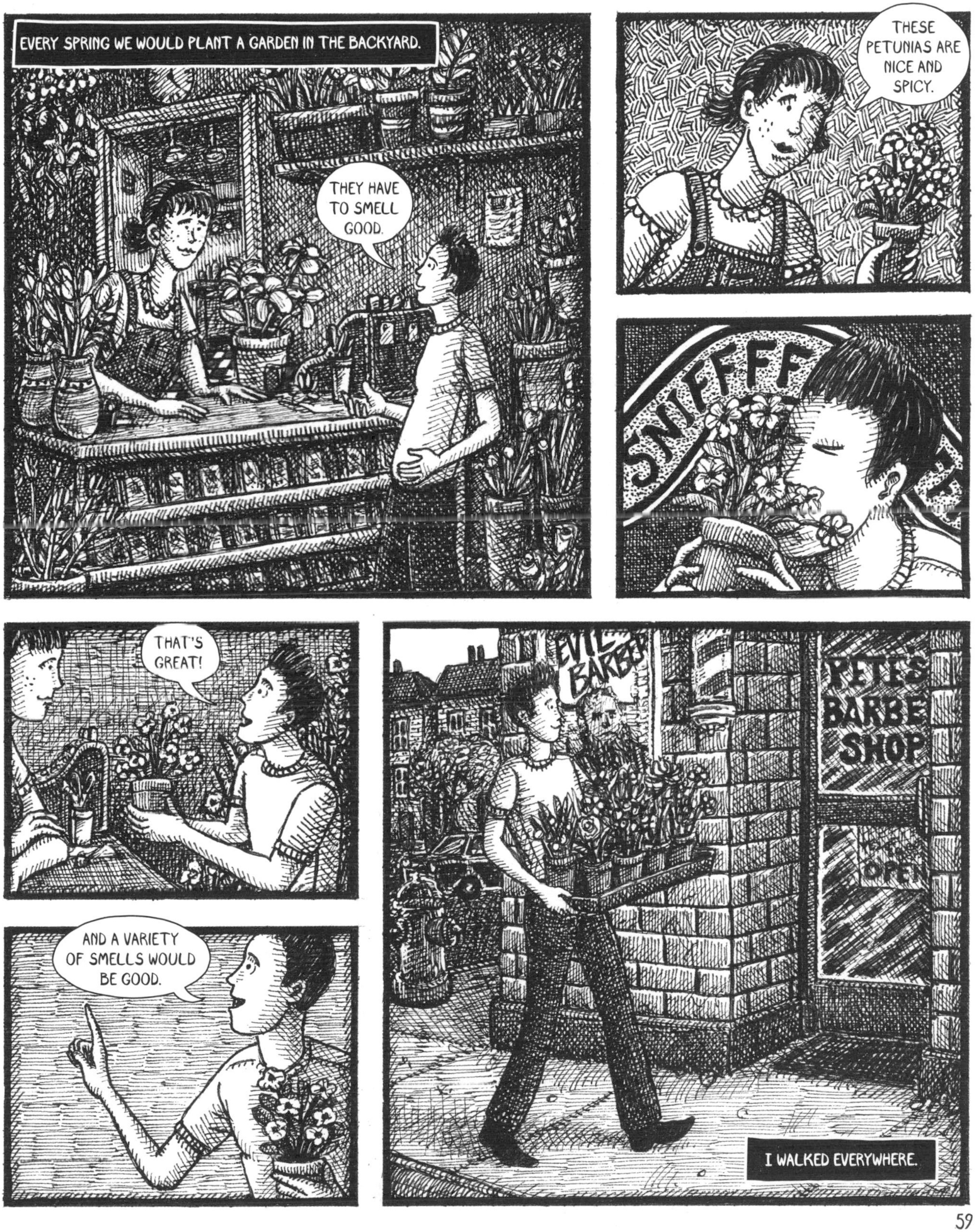
EVERY SPRING WE WOULD PLANT A GARDEN IN THE BACKYARD.
THEY HAVE TO SMELL GOOD.
THESE PETUNIAS ARE NICE AND SPICY.
SNIFFFF
THAT'S GREAT!
AND A VARIETY OF SMELLS WOULD BE GOOD.
EVIL BARBER
PETE'S BARBE SHOP
OPEN
I WALKED EVERYWHERE.

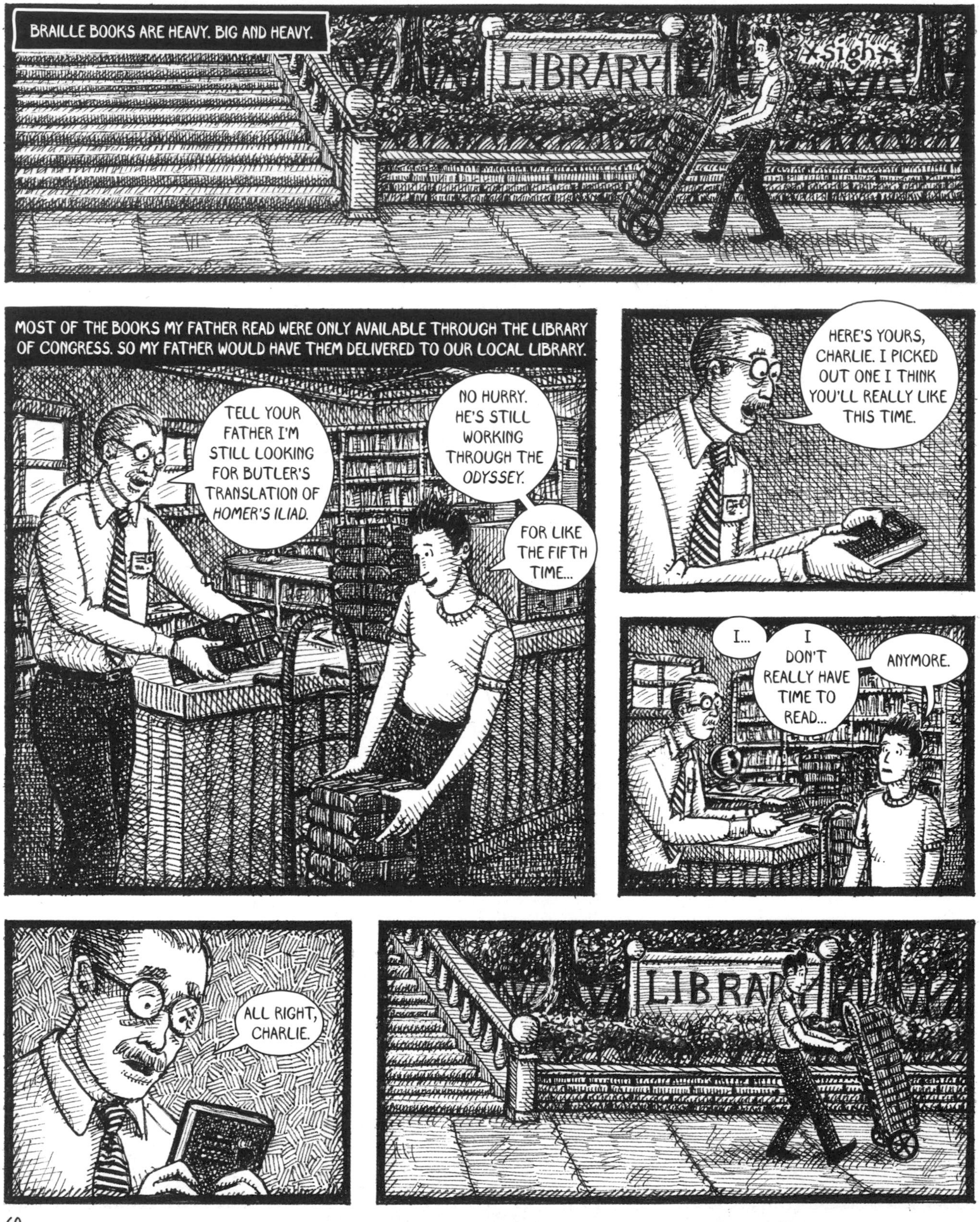
BRAILLE BOOKS ARE HEAVY. BIG AND HEAVY.
LIBRARY
sigh
MOST OF THE BOOKS MY FATHER READ WERE ONLY AVAILABLE THROUGH THE LIBRARY OF CONGRESS. SO MY FATHER WOULD HAVE THEM DELIVERED TO OUR LOCAL LIBRARY.
TELL YOUR FATHER I'M STILL LOOKING FOR BUTLER'S TRANSLATION OF HOMER'S ILIAD.
NO HURRY. HE'S STILL WORKING THROUGH THE ODYSSEY.
FOR LIKE THE FIFTH TIME...
HERE'S YOURS, CHARLIE. I PICKED OUT ONE I THINK YOU'LL REALLY LIKE THIS TIME.
I...
I DON'T REALLY HAVE TIME TO READ...
ANYMORE.
ALL RIGHT, CHARLIE.
LIBRAR

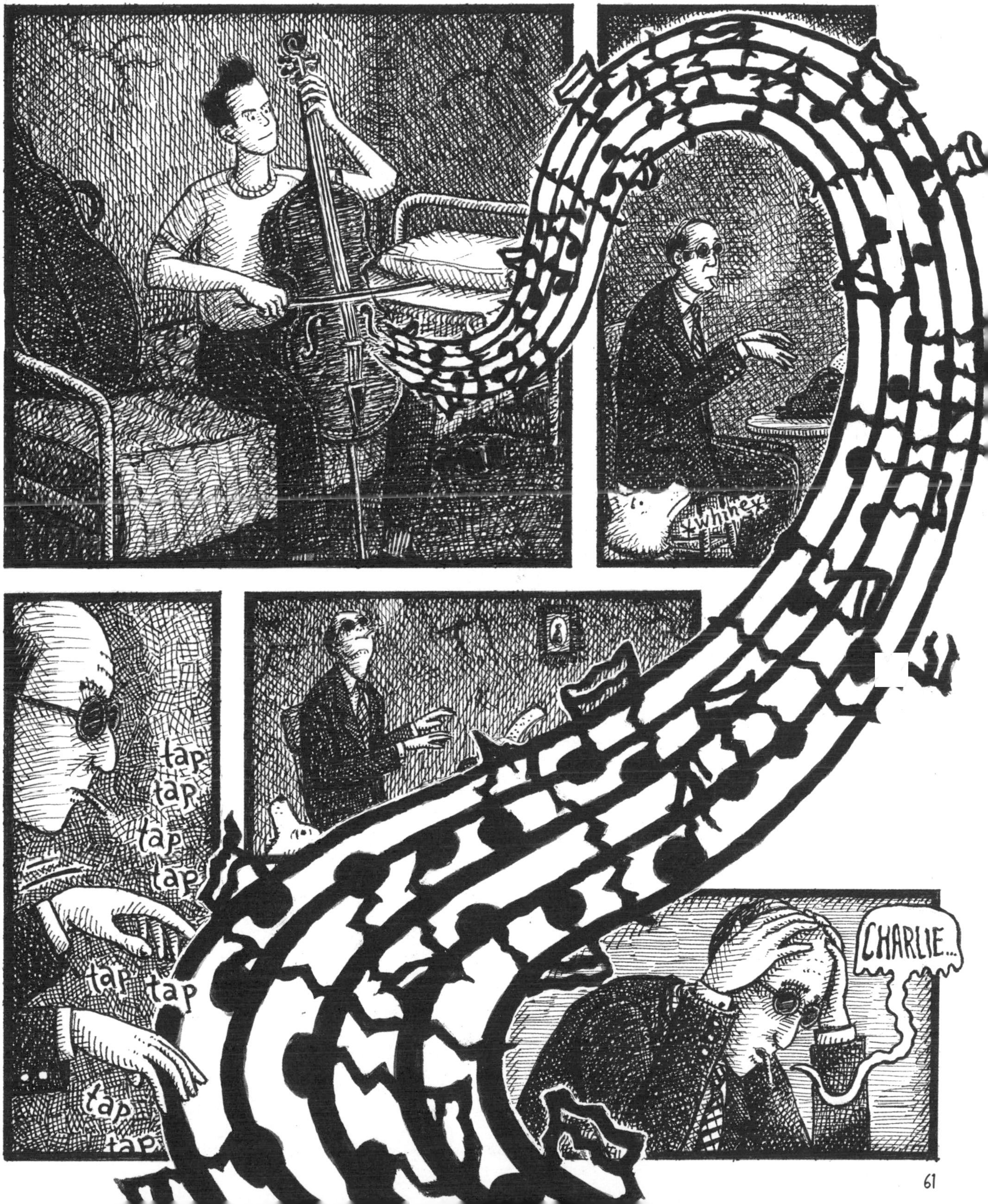

whine
tap
tap
tap
tap
tap tap
tap
CHARLIE...

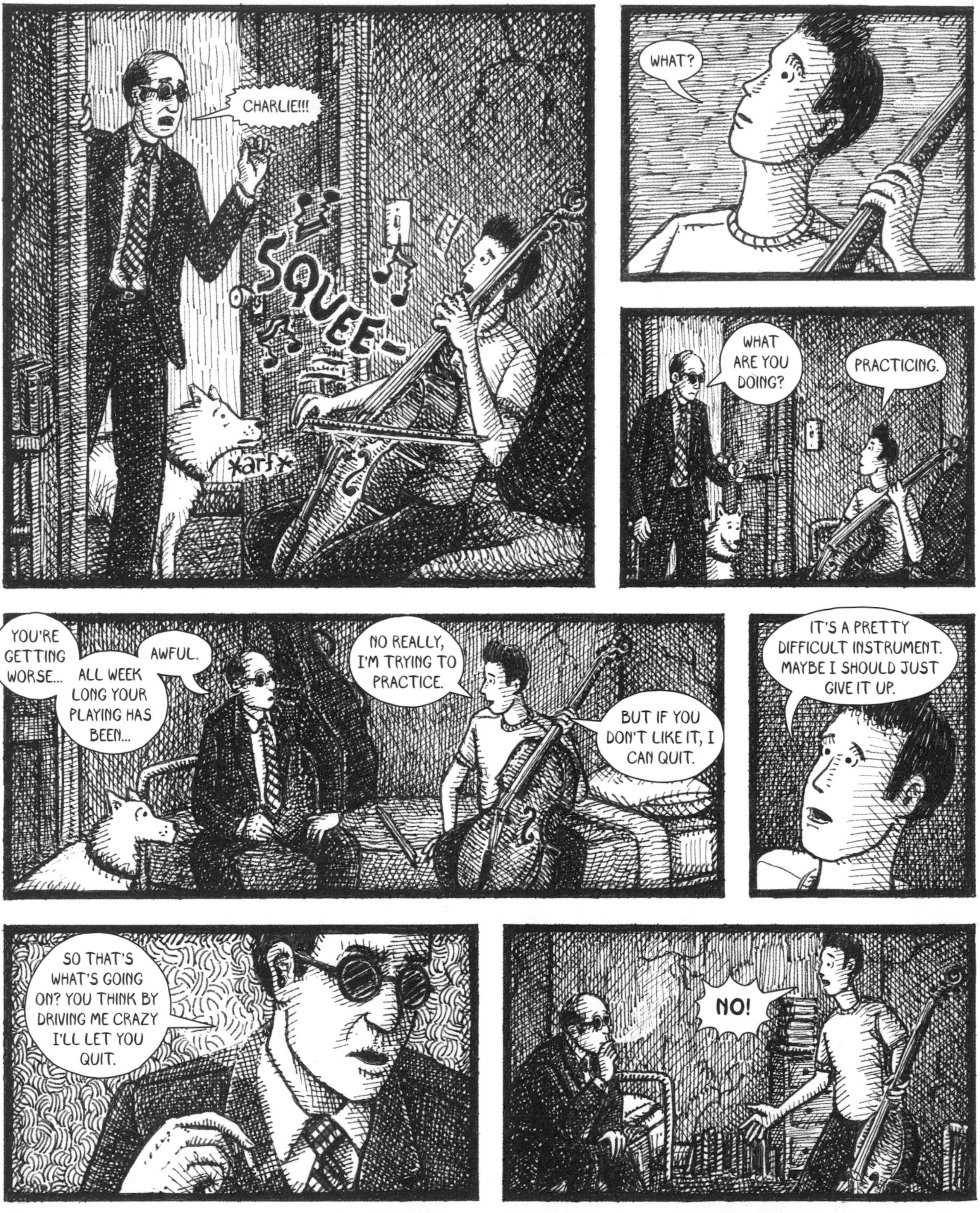
CHARLIE!!!
SQUEE-
arf
WHAT?
WHAT ARE YOU DOING?
PRACTICING.
YOU'RE GETTING WORSE...
ALL WEEK LONG YOUR PLAYING HAS BEEN...
AWFUL.
NO REALLY, I'M TRYING TO PRACTICE.
BUT IF YOU DON'T LIKE IT, I CAN QUIT.
IT'S A PRETTY DIFFICULT INSTRUMENT. MAYBE I SHOULD JUST GIVE IT UP.
SO THAT'S WHAT'S GOING ON? YOU THINK BY DRIVING ME CRAZY I'LL LET YOU QUIT.
NO!

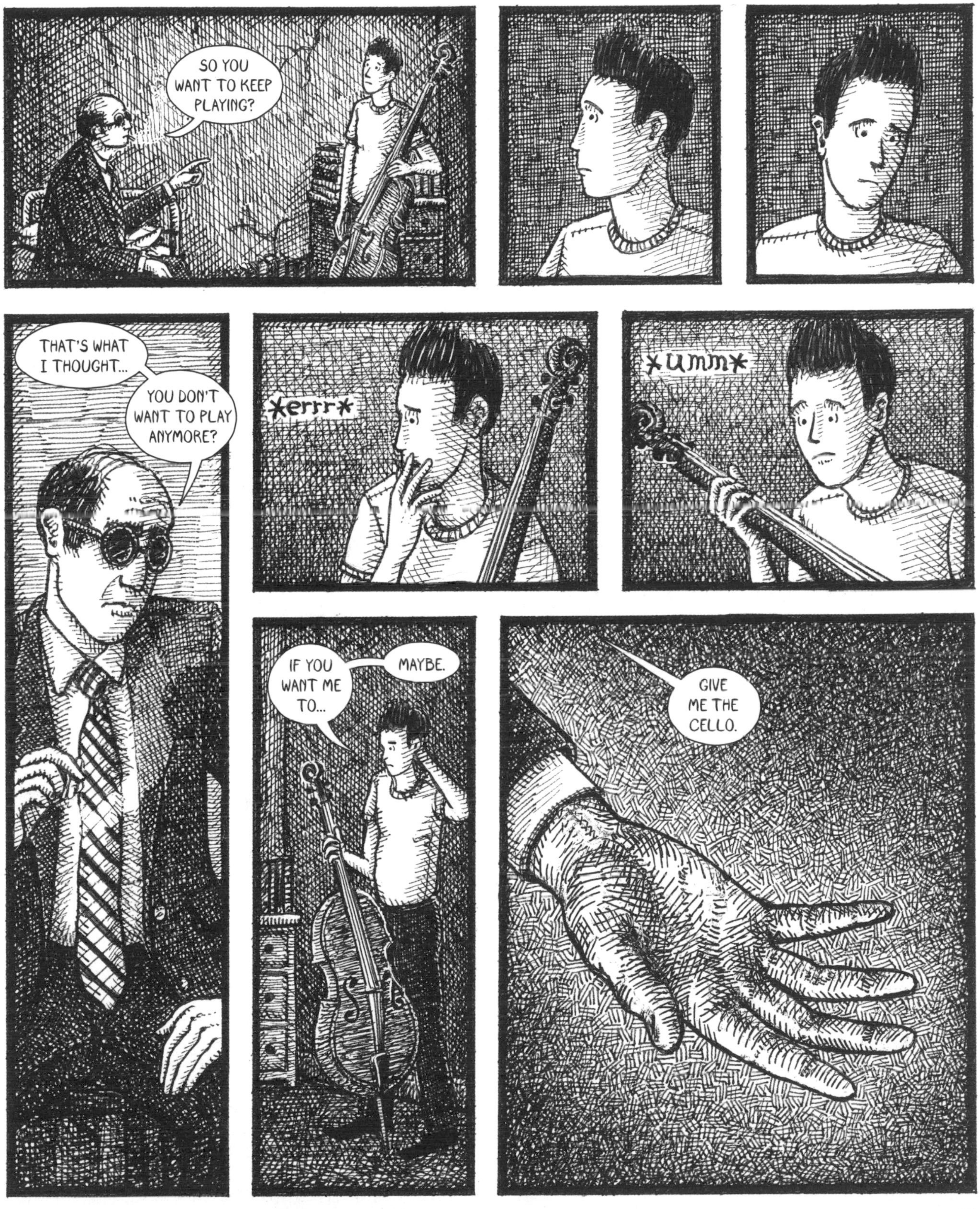
SO YOU WANT TO KEEP PLAYING?
THAT'S WHAT I THOUGHT...
YOU DON'T WANT TO PLAY ANYMORE?
errr
umm
IF YOU WANT ME TO...
MAYBE.
GIVE ME THE CELLO.

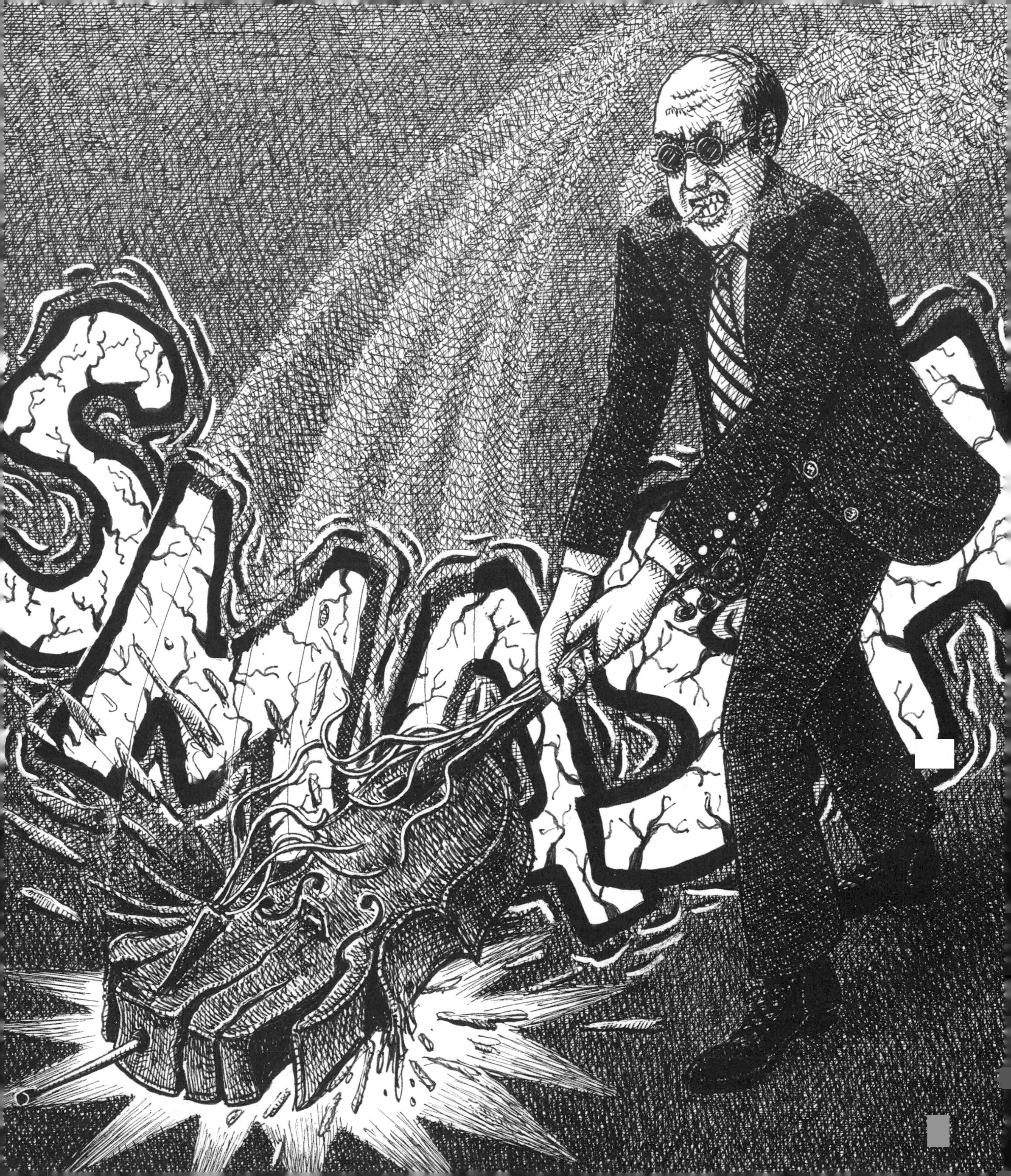

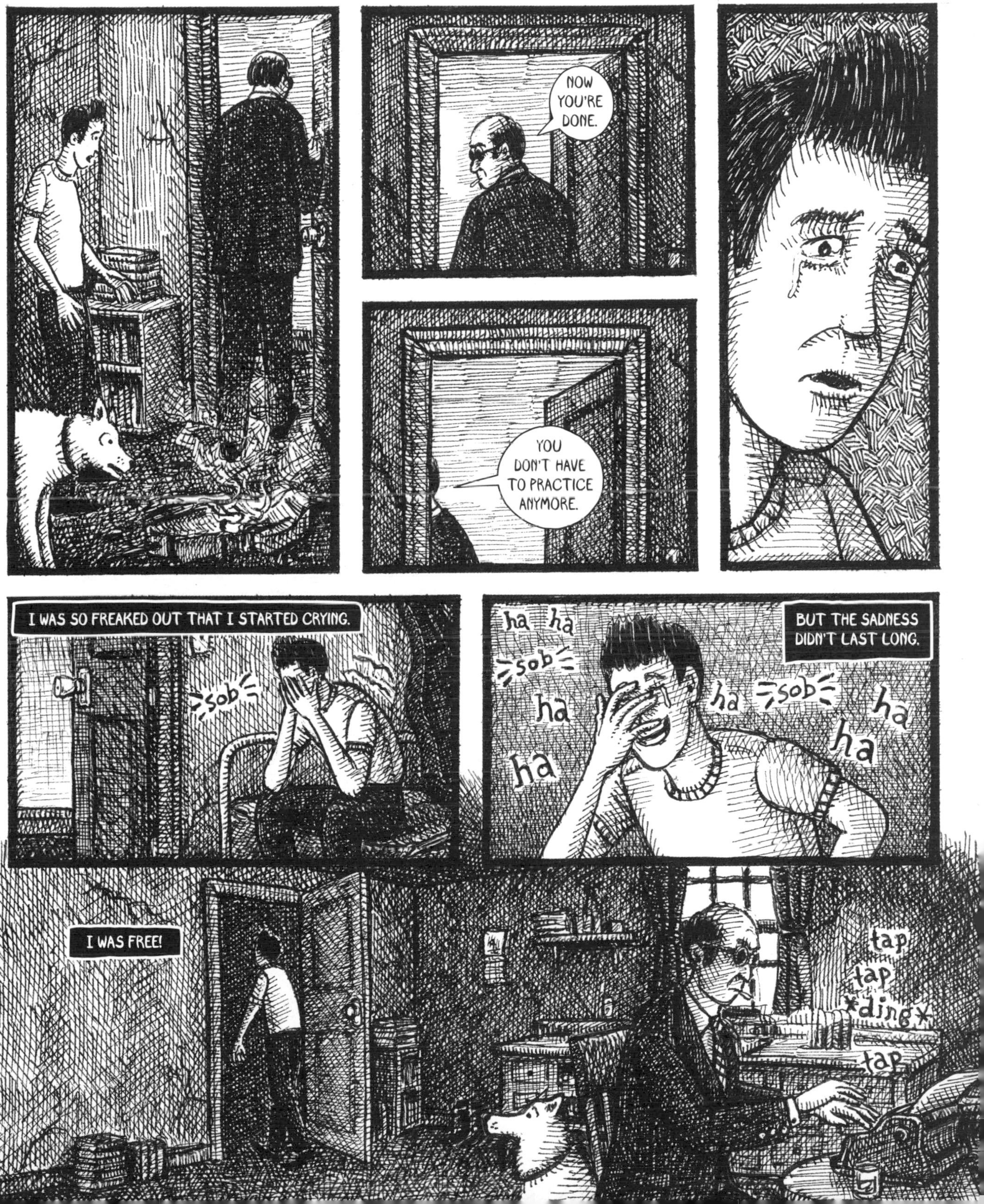
NOW YOU'RE DONE.
YOU DON'T HAVE TO PRACTICE ANYMORE.
I WAS SO FREAKED OUT THAT I STARTED CRYING.
sob
BUT THE SADNESS DIDN'T LAST LONG.
ha ha
sob
ha
ha
ha
sob
ha
ha
I WAS FREE!
tap
tap
ding
tap

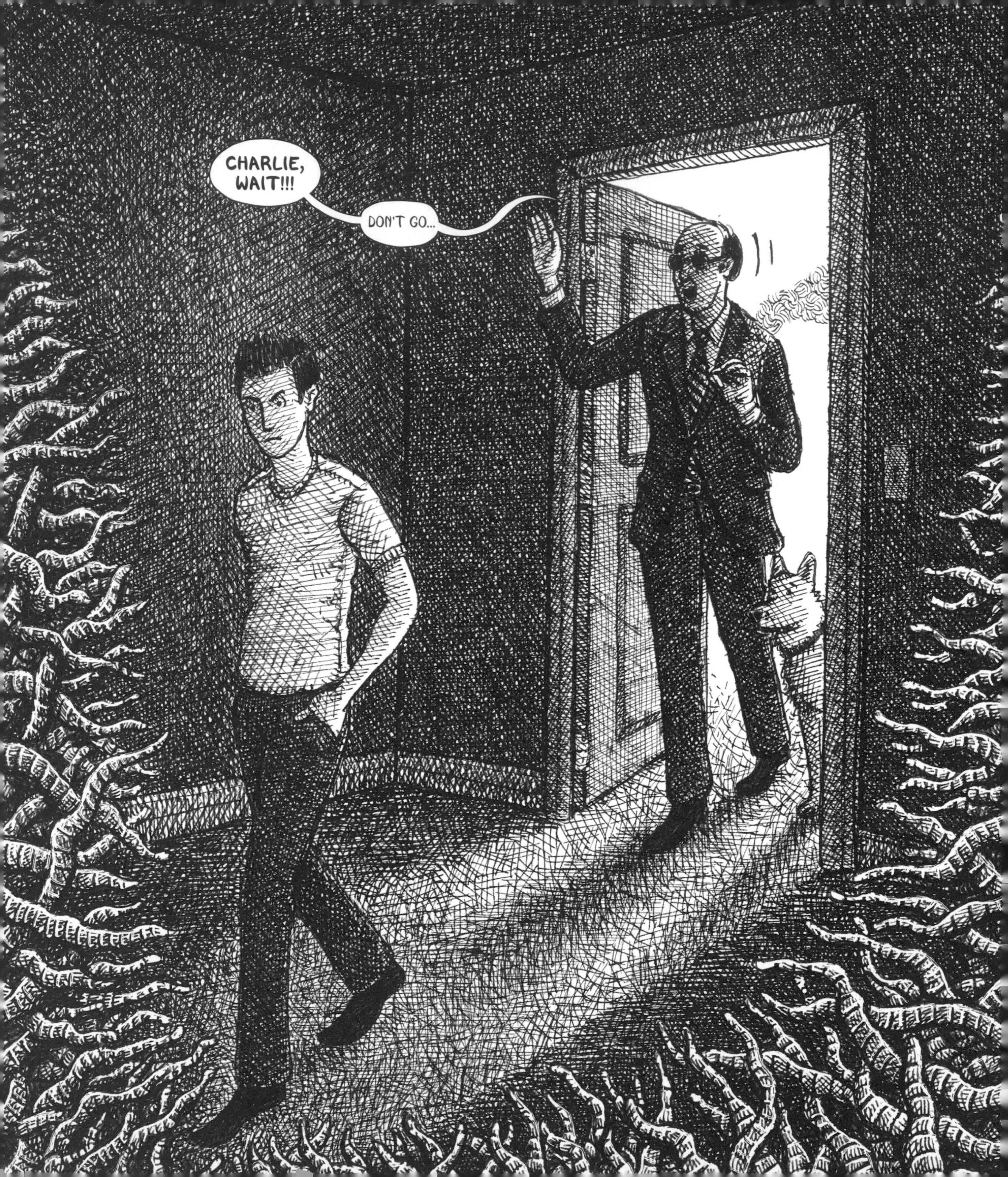
CHARLIE, WAIT!!!
DON'T GO...

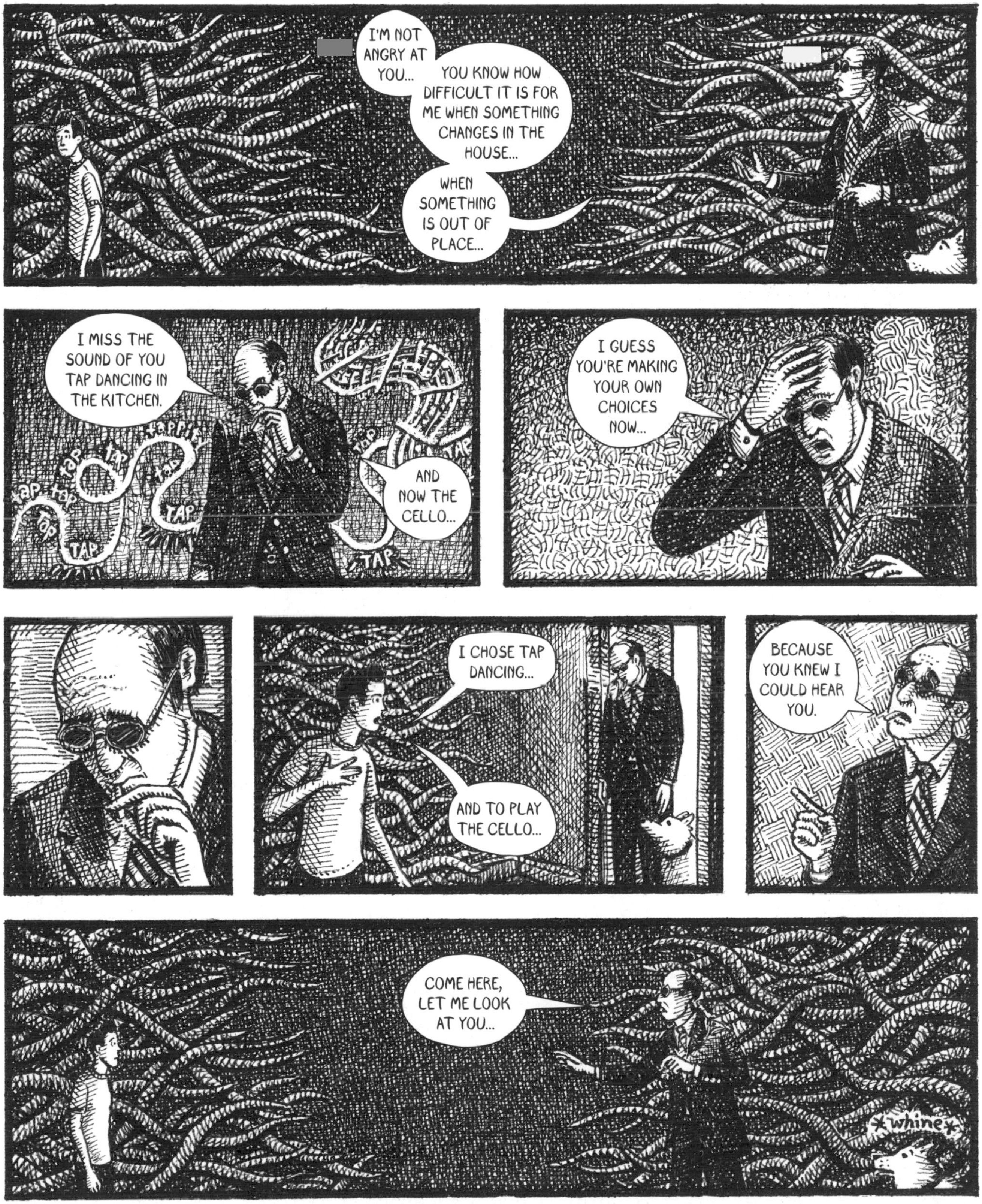
I'M NOT ANGRY AT YOU...
YOU KNOW HOW DIFFICULT IT IS FOR ME WHEN SOMETHING CHANGES IN THE HOUSE...
WHEN SOMETHING IS OUT OF PLACE...
I MISS THE SOUND OF YOU TAP DANCING IN THE KITCHEN.
AND NOW THE CELLO...
I GUESS YOU'RE MAKING YOUR OWN CHOICES NOW...
I CHOSE TAP DANCING...
AND TO PLAY THE CELLO...
BECAUSE YOU KNEW I COULD HEAR YOU.
COME HERE, LET ME LOOK AT YOU...
whine

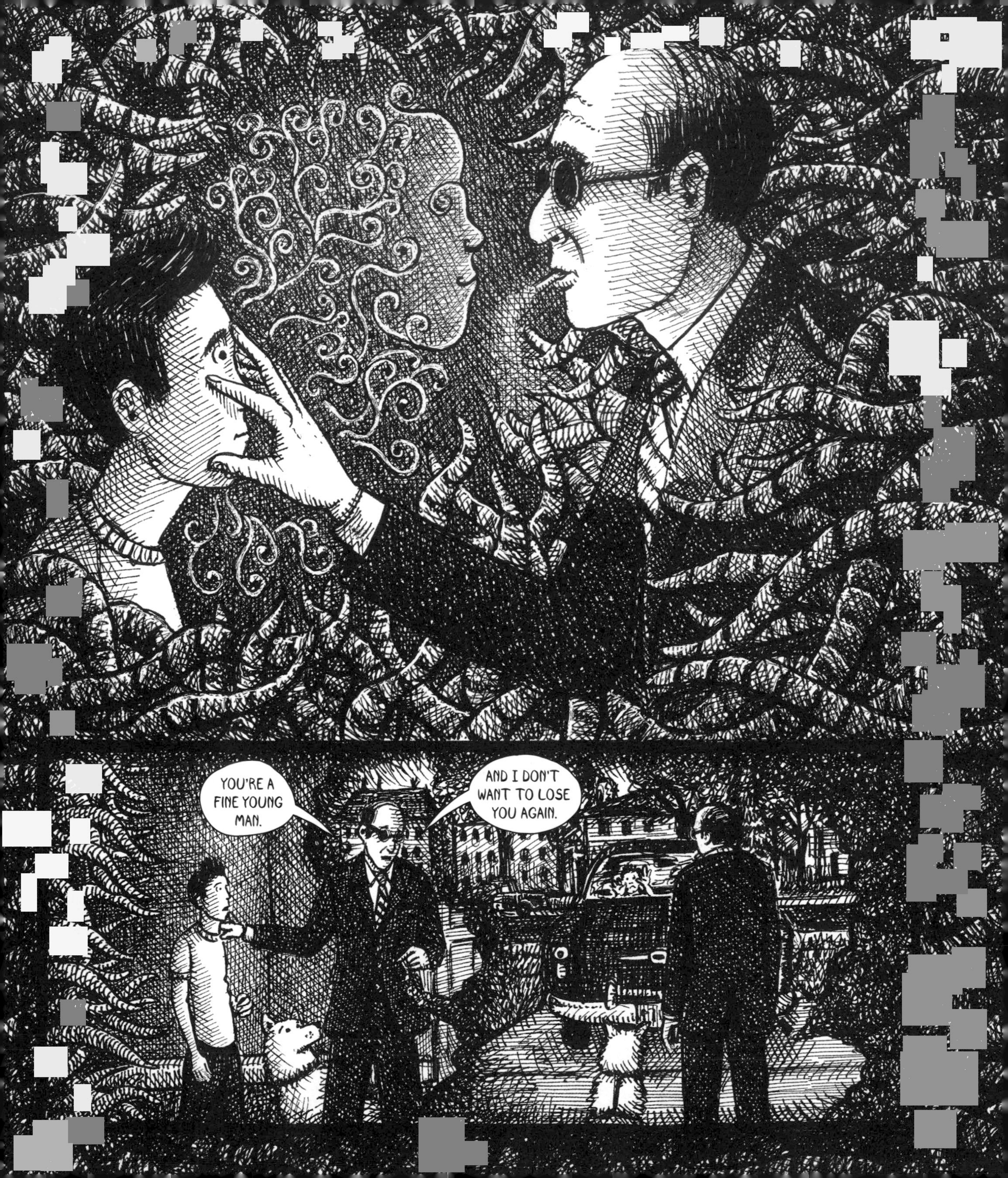
YOU'RE A FINE YOUNG MAN.
AND I DON'T WANT TO LOSE YOU AGAIN.

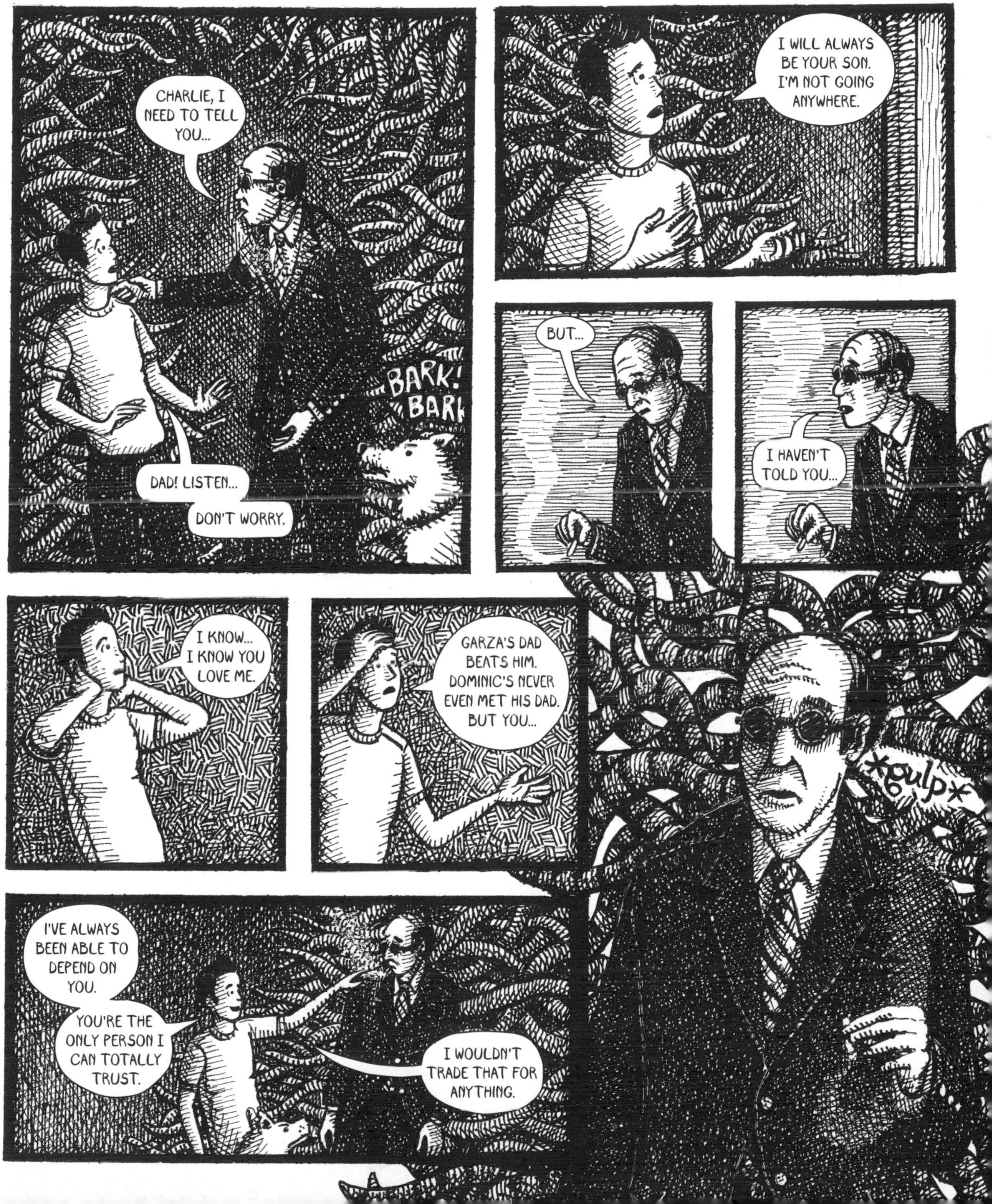
CHARLIE, I NEED TO TELL YOU...
BARK! BARK
DAD! LISTEN...
DON'T WORRY.
I WILL ALWAYS BE YOUR SON. I'M NOT GOING ANYWHERE.
BUT...
I HAVEN'T TOLD YOU...
I KNOW... I KNOW YOU LOVE ME.
GARZA'S DAD BEATS HIM. DOMINIC'S NEVER EVEN MET HIS DAD. BUT YOU...
gulp
I'VE ALWAYS BEEN ABLE TO DEPEND ON YOU.
YOU'RE THE ONLY PERSON I CAN TOTALLY TRUST.
I WOULDN'T TRADE THAT FOR ANYTHING.

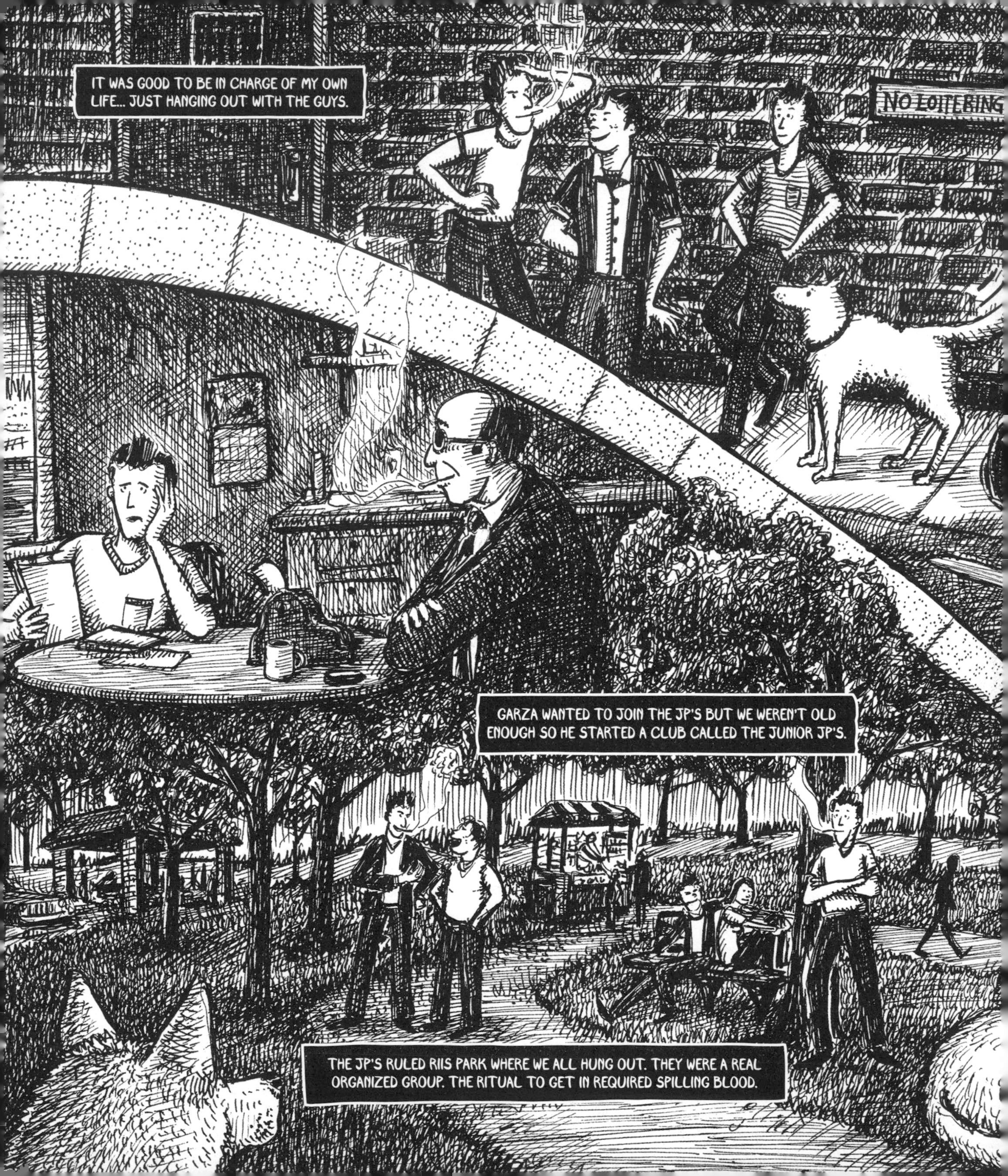
IT WAS GOOD TO BE IN CHARGE OF MY OWN LIFE... JUST HANGING OUT WITH THE GUYS.
NO LOITERING
GARZA WANTED TO JOIN THE JP'S BUT WE WEREN'T OLD ENOUGH SO HE STARTED A CLUB CALLED THE JUNIOR JP'S.
THE JP'S RULED RIIS PARK WHERE WE ALL HUNG OUT. THEY WERE A REAL ORGANIZED GROUP. THE RITUAL TO GET IN REQUIRED SPILLING BLOOD.

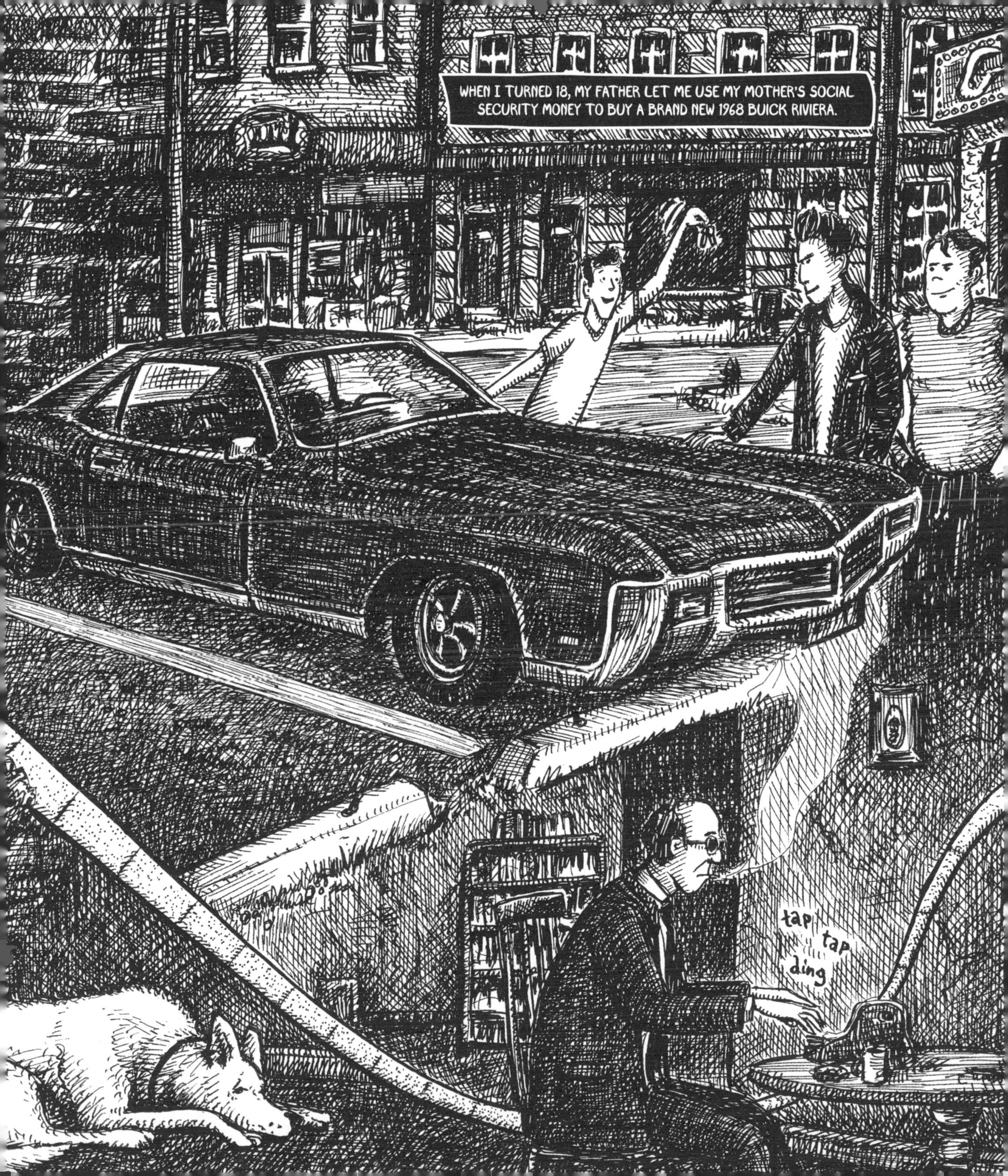
WHEN I TURNED 18, MY FATHER LET ME USE MY MOTHER'S SOCIAL SECURITY MONEY TO BUY A BRAND NEW 1968 BUICK RIVIERA.
tap
tap
ding

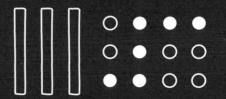

A YOUNG MAN'S TROUBLE WITH THE LAW

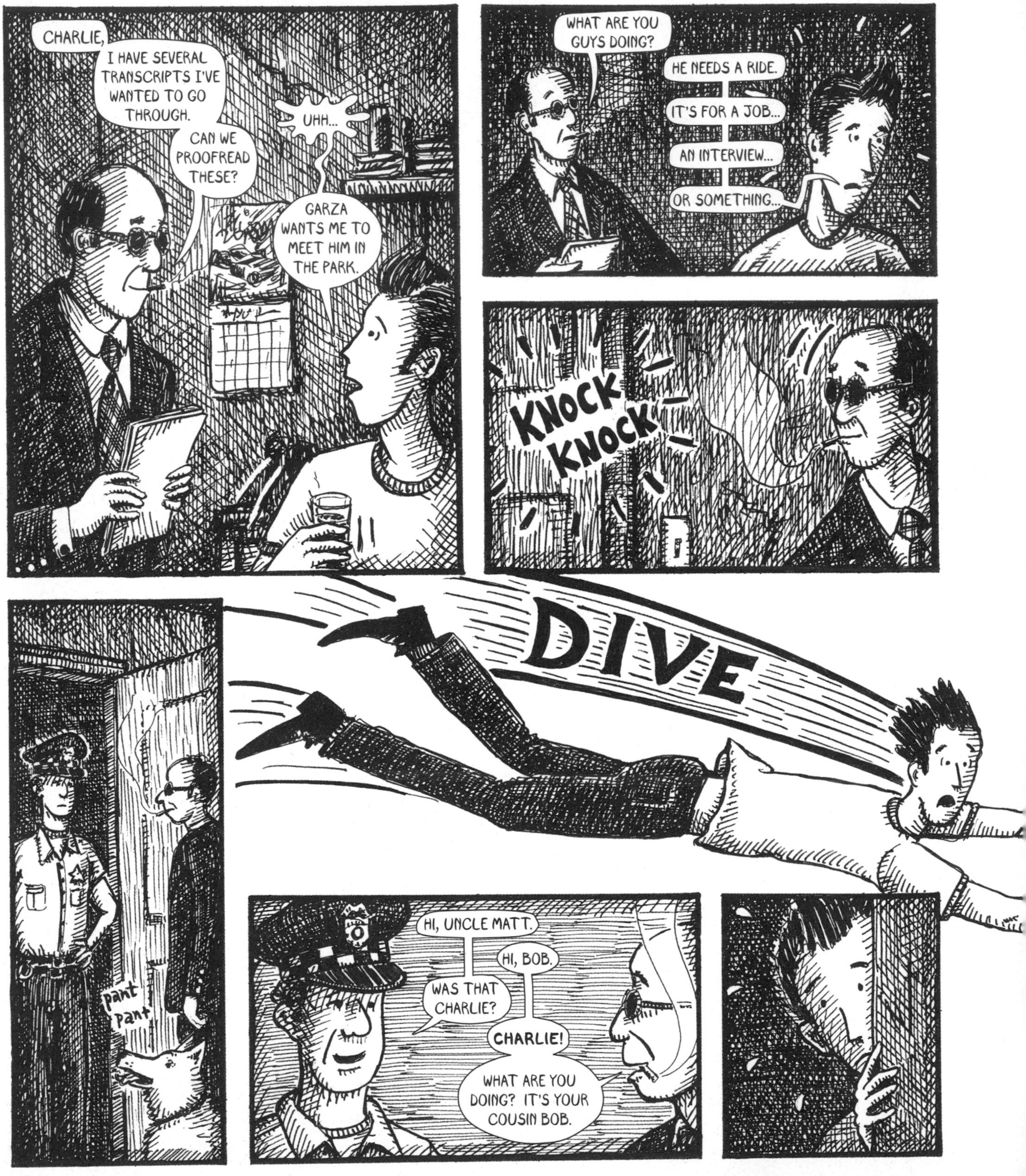

CHARLIE,
I HAVE SEVERAL TRANSCRIPTS I'VE WANTED TO GO THROUGH.
CAN WE PROOFREAD THESE?
UHH...
GARZA WANTS ME TO MEET HIM IN THE PARK.
WHAT ARE YOU GUYS DOING?
HE NEEDS A RIDE.
IT'S FOR A JOB...
AN INTERVIEW...
OR SOMETHING...
KNOCK KNOCK
DIVE
pant pant
HI, UNCLE MATT.
HI, BOB.
WAS THAT CHARLIE?
CHARLIE!
WHAT ARE YOU DOING? IT'S YOUR COUSIN BOB.

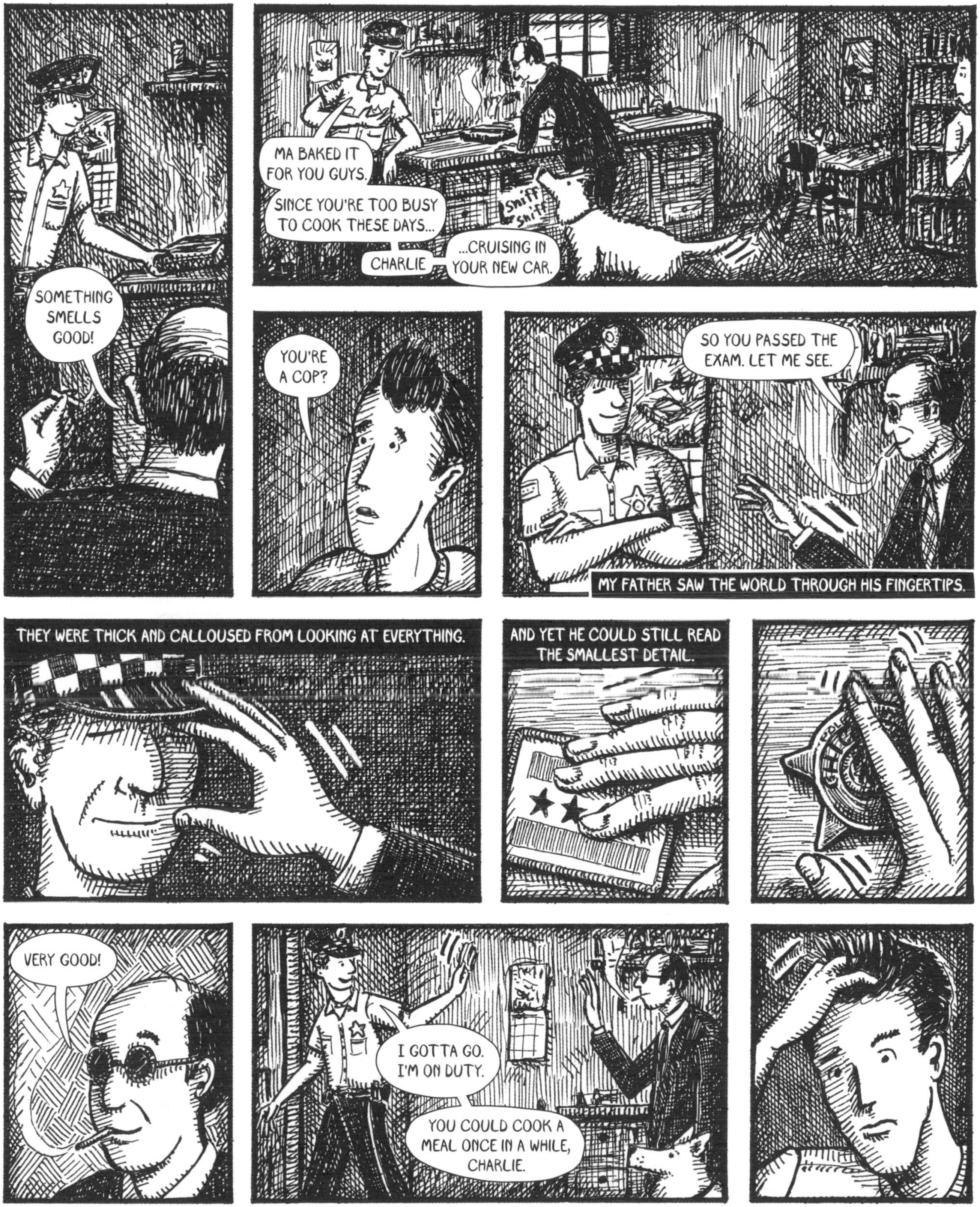
MA BAKED IT FOR YOU GUYS.
SINCE YOU'RE TOO BUSY TO COOK THESE DAYS...
CHARLIE
...CRUISING IN YOUR NEW CAR.
SNIFF SNIFF
SOMETHING SMELLS GOOD!
YOU'RE A COP?
SO YOU PASSED THE EXAM. LET ME SEE.
MY FATHER SAW THE WORLD THROUGH HIS FINGERTIPS.
THEY WERE THICK AND CALLOUSED FROM LOOKING AT EVERYTHING.
AND YET HE COULD STILL READ THE SMALLEST DETAIL.
VERY GOOD!
I GOTTA GO. I'M ON DUTY.
YOU COULD COOK A MEAL ONCE IN A WHILE, CHARLIE.

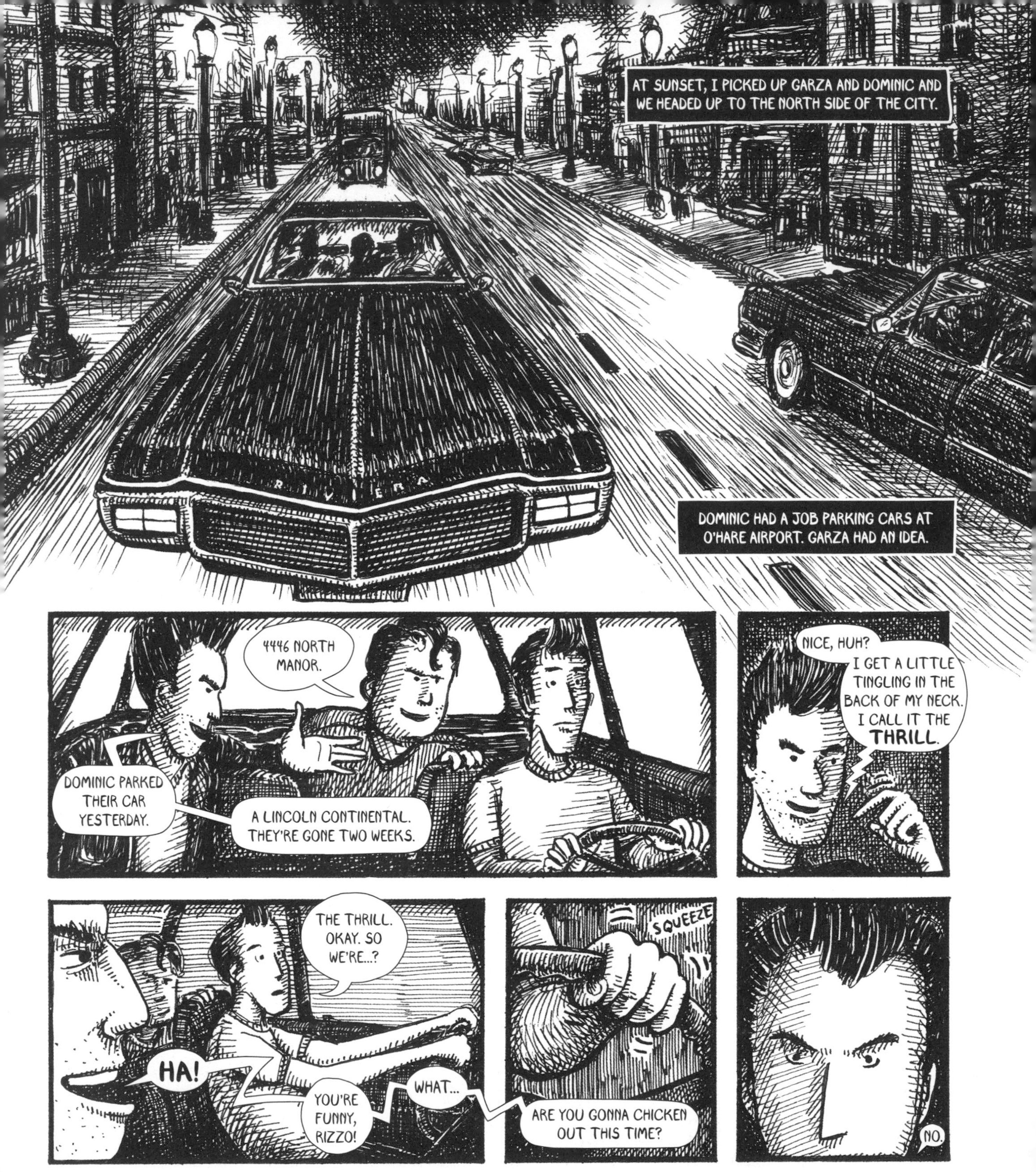
AT SUNSET, I PICKED UP GARZA AND DOMINIC AND WE HEADED UP TO THE NORTH SIDE OF THE CITY.
RIVERA
DOMINIC HAD A JOB PARKING CARS AT O'HARE AIRPORT. GARZA HAD AN IDEA.
4446 NORTH MANOR.
DOMINIC PARKED THEIR CAR YESTERDAY.
A LINCOLN CONTINENTAL. THEY'RE GONE TWO WEEKS.
NICE, HUH?
I GET A LITTLE TINGLING IN THE BACK OF MY NECK. I CALL IT THE **THRILL**.
THE THRILL. OKAY. SO WE'RE...?
HA!
YOU'RE FUNNY, RIZZO!
WHAT...
SQUEEZE
ARE YOU GONNA CHICKEN OUT THIS TIME?
NO.

SLAM
SCREECH!

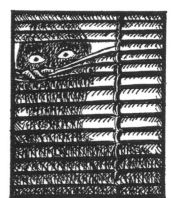

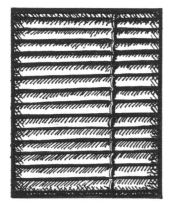

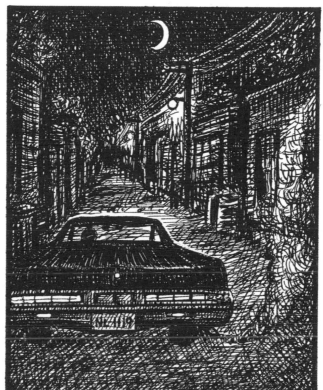

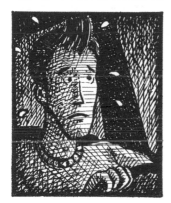

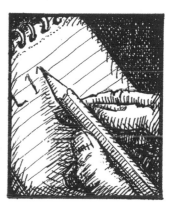

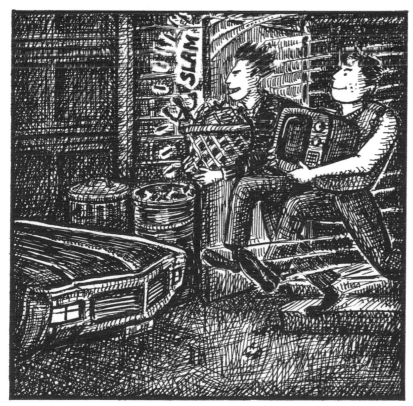

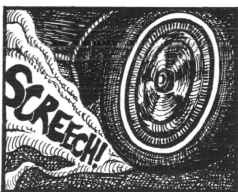

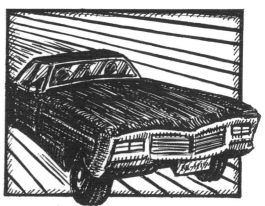

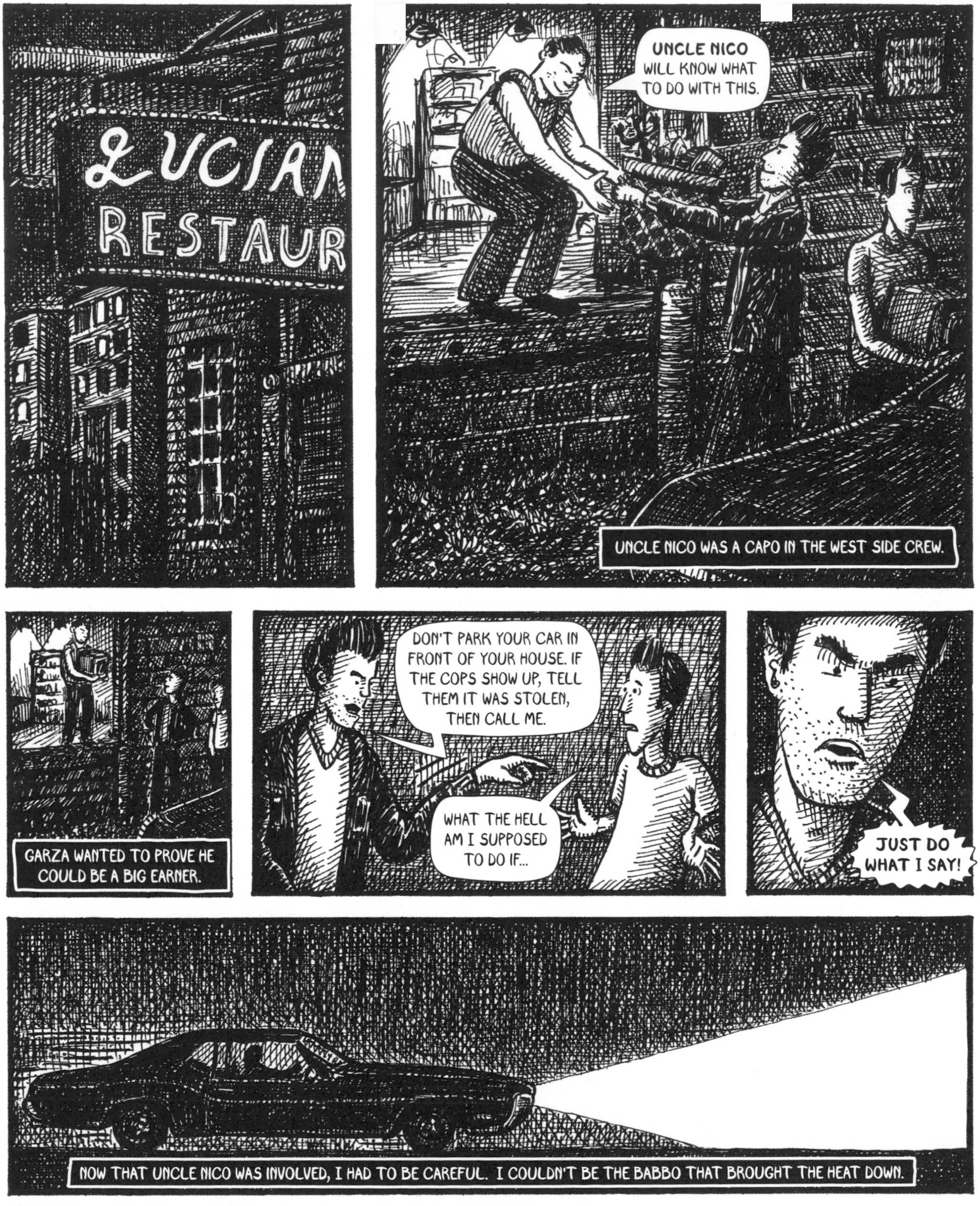
LUCIAN
RESTAUR
UNCLE NICO WILL KNOW WHAT TO DO WITH THIS.
UNCLE NICO WAS A CAPO IN THE WEST SIDE CREW.
GARZA WANTED TO PROVE HE COULD BE A BIG EARNER.
DON'T PARK YOUR CAR IN FRONT OF YOUR HOUSE. IF THE COPS SHOW UP, TELL THEM IT WAS STOLEN, THEN CALL ME.
WHAT THE HELL AM I SUPPOSED TO DO IF...
JUST DO WHAT I SAY!
NOW THAT UNCLE NICO WAS INVOLVED, I HAD TO BE CAREFUL. I COULDN'T BE THE BABBO THAT BROUGHT THE HEAT DOWN.

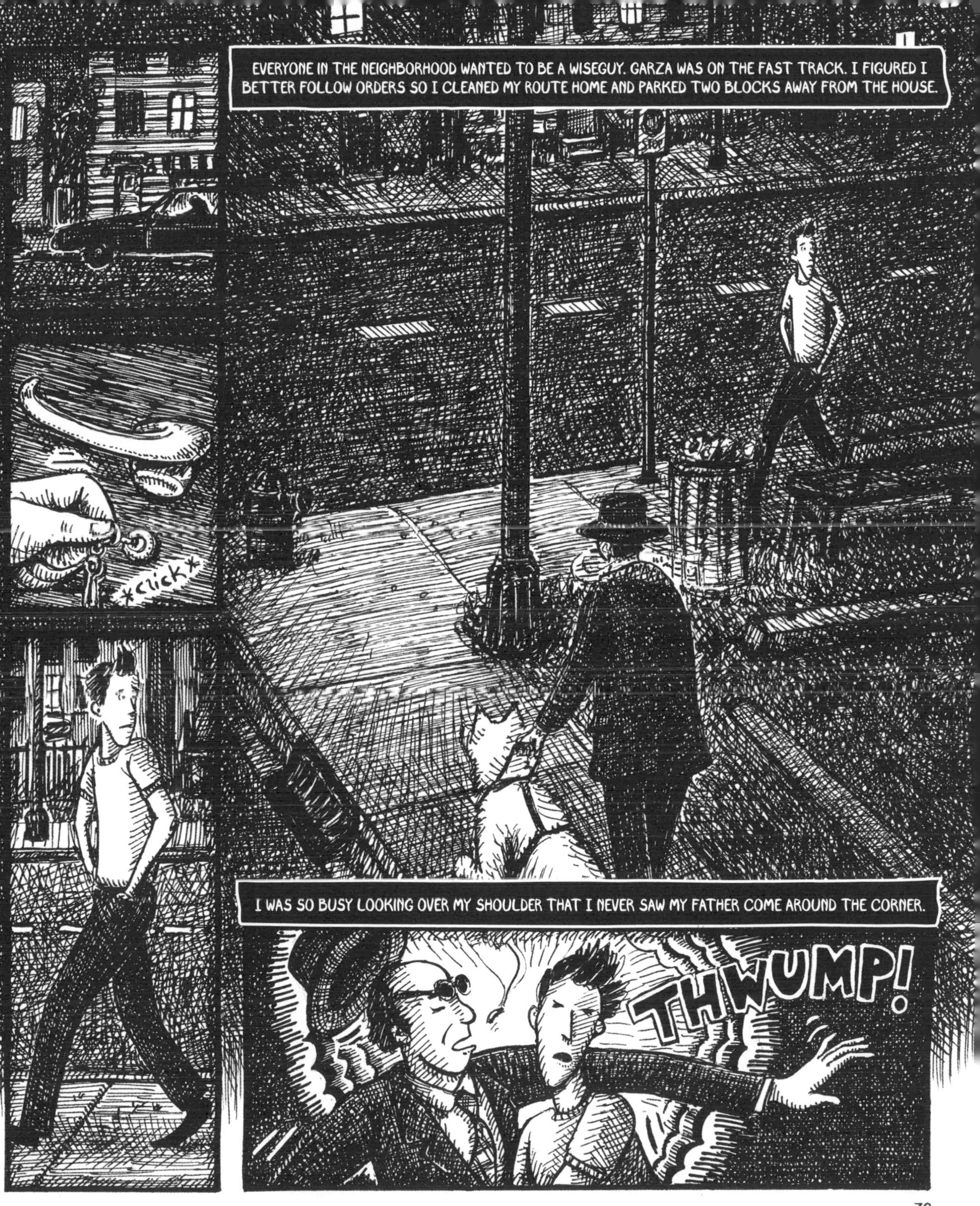
EVERYONE IN THE NEIGHBORHOOD WANTED TO BE A WISEGUY. GARZA WAS ON THE FAST TRACK. I FIGURED I BETTER FOLLOW ORDERS SO I CLEANED MY ROUTE HOME AND PARKED TWO BLOCKS AWAY FROM THE HOUSE.
CLICK
I WAS SO BUSY LOOKING OVER MY SHOULDER THAT I NEVER SAW MY FATHER COME AROUND THE CORNER.
THWUMP!

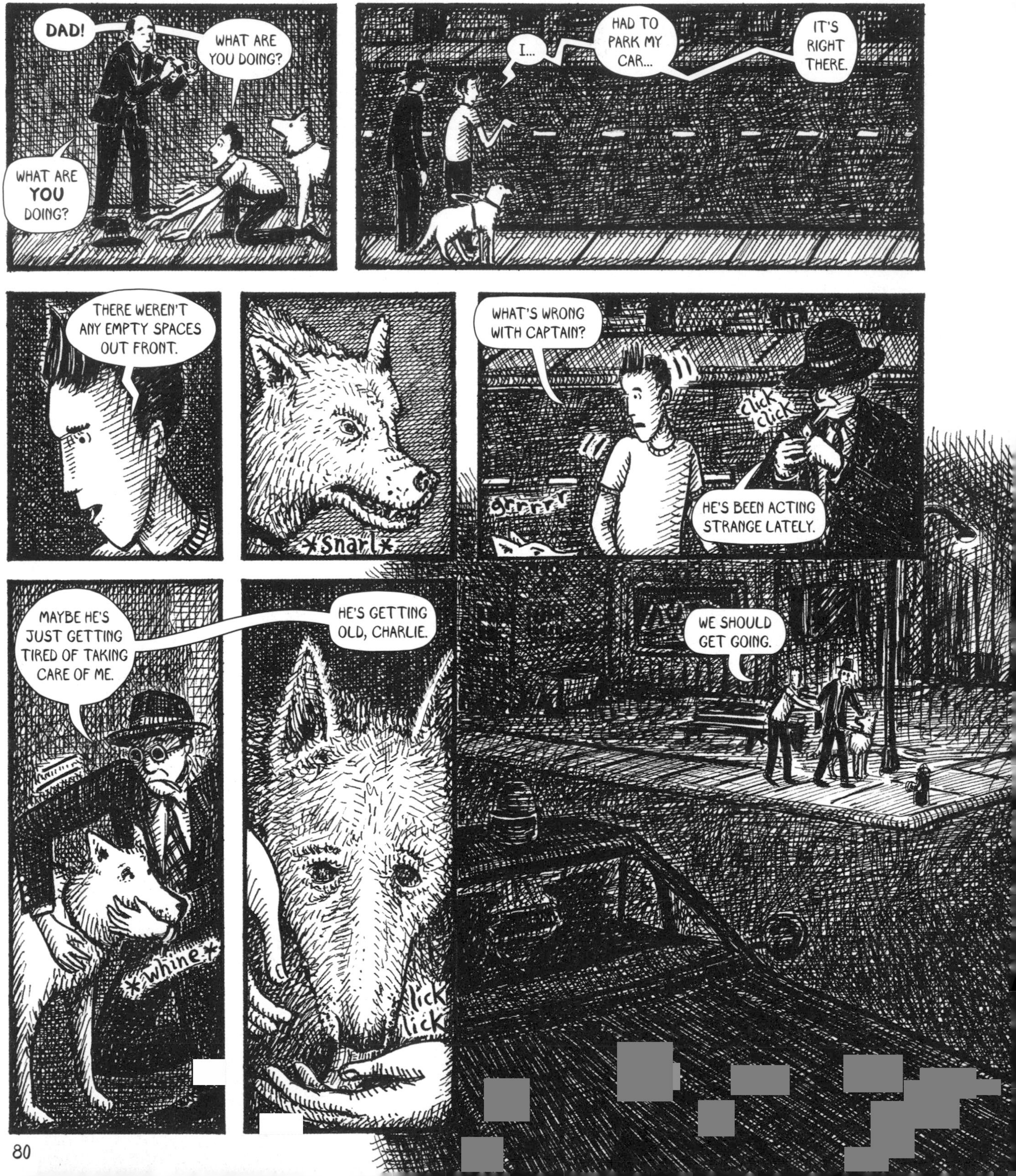
DAD!
WHAT ARE YOU DOING?
WHAT ARE YOU DOING?
I...
HAD TO PARK MY CAR...
IT'S RIGHT THERE.
THERE WEREN'T ANY EMPTY SPACES OUT FRONT.
snarl
WHAT'S WRONG WITH CAPTAIN?
grrrrr
click click
HE'S BEEN ACTING STRANGE LATELY.
MAYBE HE'S JUST GETTING TIRED OF TAKING CARE OF ME.
whine
HE'S GETTING OLD, CHARLIE.
lick lick
WE SHOULD GET GOING.

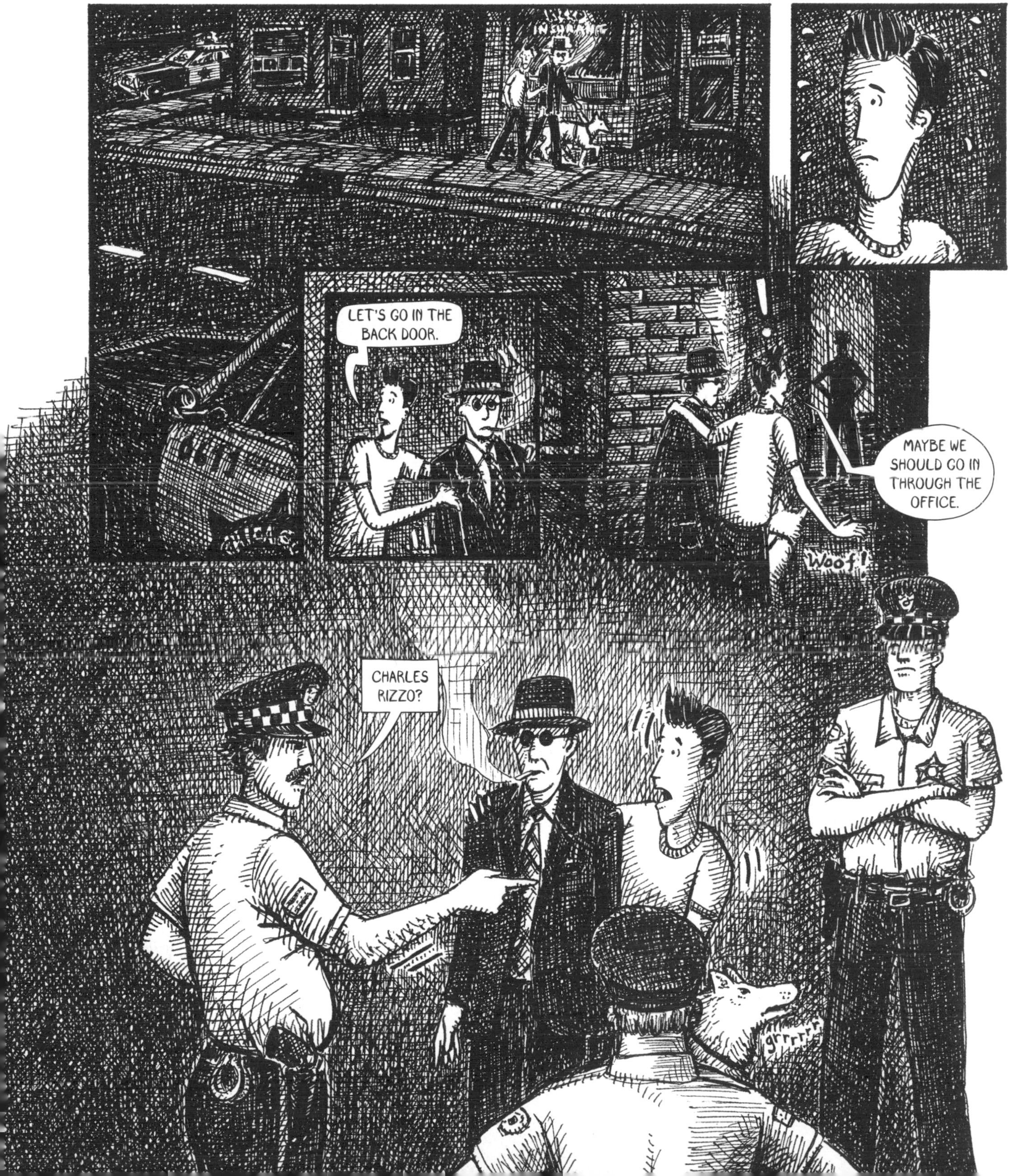
LET'S GO IN THE BACK DOOR.
MAYBE WE SHOULD GO IN THROUGH THE OFFICE.
Woof!
CHARLES RIZZO?

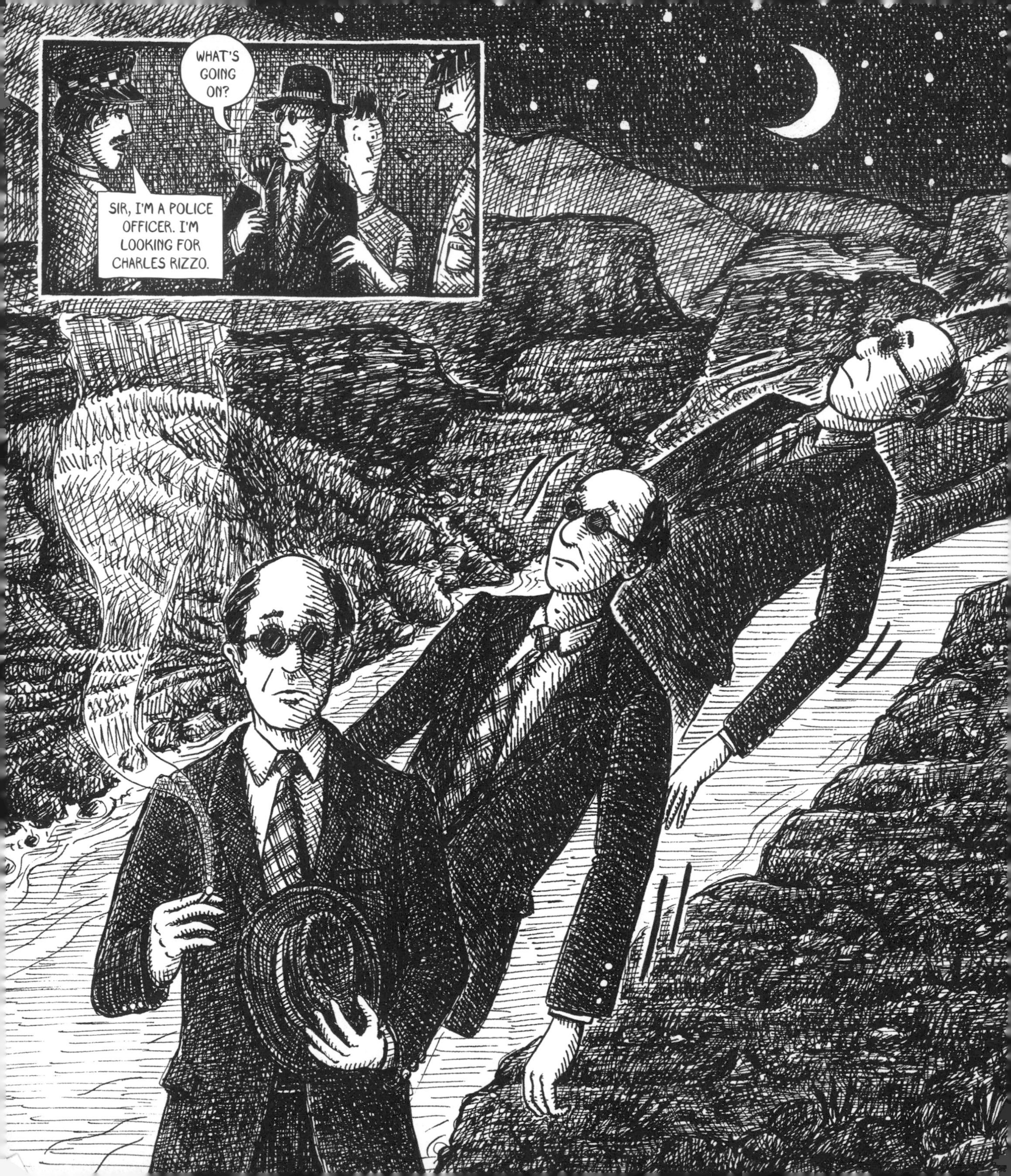
WHAT'S GOING ON?
SIR, I'M A POLICE OFFICER. I'M LOOKING FOR CHARLES RIZZO.

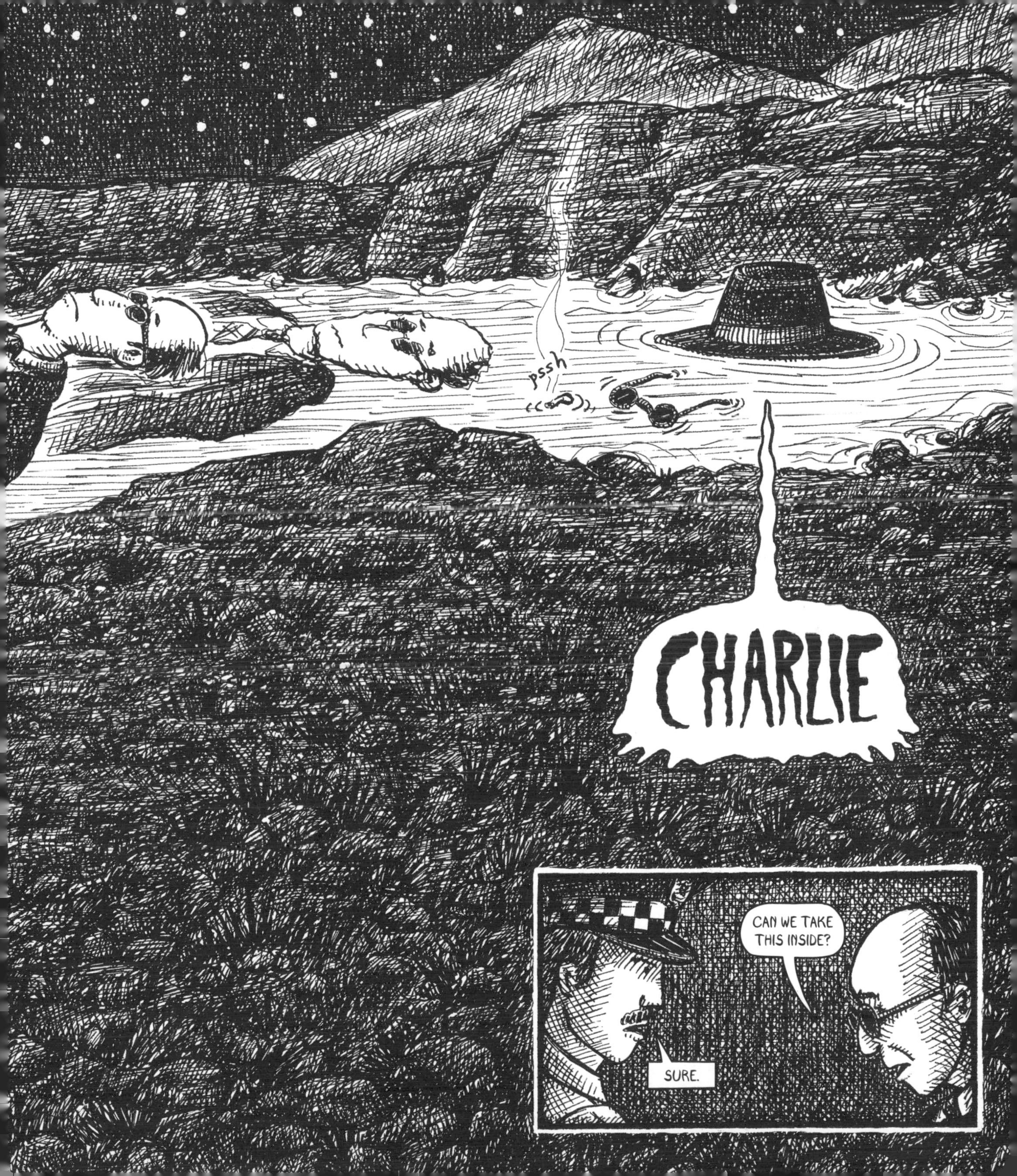
pssh
CHARLIE
CAN WE TAKE THIS INSIDE?
SURE.

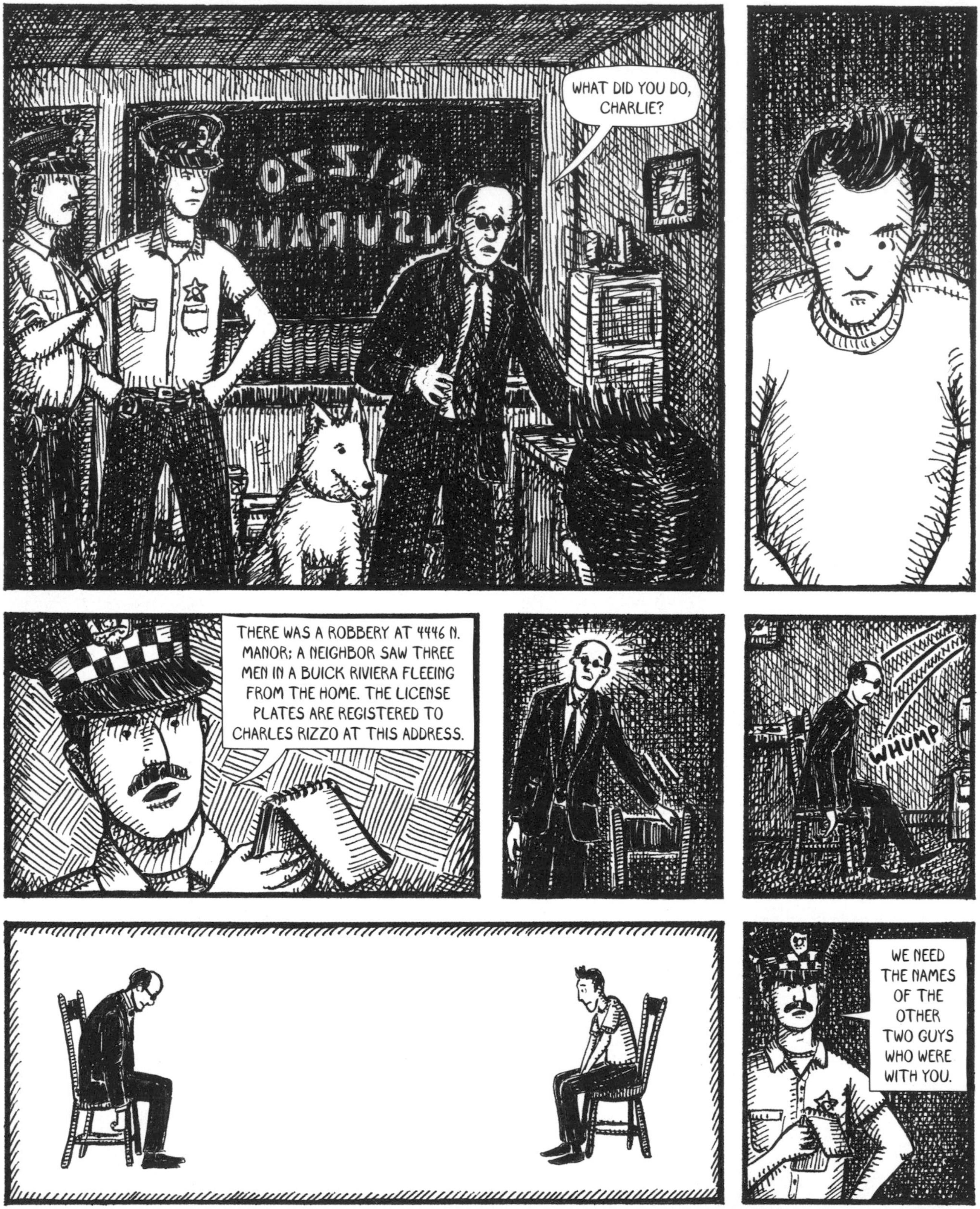

WHAT DID YOU DO, CHARLIE?
THERE WAS A ROBBERY AT 4446 N. MANOR; A NEIGHBOR SAW THREE MEN IN A BUICK RIVIERA FLEEING FROM THE HOME. THE LICENSE PLATES ARE REGISTERED TO CHARLES RIZZO AT THIS ADDRESS.
WHUMP
WE NEED THE NAMES OF THE OTHER TWO GUYS WHO WERE WITH YOU.

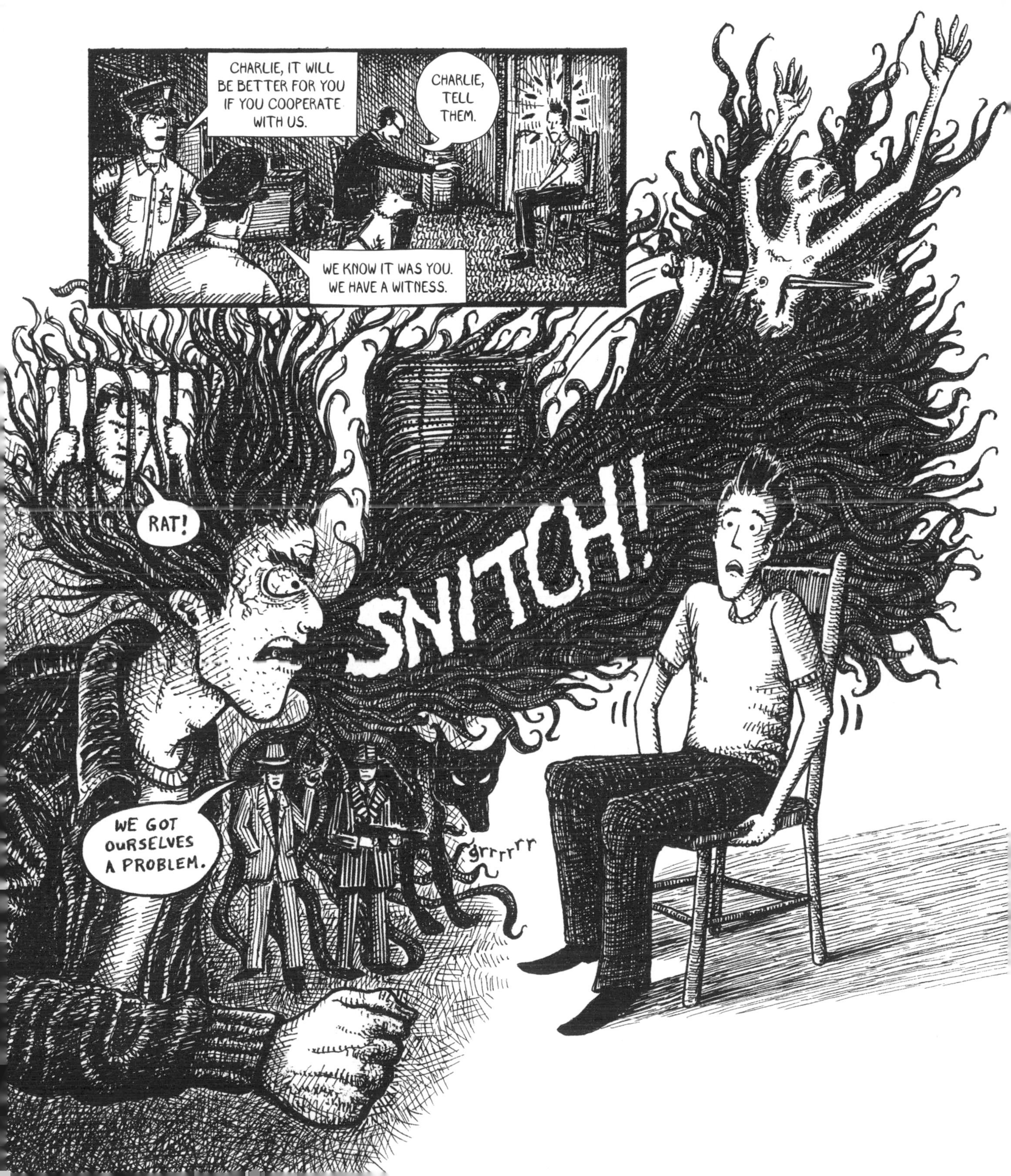
CHARLIE, IT WILL BE BETTER FOR YOU IF YOU COOPERATE WITH US.
CHARLIE, TELL THEM.
WE KNOW IT WAS YOU. WE HAVE A WITNESS.
RAT!
SNITCH!
WE GOT OURSELVES A PROBLEM.
grrrrr

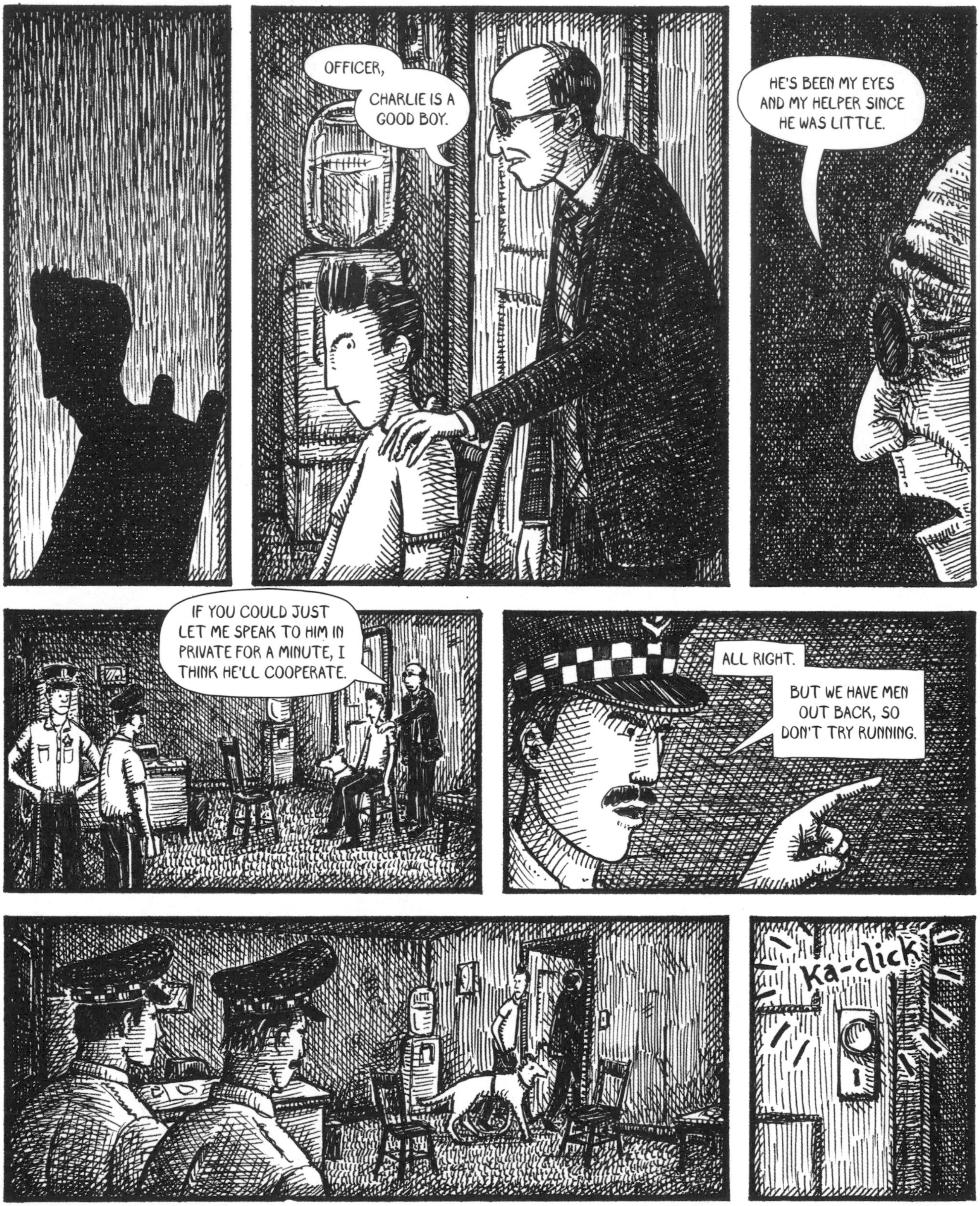

OFFICER,
CHARLIE IS A GOOD BOY.
HE'S BEEN MY EYES AND MY HELPER SINCE HE WAS LITTLE.
IF YOU COULD JUST LET ME SPEAK TO HIM IN PRIVATE FOR A MINUTE, I THINK HE'LL COOPERATE.
ALL RIGHT.
BUT WE HAVE MEN OUT BACK, SO DON'T TRY RUNNING.
Ka-click

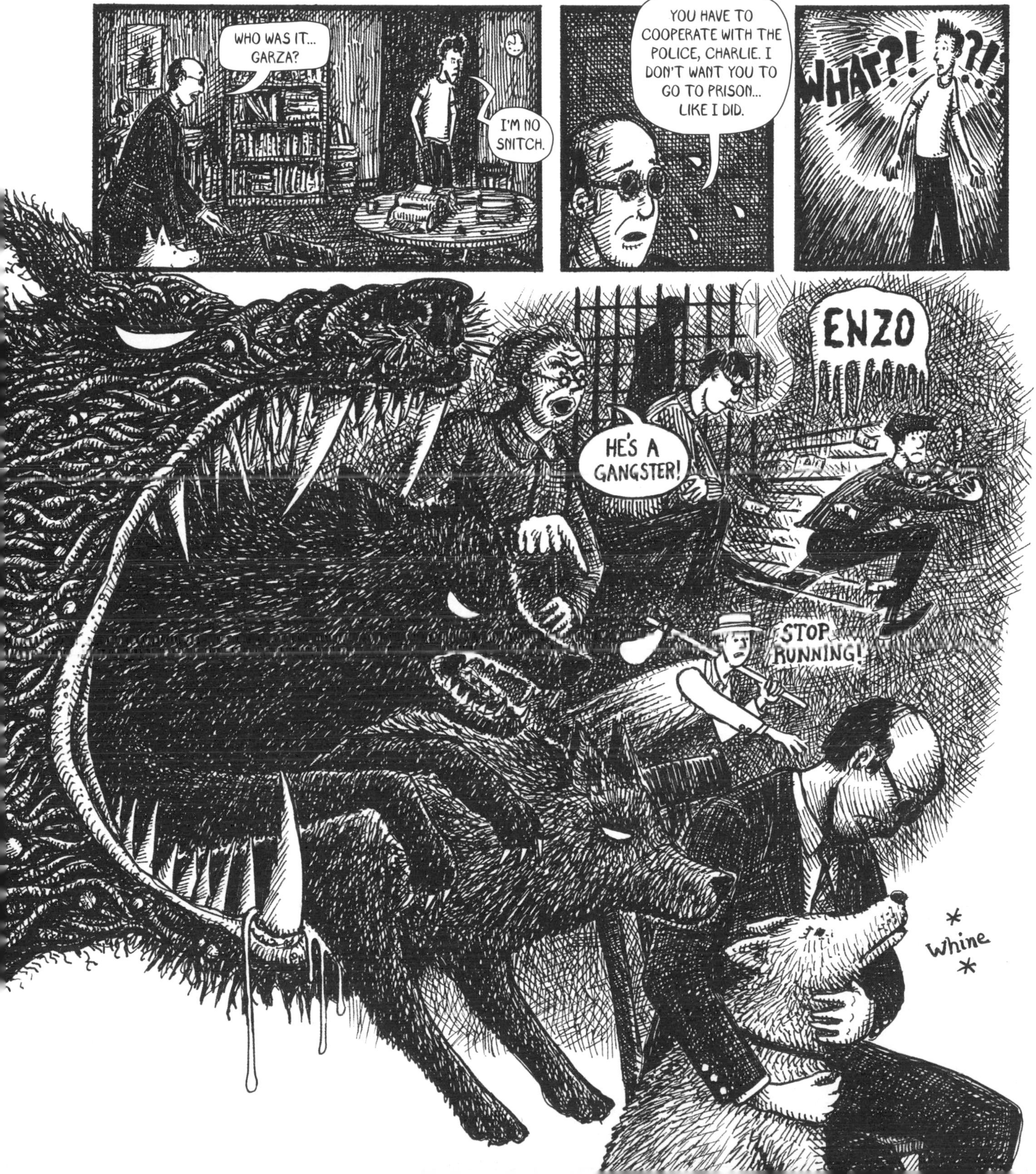
WHO WAS IT... GARZA?
I'M NO SNITCH.
YOU HAVE TO COOPERATE WITH THE POLICE, CHARLIE. I DON'T WANT YOU TO GO TO PRISON... LIKE I DID.
WHAT?! ?!
ENZO
HE'S A GANGSTER!
STOP RUNNING!
whine

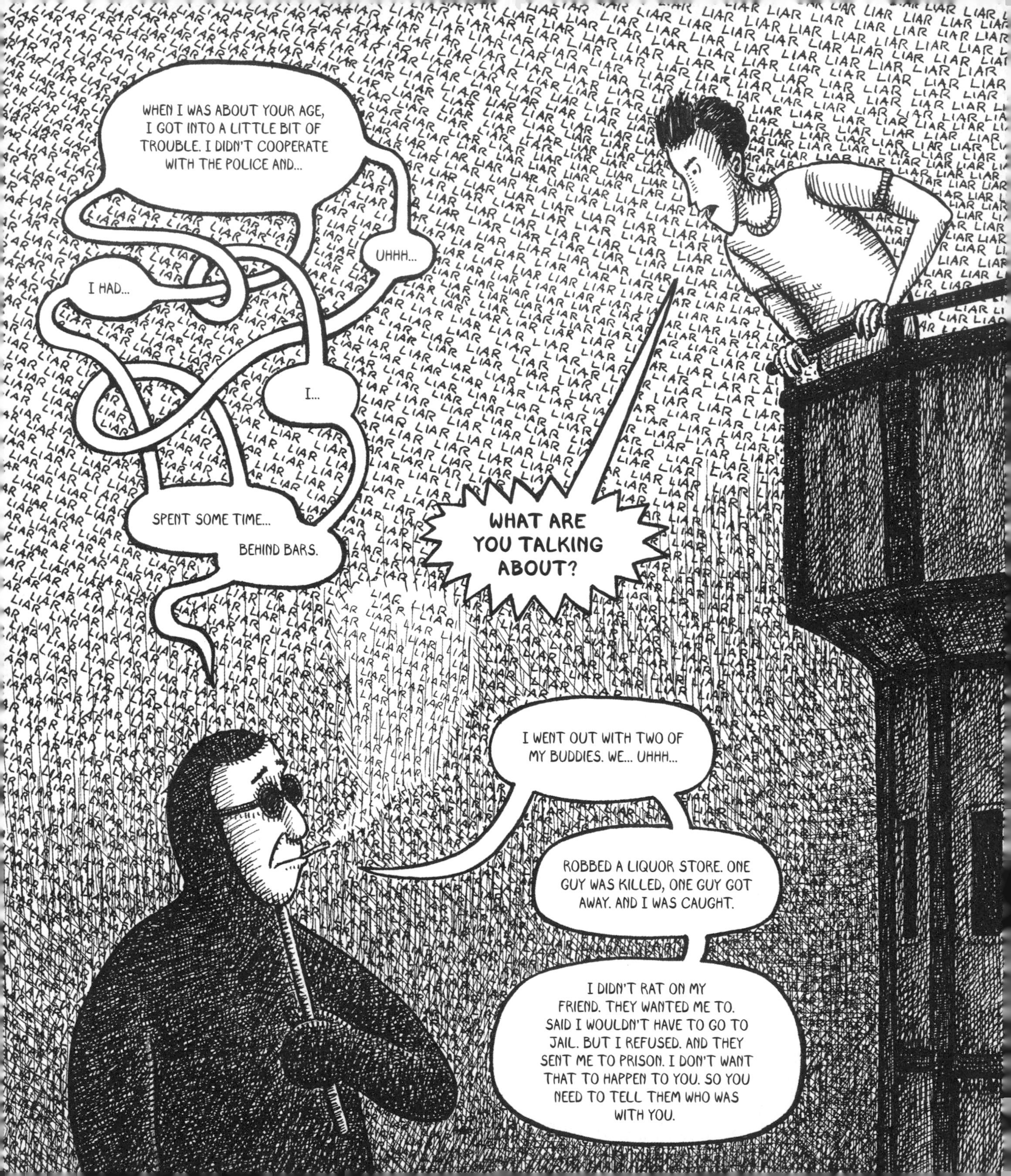
WHEN I WAS ABOUT YOUR AGE, I GOT INTO A LITTLE BIT OF TROUBLE. I DIDN'T COOPERATE WITH THE POLICE AND...
UHHH...
I HAD...
I...
SPENT SOME TIME...
BEHIND BARS.
WHAT ARE YOU TALKING ABOUT?
I WENT OUT WITH TWO OF MY BUDDIES. WE... UHHH...
ROBBED A LIQUOR STORE. ONE GUY WAS KILLED, ONE GUY GOT AWAY. AND I WAS CAUGHT.
I DIDN'T RAT ON MY FRIEND. THEY WANTED ME TO. SAID I WOULDN'T HAVE TO GO TO JAIL. BUT I REFUSED. AND THEY SENT ME TO PRISON. I DON'T WANT THAT TO HAPPEN TO YOU. SO YOU NEED TO TELL THEM WHO WAS WITH YOU.

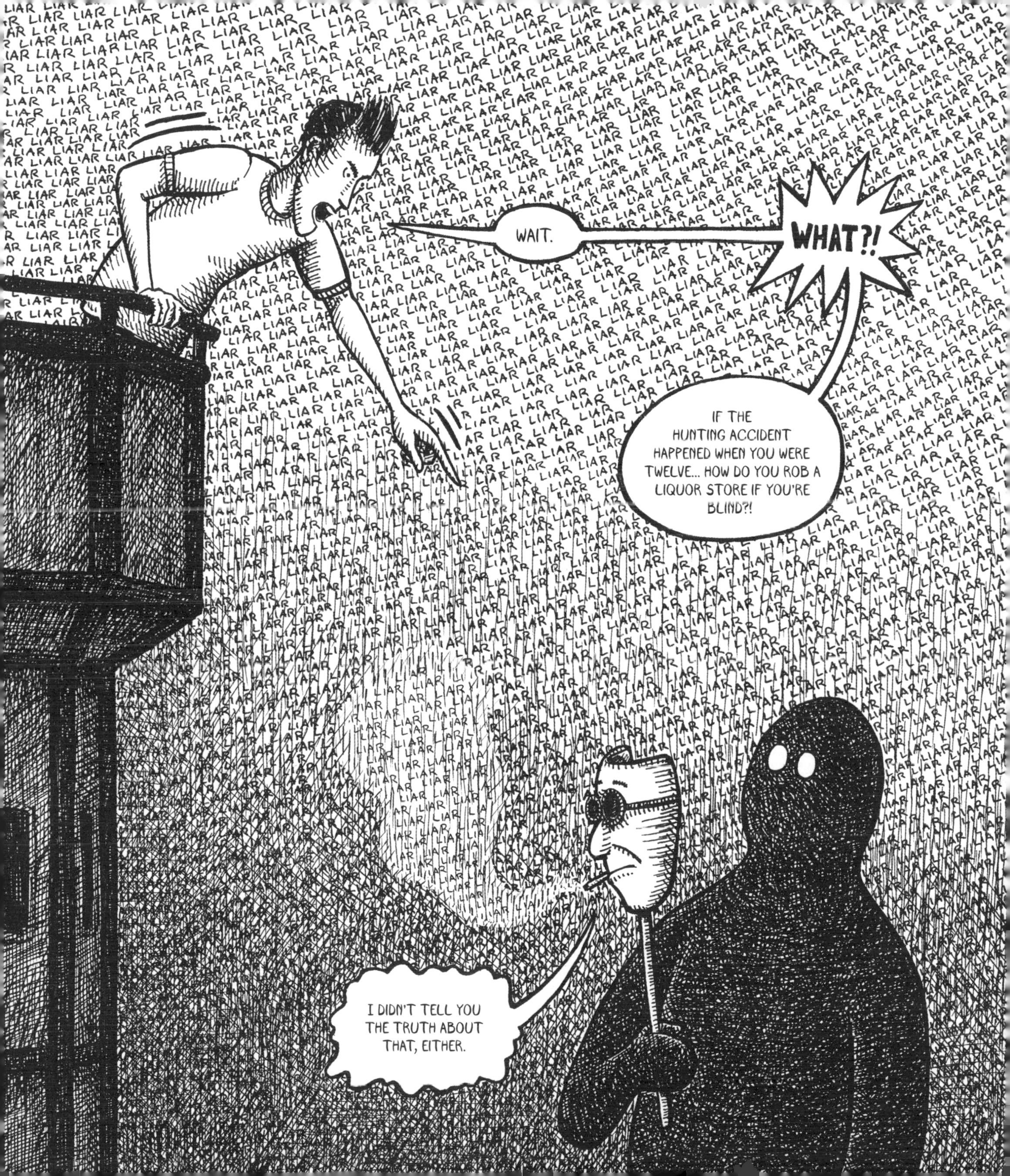
WAIT.
WHAT?!
IF THE HUNTING ACCIDENT HAPPENED WHEN YOU WERE TWELVE... HOW DO YOU ROB A LIQUOR STORE IF YOU'RE BLIND?!
I DIDN'T TELL YOU THE TRUTH ABOUT THAT, EITHER.

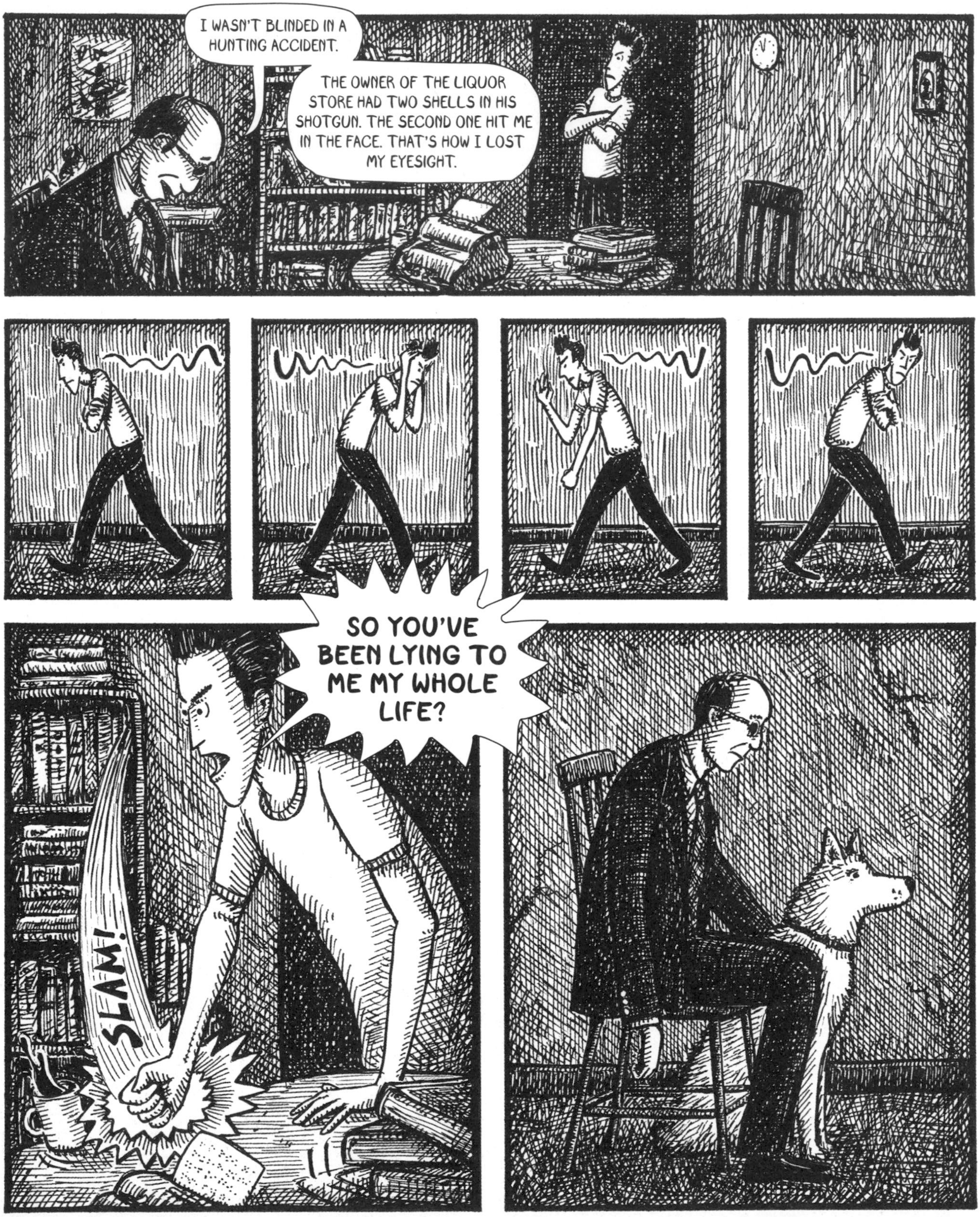
I WASN'T BLINDED IN A HUNTING ACCIDENT.
THE OWNER OF THE LIQUOR STORE HAD TWO SHELLS IN HIS SHOTGUN. THE SECOND ONE HIT ME IN THE FACE. THAT'S HOW I LOST MY EYESIGHT.
SO YOU'VE BEEN LYING TO ME MY WHOLE LIFE?
SLAM!

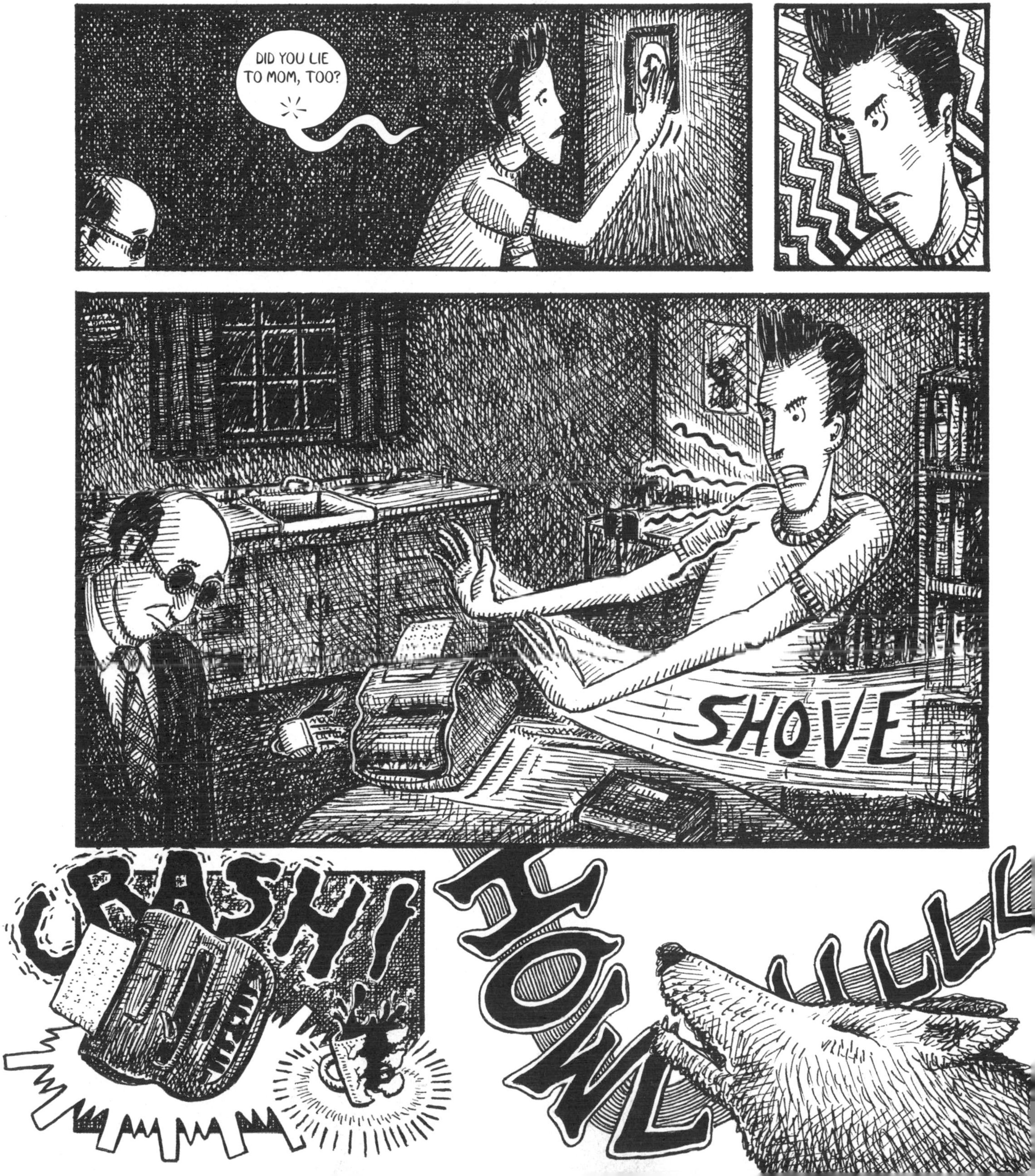
DID YOU LIE TO MOM, TOO?
SHOVE
CRASH!
HOWLLLL

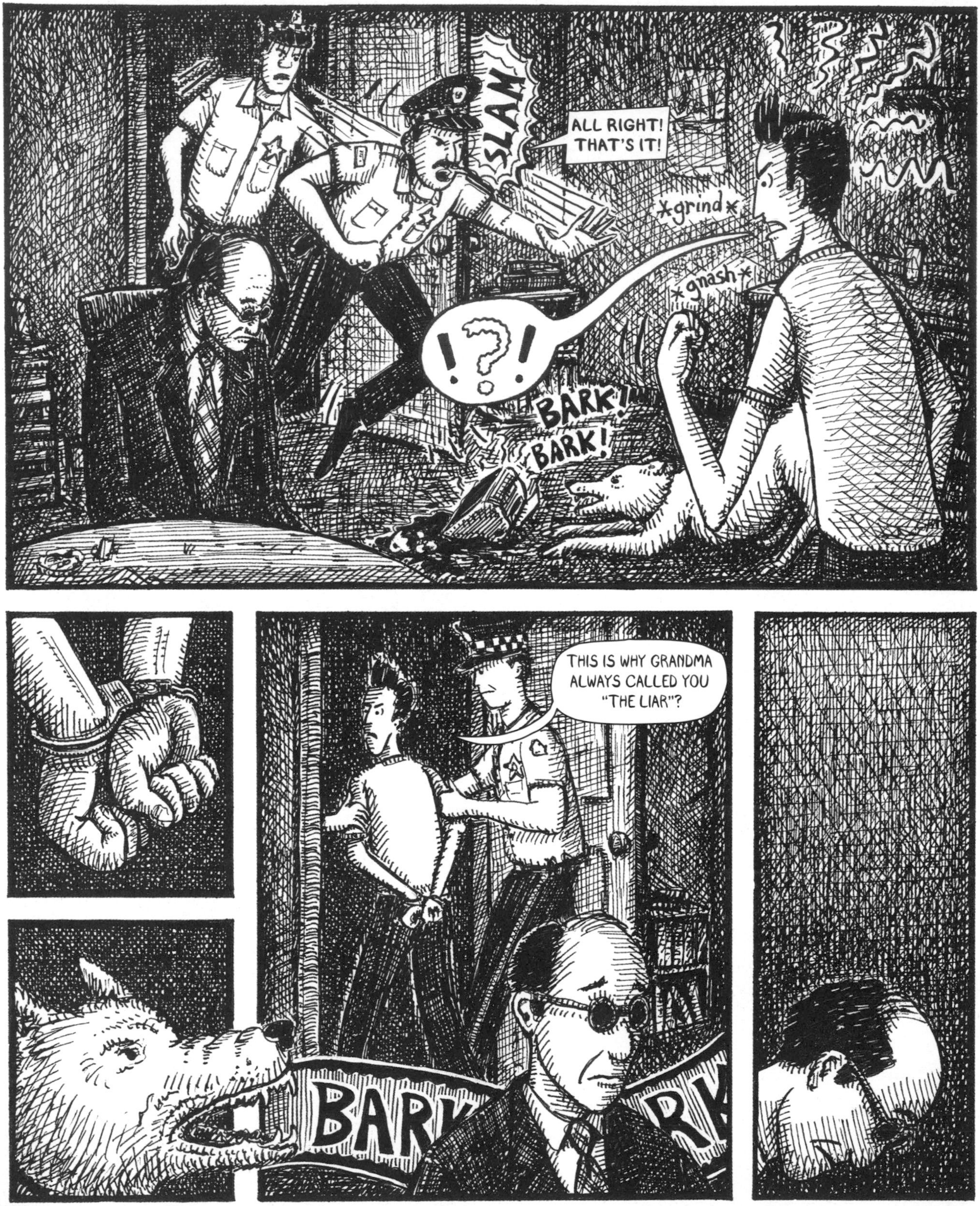
SLAM
ALL RIGHT! THAT'S IT!
grind
gnash
!?!
BARK! BARK!
THIS IS WHY GRANDMA ALWAYS CALLED YOU "THE LIAR"?
BARK

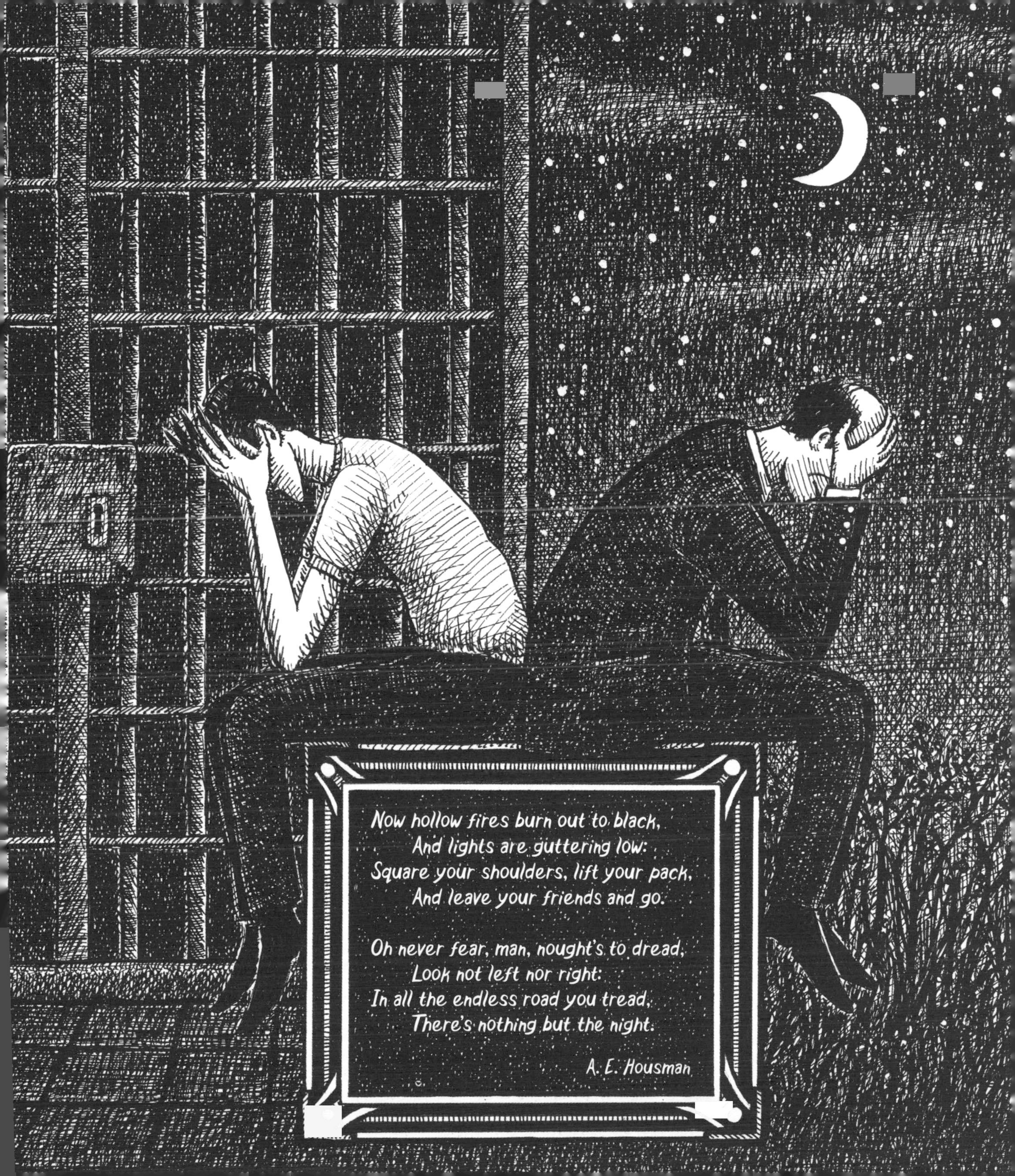
Now hollow fires burn out to black,
And lights are guttering low:
Square your shoulders, lift your pack,
And leave your friends and go.

Oh never fear, man, nought's to dread,
Look not left nor right:
In all the endless road you tread,
There's nothing but the night.

A. E. Housman

IV

CODE OF
SILENCE

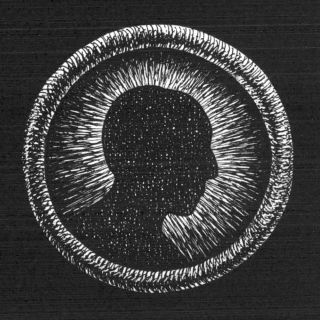

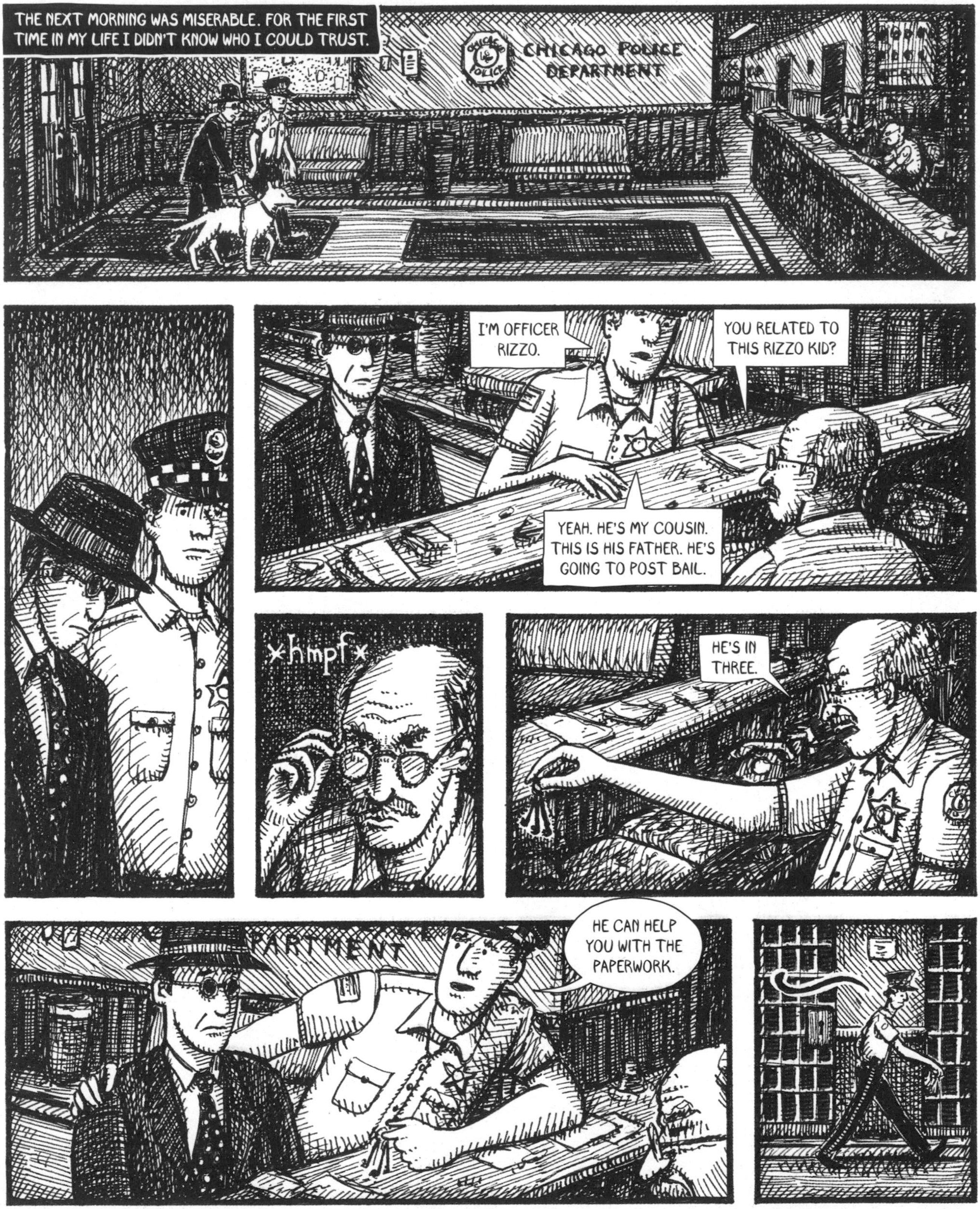
THE NEXT MORNING WAS MISERABLE. FOR THE FIRST TIME IN MY LIFE I DIDN'T KNOW WHO I COULD TRUST.
CHICAGO POLICE DEPARTMENT
I'M OFFICER RIZZO.
YOU RELATED TO THIS RIZZO KID?
YEAH. HE'S MY COUSIN. THIS IS HIS FATHER. HE'S GOING TO POST BAIL.
hmpf
HE'S IN THREE.
PARTMENT
HE CAN HELP YOU WITH THE PAPERWORK.

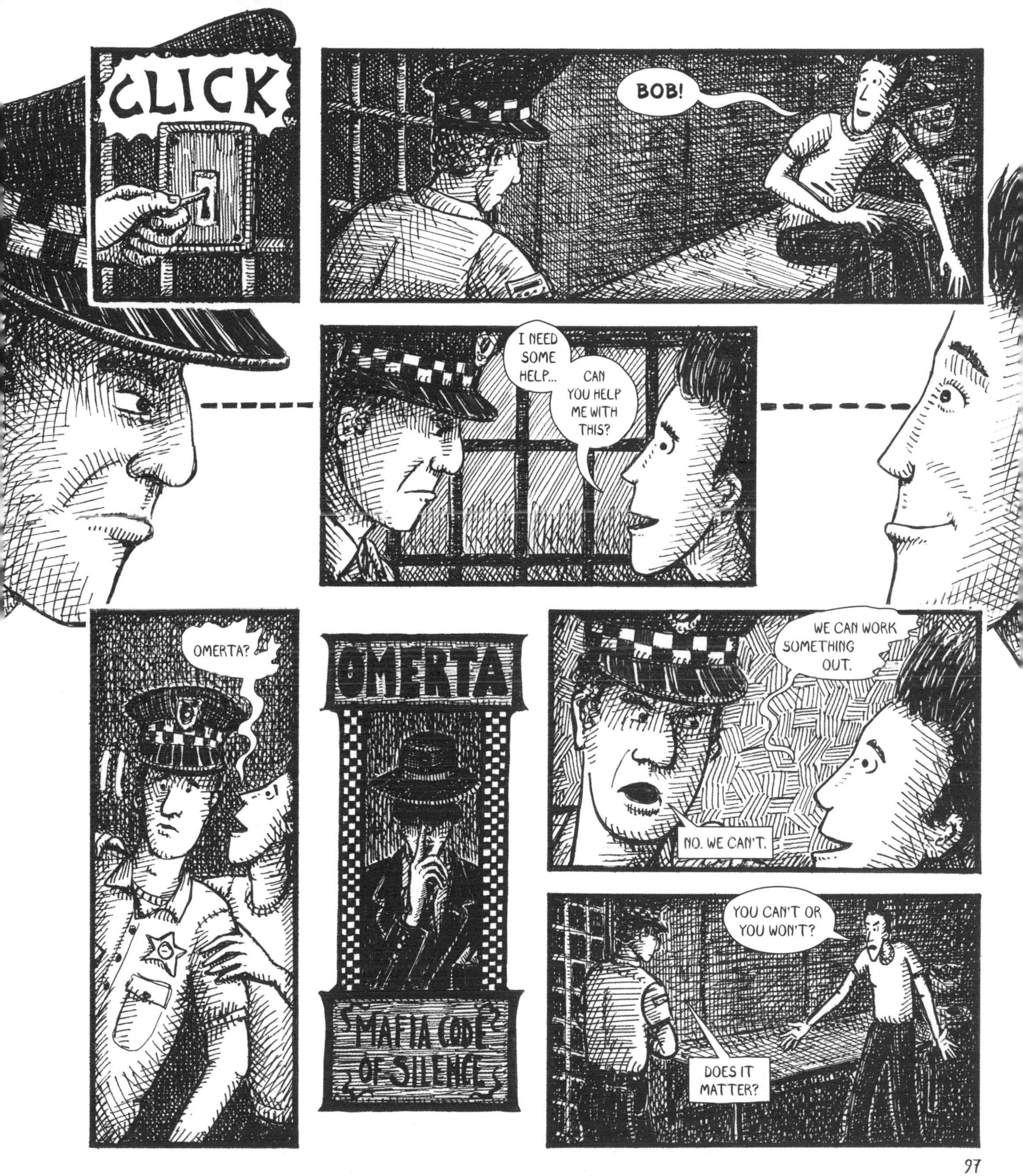
CLICK
BOB!
I NEED SOME HELP...
CAN YOU HELP ME WITH THIS?
OMERTA?
OMERTA
MAFIA CODE OF SILENCE
WE CAN WORK SOMETHING OUT.
NO. WE CAN'T.
YOU CAN'T OR YOU WON'T?
DOES IT MATTER?

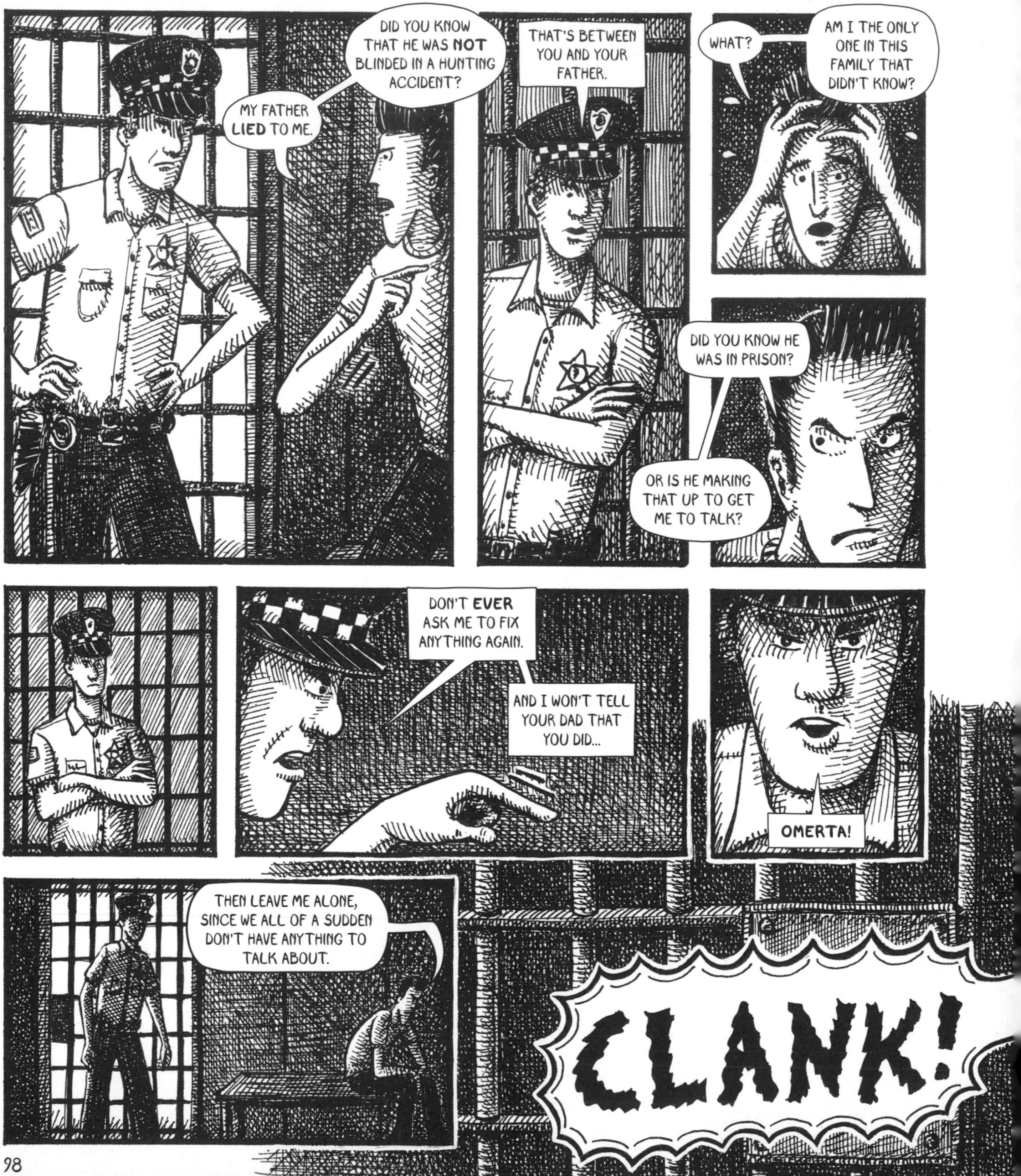
MY FATHER LIED TO ME.
DID YOU KNOW THAT HE WAS NOT BLINDED IN A HUNTING ACCIDENT?
THAT'S BETWEEN YOU AND YOUR FATHER.
WHAT?
AM I THE ONLY ONE IN THIS FAMILY THAT DIDN'T KNOW?
DID YOU KNOW HE WAS IN PRISON?
OR IS HE MAKING THAT UP TO GET ME TO TALK?
DON'T EVER ASK ME TO FIX ANYTHING AGAIN.
AND I WON'T TELL YOUR DAD THAT YOU DID...
OMERTA!
THEN LEAVE ME ALONE, SINCE WE ALL OF A SUDDEN DON'T HAVE ANYTHING TO TALK ABOUT.
CLANK!

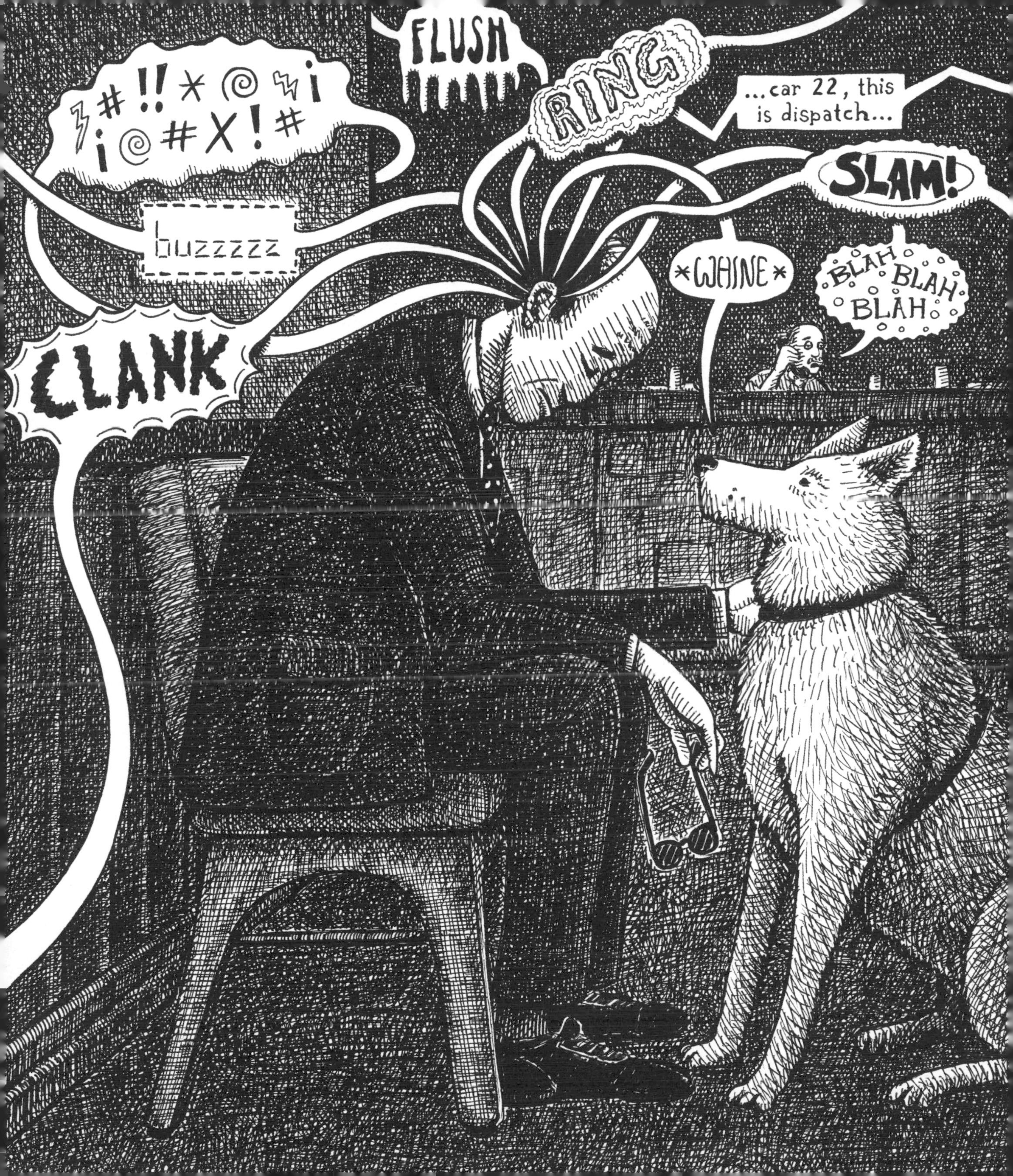
FLUSH
RING
...car 22, this is dispatch...
SLAM!
buzzzzz
WHINE
BLAH BLAH BLAH
CLANK

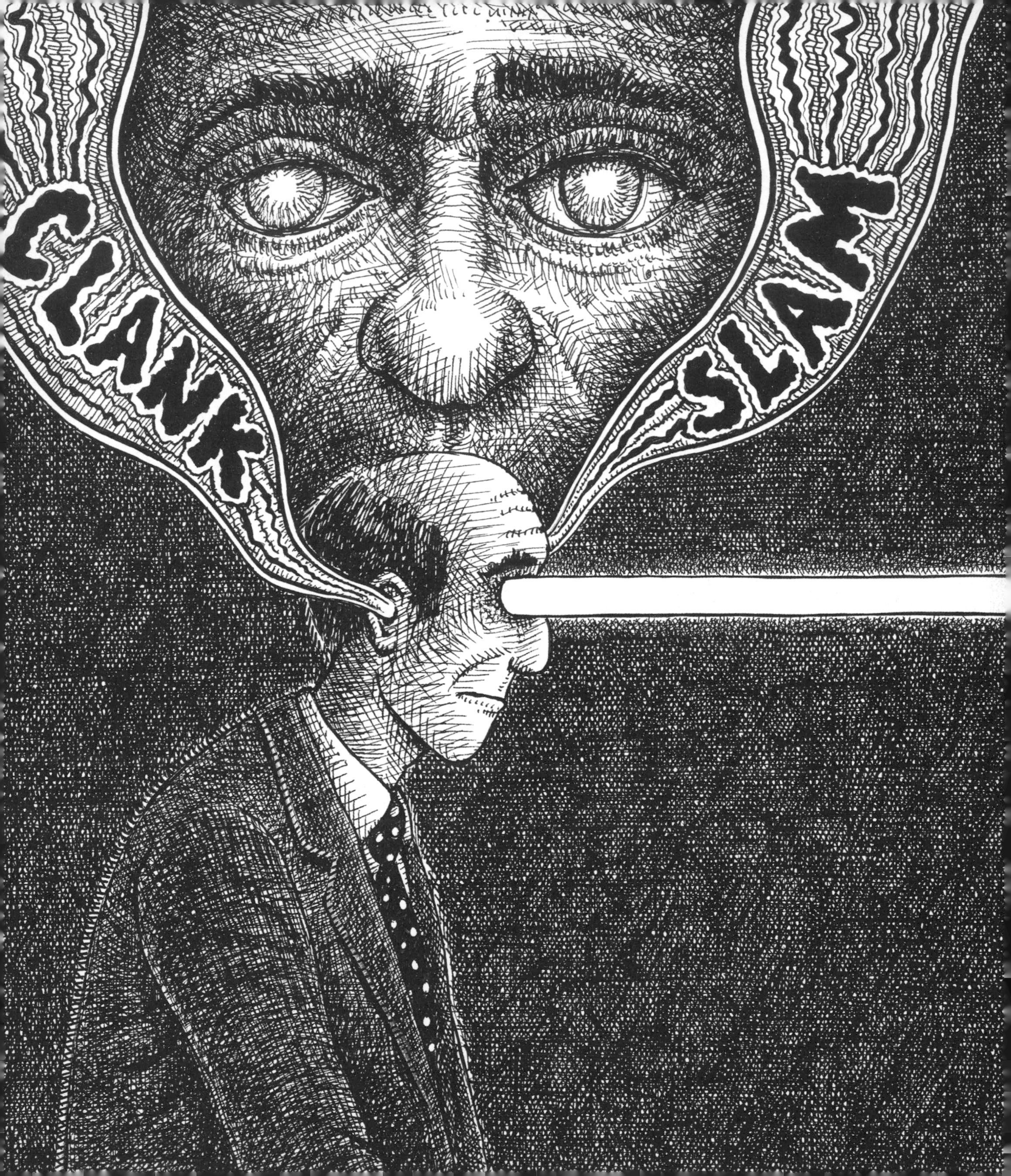
CLANK
SLAM

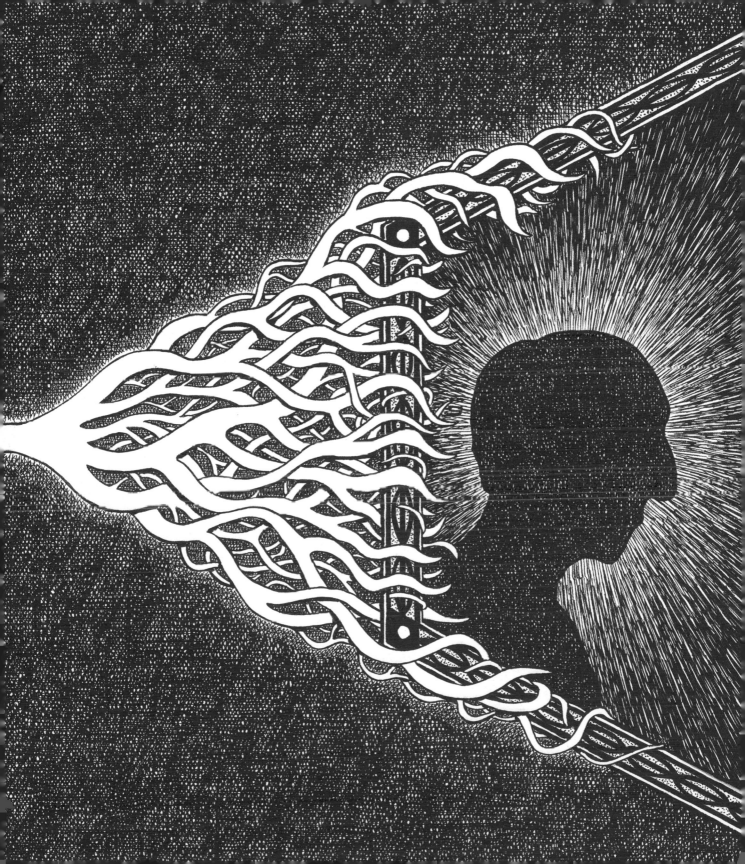

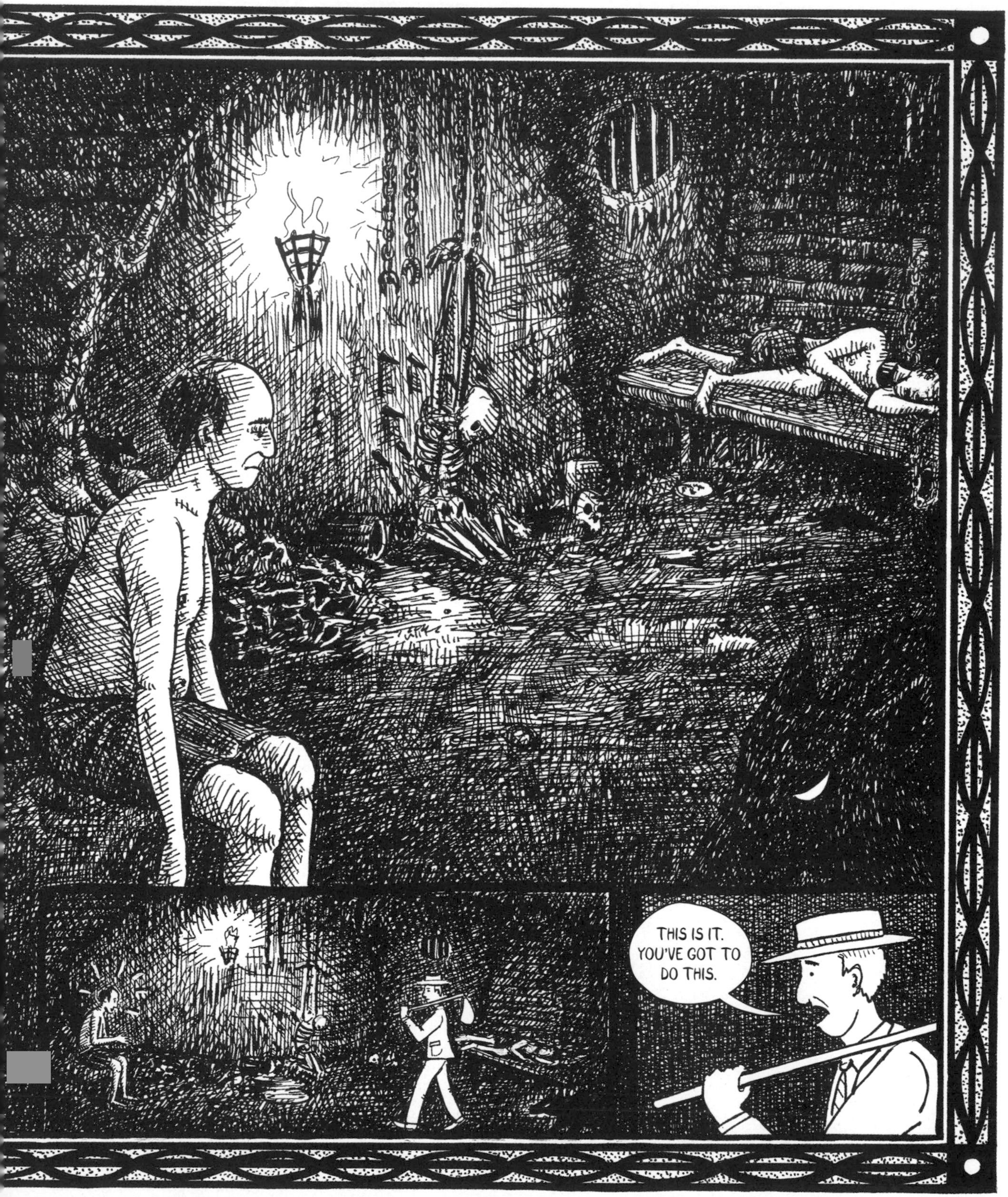
THIS IS IT. YOU'VE GOT TO DO THIS.

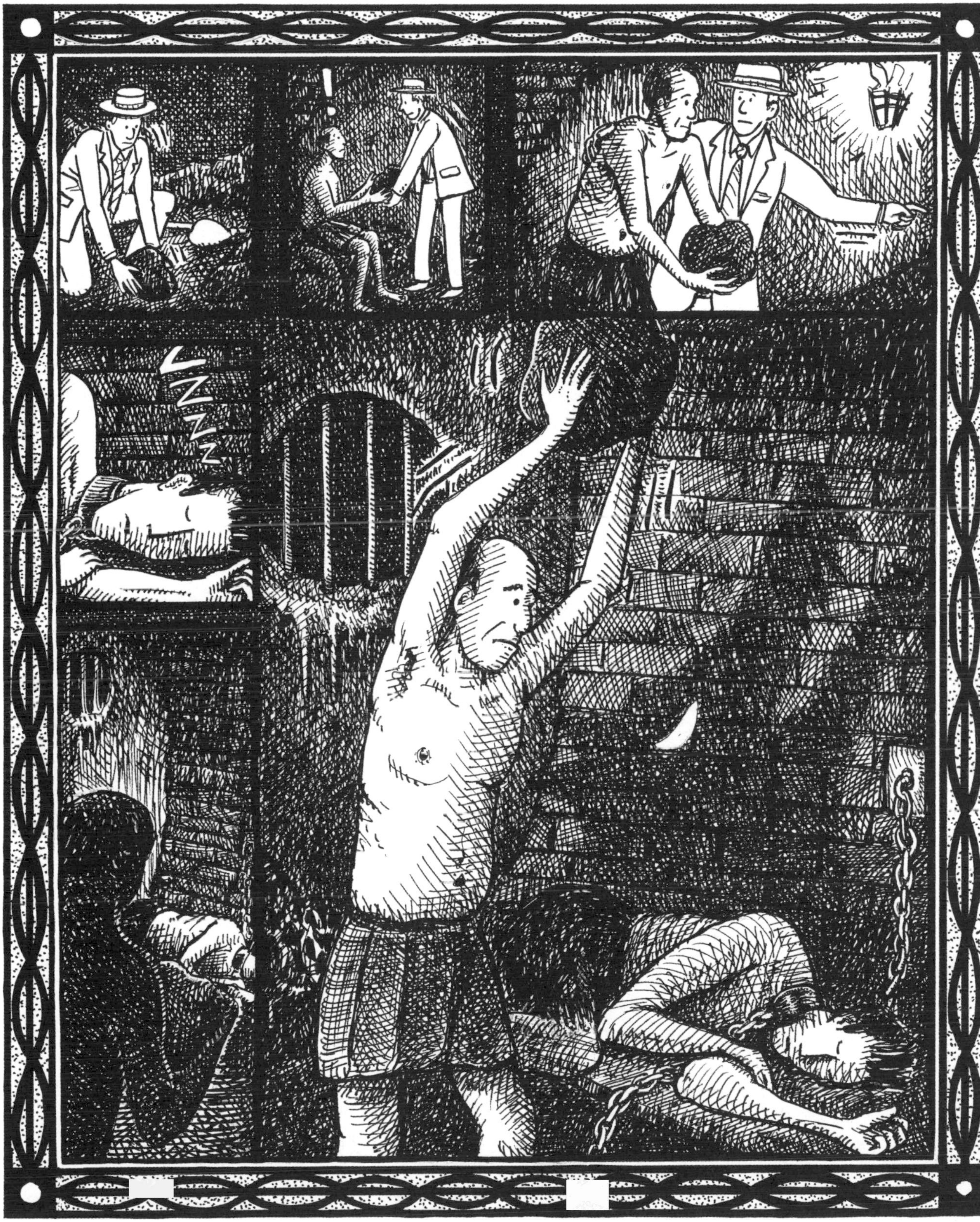
!
ZZZZ

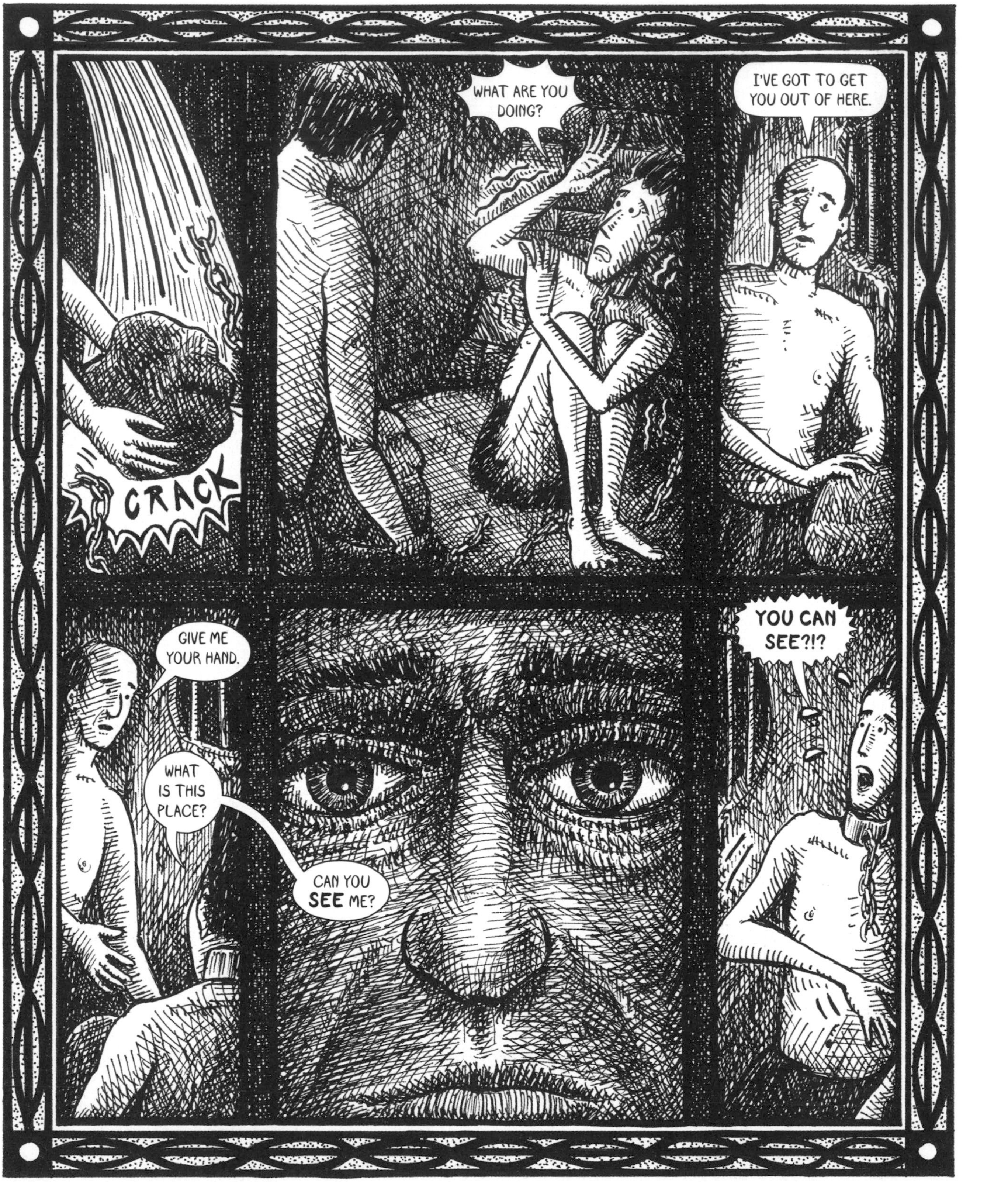
CRACK
WHAT ARE YOU DOING?
I'VE GOT TO GET YOU OUT OF HERE.
GIVE ME YOUR HAND.
WHAT IS THIS PLACE?
CAN YOU SEE ME?
YOU CAN SEE?!?

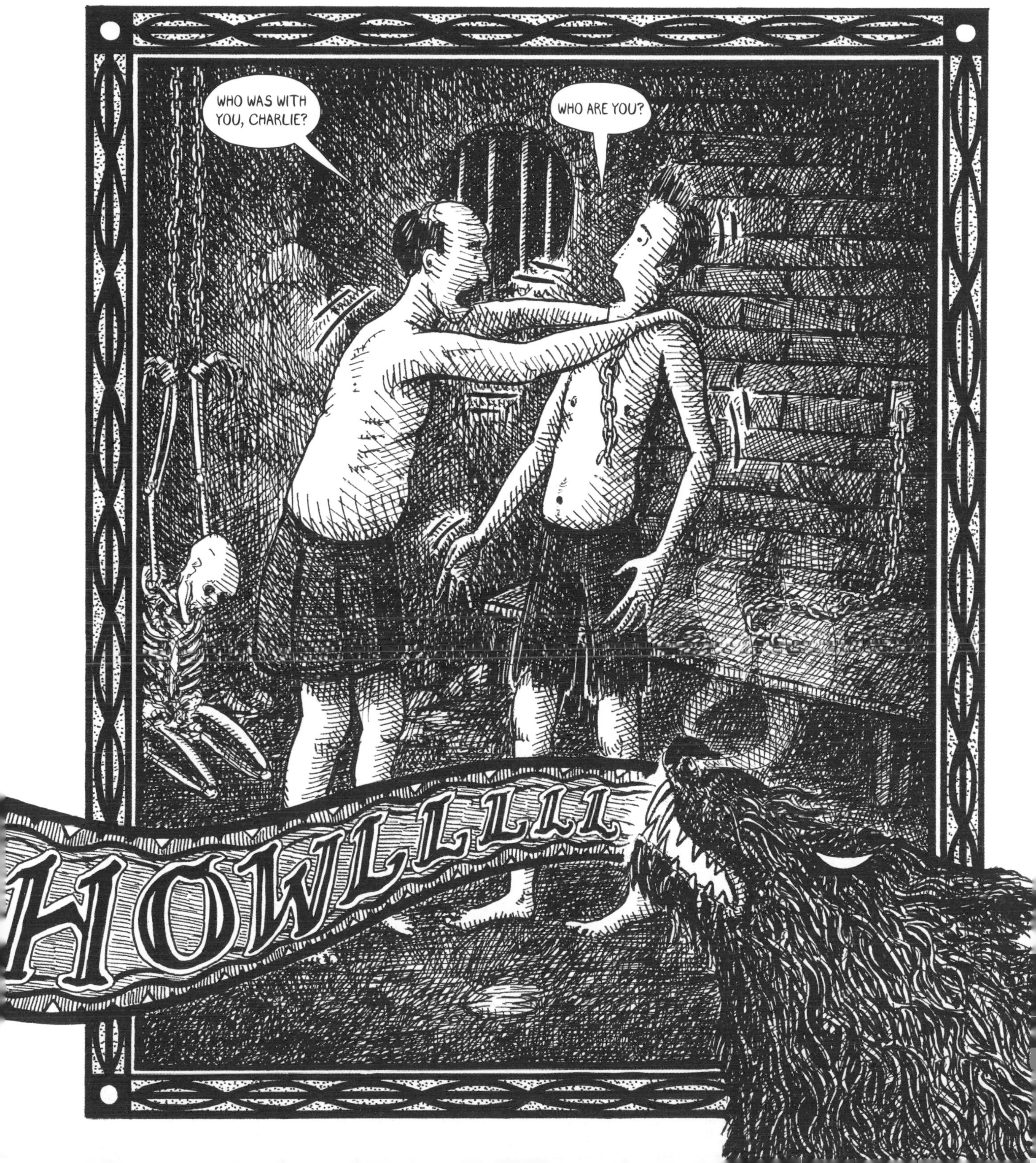
WHO WAS WITH YOU, CHARLIE?
WHO ARE YOU?
HOWLLLLL

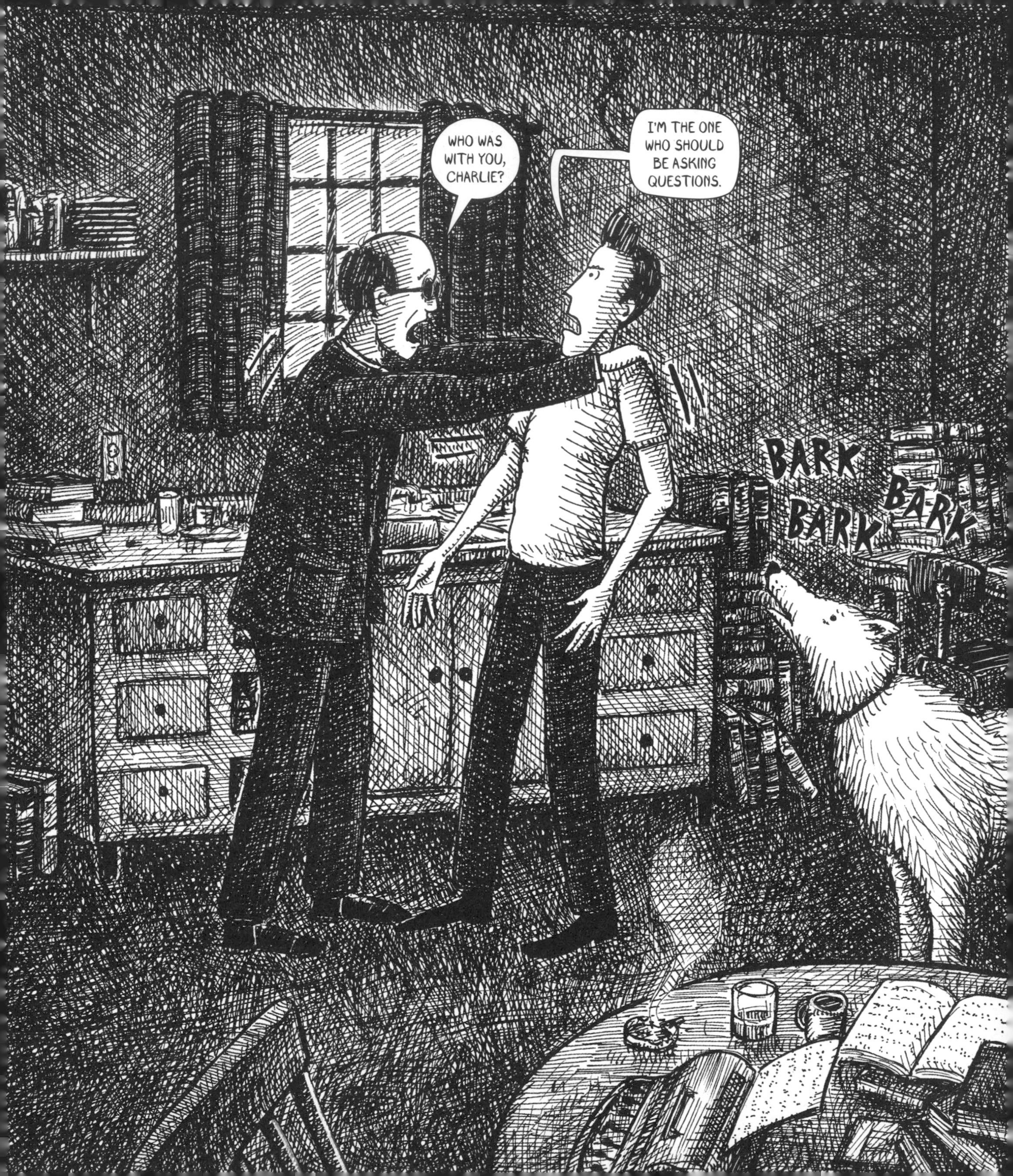
WHO WAS WITH YOU, CHARLIE?
I'M THE ONE WHO SHOULD BE ASKING QUESTIONS.
BARK
BARK
BARK

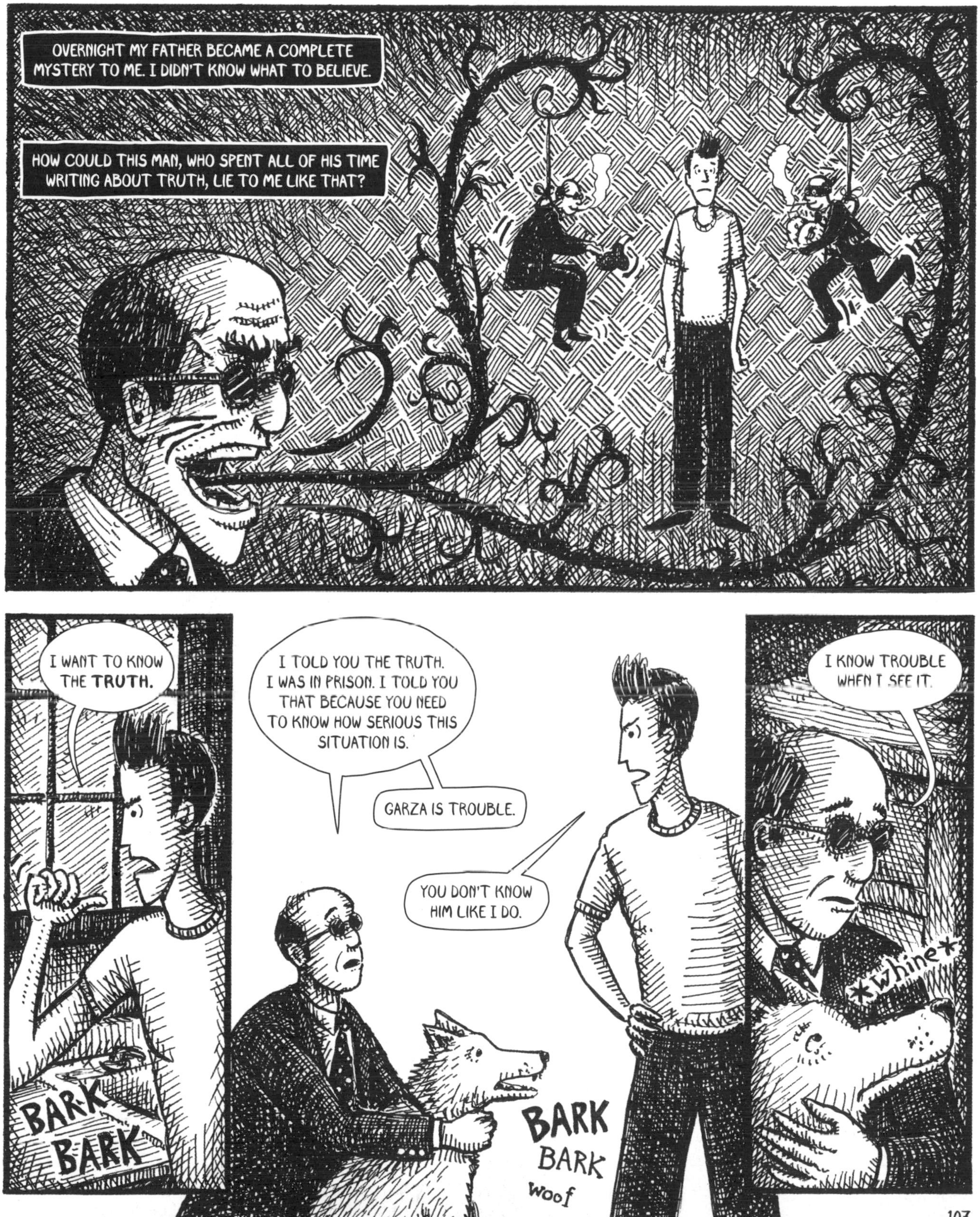

OVERNIGHT MY FATHER BECAME A COMPLETE MYSTERY TO ME. I DIDN'T KNOW WHAT TO BELIEVE.
HOW COULD THIS MAN, WHO SPENT ALL OF HIS TIME WRITING ABOUT TRUTH, LIE TO ME LIKE THAT?
I WANT TO KNOW THE **TRUTH.**
BARK BARK
I TOLD YOU THE TRUTH. I WAS IN PRISON. I TOLD YOU THAT BECAUSE YOU NEED TO KNOW HOW SERIOUS THIS SITUATION IS.
GARZA IS TROUBLE.
YOU DON'T KNOW HIM LIKE I DO.
BARK
BARK
woof
I KNOW TROUBLE WHEN I SEE IT.
whine

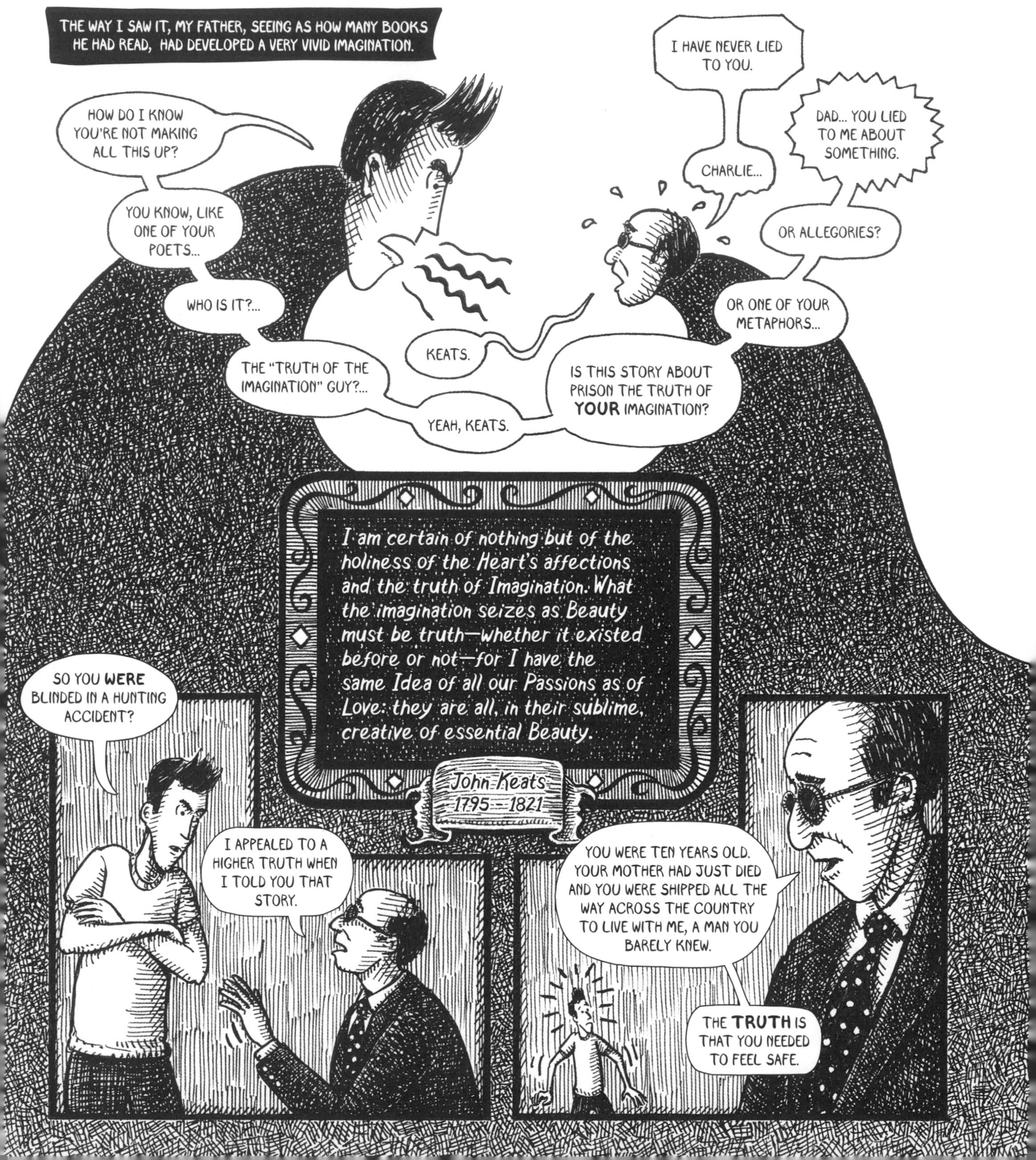
THE WAY I SAW IT, MY FATHER, SEEING AS HOW MANY BOOKS HE HAD READ, HAD DEVELOPED A VERY VIVID IMAGINATION.
HOW DO I KNOW YOU'RE NOT MAKING ALL THIS UP?
YOU KNOW, LIKE ONE OF YOUR POETS...
WHO IS IT?...
THE "TRUTH OF THE IMAGINATION" GUY?...
KEATS.
YEAH, KEATS.
IS THIS STORY ABOUT PRISON THE TRUTH OF **YOUR** IMAGINATION?
I HAVE NEVER LIED TO YOU.
CHARLIE...
DAD... YOU LIED TO ME ABOUT SOMETHING.
OR ALLEGORIES?
OR ONE OF YOUR METAPHORS...
I am certain of nothing but of the holiness of the Heart's affections and the truth of Imagination. What the imagination seizes as Beauty must be truth—whether it existed before or not—for I have the same Idea of all our Passions as of Love: they are all, in their sublime, creative of essential Beauty.
John Keats 1795 - 1821
SO YOU **WERE** BLINDED IN A HUNTING ACCIDENT?
I APPEALED TO A HIGHER TRUTH WHEN I TOLD YOU THAT STORY.
YOU WERE TEN YEARS OLD. YOUR MOTHER HAD JUST DIED AND YOU WERE SHIPPED ALL THE WAY ACROSS THE COUNTRY TO LIVE WITH ME, A MAN YOU BARELY KNEW.
THE **TRUTH** IS THAT YOU NEEDED TO FEEL SAFE.

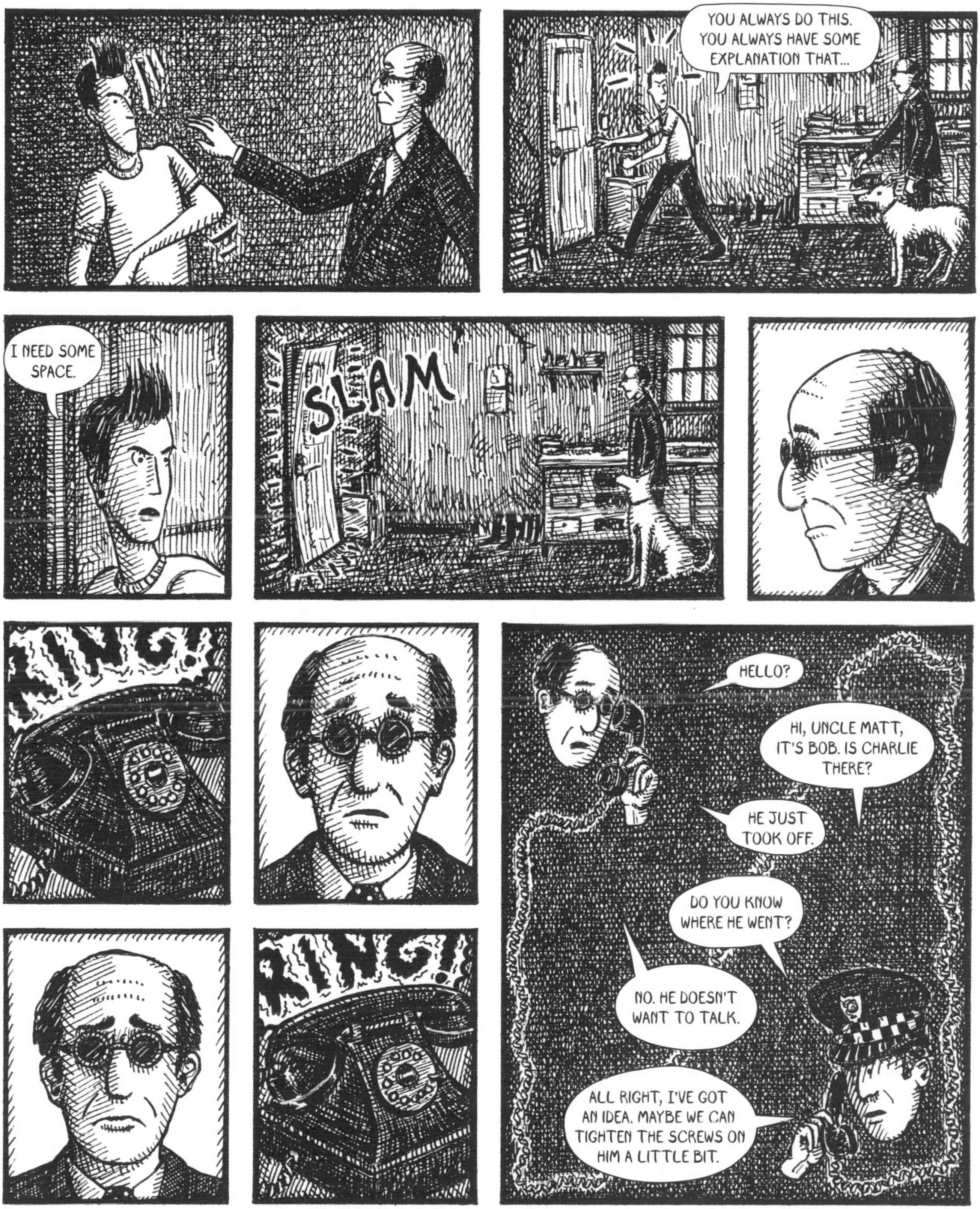
YOU ALWAYS DO THIS. YOU ALWAYS HAVE SOME EXPLANATION THAT...
I NEED SOME SPACE.
SLAM
RING!
HELLO?
HI, UNCLE MATT, IT'S BOB. IS CHARLIE THERE?
HE JUST TOOK OFF.
DO YOU KNOW WHERE HE WENT?
NO. HE DOESN'T WANT TO TALK.
RING!
ALL RIGHT, I'VE GOT AN IDEA. MAYBE WE CAN TIGHTEN THE SCREWS ON HIM A LITTLE BIT.

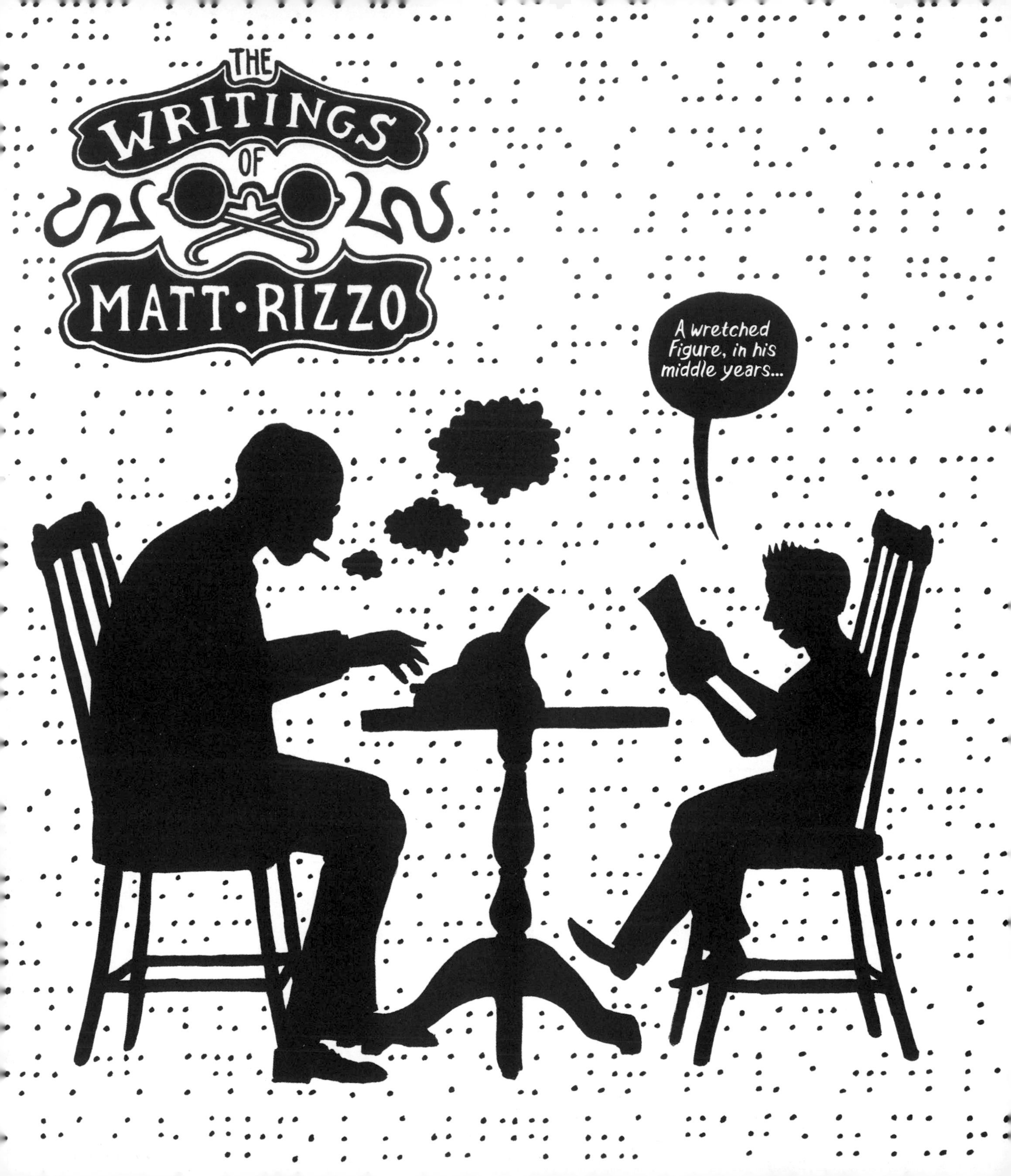
THE WRITINGS OF MATT·RIZZO
A wretched Figure, in his middle years...

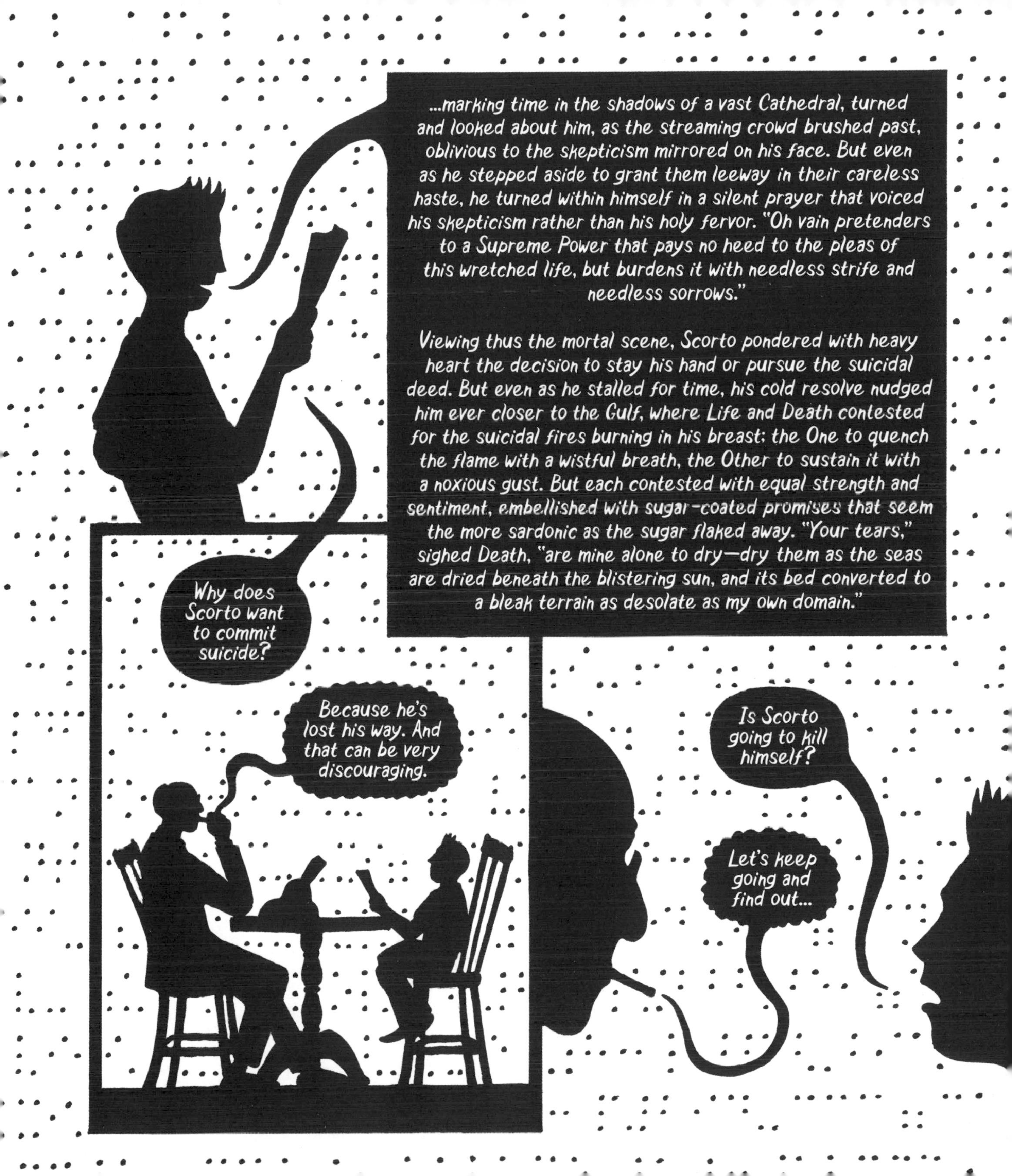
...marking time in the shadows of a vast Cathedral, turned and looked about him, as the streaming crowd brushed past, oblivious to the skepticism mirrored on his face. But even as he stepped aside to grant them leeway in their careless haste, he turned within himself in a silent prayer that voiced his skepticism rather than his holy fervor. "Oh vain pretenders to a Supreme Power that pays no heed to the pleas of this wretched life, but burdens it with needless strife and needless sorrows."
Viewing thus the mortal scene, Scorto pondered with heavy heart the decision to stay his hand or pursue the suicidal deed. But even as he stalled for time, his cold resolve nudged him ever closer to the Gulf, where Life and Death contested for the suicidal fires burning in his breast: the One to quench the flame with a wistful breath, the Other to sustain it with a noxious gust. But each contested with equal strength and sentiment, embellished with sugar-coated promises that seem the more sardonic as the sugar flaked away. "Your tears," sighed Death, "are mine alone to dry—dry them as the seas are dried beneath the blistering sun, and its bed converted to a bleak terrain as desolate as my own domain."
Why does Scorto want to commit suicide?
Because he's lost his way. And that can be very discouraging.
Is Scorto going to kill himself?
Let's keep going and find out...

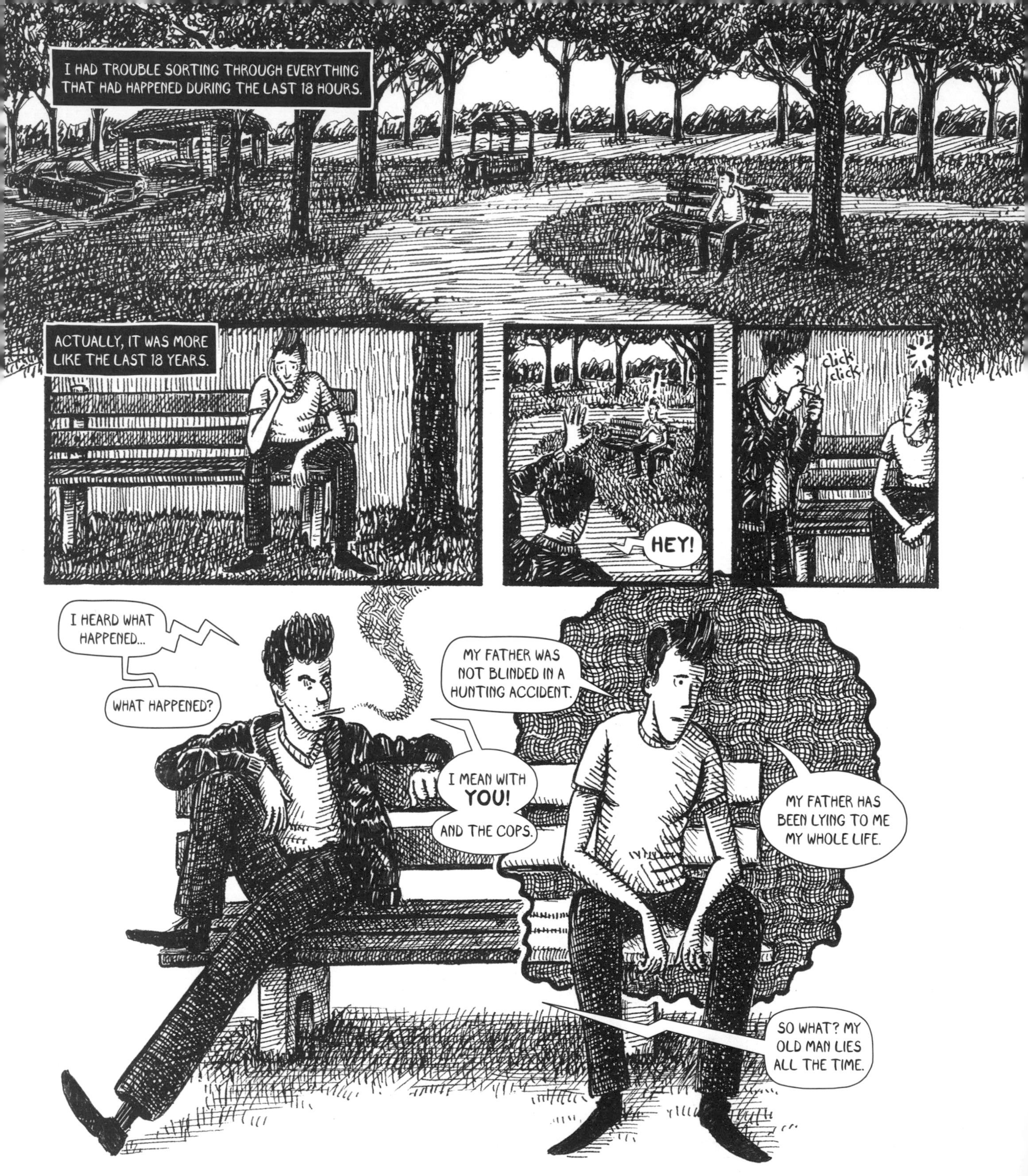

I HAD TROUBLE SORTING THROUGH EVERYTHING THAT HAD HAPPENED DURING THE LAST 18 HOURS.
ACTUALLY, IT WAS MORE LIKE THE LAST 18 YEARS.
HEY!
click click
I HEARD WHAT HAPPENED...
WHAT HAPPENED?
I MEAN WITH YOU!
AND THE COPS.
MY FATHER WAS NOT BLINDED IN A HUNTING ACCIDENT.
MY FATHER HAS BEEN LYING TO ME MY WHOLE LIFE.
SO WHAT? MY OLD MAN LIES ALL THE TIME.

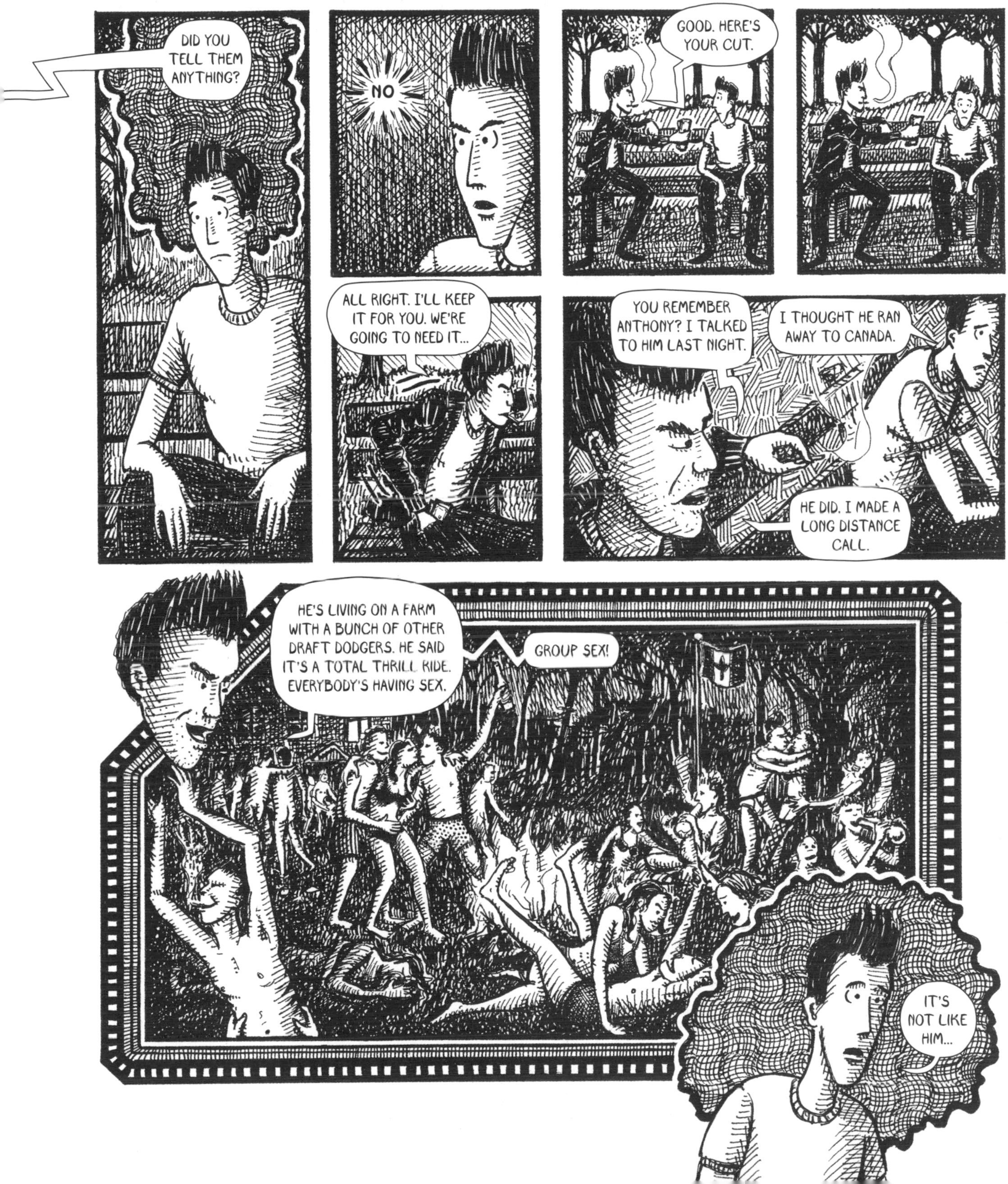
DID YOU TELL THEM ANYTHING?
NO
GOOD. HERE'S YOUR CUT.
ALL RIGHT. I'LL KEEP IT FOR YOU. WE'RE GOING TO NEED IT...
YOU REMEMBER ANTHONY? I TALKED TO HIM LAST NIGHT.
I THOUGHT HE RAN AWAY TO CANADA.
HE DID. I MADE A LONG DISTANCE CALL.
HE'S LIVING ON A FARM WITH A BUNCH OF OTHER DRAFT DODGERS. HE SAID IT'S A TOTAL THRILL RIDE. EVERYBODY'S HAVING SEX.
GROUP SEX!
IT'S NOT LIKE HIM...

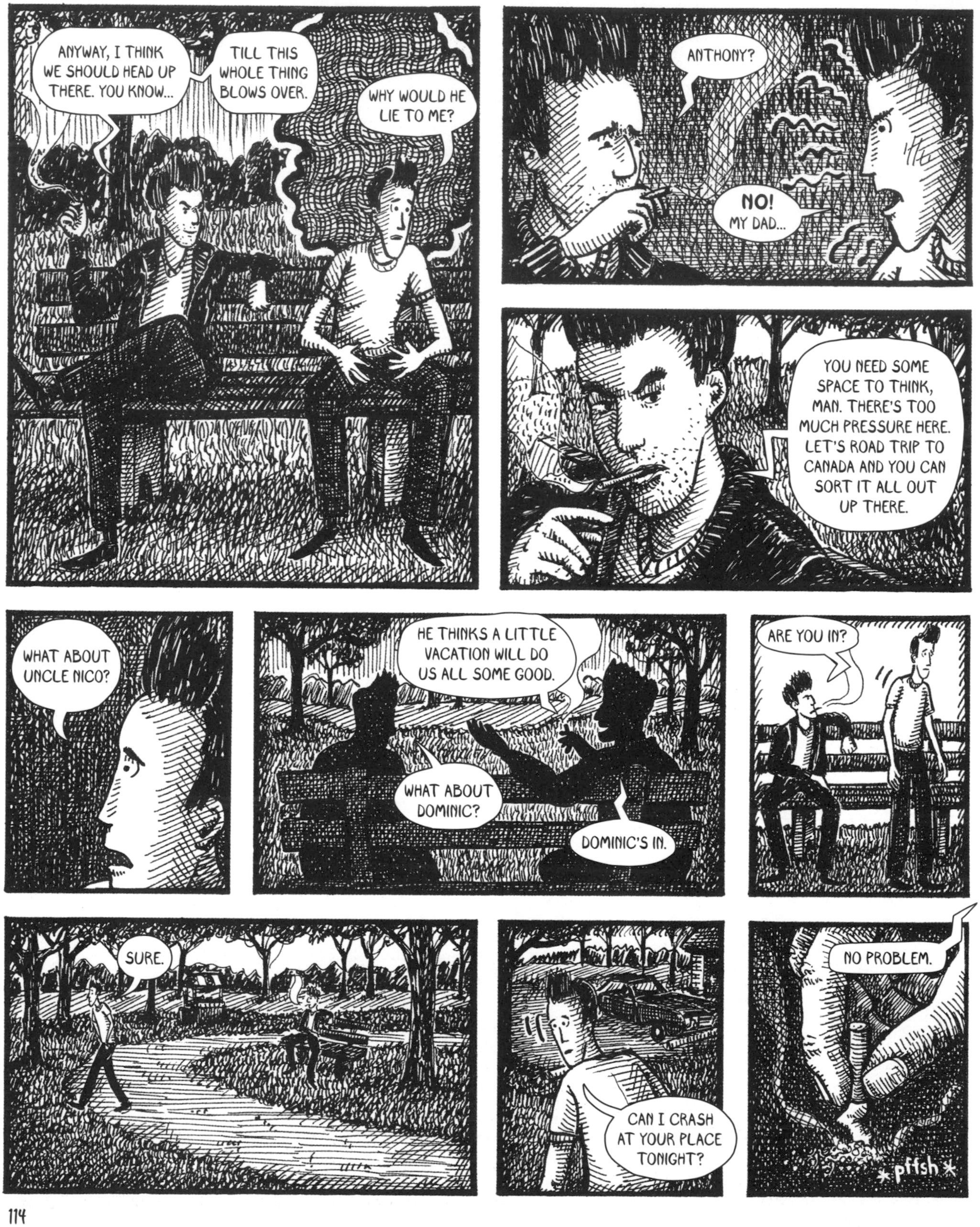
ANYWAY, I THINK WE SHOULD HEAD UP THERE. YOU KNOW...
TILL THIS WHOLE THING BLOWS OVER.
WHY WOULD HE LIE TO ME?
ANTHONY?
NO! MY DAD...
YOU NEED SOME SPACE TO THINK, MAN. THERE'S TOO MUCH PRESSURE HERE. LET'S ROAD TRIP TO CANADA AND YOU CAN SORT IT ALL OUT UP THERE.
WHAT ABOUT UNCLE NICO?
HE THINKS A LITTLE VACATION WILL DO US ALL SOME GOOD.
WHAT ABOUT DOMINIC?
DOMINIC'S IN.
ARE YOU IN?
SURE.
CAN I CRASH AT YOUR PLACE TONIGHT?
NO PROBLEM.
pfsh

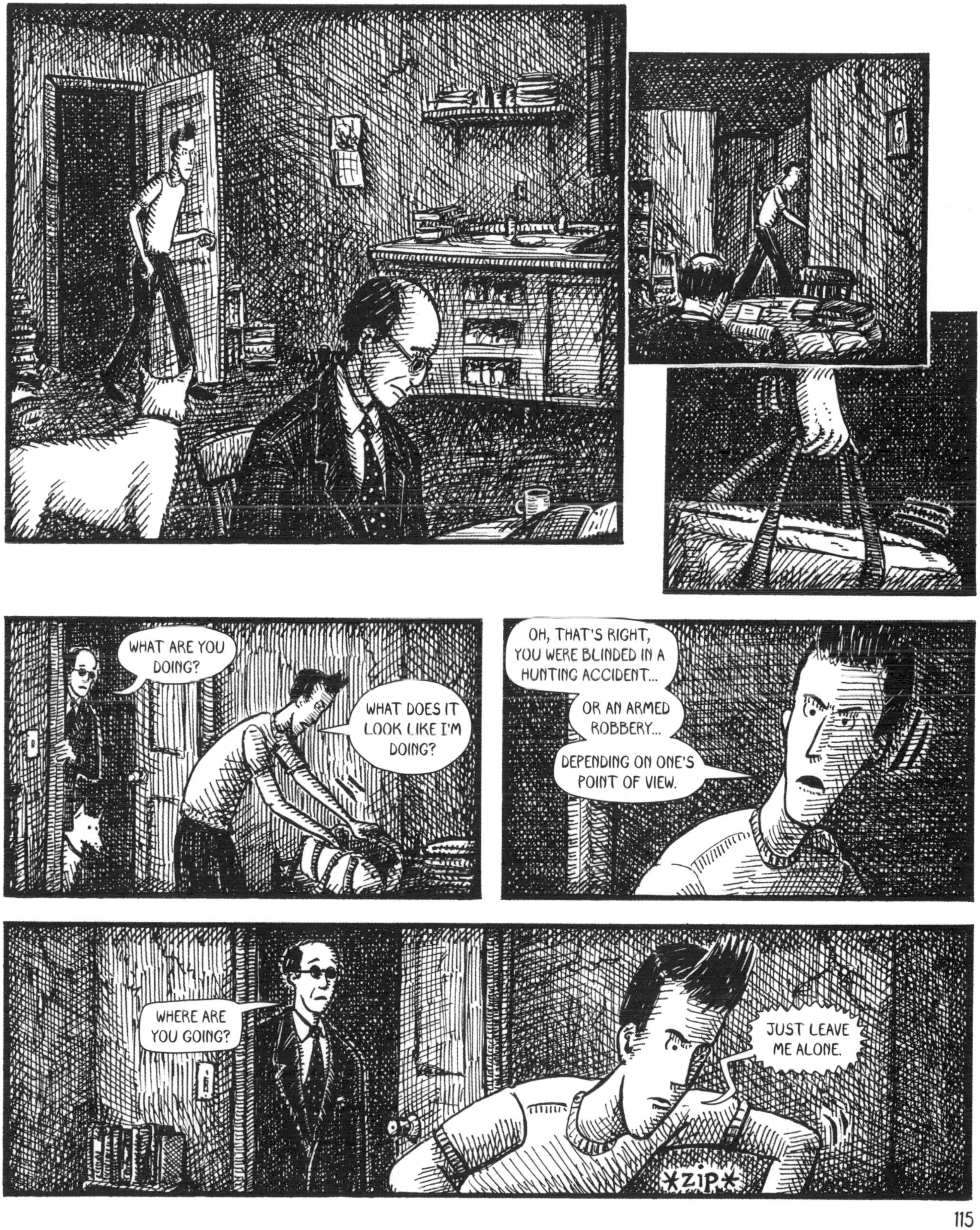
WHAT ARE YOU DOING?
WHAT DOES IT LOOK LIKE I'M DOING?
OH, THAT'S RIGHT, YOU WERE BLINDED IN A HUNTING ACCIDENT...
OR AN ARMED ROBBERY...
DEPENDING ON ONE'S POINT OF VIEW.
WHERE ARE YOU GOING?
JUST LEAVE ME ALONE.
ZIP

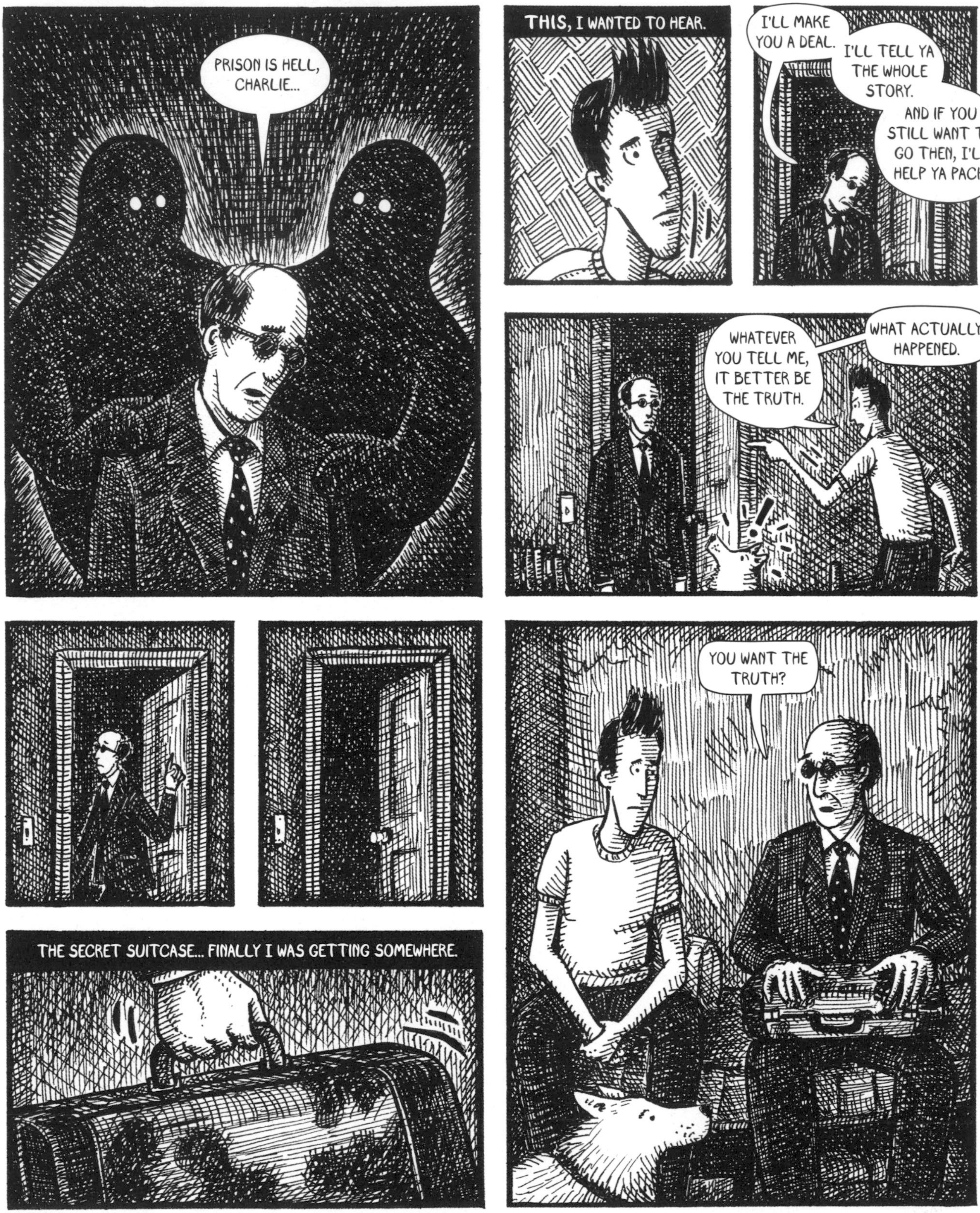
PRISON IS HELL, CHARLIE...
THIS, I WANTED TO HEAR.
I'LL MAKE YOU A DEAL.
I'LL TELL YA THE WHOLE STORY.
AND IF YOU STILL WANT TO GO THEN, I'LL HELP YA PACK.
WHATEVER YOU TELL ME, IT BETTER BE THE TRUTH.
WHAT ACTUALLY HAPPENED.
THE SECRET SUITCASE... FINALLY I WAS GETTING SOMEWHERE.
YOU WANT THE TRUTH?

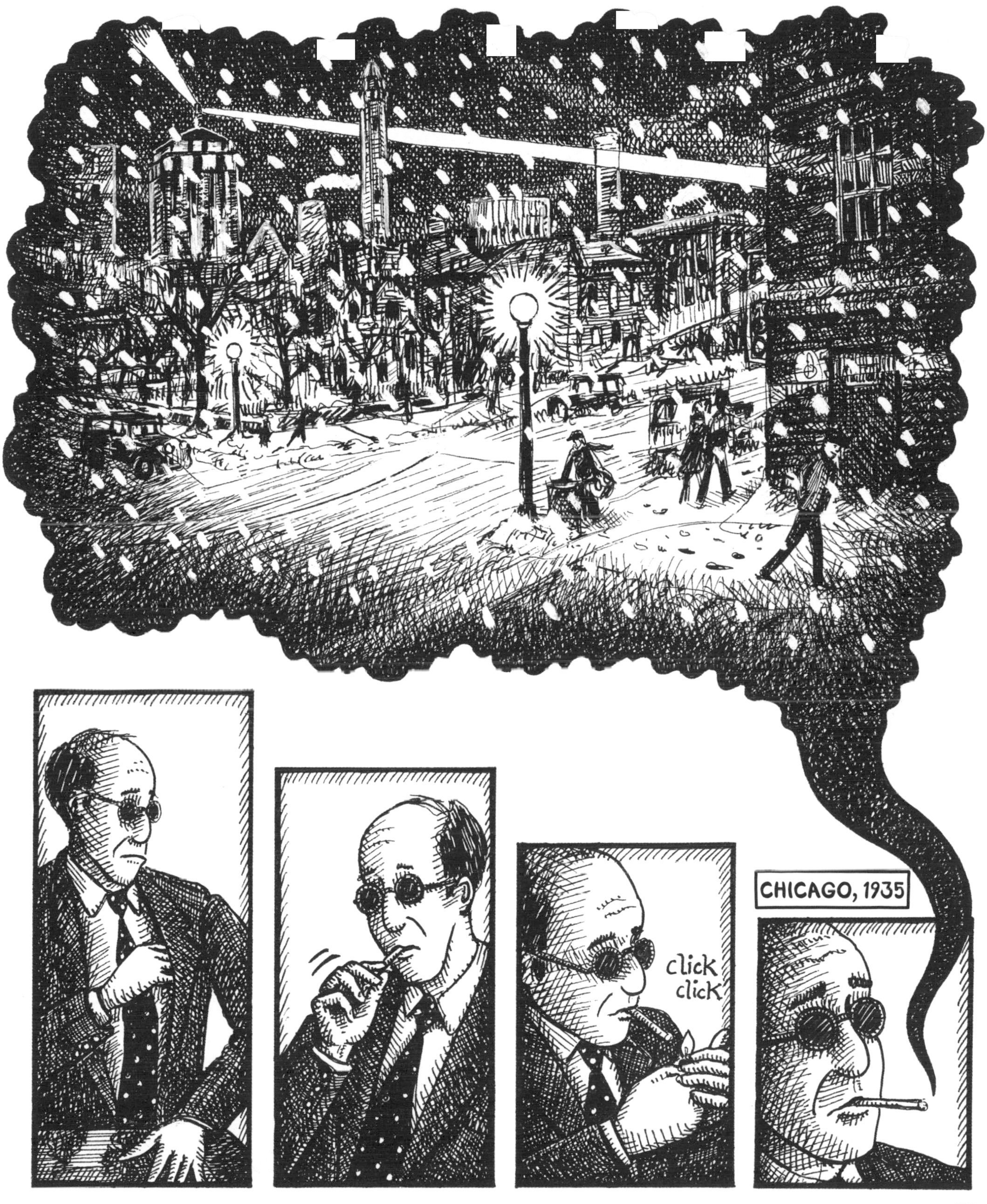
click
click
CHICAGO, 1935

V

THE TRUTH

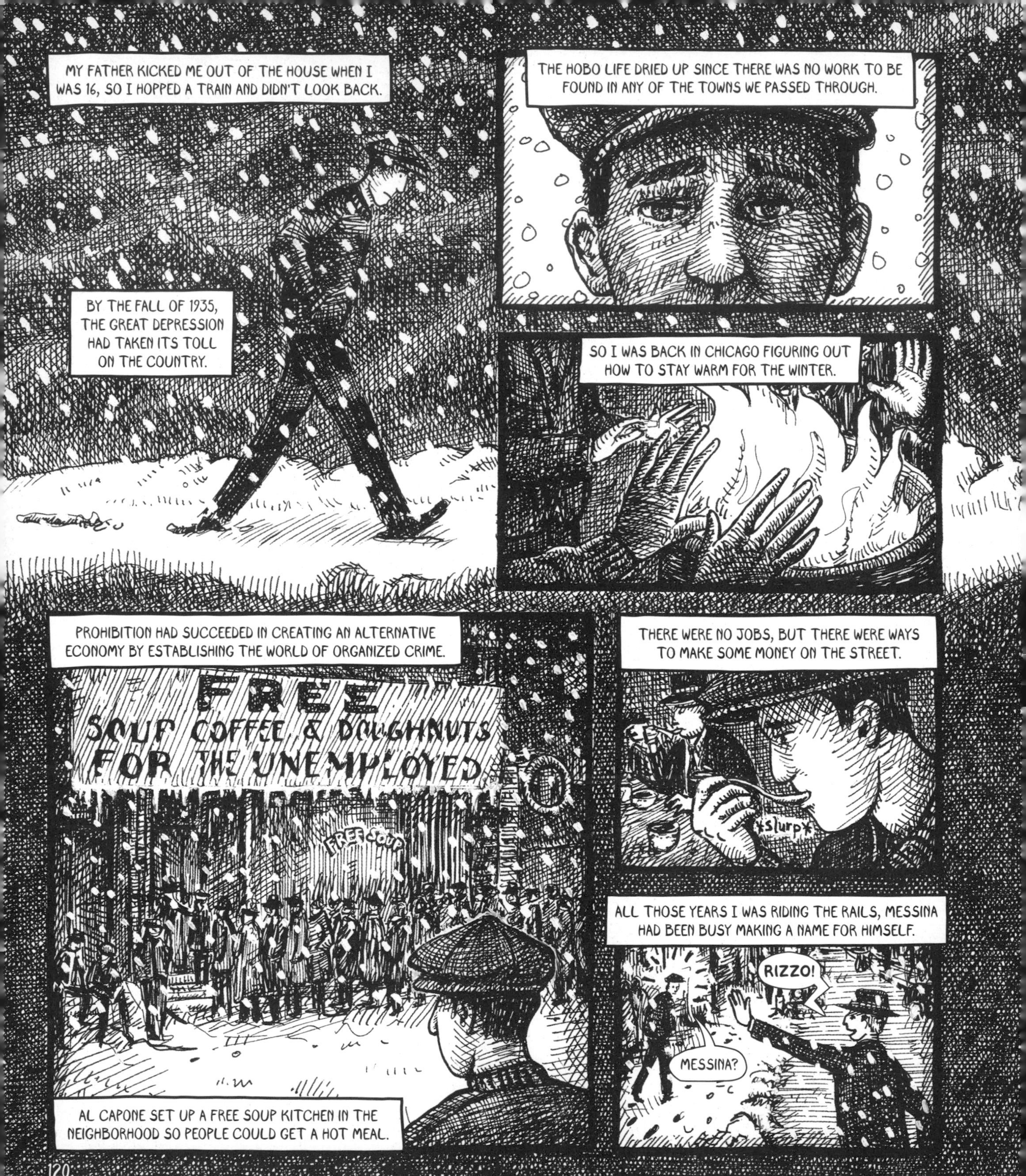

MY FATHER KICKED ME OUT OF THE HOUSE WHEN I WAS 16, SO I HOPPED A TRAIN AND DIDN'T LOOK BACK.
BY THE FALL OF 1935, THE GREAT DEPRESSION HAD TAKEN ITS TOLL ON THE COUNTRY.
THE HOBO LIFE DRIED UP SINCE THERE WAS NO WORK TO BE FOUND IN ANY OF THE TOWNS WE PASSED THROUGH.
SO I WAS BACK IN CHICAGO FIGURING OUT HOW TO STAY WARM FOR THE WINTER.
PROHIBITION HAD SUCCEEDED IN CREATING AN ALTERNATIVE ECONOMY BY ESTABLISHING THE WORLD OF ORGANIZED CRIME.
FREE
SOUP COFFEE & DOUGHNUTS
FOR THE UNEMPLOYED
FREE SOUP
AL CAPONE SET UP A FREE SOUP KITCHEN IN THE NEIGHBORHOOD SO PEOPLE COULD GET A HOT MEAL.
THERE WERE NO JOBS, BUT THERE WERE WAYS TO MAKE SOME MONEY ON THE STREET.
slurp
ALL THOSE YEARS I WAS RIDING THE RAILS, MESSINA HAD BEEN BUSY MAKING A NAME FOR HIMSELF.
RIZZO!
MESSINA?

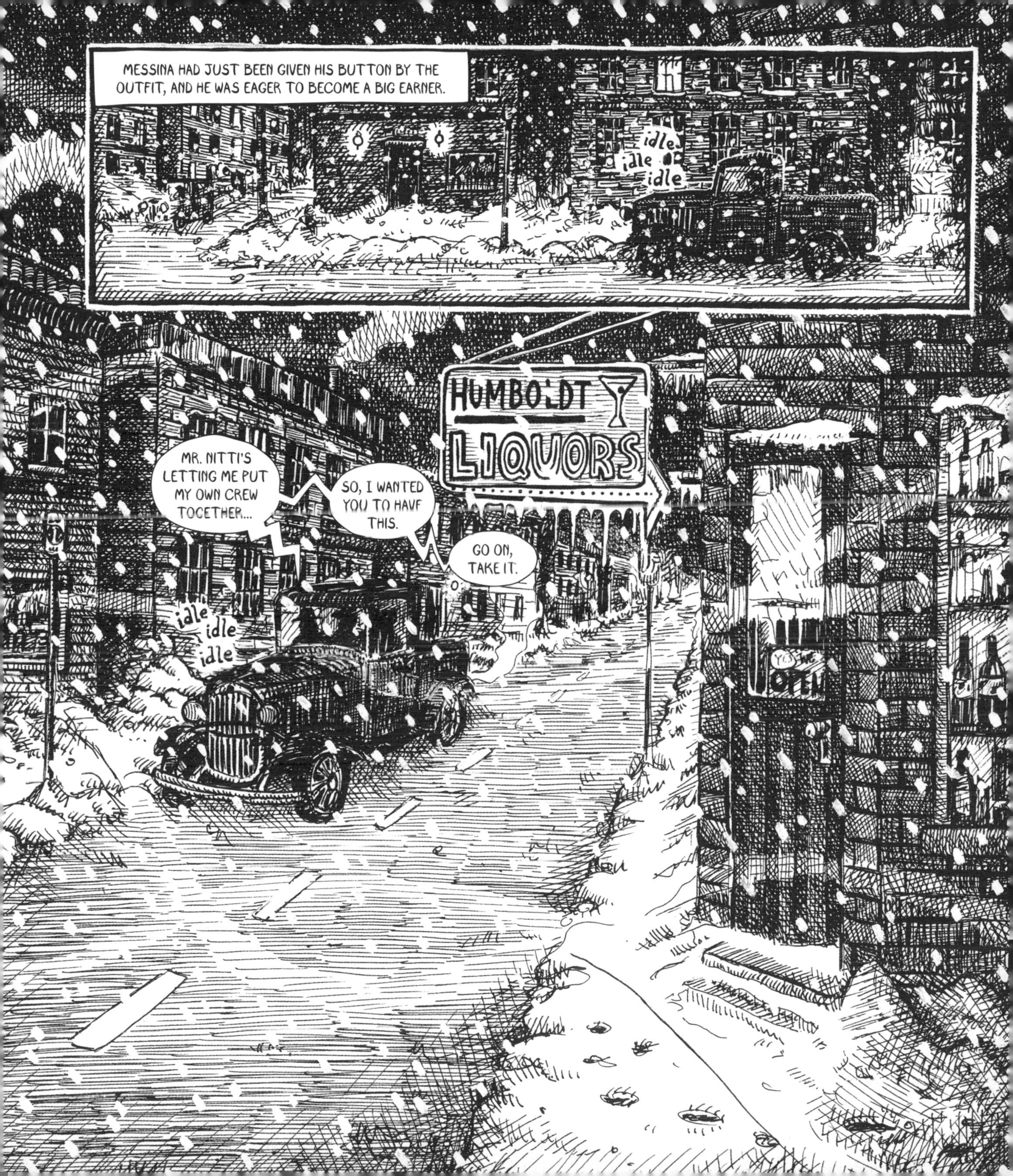
MESSINA HAD JUST BEEN GIVEN HIS BUTTON BY THE OUTFIT, AND HE WAS EAGER TO BECOME A BIG EARNER.
idle idle idle
HUMBOLDT LIQUORS
MR. NITTI'S LETTING ME PUT MY OWN CREW TOGETHER...
SO, I WANTED YOU TO HAVE THIS.
GO ON, TAKE IT.
idle idle idle
OPEN

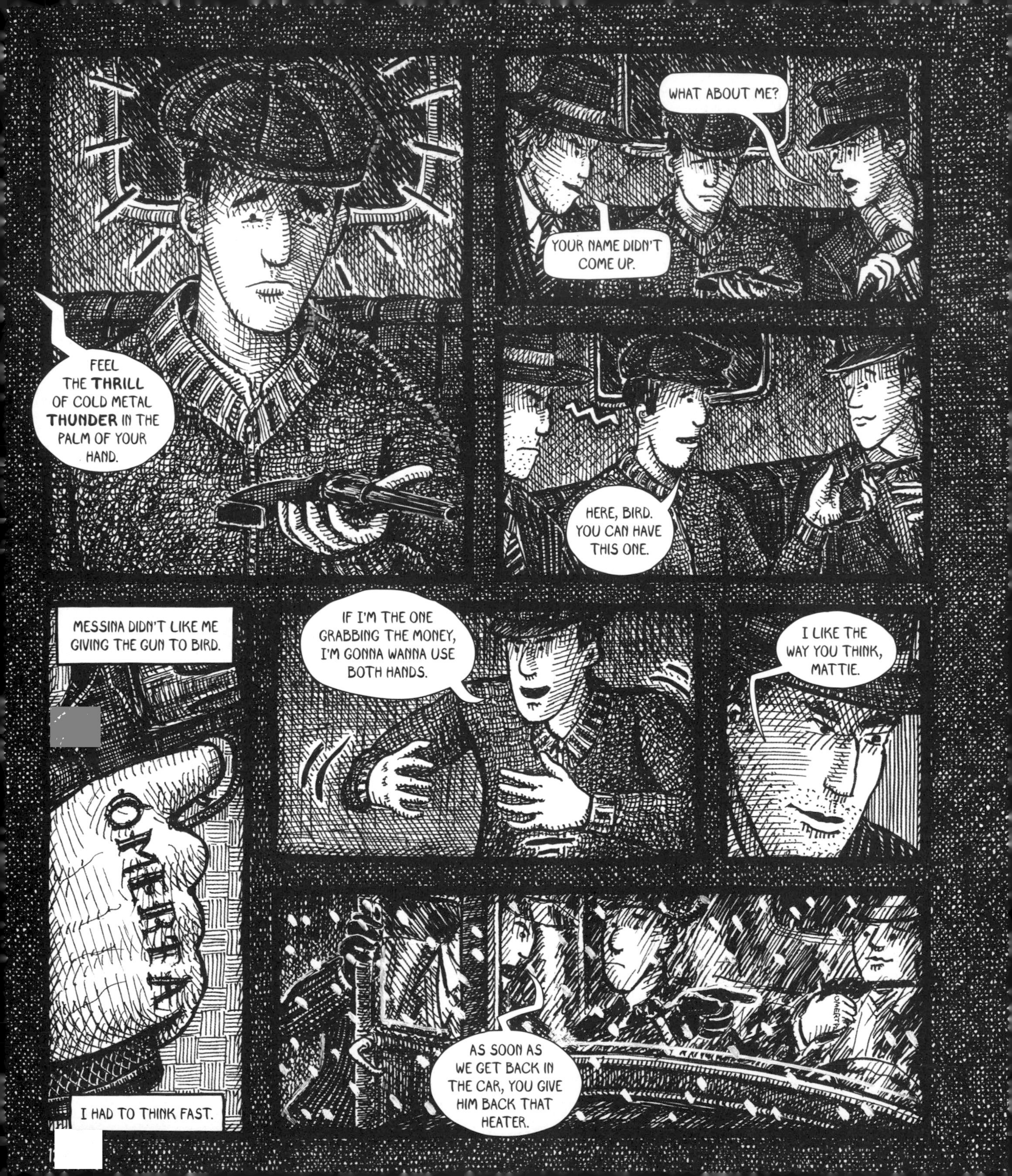
FEEL THE THRILL OF COLD METAL THUNDER IN THE PALM OF YOUR HAND.
WHAT ABOUT ME?
YOUR NAME DIDN'T COME UP.
HERE, BIRD. YOU CAN HAVE THIS ONE.
MESSINA DIDN'T LIKE ME GIVING THE GUN TO BIRD.
OMERTA
I HAD TO THINK FAST.
IF I'M THE ONE GRABBING THE MONEY, I'M GONNA WANNA USE BOTH HANDS.
I LIKE THE WAY YOU THINK, MATTIE.
AS SOON AS WE GET BACK IN THE CAR, YOU GIVE HIM BACK THAT HEATER.

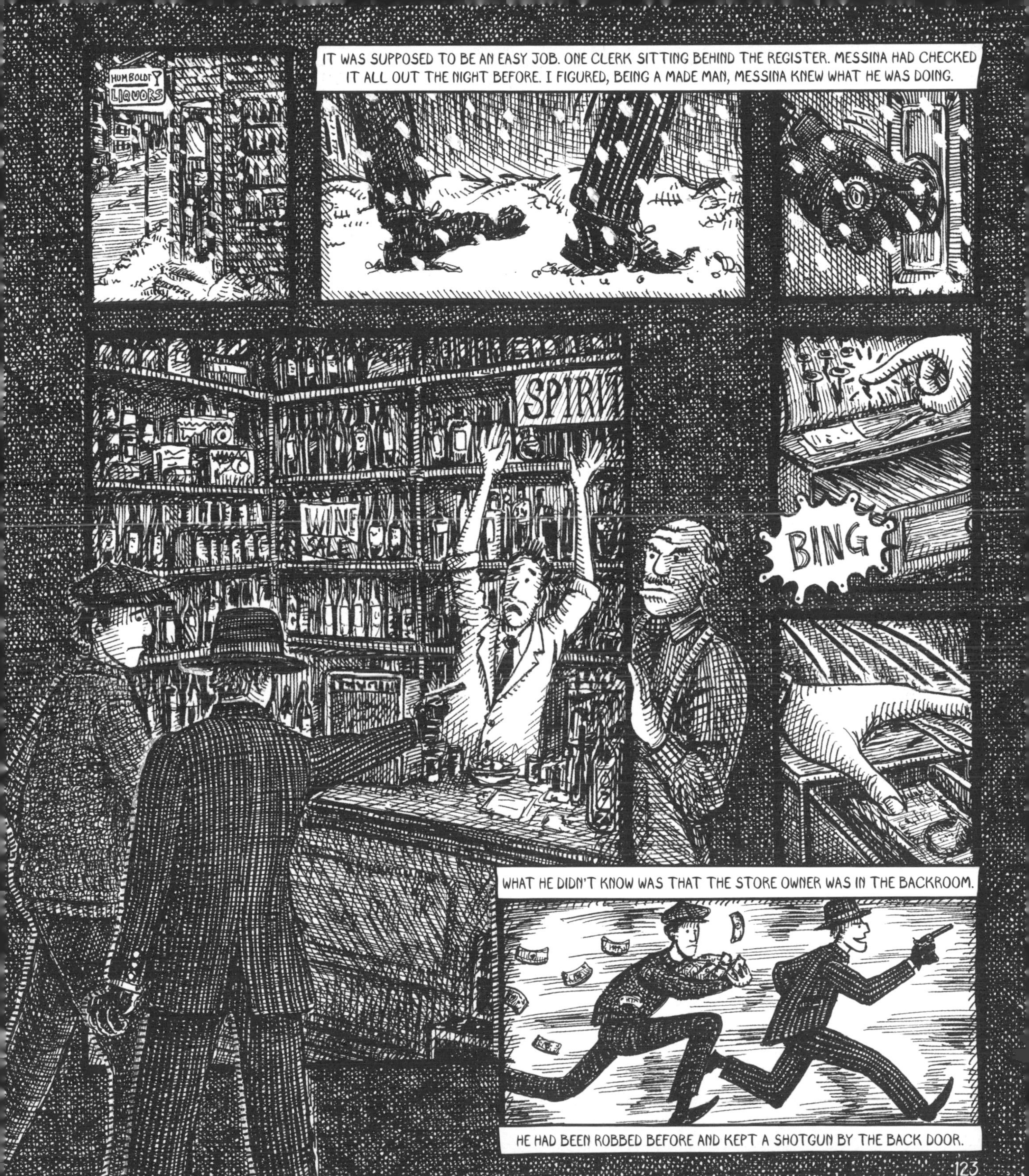
HUMBOLDT LIQUORS
IT WAS SUPPOSED TO BE AN EASY JOB. ONE CLERK SITTING BEHIND THE REGISTER. MESSINA HAD CHECKED IT ALL OUT THE NIGHT BEFORE. I FIGURED, BEING A MADE MAN, MESSINA KNEW WHAT HE WAS DOING.
SPIRI
WINE SALE
BING
WHAT HE DIDN'T KNOW WAS THAT THE STORE OWNER WAS IN THE BACKROOM.
HE HAD BEEN ROBBED BEFORE AND KEPT A SHOTGUN BY THE BACK DOOR.

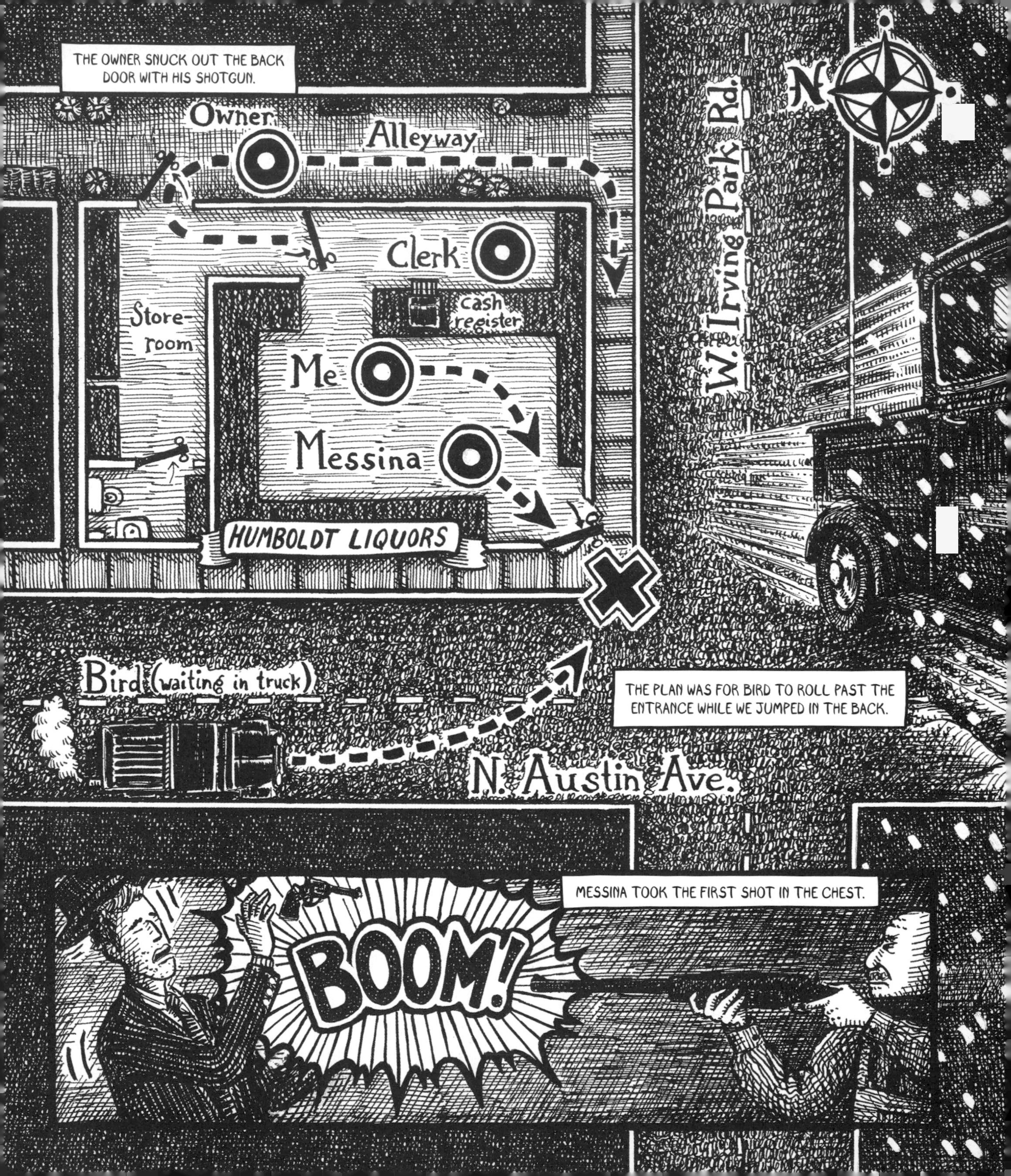
THE OWNER SNUCK OUT THE BACK DOOR WITH HIS SHOTGUN.
Owner
Alleyway
Clerk
cash register
Store-room
Me
Messina
HUMBOLDT LIQUORS
W. Irving Park Rd.
N
Bird (waiting in truck)
THE PLAN WAS FOR BIRD TO ROLL PAST THE ENTRANCE WHILE WE JUMPED IN THE BACK.
N. Austin Ave.
MESSINA TOOK THE FIRST SHOT IN THE CHEST.
BOOM!

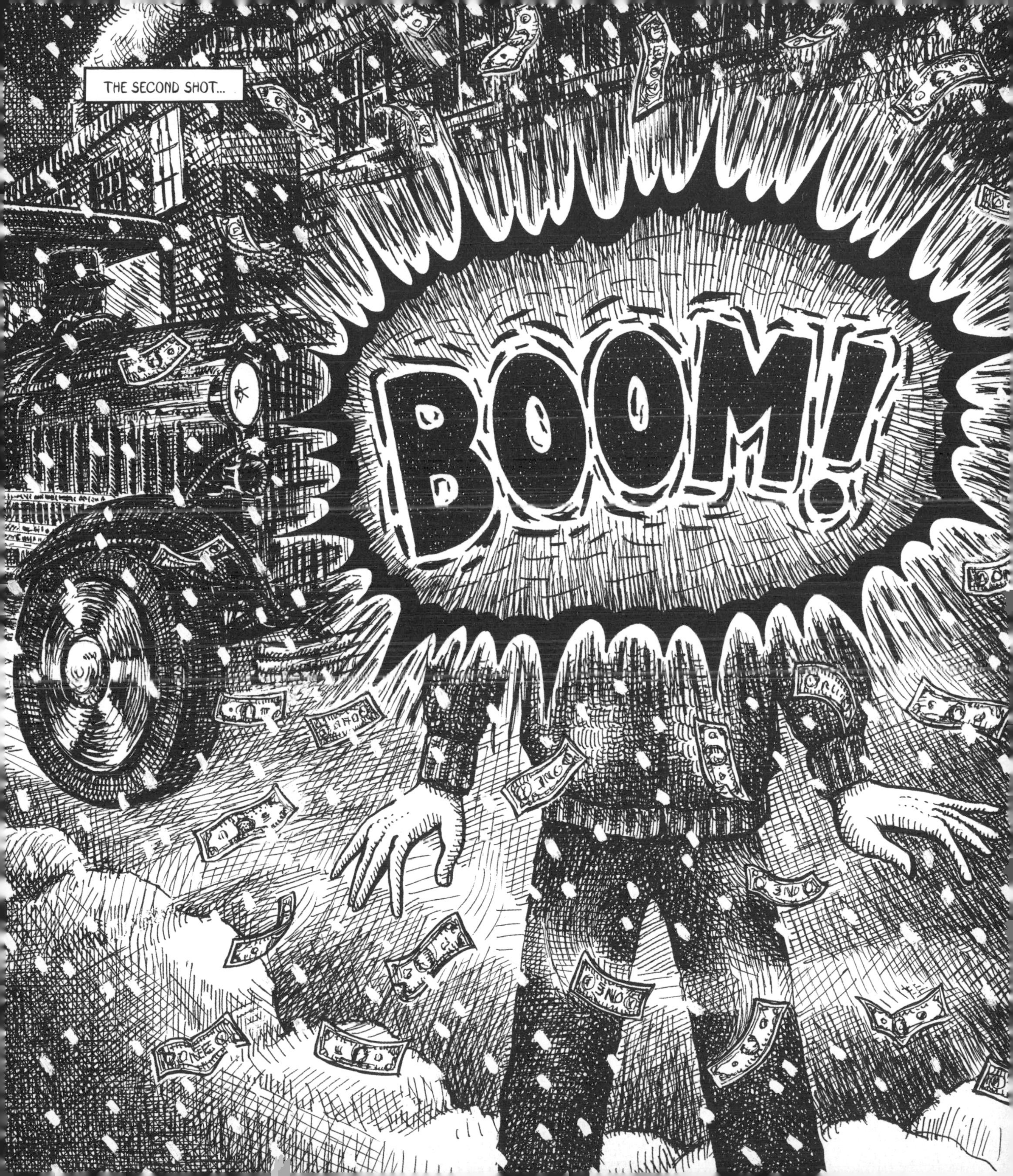
THE SECOND SHOT...
BOOM!

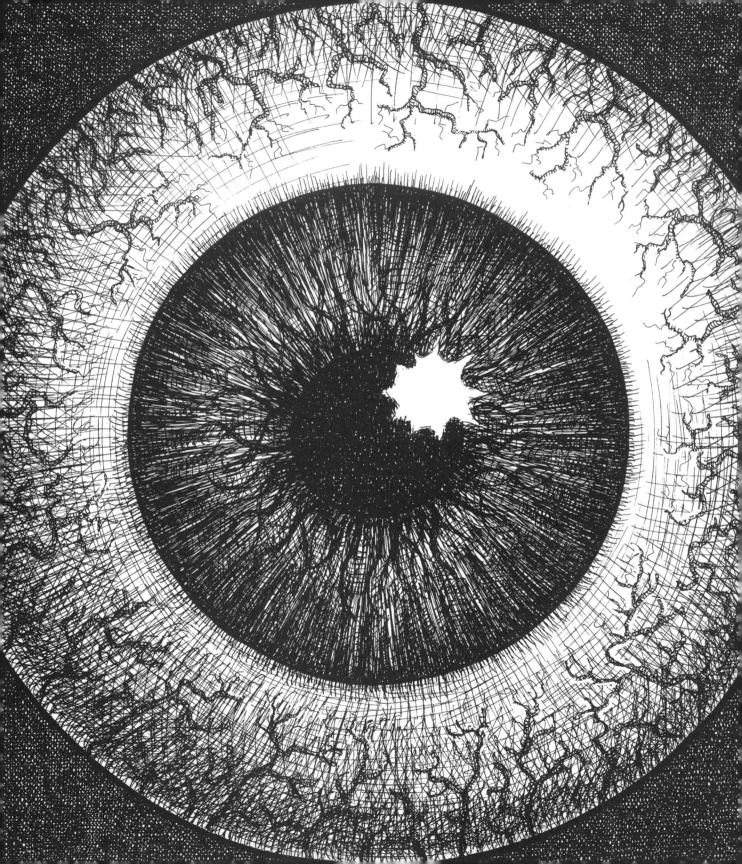

YOUR HONOR, THE STATE WOULD LIKE TO ACKNOWLEDGE THAT THIS BOY HAS REFUSED TO COOPERATE.
IS THAT RIGHT, MR. RIZZO?
YOU WOULD RATHER GO TO JAIL THAN COOPERATE WITH THE STATE'S ATTORNEY?
MR. RIZZO, DO YOU HAVE A RESPONSE?
THEN IT BECOMES THE BURDEN OF THE STATE TO PASS SENTENCE.
I HEREBY SENTENCE YOU ONE YEAR TO LIFE AT STATEVILLE PRISON.

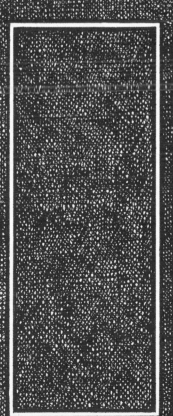

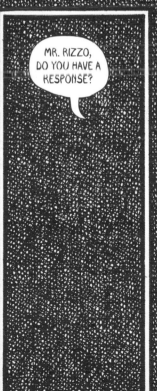

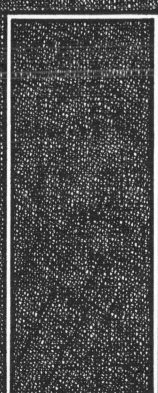

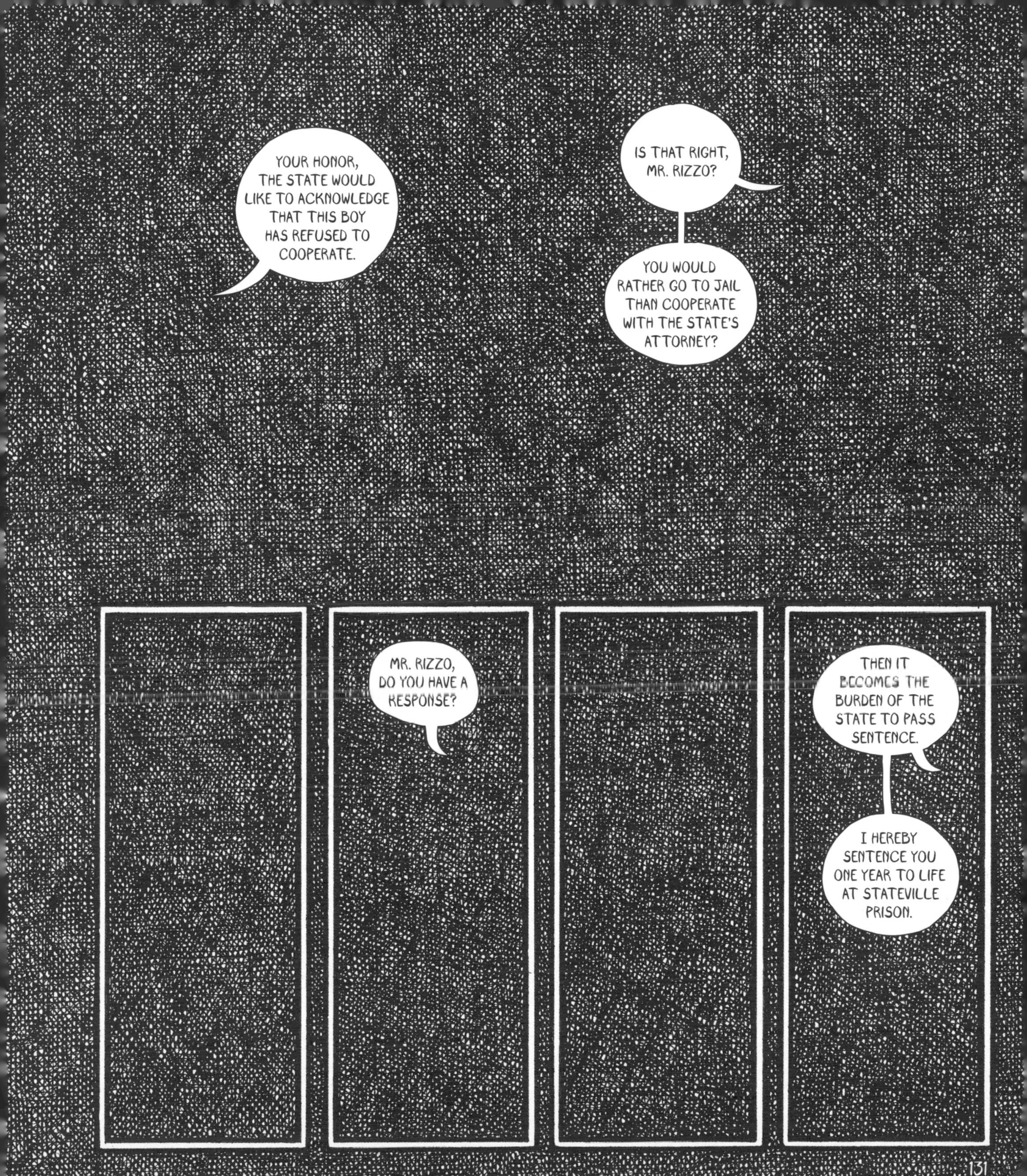

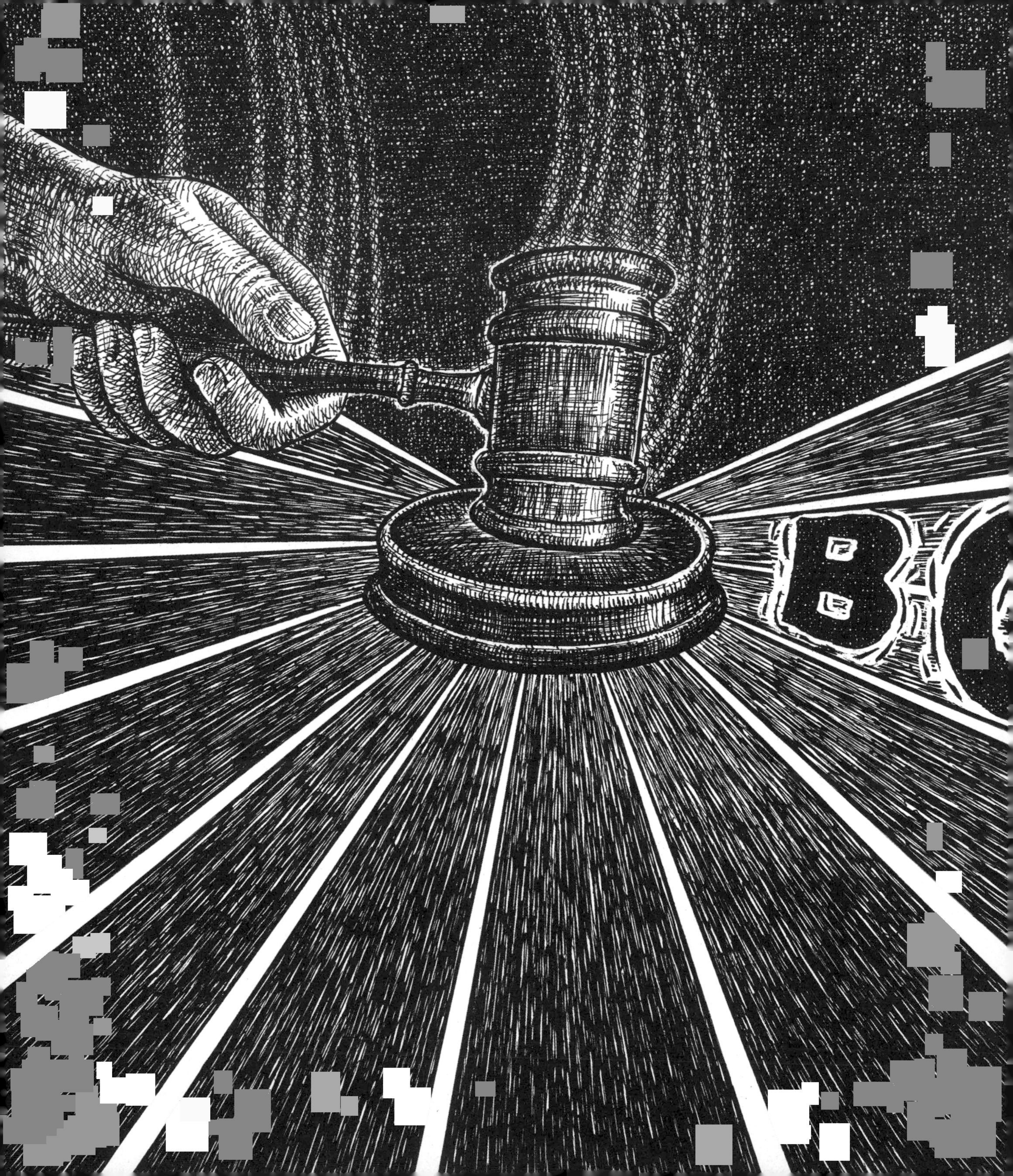

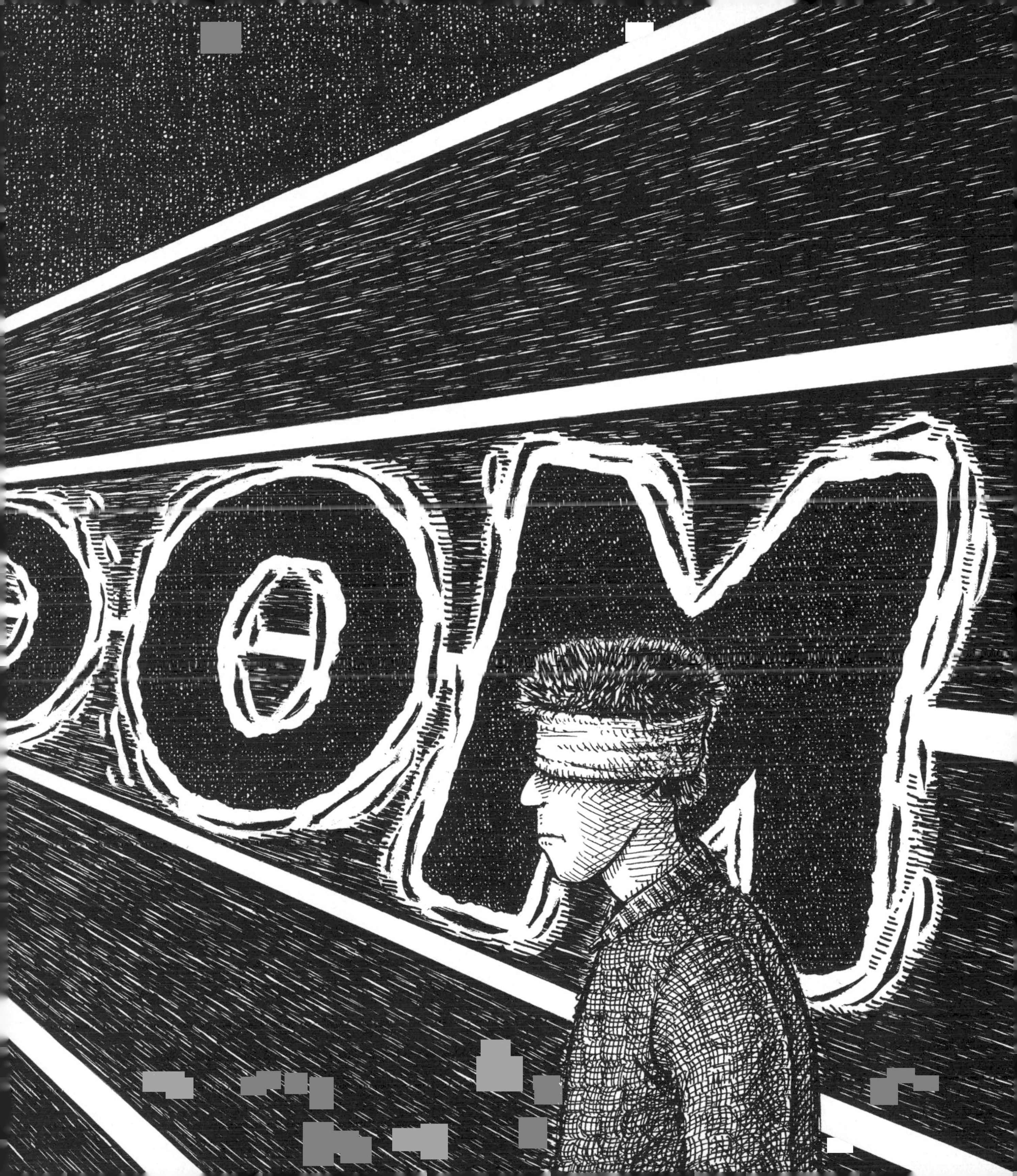

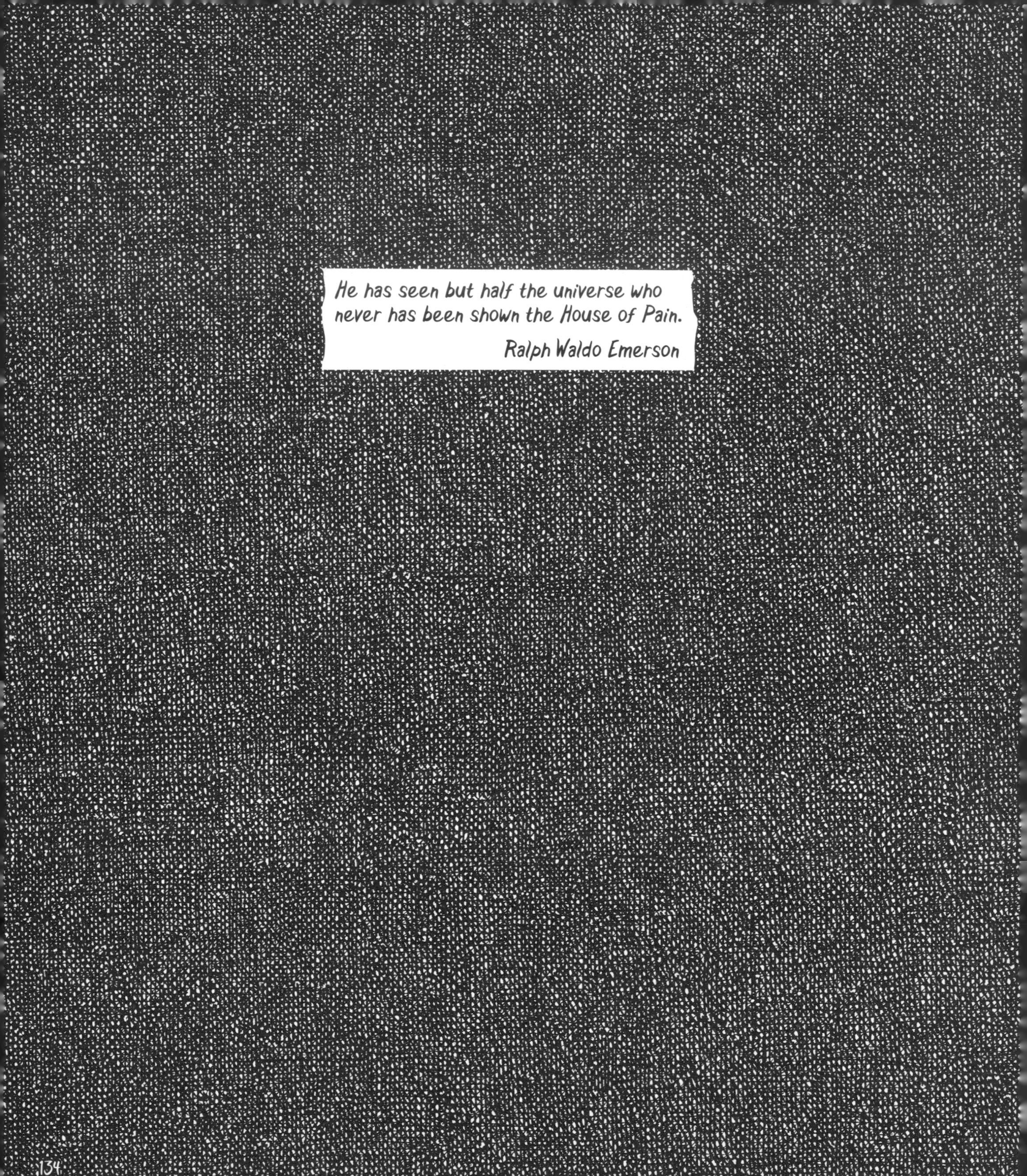
He has seen but half the universe who never has been shown the House of Pain.
Ralph Waldo Emerson

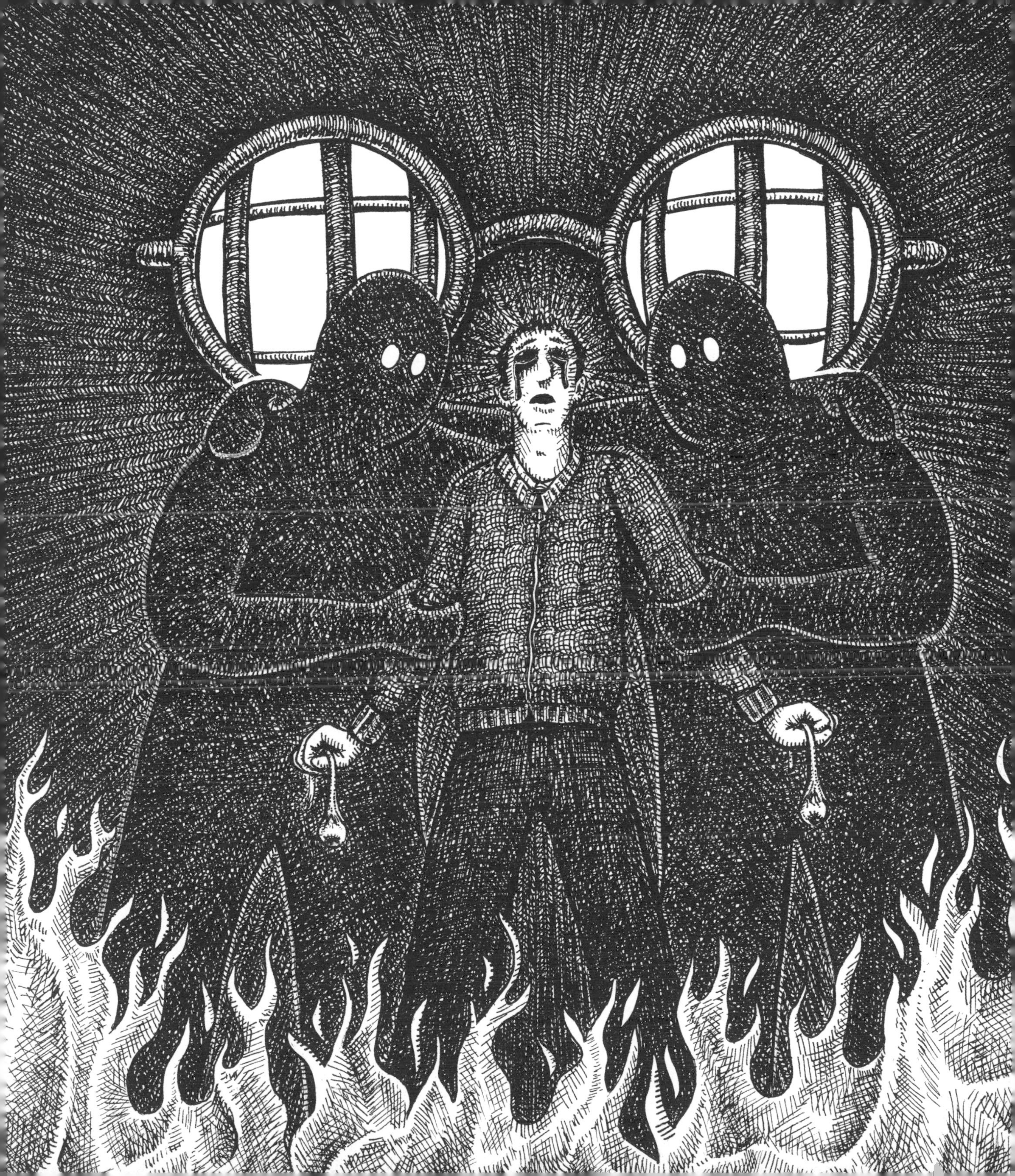

VI :::
NATHAN LEOPOLD

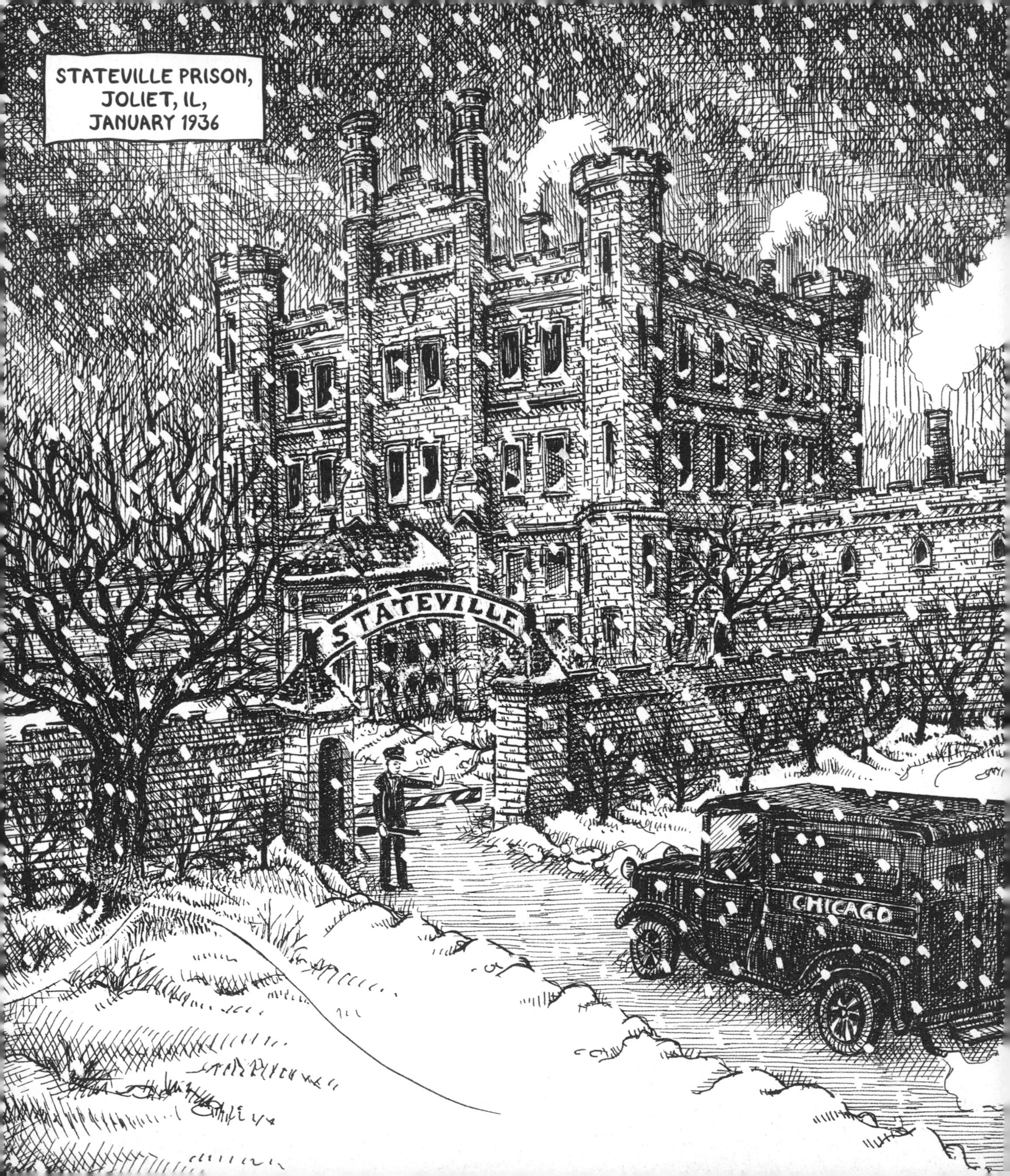
STATEVILLE PRISON, JOLIET, IL, JANUARY 1936
STATEVILLE
CHICAGO

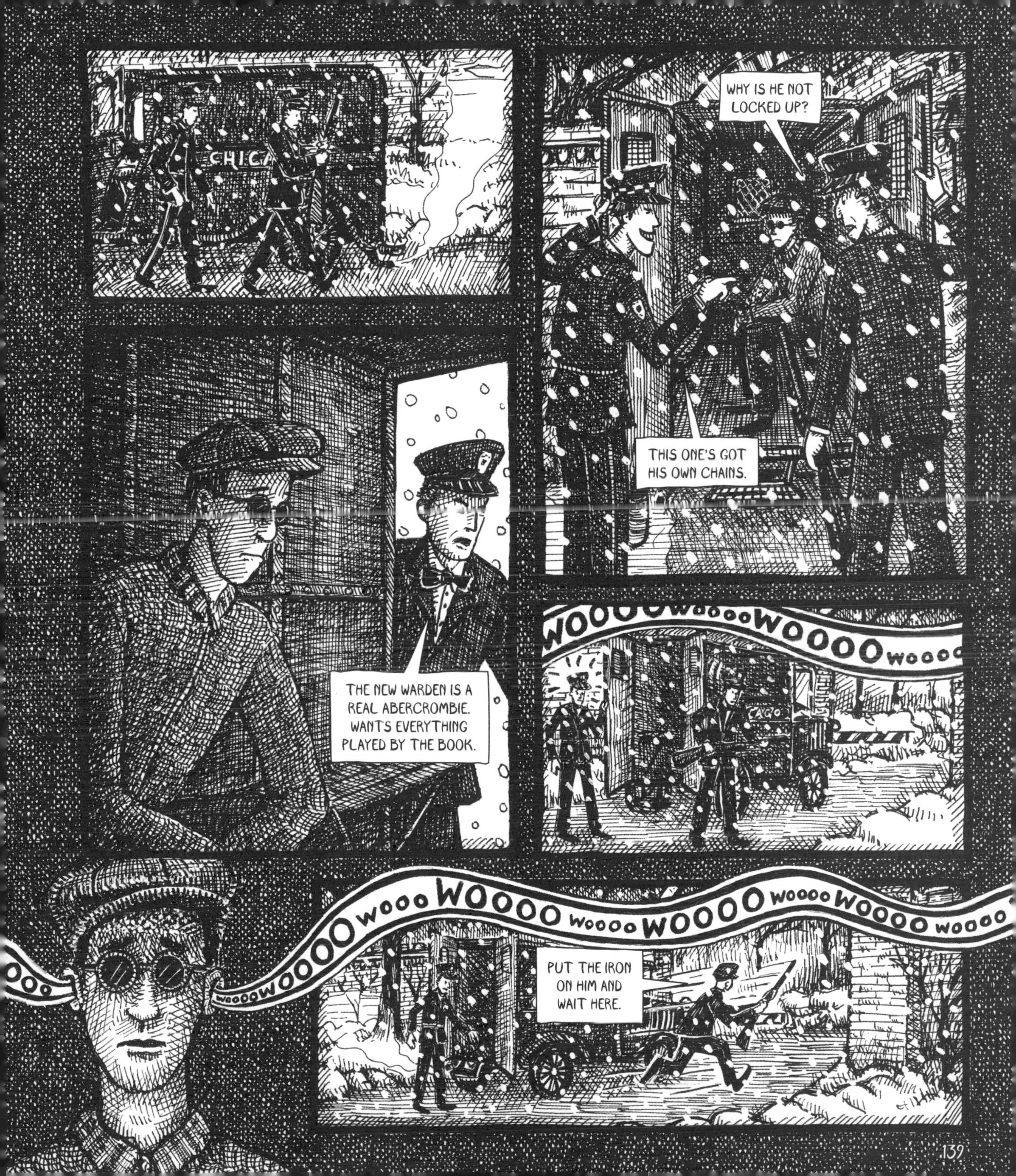
CHICA
WHY IS HE NOT LOCKED UP?
THIS ONE'S GOT HIS OWN CHAINS.
THE NEW WARDEN IS A REAL ABERCROMBIE. WANTS EVERYTHING PLAYED BY THE BOOK.
WOOOOwooooWOOOOwoooo
woooWOOOOwooooWOOOOwooooWOOOOwoooo
oooowoooWOOOO
PUT THE IRON ON HIM AND WAIT HERE.

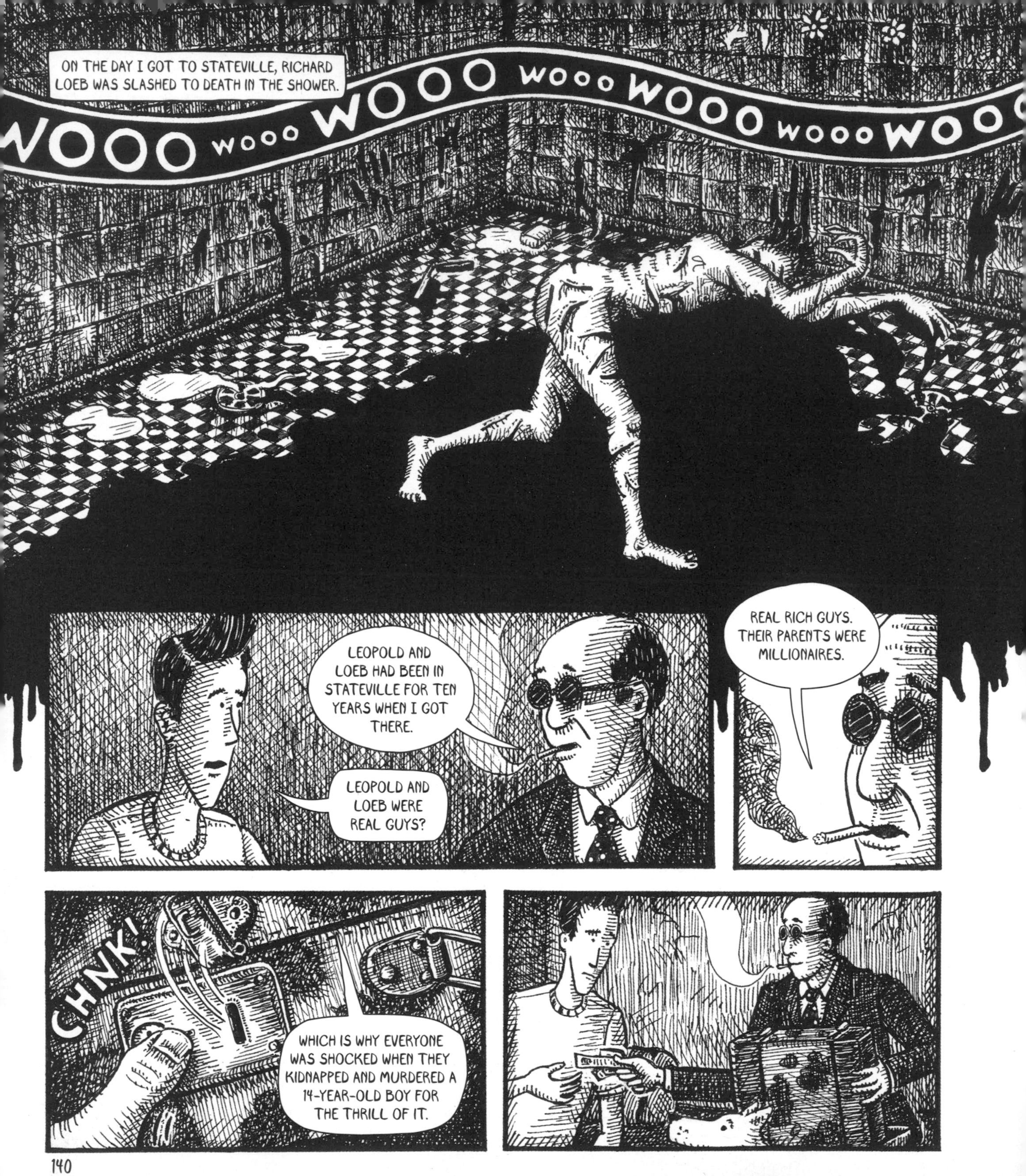
ON THE DAY I GOT TO STATEVILLE, RICHARD LOEB WAS SLASHED TO DEATH IN THE SHOWER.
WOOO wooo WOOO WOOO wooo WOOO wooo WOO
LEOPOLD AND LOEB HAD BEEN IN STATEVILLE FOR TEN YEARS WHEN I GOT THERE.
LEOPOLD AND LOEB WERE REAL GUYS?
REAL RICH GUYS. THEIR PARENTS WERE MILLIONAIRES.
CHNK!
WHICH IS WHY EVERYONE WAS SHOCKED WHEN THEY KIDNAPPED AND MURDERED A 14-YEAR-OLD BOY FOR THE THRILL OF IT.

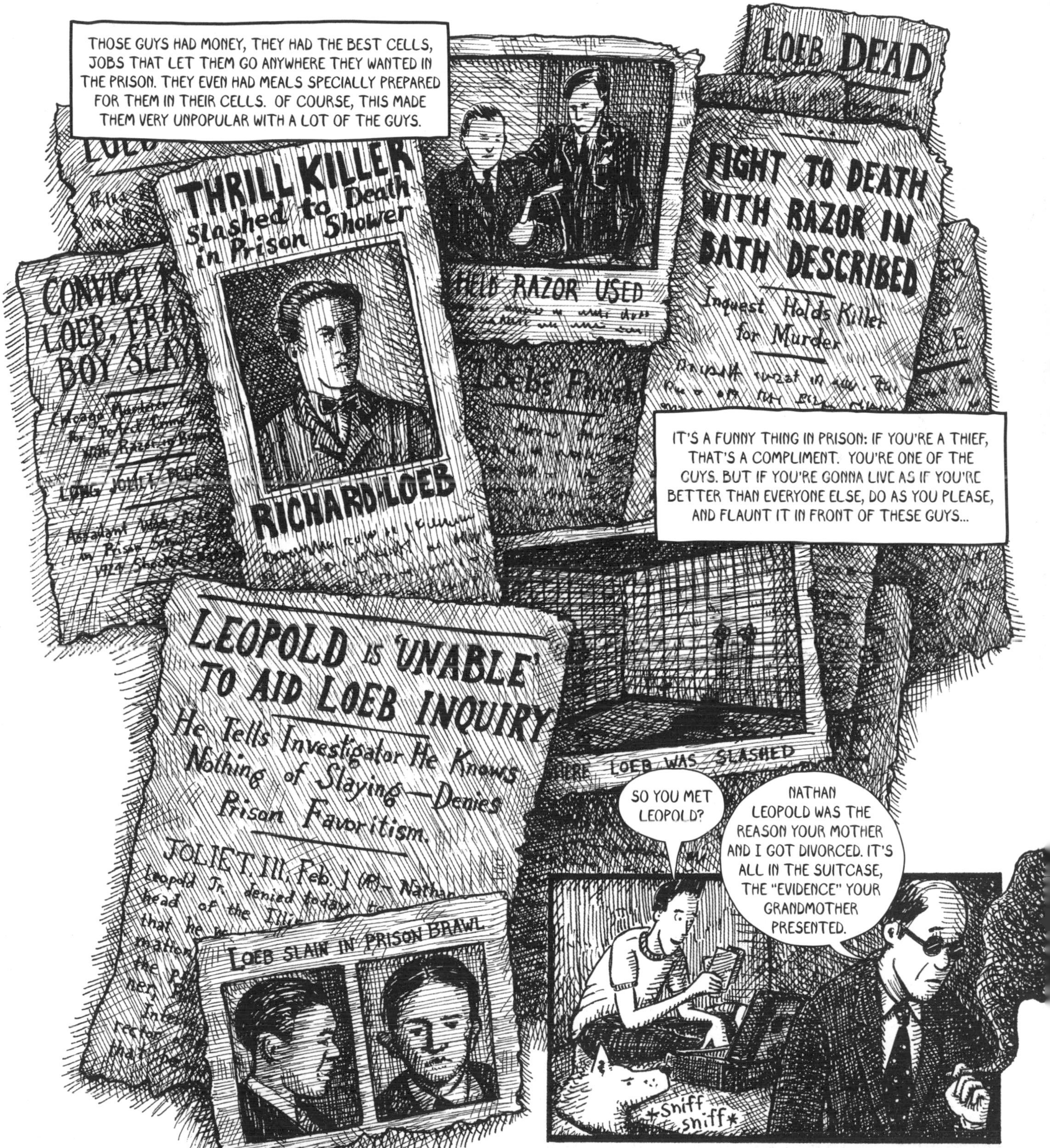
THOSE GUYS HAD MONEY, THEY HAD THE BEST CELLS, JOBS THAT LET THEM GO ANYWHERE THEY WANTED IN THE PRISON. THEY EVEN HAD MEALS SPECIALLY PREPARED FOR THEM IN THEIR CELLS. OF COURSE, THIS MADE THEM VERY UNPOPULAR WITH A LOT OF THE GUYS.
LOEB DEAD
THRILL KILLER
Slashed to Death in Prison Shower
RICHARD LOEB
HELD RAZOR USED
FIGHT TO DEATH WITH RAZOR IN BATH DESCRIBED
Inquest Holds Killer for Murder
IT'S A FUNNY THING IN PRISON: IF YOU'RE A THIEF, THAT'S A COMPLIMENT. YOU'RE ONE OF THE GUYS. BUT IF YOU'RE GONNA LIVE AS IF YOU'RE BETTER THAN EVERYONE ELSE, DO AS YOU PLEASE, AND FLAUNT IT IN FRONT OF THESE GUYS...
LEOPOLD IS 'UNABLE' TO AID LOEB INQUIRY
He Tells Investigator He Knows Nothing of Slaying—Denies Prison Favoritism.
LOEB SLAIN IN PRISON BRAWL
LOEB WAS SLASHED
SO YOU MET LEOPOLD?
NATHAN LEOPOLD WAS THE REASON YOUR MOTHER AND I GOT DIVORCED. IT'S ALL IN THE SUITCASE, THE "EVIDENCE" YOUR GRANDMOTHER PRESENTED.
sniff sniff

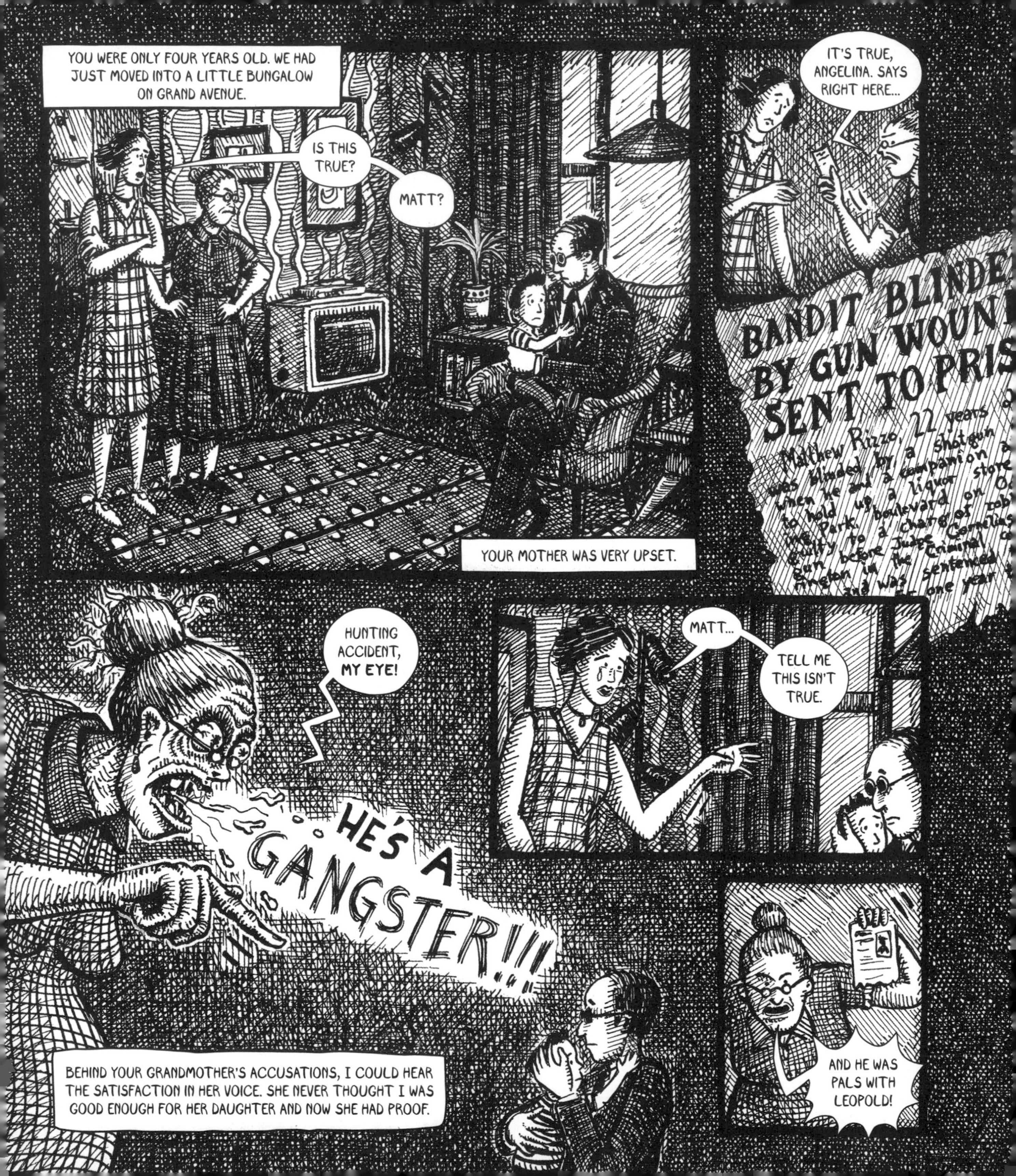
YOU WERE ONLY FOUR YEARS OLD. WE HAD JUST MOVED INTO A LITTLE BUNGALOW ON GRAND AVENUE.
IS THIS TRUE?
MATT?
YOUR MOTHER WAS VERY UPSET.
IT'S TRUE, ANGELINA. SAYS RIGHT HERE...
BANDIT BLINDE
BY GUN WOUN
SENT TO PRIS
Matthew Rizzo, 22 years
was blinded by a shotgun
when he and a companion
to hold up a liquor store
Park boulevard on
HUNTING ACCIDENT, **MY EYE!**
HE'S A GANGSTER!!!
MATT...
TELL ME THIS ISN'T TRUE.
BEHIND YOUR GRANDMOTHER'S ACCUSATIONS, I COULD HEAR THE SATISFACTION IN HER VOICE. SHE NEVER THOUGHT I WAS GOOD ENOUGH FOR HER DAUGHTER AND NOW SHE HAD PROOF.
AND HE WAS PALS WITH LEOPOLD!

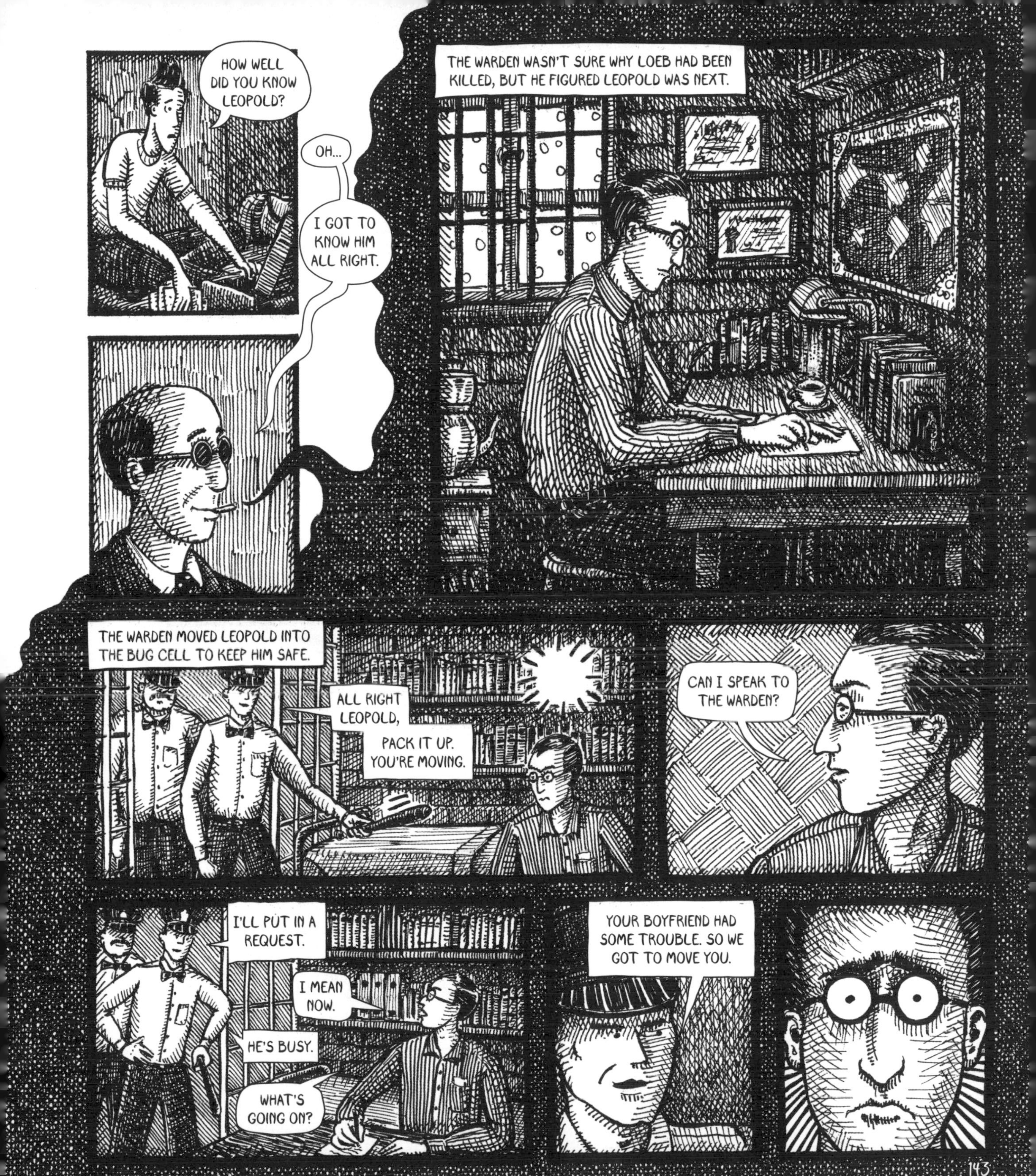
HOW WELL DID YOU KNOW LEOPOLD?
OH...
I GOT TO KNOW HIM ALL RIGHT.
THE WARDEN WASN'T SURE WHY LOEB HAD BEEN KILLED, BUT HE FIGURED LEOPOLD WAS NEXT.
THE WARDEN MOVED LEOPOLD INTO THE BUG CELL TO KEEP HIM SAFE.
ALL RIGHT LEOPOLD,
PACK IT UP. YOU'RE MOVING.
CAN I SPEAK TO THE WARDEN?
I'LL PUT IN A REQUEST.
I MEAN NOW.
HE'S BUSY.
WHAT'S GOING ON?
YOUR BOYFRIEND HAD SOME TROUBLE. SO WE GOT TO MOVE YOU.

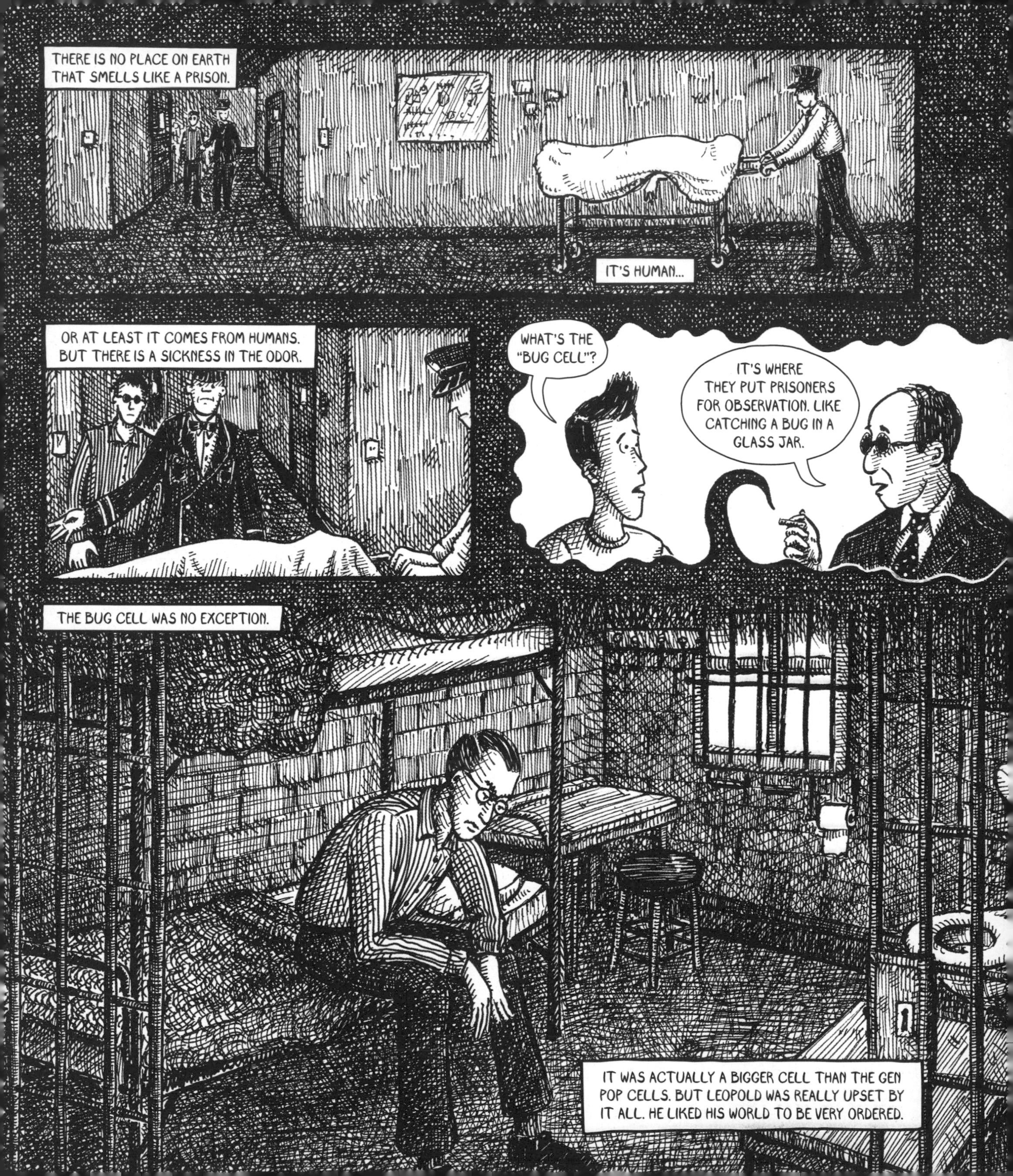
THERE IS NO PLACE ON EARTH THAT SMELLS LIKE A PRISON.
IT'S HUMAN...
OR AT LEAST IT COMES FROM HUMANS. BUT THERE IS A SICKNESS IN THE ODOR.
WHAT'S THE "BUG CELL"?
IT'S WHERE THEY PUT PRISONERS FOR OBSERVATION. LIKE CATCHING A BUG IN A GLASS JAR.
THE BUG CELL WAS NO EXCEPTION.
IT WAS ACTUALLY A BIGGER CELL THAN THE GEN POP CELLS. BUT LEOPOLD WAS REALLY UPSET BY IT ALL. HE LIKED HIS WORLD TO BE VERY ORDERED.

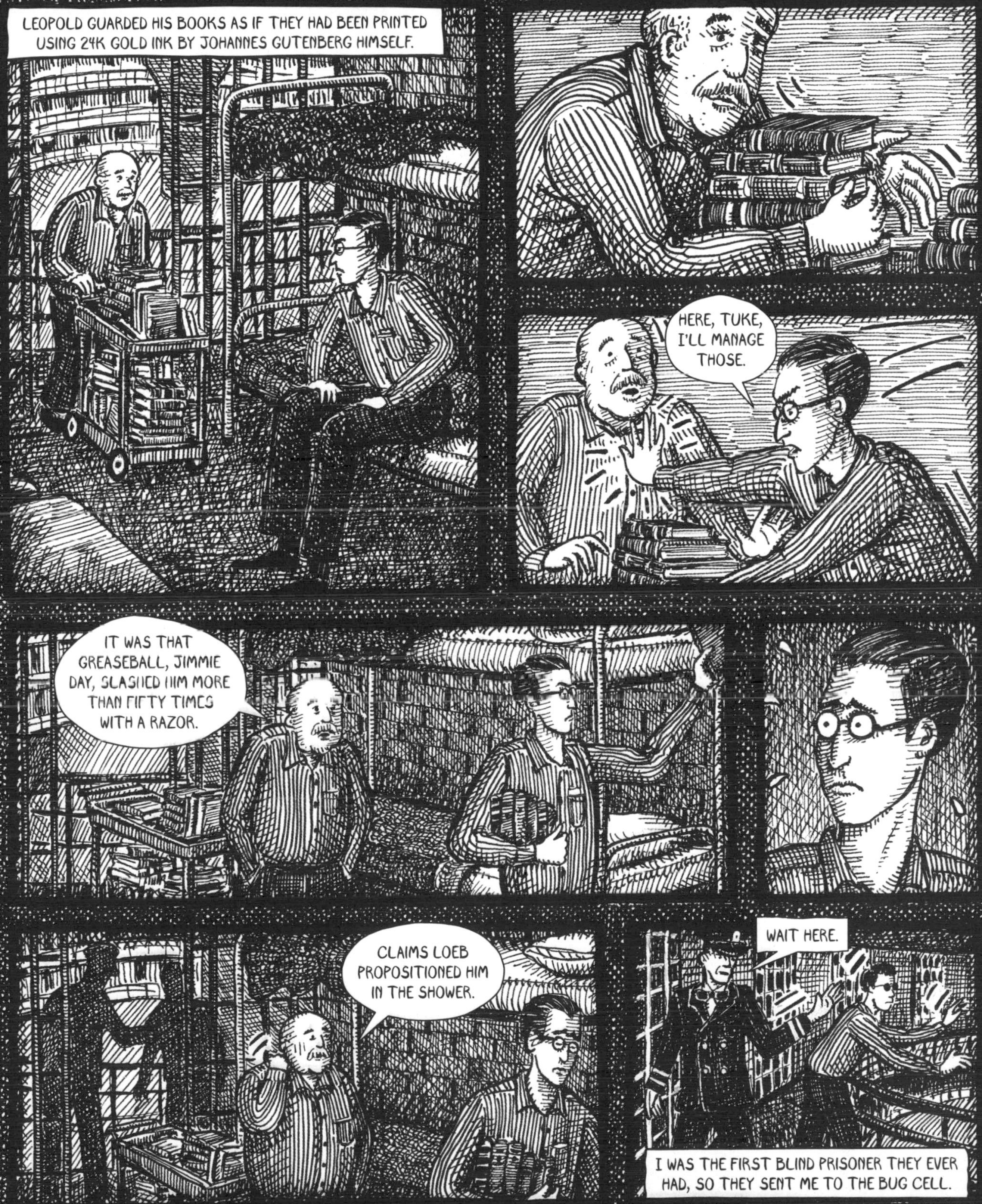
LEOPOLD GUARDED HIS BOOKS AS IF THEY HAD BEEN PRINTED USING 24K GOLD INK BY JOHANNES GUTENBERG HIMSELF.
HERE, TUKE, I'LL MANAGE THOSE.
IT WAS THAT GREASEBALL, JIMMIE DAY, SLASHED HIM MORE THAN FIFTY TIMES WITH A RAZOR.
CLAIMS LOEB PROPOSITIONED HIM IN THE SHOWER.
WAIT HERE.
I WAS THE FIRST BLIND PRISONER THEY EVER HAD, SO THEY SENT ME TO THE BUG CELL.

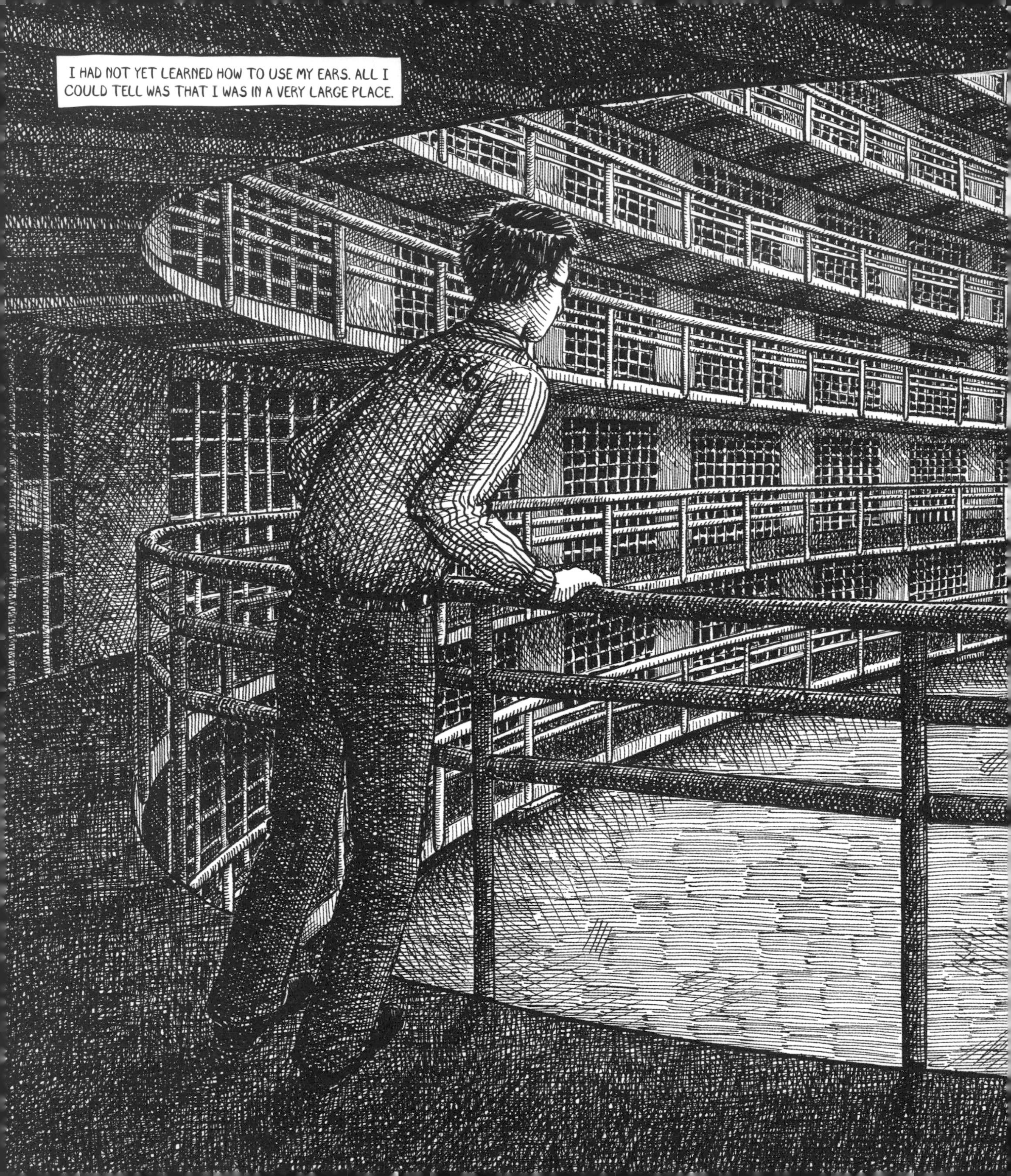
I HAD NOT YET LEARNED HOW TO USE MY EARS. ALL I COULD TELL WAS THAT I WAS IN A VERY LARGE PLACE.

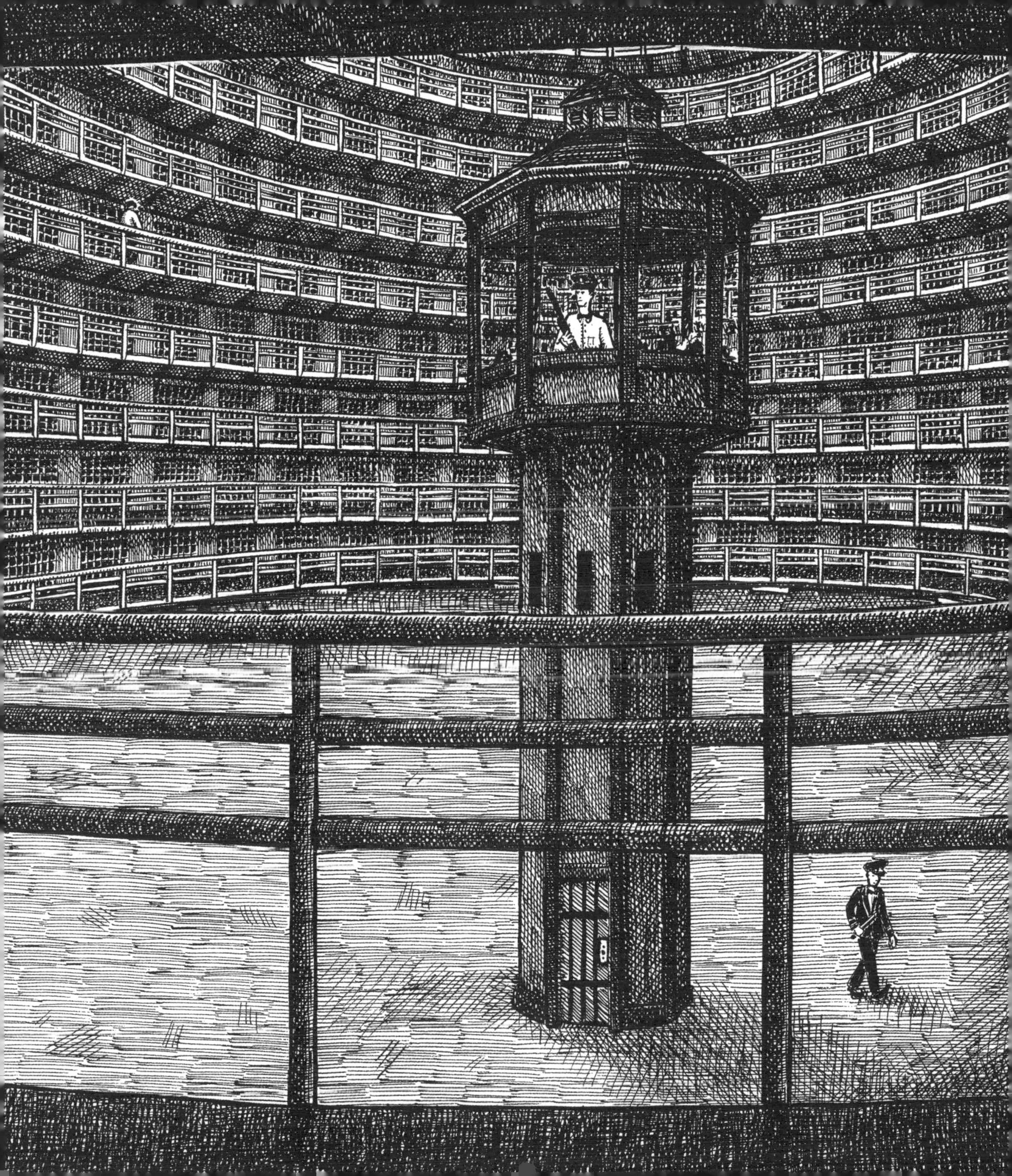

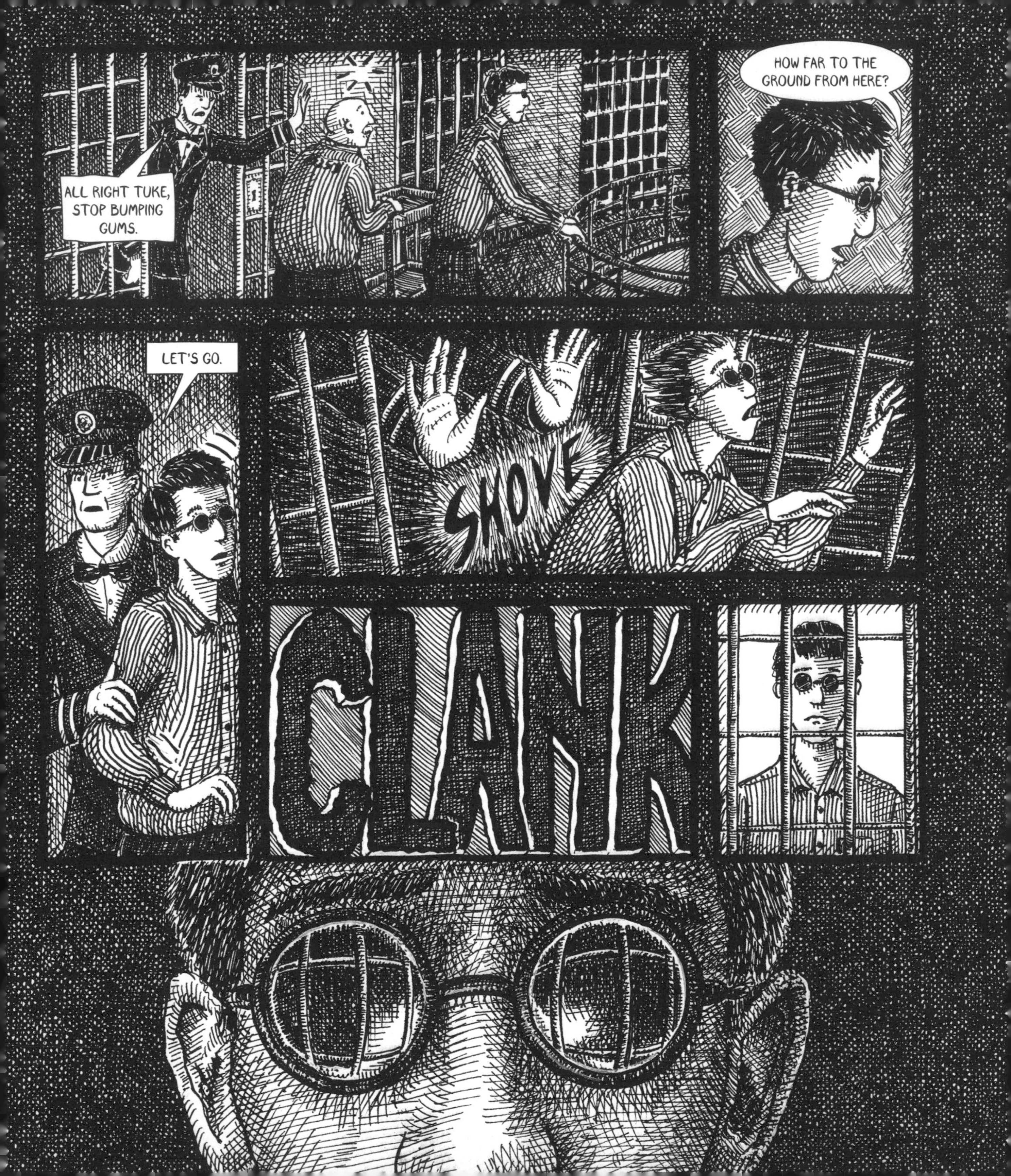
ALL RIGHT TUKE, STOP BUMPING GUMS.
HOW FAR TO THE GROUND FROM HERE?
LET'S GO.
SHOVE
CLANK

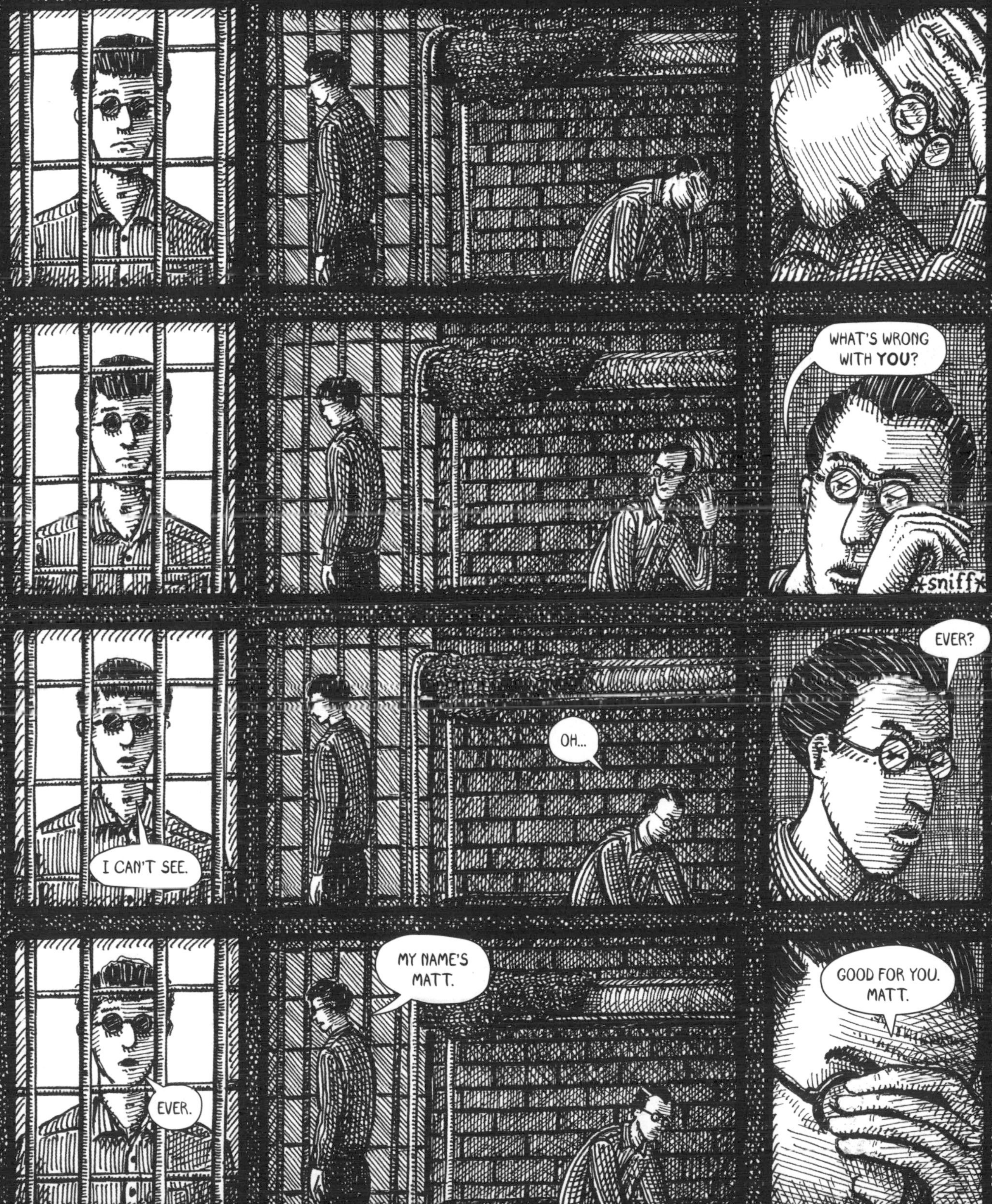
WHAT'S WRONG WITH YOU?
sniff
I CAN'T SEE.
OH...
EVER?
EVER.
MY NAME'S MATT.
GOOD FOR YOU. MATT.

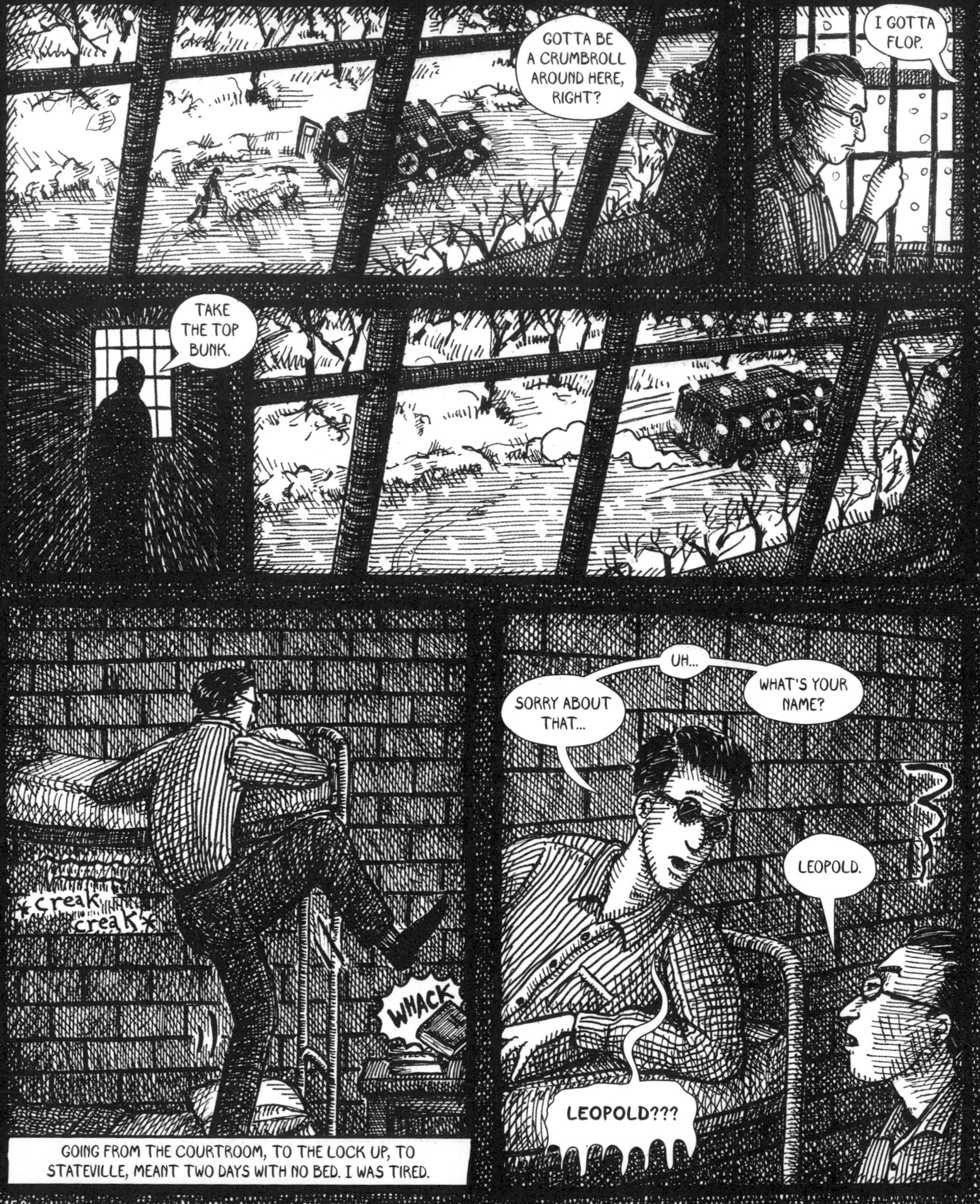
GOTTA BE A CRUMBROLL AROUND HERE, RIGHT?
I GOTTA FLOP.
TAKE THE TOP BUNK.
creak creak
WHACK
GOING FROM THE COURTROOM, TO THE LOCK UP, TO STATEVILLE, MEANT TWO DAYS WITH NO BED. I WAS TIRED.
SORRY ABOUT THAT...
UH...
WHAT'S YOUR NAME?
LEOPOLD.
LEOPOLD???

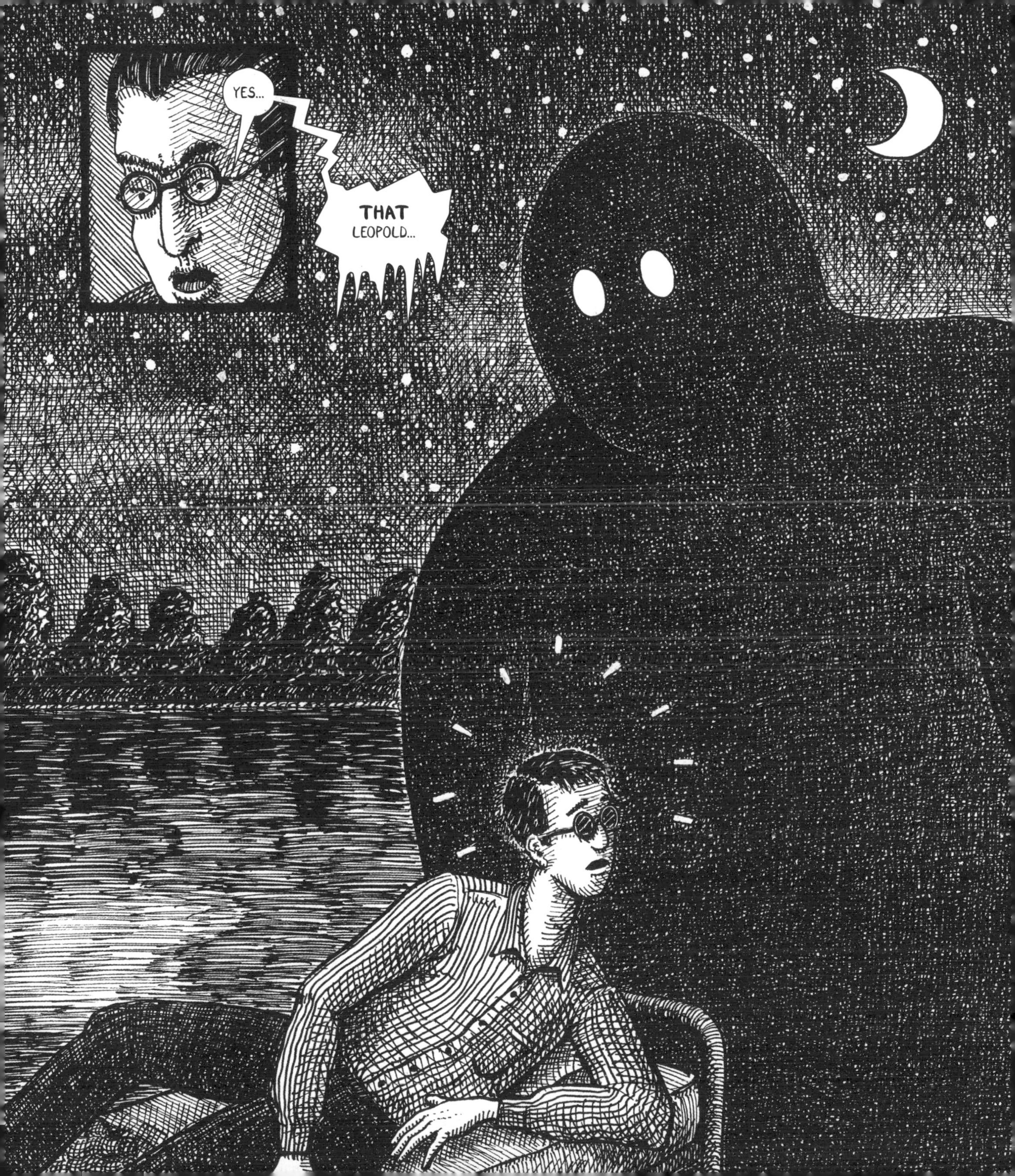
YES...
THAT LEOPOLD...

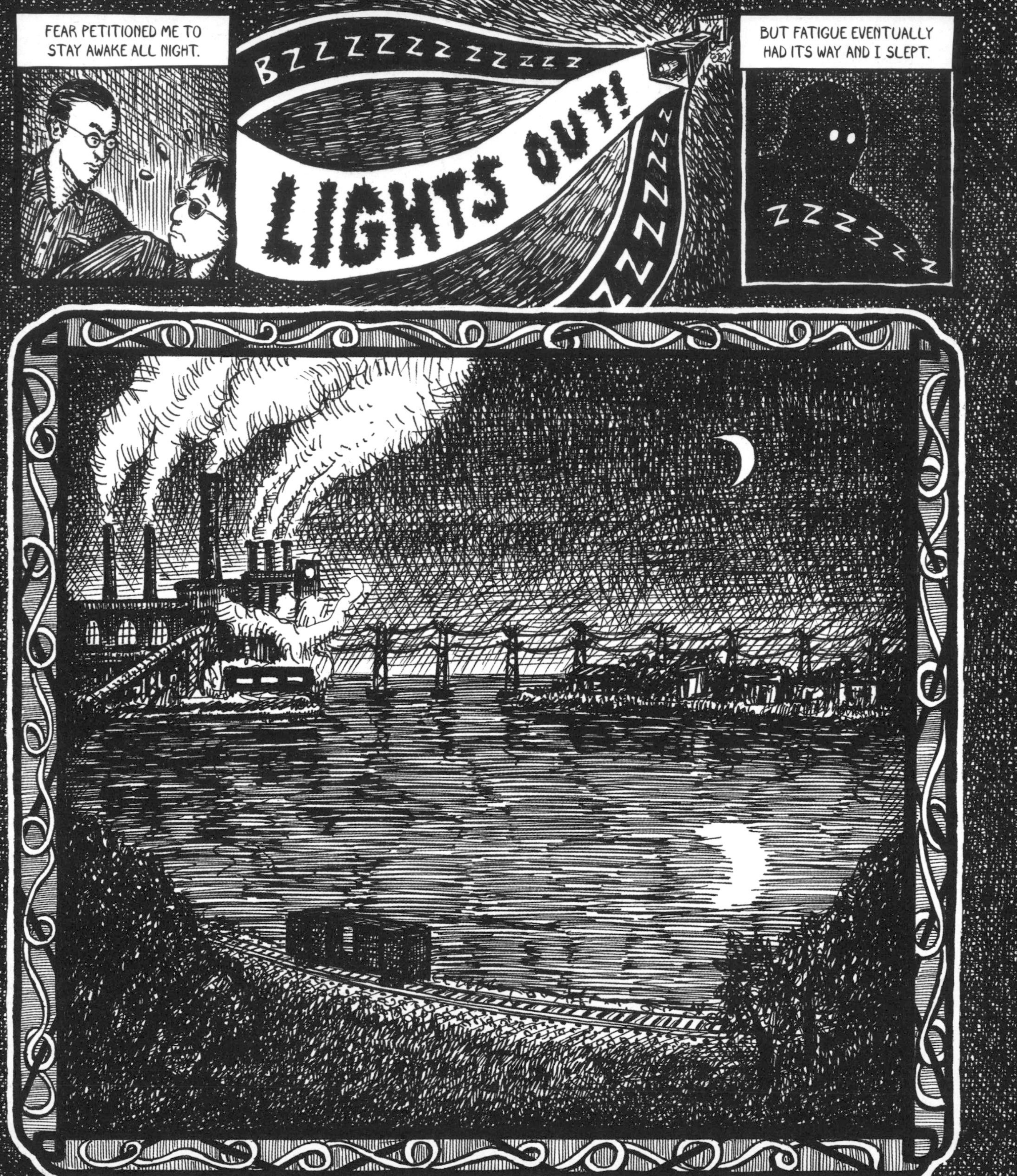
FEAR PETITIONED ME TO STAY AWAKE ALL NIGHT.
BZZZZZZZZZZZZZ
LIGHTS OUT!
BUT FATIGUE EVENTUALLY HAD ITS WAY AND I SLEPT.
ZZZZZZZ

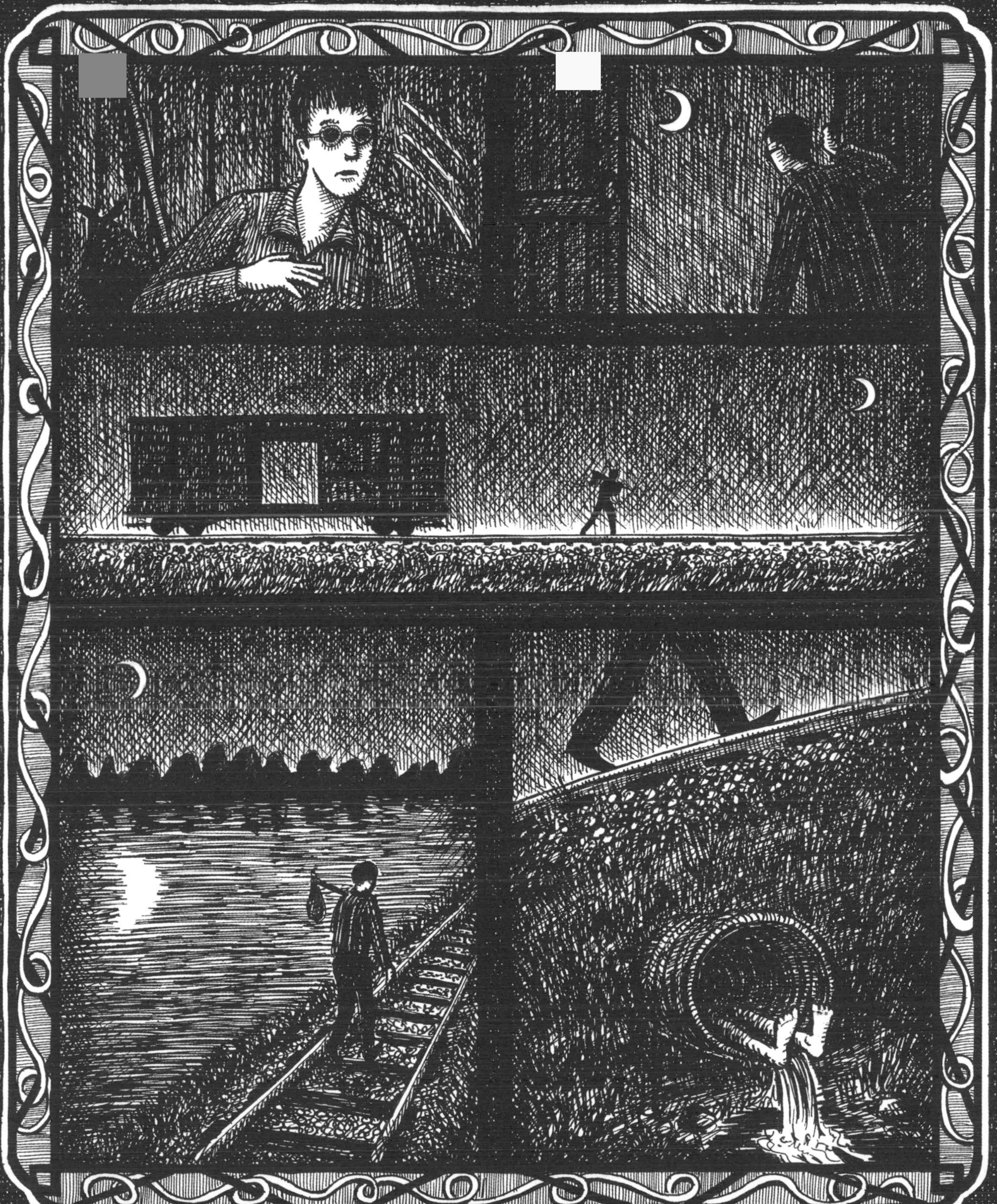

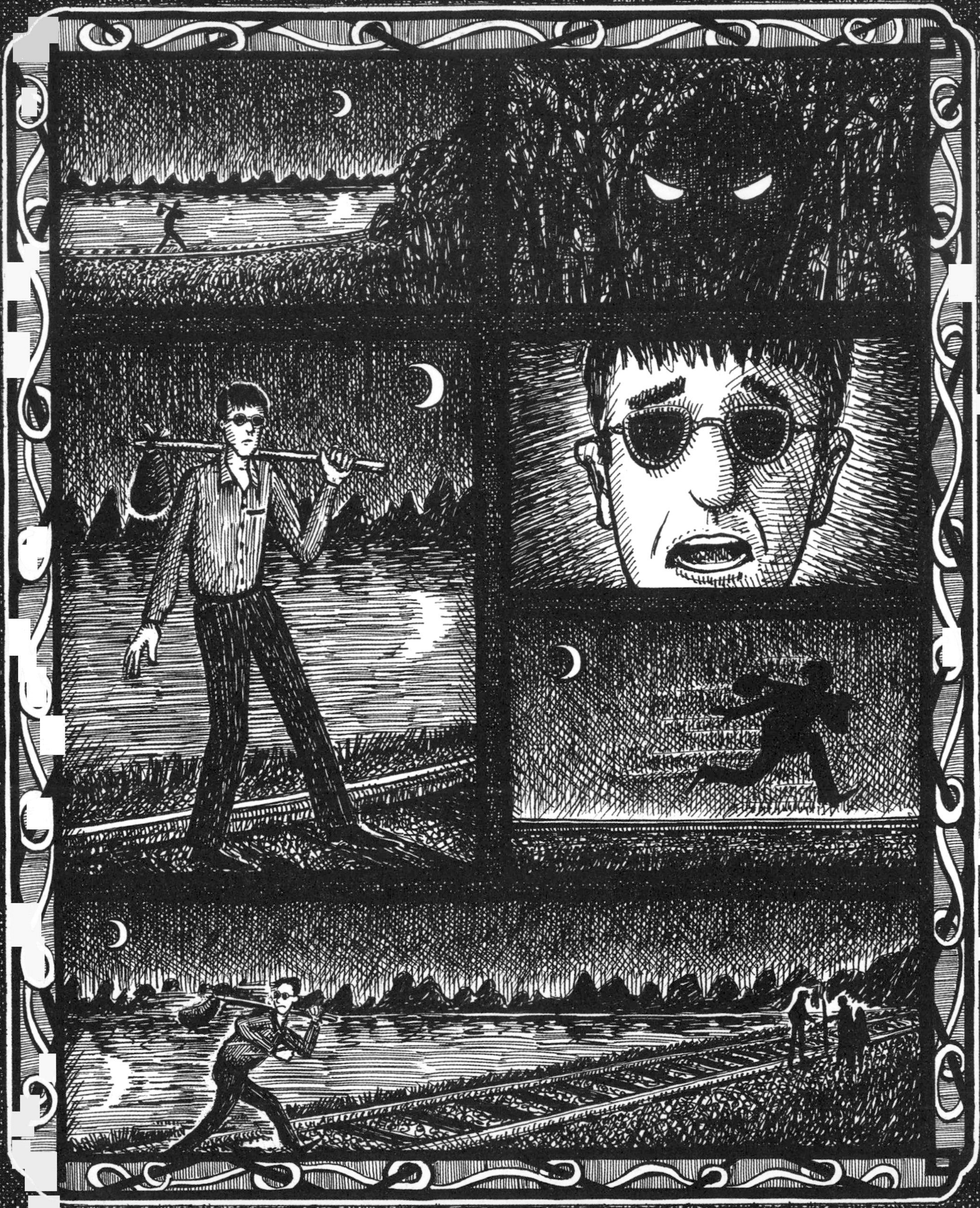

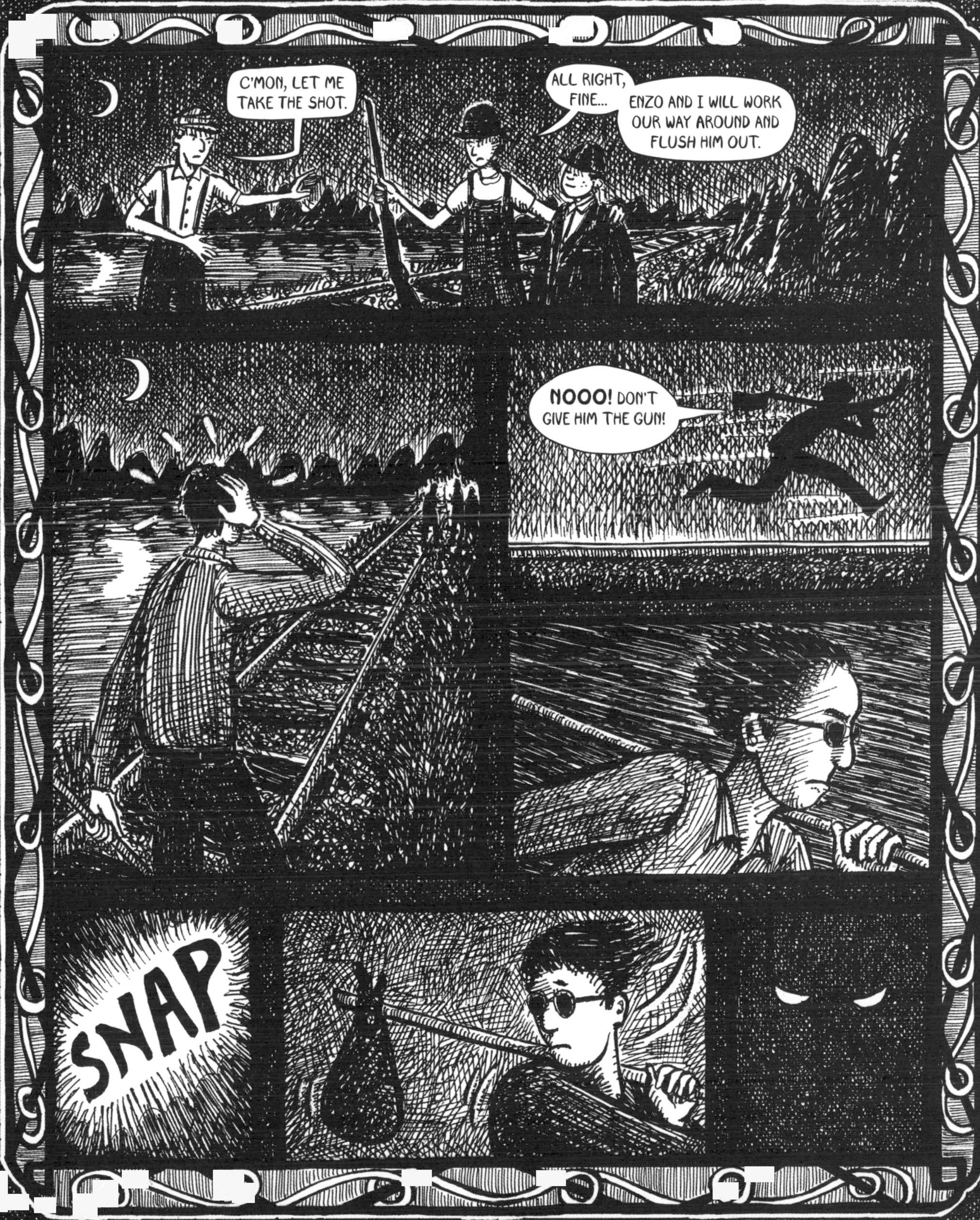
C'MON, LET ME TAKE THE SHOT.
ALL RIGHT, FINE...
ENZO AND I WILL WORK OUR WAY AROUND AND FLUSH HIM OUT.
NOOO! DON'T GIVE HIM THE GUN!
SNAP

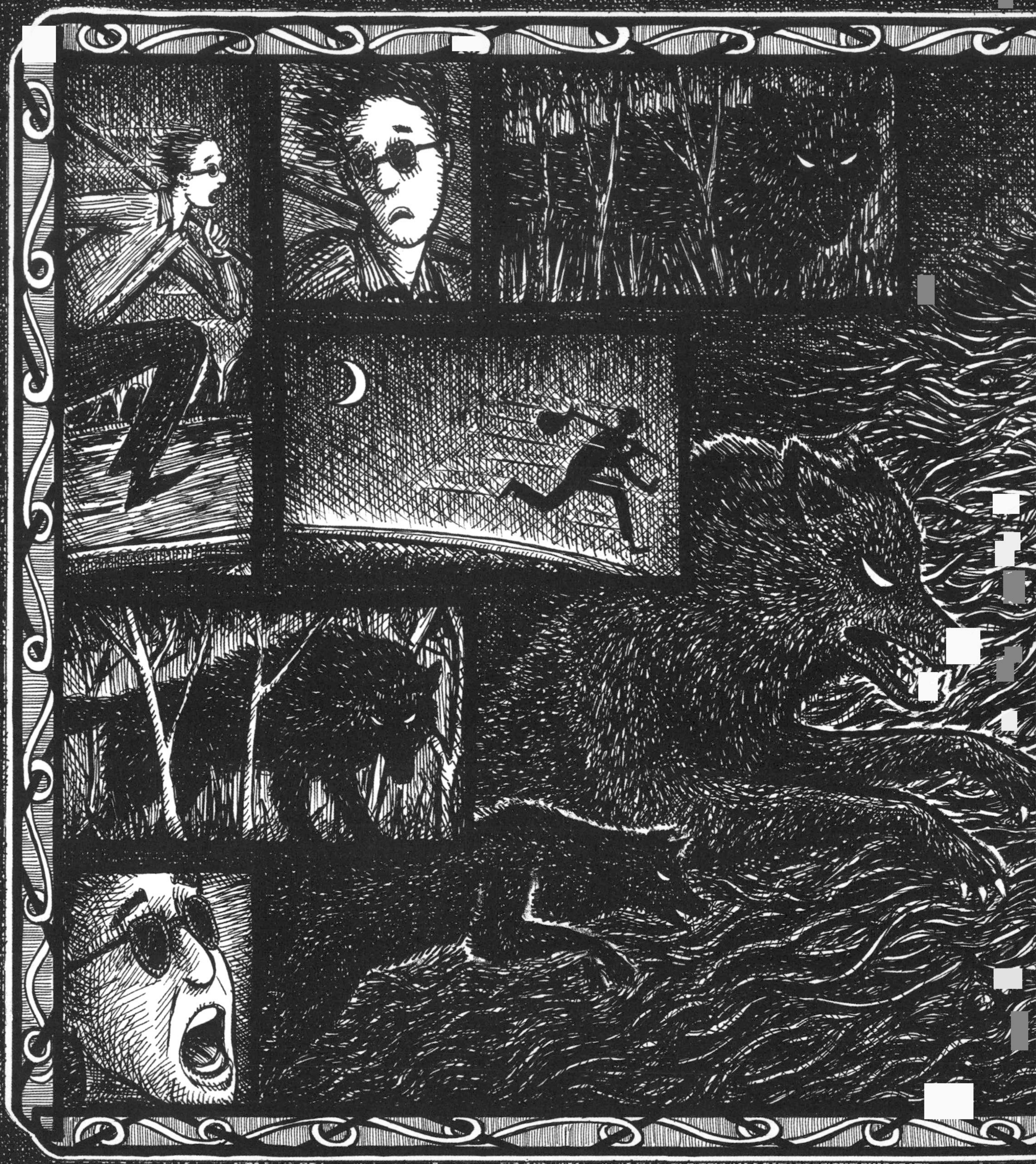

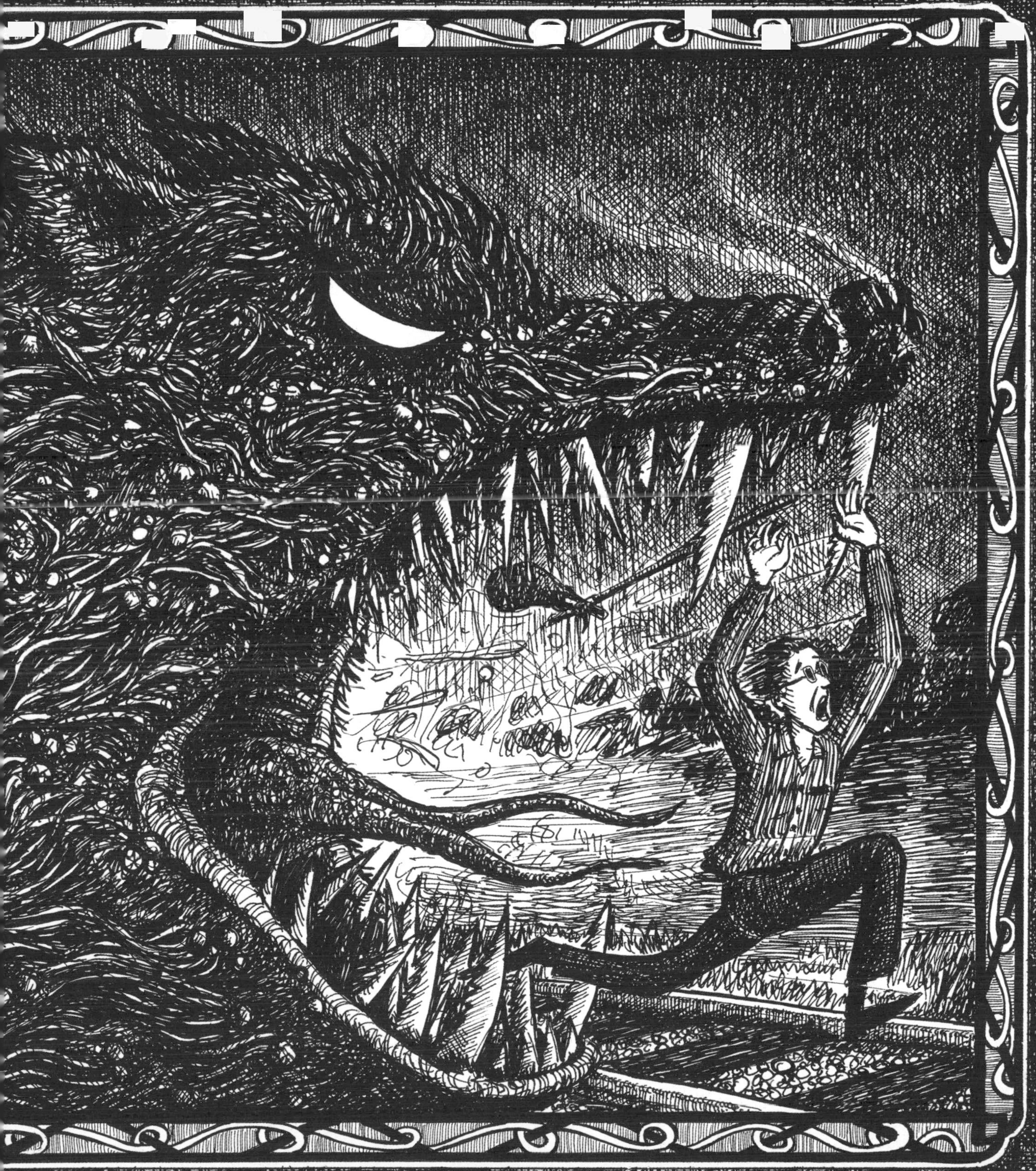

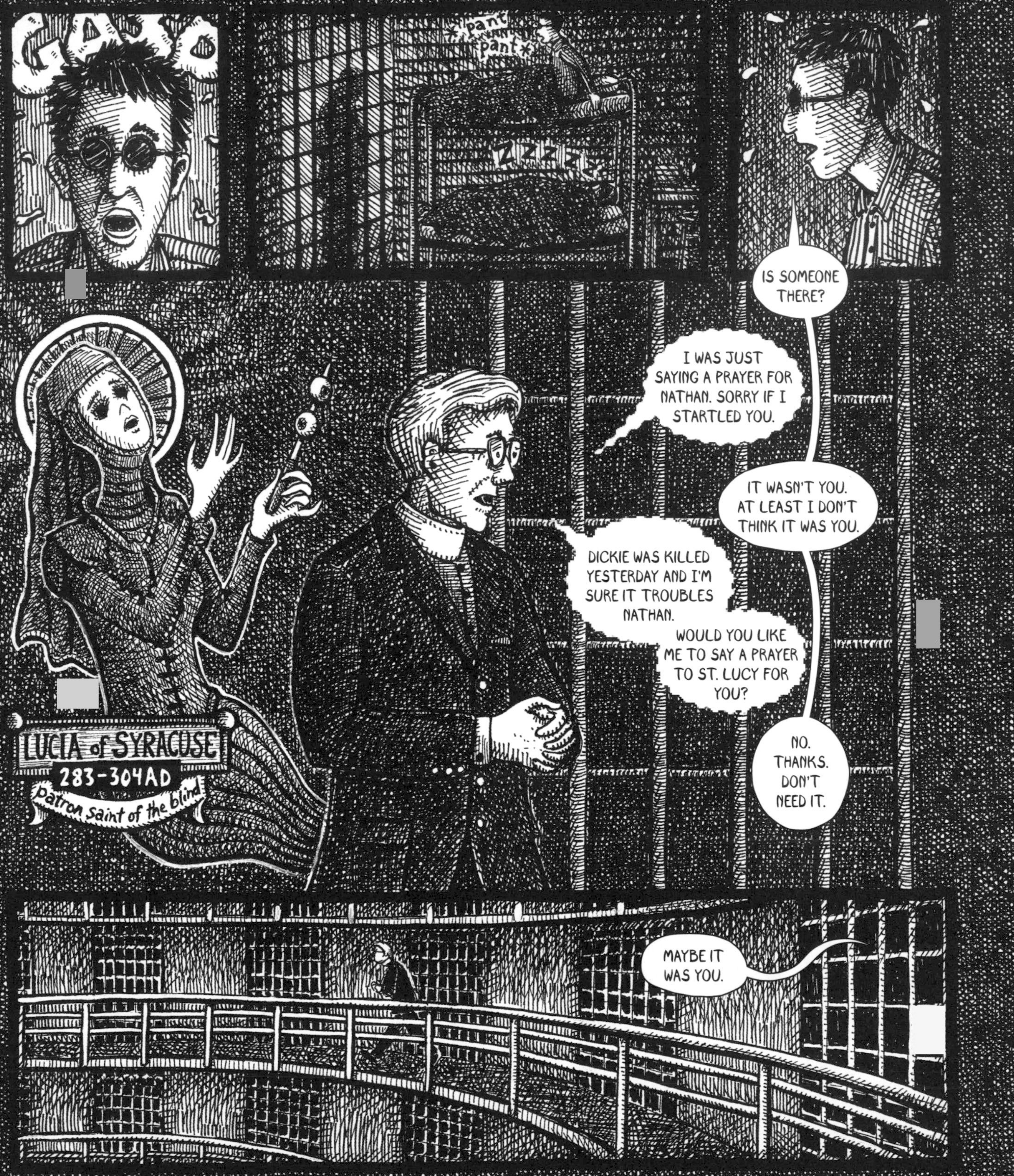
GASP
pant pant
ZZZZ
IS SOMEONE THERE?
I WAS JUST SAYING A PRAYER FOR NATHAN. SORRY IF I STARTLED YOU.
IT WASN'T YOU. AT LEAST I DON'T THINK IT WAS YOU.
DICKIE WAS KILLED YESTERDAY AND I'M SURE IT TROUBLES NATHAN.
WOULD YOU LIKE ME TO SAY A PRAYER TO ST. LUCY FOR YOU?
NO. THANKS. DON'T NEED IT.
LUCIA of SYRACUSE
283-304AD
Patron saint of the blind
MAYBE IT WAS YOU.

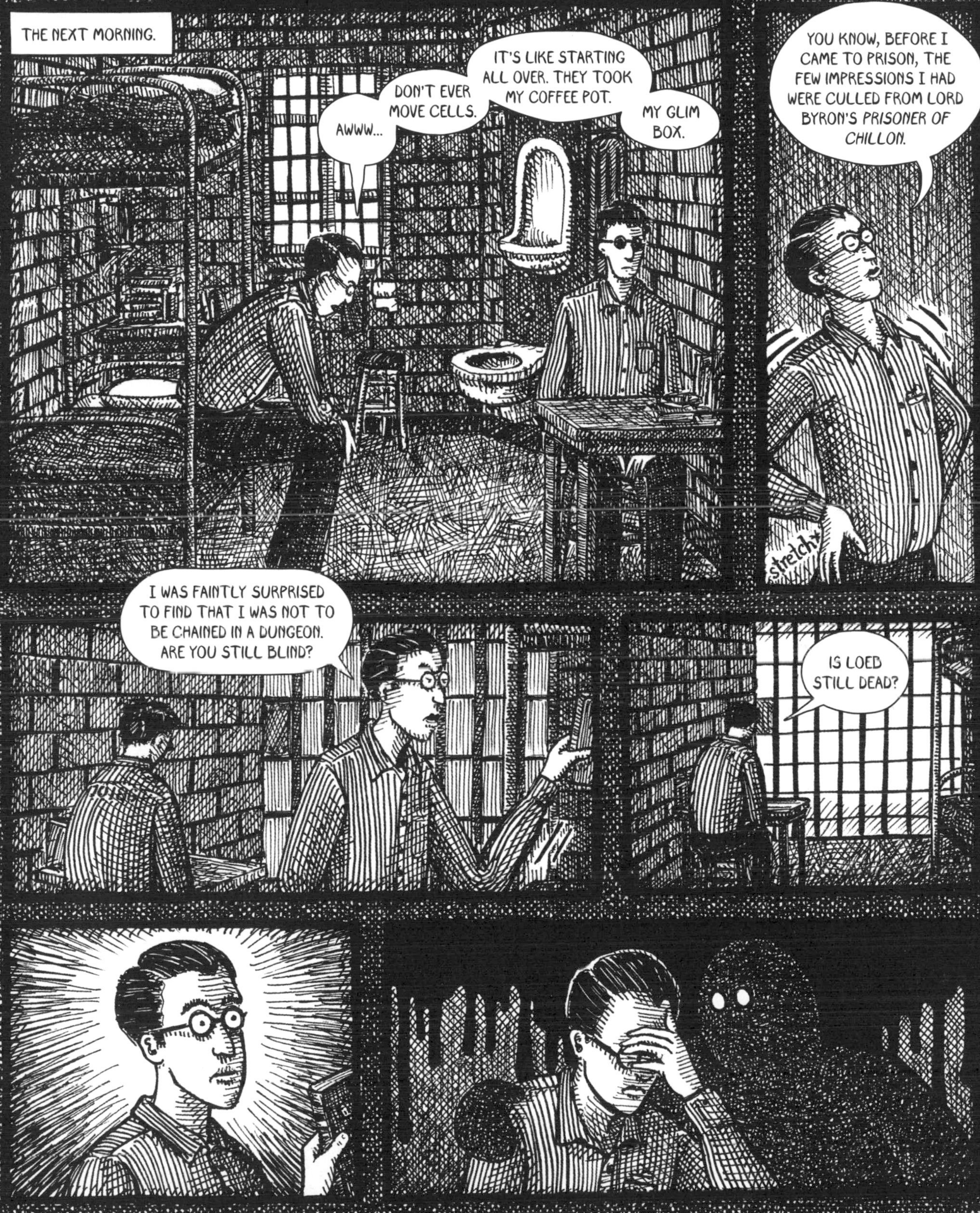

THE NEXT MORNING.
AWWW...
DON'T EVER MOVE CELLS.
IT'S LIKE STARTING ALL OVER. THEY TOOK MY COFFEE POT.
MY GLIM BOX.
YOU KNOW, BEFORE I CAME TO PRISON, THE FEW IMPRESSIONS I HAD WERE CULLED FROM LORD BYRON'S *PRISONER OF CHILLON*.
stretch
I WAS FAINTLY SURPRISED TO FIND THAT I WAS NOT TO BE CHAINED IN A DUNGEON. ARE YOU STILL BLIND?
IS LOEB STILL DEAD?

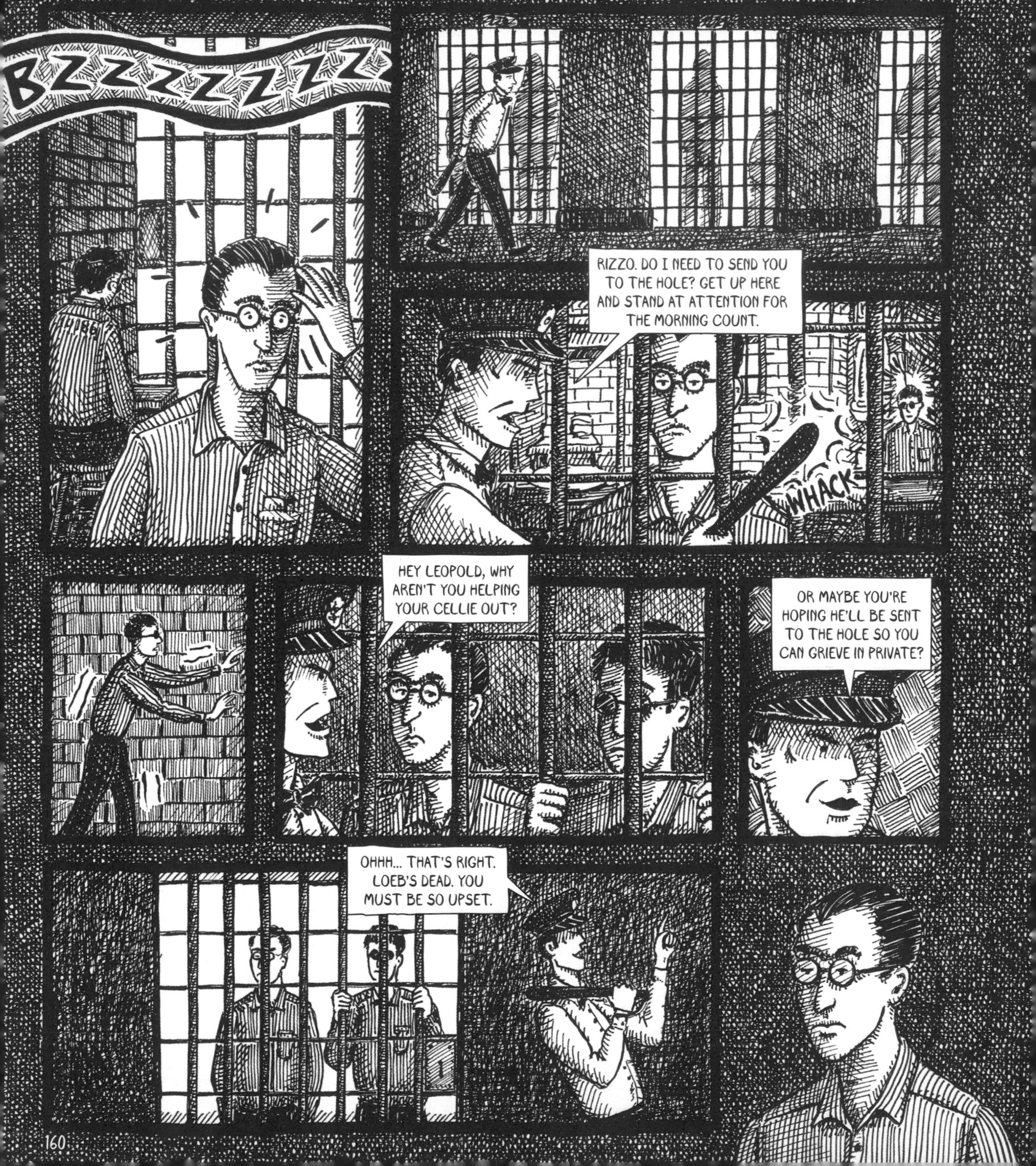
BZZZZZZZZ
RIZZO. DO I NEED TO SEND YOU TO THE HOLE? GET UP HERE AND STAND AT ATTENTION FOR THE MORNING COUNT.
WHACK
HEY LEOPOLD, WHY AREN'T YOU HELPING YOUR CELLIE OUT?
OR MAYBE YOU'RE HOPING HE'LL BE SENT TO THE HOLE SO YOU CAN GRIEVE IN PRIVATE?
OHHH... THAT'S RIGHT. LOEB'S DEAD. YOU MUST BE SO UPSET.

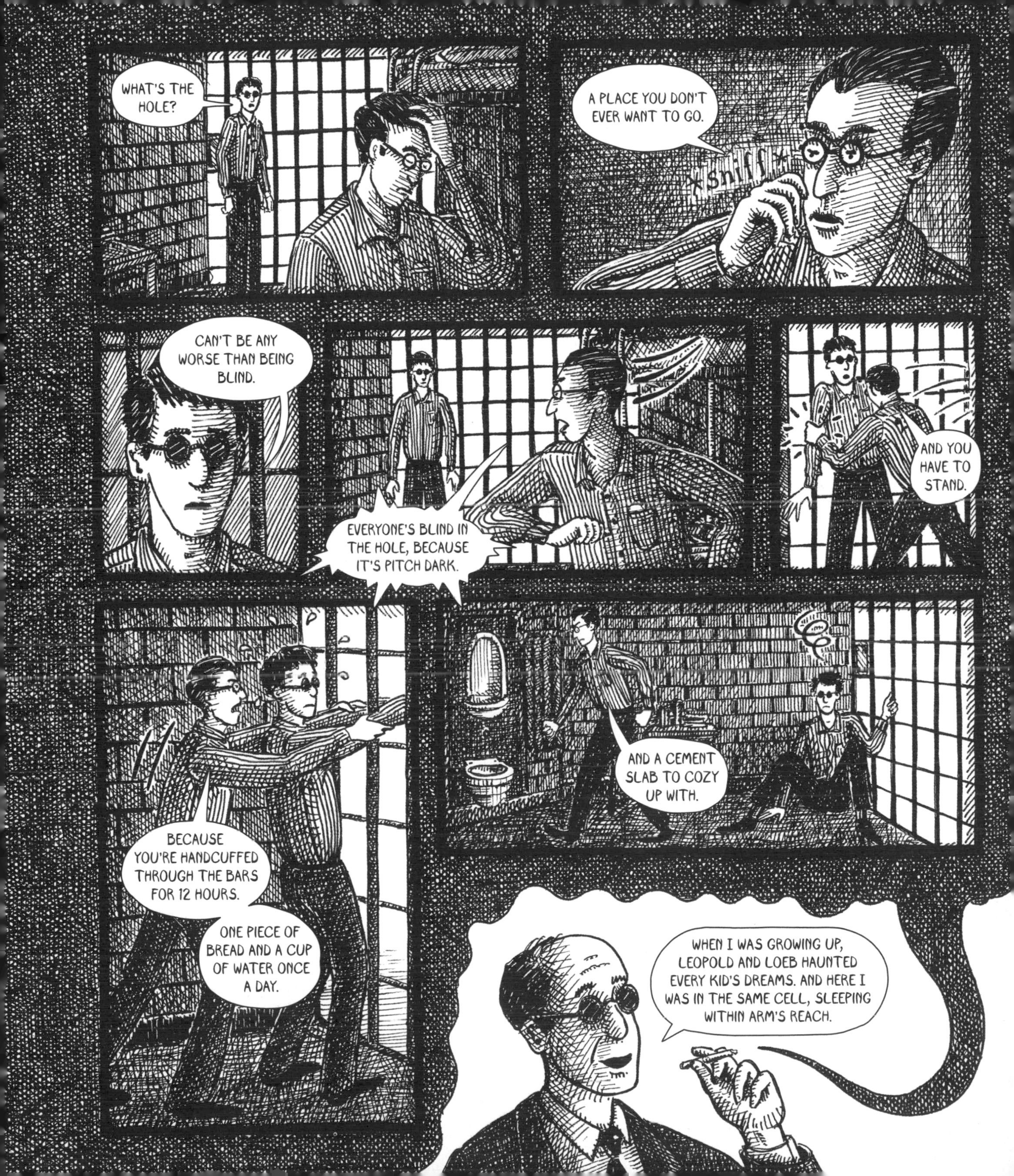
WHAT'S THE HOLE?
A PLACE YOU DON'T EVER WANT TO GO.
SNIFF
CAN'T BE ANY WORSE THAN BEING BLIND.
EVERYONE'S BLIND IN THE HOLE, BECAUSE IT'S PITCH DARK.
AND YOU HAVE TO STAND.
BECAUSE YOU'RE HANDCUFFED THROUGH THE BARS FOR 12 HOURS.
ONE PIECE OF BREAD AND A CUP OF WATER ONCE A DAY.
AND A CEMENT SLAB TO COZY UP WITH.
WHEN I WAS GROWING UP, LEOPOLD AND LOEB HAUNTED EVERY KID'S DREAMS. AND HERE I WAS IN THE SAME CELL, SLEEPING WITHIN ARM'S REACH.

VII ⠿

THE DARKNESS

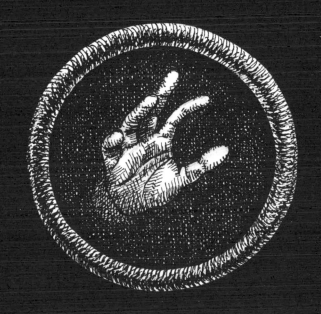

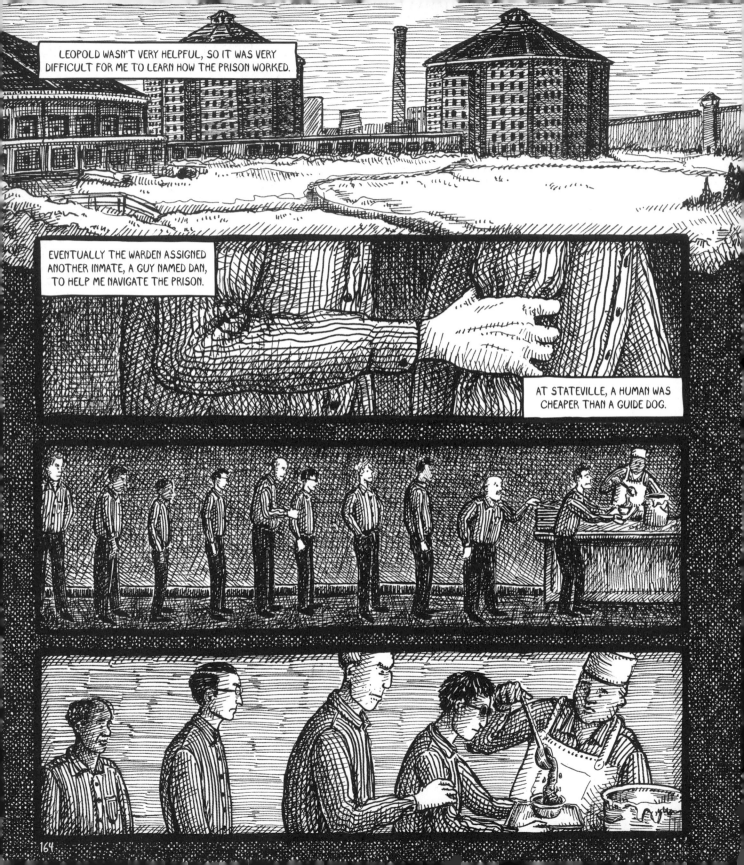

LEOPOLD WASN'T VERY HELPFUL, SO IT WAS VERY DIFFICULT FOR ME TO LEARN HOW THE PRISON WORKED.

EVENTUALLY THE WARDEN ASSIGNED ANOTHER INMATE, A GUY NAMED DAN, TO HELP ME NAVIGATE THE PRISON.

AT STATEVILLE, A HUMAN WAS CHEAPER THAN A GUIDE DOG.

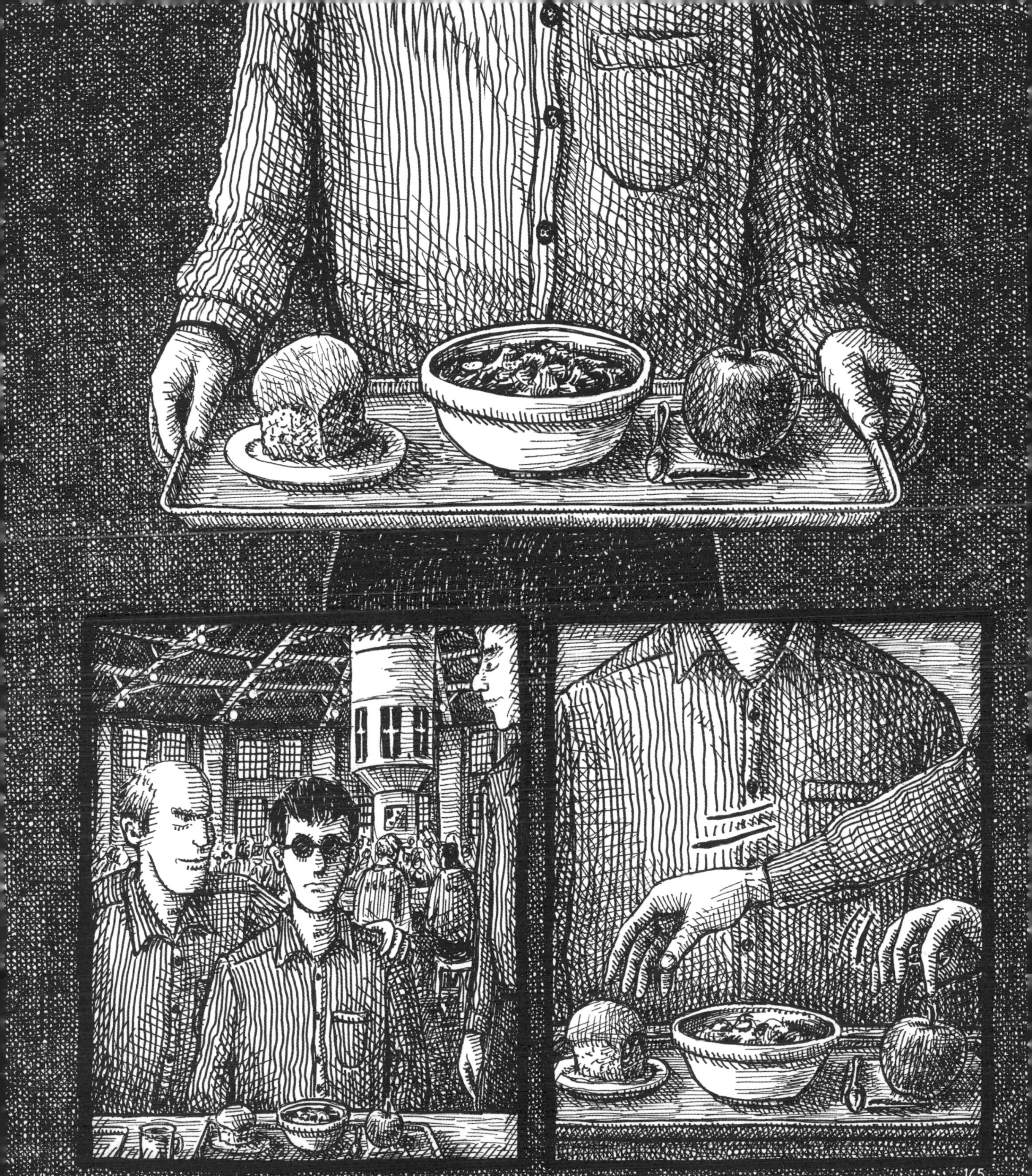

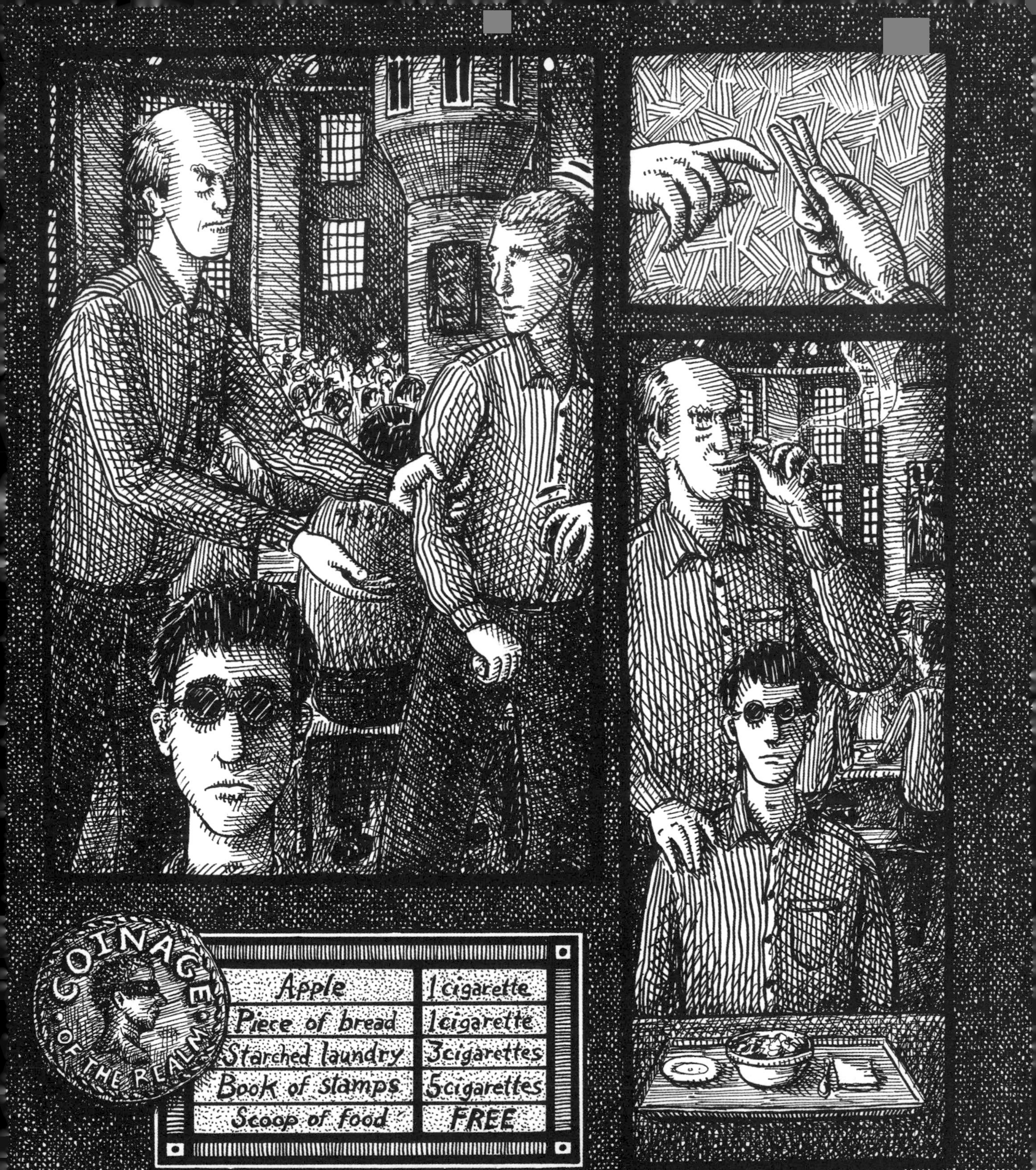

COINAGE OF THE REALM
Apple 1 cigarette
Piece of bread 1 cigarette
Starched laundry 3 cigarettes
Book of stamps 5 cigarettes
Scoop of food FREE

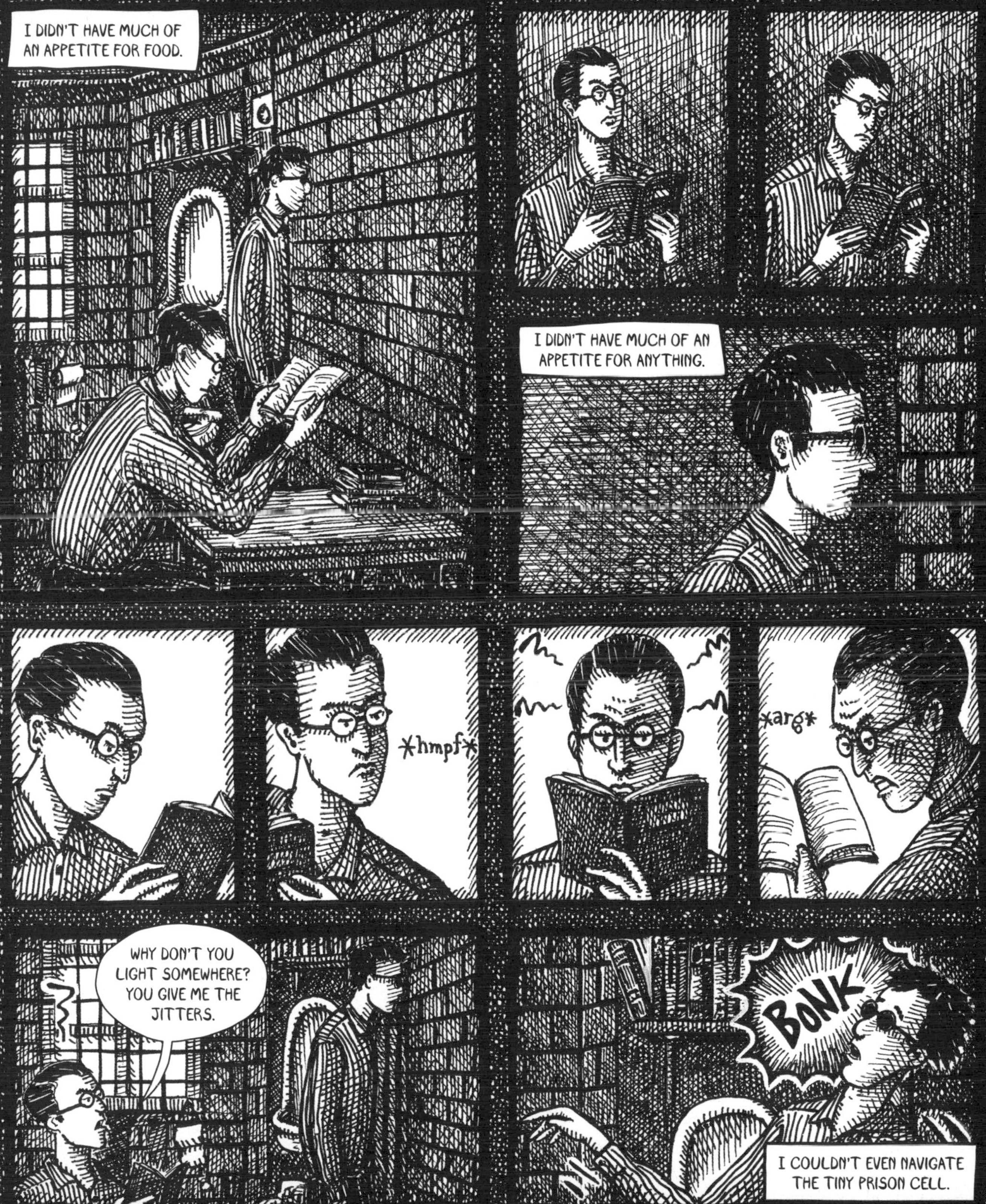
I DIDN'T HAVE MUCH OF AN APPETITE FOR FOOD.
I DIDN'T HAVE MUCH OF AN APPETITE FOR ANYTHING.
hmpf
arg
WHY DON'T YOU LIGHT SOMEWHERE? YOU GIVE ME THE JITTERS.
BONK
I COULDN'T EVEN NAVIGATE THE TINY PRISON CELL.

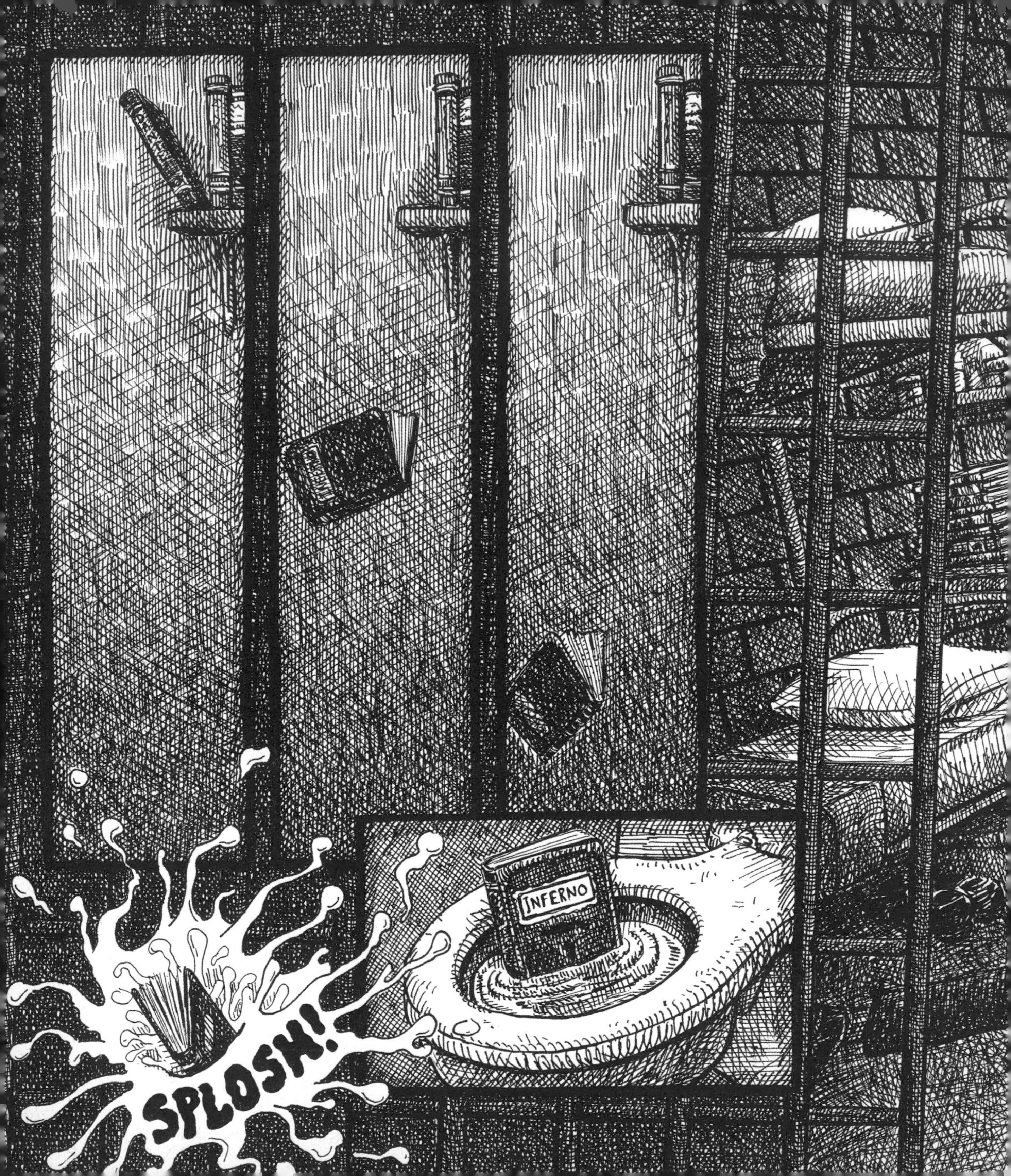
INFERNO
SPLOSH!

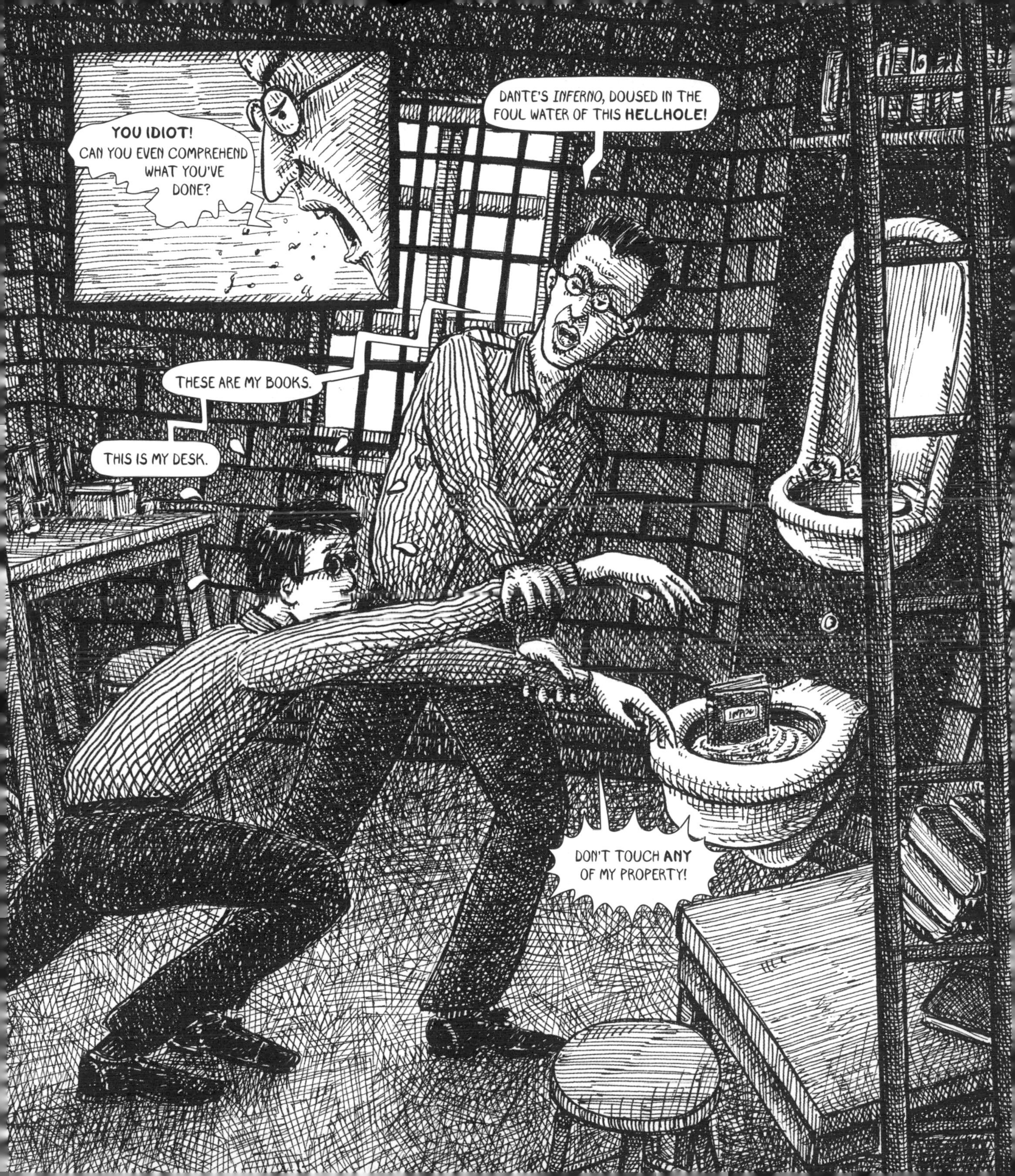
YOU IDIOT! CAN YOU EVEN COMPREHEND WHAT YOU'VE DONE?
DANTE'S *INFERNO*, DOUSED IN THE FOUL WATER OF THIS **HELLHOLE!**
THESE ARE MY BOOKS.
THIS IS MY DESK.
DON'T TOUCH **ANY** OF MY PROPERTY!

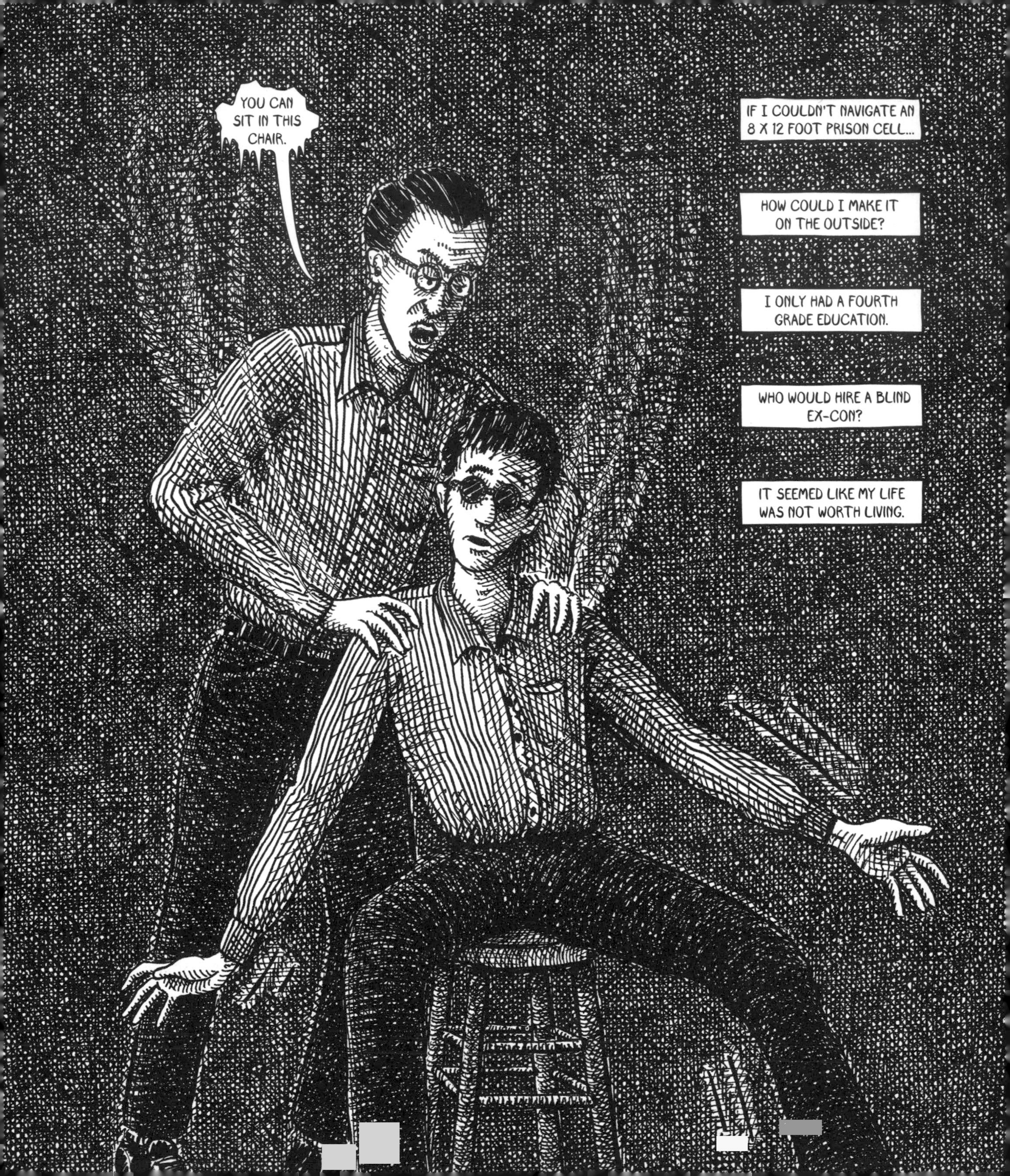
YOU CAN SIT IN THIS CHAIR.
IF I COULDN'T NAVIGATE AN 8 X 12 FOOT PRISON CELL...
HOW COULD I MAKE IT ON THE OUTSIDE?
I ONLY HAD A FOURTH GRADE EDUCATION.
WHO WOULD HIRE A BLIND EX-CON?
IT SEEMED LIKE MY LIFE WAS NOT WORTH LIVING.

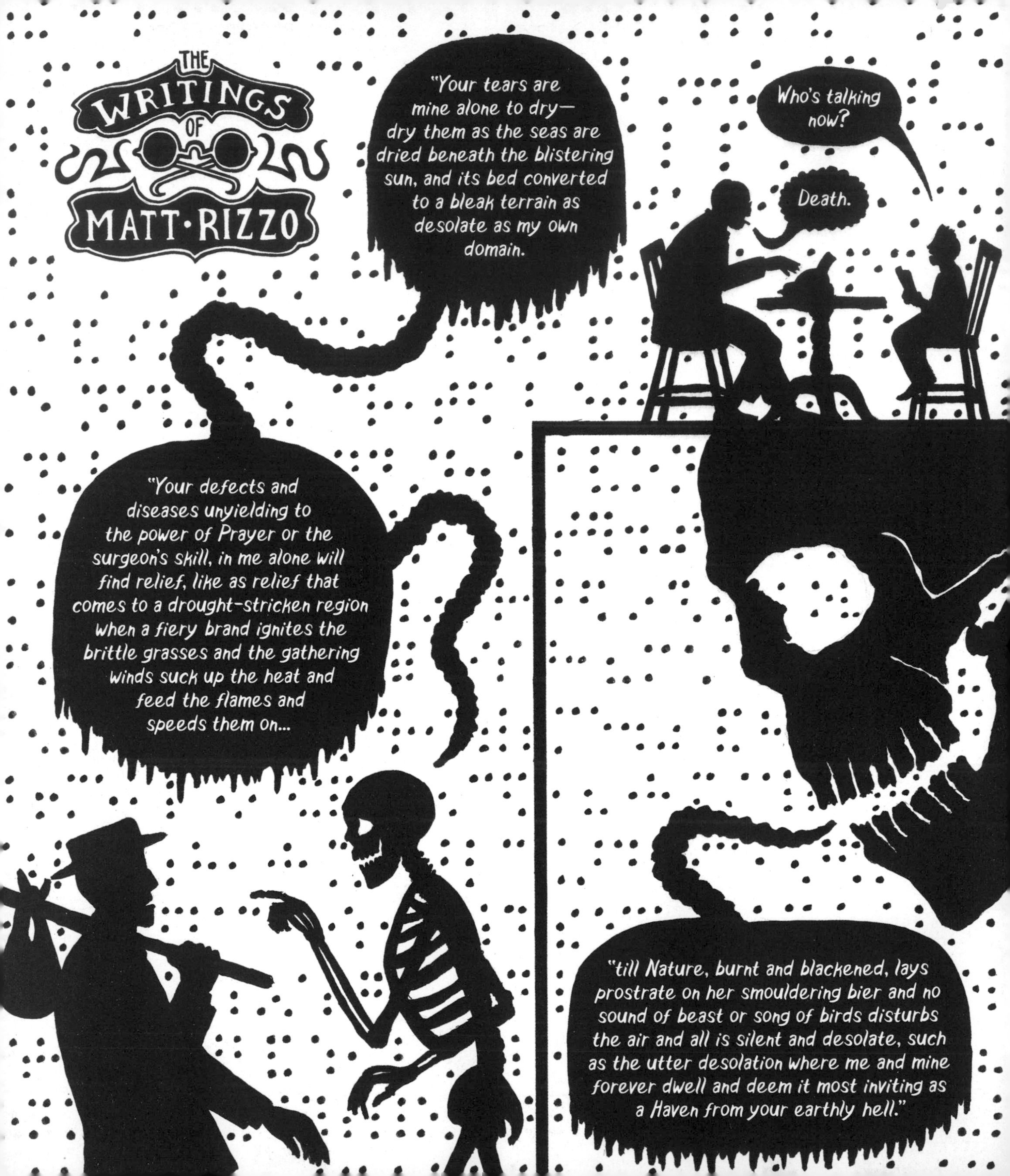
THE WRITINGS OF MATT·RIZZO
"Your tears are mine alone to dry—dry them as the seas are dried beneath the blistering sun, and its bed converted to a bleak terrain as desolate as my own domain.
Who's talking now?
Death.
"Your defects and diseases unyielding to the power of Prayer or the surgeon's skill, in me alone will find relief, like as relief that comes to a drought-stricken region when a fiery brand ignites the brittle grasses and the gathering winds suck up the heat and feed the flames and speeds them on...
"till Nature, burnt and blackened, lays prostrate on her smouldering bier and no sound of beast or song of birds disturbs the air and all is silent and desolate, such as the utter desolation where me and mine forever dwell and deem it most inviting as a Haven from your earthly hell."

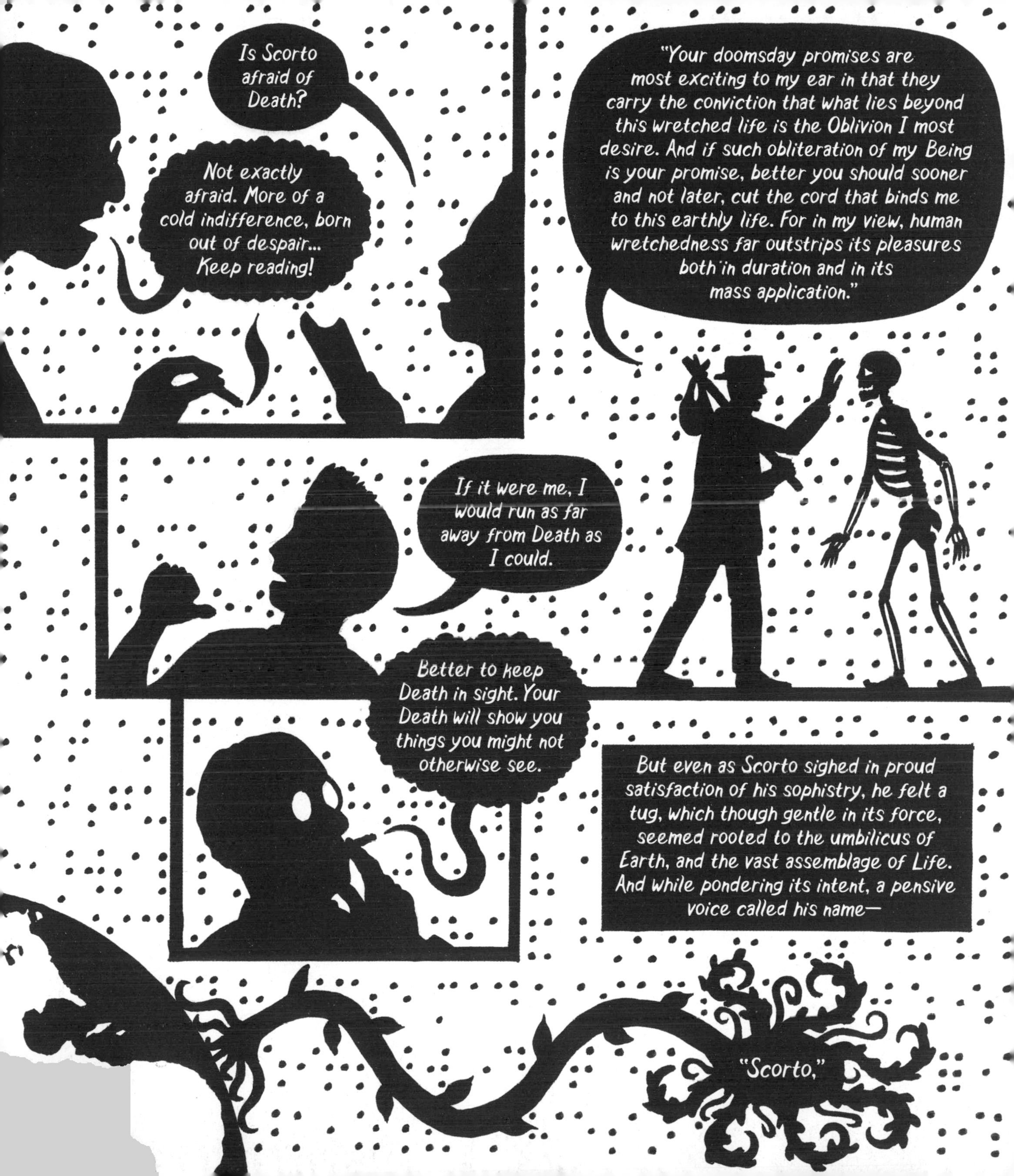
Is Scorto afraid of Death?
Not exactly afraid. More of a cold indifference, born out of despair... Keep reading!
"Your doomsday promises are most exciting to my ear in that they carry the conviction that what lies beyond this wretched life is the Oblivion I most desire. And if such obliteration of my Being is your promise, better you should sooner and not later, cut the cord that binds me to this earthly life. For in my view, human wretchedness far outstrips its pleasures both in duration and in its mass application."
If it were me, I would run as far away from Death as I could.
Better to keep Death in sight. Your Death will show you things you might not otherwise see.
But even as Scorto sighed in proud satisfaction of his sophistry, he felt a tug, which though gentle in its force, seemed rooted to the umbilicus of Earth, and the vast assemblage of Life. And while pondering its intent, a pensive voice called his name—
"Scorto,"

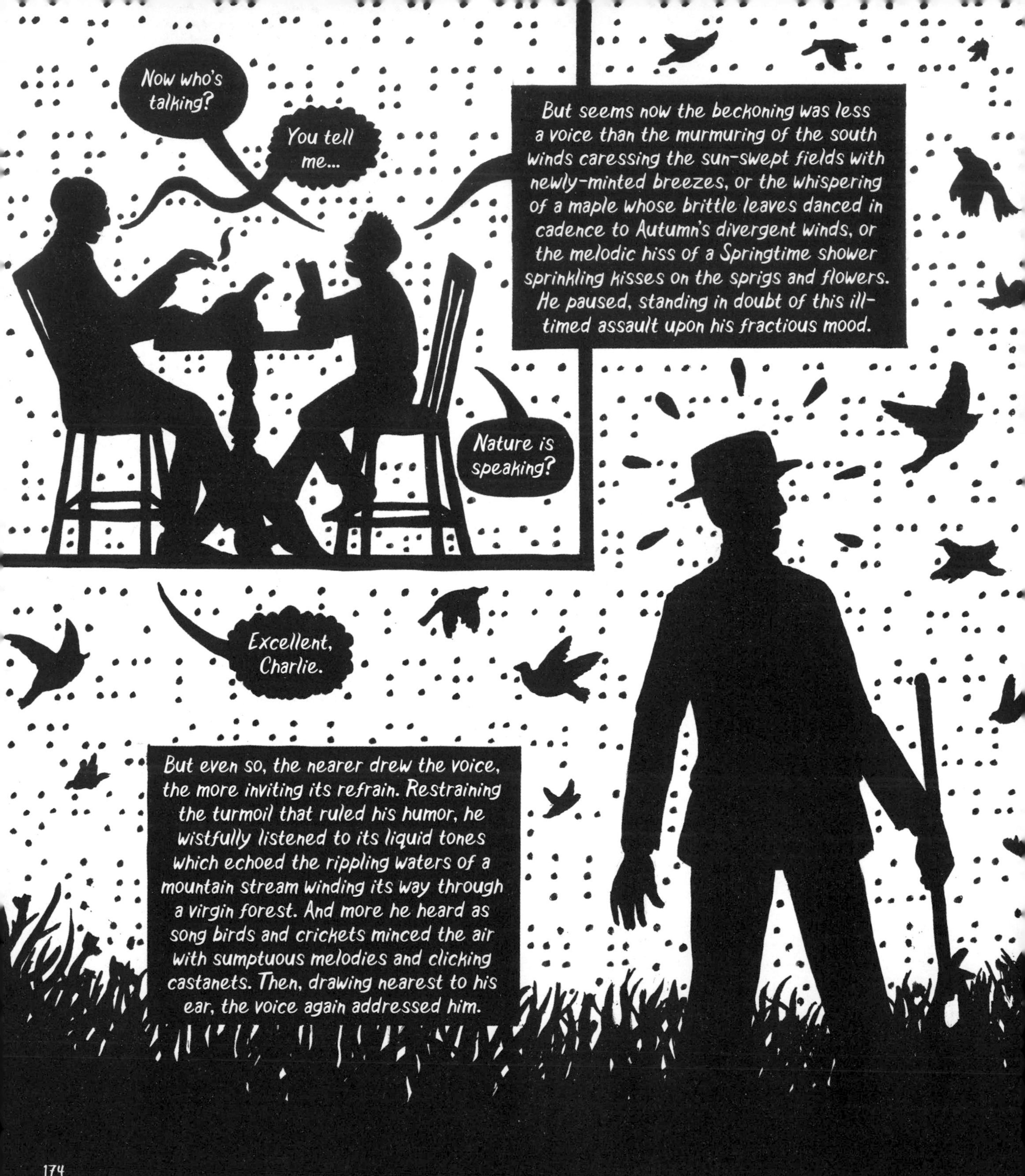

Now who's talking?
You tell me...
But seems now the beckoning was less a voice than the murmuring of the south winds caressing the sun-swept fields with newly-minted breezes, or the whispering of a maple whose brittle leaves danced in cadence to Autumn's divergent winds, or the melodic hiss of a Springtime shower sprinkling kisses on the sprigs and flowers. He paused, standing in doubt of this ill-timed assault upon his fractious mood.
Nature is speaking?
Excellent, Charlie.
But even so, the nearer drew the voice, the more inviting its refrain. Restraining the turmoil that ruled his humor, he wistfully listened to its liquid tones which echoed the rippling waters of a mountain stream winding its way through a virgin forest. And more he heard as song birds and crickets minced the air with sumptuous melodies and clicking castanets. Then, drawing nearest to his ear, the voice again addressed him.

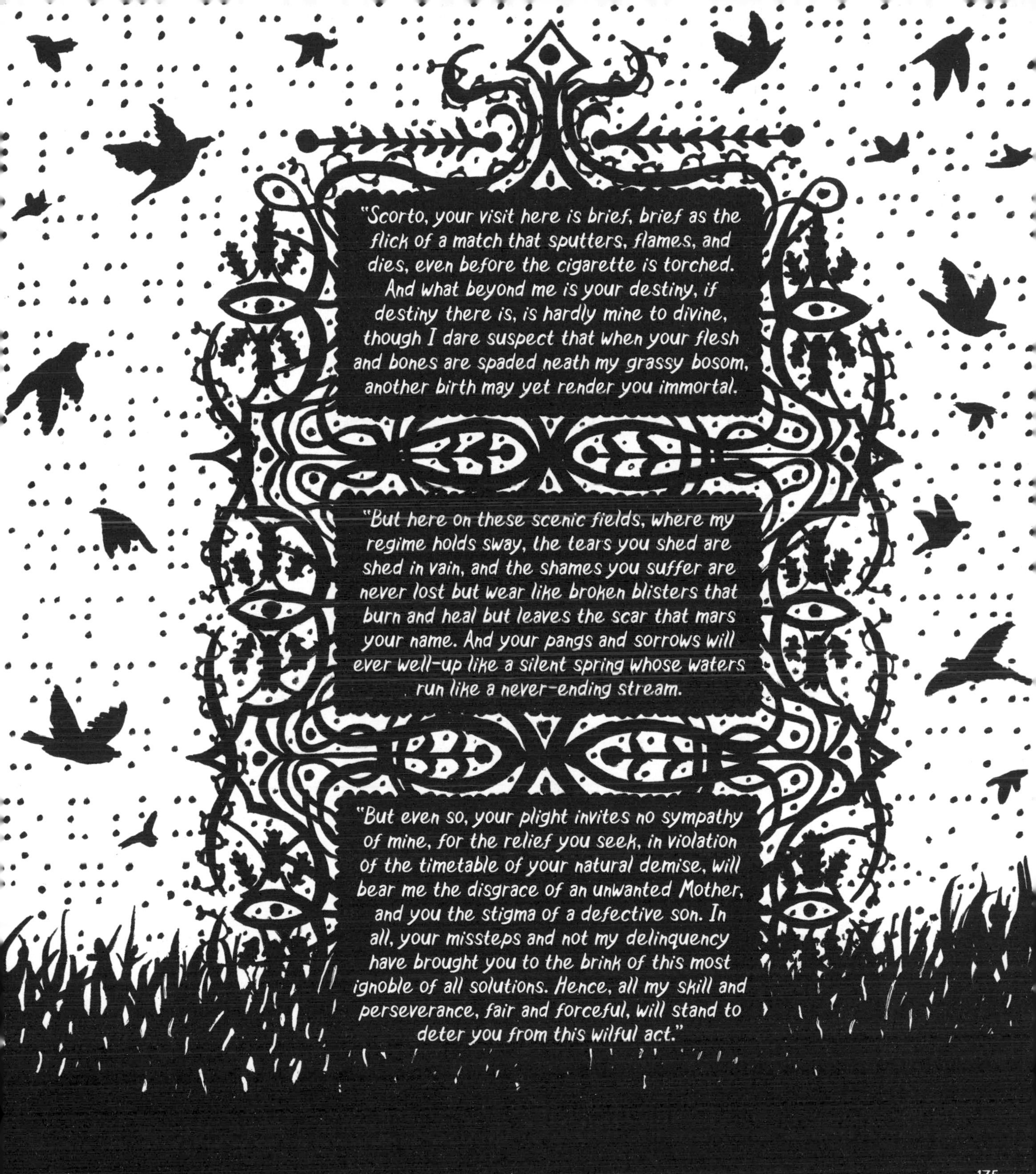
"Scorto, your visit here is brief, brief as the flick of a match that sputters, flames, and dies, even before the cigarette is torched. And what beyond me is your destiny, if destiny there is, is hardly mine to divine, though I dare suspect that when your flesh and bones are spaded neath my grassy bosom, another birth may yet render you immortal.
"But here on these scenic fields, where my regime holds sway, the tears you shed are shed in vain, and the shames you suffer are never lost but wear like broken blisters that burn and heal but leaves the scar that mars your name. And your pangs and sorrows will ever well-up like a silent spring whose waters run like a never-ending stream.
"But even so, your plight invites no sympathy of mine, for the relief you seek, in violation of the timetable of your natural demise, will bear me the disgrace of an unwanted Mother, and you the stigma of a defective son. In all, your missteps and not my delinquency have brought you to the brink of this most ignoble of all solutions. Hence, all my skill and perseverance, fair and forceful, will stand to deter you from this wilful act."

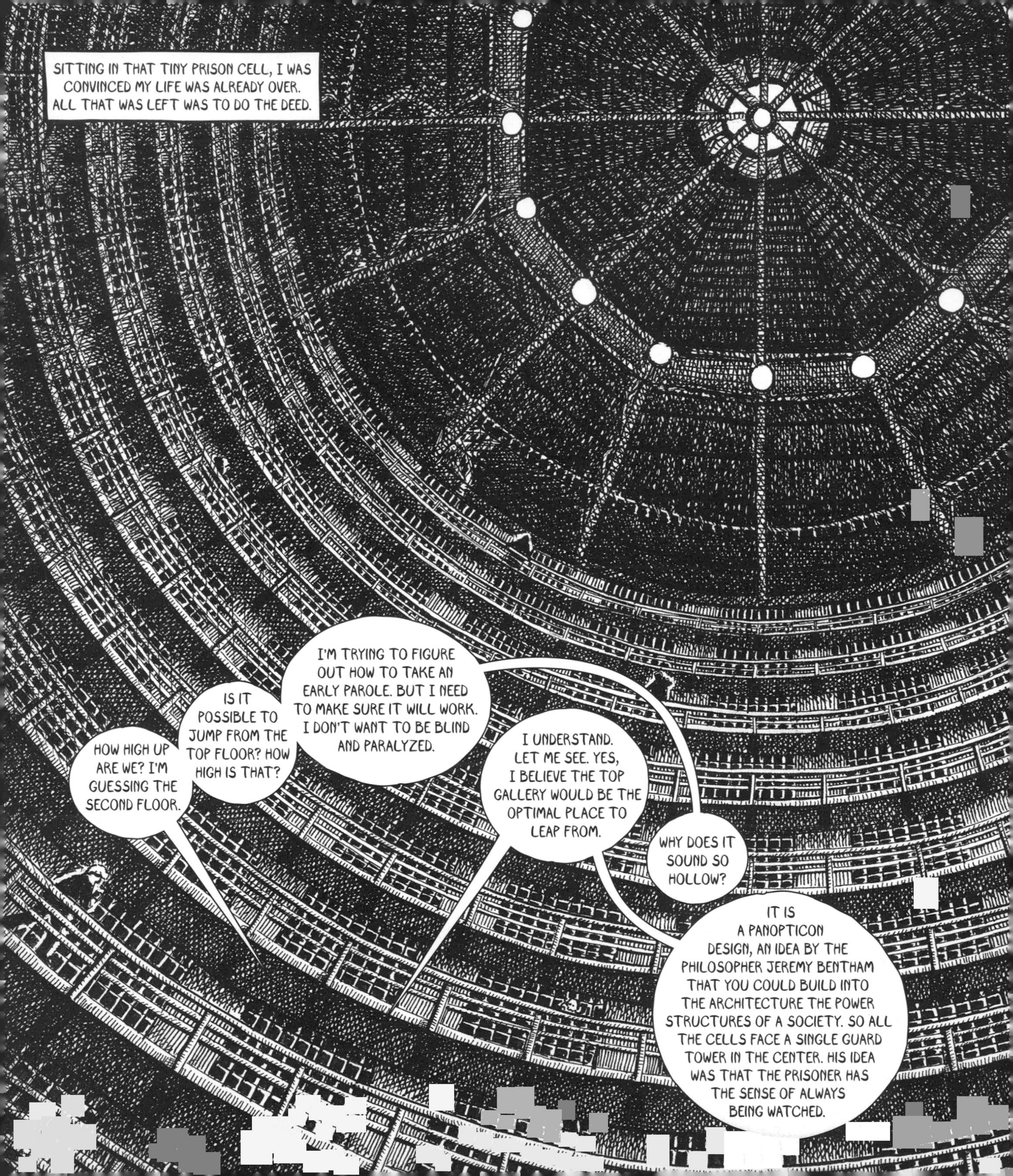
SITTING IN THAT TINY PRISON CELL, I WAS CONVINCED MY LIFE WAS ALREADY OVER. ALL THAT WAS LEFT WAS TO DO THE DEED.
HOW HIGH UP ARE WE? I'M GUESSING THE SECOND FLOOR.
IS IT POSSIBLE TO JUMP FROM THE TOP FLOOR? HOW HIGH IS THAT?
I'M TRYING TO FIGURE OUT HOW TO TAKE AN EARLY PAROLE. BUT I NEED TO MAKE SURE IT WILL WORK. I DON'T WANT TO BE BLIND AND PARALYZED.
I UNDERSTAND. LET ME SEE. YES, I BELIEVE THE TOP GALLERY WOULD BE THE OPTIMAL PLACE TO LEAP FROM.
WHY DOES IT SOUND SO HOLLOW?
IT IS A PANOPTICON DESIGN, AN IDEA BY THE PHILOSOPHER JEREMY BENTHAM THAT YOU COULD BUILD INTO THE ARCHITECTURE THE POWER STRUCTURES OF A SOCIETY. SO ALL THE CELLS FACE A SINGLE GUARD TOWER IN THE CENTER. HIS IDEA WAS THAT THE PRISONER HAS THE SENSE OF ALWAYS BEING WATCHED.

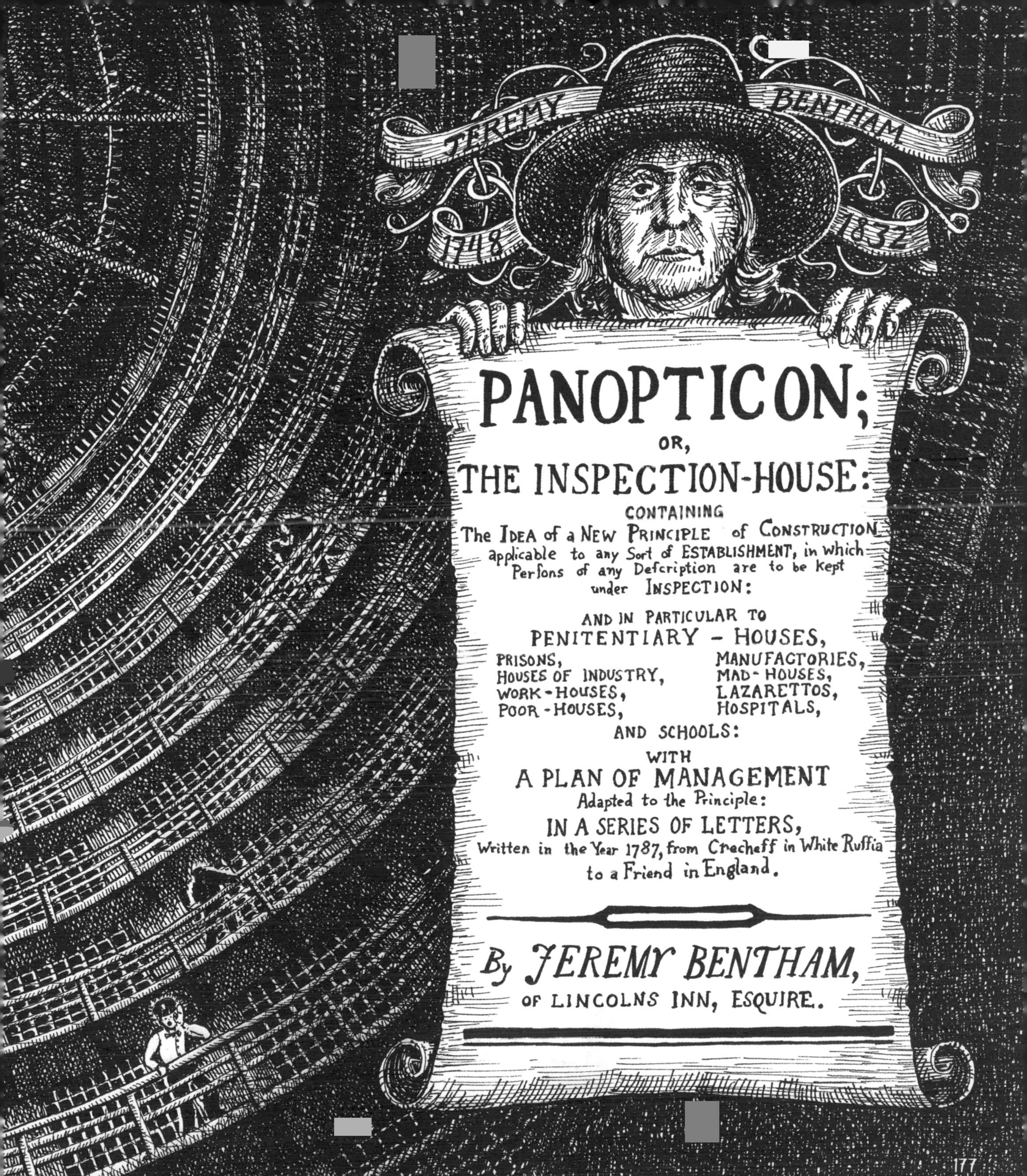
JEREMY BENTHAM
1748
1832
PANOPTICON;
OR,
THE INSPECTION-HOUSE:
CONTAINING
The IDEA of a NEW PRINCIPLE of CONSTRUCTION
applicable to any Sort of ESTABLISHMENT, in which
Perfons of any Defcription are to be kept
under INSPECTION:
AND IN PARTICULAR TO
PENITENTIARY - HOUSES,
PRISONS,
HOUSES OF INDUSTRY,
WORK-HOUSES,
POOR-HOUSES,
MANUFACTORIES,
MAD-HOUSES,
LAZARETTOS,
HOSPITALS,
AND SCHOOLS:
WITH
A PLAN OF MANAGEMENT
Adapted to the Principle:
IN A SERIES OF LETTERS,
Written in the Year 1787, from Crecheff in White Ruffia
to a Friend in England.
By JEREMY BENTHAM,
OF LINCOLNS INN, ESQUIRE.

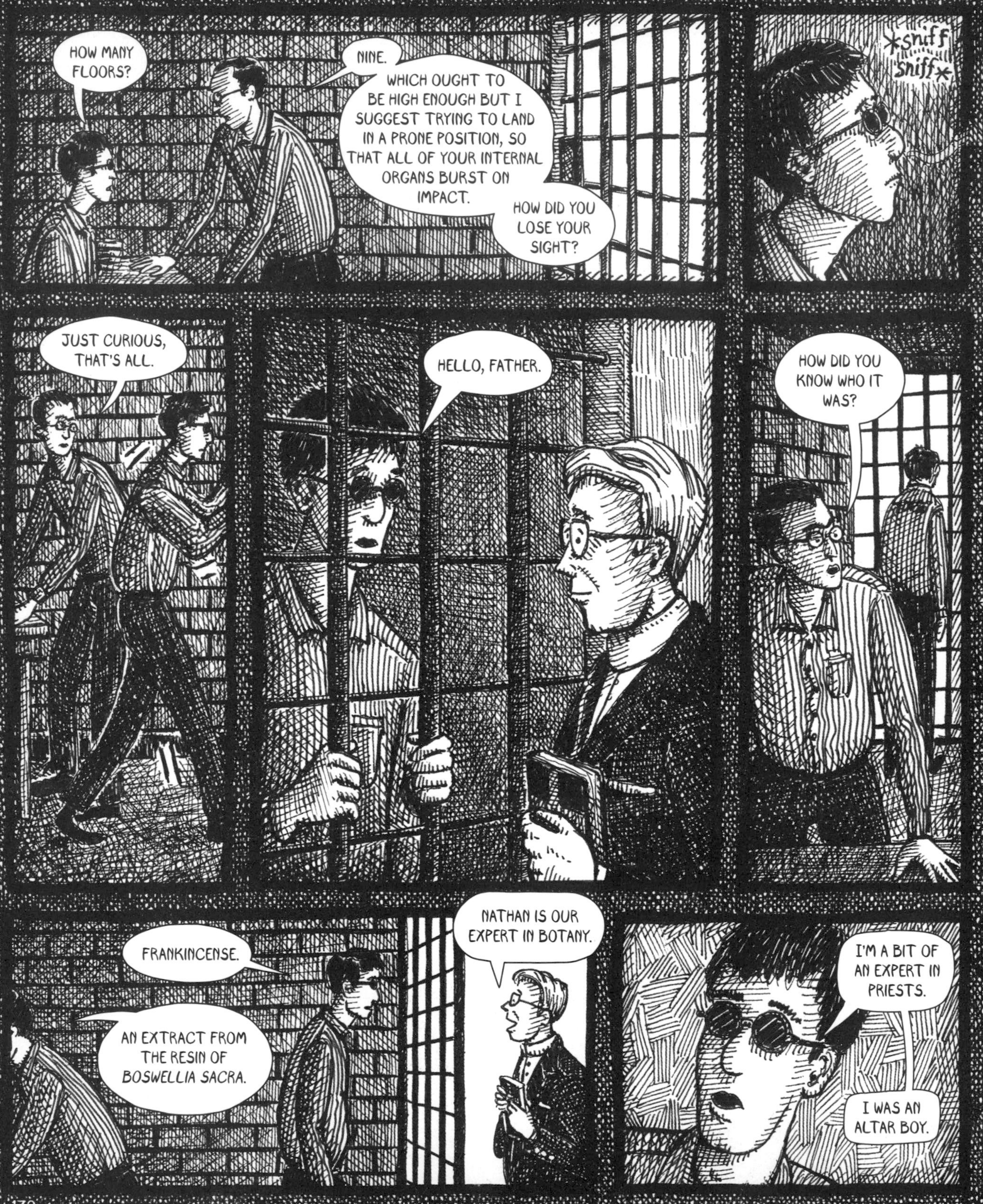
HOW MANY FLOORS?
NINE.
WHICH OUGHT TO BE HIGH ENOUGH BUT I SUGGEST TRYING TO LAND IN A PRONE POSITION, SO THAT ALL OF YOUR INTERNAL ORGANS BURST ON IMPACT.
HOW DID YOU LOSE YOUR SIGHT?
sniff sniff
JUST CURIOUS, THAT'S ALL.
HELLO, FATHER.
HOW DID YOU KNOW WHO IT WAS?
FRANKINCENSE.
AN EXTRACT FROM THE RESIN OF BOSWELLIA SACRA.
NATHAN IS OUR EXPERT IN BOTANY.
I'M A BIT OF AN EXPERT IN PRIESTS.
I WAS AN ALTAR BOY.

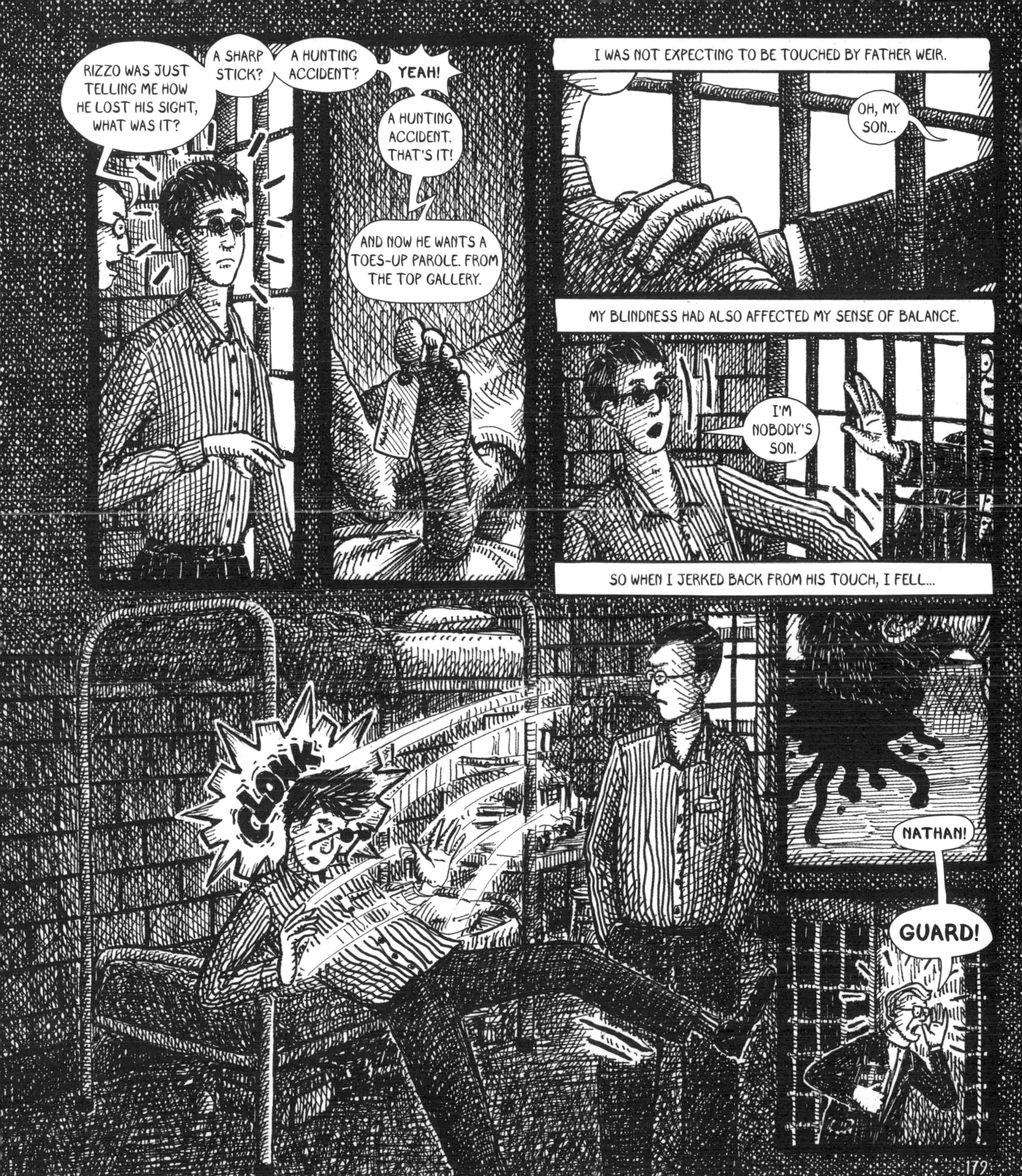

RIZZO WAS JUST TELLING ME HOW HE LOST HIS SIGHT, WHAT WAS IT?
A SHARP STICK?
A HUNTING ACCIDENT?
YEAH!
A HUNTING ACCIDENT. THAT'S IT!
AND NOW HE WANTS A TOES-UP PAROLE. FROM THE TOP GALLERY.
I WAS NOT EXPECTING TO BE TOUCHED BY FATHER WEIR.
OH, MY SON...
MY BLINDNESS HAD ALSO AFFECTED MY SENSE OF BALANCE.
I'M NOBODY'S SON.
SO WHEN I JERKED BACK FROM HIS TOUCH, I FELL...
CLONK
NATHAN!
GUARD!

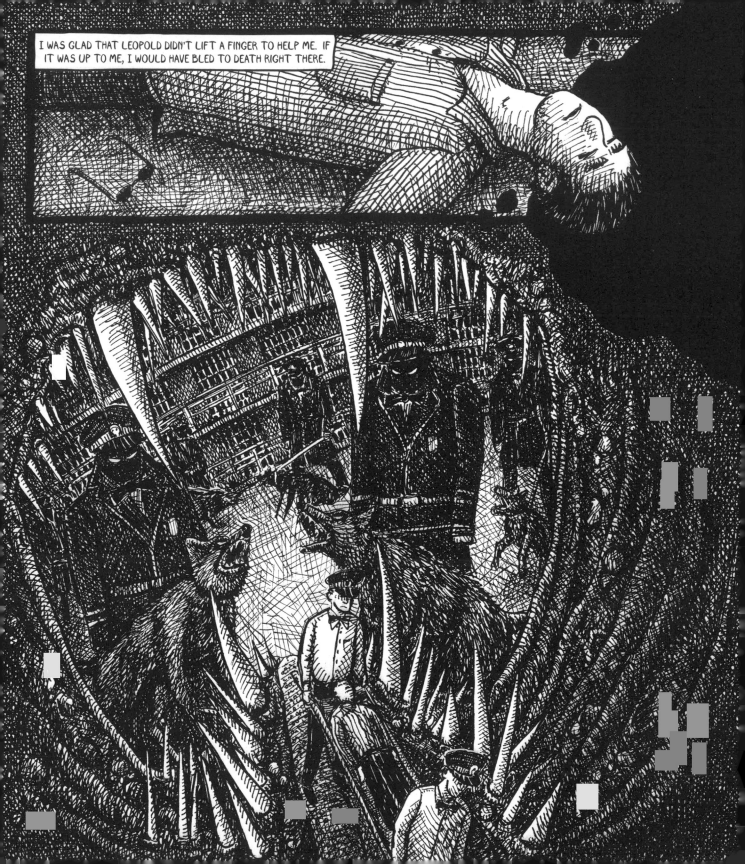

I WAS GLAD THAT LEOPOLD DIDN'T LIFT A FINGER TO HELP ME. IF IT WAS UP TO ME, I WOULD HAVE BLED TO DEATH RIGHT THERE.

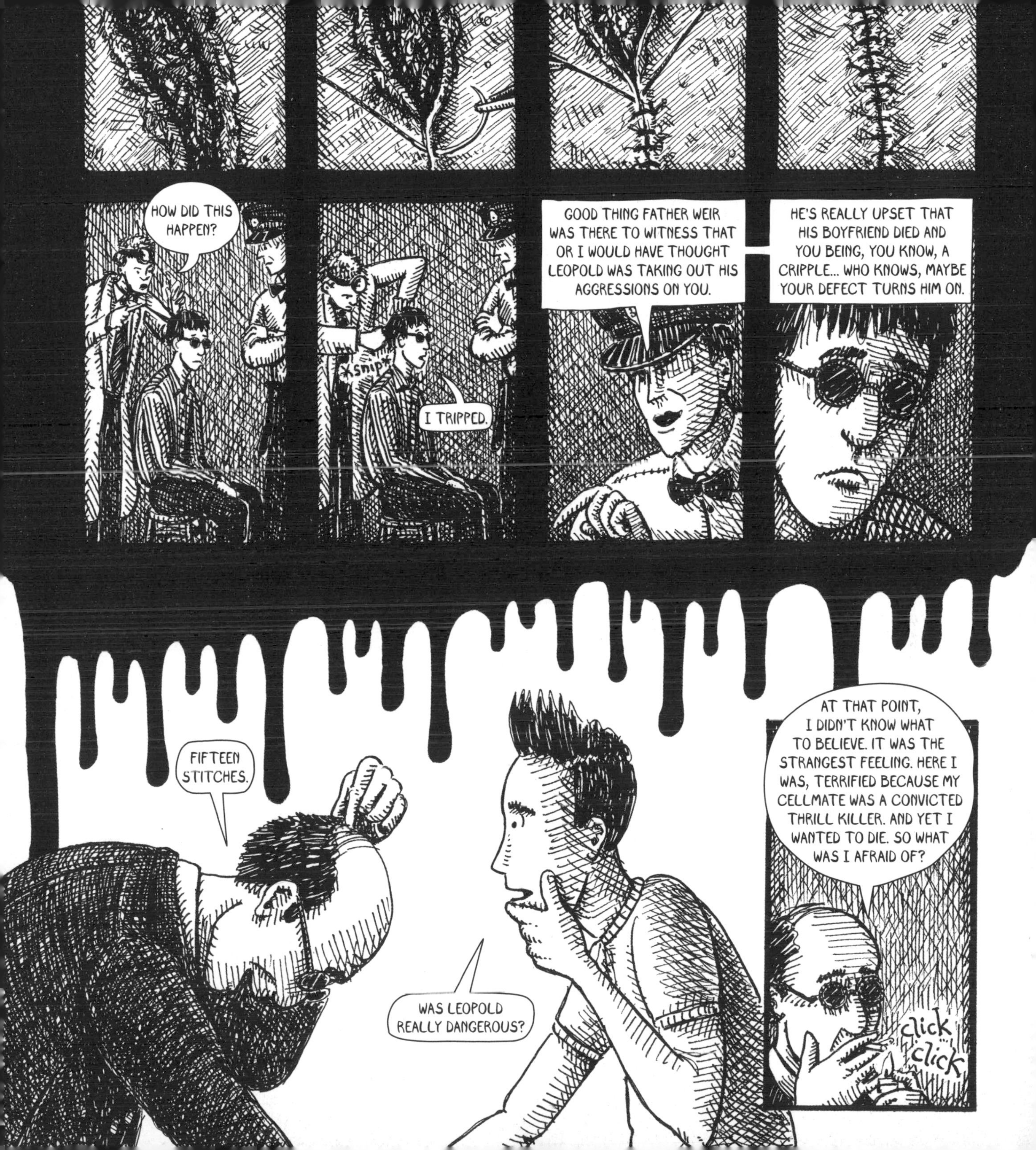
HOW DID THIS HAPPEN?
SNIP
I TRIPPED.
GOOD THING FATHER WEIR WAS THERE TO WITNESS THAT OR I WOULD HAVE THOUGHT LEOPOLD WAS TAKING OUT HIS AGGRESSIONS ON YOU.
HE'S REALLY UPSET THAT HIS BOYFRIEND DIED AND YOU BEING, YOU KNOW, A CRIPPLE... WHO KNOWS, MAYBE YOUR DEFECT TURNS HIM ON.
FIFTEEN STITCHES.
WAS LEOPOLD REALLY DANGEROUS?
AT THAT POINT, I DIDN'T KNOW WHAT TO BELIEVE. IT WAS THE STRANGEST FEELING. HERE I WAS, TERRIFIED BECAUSE MY CELLMATE WAS A CONVICTED THRILL KILLER. AND YET I WANTED TO DIE. SO WHAT WAS I AFRAID OF?
click... click

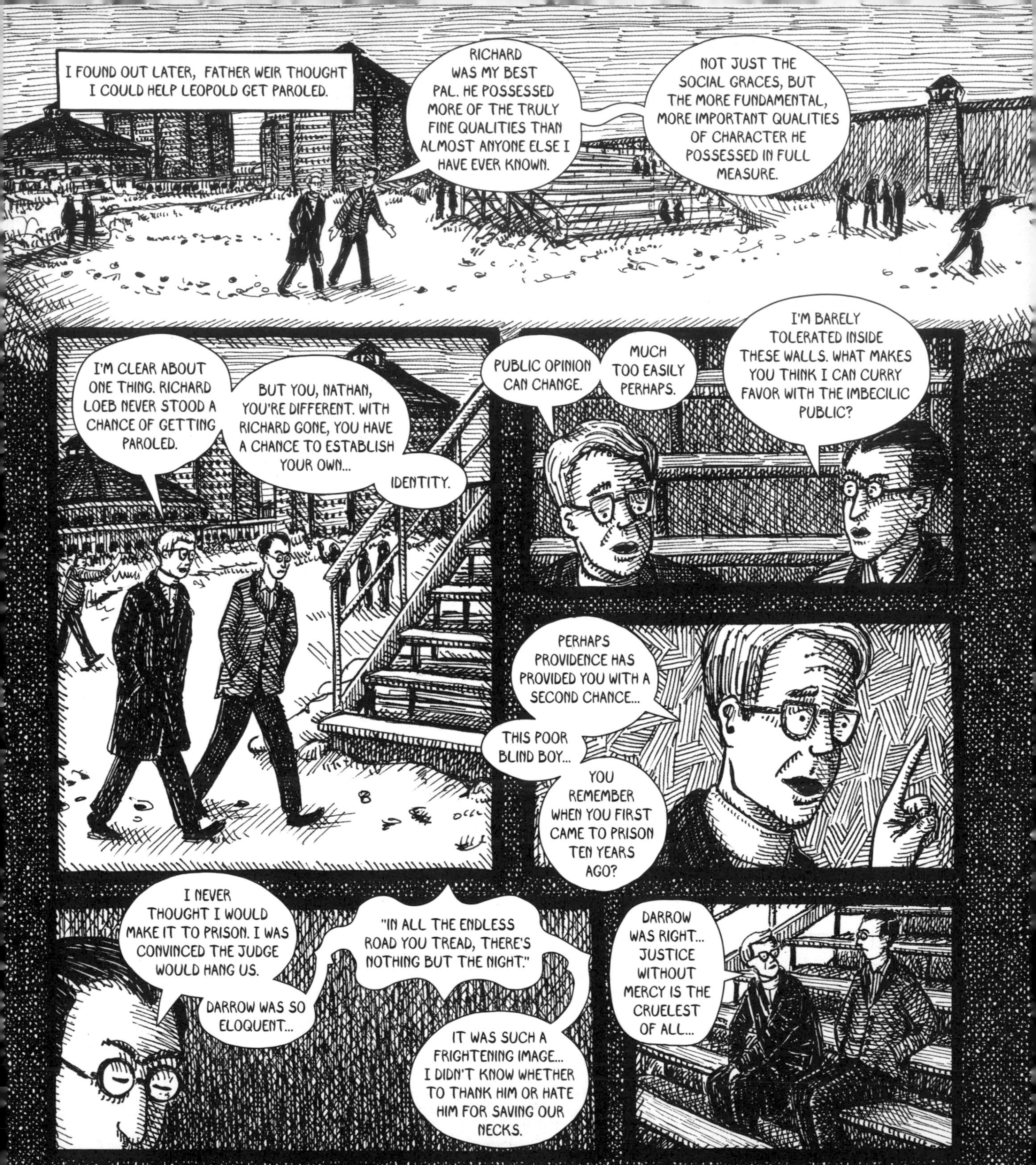
I FOUND OUT LATER, FATHER WEIR THOUGHT I COULD HELP LEOPOLD GET PAROLED.
RICHARD WAS MY BEST PAL. HE POSSESSED MORE OF THE TRULY FINE QUALITIES THAN ALMOST ANYONE ELSE I HAVE EVER KNOWN.
NOT JUST THE SOCIAL GRACES, BUT THE MORE FUNDAMENTAL, MORE IMPORTANT QUALITIES OF CHARACTER HE POSSESSED IN FULL MEASURE.
I'M CLEAR ABOUT ONE THING. RICHARD LOEB NEVER STOOD A CHANCE OF GETTING PAROLED.
BUT YOU, NATHAN, YOU'RE DIFFERENT. WITH RICHARD GONE, YOU HAVE A CHANCE TO ESTABLISH YOUR OWN...
IDENTITY.
PUBLIC OPINION CAN CHANGE.
MUCH TOO EASILY PERHAPS.
I'M BARELY TOLERATED INSIDE THESE WALLS. WHAT MAKES YOU THINK I CAN CURRY FAVOR WITH THE IMBECILIC PUBLIC?
PERHAPS PROVIDENCE HAS PROVIDED YOU WITH A SECOND CHANCE...
THIS POOR BLIND BOY...
YOU REMEMBER WHEN YOU FIRST CAME TO PRISON TEN YEARS AGO?
I NEVER THOUGHT I WOULD MAKE IT TO PRISON. I WAS CONVINCED THE JUDGE WOULD HANG US.
DARROW WAS SO ELOQUENT...
"IN ALL THE ENDLESS ROAD YOU TREAD, THERE'S NOTHING BUT THE NIGHT."
IT WAS SUCH A FRIGHTENING IMAGE... I DIDN'T KNOW WHETHER TO THANK HIM OR HATE HIM FOR SAVING OUR NECKS.
DARROW WAS RIGHT... JUSTICE WITHOUT MERCY IS THE CRUELEST OF ALL...

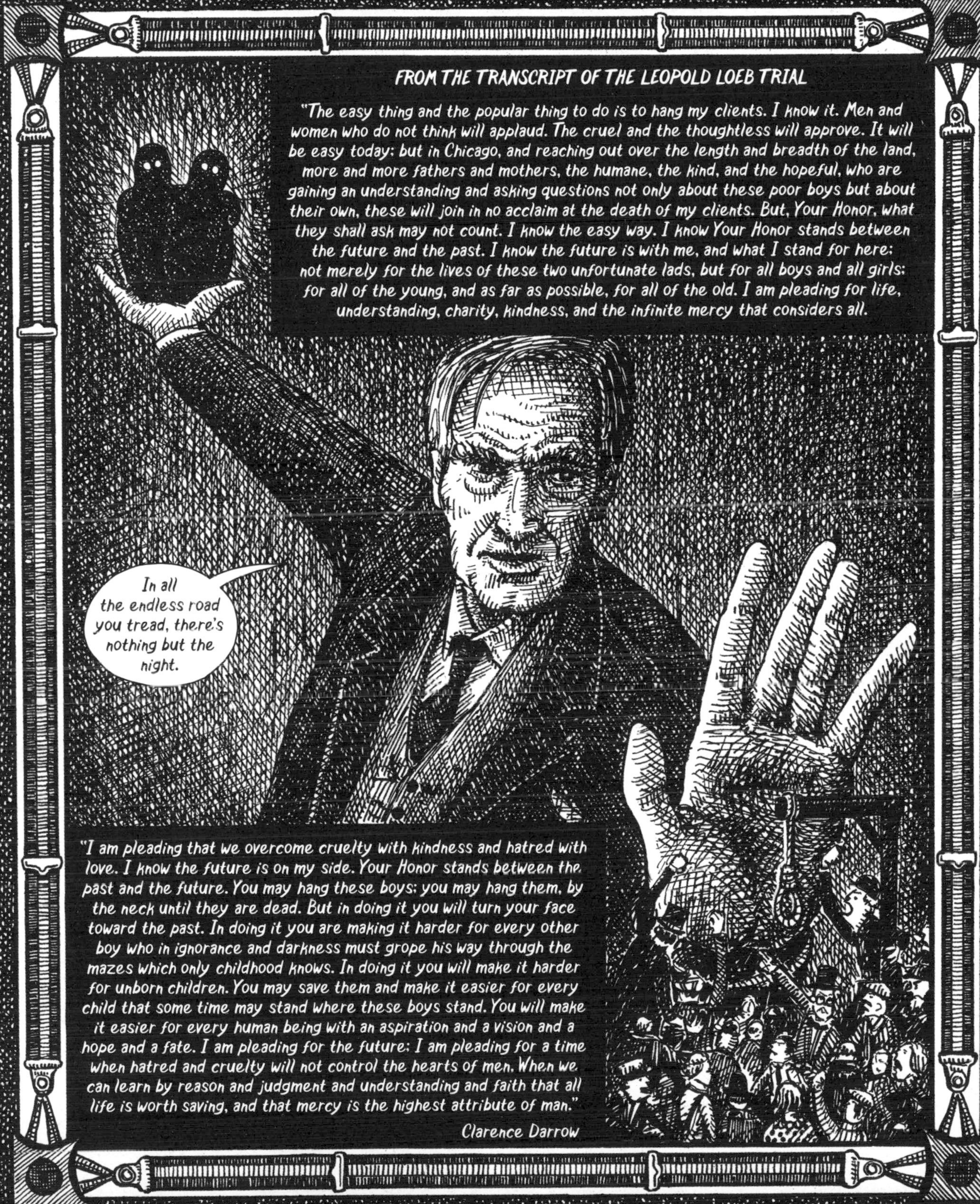
FROM THE TRANSCRIPT OF THE LEOPOLD LOEB TRIAL
"The easy thing and the popular thing to do is to hang my clients. I know it. Men and women who do not think will applaud. The cruel and the thoughtless will approve. It will be easy today; but in Chicago, and reaching out over the length and breadth of the land, more and more fathers and mothers, the humane, the kind, and the hopeful, who are gaining an understanding and asking questions not only about these poor boys but about their own, these will join in no acclaim at the death of my clients. But, Your Honor, what they shall ask may not count. I know the easy way. I know Your Honor stands between the future and the past. I know the future is with me, and what I stand for here; not merely for the lives of these two unfortunate lads, but for all boys and all girls; for all of the young, and as far as possible, for all of the old. I am pleading for life, understanding, charity, kindness, and the infinite mercy that considers all.
In all the endless road you tread, there's nothing but the night.
"I am pleading that we overcome cruelty with kindness and hatred with love. I know the future is on my side. Your Honor stands between the past and the future. You may hang these boys; you may hang them by the neck until they are dead. But in doing it you will turn your face toward the past. In doing it you are making it harder for every other boy who in ignorance and darkness must grope his way through the mazes which only childhood knows. In doing it you will make it harder for unborn children. You may save them and make it easier for every child that some time may stand where these boys stand. You will make it easier for every human being with an aspiration and a vision and a hope and a fate. I am pleading for the future; I am pleading for a time when hatred and cruelty will not control the hearts of men. When we can learn by reason and judgment and understanding and faith that all life is worth saving, and that mercy is the highest attribute of man."
Clarence Darrow

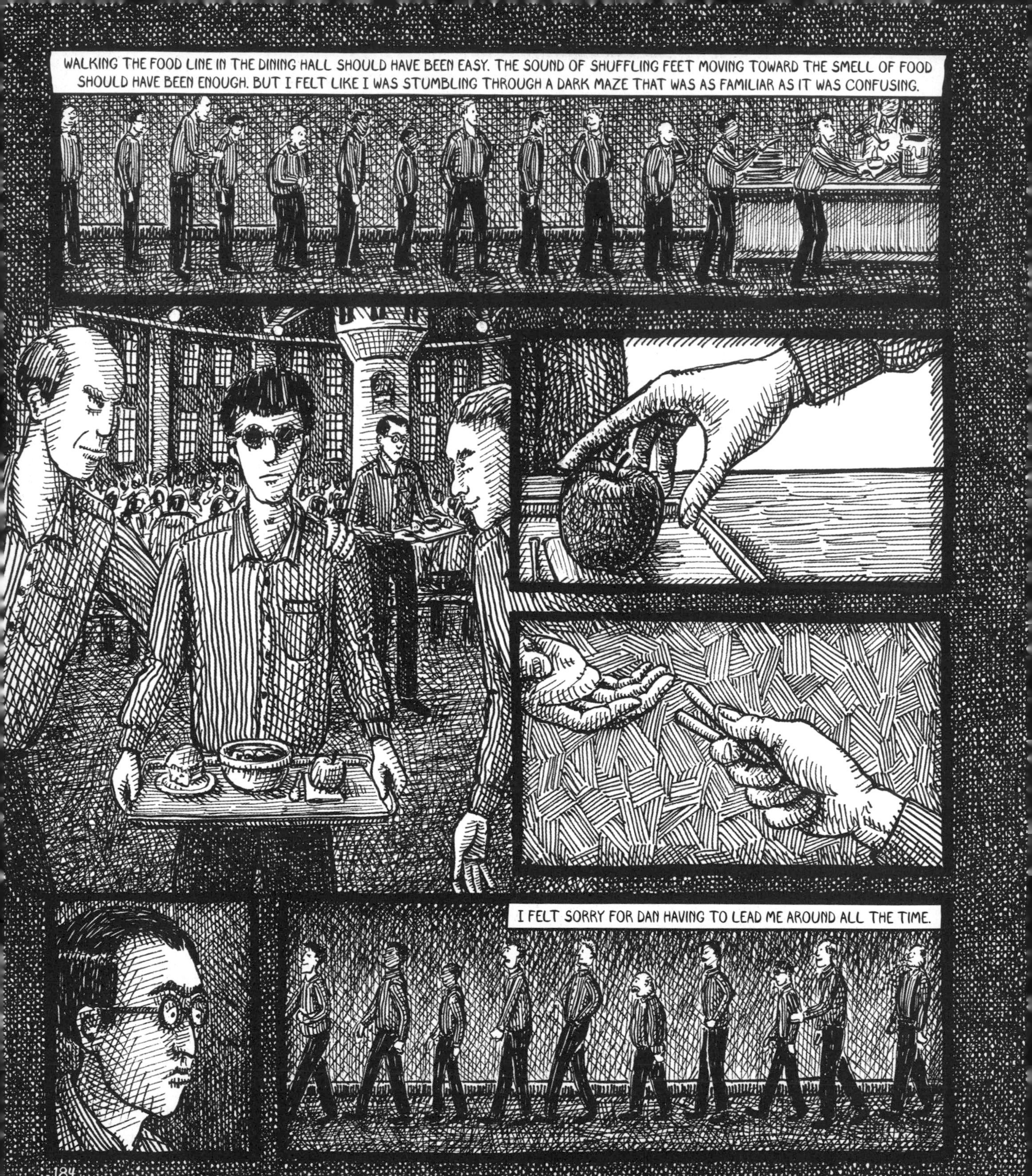
WALKING THE FOOD LINE IN THE DINING HALL SHOULD HAVE BEEN EASY. THE SOUND OF SHUFFLING FEET MOVING TOWARD THE SMELL OF FOOD SHOULD HAVE BEEN ENOUGH. BUT I FELT LIKE I WAS STUMBLING THROUGH A DARK MAZE THAT WAS AS FAMILIAR AS IT WAS CONFUSING.
I FELT SORRY FOR DAN HAVING TO LEAD ME AROUND ALL THE TIME.

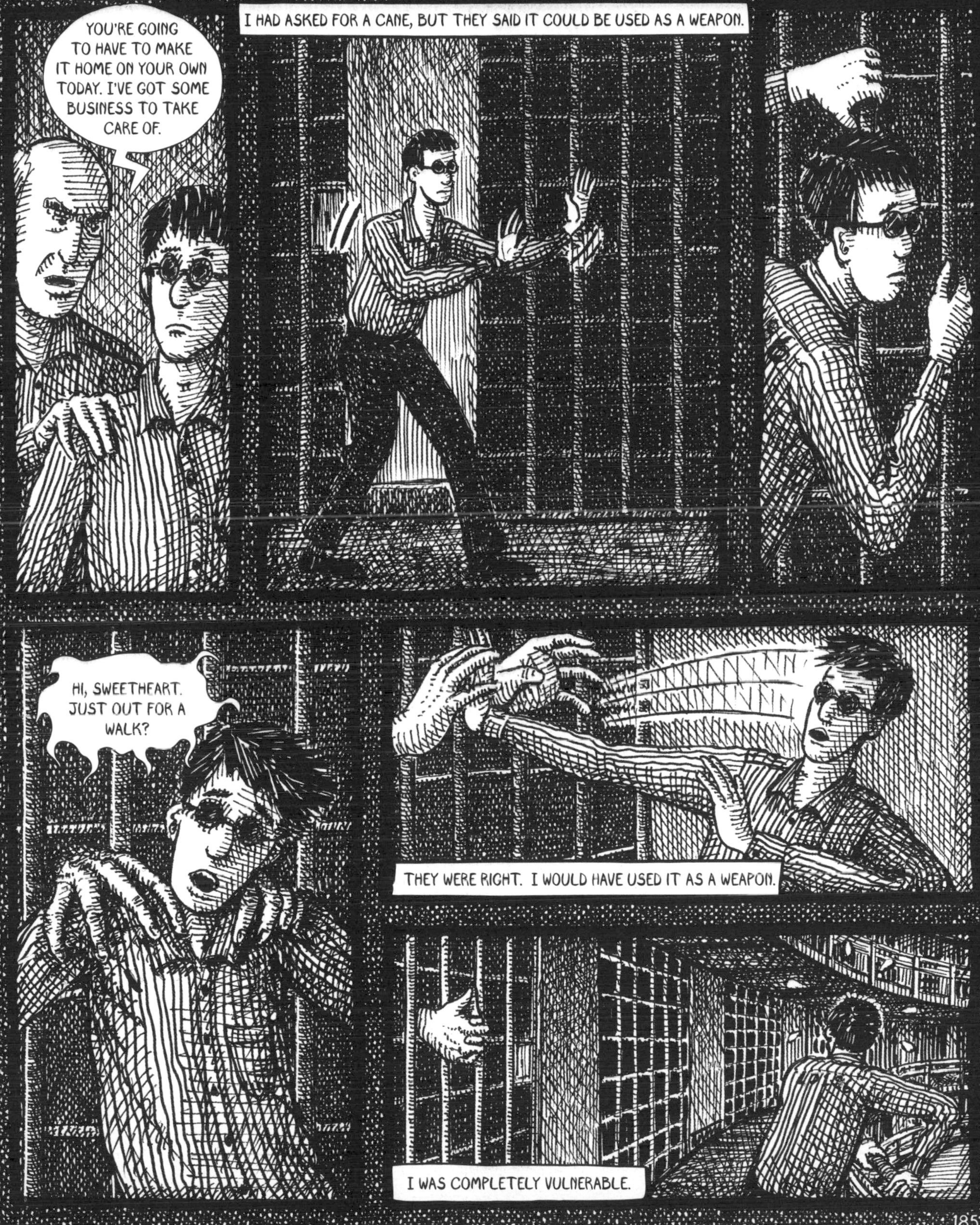

YOU'RE GOING TO HAVE TO MAKE IT HOME ON YOUR OWN TODAY. I'VE GOT SOME BUSINESS TO TAKE CARE OF.
I HAD ASKED FOR A CANE, BUT THEY SAID IT COULD BE USED AS A WEAPON.
HI, SWEETHEART. JUST OUT FOR A WALK?
THEY WERE RIGHT. I WOULD HAVE USED IT AS A WEAPON.
I WAS COMPLETELY VULNERABLE.

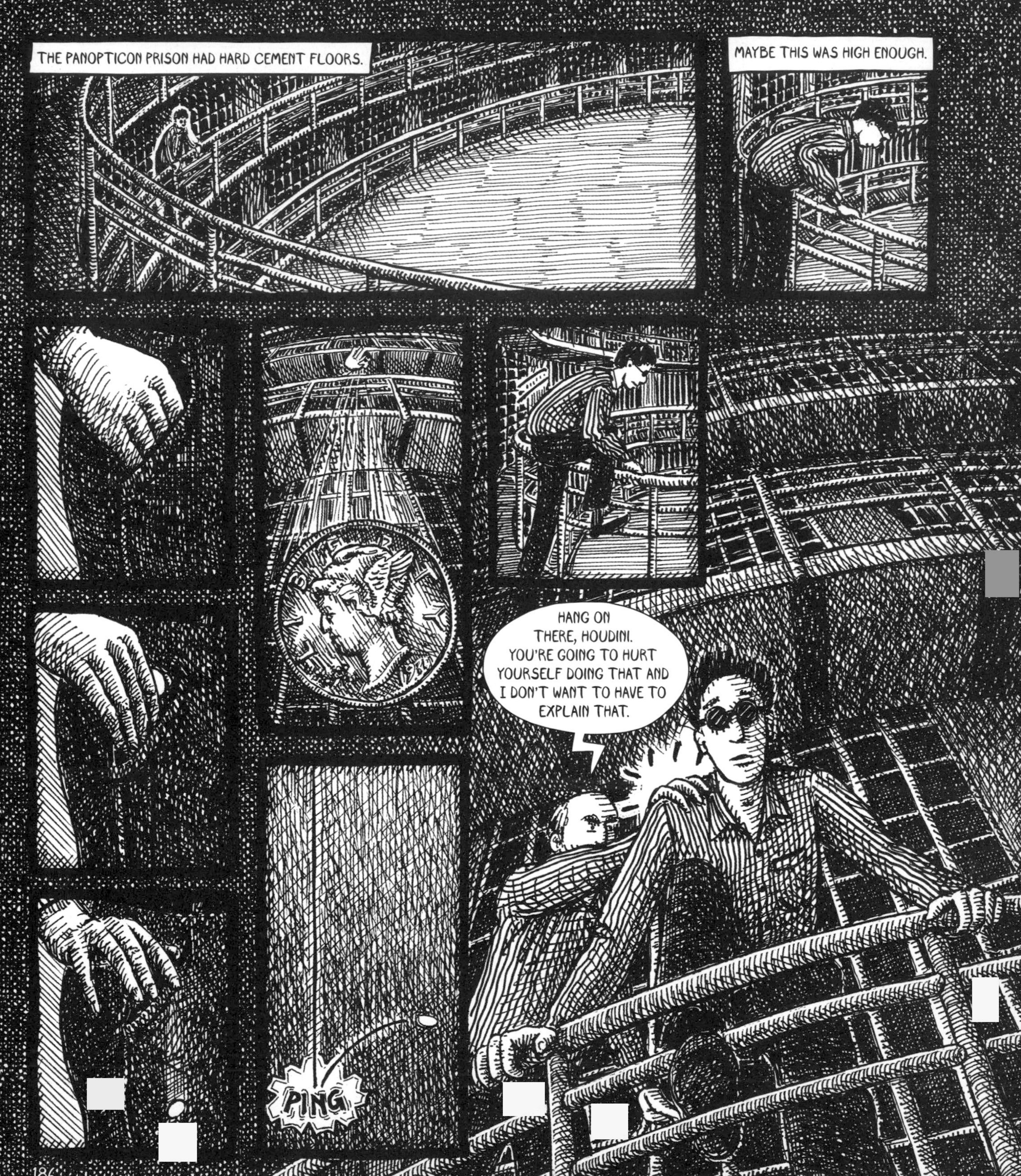

THE PANOPTICON PRISON HAD HARD CEMENT FLOORS.
MAYBE THIS WAS HIGH ENOUGH.
PING
HANG ON THERE, HOUDINI. YOU'RE GOING TO HURT YOURSELF DOING THAT AND I DON'T WANT TO HAVE TO EXPLAIN THAT.

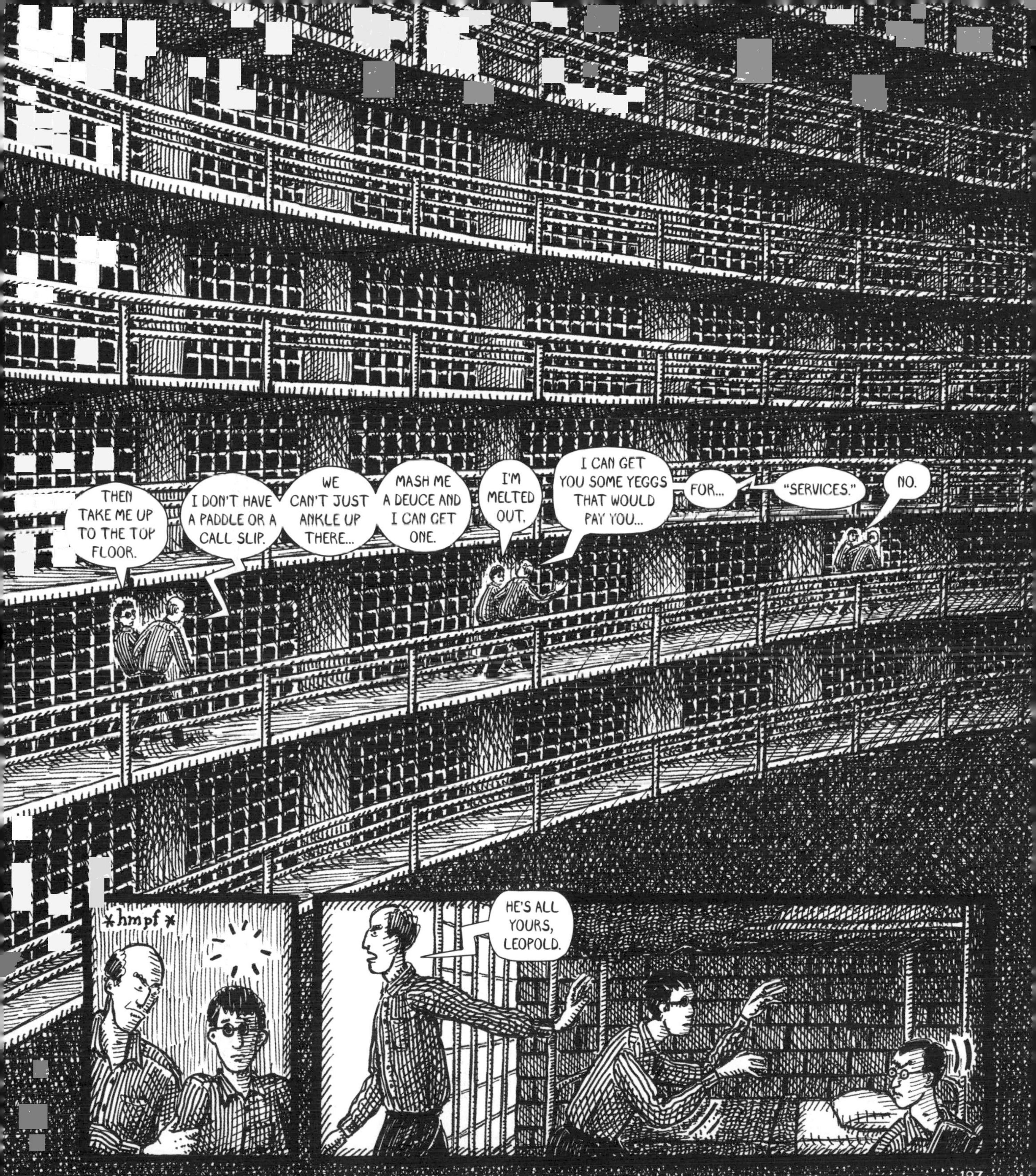
THEN TAKE ME UP TO THE TOP FLOOR.
I DON'T HAVE A PADDLE OR A CALL SLIP.
WE CAN'T JUST ANKLE UP THERE...
MASH ME A DEUCE AND I CAN GET ONE.
I'M MELTED OUT.
I CAN GET YOU SOME YEGGS THAT WOULD PAY YOU...
FOR...
"SERVICES."
NO.
hmpf
HE'S ALL YOURS, LEOPOLD.

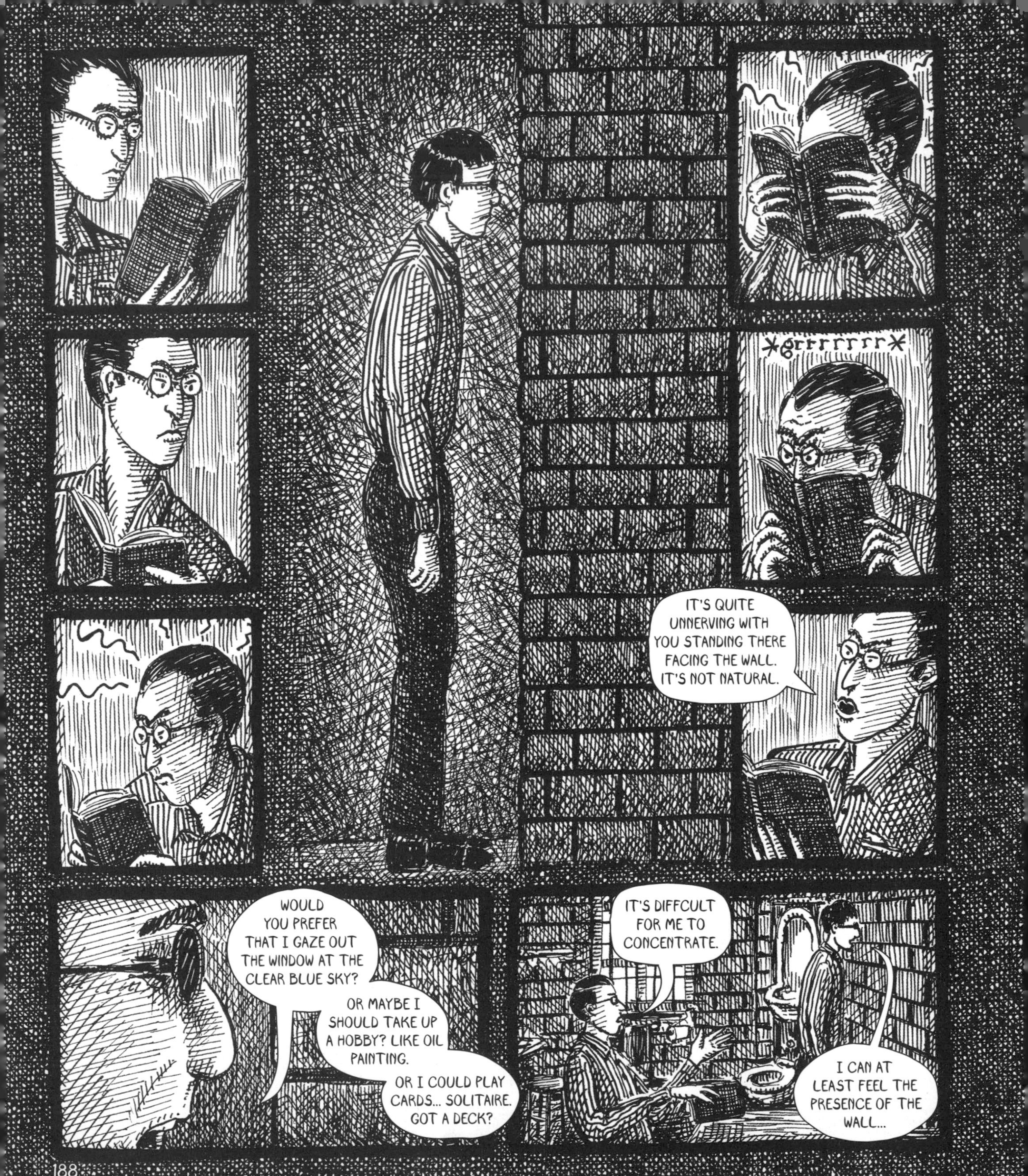
grrrrrrr
IT'S QUITE UNNERVING WITH YOU STANDING THERE FACING THE WALL. IT'S NOT NATURAL.
WOULD YOU PREFER THAT I GAZE OUT THE WINDOW AT THE CLEAR BLUE SKY?
OR MAYBE I SHOULD TAKE UP A HOBBY? LIKE OIL PAINTING.
OR I COULD PLAY CARDS... SOLITAIRE. GOT A DECK?
IT'S DIFFCULT FOR ME TO CONCENTRATE.
I CAN AT LEAST FEEL THE PRESENCE OF THE WALL...

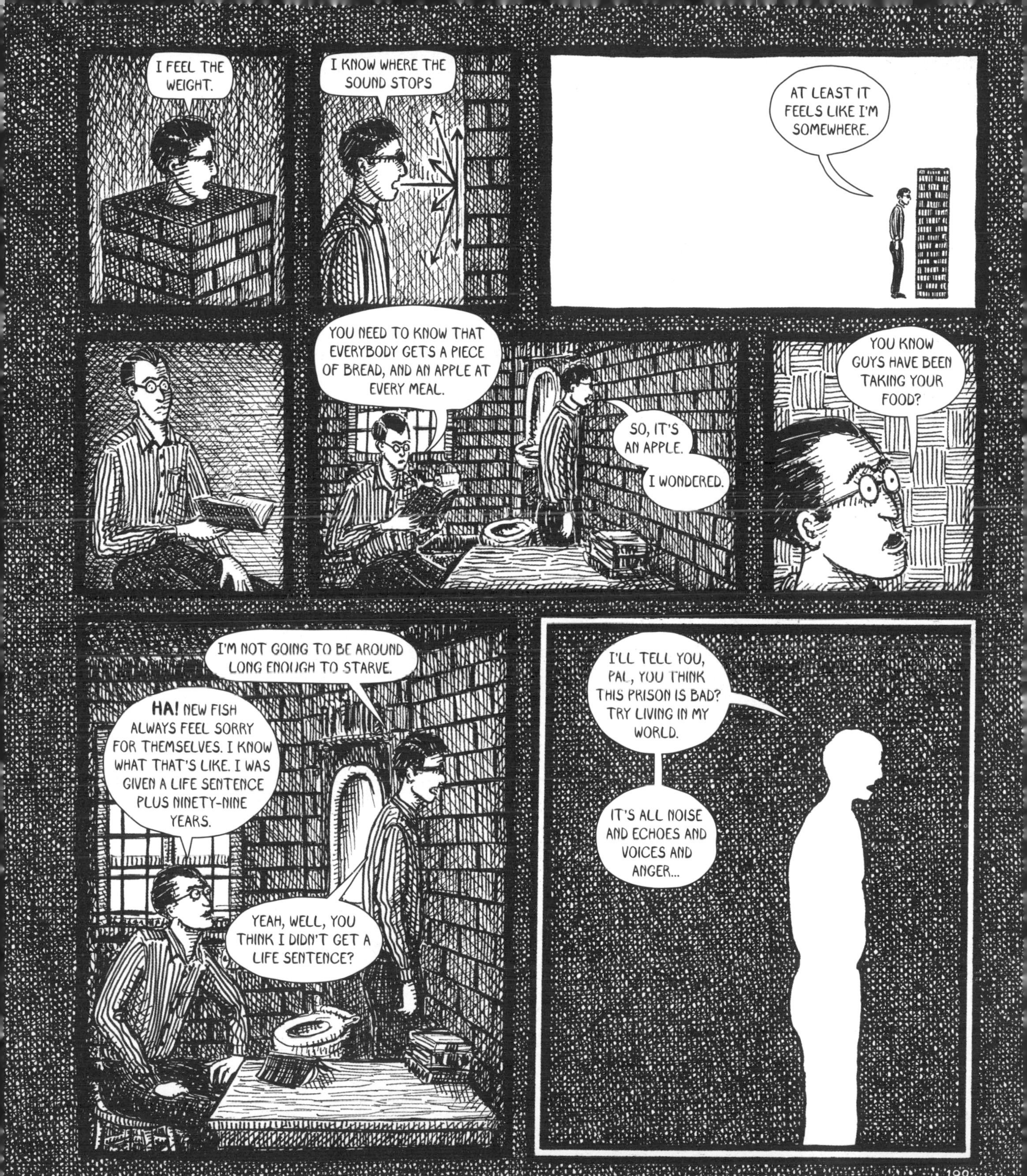
I FEEL THE WEIGHT.
I KNOW WHERE THE SOUND STOPS
AT LEAST IT FEELS LIKE I'M SOMEWHERE.
YOU NEED TO KNOW THAT EVERYBODY GETS A PIECE OF BREAD, AND AN APPLE AT EVERY MEAL.
SO, IT'S AN APPLE.
I WONDERED.
YOU KNOW GUYS HAVE BEEN TAKING YOUR FOOD?
I'M NOT GOING TO BE AROUND LONG ENOUGH TO STARVE.
HA! NEW FISH ALWAYS FEEL SORRY FOR THEMSELVES. I KNOW WHAT THAT'S LIKE. I WAS GIVEN A LIFE SENTENCE PLUS NINETY-NINE YEARS.
YEAH, WELL, YOU THINK I DIDN'T GET A LIFE SENTENCE?
I'LL TELL YOU, PAL, YOU THINK THIS PRISON IS BAD? TRY LIVING IN MY WORLD.
IT'S ALL NOISE AND ECHOES AND VOICES AND ANGER...

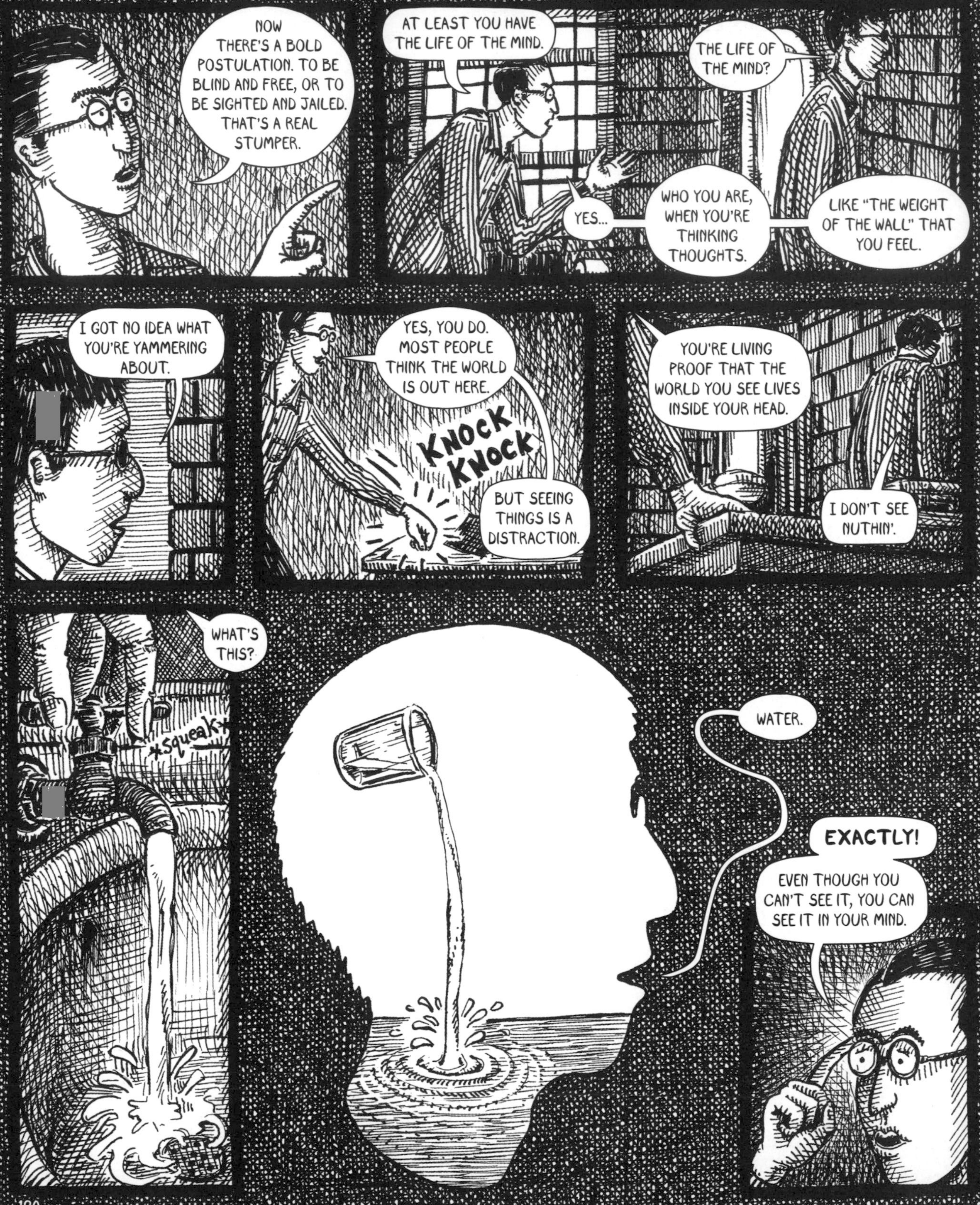

NOW THERE'S A BOLD POSTULATION. TO BE BLIND AND FREE, OR TO BE SIGHTED AND JAILED. THAT'S A REAL STUMPER.
AT LEAST YOU HAVE THE LIFE OF THE MIND.
THE LIFE OF THE MIND?
YES...
WHO YOU ARE, WHEN YOU'RE THINKING THOUGHTS.
LIKE "THE WEIGHT OF THE WALL" THAT YOU FEEL.
I GOT NO IDEA WHAT YOU'RE YAMMERING ABOUT.
YES, YOU DO. MOST PEOPLE THINK THE WORLD IS OUT HERE.
KNOCK KNOCK
BUT SEEING THINGS IS A DISTRACTION.
YOU'RE LIVING PROOF THAT THE WORLD YOU SEE LIVES INSIDE YOUR HEAD.
I DON'T SEE NUTHIN'.
WHAT'S THIS?
squeak
WATER.
EXACTLY!
EVEN THOUGH YOU CAN'T SEE IT, YOU CAN SEE IT IN YOUR MIND.

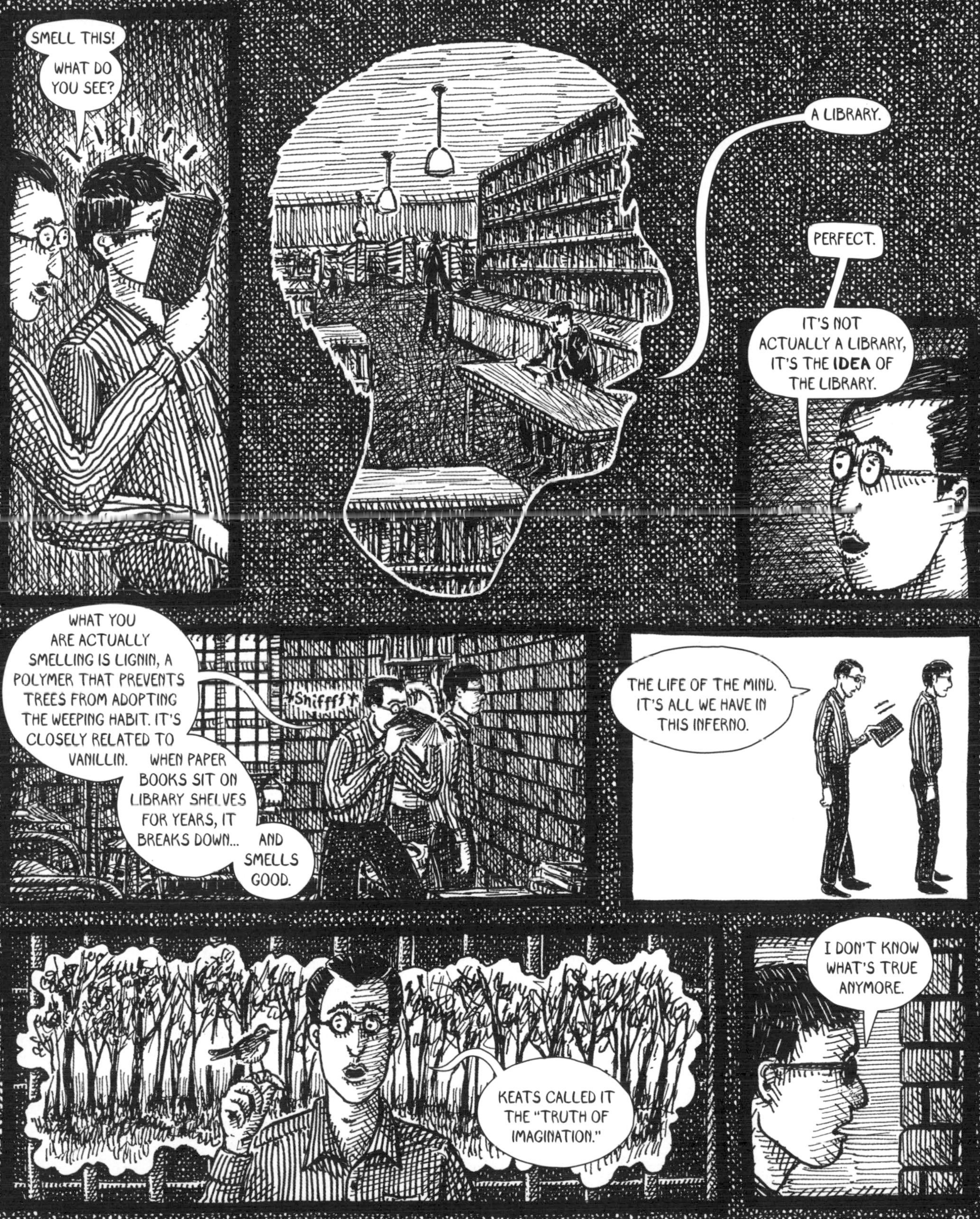
SMELL THIS!
WHAT DO YOU SEE?
A LIBRARY.
PERFECT.
IT'S NOT ACTUALLY A LIBRARY, IT'S THE **IDEA** OF THE LIBRARY.
WHAT YOU ARE ACTUALLY SMELLING IS LIGNIN, A POLYMER THAT PREVENTS TREES FROM ADOPTING THE WEEPING HABIT. IT'S CLOSELY RELATED TO VANILLIN.
SNIFFFF
WHEN PAPER BOOKS SIT ON LIBRARY SHELVES FOR YEARS, IT BREAKS DOWN...
AND SMELLS GOOD.
THE LIFE OF THE MIND. IT'S ALL WE HAVE IN THIS INFERNO.
KEATS CALLED IT THE "TRUTH OF IMAGINATION."
I DON'T KNOW WHAT'S TRUE ANYMORE.

I SAY GIVE IT SOME TIME, THAT'S WHAT I DID.

WHEN I FIRST GOT HERE, ALL I COULD THINK ABOUT WAS HOW TO KICK THE BUCKET.

WHY DIDN'T YOU GO THROUGH WITH IT?

AT FIRST, I COULDN'T DO THAT TO MY FATHER.

HE WORKED SO HARD TO KEEP ME FROM HANGING. AND NOW HE'S COME TO VISIT ME EVERY OTHER WEEK FOR TEN YEARS. I THOUGHT MAYBE I WOULD WAIT UNTIL HE DIES, BUT...

I DON'T HAVE THAT PROBLEM.

MY FATHER WAS THE ANGRY ICEMAN.

WHEN I WAS TEN, I TRIED TO HANG ONE OF THE ICE BLOCKS BY MYSELF.

IT WAS TOO HEAVY AND WHEN IT SLID OFF THE CART I TRIED TO CATCH IT.

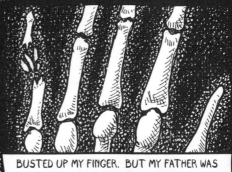

BUSTED UP MY FINGER. BUT MY FATHER WAS ANGRY BECAUSE THE BLOCK OF ICE BUSTED.

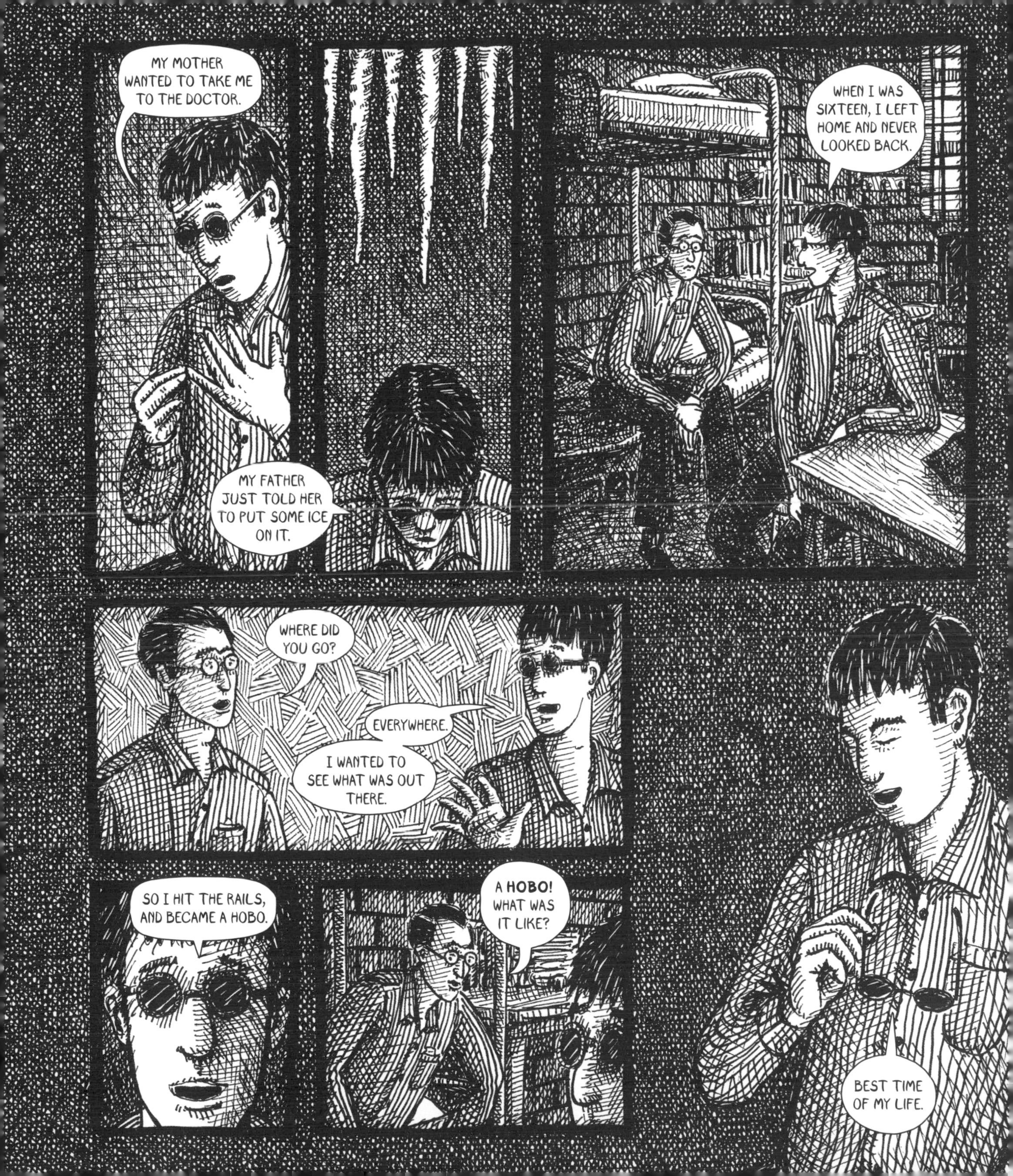
MY MOTHER WANTED TO TAKE ME TO THE DOCTOR.
MY FATHER JUST TOLD HER TO PUT SOME ICE ON IT.
WHEN I WAS SIXTEEN, I LEFT HOME AND NEVER LOOKED BACK.
WHERE DID YOU GO?
EVERYWHERE.
I WANTED TO SEE WHAT WAS OUT THERE.
SO I HIT THE RAILS, AND BECAME A HOBO.
A **HOBO!** WHAT WAS IT LIKE?
BEST TIME OF MY LIFE.

VIII

PLATO'S CAVE

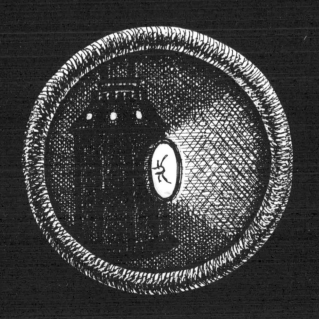

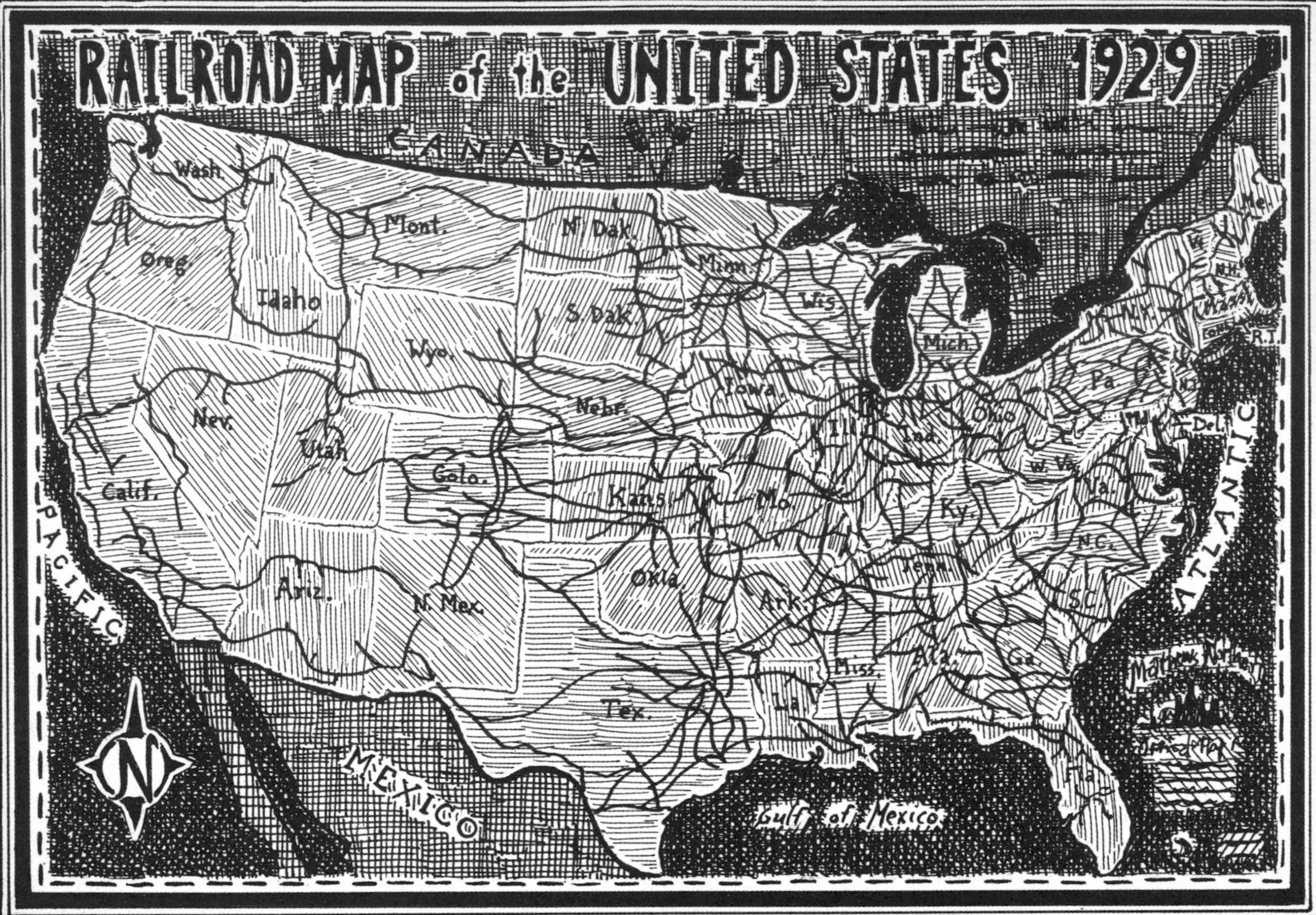
RAILROAD MAP of the UNITED STATES 1929
CANADA
PACIFIC
ATLANTIC
MEXICO
Gulf of Mexico
Wash.
Oreg.
Idaho
Mont.
N. Dak.
S. Dak.
Wyo.
Nev.
Utah
Calif.
Colo.
Nebr.
Kans.
Ariz.
N. Mex.
Okla.
Tex.
Minn.
Wis.
Iowa
Mo.
Ark.
La.
Miss.
Ala.
Ga.
Fla.
Ill.
Ind.
Ohio
Mich.
Ky.
Tenn.
W. Va.
Va.
N.C.
S.C.
Pa.
Del.
N.Y.
Me.
R.I.
N

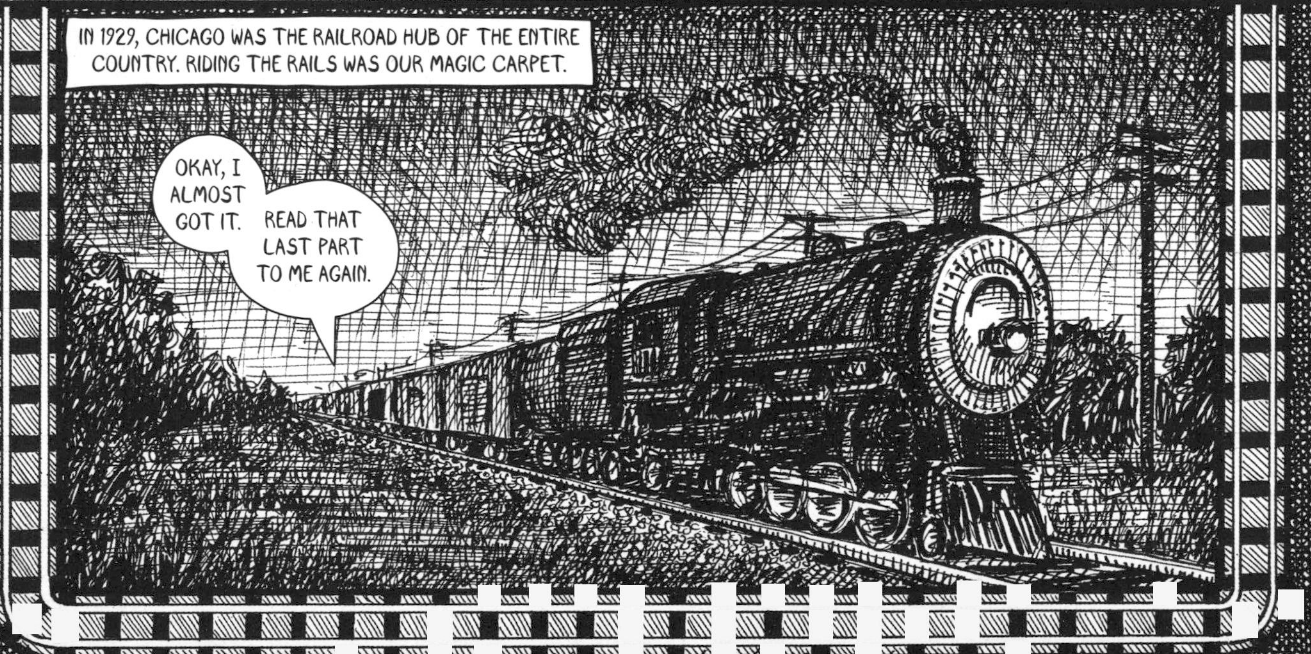
IN 1929, CHICAGO WAS THE RAILROAD HUB OF THE ENTIRE COUNTRY. RIDING THE RAILS WAS OUR MAGIC CARPET.
OKAY, I ALMOST GOT IT.
READ THAT LAST PART TO ME AGAIN.

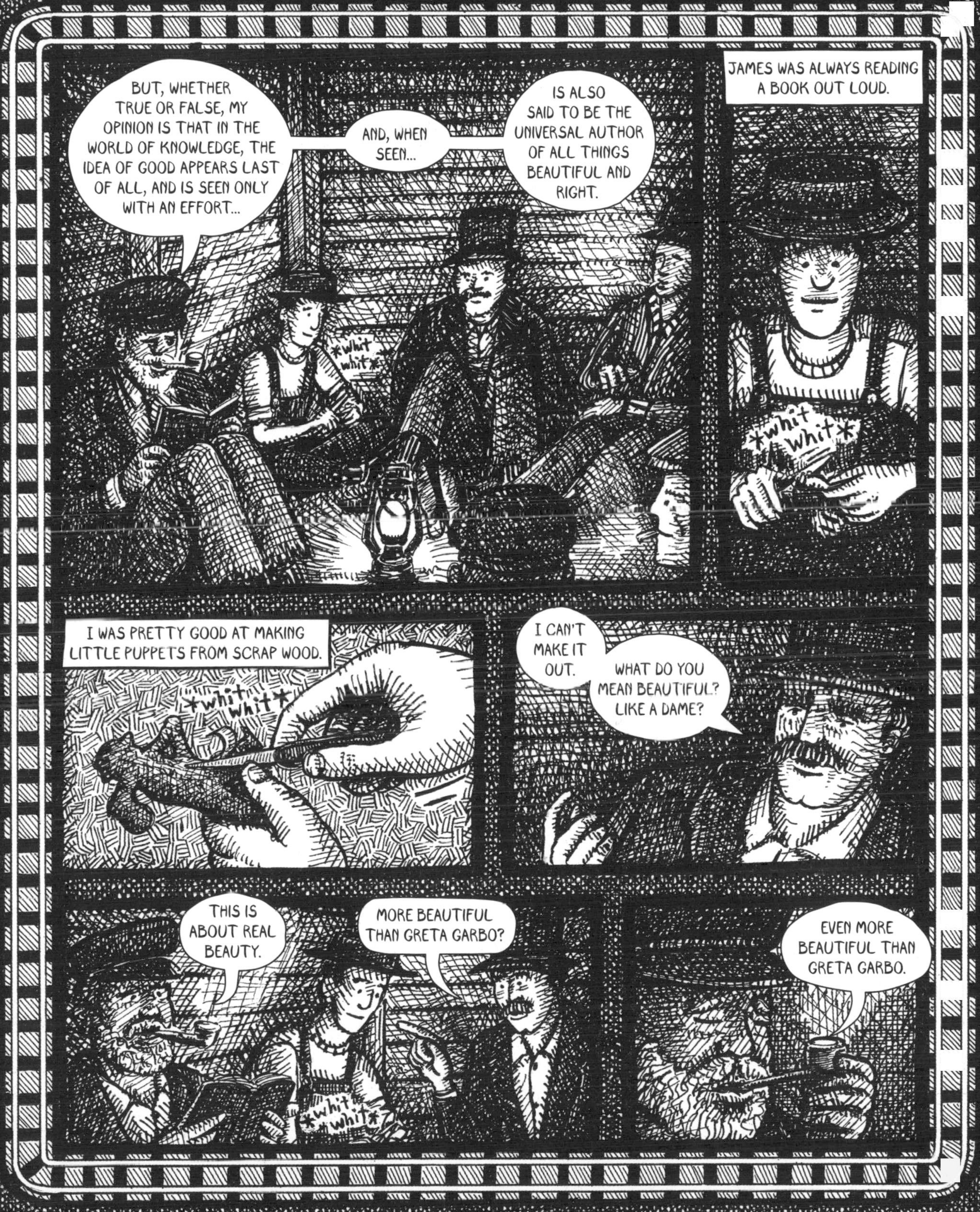

BUT, WHETHER TRUE OR FALSE, MY OPINION IS THAT IN THE WORLD OF KNOWLEDGE, THE IDEA OF GOOD APPEARS LAST OF ALL, AND IS SEEN ONLY WITH AN EFFORT...
AND, WHEN SEEN...
IS ALSO SAID TO BE THE UNIVERSAL AUTHOR OF ALL THINGS BEAUTIFUL AND RIGHT.
whit whit
JAMES WAS ALWAYS READING A BOOK OUT LOUD.
whit whit
I WAS PRETTY GOOD AT MAKING LITTLE PUPPETS FROM SCRAP WOOD.
whit whit
I CAN'T MAKE IT OUT.
WHAT DO YOU MEAN BEAUTIFUL? LIKE A DAME?
THIS IS ABOUT REAL BEAUTY.
MORE BEAUTIFUL THAN GRETA GARBO?
whit whit
EVEN MORE BEAUTIFUL THAN GRETA GARBO.

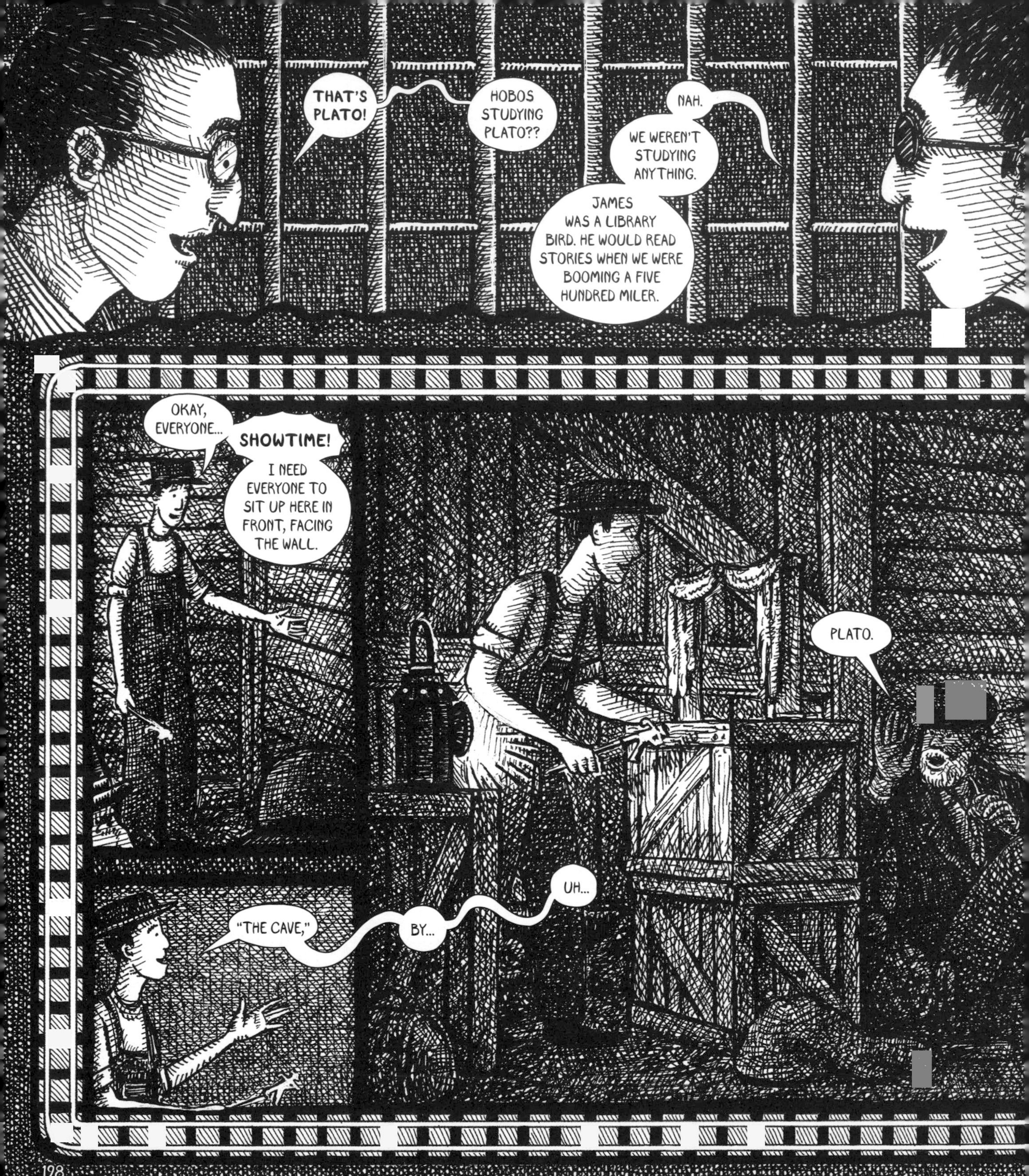
THAT'S PLATO!
HOBOS STUDYING PLATO??
NAH.
WE WEREN'T STUDYING ANYTHING.
JAMES WAS A LIBRARY BIRD. HE WOULD READ STORIES WHEN WE WERE BOOMING A FIVE HUNDRED MILER.
OKAY, EVERYONE...
SHOWTIME!
I NEED EVERYONE TO SIT UP HERE IN FRONT, FACING THE WALL.
PLATO.
"THE CAVE,"
BY...
UH...

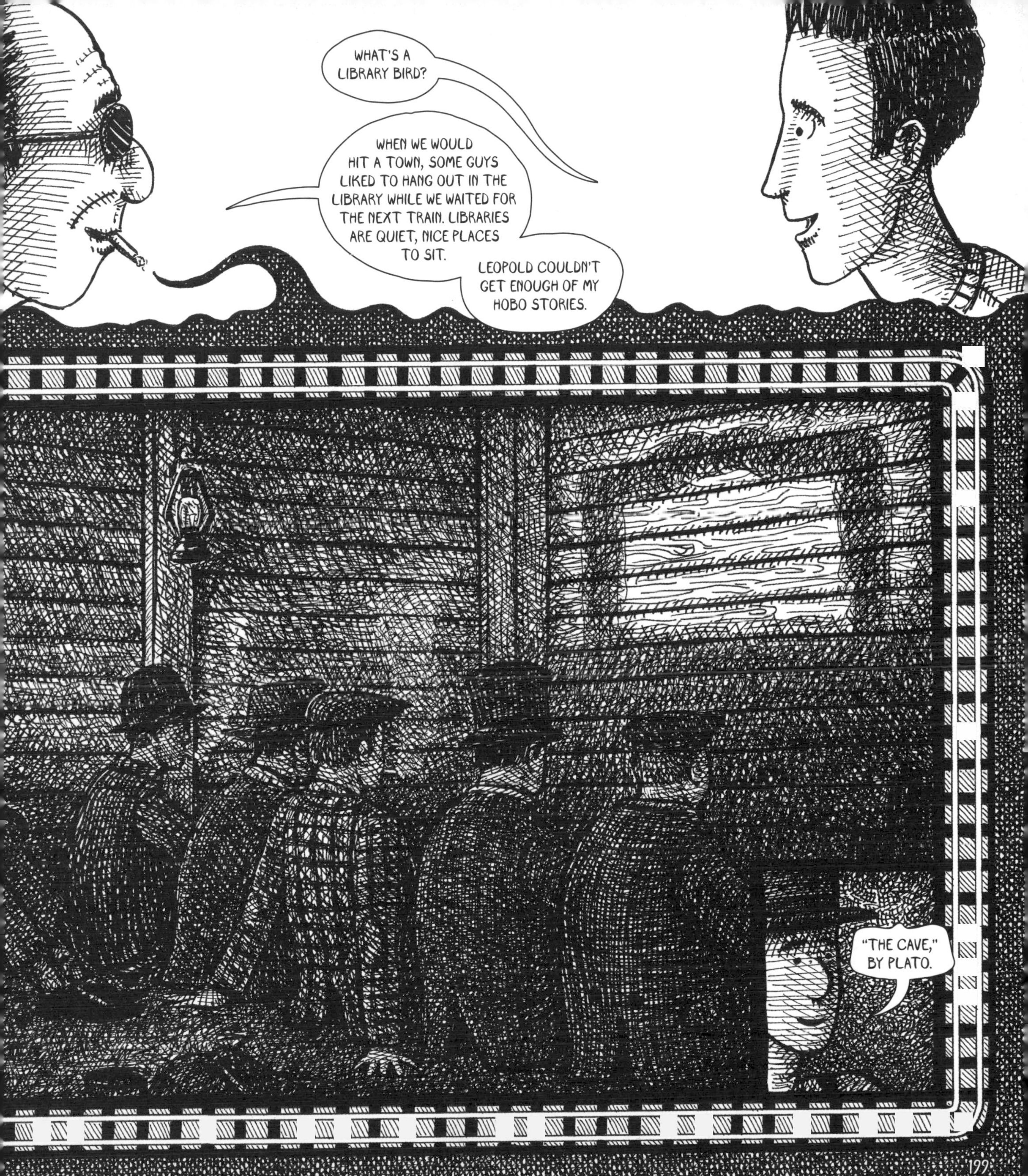
WHAT'S A LIBRARY BIRD?
WHEN WE WOULD HIT A TOWN, SOME GUYS LIKED TO HANG OUT IN THE LIBRARY WHILE WE WAITED FOR THE NEXT TRAIN. LIBRARIES ARE QUIET, NICE PLACES TO SIT.
LEOPOLD COULDN'T GET ENOUGH OF MY HOBO STORIES.
"THE CAVE," BY PLATO.

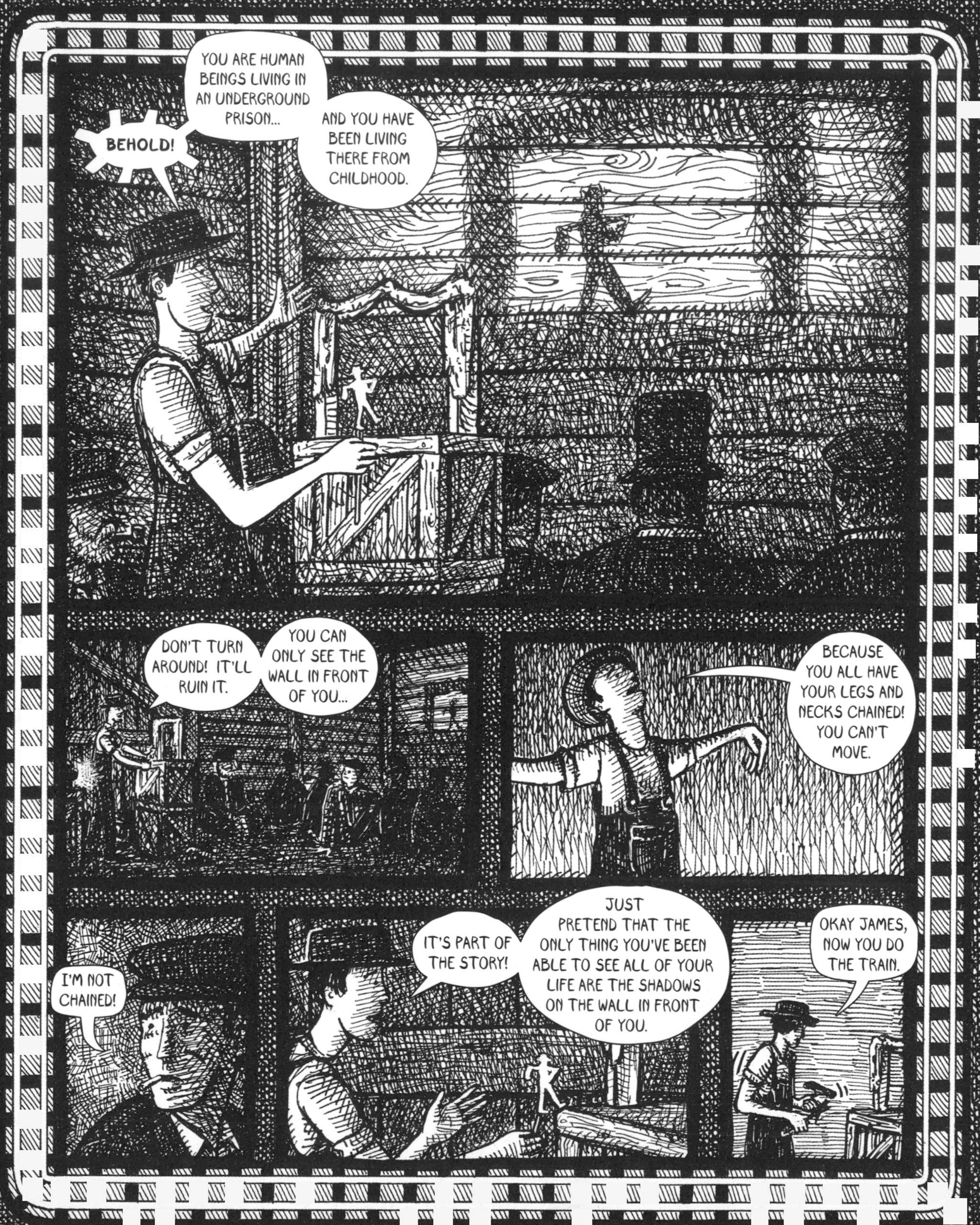
BEHOLD!
YOU ARE HUMAN BEINGS LIVING IN AN UNDERGROUND PRISON...
AND YOU HAVE BEEN LIVING THERE FROM CHILDHOOD.
DON'T TURN AROUND! IT'LL RUIN IT.
YOU CAN ONLY SEE THE WALL IN FRONT OF YOU...
BECAUSE YOU ALL HAVE YOUR LEGS AND NECKS CHAINED! YOU CAN'T MOVE.
I'M NOT CHAINED!
IT'S PART OF THE STORY!
JUST PRETEND THAT THE ONLY THING YOU'VE BEEN ABLE TO SEE ALL OF YOUR LIFE ARE THE SHADOWS ON THE WALL IN FRONT OF YOU.
OKAY JAMES, NOW YOU DO THE TRAIN.

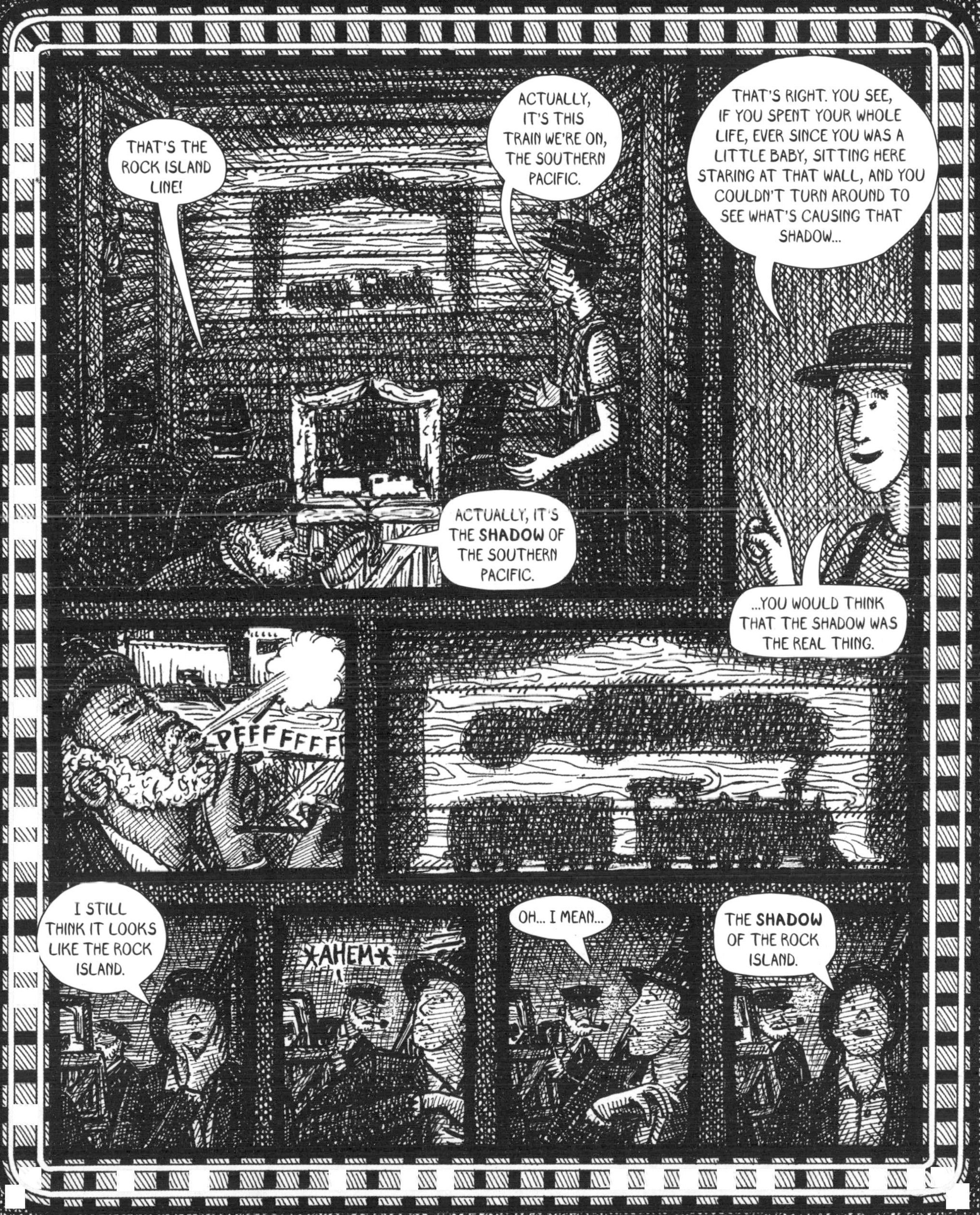
THAT'S THE ROCK ISLAND LINE!
ACTUALLY, IT'S THIS TRAIN WE'RE ON, THE SOUTHERN PACIFIC.
ACTUALLY, IT'S THE **SHADOW** OF THE SOUTHERN PACIFIC.
THAT'S RIGHT. YOU SEE, IF YOU SPENT YOUR WHOLE LIFE, EVER SINCE YOU WAS A LITTLE BABY, SITTING HERE STARING AT THAT WALL, AND YOU COULDN'T TURN AROUND TO SEE WHAT'S CAUSING THAT SHADOW...
...YOU WOULD THINK THAT THE SHADOW WAS THE REAL THING.
PFFFFFFF
I STILL THINK IT LOOKS LIKE THE ROCK ISLAND.
AHEM
OH... I MEAN...
THE **SHADOW** OF THE ROCK ISLAND.

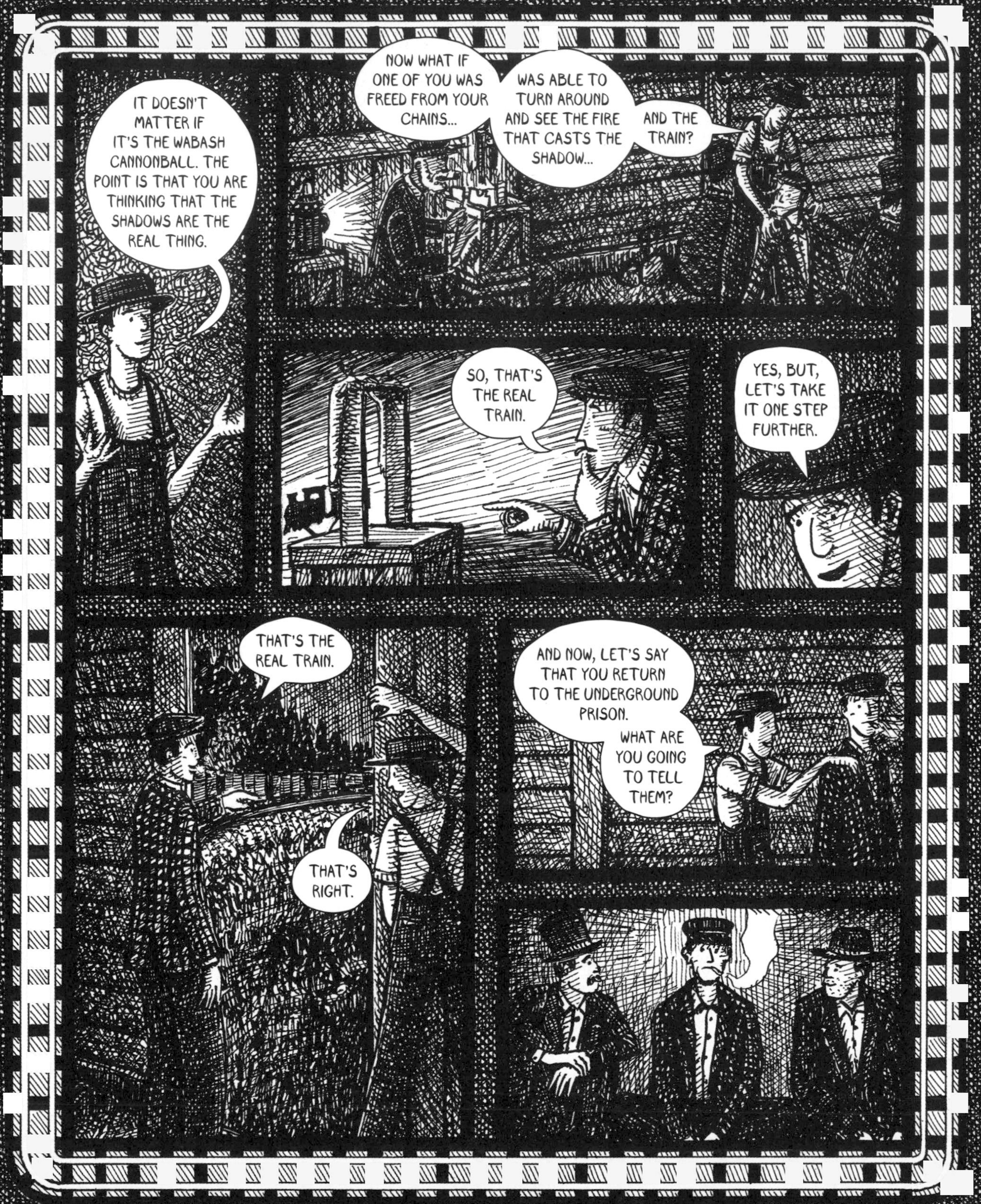
IT DOESN'T MATTER IF IT'S THE WABASH CANNONBALL. THE POINT IS THAT YOU ARE THINKING THAT THE SHADOWS ARE THE REAL THING.
NOW WHAT IF ONE OF YOU WAS FREED FROM YOUR CHAINS...
WAS ABLE TO TURN AROUND AND SEE THE FIRE THAT CASTS THE SHADOW...
AND THE TRAIN?
SO, THAT'S THE REAL TRAIN.
YES, BUT, LET'S TAKE IT ONE STEP FURTHER.
THAT'S THE REAL TRAIN.
THAT'S RIGHT.
AND NOW, LET'S SAY THAT YOU RETURN TO THE UNDERGROUND PRISON.
WHAT ARE YOU GOING TO TELL THEM?

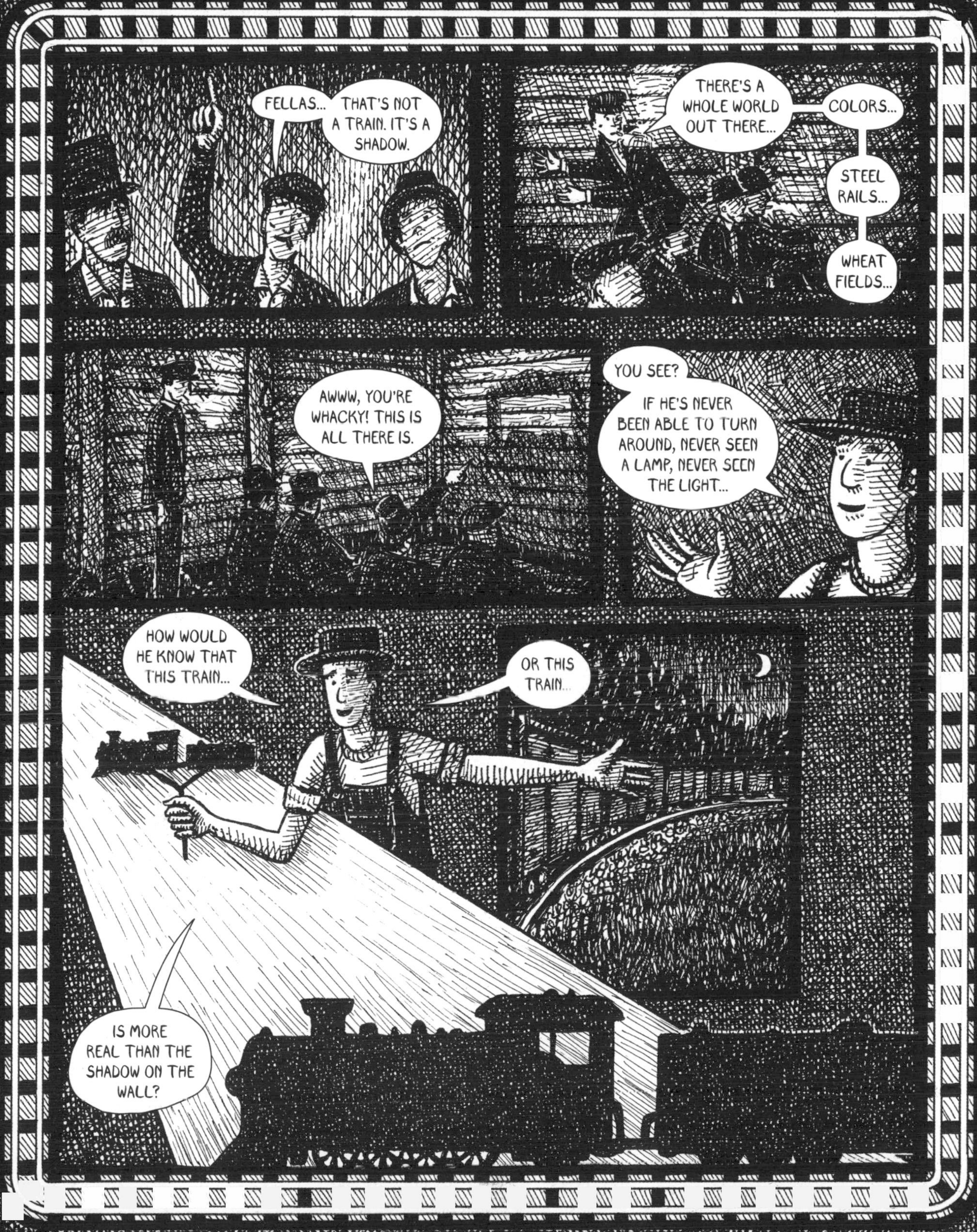
FELLAS...
THAT'S NOT A TRAIN. IT'S A SHADOW.
THERE'S A WHOLE WORLD OUT THERE...
COLORS...
STEEL RAILS...
WHEAT FIELDS...
AWWW, YOU'RE WHACKY! THIS IS ALL THERE IS.
YOU SEE?
IF HE'S NEVER BEEN ABLE TO TURN AROUND, NEVER SEEN A LAMP, NEVER SEEN THE LIGHT...
HOW WOULD HE KNOW THAT THIS TRAIN...
OR THIS TRAIN...
IS MORE REAL THAN THE SHADOW ON THE WALL?

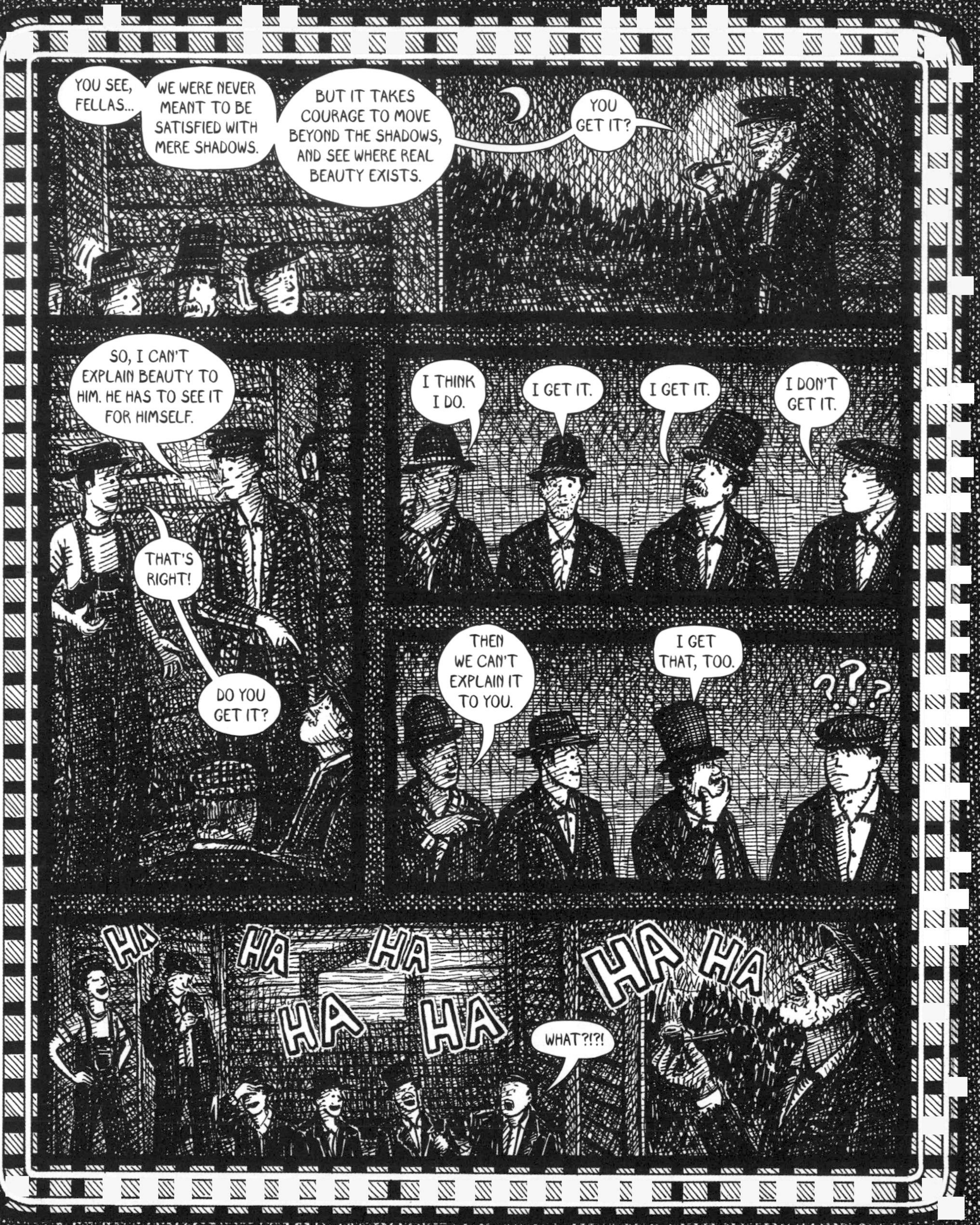

YOU SEE, FELLAS...
WE WERE NEVER MEANT TO BE SATISFIED WITH MERE SHADOWS.
BUT IT TAKES COURAGE TO MOVE BEYOND THE SHADOWS, AND SEE WHERE REAL BEAUTY EXISTS.
YOU GET IT?
SO, I CAN'T EXPLAIN BEAUTY TO HIM. HE HAS TO SEE IT FOR HIMSELF.
THAT'S RIGHT!
DO YOU GET IT?
I THINK I DO.
I GET IT.
I GET IT.
I DON'T GET IT.
THEN WE CAN'T EXPLAIN IT TO YOU.
I GET THAT, TOO.
???
HA HA HA HA HA
WHAT?!?!
HA HA HA

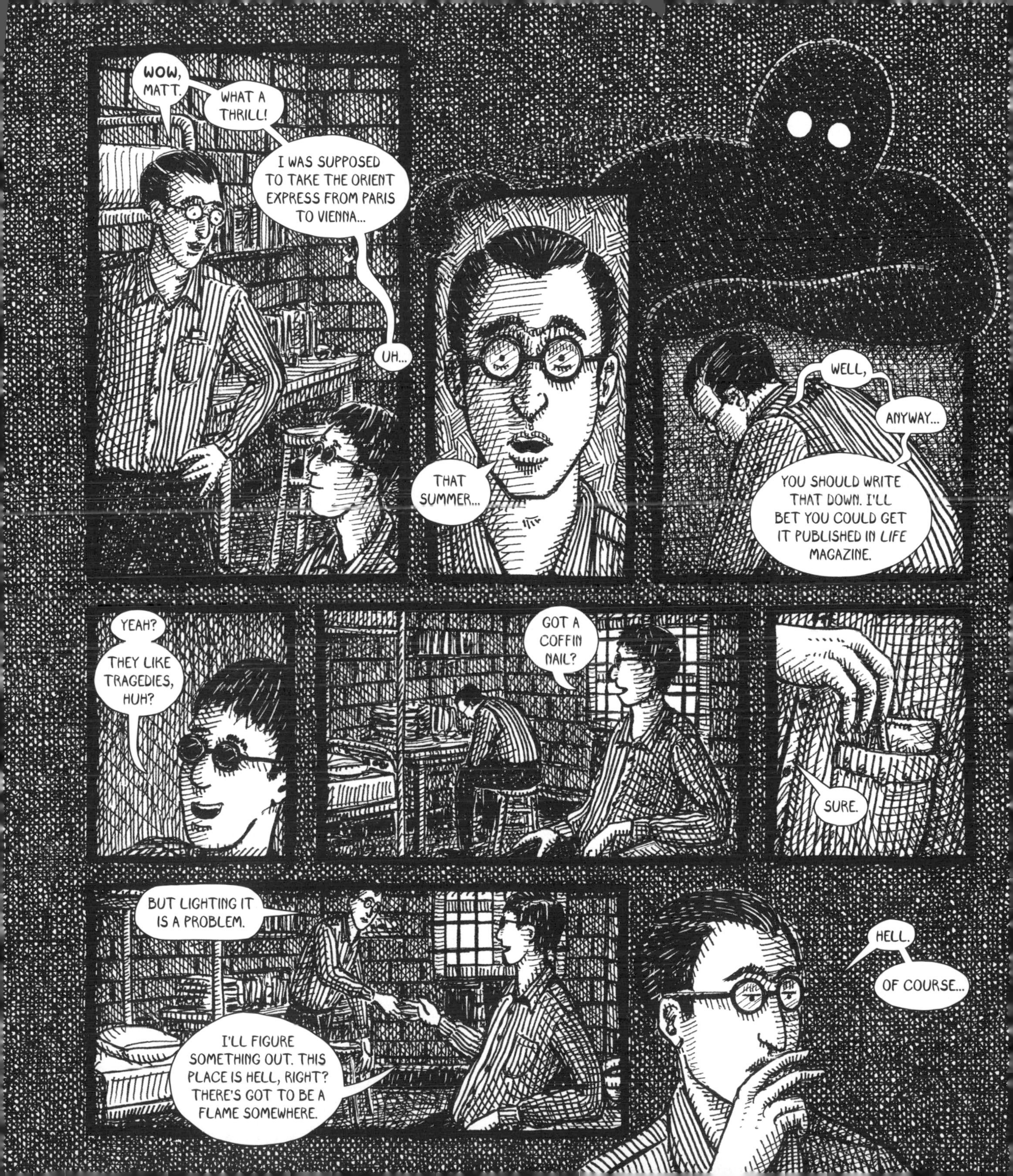
WOW, MATT.
WHAT A THRILL!
I WAS SUPPOSED TO TAKE THE ORIENT EXPRESS FROM PARIS TO VIENNA...
UH...
THAT SUMMER...
WELL,
ANYWAY...
YOU SHOULD WRITE THAT DOWN. I'LL BET YOU COULD GET IT PUBLISHED IN *LIFE* MAGAZINE.
YEAH?
THEY LIKE TRAGEDIES, HUH?
GOT A COFFIN NAIL?
SURE.
BUT LIGHTING IT IS A PROBLEM.
I'LL FIGURE SOMETHING OUT. THIS PLACE IS HELL, RIGHT? THERE'S GOT TO BE A FLAME SOMEWHERE.
HELL.
OF COURSE...

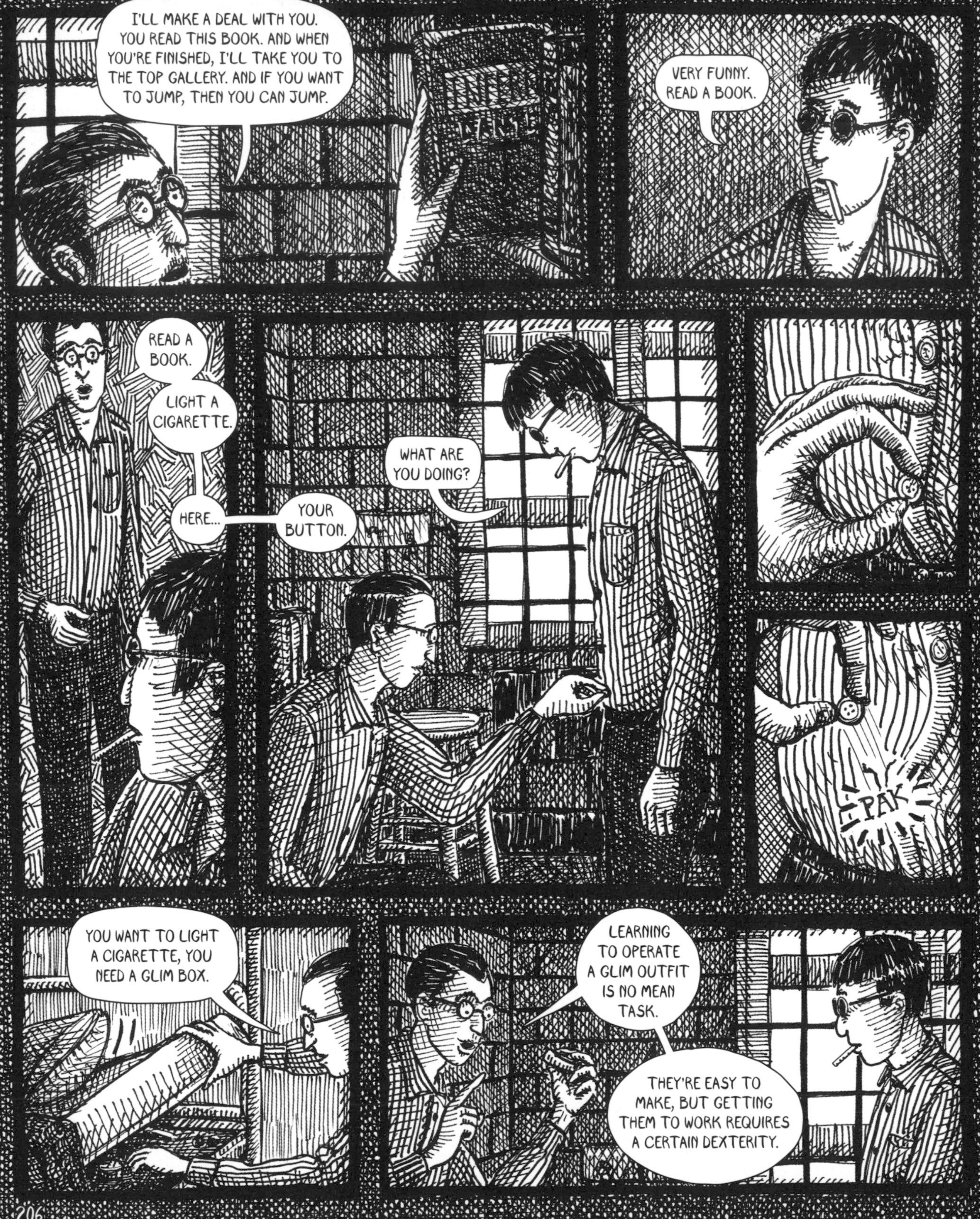
I'LL MAKE A DEAL WITH YOU. YOU READ THIS BOOK. AND WHEN YOU'RE FINISHED, I'LL TAKE YOU TO THE TOP GALLERY. AND IF YOU WANT TO JUMP, THEN YOU CAN JUMP.
VERY FUNNY. READ A BOOK.
READ A BOOK.
LIGHT A CIGARETTE.
HERE...
YOUR BUTTON.
WHAT ARE YOU DOING?
PAK
YOU WANT TO LIGHT A CIGARETTE, YOU NEED A GLIM BOX.
LEARNING TO OPERATE A GLIM OUTFIT IS NO MEAN TASK.
THEY'RE EASY TO MAKE, BUT GETTING THEM TO WORK REQUIRES A CERTAIN DEXTERITY.

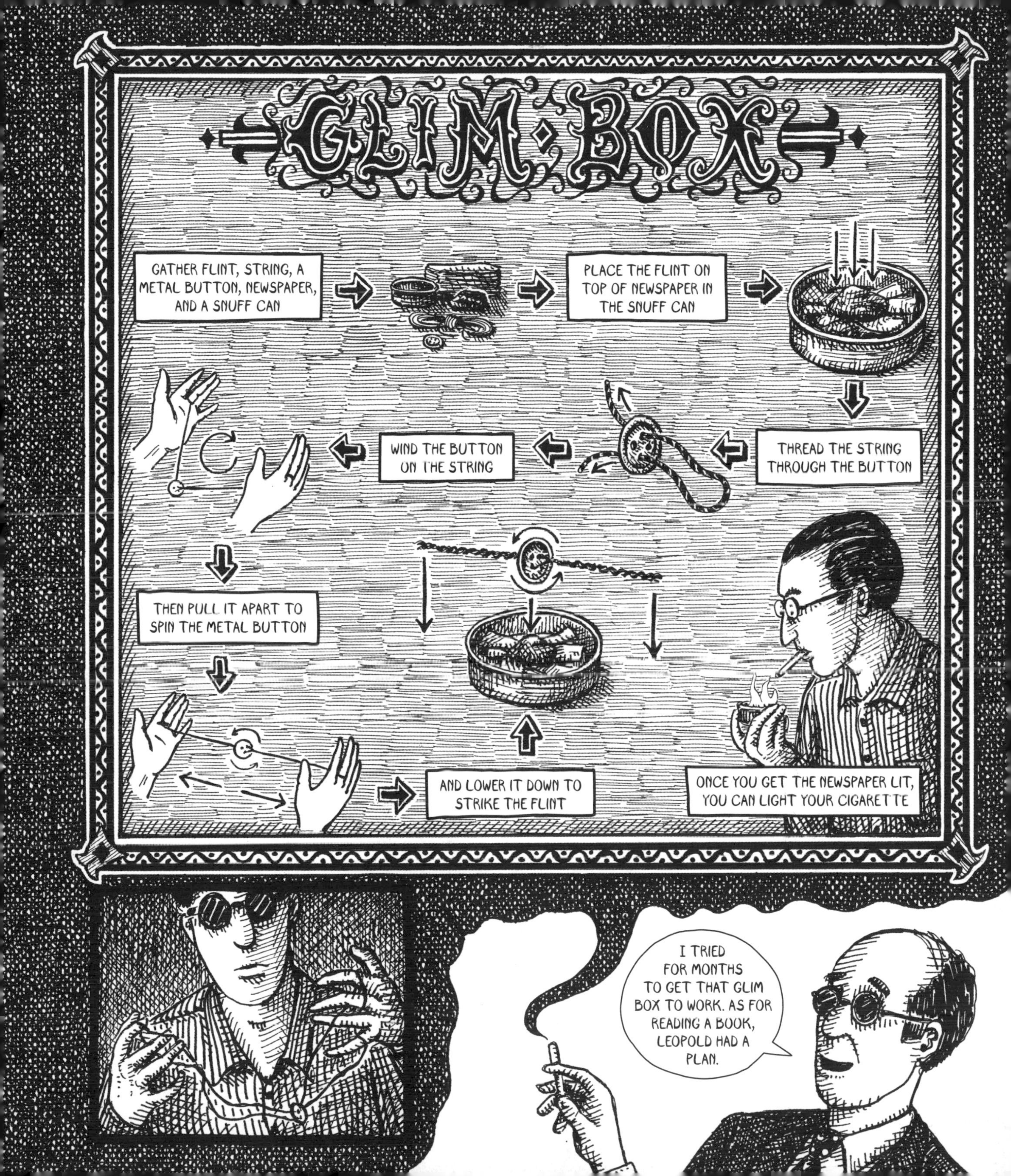
GLIM BOX
GATHER FLINT, STRING, A METAL BUTTON, NEWSPAPER, AND A SNUFF CAN
PLACE THE FLINT ON TOP OF NEWSPAPER IN THE SNUFF CAN
THREAD THE STRING THROUGH THE BUTTON
WIND THE BUTTON ON THE STRING
THEN PULL IT APART TO SPIN THE METAL BUTTON
AND LOWER IT DOWN TO STRIKE THE FLINT
ONCE YOU GET THE NEWSPAPER LIT, YOU CAN LIGHT YOUR CIGARETTE
I TRIED FOR MONTHS TO GET THAT GLIM BOX TO WORK. AS FOR READING A BOOK, LEOPOLD HAD A PLAN.

IX

THE INFERNO

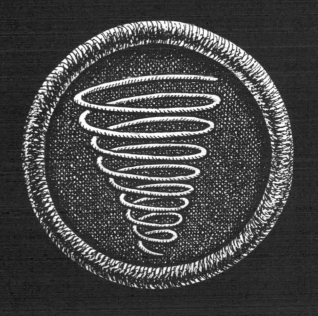

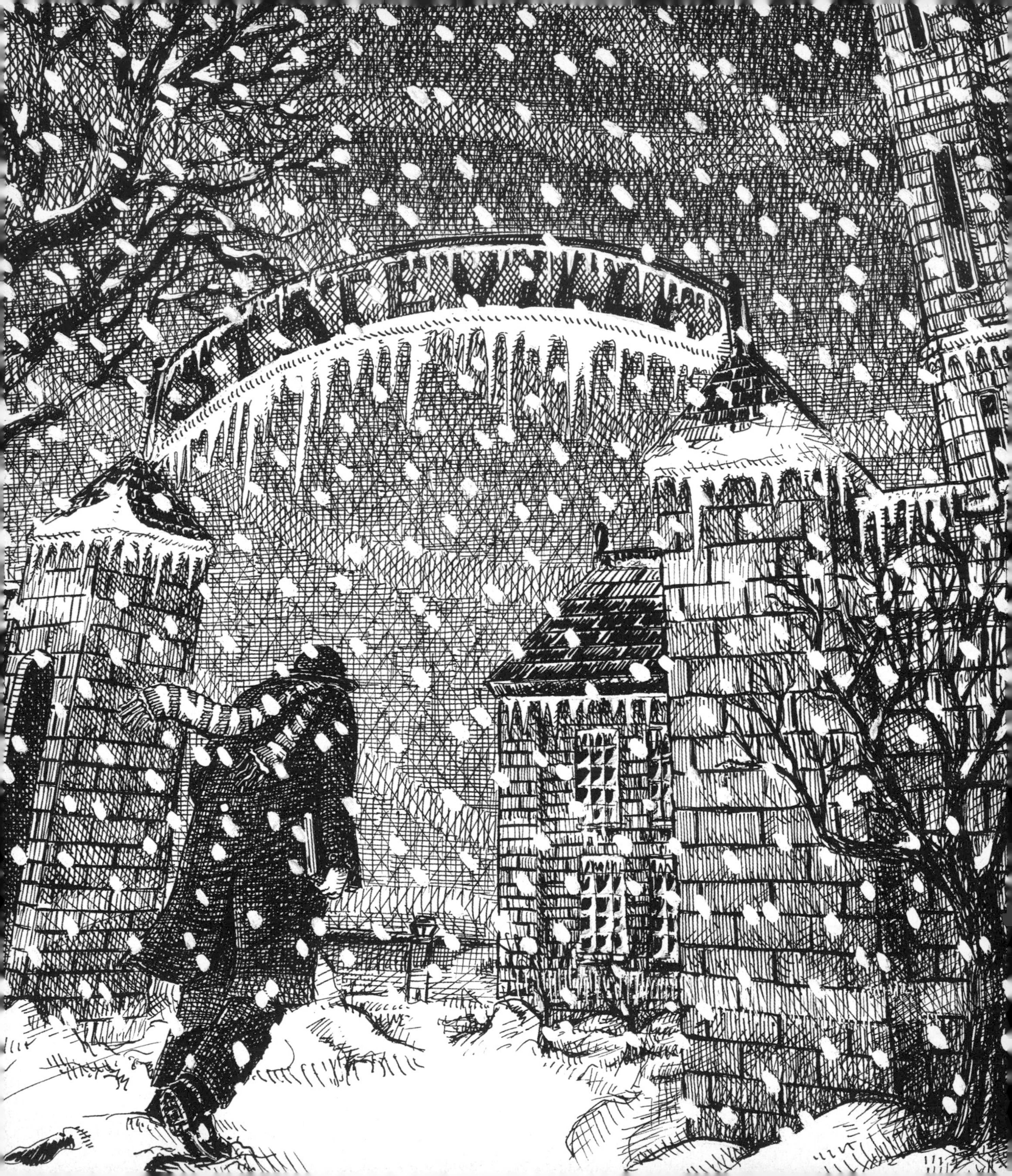

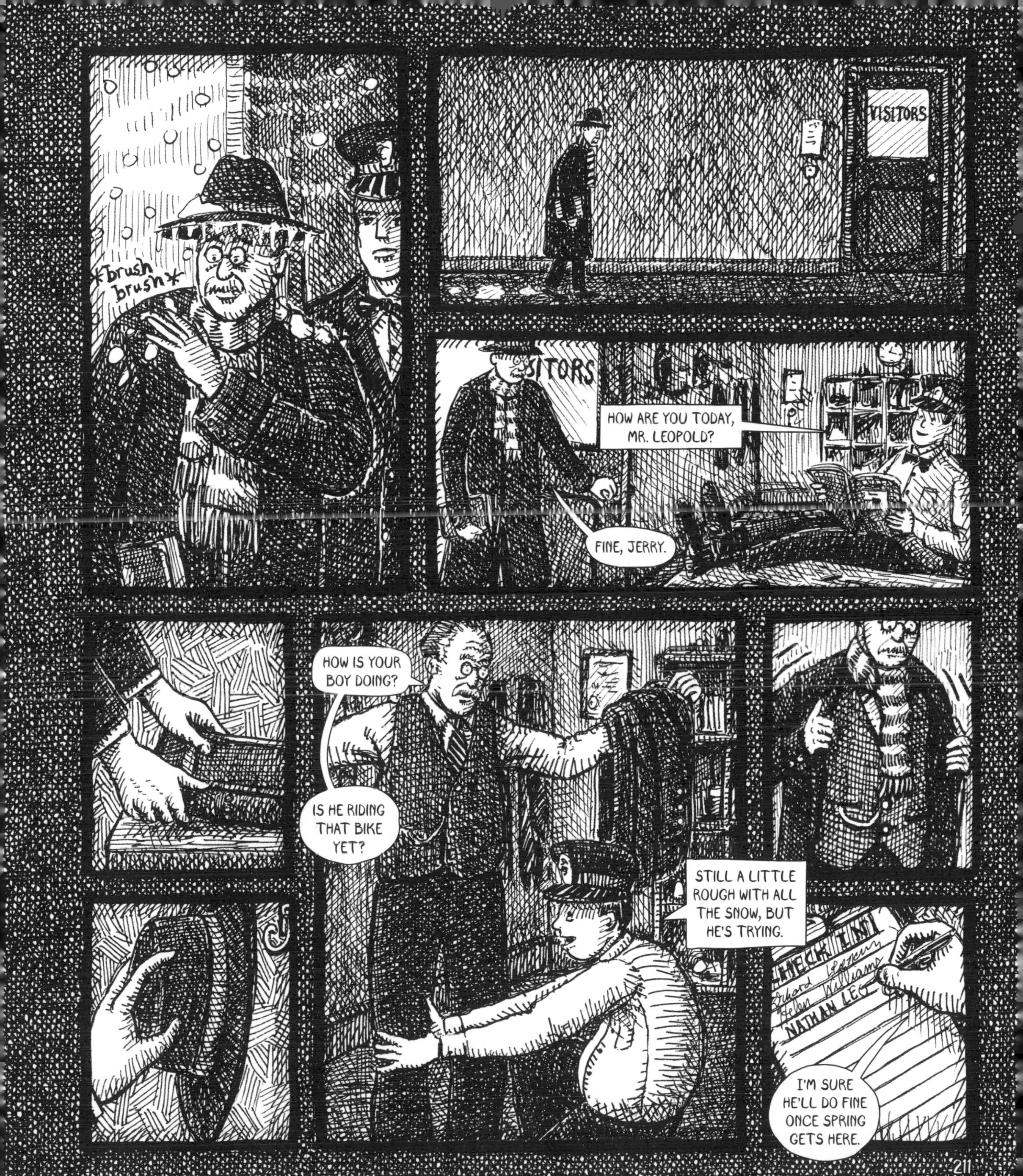
brush brush
VISITORS
HOW ARE YOU TODAY, MR. LEOPOLD?
FINE, JERRY.
HOW IS YOUR BOY DOING?
IS HE RIDING THAT BIKE YET?
STILL A LITTLE ROUGH WITH ALL THE SNOW, BUT HE'S TRYING.
I'M SURE HE'LL DO FINE ONCE SPRING GETS HERE.

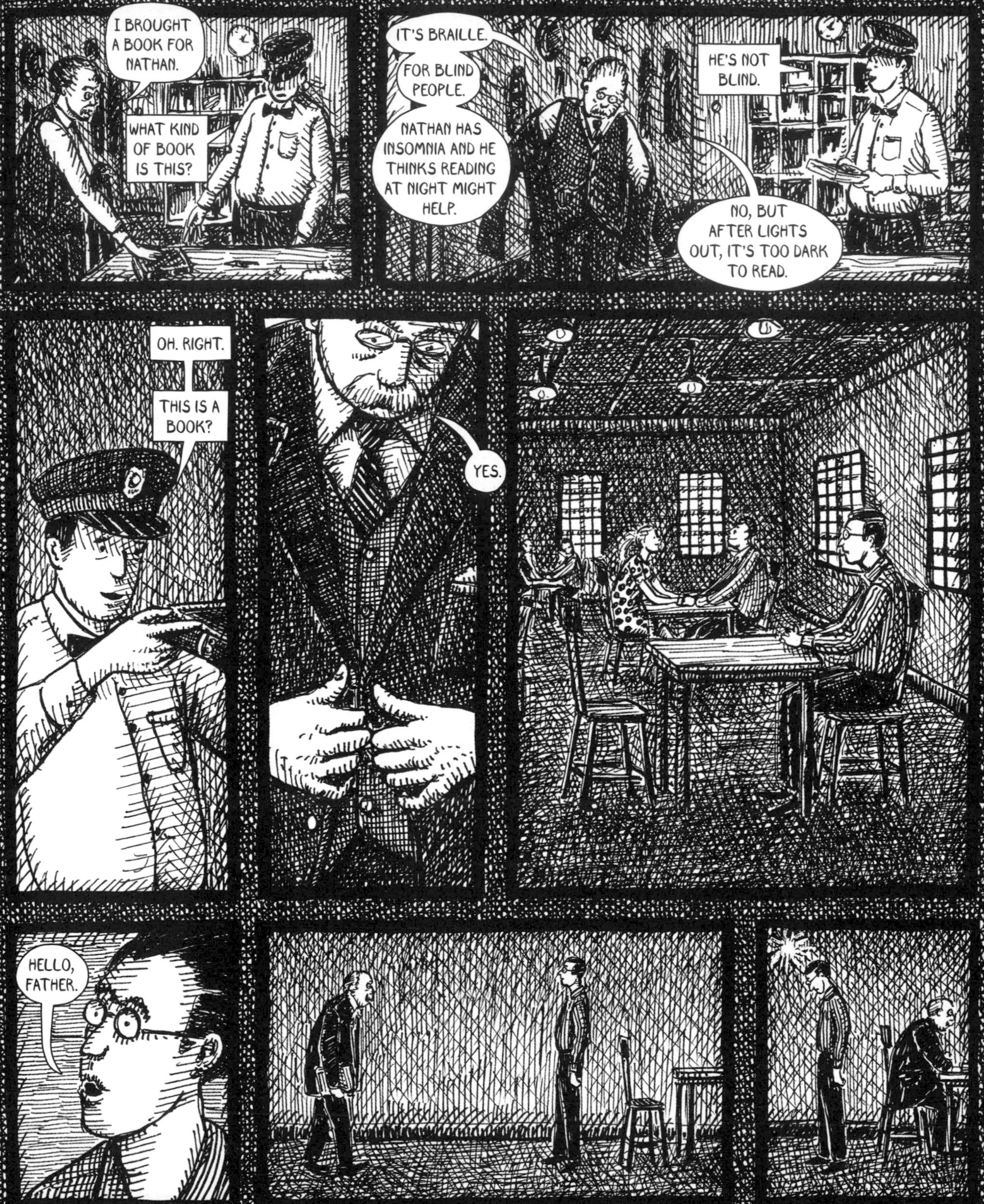
I BROUGHT A BOOK FOR NATHAN.
WHAT KIND OF BOOK IS THIS?
IT'S BRAILLE.
FOR BLIND PEOPLE.
NATHAN HAS INSOMNIA AND HE THINKS READING AT NIGHT MIGHT HELP.
HE'S NOT BLIND.
NO, BUT AFTER LIGHTS OUT, IT'S TOO DARK TO READ.
OH. RIGHT.
THIS IS A BOOK?
YES.
HELLO, FATHER.

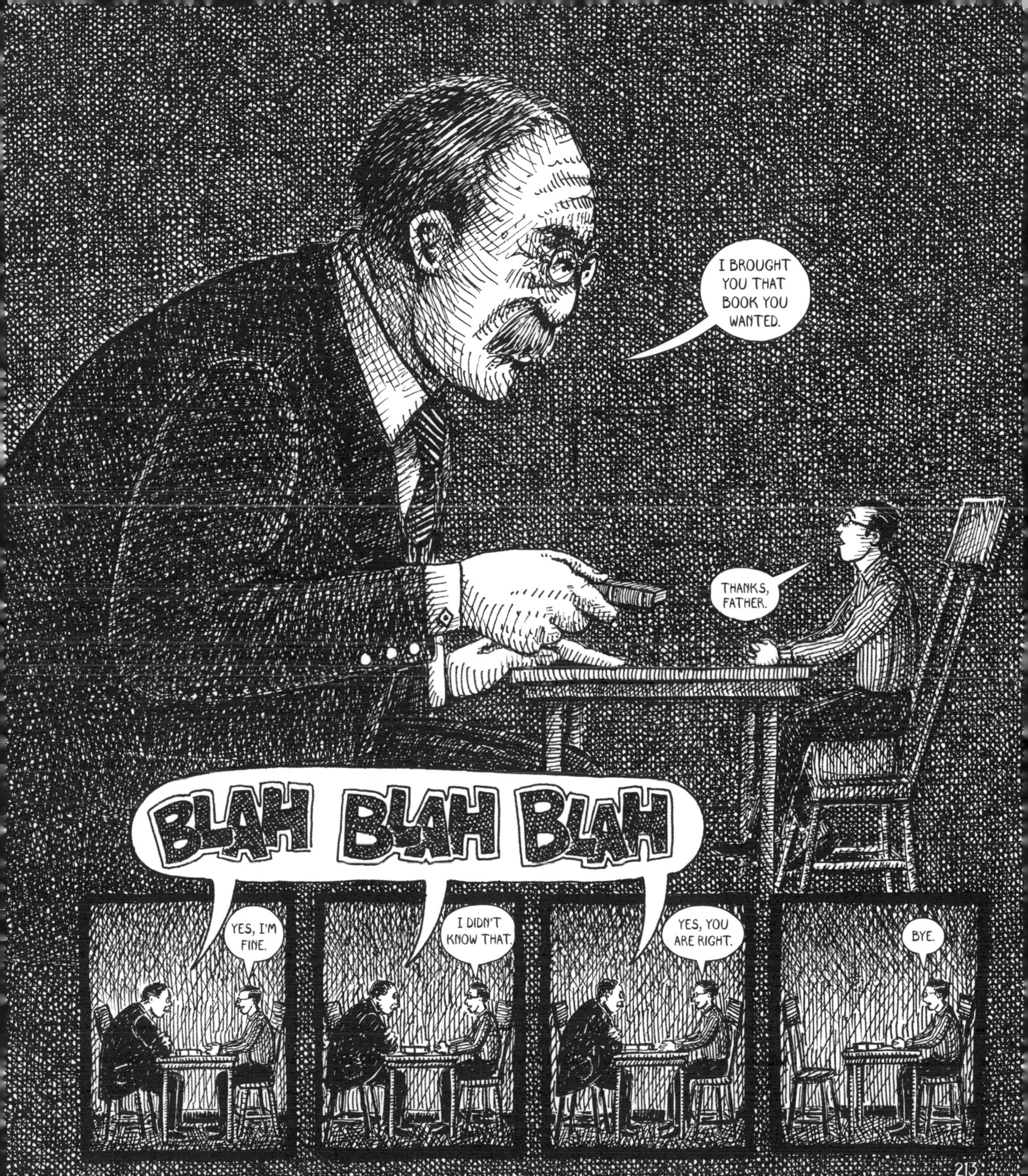
I BROUGHT YOU THAT BOOK YOU WANTED.
THANKS, FATHER.
BLAH BLAH BLAH
YES, I'M FINE.
I DIDN'T KNOW THAT.
YES, YOU ARE RIGHT.
BYE.

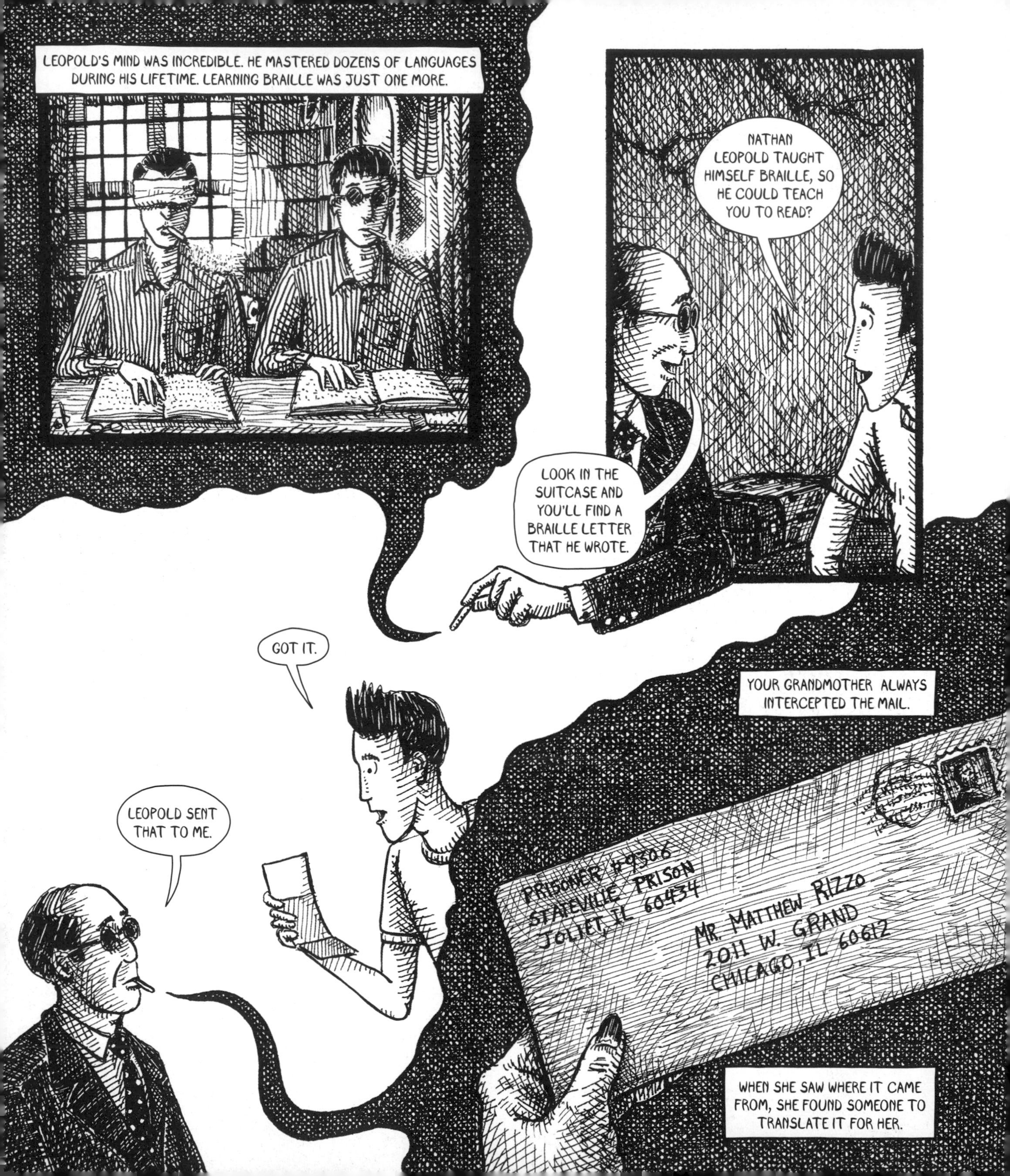
LEOPOLD'S MIND WAS INCREDIBLE. HE MASTERED DOZENS OF LANGUAGES DURING HIS LIFETIME. LEARNING BRAILLE WAS JUST ONE MORE.
NATHAN LEOPOLD TAUGHT HIMSELF BRAILLE, SO HE COULD TEACH YOU TO READ?
LOOK IN THE SUITCASE AND YOU'LL FIND A BRAILLE LETTER THAT HE WROTE.
GOT IT.
YOUR GRANDMOTHER ALWAYS INTERCEPTED THE MAIL.
LEOPOLD SENT THAT TO ME.
PRISONER #9306
STATEVILLE PRISON
JOLIET, IL 60434
MR. MATTHEW RIZZO
2011 W. GRAND
CHICAGO, IL 60612
WHEN SHE SAW WHERE IT CAME FROM, SHE FOUND SOMEONE TO TRANSLATE IT FOR HER.

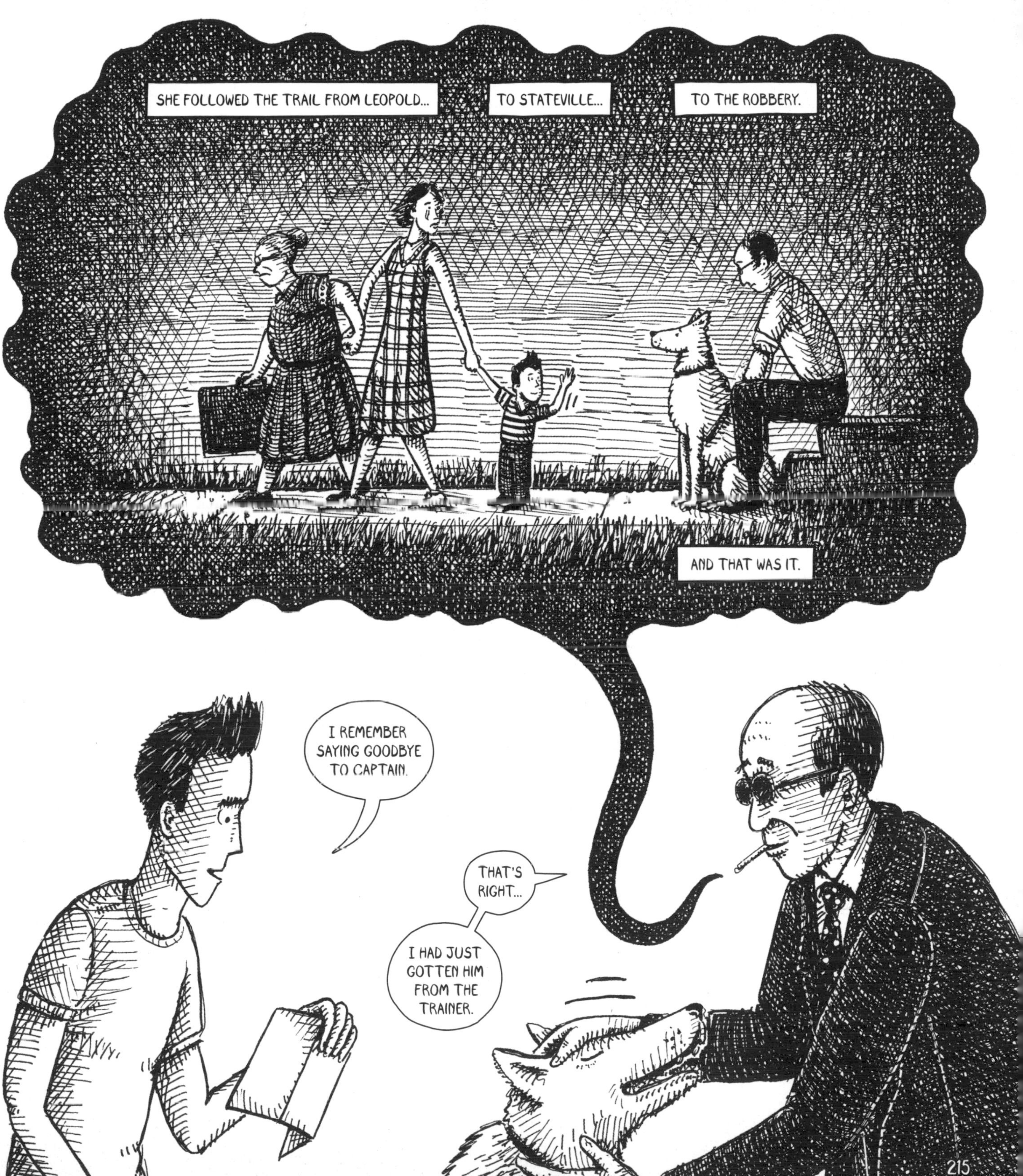
SHE FOLLOWED THE TRAIL FROM LEOPOLD...
TO STATEVILLE...
TO THE ROBBERY.
AND THAT WAS IT.
I REMEMBER SAYING GOODBYE TO CAPTAIN.
THAT'S RIGHT...
I HAD JUST GOTTEN HIM FROM THE TRAINER.

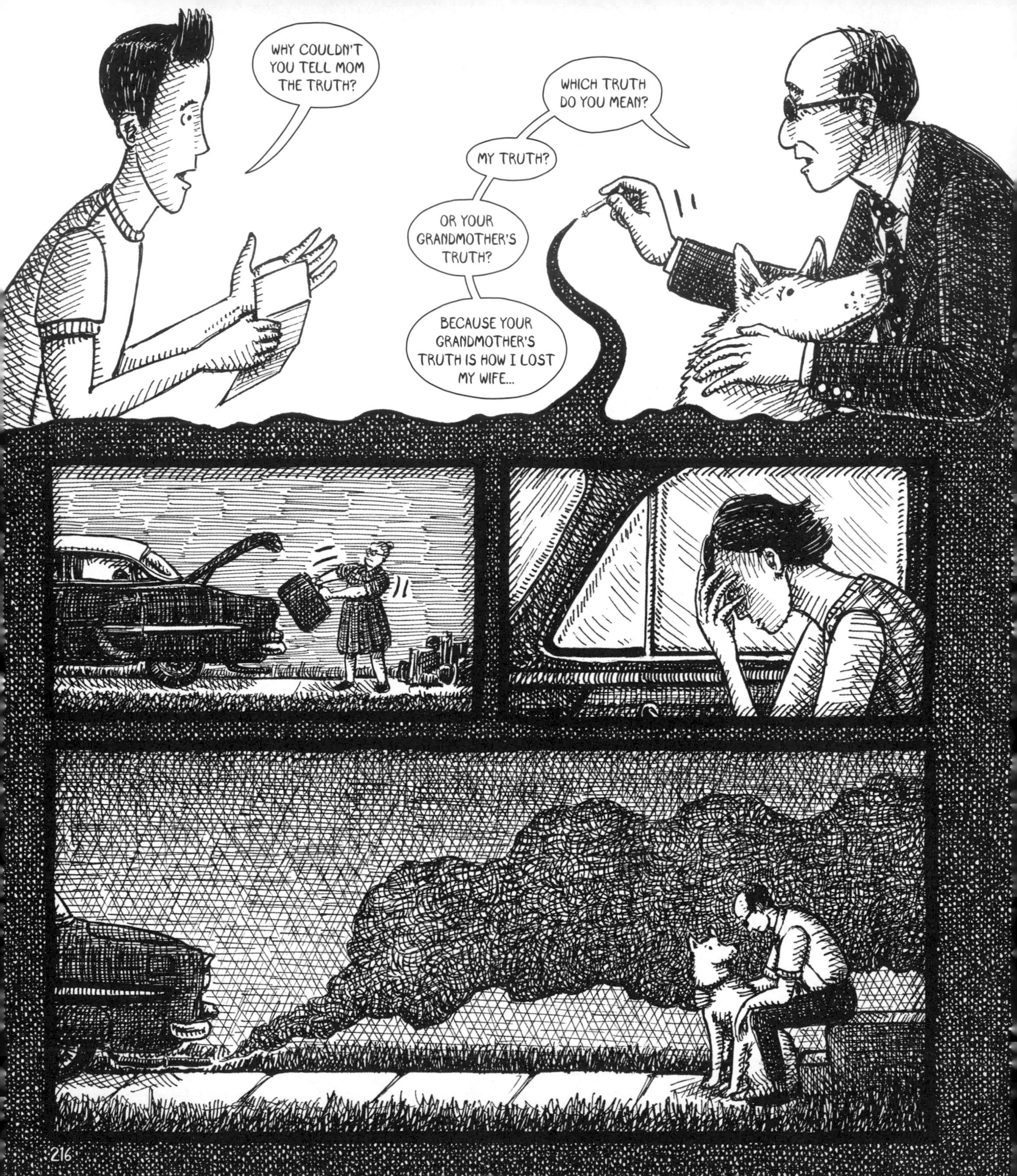
WHY COULDN'T YOU TELL MOM THE TRUTH?
WHICH TRUTH DO YOU MEAN?
MY TRUTH?
OR YOUR GRANDMOTHER'S TRUTH?
BECAUSE YOUR GRANDMOTHER'S TRUTH IS HOW I LOST MY WIFE...

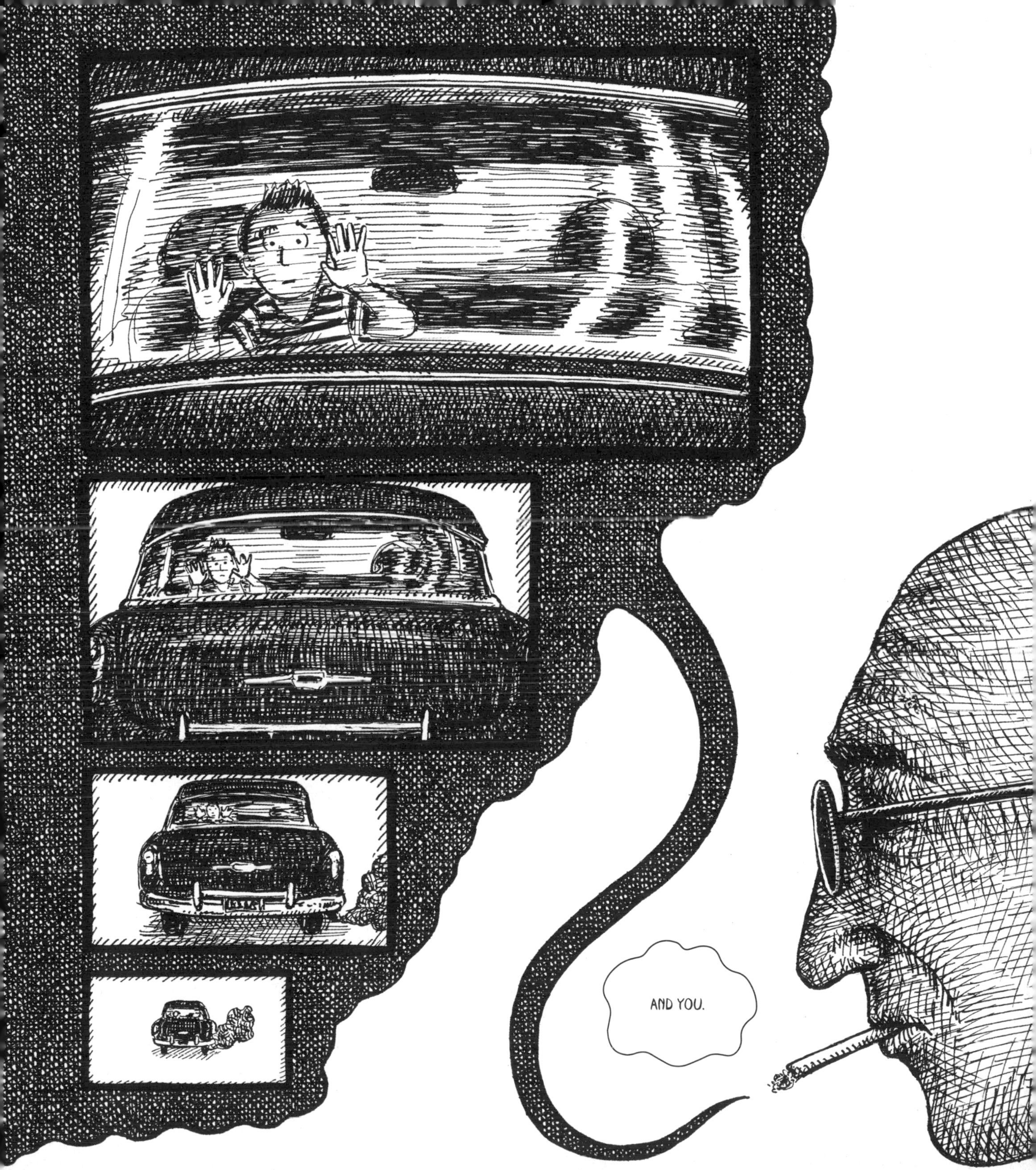
AND YOU.

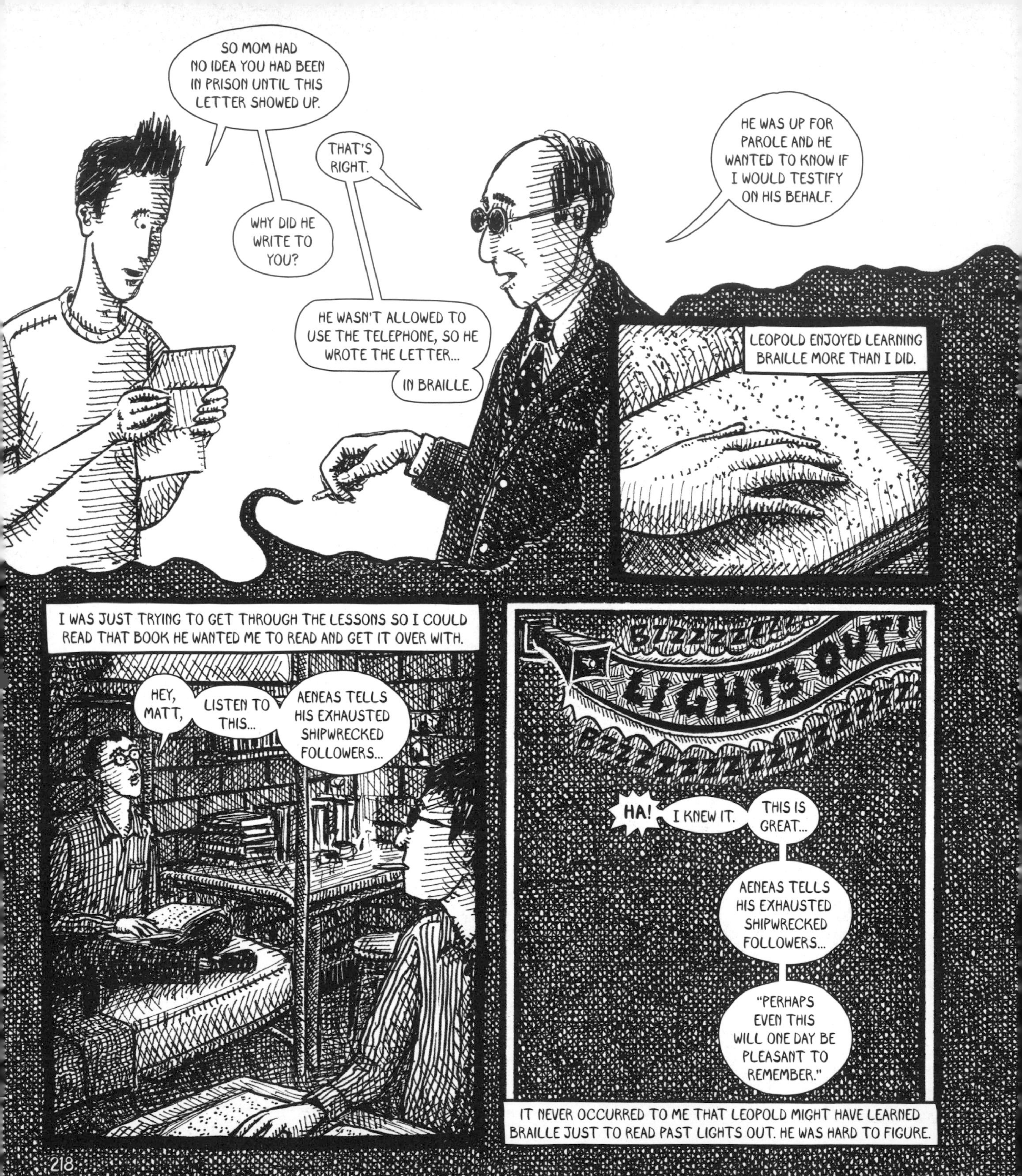

SO MOM HAD NO IDEA YOU HAD BEEN IN PRISON UNTIL THIS LETTER SHOWED UP.
THAT'S RIGHT.
WHY DID HE WRITE TO YOU?
HE WAS UP FOR PAROLE AND HE WANTED TO KNOW IF I WOULD TESTIFY ON HIS BEHALF.
HE WASN'T ALLOWED TO USE THE TELEPHONE, SO HE WROTE THE LETTER...
IN BRAILLE.
LEOPOLD ENJOYED LEARNING BRAILLE MORE THAN I DID.
I WAS JUST TRYING TO GET THROUGH THE LESSONS SO I COULD READ THAT BOOK HE WANTED ME TO READ AND GET IT OVER WITH.
HEY, MATT,
LISTEN TO THIS...
AENEAS TELLS HIS EXHAUSTED SHIPWRECKED FOLLOWERS...
BZZZZZZ
LIGHTS OUT!
BZZZZZZZZZZZZZZZZZZ
HA!
I KNEW IT.
THIS IS GREAT...
AENEAS TELLS HIS EXHAUSTED SHIPWRECKED FOLLOWERS...
"PERHAPS EVEN THIS WILL ONE DAY BE PLEASANT TO REMEMBER."
IT NEVER OCCURRED TO ME THAT LEOPOLD MIGHT HAVE LEARNED BRAILLE JUST TO READ PAST LIGHTS OUT. HE WAS HARD TO FIGURE.

A WEEK LATER...

DELIVERY.

THE BLIND BOOK YOU WANTED.

THIS IS YOUR BOOK, MATT.

YOU CAN READ IT DURING THE DAY, BUT I GET IT AT NIGHT.

DEAL?

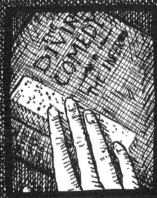

HOW MANY DEALS ARE WE GOING TO MAKE OVER THIS BOOK?

RIGHT.

YOU WANT TO TAKE A BRODIE WHEN YOU'RE FINISHED.

DANTE'S...

DIVINE COMEDY.

SO, IT'S FUNNY?

NO, IT'S NOT FUNNY...

WELL, IT IS,

BUT NOT LIKE THAT.

MIRTHFUL,

PERHAPS.

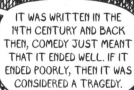

IT WAS WRITTEN IN THE 14TH CENTURY AND BACK THEN, COMEDY JUST MEANT THAT IT ENDED WELL. IF IT ENDED POORLY, THEN IT WAS CONSIDERED A TRAGEDY.

IT'S ABOUT A MAN WHO HAS LOST HIS WAY.

219

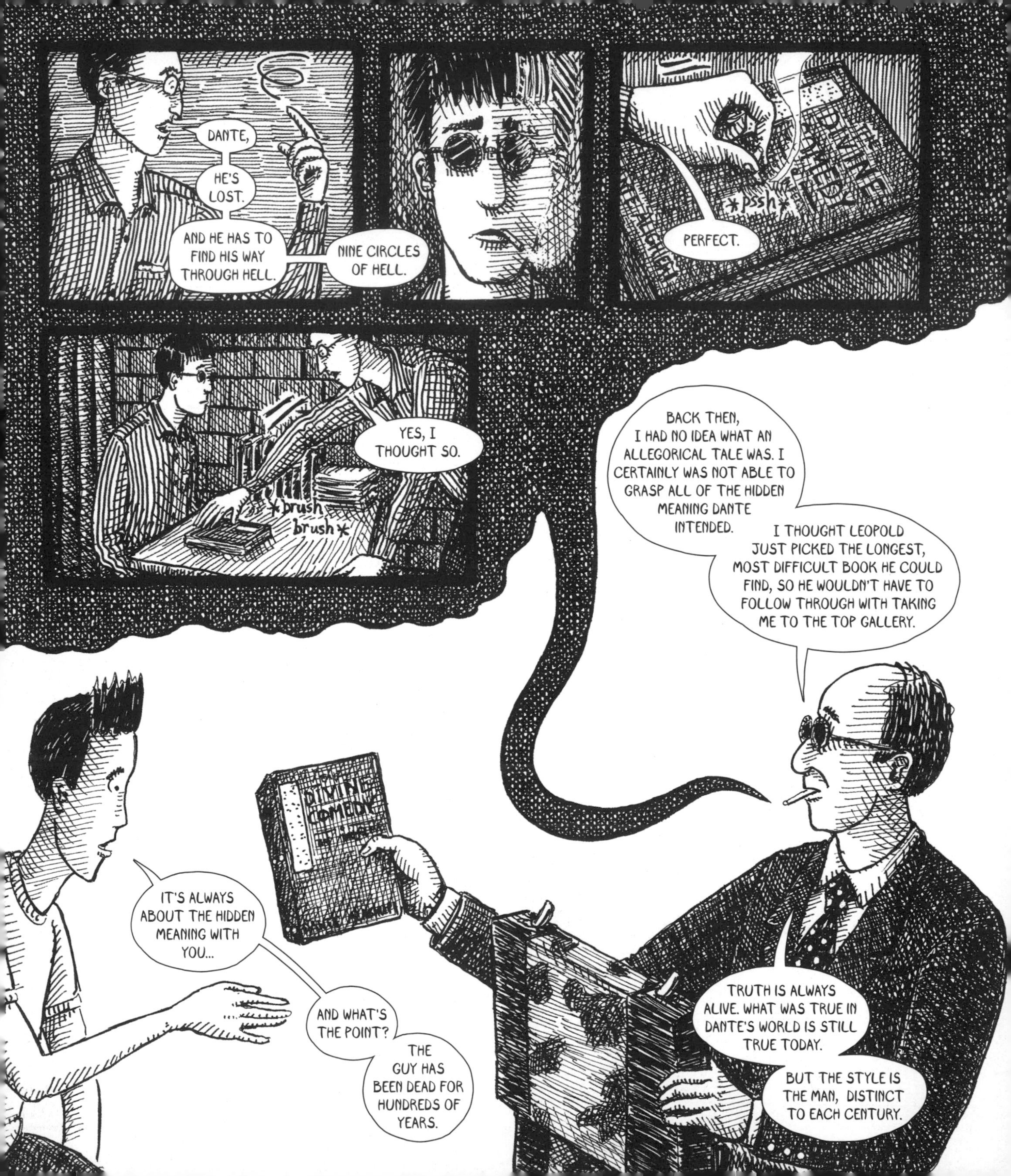
DANTE,
HE'S LOST.
AND HE HAS TO FIND HIS WAY THROUGH HELL.
NINE CIRCLES OF HELL.
pssh
PERFECT.
YES, I THOUGHT SO.
brush brush
BACK THEN, I HAD NO IDEA WHAT AN ALLEGORICAL TALE WAS. I CERTAINLY WAS NOT ABLE TO GRASP ALL OF THE HIDDEN MEANING DANTE INTENDED.
I THOUGHT LEOPOLD JUST PICKED THE LONGEST, MOST DIFFICULT BOOK HE COULD FIND, SO HE WOULDN'T HAVE TO FOLLOW THROUGH WITH TAKING ME TO THE TOP GALLERY.
DIVINE COMEDY
IT'S ALWAYS ABOUT THE HIDDEN MEANING WITH YOU...
AND WHAT'S THE POINT?
THE GUY HAS BEEN DEAD FOR HUNDREDS OF YEARS.
TRUTH IS ALWAYS ALIVE. WHAT WAS TRUE IN DANTE'S WORLD IS STILL TRUE TODAY.
BUT THE STYLE IS THE MAN, DISTINCT TO EACH CENTURY.

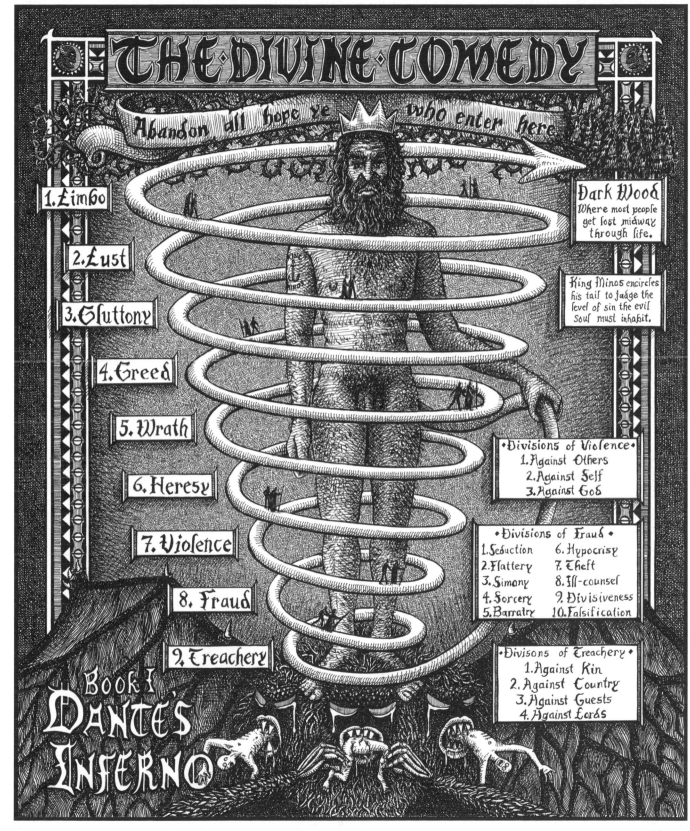

THE·DIVINE·COMEDY

Abandon all hope ye who enter here

1. Limbo
2. Lust
3. Gluttony
4. Greed
5. Wrath
6. Heresy
7. Violence
8. Fraud
9. Treachery

Dark Wood Where most people get lost midway through life.

King Minos encircles his tail to judge the level of sin the evil soul must inhabit.

•Divisions of Violence•
1. Against Others
2. Against Self
3. Against God

•Divisions of Fraud•
1. Seduction
2. Flattery
3. Simony
4. Sorcery
5. Barratry
6. Hypocrisy
7. Theft
8. Ill-counsel
9. Divisiveness
10. Falsification

•Divisons of Treachery•
1. Against Kin
2. Against Country
3. Against Guests
4. Against Lords

Book I
DANTE'S
INFERNO

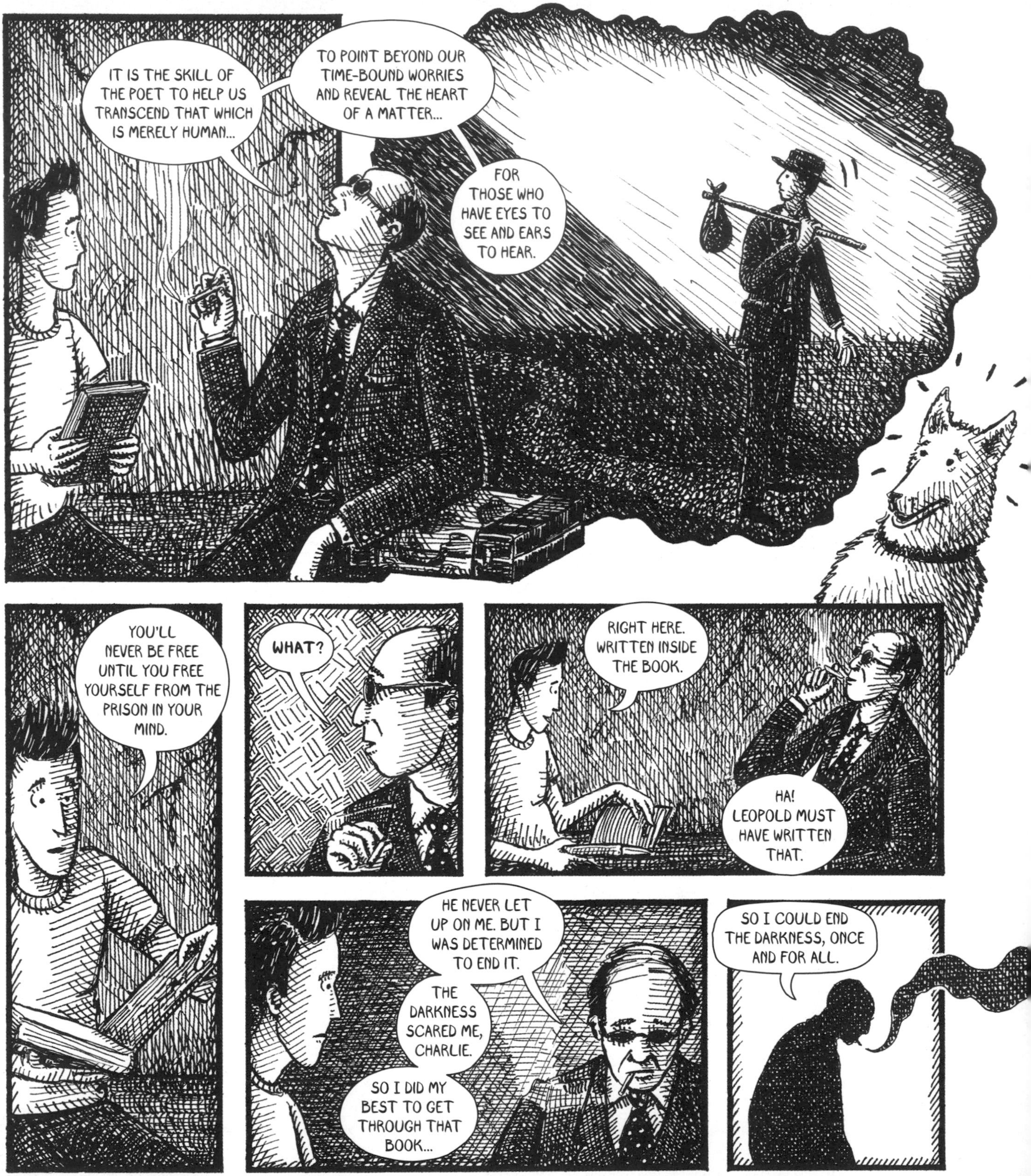
IT IS THE SKILL OF THE POET TO HELP US TRANSCEND THAT WHICH IS MERELY HUMAN...
TO POINT BEYOND OUR TIME-BOUND WORRIES AND REVEAL THE HEART OF A MATTER...
FOR THOSE WHO HAVE EYES TO SEE AND EARS TO HEAR.
YOU'LL NEVER BE FREE UNTIL YOU FREE YOURSELF FROM THE PRISON IN YOUR MIND.
WHAT?
RIGHT HERE. WRITTEN INSIDE THE BOOK.
HA! LEOPOLD MUST HAVE WRITTEN THAT.
HE NEVER LET UP ON ME. BUT I WAS DETERMINED TO END IT.
THE DARKNESS SCARED ME, CHARLIE.
SO I DID MY BEST TO GET THROUGH THAT BOOK...
SO I COULD END THE DARKNESS, ONCE AND FOR ALL.

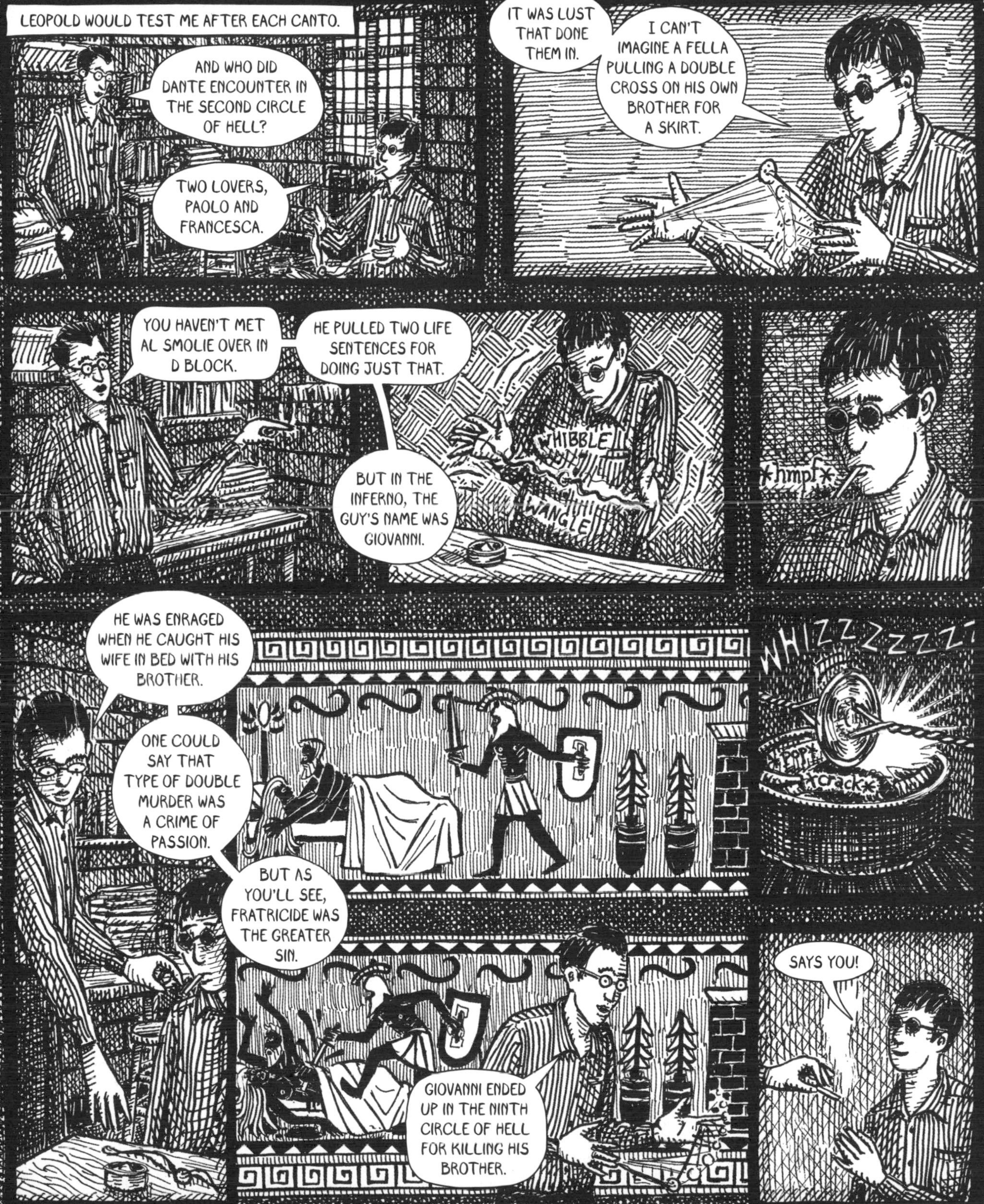
LEOPOLD WOULD TEST ME AFTER EACH CANTO.
AND WHO DID DANTE ENCOUNTER IN THE SECOND CIRCLE OF HELL?
TWO LOVERS, PAOLO AND FRANCESCA.
IT WAS LUST THAT DONE THEM IN.
I CAN'T IMAGINE A FELLA PULLING A DOUBLE CROSS ON HIS OWN BROTHER FOR A SKIRT.
YOU HAVEN'T MET AL SMOLIE OVER IN D BLOCK.
HE PULLED TWO LIFE SENTENCES FOR DOING JUST THAT.
BUT IN THE INFERNO, THE GUY'S NAME WAS GIOVANNI.
WHIBBLE
WANGLE
hmpf
HE WAS ENRAGED WHEN HE CAUGHT HIS WIFE IN BED WITH HIS BROTHER.
ONE COULD SAY THAT TYPE OF DOUBLE MURDER WAS A CRIME OF PASSION.
BUT AS YOU'LL SEE, FRATRICIDE WAS THE GREATER SIN.
WHIZZZZZZZ
pop
crack
GIOVANNI ENDED UP IN THE NINTH CIRCLE OF HELL FOR KILLING HIS BROTHER.
SAYS YOU!

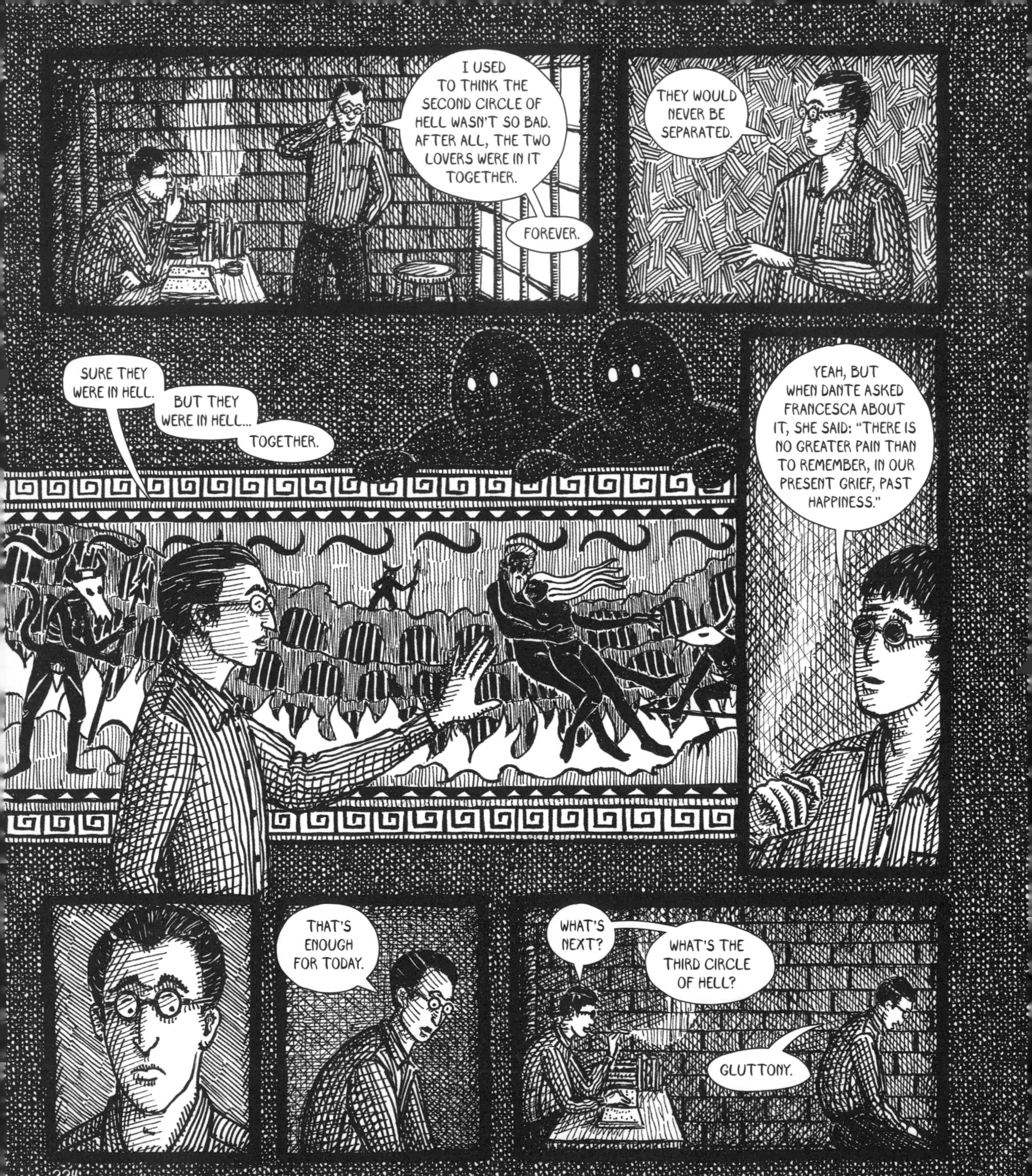
I USED TO THINK THE SECOND CIRCLE OF HELL WASN'T SO BAD. AFTER ALL, THE TWO LOVERS WERE IN IT TOGETHER.
FOREVER.
THEY WOULD NEVER BE SEPARATED.
SURE THEY WERE IN HELL.
BUT THEY WERE IN HELL...
TOGETHER.
YEAH, BUT WHEN DANTE ASKED FRANCESCA ABOUT IT, SHE SAID: "THERE IS NO GREATER PAIN THAN TO REMEMBER, IN OUR PRESENT GRIEF, PAST HAPPINESS."
THAT'S ENOUGH FOR TODAY.
WHAT'S NEXT?
WHAT'S THE THIRD CIRCLE OF HELL?
GLUTTONY.

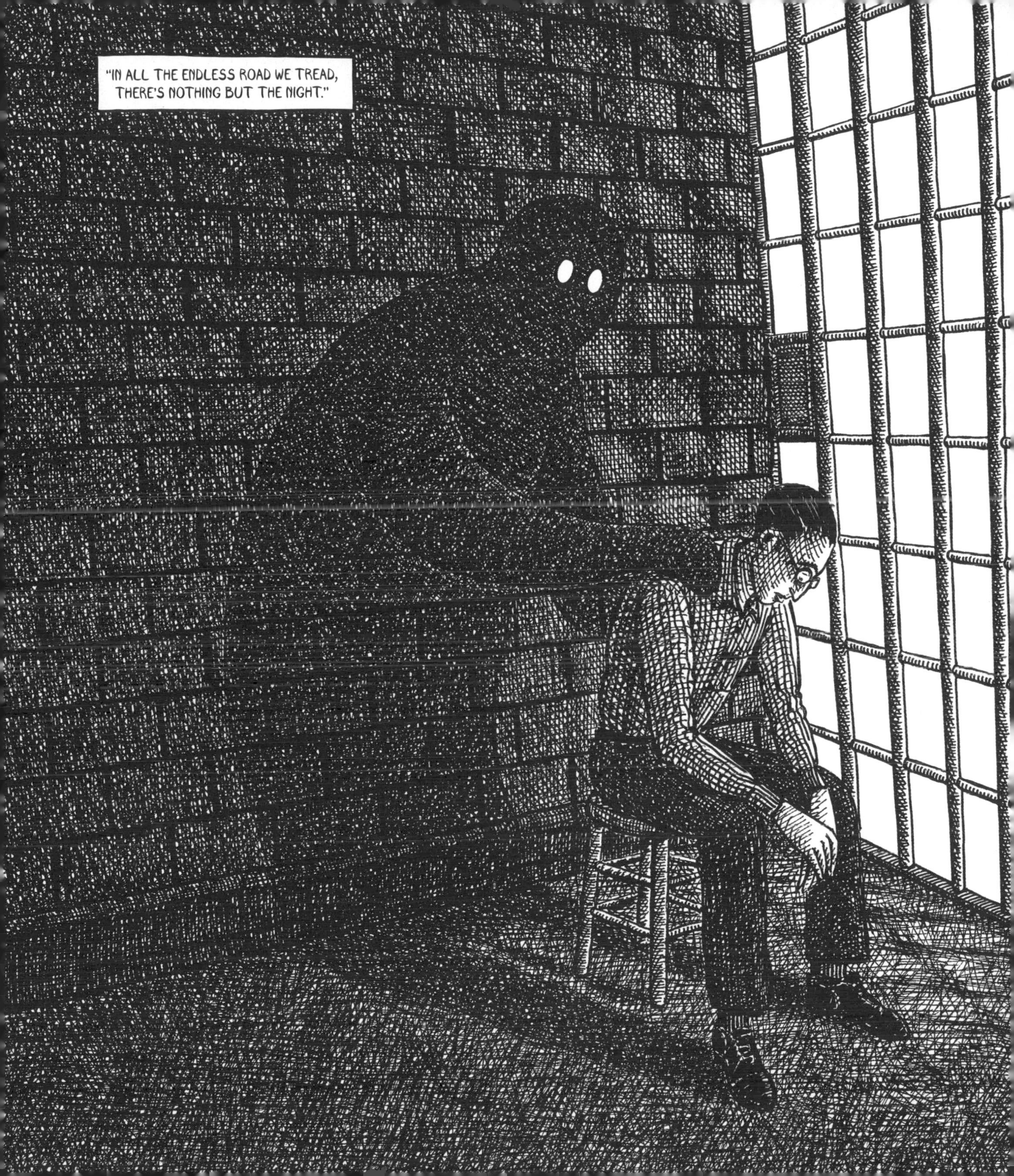
"IN ALL THE ENDLESS ROAD WE TREAD, THERE'S NOTHING BUT THE NIGHT."

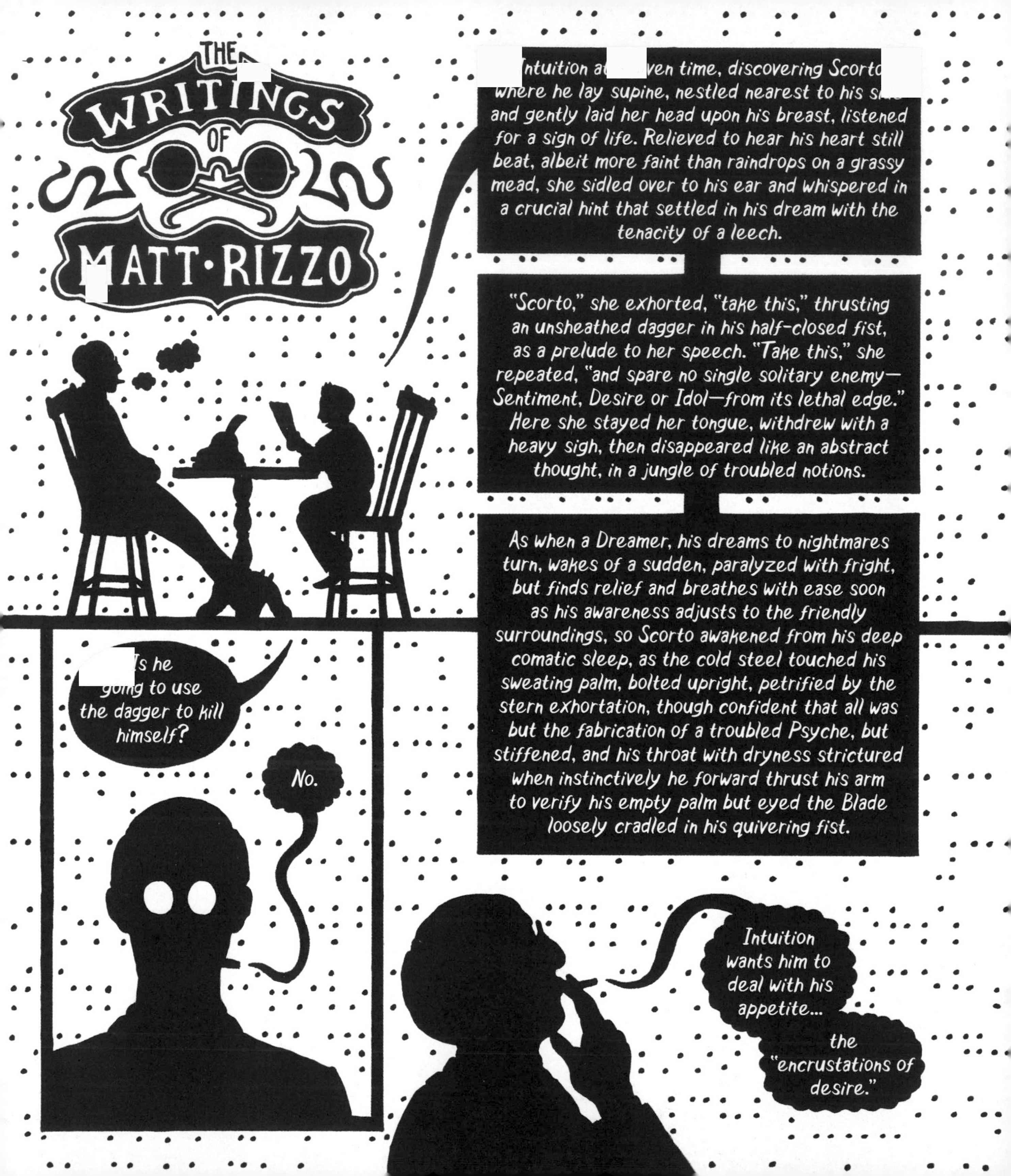
THE WRITINGS OF MATT·RIZZO
ntuition a ven time, discovering Scorto where he lay supine, nestled nearest to his s and gently laid her head upon his breast, listened for a sign of life. Relieved to hear his heart still beat, albeit more faint than raindrops on a grassy mead, she sidled over to his ear and whispered in a crucial hint that settled in his dream with the tenacity of a leech.
"Scorto," she exhorted, "take this," thrusting an unsheathed dagger in his half-closed fist, as a prelude to her speech. "Take this," she repeated, "and spare no single solitary enemy—Sentiment, Desire or Idol—from its lethal edge." Here she stayed her tongue, withdrew with a heavy sigh, then disappeared like an abstract thought, in a jungle of troubled notions.
As when a Dreamer, his dreams to nightmares turn, wakes of a sudden, paralyzed with fright, but finds relief and breathes with ease soon as his awareness adjusts to the friendly surroundings, so Scorto awakened from his deep comatic sleep, as the cold steel touched his sweating palm, bolted upright, petrified by the stern exhortation, though confident that all was but the fabrication of a troubled Psyche, but stiffened, and his throat with dryness strictured when instinctively he forward thrust his arm to verify his empty palm but eyed the Blade loosely cradled in his quivering fist.
s he to use the dagger to kill himself?
No.
Intuition wants him to deal with his appetite...
the "encrustations of desire."

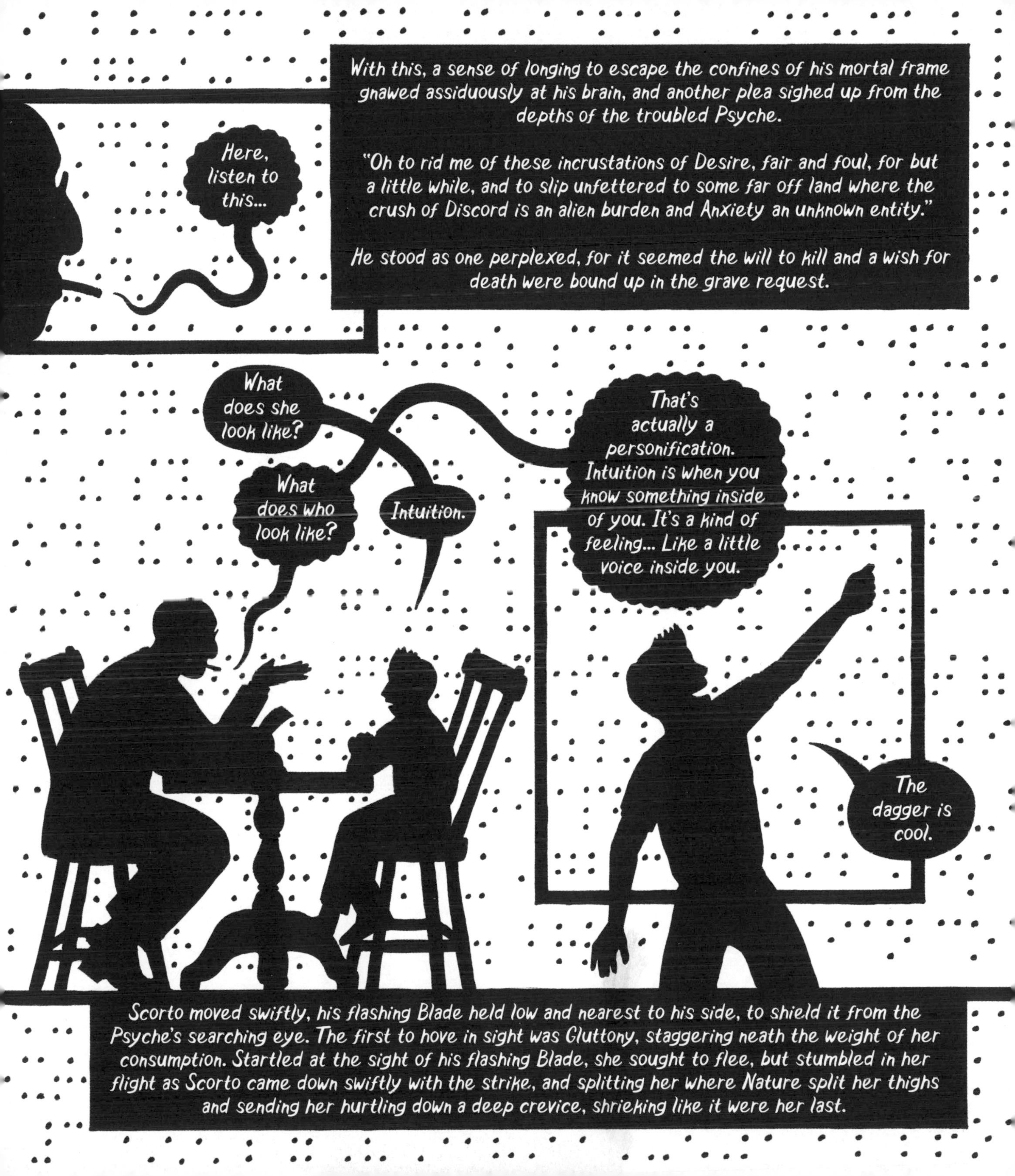
With this, a sense of longing to escape the confines of his mortal frame gnawed assiduously at his brain, and another plea sighed up from the depths of the troubled Psyche.
"Oh to rid me of these incrustations of Desire, fair and foul, for but a little while, and to slip unfettered to some far off land where the crush of Discord is an alien burden and Anxiety an unknown entity."
He stood as one perplexed, for it seemed the will to kill and a wish for death were bound up in the grave request.
Here, listen to this...
What does she look like?
What does who look like?
Intuition.
That's actually a personification. Intuition is when you know something inside of you. It's a kind of feeling... Like a little voice inside you.
The dagger is cool.
Scorto moved swiftly, his flashing Blade held low and nearest to his side, to shield it from the Psyche's searching eye. The first to hove in sight was Gluttony, staggering neath the weight of her consumption. Startled at the sight of his flashing Blade, she sought to flee, but stumbled in her flight as Scorto came down swiftly with the strike, and splitting her where Nature split her thighs and sending her hurtling down a deep crevice, shrieking like it were her last.

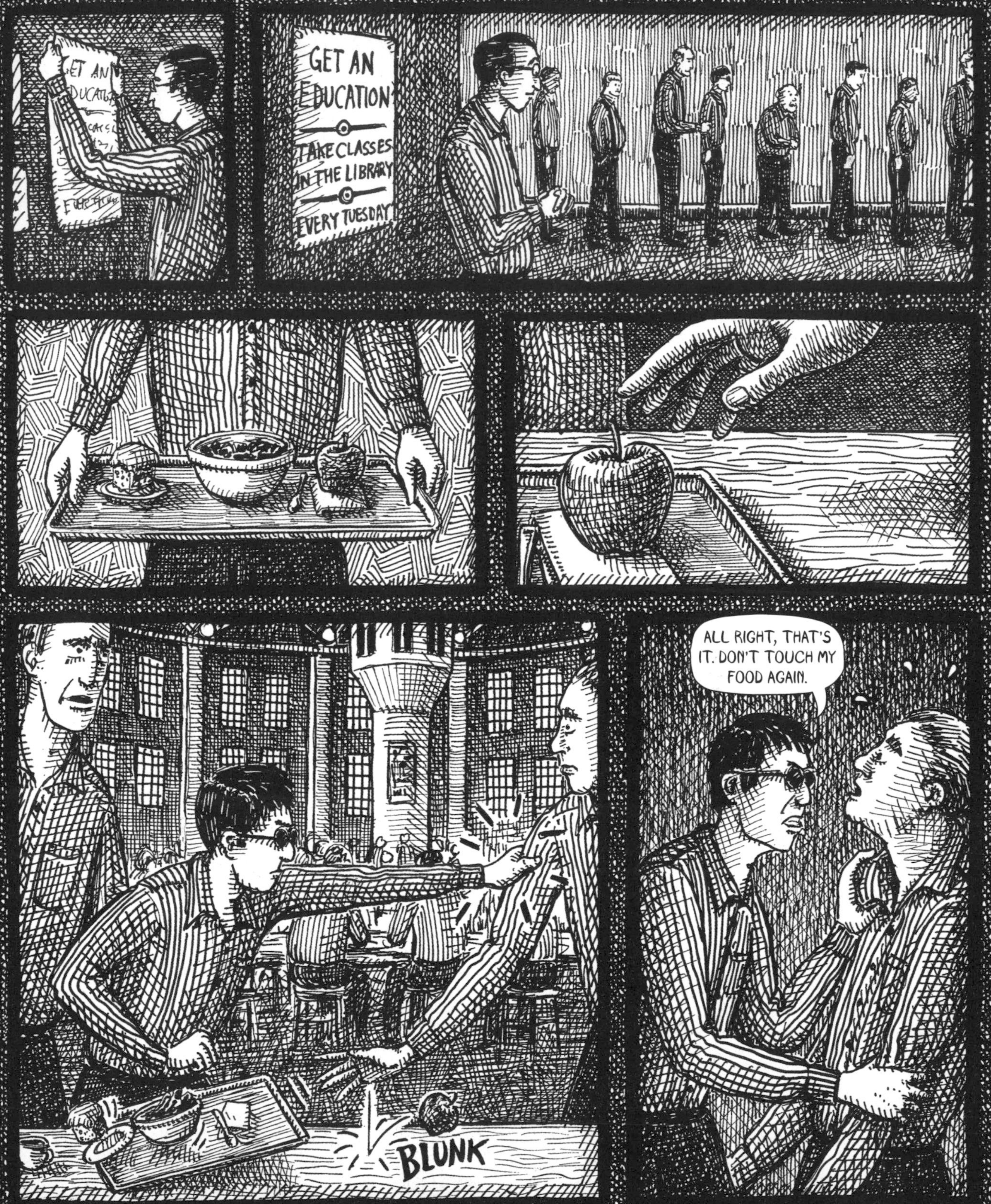
GET AN EDUCATION
TAKE CLASSES IN THE LIBRARY
EVERY TUESDAY
BLUNK
ALL RIGHT, THAT'S IT. DON'T TOUCH MY FOOD AGAIN.

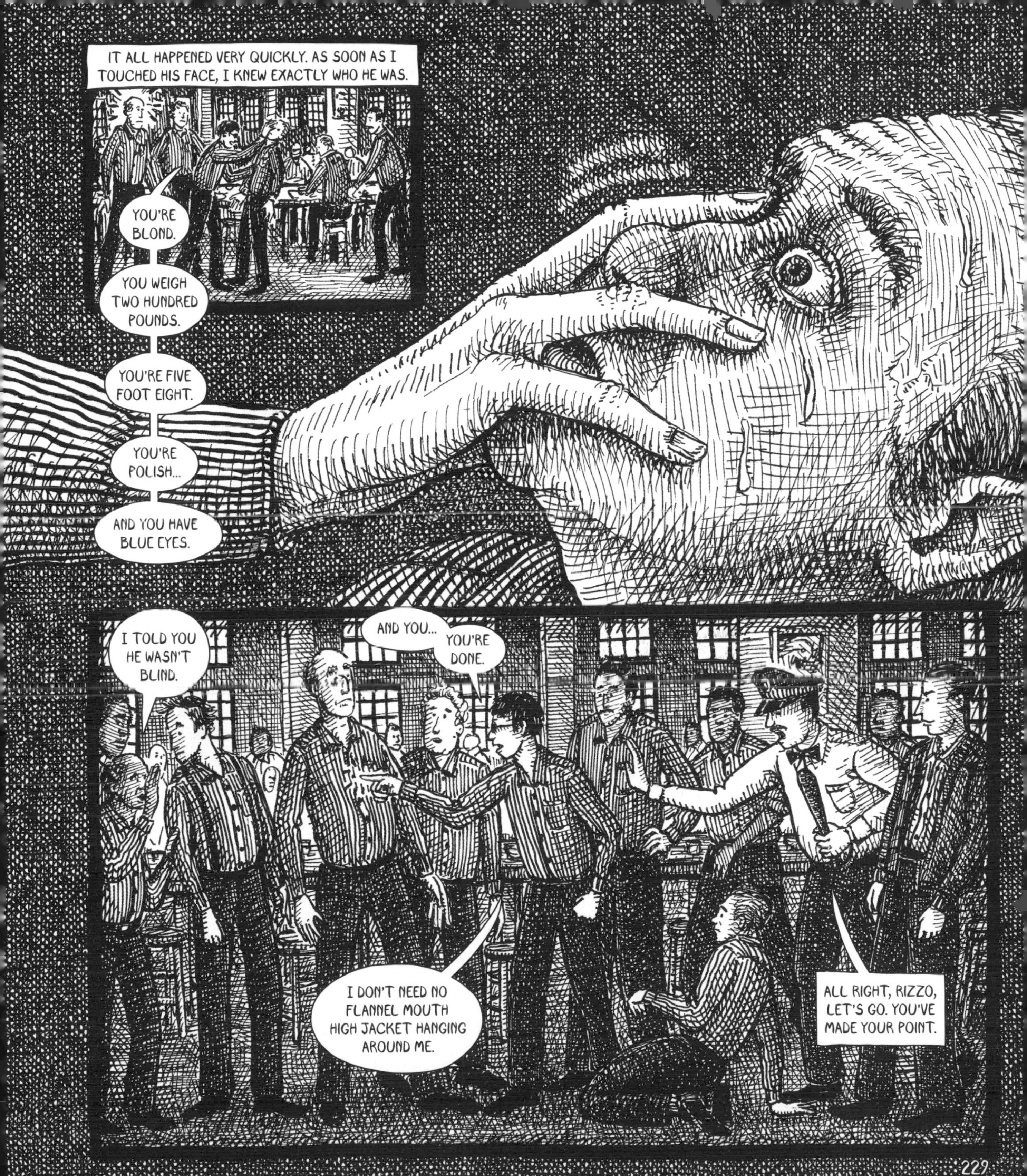
IT ALL HAPPENED VERY QUICKLY. AS SOON AS I TOUCHED HIS FACE, I KNEW EXACTLY WHO HE WAS.
YOU'RE BLOND.
YOU WEIGH TWO HUNDRED POUNDS.
YOU'RE FIVE FOOT EIGHT.
YOU'RE POLISH...
AND YOU HAVE BLUE EYES.
I TOLD YOU HE WASN'T BLIND.
AND YOU...
YOU'RE DONE.
I DON'T NEED NO FLANNEL MOUTH HIGH JACKET HANGING AROUND ME.
ALL RIGHT, RIZZO, LET'S GO. YOU'VE MADE YOUR POINT.

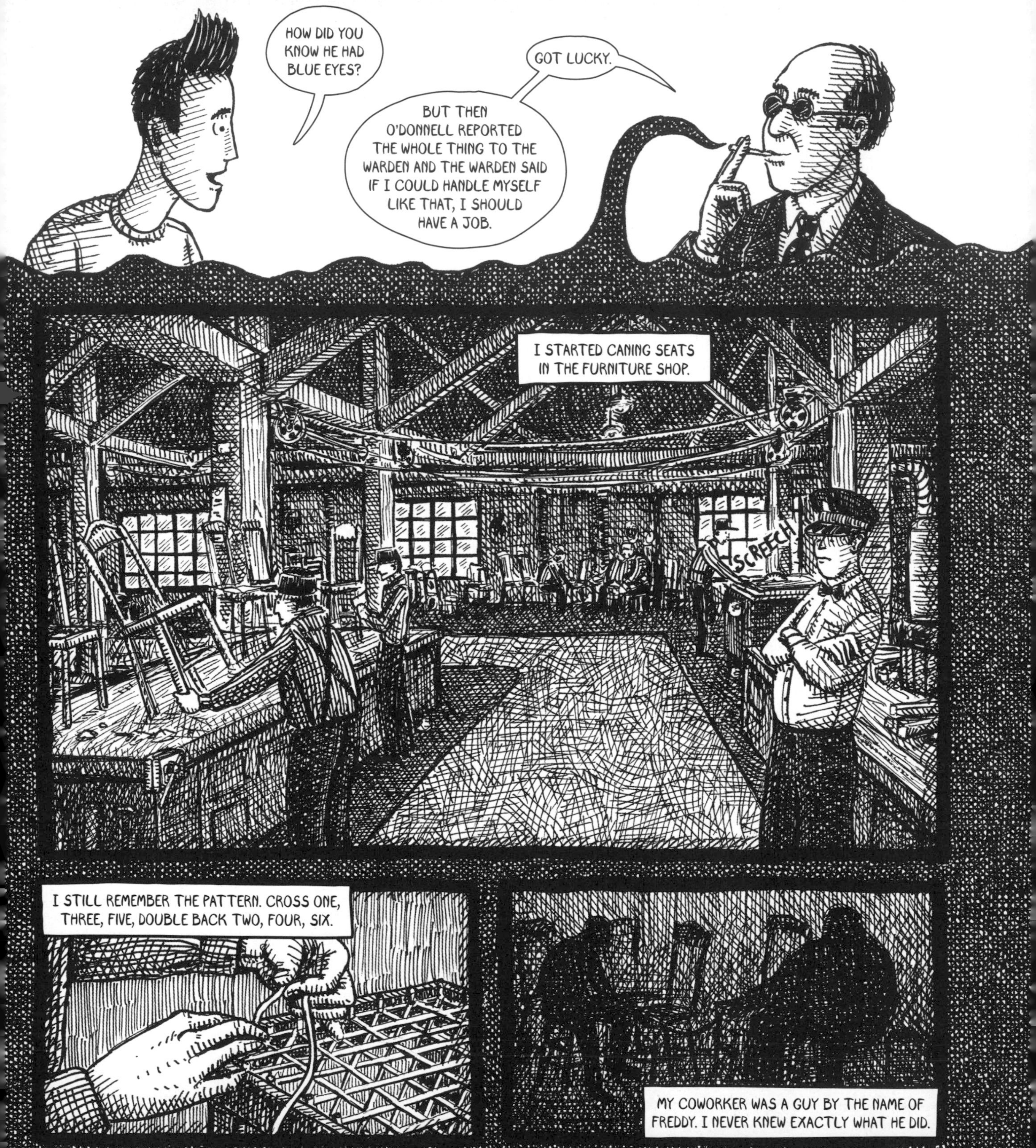
HOW DID YOU KNOW HE HAD BLUE EYES?
GOT LUCKY.
BUT THEN O'DONNELL REPORTED THE WHOLE THING TO THE WARDEN AND THE WARDEN SAID IF I COULD HANDLE MYSELF LIKE THAT, I SHOULD HAVE A JOB.
I STARTED CANING SEATS IN THE FURNITURE SHOP.
SCREECH
I STILL REMEMBER THE PATTERN. CROSS ONE, THREE, FIVE, DOUBLE BACK TWO, FOUR, SIX.
MY COWORKER WAS A GUY BY THE NAME OF FREDDY. I NEVER KNEW EXACTLY WHAT HE DID.

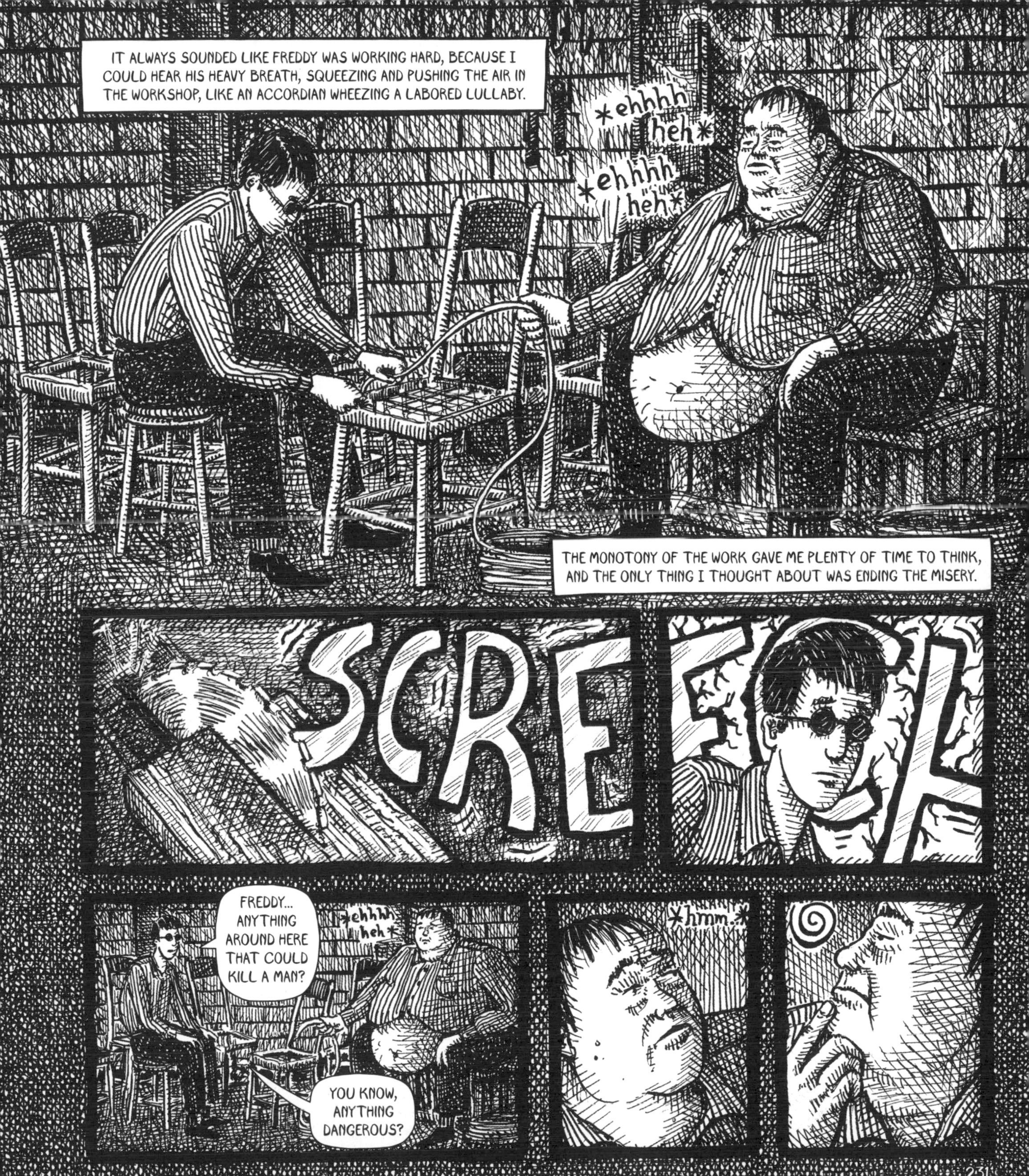
IT ALWAYS SOUNDED LIKE FREDDY WAS WORKING HARD, BECAUSE I COULD HEAR HIS HEAVY BREATH, SQUEEZING AND PUSHING THE AIR IN THE WORKSHOP, LIKE AN ACCORDIAN WHEEZING A LABORED LULLABY.
ehhhh heh
ehhhh heh
THE MONOTONY OF THE WORK GAVE ME PLENTY OF TIME TO THINK, AND THE ONLY THING I THOUGHT ABOUT WAS ENDING THE MISERY.
SCREECH
FREDDY... ANYTHING AROUND HERE THAT COULD KILL A MAN?
ehhhh heh
YOU KNOW, ANYTHING DANGEROUS?
hmm

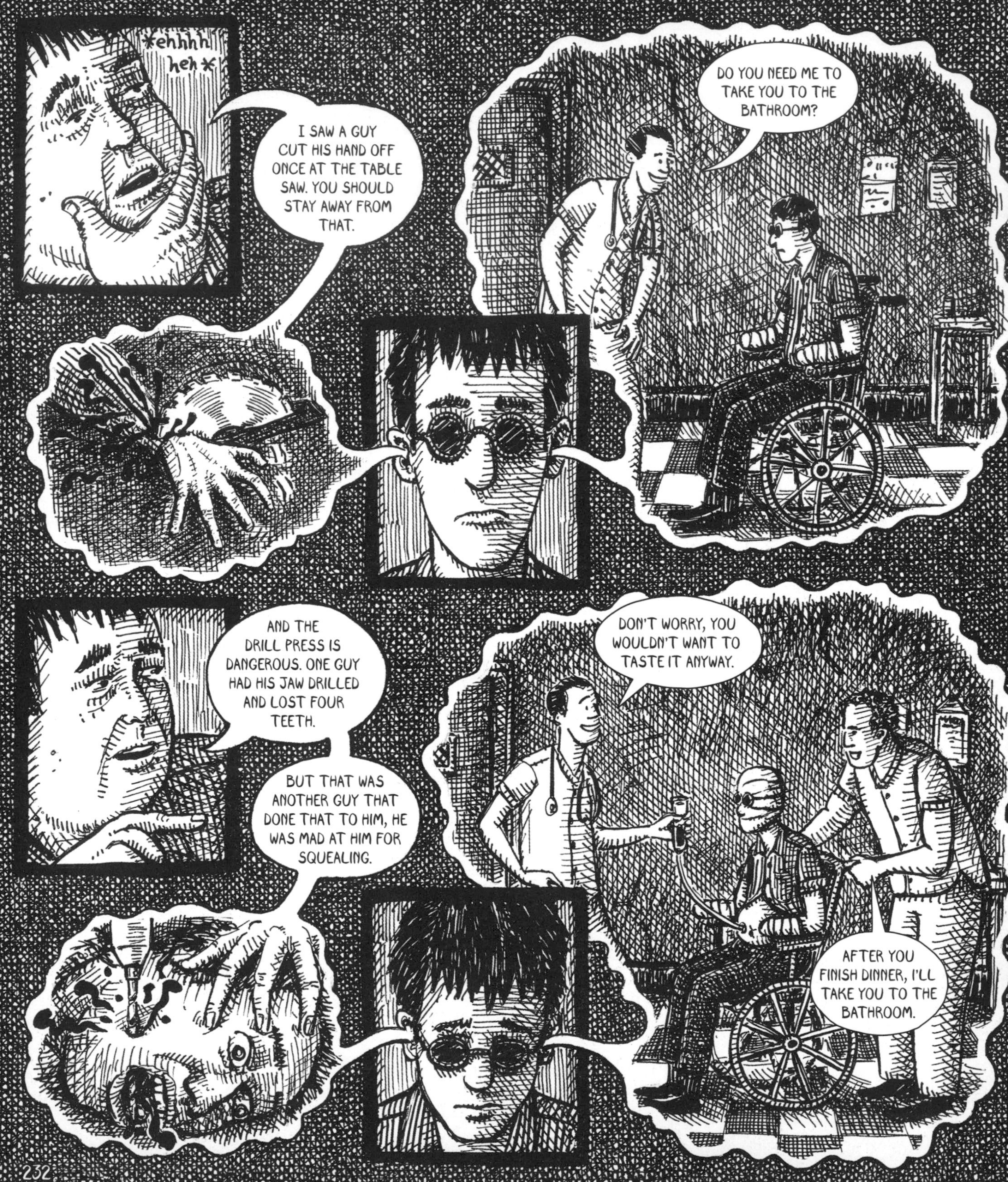
ehhhh heh
I SAW A GUY CUT HIS HAND OFF ONCE AT THE TABLE SAW. YOU SHOULD STAY AWAY FROM THAT.
DO YOU NEED ME TO TAKE YOU TO THE BATHROOM?
AND THE DRILL PRESS IS DANGEROUS. ONE GUY HAD HIS JAW DRILLED AND LOST FOUR TEETH.
BUT THAT WAS ANOTHER GUY THAT DONE THAT TO HIM, HE WAS MAD AT HIM FOR SQUEALING.
DON'T WORRY, YOU WOULDN'T WANT TO TASTE IT ANYWAY.
AFTER YOU FINISH DINNER, I'LL TAKE YOU TO THE BATHROOM.

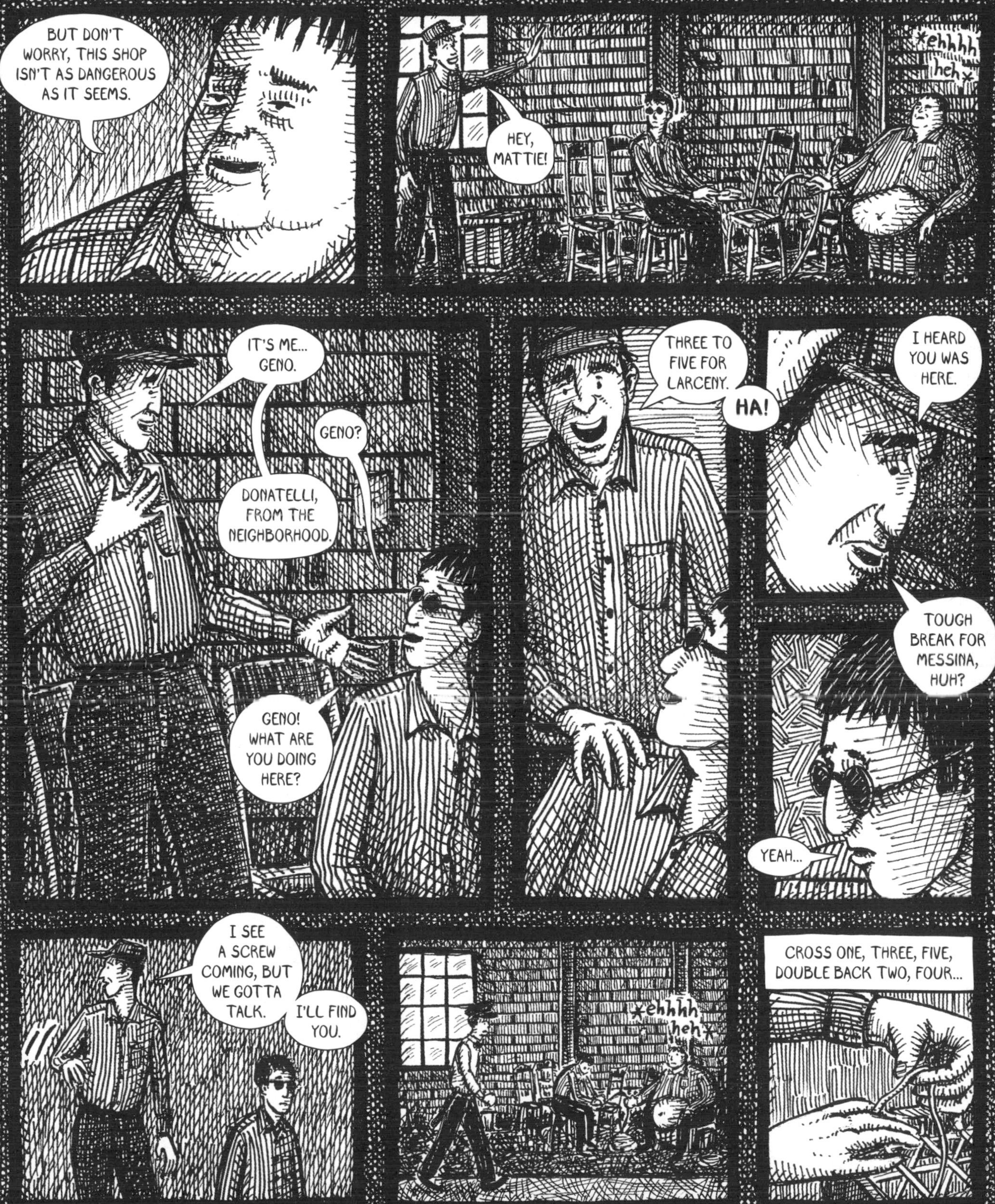
BUT DON'T WORRY, THIS SHOP ISN'T AS DANGEROUS AS IT SEEMS.
HEY, MATTIE!
ehhhh heh
IT'S ME... GENO.
GENO?
DONATELLI, FROM THE NEIGHBORHOOD.
GENO! WHAT ARE YOU DOING HERE?
THREE TO FIVE FOR LARCENY.
HA!
I HEARD YOU WAS HERE.
TOUGH BREAK FOR MESSINA, HUH?
YEAH...
I SEE A SCREW COMING, BUT WE GOTTA TALK.
I'LL FIND YOU.
ehhhh heh
CROSS ONE, THREE, FIVE, DOUBLE BACK TWO, FOUR...

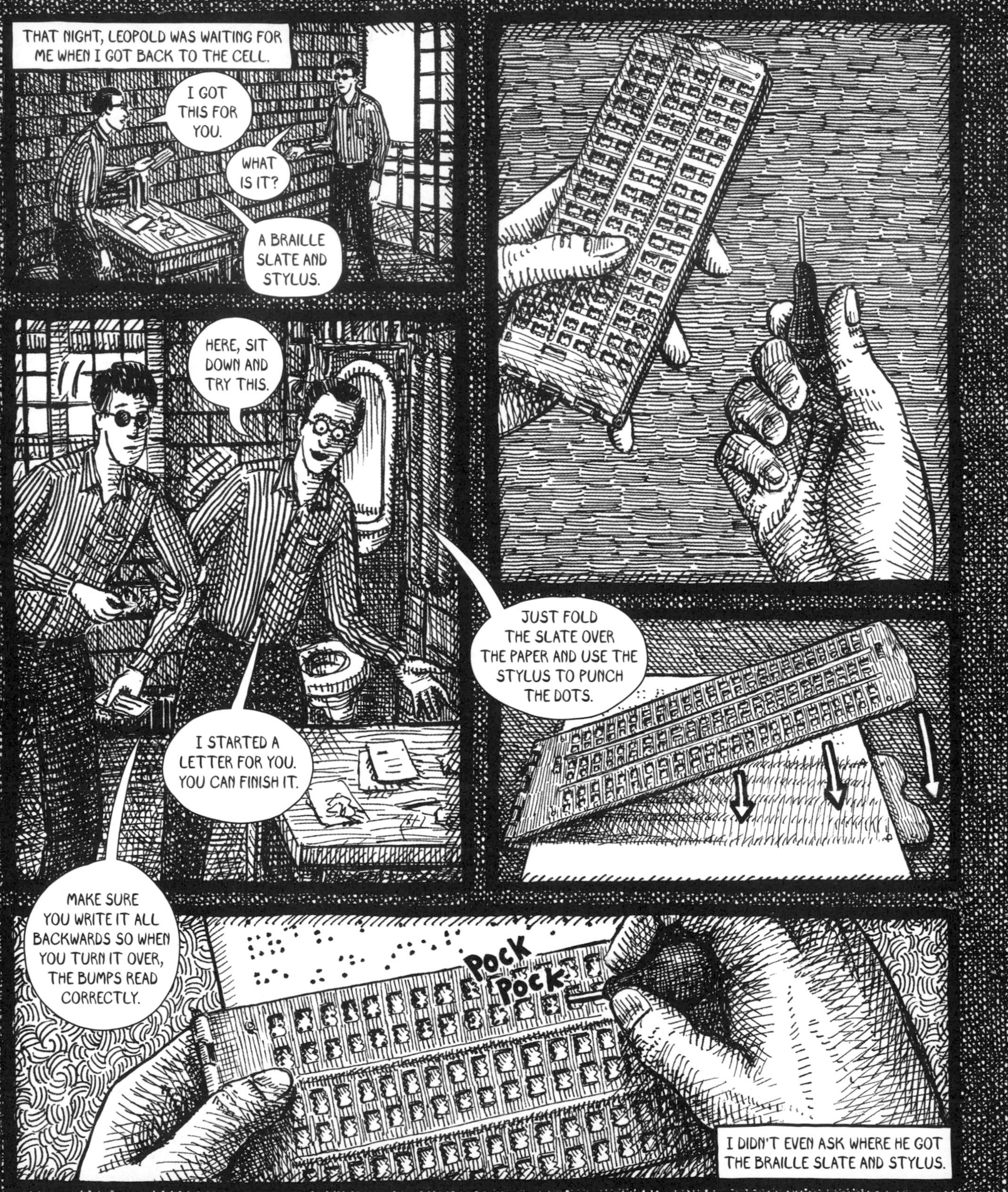
THAT NIGHT, LEOPOLD WAS WAITING FOR ME WHEN I GOT BACK TO THE CELL.
I GOT THIS FOR YOU.
WHAT IS IT?
A BRAILLE SLATE AND STYLUS.
HERE, SIT DOWN AND TRY THIS.
I STARTED A LETTER FOR YOU. YOU CAN FINISH IT.
JUST FOLD THE SLATE OVER THE PAPER AND USE THE STYLUS TO PUNCH THE DOTS.
MAKE SURE YOU WRITE IT ALL BACKWARDS SO WHEN YOU TURN IT OVER, THE BUMPS READ CORRECTLY.
POCK
POCK
I DIDN'T EVEN ASK WHERE HE GOT THE BRAILLE SLATE AND STYLUS.

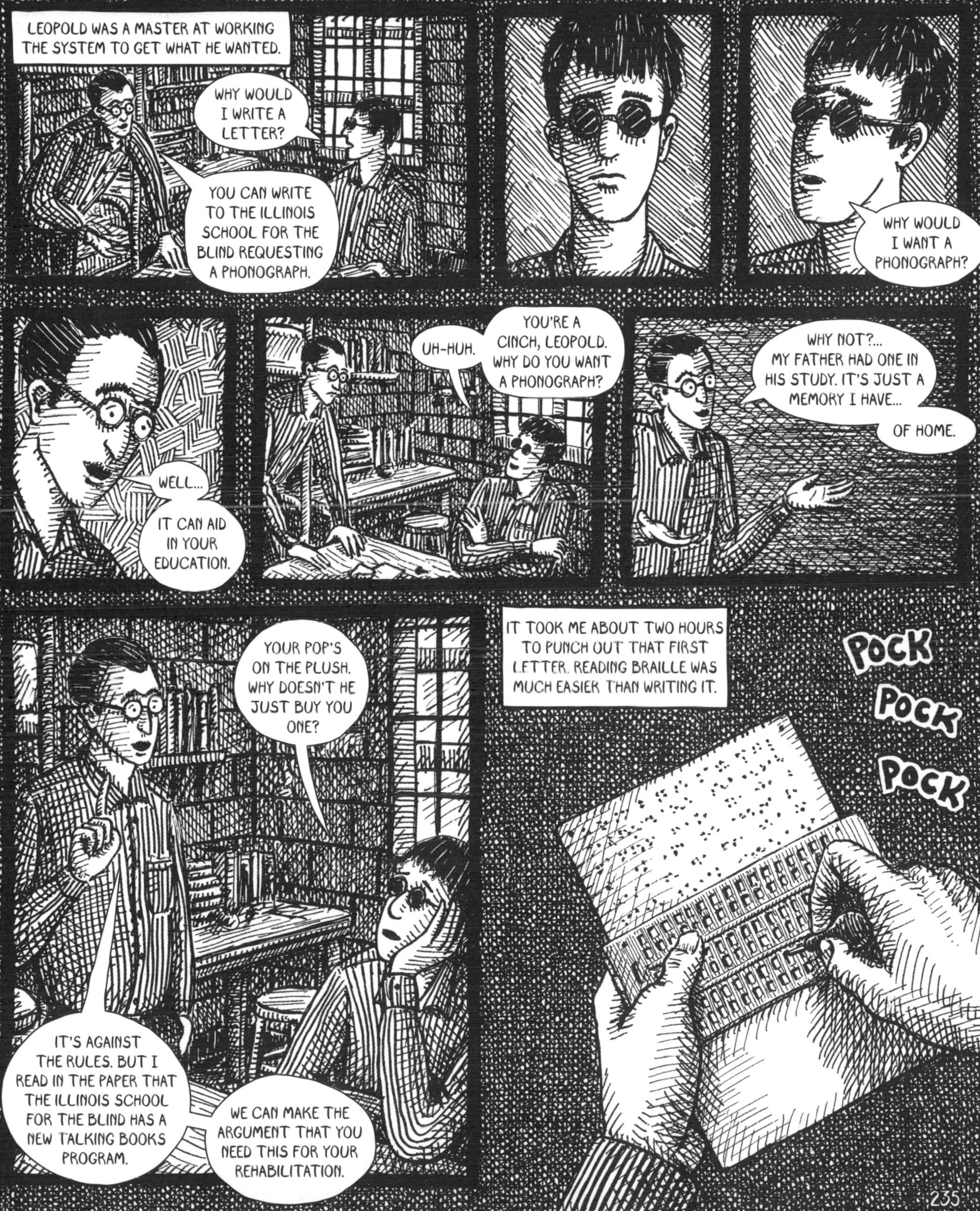
LEOPOLD WAS A MASTER AT WORKING THE SYSTEM TO GET WHAT HE WANTED.
WHY WOULD I WRITE A LETTER?
YOU CAN WRITE TO THE ILLINOIS SCHOOL FOR THE BLIND REQUESTING A PHONOGRAPH.
WHY WOULD I WANT A PHONOGRAPH?
WELL...
IT CAN AID IN YOUR EDUCATION.
UH-HUH.
YOU'RE A CINCH, LEOPOLD. WHY DO YOU WANT A PHONOGRAPH?
WHY NOT?... MY FATHER HAD ONE IN HIS STUDY. IT'S JUST A MEMORY I HAVE...
OF HOME.
YOUR POP'S ON THE PLUSH. WHY DOESN'T HE JUST BUY YOU ONE?
IT'S AGAINST THE RULES. BUT I READ IN THE PAPER THAT THE ILLINOIS SCHOOL FOR THE BLIND HAS A NEW TALKING BOOKS PROGRAM.
WE CAN MAKE THE ARGUMENT THAT YOU NEED THIS FOR YOUR REHABILITATION.
IT TOOK ME ABOUT TWO HOURS TO PUNCH OUT THAT FIRST LETTER. READING BRAILLE WAS MUCH EASIER THAN WRITING IT.
POCK
POCK
POCK

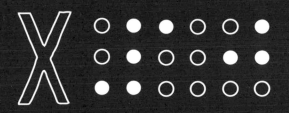

X

THE ÜBERMENSCH

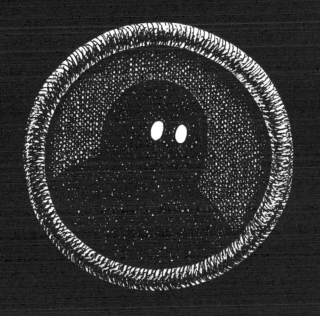

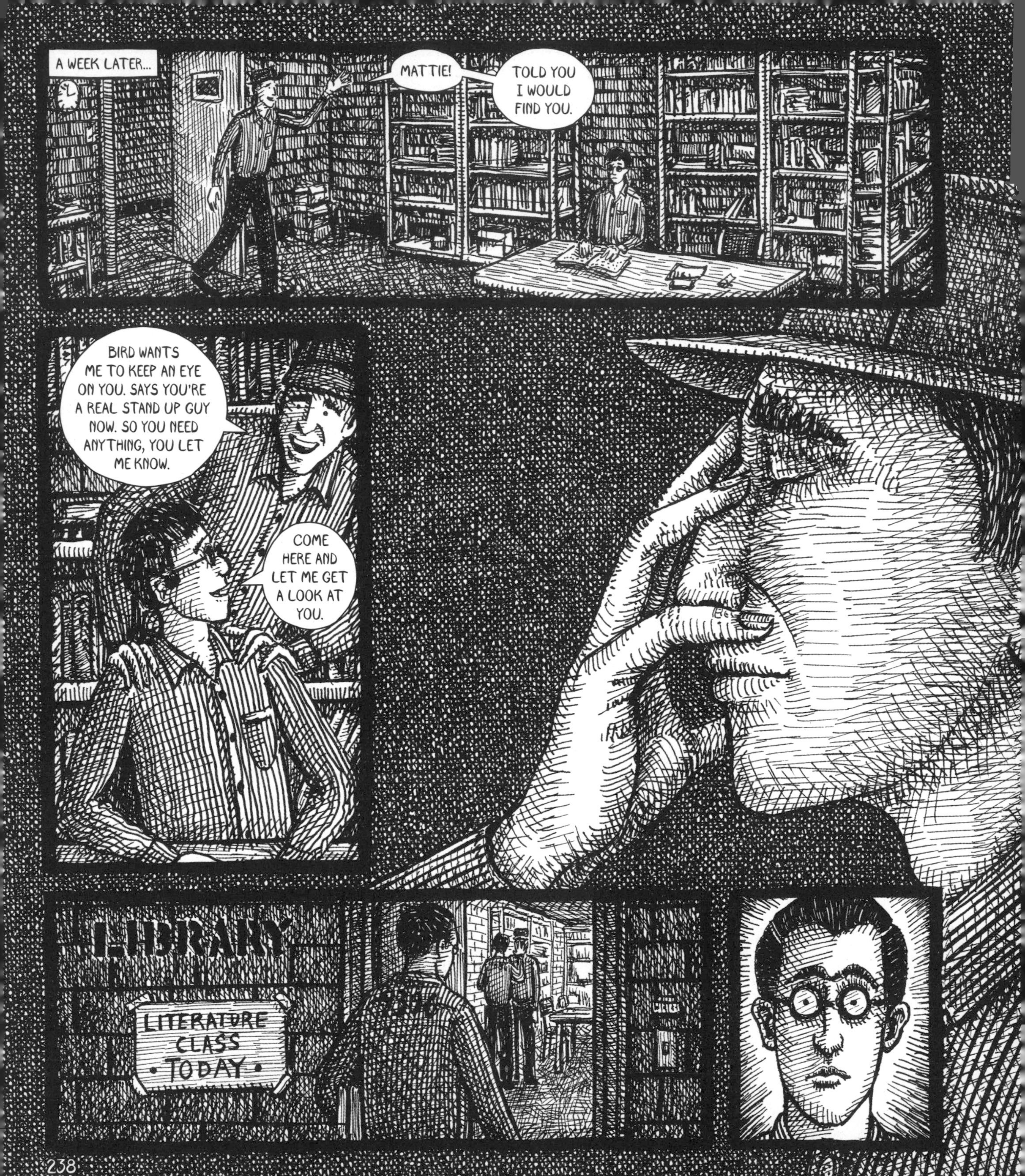
A WEEK LATER...
MATTIE!
TOLD YOU I WOULD FIND YOU.
BIRD WANTS ME TO KEEP AN EYE ON YOU. SAYS YOU'RE A REAL STAND UP GUY NOW. SO YOU NEED ANYTHING, YOU LET ME KNOW.
COME HERE AND LET ME GET A LOOK AT YOU.
LIBRARY
LITERATURE CLASS TODAY

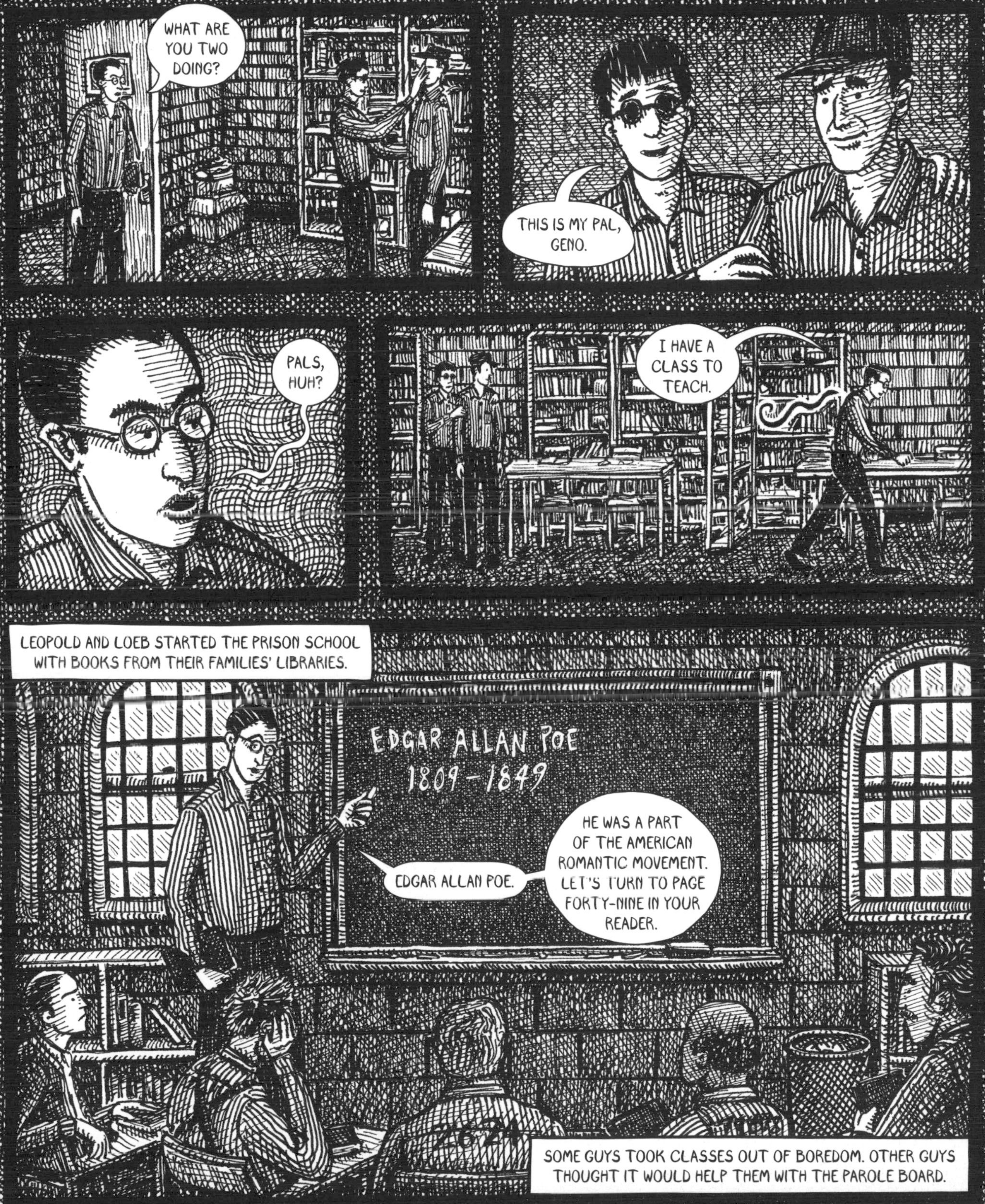
WHAT ARE YOU TWO DOING?
THIS IS MY PAL, GENO.
PALS, HUH?
I HAVE A CLASS TO TEACH.
LEOPOLD AND LOEB STARTED THE PRISON SCHOOL WITH BOOKS FROM THEIR FAMILIES' LIBRARIES.
EDGAR ALLAN POE
1809–1849
EDGAR ALLAN POE.
HE WAS A PART OF THE AMERICAN ROMANTIC MOVEMENT. LET'S TURN TO PAGE FORTY-NINE IN YOUR READER.
SOME GUYS TOOK CLASSES OUT OF BOREDOM. OTHER GUYS THOUGHT IT WOULD HELP THEM WITH THE PAROLE BOARD.

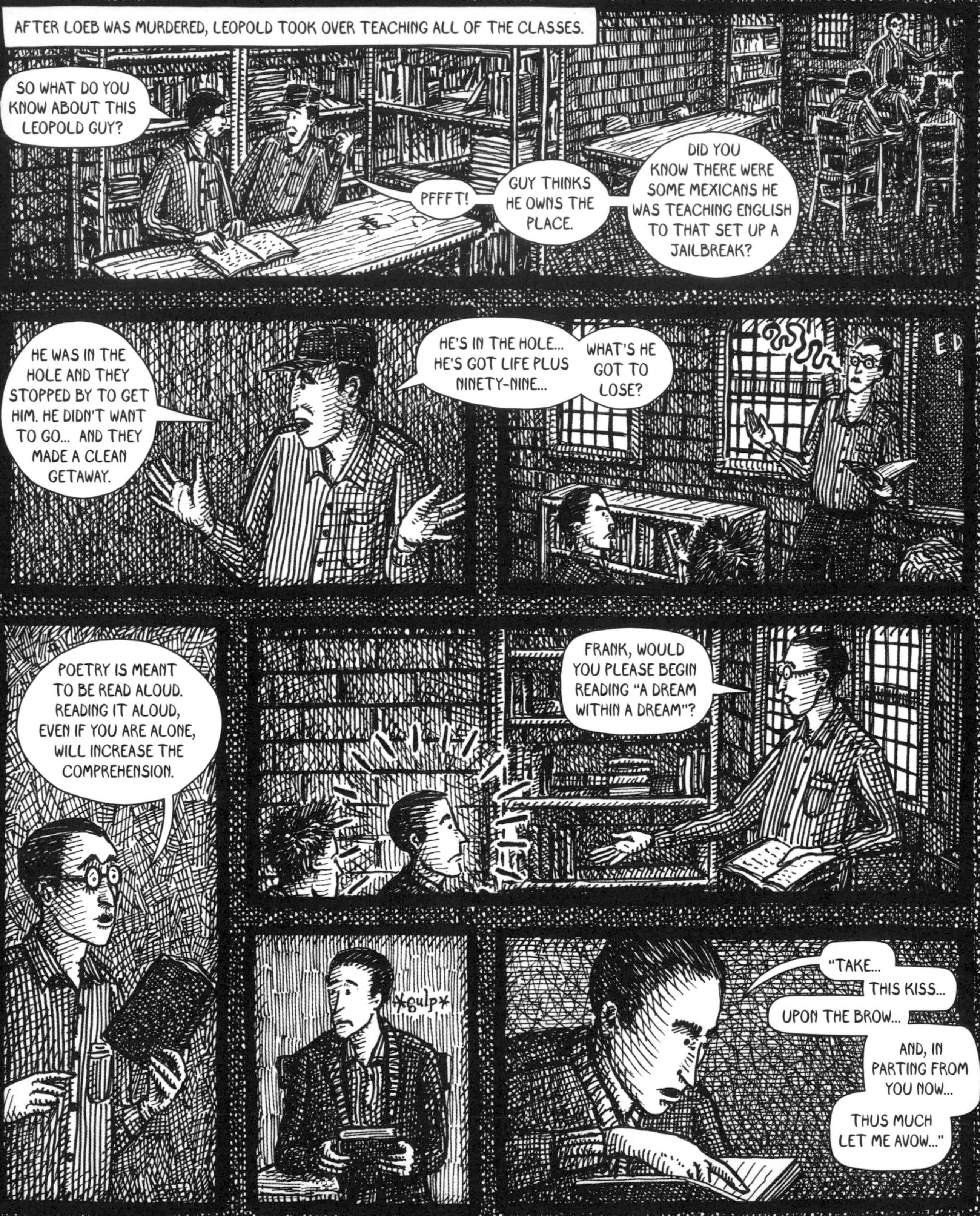
AFTER LOEB WAS MURDERED, LEOPOLD TOOK OVER TEACHING ALL OF THE CLASSES.
SO WHAT DO YOU KNOW ABOUT THIS LEOPOLD GUY?
PFFFT!
GUY THINKS HE OWNS THE PLACE.
DID YOU KNOW THERE WERE SOME MEXICANS HE WAS TEACHING ENGLISH TO THAT SET UP A JAILBREAK?
HE WAS IN THE HOLE AND THEY STOPPED BY TO GET HIM. HE DIDN'T WANT TO GO... AND THEY MADE A CLEAN GETAWAY.
HE'S IN THE HOLE... HE'S GOT LIFE PLUS NINETY-NINE...
WHAT'S HE GOT TO LOSE?
POETRY IS MEANT TO BE READ ALOUD. READING IT ALOUD, EVEN IF YOU ARE ALONE, WILL INCREASE THE COMPREHENSION.
FRANK, WOULD YOU PLEASE BEGIN READING "A DREAM WITHIN A DREAM"?
gulp
"TAKE...
THIS KISS...
UPON THE BROW...
AND, IN PARTING FROM YOU NOW...
THUS MUCH LET ME AVOW..."

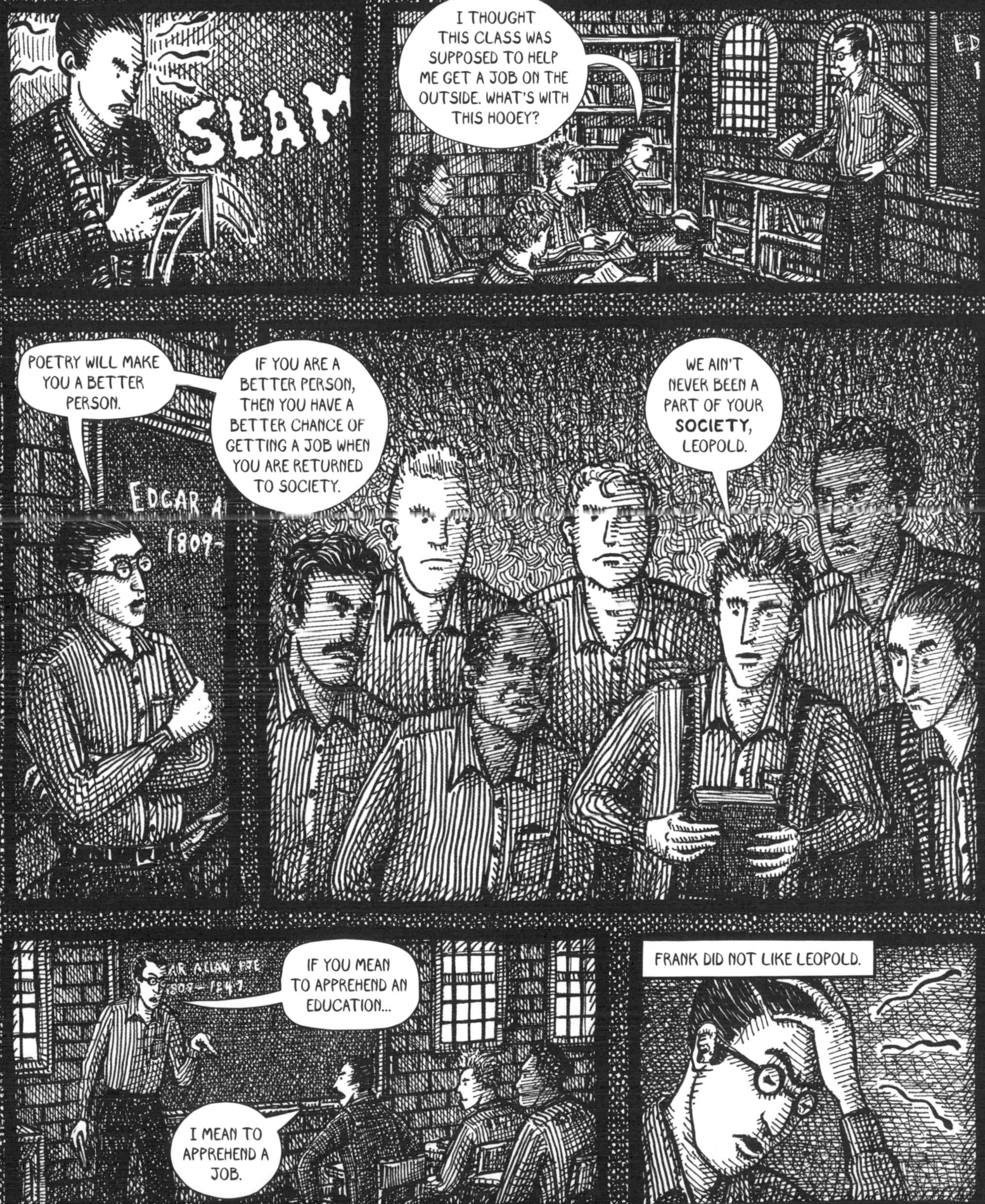

SLAM
I THOUGHT THIS CLASS WAS SUPPOSED TO HELP ME GET A JOB ON THE OUTSIDE. WHAT'S WITH THIS HOOEY?
POETRY WILL MAKE YOU A BETTER PERSON.
IF YOU ARE A BETTER PERSON, THEN YOU HAVE A BETTER CHANCE OF GETTING A JOB WHEN YOU ARE RETURNED TO SOCIETY.
WE AIN'T NEVER BEEN A PART OF YOUR **SOCIETY**, LEOPOLD.
IF YOU MEAN TO APPREHEND AN EDUCATION...
I MEAN TO APPREHEND A JOB.
FRANK DID NOT LIKE LEOPOLD.

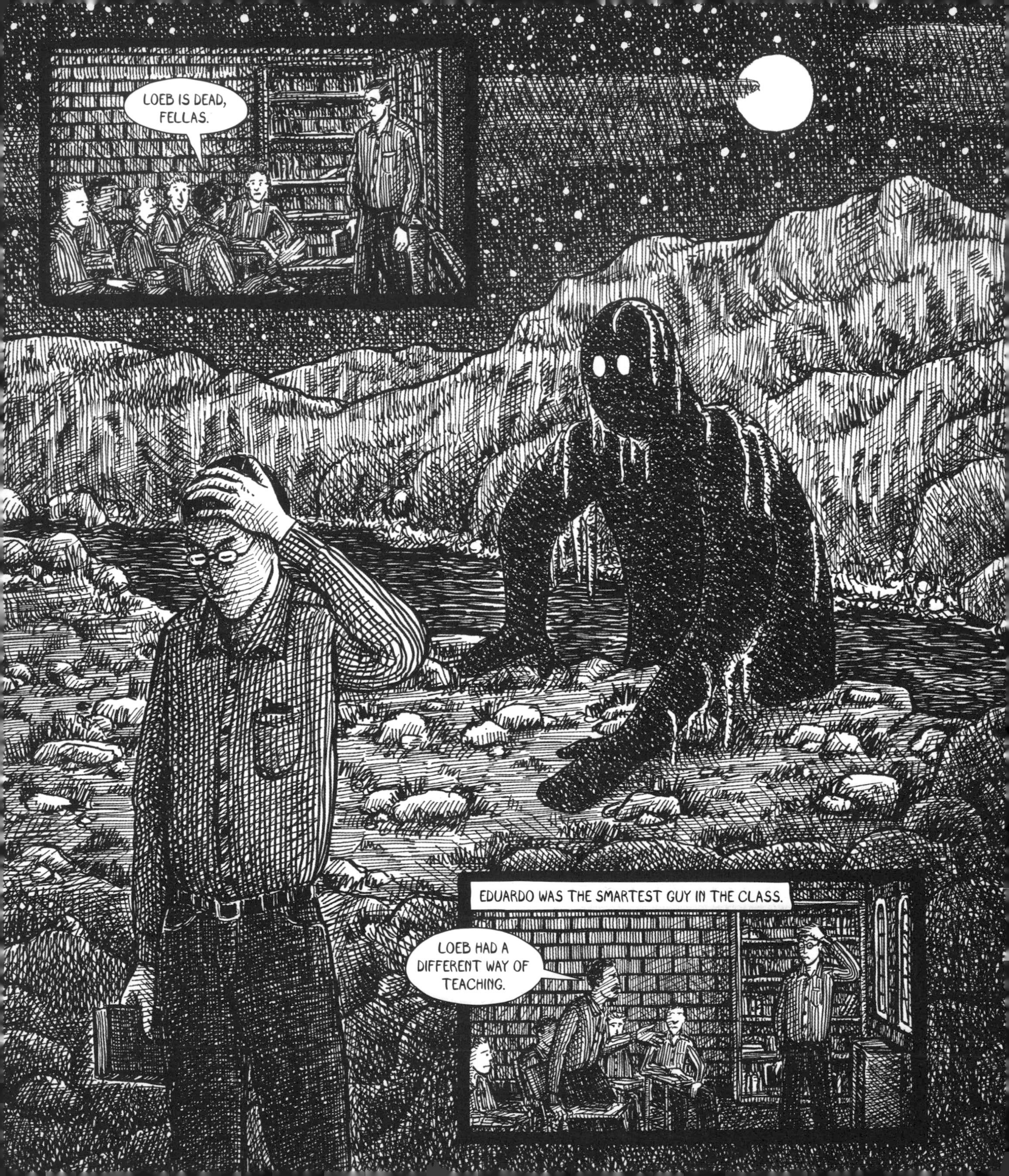
LOEB IS DEAD, FELLAS.
EDUARDO WAS THE SMARTEST GUY IN THE CLASS.
LOEB HAD A DIFFERENT WAY OF TEACHING.

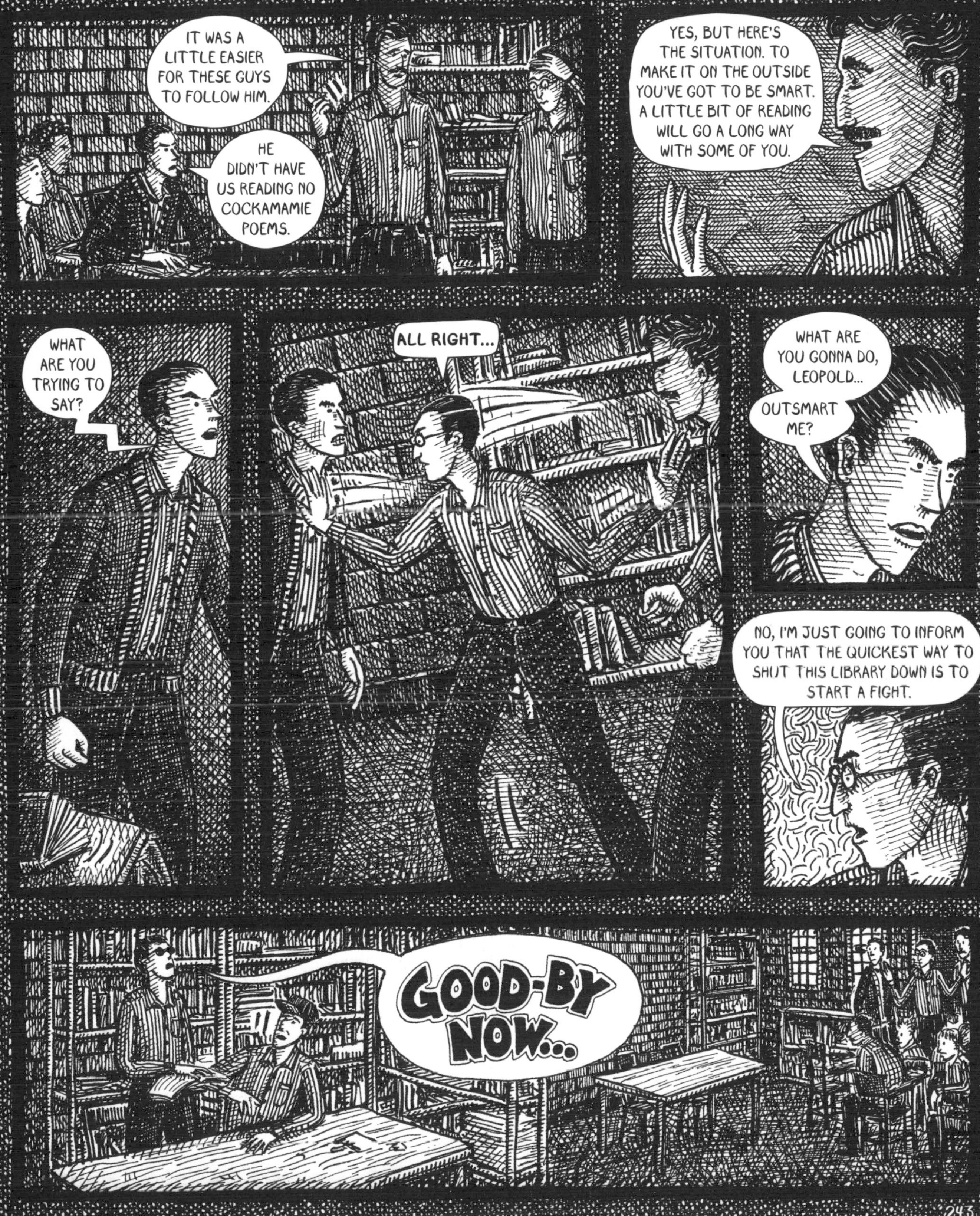
IT WAS A LITTLE EASIER FOR THESE GUYS TO FOLLOW HIM.
HE DIDN'T HAVE US READING NO COCKAMAMIE POEMS.
YES, BUT HERE'S THE SITUATION. TO MAKE IT ON THE OUTSIDE YOU'VE GOT TO BE SMART. A LITTLE BIT OF READING WILL GO A LONG WAY WITH SOME OF YOU.
WHAT ARE YOU TRYING TO SAY?
ALL RIGHT...
WHAT ARE YOU GONNA DO, LEOPOLD...
OUTSMART ME?
NO, I'M JUST GOING TO INFORM YOU THAT THE QUICKEST WAY TO SHUT THIS LIBRARY DOWN IS TO START A FIGHT.
GOOD-BY NOW...

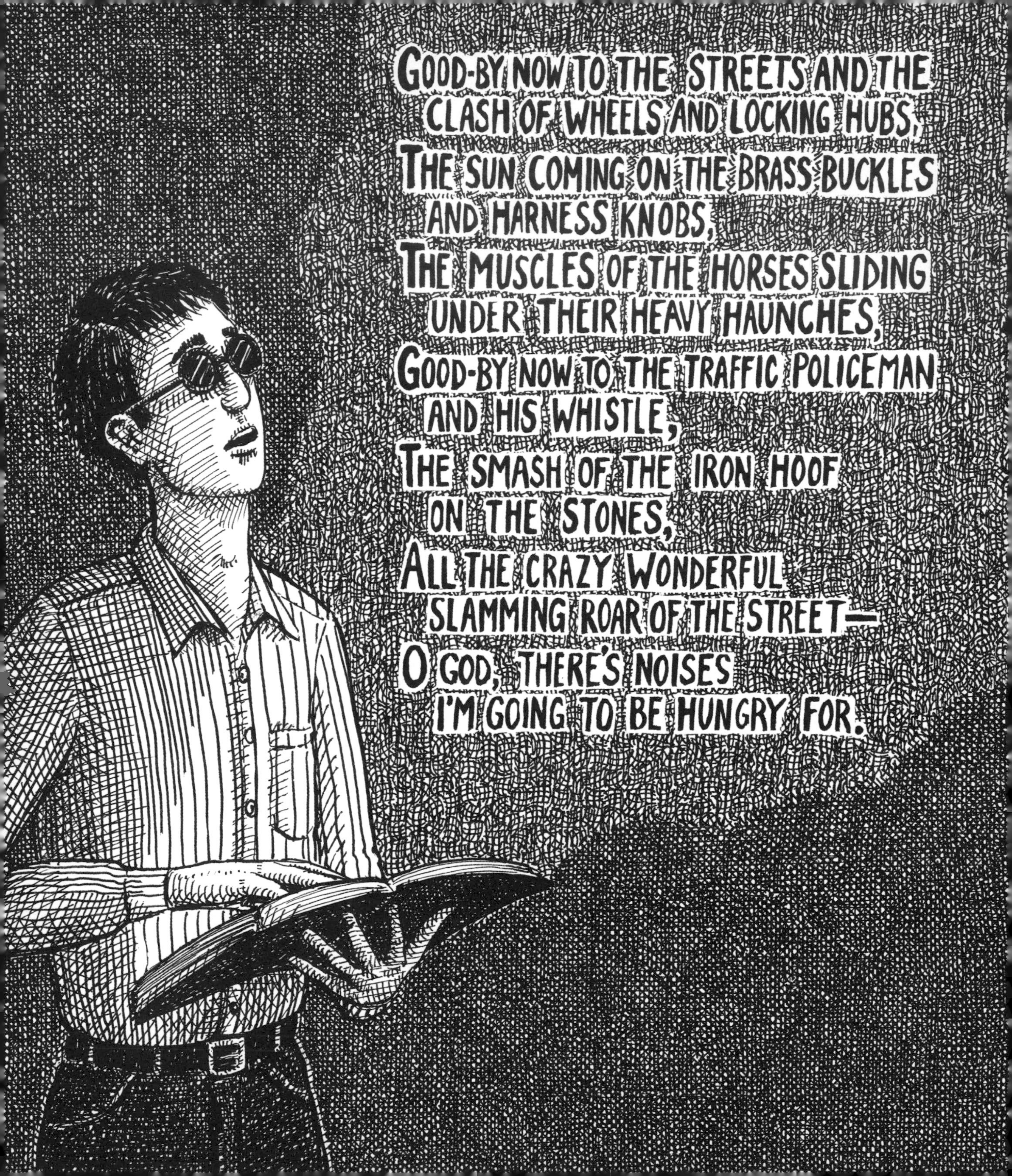
GOOD-BY NOW TO THE STREETS AND THE CLASH OF WHEELS AND LOCKING HUBS,
THE SUN COMING ON THE BRASS BUCKLES AND HARNESS KNOBS,
THE MUSCLES OF THE HORSES SLIDING UNDER THEIR HEAVY HAUNCHES,
GOOD-BY NOW TO THE TRAFFIC POLICEMAN AND HIS WHISTLE,
THE SMASH OF THE IRON HOOF ON THE STONES,
ALL THE CRAZY WONDERFUL SLAMMING ROAR OF THE STREET—
O GOD, THERE'S NOISES I'M GOING TO BE HUNGRY FOR.

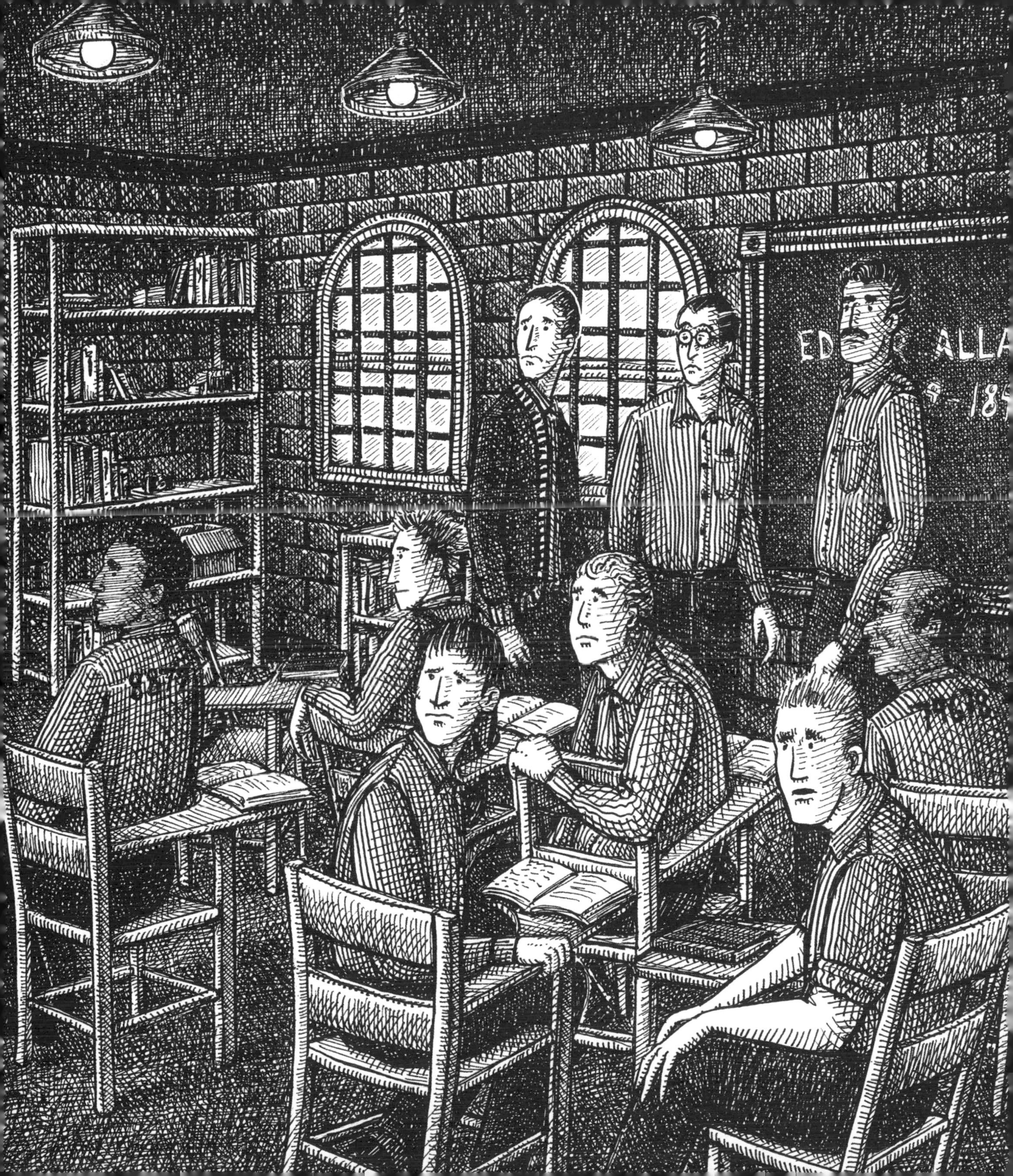

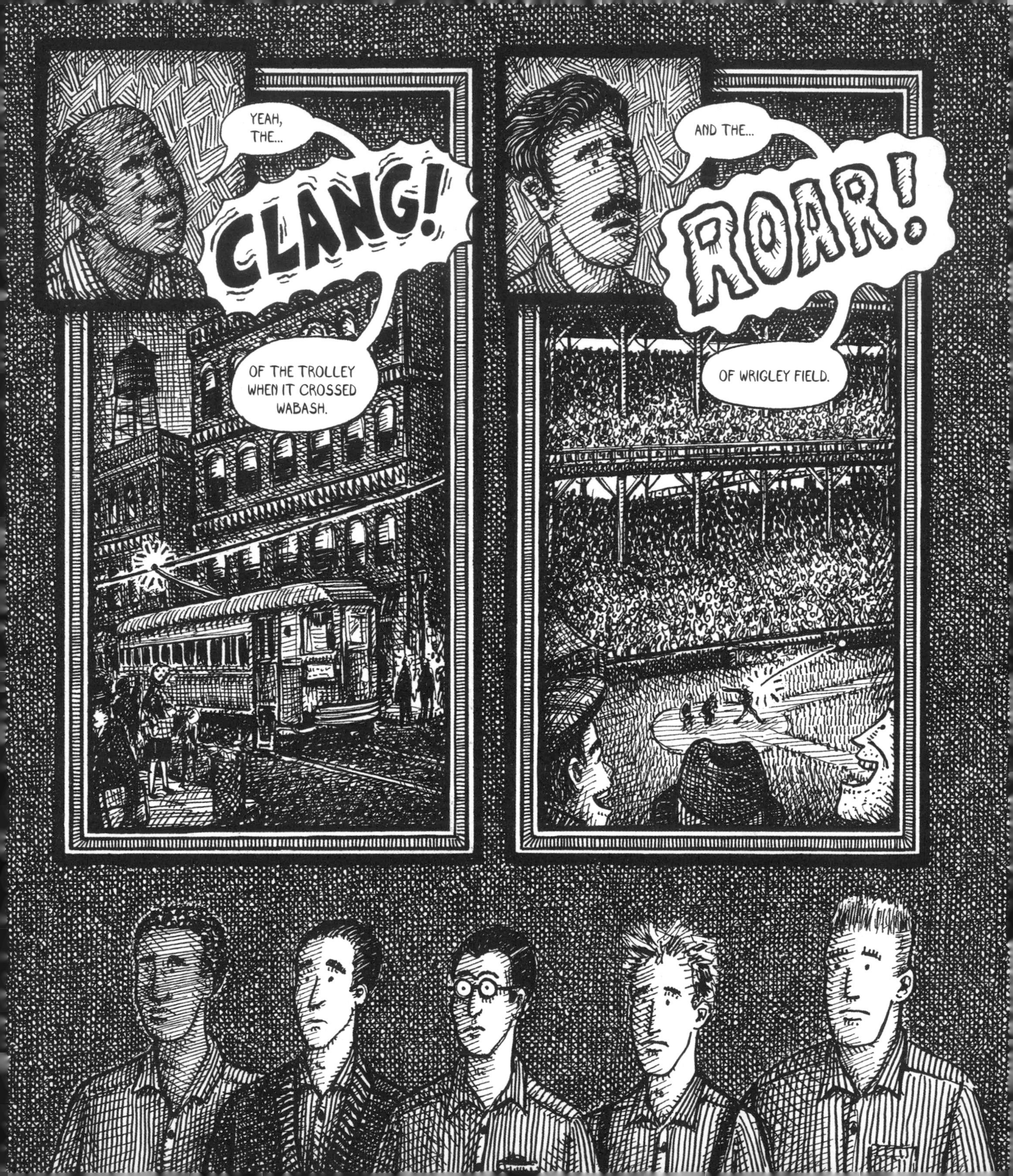
YEAH, THE...
CLANG!
OF THE TROLLEY WHEN IT CROSSED WABASH.
AND THE...
ROAR!
OF WRIGLEY FIELD.

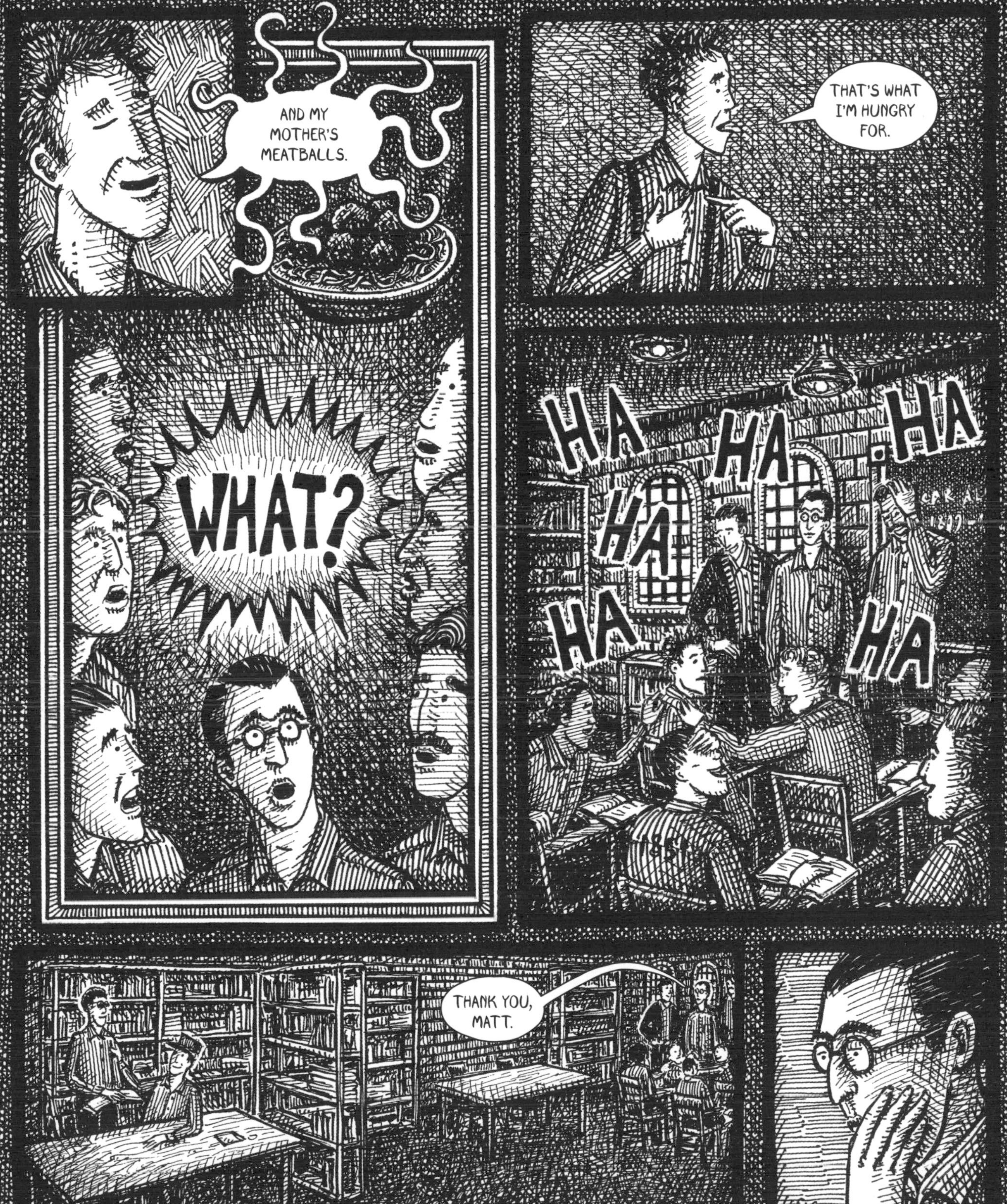
AND MY MOTHER'S MEATBALLS.
THAT'S WHAT I'M HUNGRY FOR.
WHAT?
HA HA HA HA HA HA
THANK YOU, MATT.

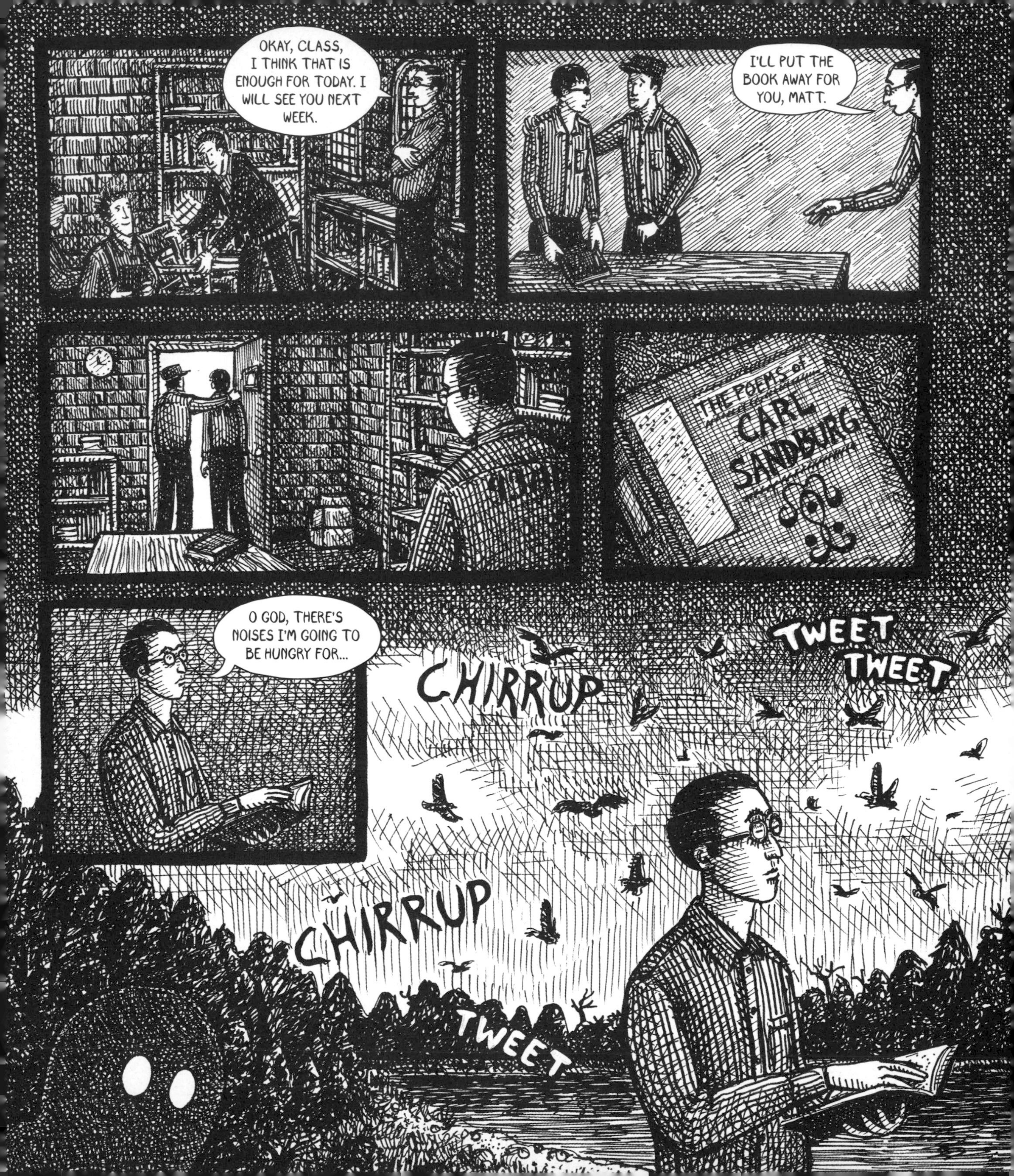
OKAY, CLASS, I THINK THAT IS ENOUGH FOR TODAY. I WILL SEE YOU NEXT WEEK.
I'LL PUT THE BOOK AWAY FOR YOU, MATT.
THE POEMS of CARL SANDBURG
O GOD, THERE'S NOISES I'M GOING TO BE HUNGRY FOR...
CHIRRUP
TWEET TWEET
CHIRRUP
TWEET

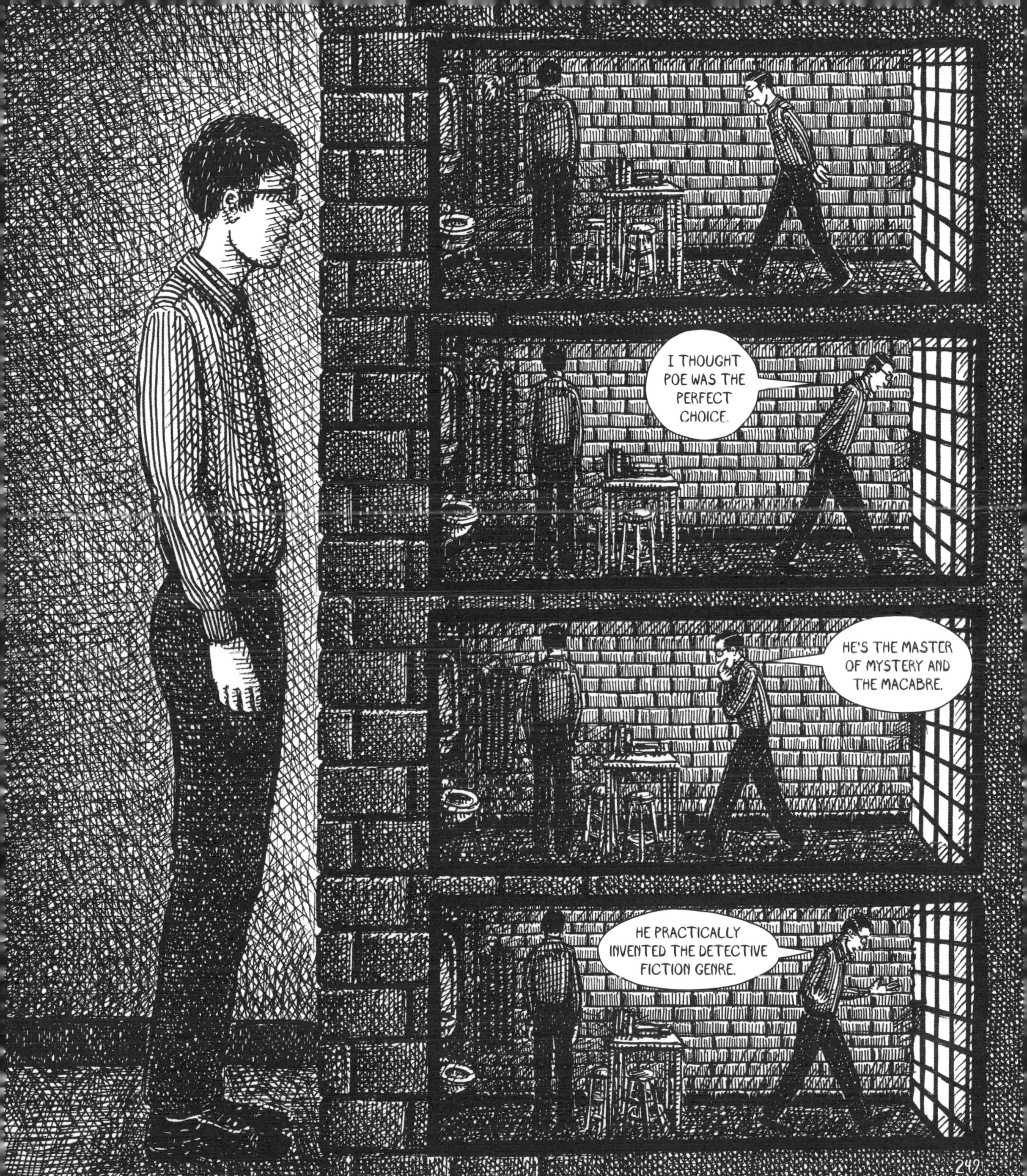
I THOUGHT POE WAS THE PERFECT CHOICE.
HE'S THE MASTER OF MYSTERY AND THE MACABRE.
HE PRACTICALLY INVENTED THE DETECTIVE FICTION GENRE.

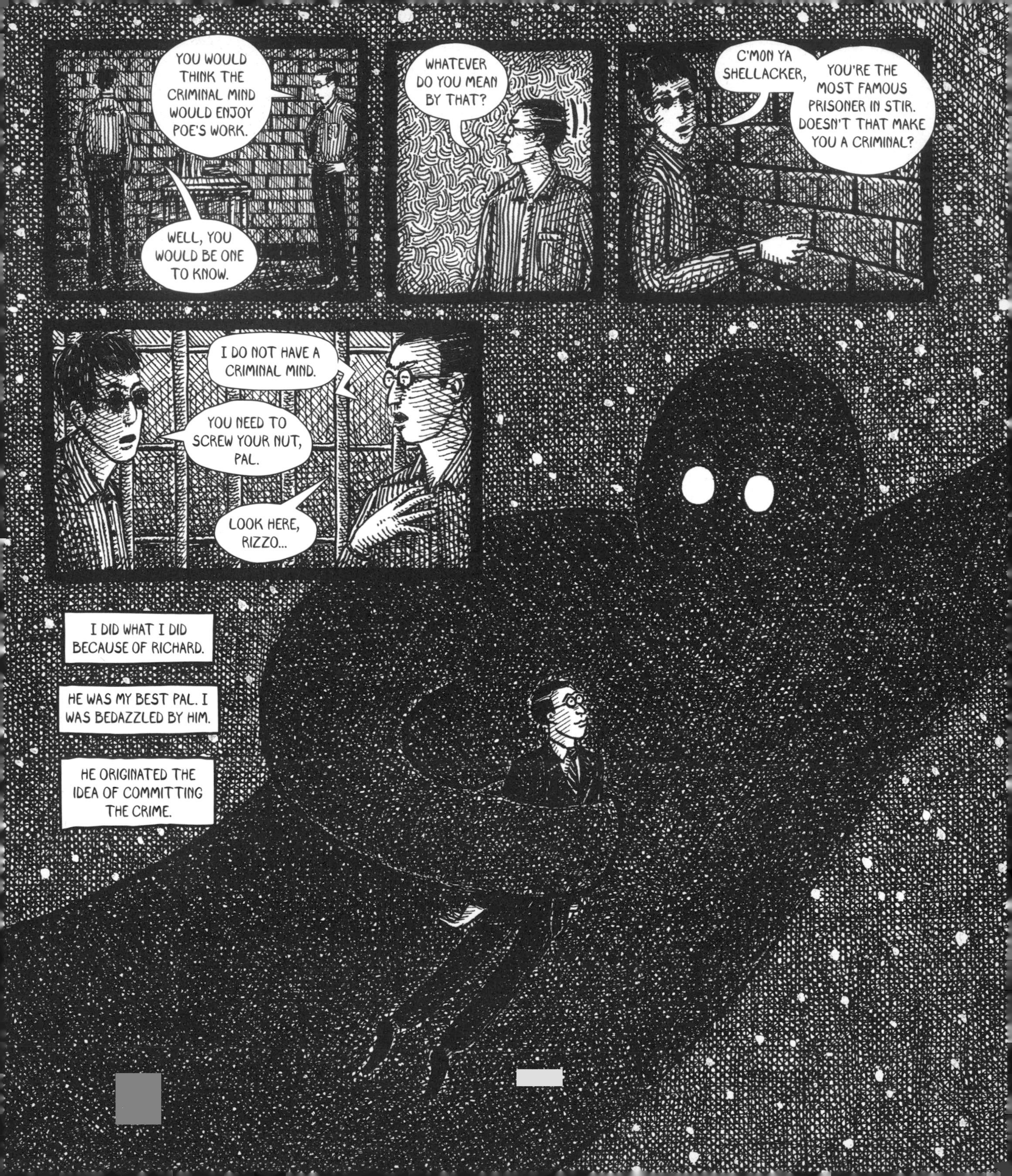
YOU WOULD THINK THE CRIMINAL MIND WOULD ENJOY POE'S WORK.
WELL, YOU WOULD BE ONE TO KNOW.
WHATEVER DO YOU MEAN BY THAT?
C'MON YA SHELLACKER,
YOU'RE THE MOST FAMOUS PRISONER IN STIR. DOESN'T THAT MAKE YOU A CRIMINAL?
I DO NOT HAVE A CRIMINAL MIND.
YOU NEED TO SCREW YOUR NUT, PAL.
LOOK HERE, RIZZO...
I DID WHAT I DID BECAUSE OF RICHARD.
HE WAS MY BEST PAL. I WAS BEDAZZLED BY HIM.
HE ORIGINATED THE IDEA OF COMMITTING THE CRIME.

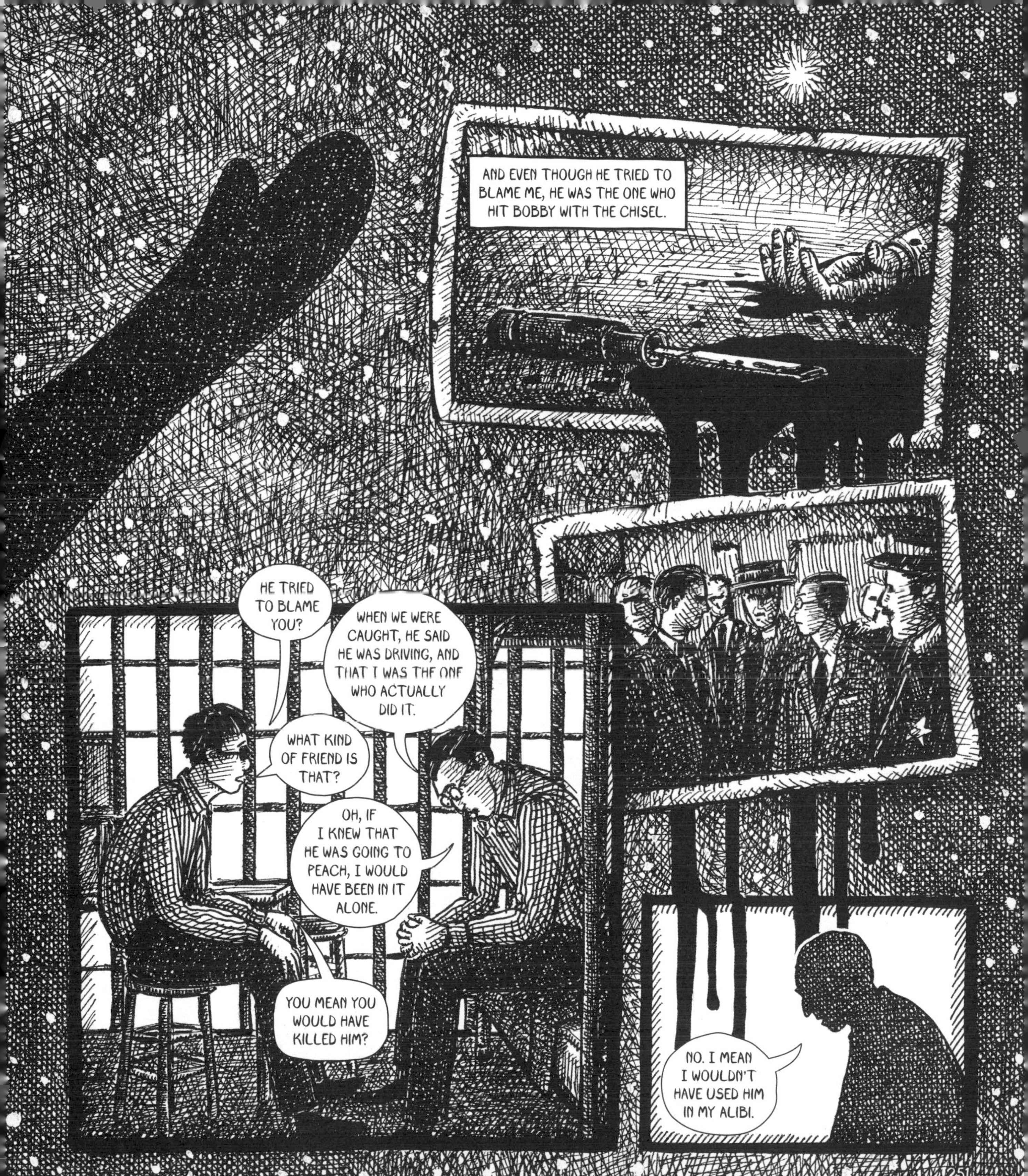

AND EVEN THOUGH HE TRIED TO BLAME ME, HE WAS THE ONE WHO HIT BOBBY WITH THE CHISEL.
HE TRIED TO BLAME YOU?
WHEN WE WERE CAUGHT, HE SAID HE WAS DRIVING, AND THAT I WAS THE ONE WHO ACTUALLY DID IT.
WHAT KIND OF FRIEND IS THAT?
OH, IF I KNEW THAT HE WAS GOING TO PEACH, I WOULD HAVE BEEN IN IT ALONE.
YOU MEAN YOU WOULD HAVE KILLED HIM?
NO. I MEAN I WOULDN'T HAVE USED HIM IN MY ALIBI.

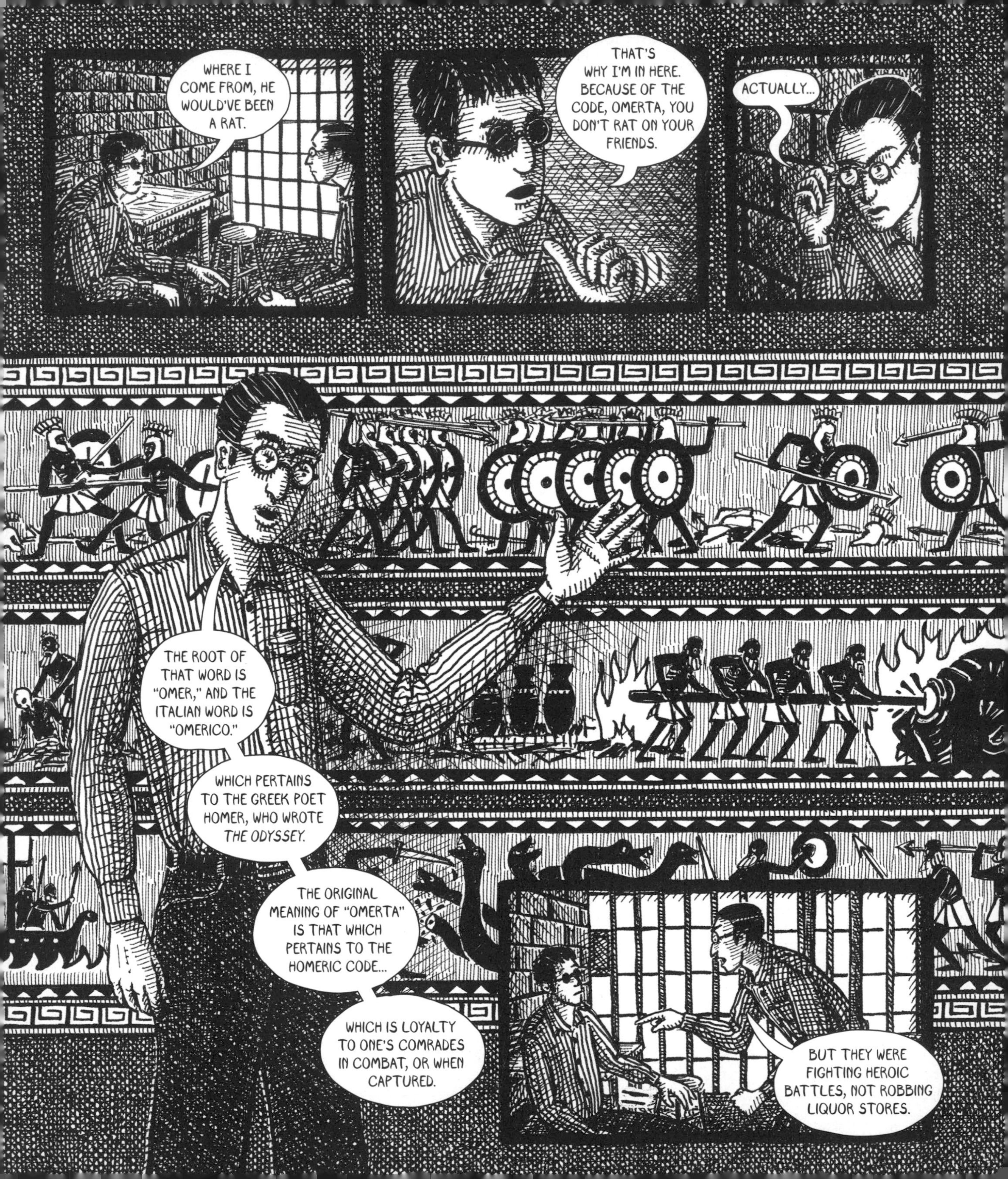
WHERE I COME FROM, HE WOULD'VE BEEN A RAT.
THAT'S WHY I'M IN HERE. BECAUSE OF THE CODE, OMERTA, YOU DON'T RAT ON YOUR FRIENDS.
ACTUALLY...
THE ROOT OF THAT WORD IS "OMER," AND THE ITALIAN WORD IS "OMERICO."
WHICH PERTAINS TO THE GREEK POET HOMER, WHO WROTE *THE ODYSSEY.*
THE ORIGINAL MEANING OF "OMERTA" IS THAT WHICH PERTAINS TO THE HOMERIC CODE...
WHICH IS LOYALTY TO ONE'S COMRADES IN COMBAT, OR WHEN CAPTURED.
BUT THEY WERE FIGHTING HEROIC BATTLES, NOT ROBBING LIQUOR STORES.

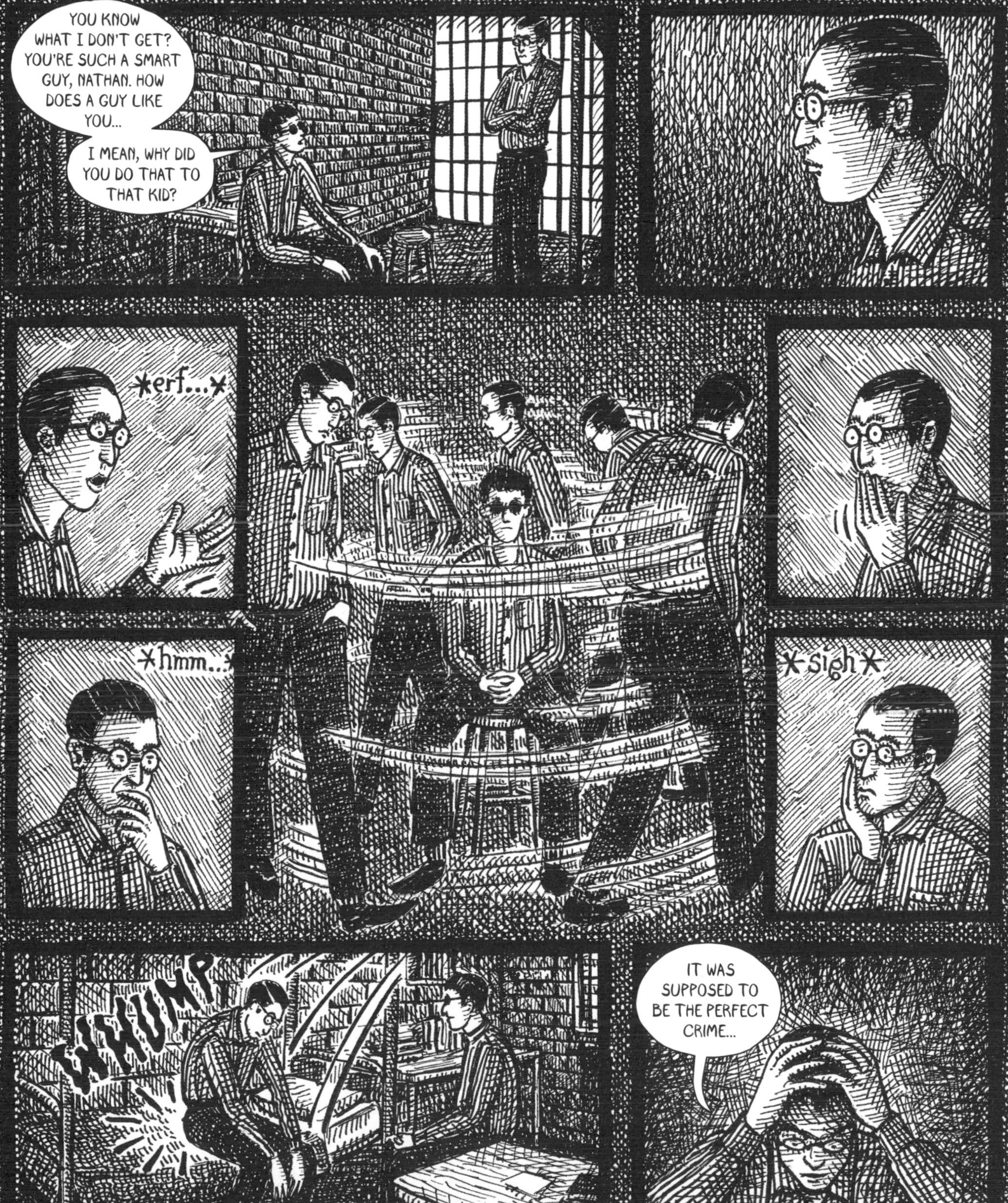
YOU KNOW WHAT I DON'T GET? YOU'RE SUCH A SMART GUY, NATHAN. HOW DOES A GUY LIKE YOU...
I MEAN, WHY DID YOU DO THAT TO THAT KID?
erf...
hmm...
sigh
WHUMP
IT WAS SUPPOSED TO BE THE PERFECT CRIME...

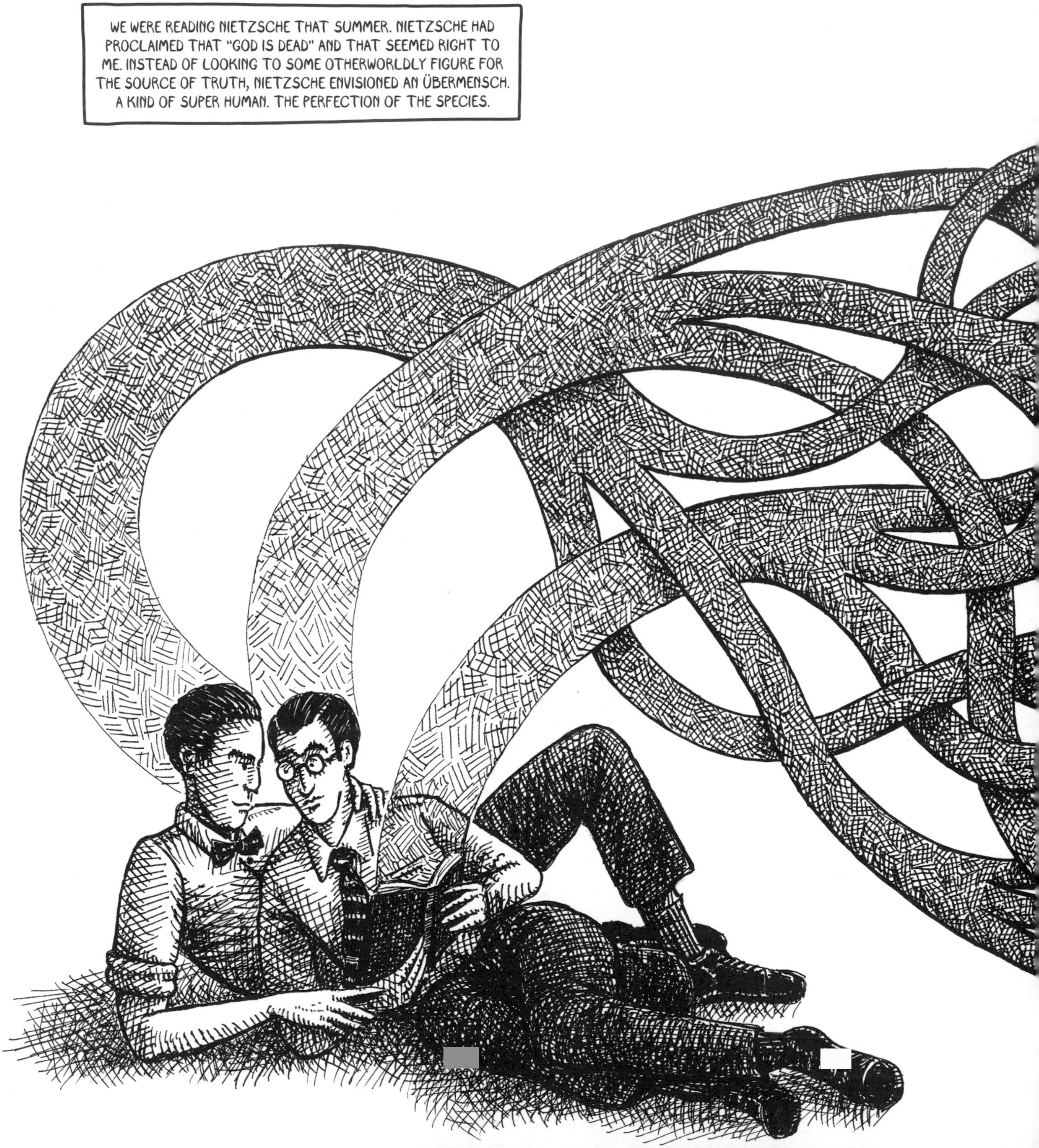
WE WERE READING NIETZSCHE THAT SUMMER. NIETZSCHE HAD PROCLAIMED THAT "GOD IS DEAD" AND THAT SEEMED RIGHT TO ME. INSTEAD OF LOOKING TO SOME OTHERWORLDLY FIGURE FOR THE SOURCE OF TRUTH, NIETZSCHE ENVISIONED AN ÜBERMENSCH. A KIND OF SUPER HUMAN. THE PERFECTION OF THE SPECIES.

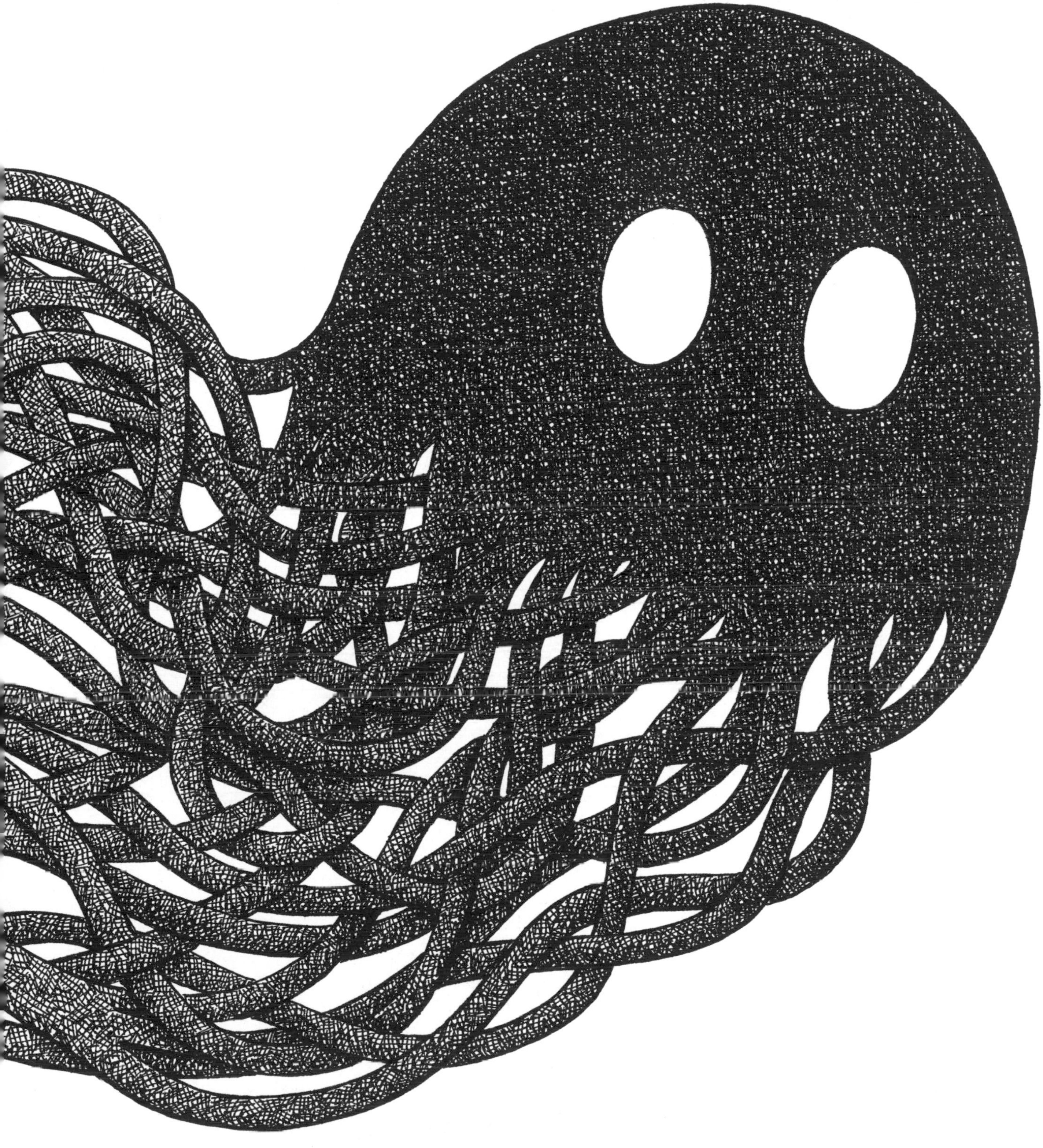

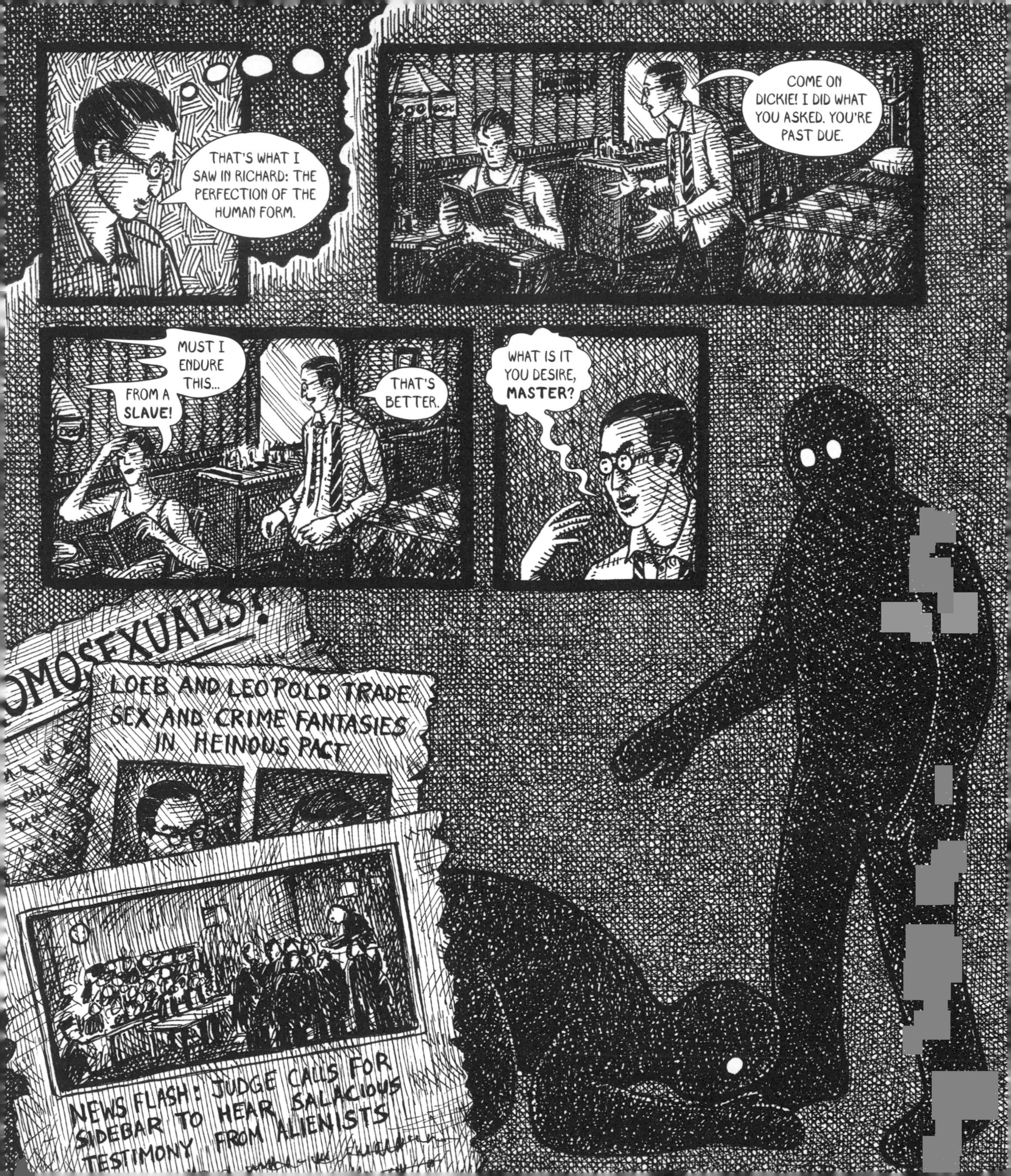
THAT'S WHAT I SAW IN RICHARD: THE PERFECTION OF THE HUMAN FORM.
COME ON DICKIE! I DID WHAT YOU ASKED. YOU'RE PAST DUE.
MUST I ENDURE THIS...
FROM A SLAVE!
THAT'S BETTER.
WHAT IS IT YOU DESIRE, MASTER?
OMOSEXUALS!
LOEB AND LEOPOLD TRADE SEX AND CRIME FANTASIES IN HEINOUS PACT
NEWS FLASH: JUDGE CALLS FOR SIDEBAR TO HEAR SALACIOUS TESTIMONY FROM ALIENISTS

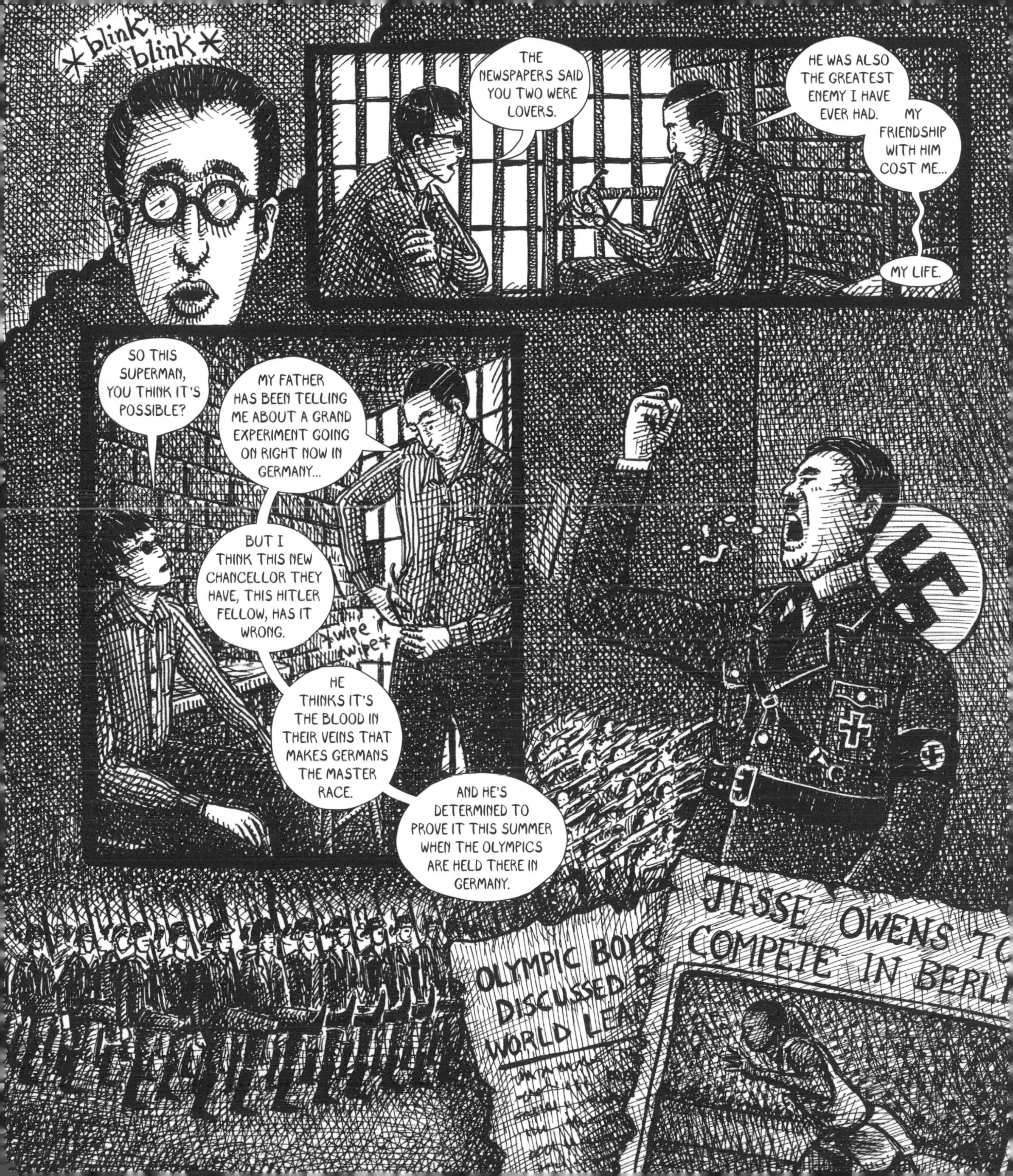
blink blink
THE NEWSPAPERS SAID YOU TWO WERE LOVERS.
HE WAS ALSO THE GREATEST ENEMY I HAVE EVER HAD.
MY FRIENDSHIP WITH HIM COST ME...
MY LIFE.
SO THIS SUPERMAN, YOU THINK IT'S POSSIBLE?
MY FATHER HAS BEEN TELLING ME ABOUT A GRAND EXPERIMENT GOING ON RIGHT NOW IN GERMANY...
BUT I THINK THIS NEW CHANCELLOR THEY HAVE, THIS HITLER FELLOW, HAS IT WRONG.
wipe wipe
HE THINKS IT'S THE BLOOD IN THEIR VEINS THAT MAKES GERMANS THE MASTER RACE.
AND HE'S DETERMINED TO PROVE IT THIS SUMMER WHEN THE OLYMPICS ARE HELD THERE IN GERMANY.
OLYMPIC BOYC DISCUSSED B WORLD LEA
JESSE OWENS TO COMPETE IN BERL

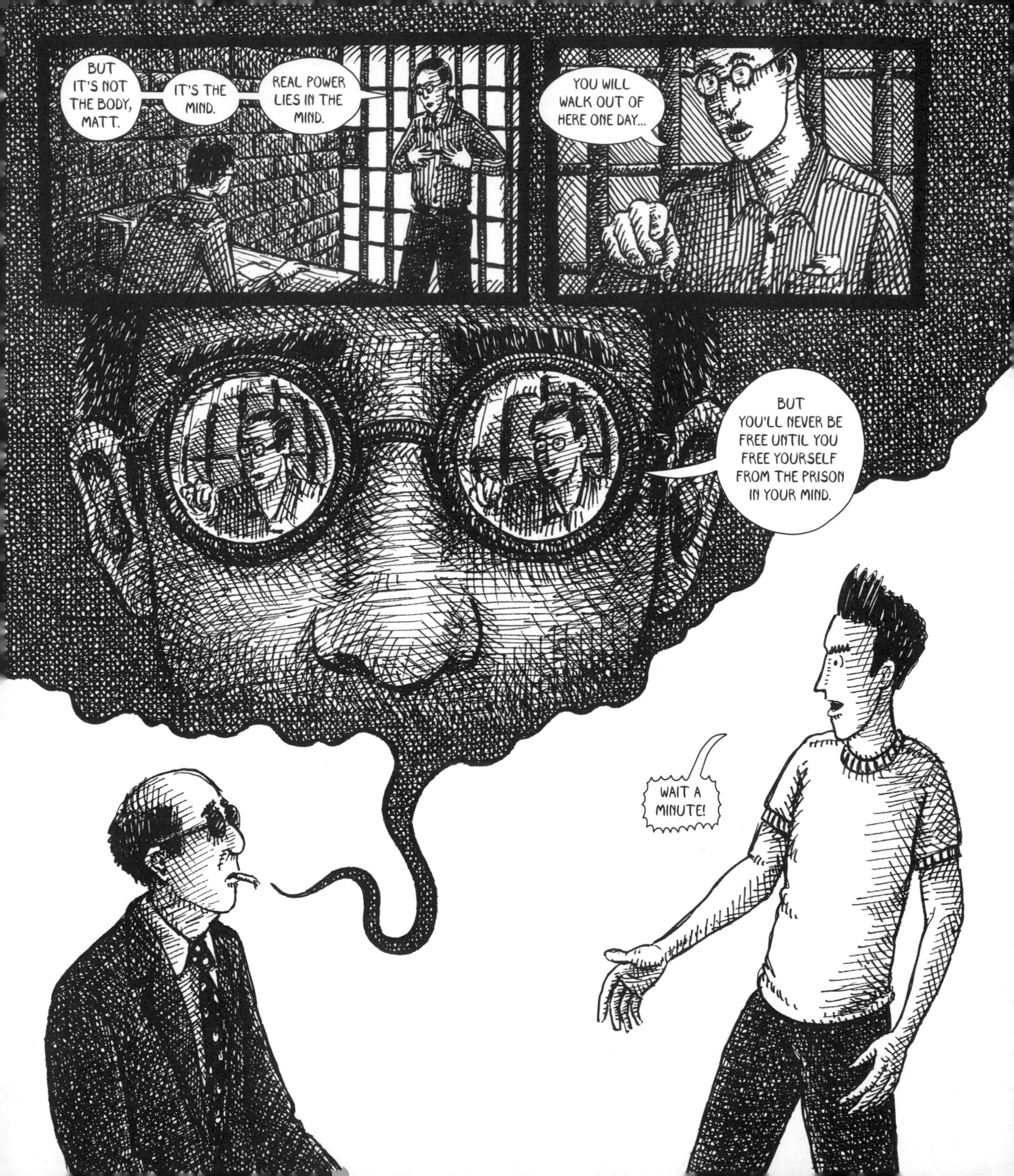
BUT IT'S NOT THE BODY, MATT.
IT'S THE MIND.
REAL POWER LIES IN THE MIND.
YOU WILL WALK OUT OF HERE ONE DAY...
BUT YOU'LL NEVER BE FREE UNTIL YOU FREE YOURSELF FROM THE PRISON IN YOUR MIND.
WAIT A MINUTE!

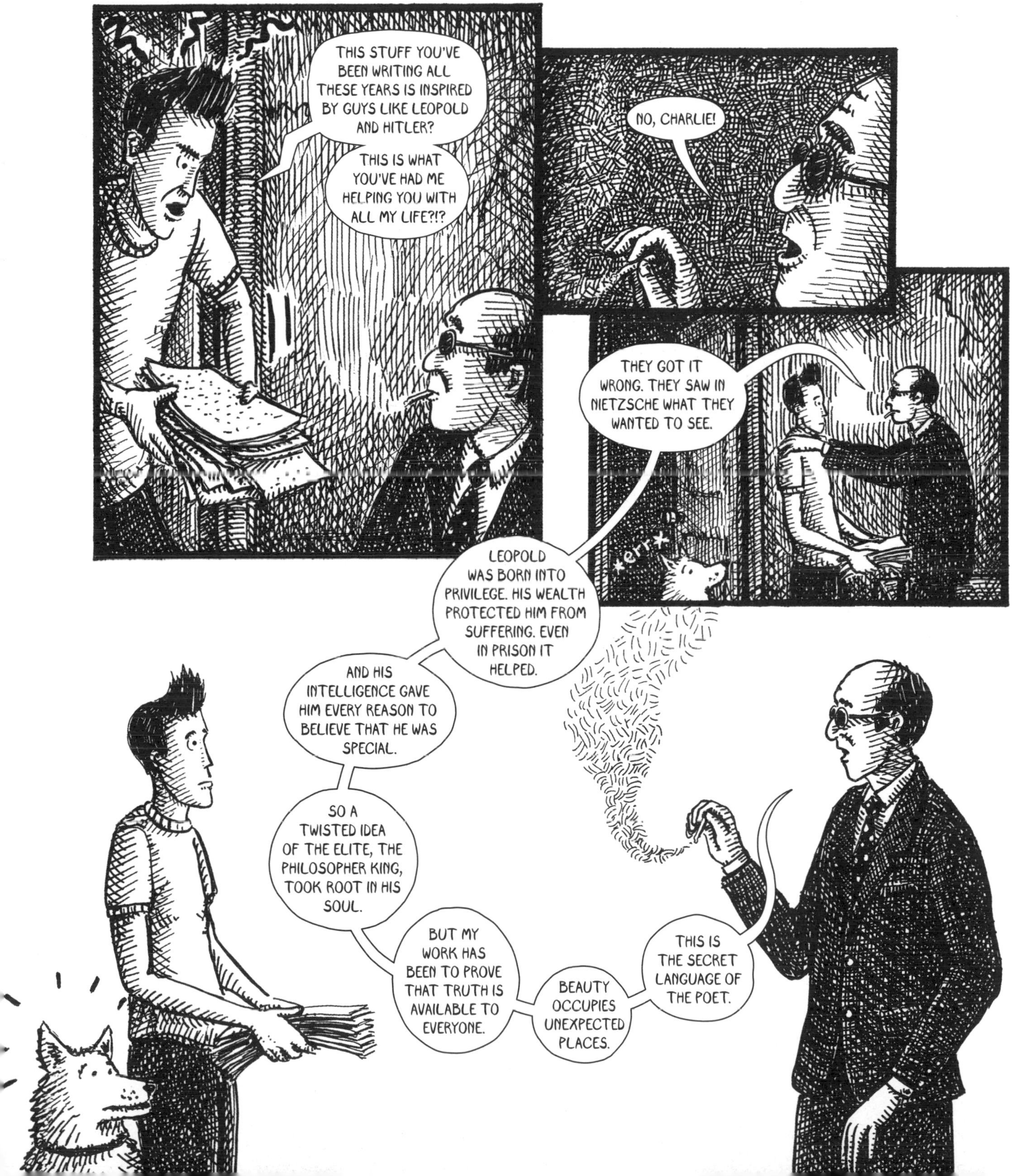

THIS STUFF YOU'VE BEEN WRITING ALL THESE YEARS IS INSPIRED BY GUYS LIKE LEOPOLD AND HITLER?
THIS IS WHAT YOU'VE HAD ME HELPING YOU WITH ALL MY LIFE?!?
NO, CHARLIE!
THEY GOT IT WRONG. THEY SAW IN NIETZSCHE WHAT THEY WANTED TO SEE.
err
LEOPOLD WAS BORN INTO PRIVILEGE. HIS WEALTH PROTECTED HIM FROM SUFFERING. EVEN IN PRISON IT HELPED.
AND HIS INTELLIGENCE GAVE HIM EVERY REASON TO BELIEVE THAT HE WAS SPECIAL.
SO A TWISTED IDEA OF THE ELITE, THE PHILOSOPHER KING, TOOK ROOT IN HIS SOUL.
BUT MY WORK HAS BEEN TO PROVE THAT TRUTH IS AVAILABLE TO EVERYONE.
BEAUTY OCCUPIES UNEXPECTED PLACES.
THIS IS THE SECRET LANGUAGE OF THE POET.

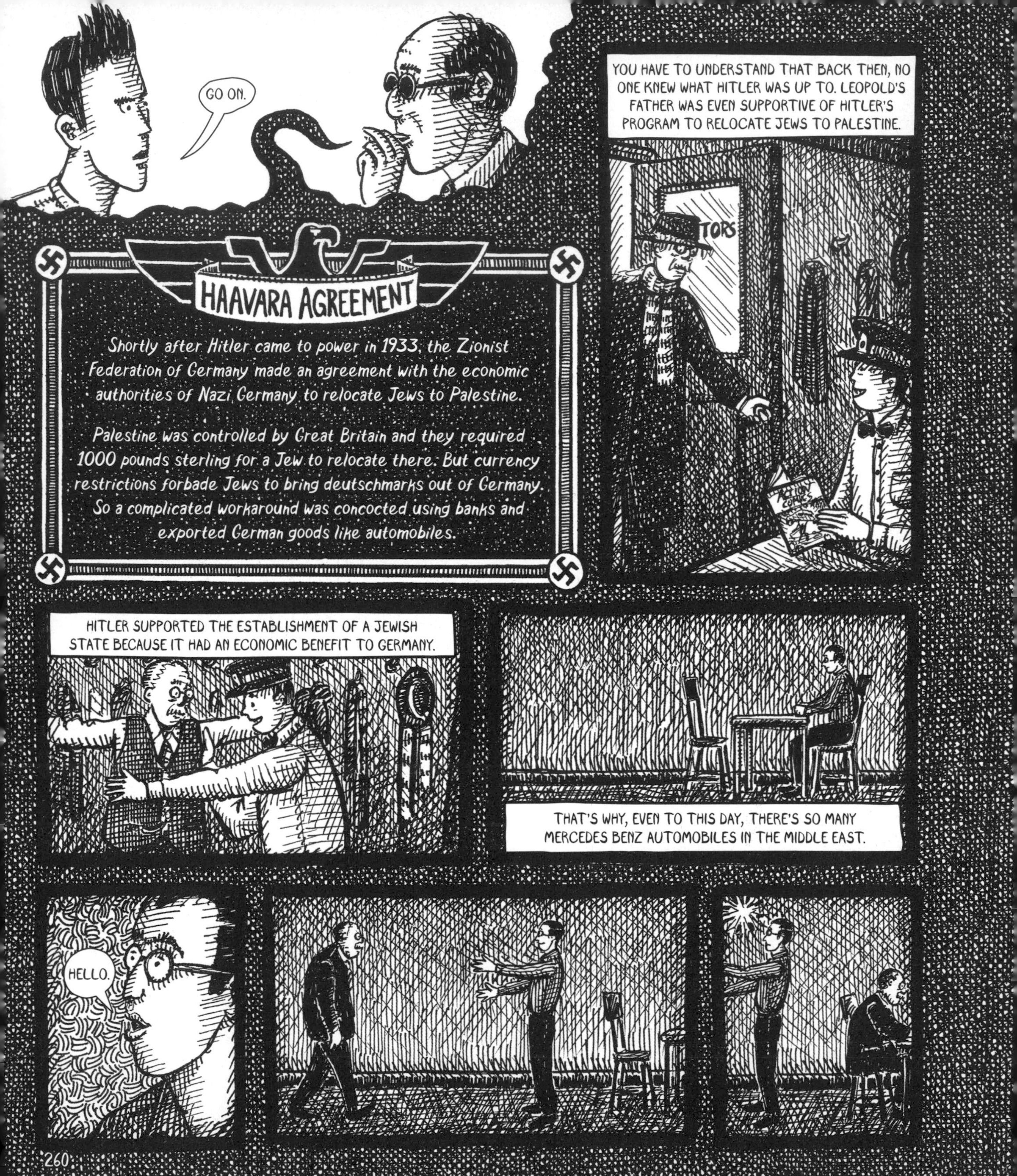

GO ON.
YOU HAVE TO UNDERSTAND THAT BACK THEN, NO ONE KNEW WHAT HITLER WAS UP TO. LEOPOLD'S FATHER WAS EVEN SUPPORTIVE OF HITLER'S PROGRAM TO RELOCATE JEWS TO PALESTINE.
HAAVARA AGREEMENT
Shortly after Hitler came to power in 1933, the Zionist Federation of Germany made an agreement with the economic authorities of Nazi Germany to relocate Jews to Palestine.
Palestine was controlled by Great Britain and they required 1000 pounds sterling for a Jew to relocate there. But currency restrictions forbade Jews to bring deutschmarks out of Germany. So a complicated workaround was concocted using banks and exported German goods like automobiles.
TORS
HITLER SUPPORTED THE ESTABLISHMENT OF A JEWISH STATE BECAUSE IT HAD AN ECONOMIC BENEFIT TO GERMANY.
THAT'S WHY, EVEN TO THIS DAY, THERE'S SO MANY MERCEDES BENZ AUTOMOBILES IN THE MIDDLE EAST.
HELLO.

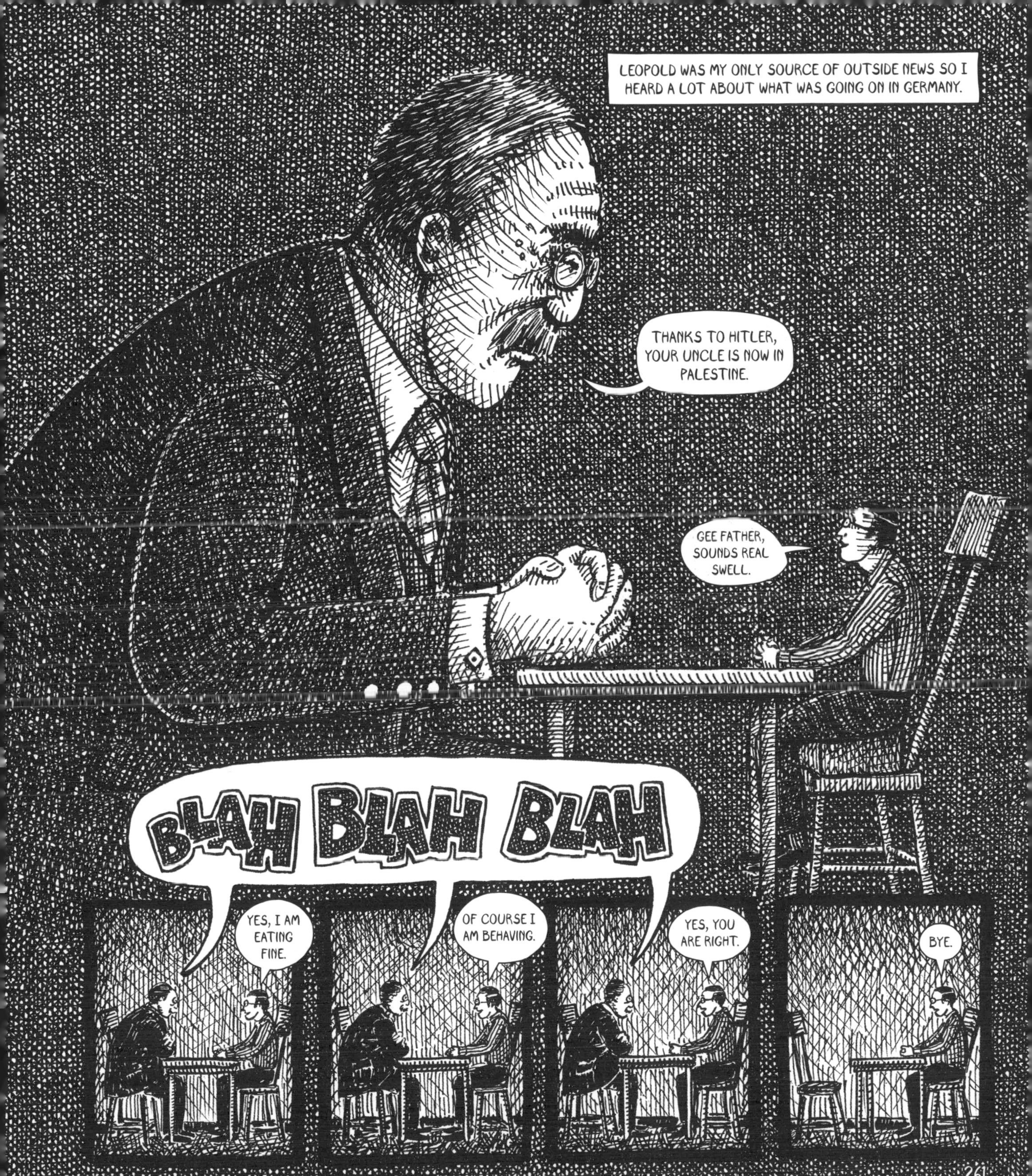

LEOPOLD WAS MY ONLY SOURCE OF OUTSIDE NEWS SO I HEARD A LOT ABOUT WHAT WAS GOING ON IN GERMANY.
THANKS TO HITLER, YOUR UNCLE IS NOW IN PALESTINE.
GEE FATHER, SOUNDS REAL SWELL.
BLAH BLAH BLAH
YES, I AM EATING FINE.
OF COURSE I AM BEHAVING.
YES, YOU ARE RIGHT.
BYE.

XI

PRINCIPLES OF SOUND

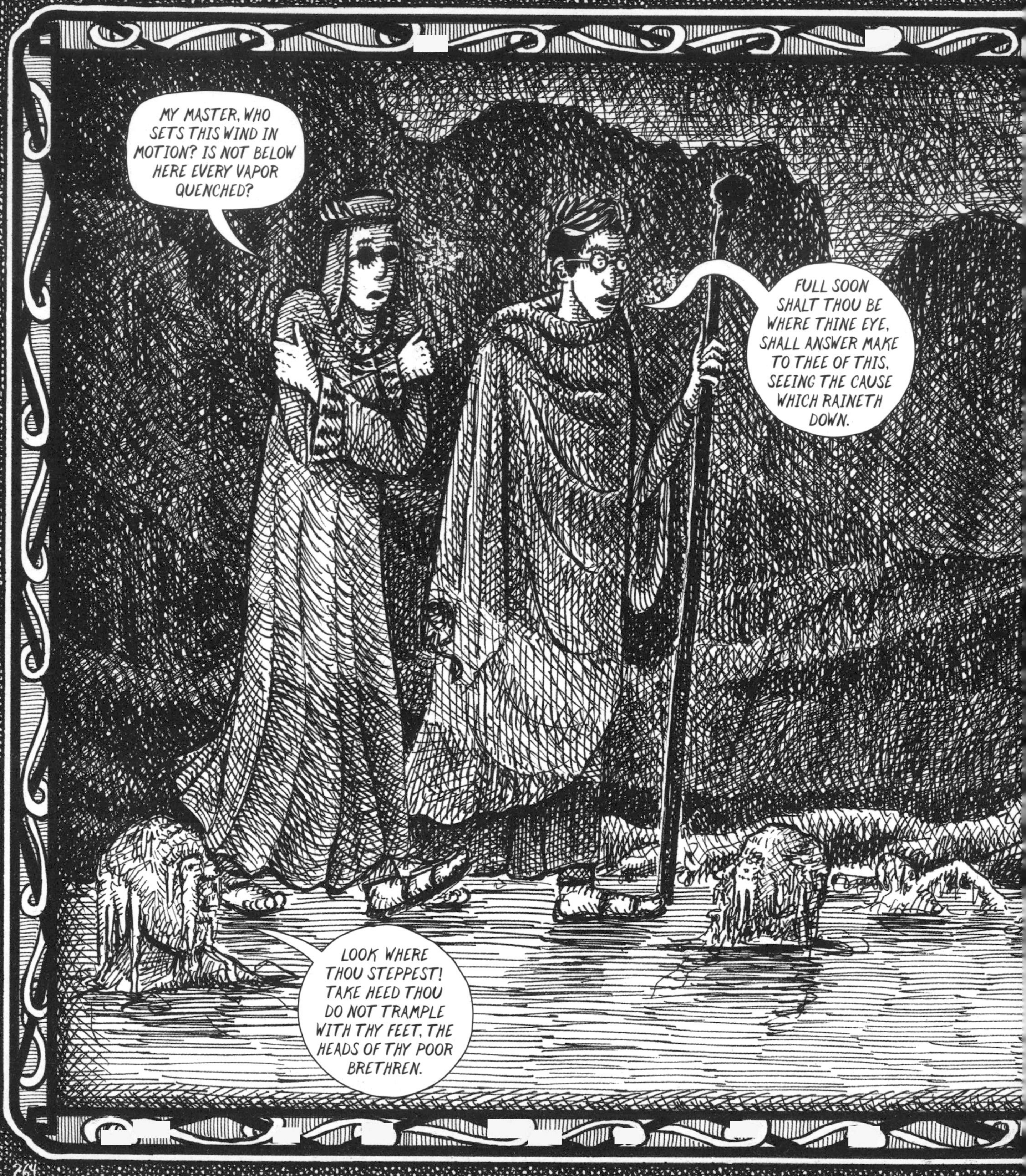
MY MASTER, WHO SETS THIS WIND IN MOTION? IS NOT BELOW HERE EVERY VAPOR QUENCHED?
FULL SOON SHALT THOU BE WHERE THINE EYE, SHALL ANSWER MAKE TO THEE OF THIS, SEEING THE CAUSE WHICH RAINETH DOWN.
LOOK WHERE THOU STEPPEST! TAKE HEED THOU DO NOT TRAMPLE WITH THY FEET, THE HEADS OF THY POOR BRETHREN.

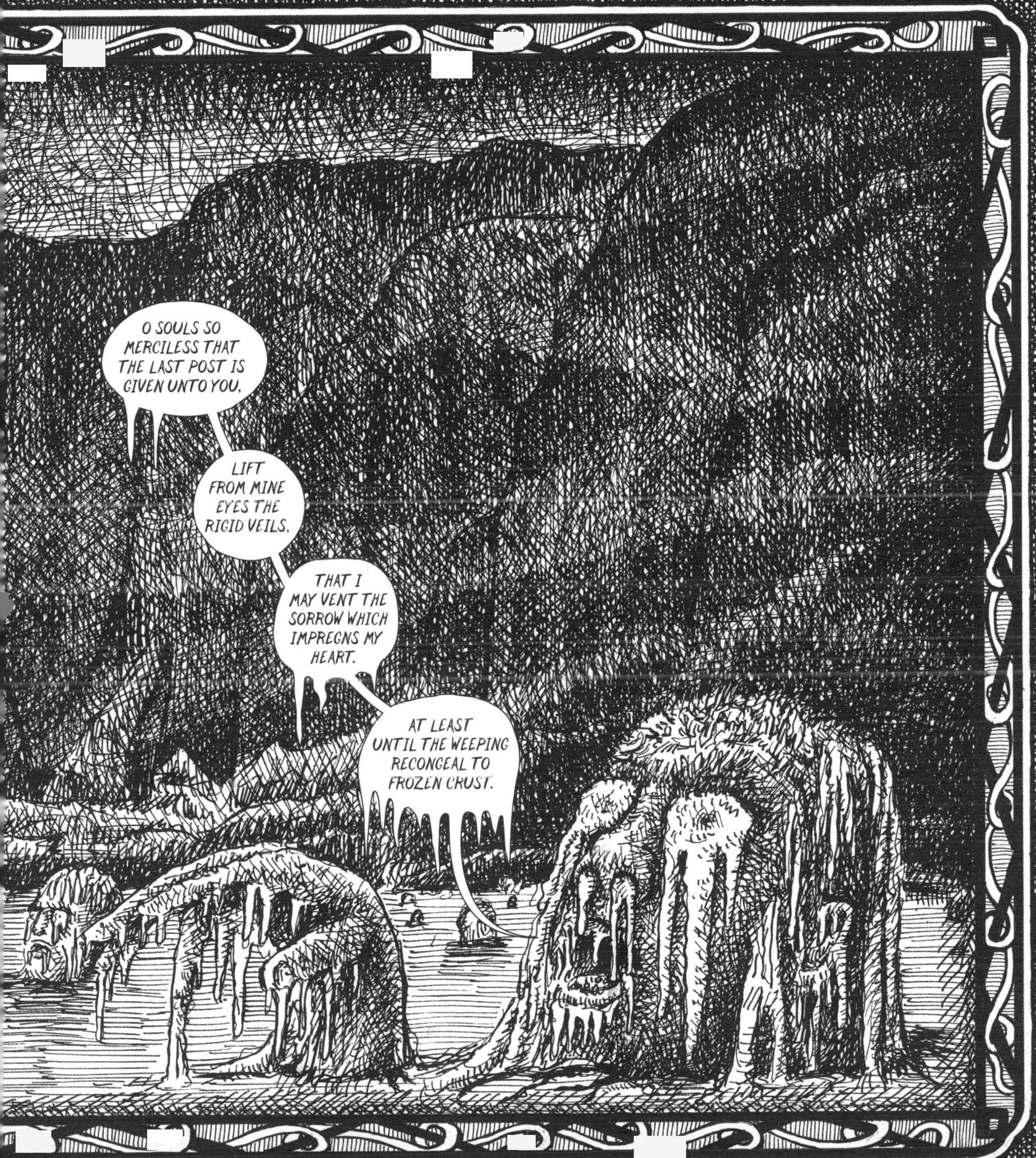
O SOULS SO MERCILESS THAT THE LAST POST IS GIVEN UNTO YOU,
LIFT FROM MINE EYES THE RIGID VEILS,
THAT I MAY VENT THE SORROW WHICH IMPREGNS MY HEART.
AT LEAST UNTIL THE WEEPING RECONGEAL TO FROZEN CRUST.

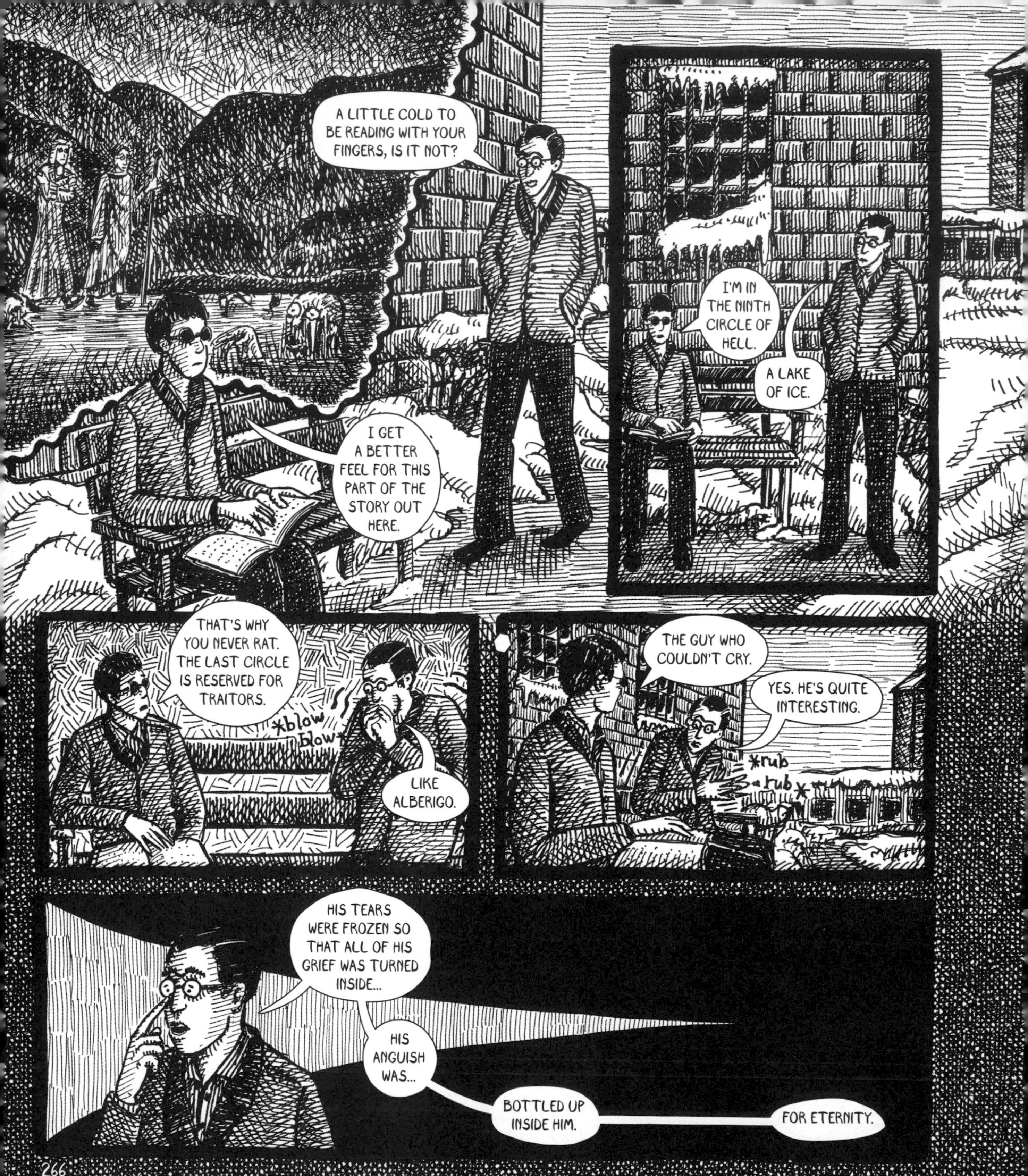
A LITTLE COLD TO BE READING WITH YOUR FINGERS, IS IT NOT?
I GET A BETTER FEEL FOR THIS PART OF THE STORY OUT HERE.
I'M IN THE NINTH CIRCLE OF HELL.
A LAKE OF ICE.
THAT'S WHY YOU NEVER RAT. THE LAST CIRCLE IS RESERVED FOR TRAITORS.
blow blow
LIKE ALBERIGO.
THE GUY WHO COULDN'T CRY.
YES. HE'S QUITE INTERESTING.
rub rub
HIS TEARS WERE FROZEN SO THAT ALL OF HIS GRIEF WAS TURNED INSIDE...
HIS ANGUISH WAS...
BOTTLED UP INSIDE HIM.
FOR ETERNITY.

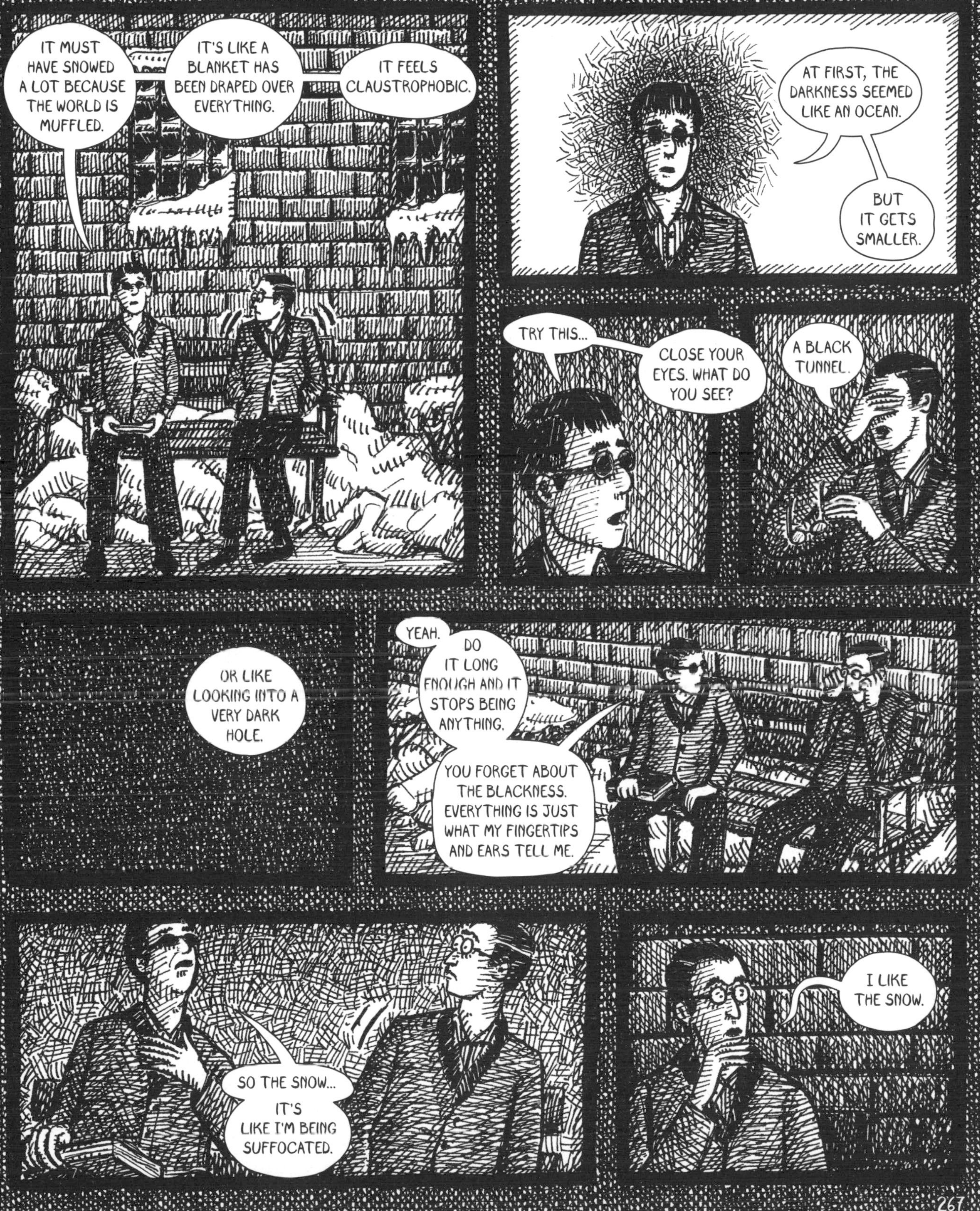
IT MUST HAVE SNOWED A LOT BECAUSE THE WORLD IS MUFFLED.
IT'S LIKE A BLANKET HAS BEEN DRAPED OVER EVERYTHING.
IT FEELS CLAUSTROPHOBIC.
AT FIRST, THE DARKNESS SEEMED LIKE AN OCEAN.
BUT IT GETS SMALLER.
TRY THIS...
CLOSE YOUR EYES. WHAT DO YOU SEE?
A BLACK TUNNEL.
OR LIKE LOOKING INTO A VERY DARK HOLE.
YEAH.
DO IT LONG ENOUGH AND IT STOPS BEING ANYTHING.
YOU FORGET ABOUT THE BLACKNESS. EVERYTHING IS JUST WHAT MY FINGERTIPS AND EARS TELL ME.
SO THE SNOW...
IT'S LIKE I'M BEING SUFFOCATED.
I LIKE THE SNOW.

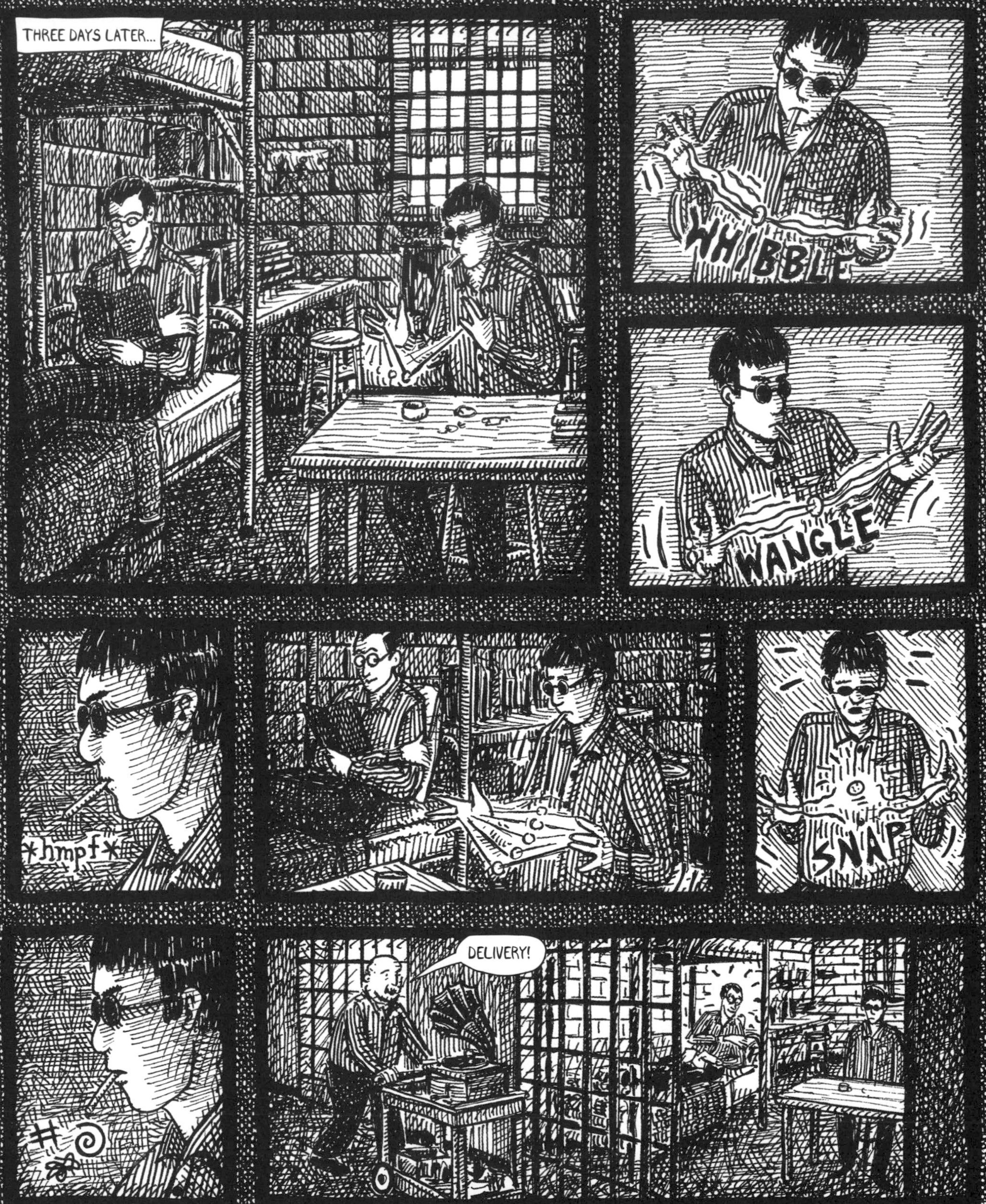
THREE DAYS LATER...
WHIBBLE
WANGLE
hmpf
SNAP
DELIVERY!

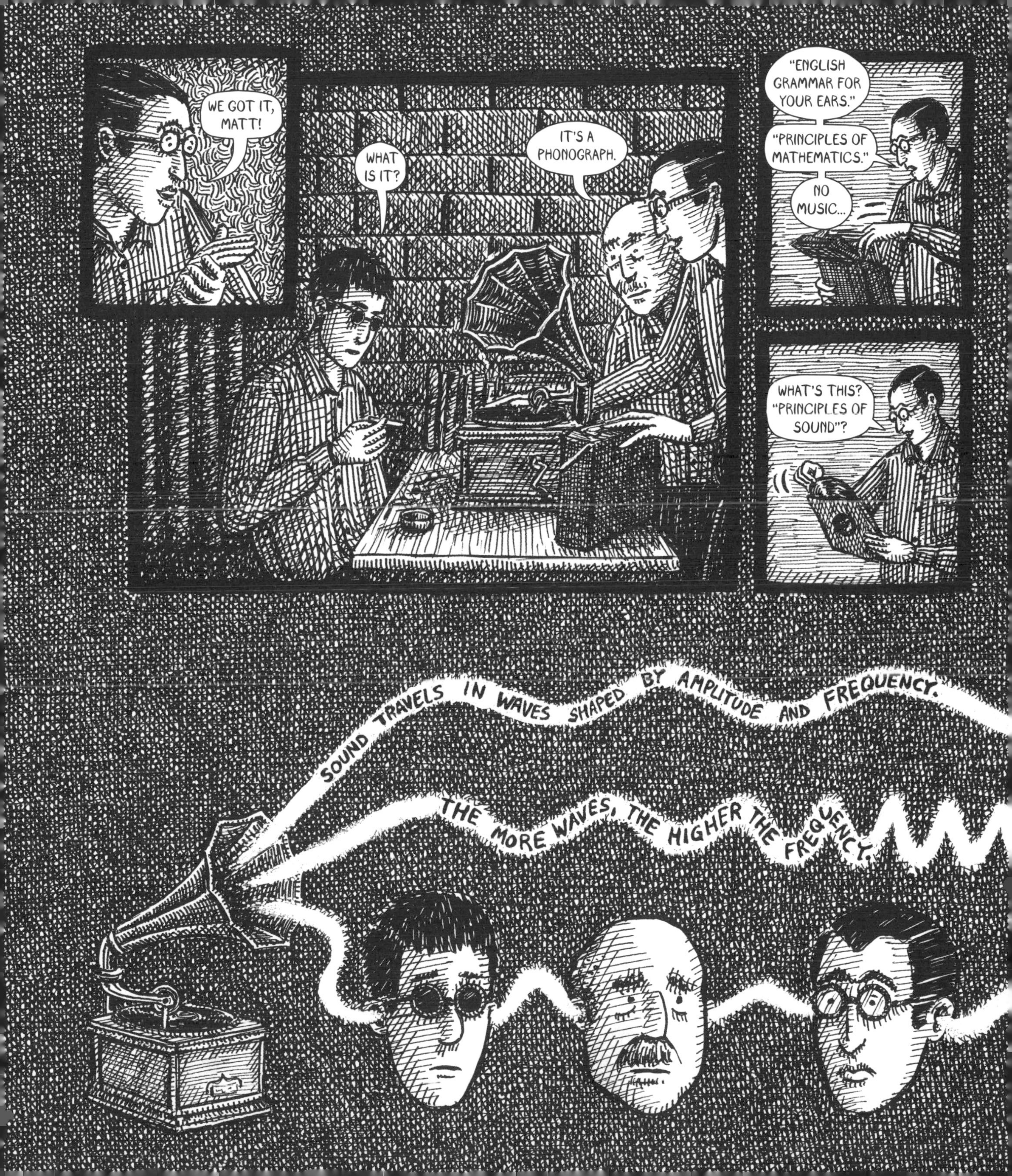
WE GOT IT, MATT!
WHAT IS IT?
IT'S A PHONOGRAPH.
"ENGLISH GRAMMAR FOR YOUR EARS."
"PRINCIPLES OF MATHEMATICS."
NO MUSIC...
WHAT'S THIS? "PRINCIPLES OF SOUND"?
SOUND TRAVELS IN WAVES SHAPED BY AMPLITUDE AND FREQUENCY.
THE MORE WAVES, THE HIGHER THE FREQUENCY.

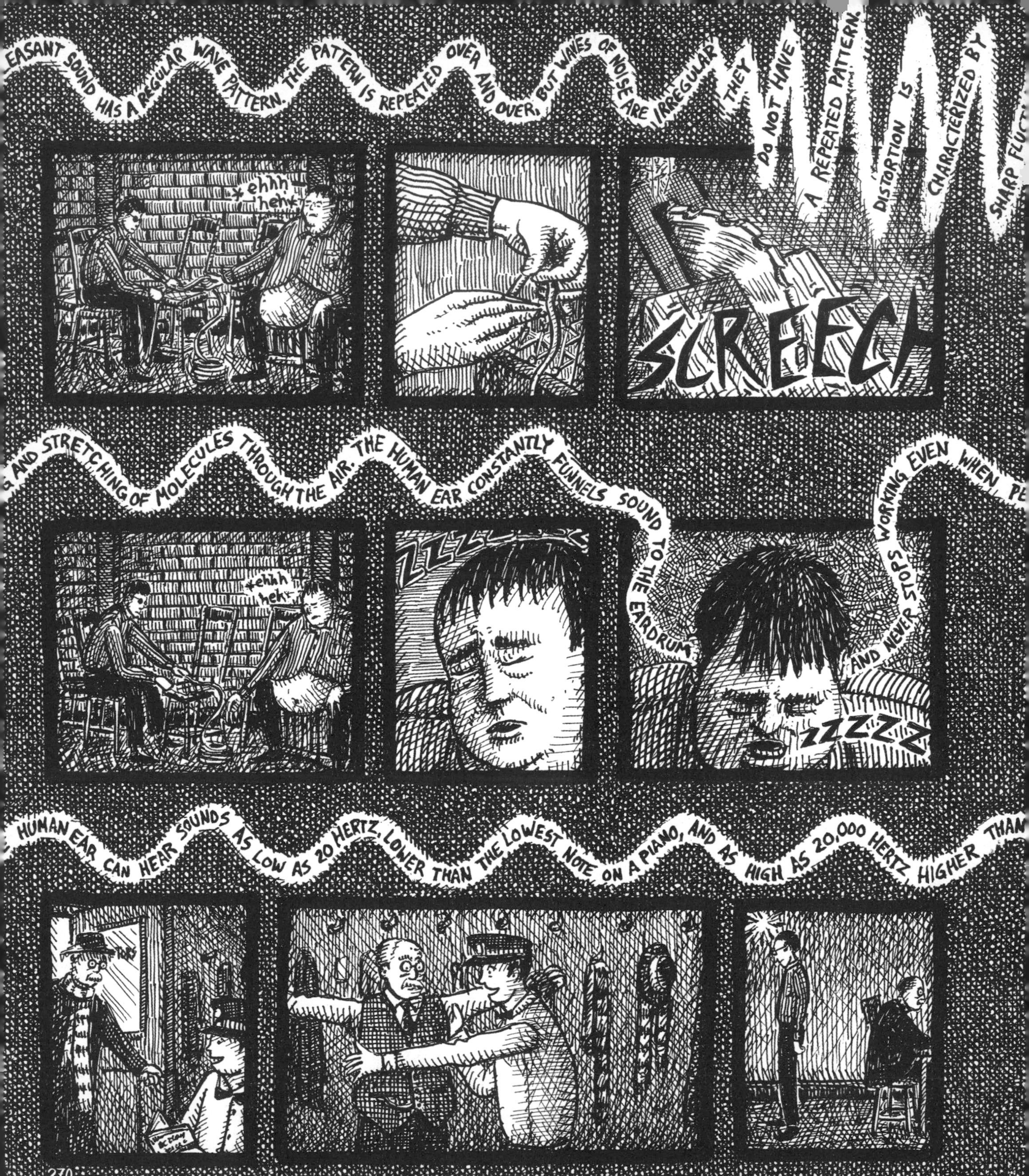
EASANT SOUND HAS A REGULAR WAVE PATTERN. THE PATTERN IS REPEATED OVER AND OVER, BUT WAVES OF NOISE ARE IRREGULAR. THEY DO NOT HAVE A REPEATED PATTERN. DISTORTION IS CHARACTERIZED BY SHARP FLUC
ehhh heh
SCREECH
AND STRETCHING OF MOLECULES THROUGH THE AIR. THE HUMAN EAR CONSTANTLY FUNNELS SOUND TO THE EARDRUM AND NEVER STOPS WORKING EVEN WHEN PE
ehhh heh
ZZZZZ
ZZZZZ
HUMAN EAR CAN HEAR SOUNDS AS LOW AS 20 HERTZ, LOWER THAN THE LOWEST NOTE ON A PIANO, AND AS HIGH AS 20,000 HERTZ HIGHER THAN

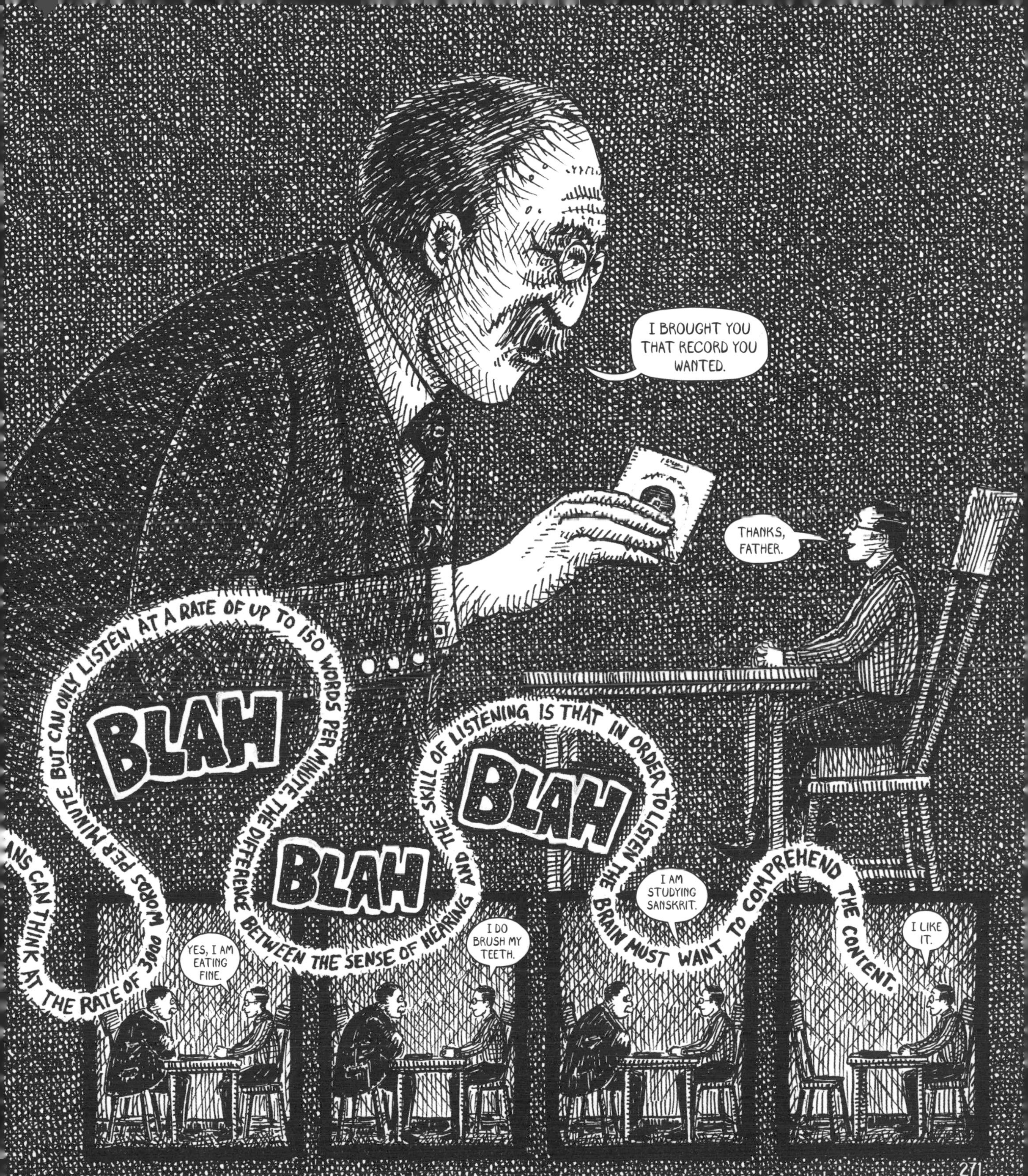
I BROUGHT YOU THAT RECORD YOU WANTED.
THANKS, FATHER.
ANS CAN THINK AT THE RATE OF 3,000 WORDS PER MINUTE BUT CAN ONLY LISTEN AT A RATE OF UP TO 150 WORDS PER MINUTE. THE DIFFERENCE BETWEEN THE SENSE OF HEARING AND THE SKILL OF LISTENING IS THAT IN ORDER TO LISTEN THE BRAIN MUST WANT TO COMPREHEND THE CONTENT.
BLAH
BLAH
BLAH
YES, I AM EATING FINE.
I DO BRUSH MY TEETH.
I AM STUDYING SANSKRIT.
I LIKE IT.

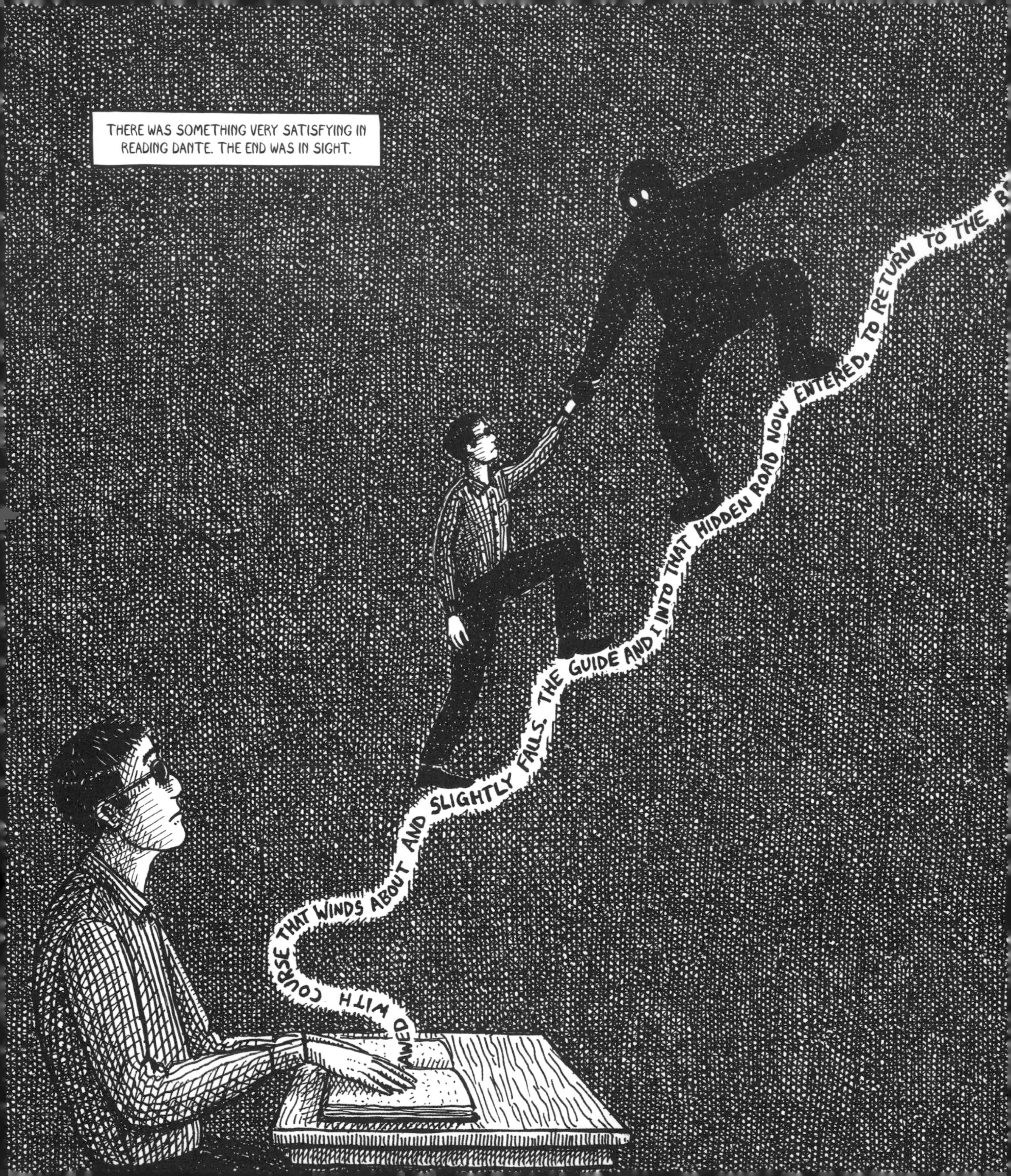
THERE WAS SOMETHING VERY SATISFYING IN READING DANTE. THE END WAS IN SIGHT.
AMED WITH COURSE THAT WINDS ABOUT AND SLIGHTLY FALLS. THE GUIDE AND I INTO THAT HIDDEN ROAD NOW ENTERED, TO RETURN TO THE B

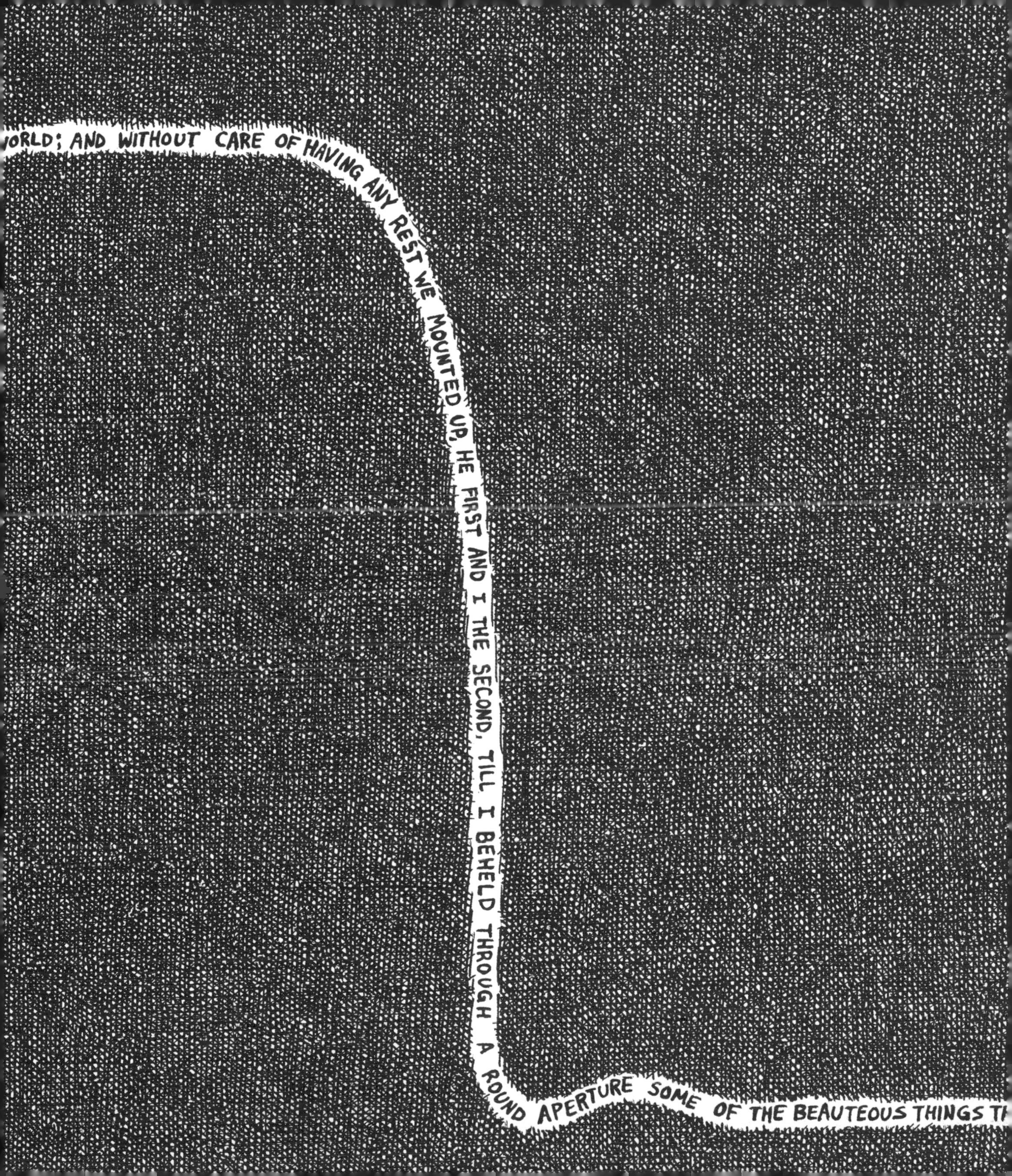
WORLD; AND WITHOUT CARE OF HAVING ANY REST WE MOUNTED UP, HE FIRST AND I THE SECOND, TILL I BEHELD THROUGH A ROUND APERTURE SOME OF THE BEAUTEOUS THINGS TH

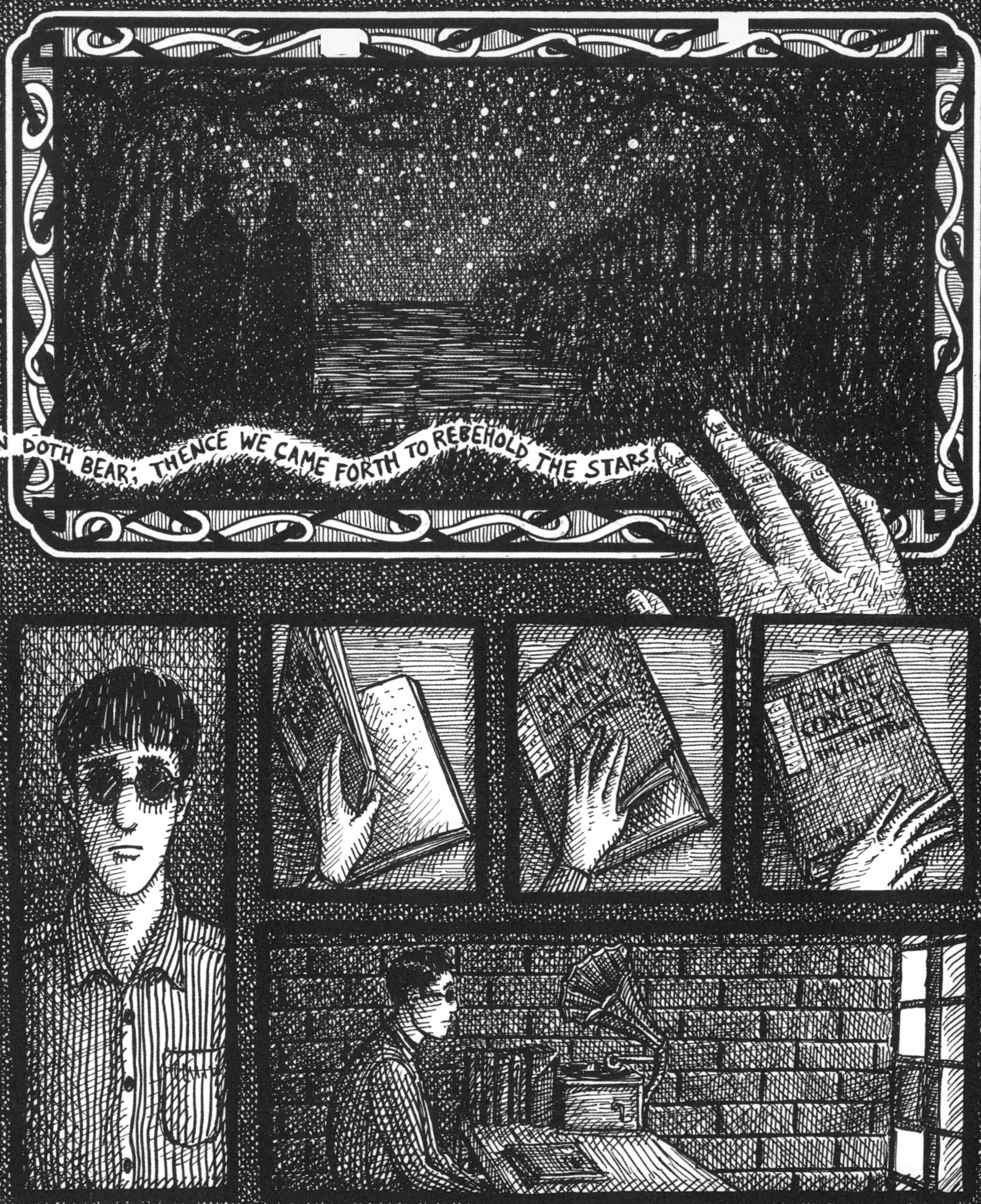
VEN DOTH BEAR; THENCE WE CAME FORTH TO REBEHOLD THE STARS.
DIVINE COMEDY

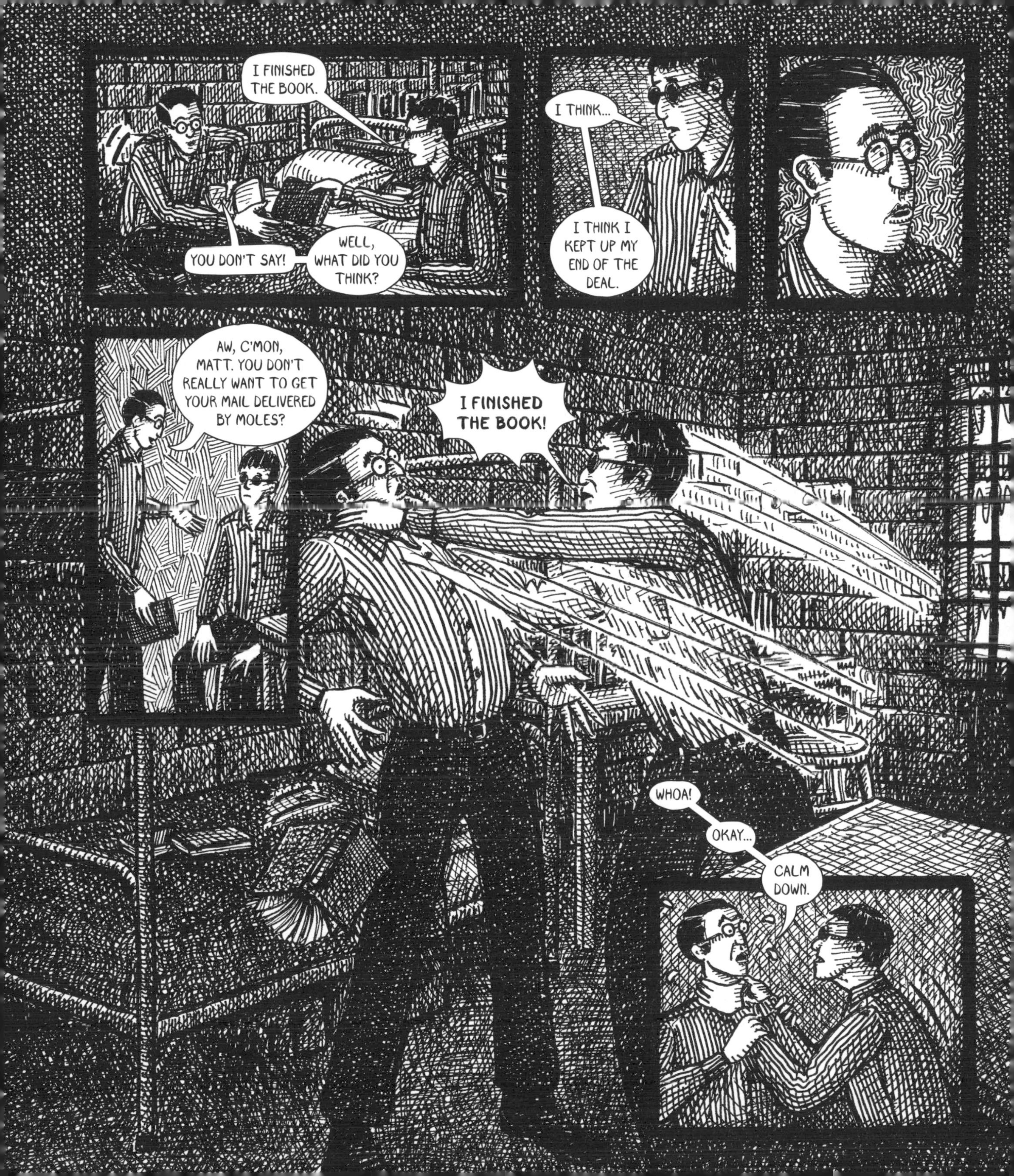
I FINISHED THE BOOK.
YOU DON'T SAY!
WELL, WHAT DID YOU THINK?
I THINK...
I THINK I KEPT UP MY END OF THE DEAL.
AW, C'MON, MATT. YOU DON'T REALLY WANT TO GET YOUR MAIL DELIVERED BY MOLES?
I FINISHED THE BOOK!
WHOA!
OKAY...
CALM DOWN.

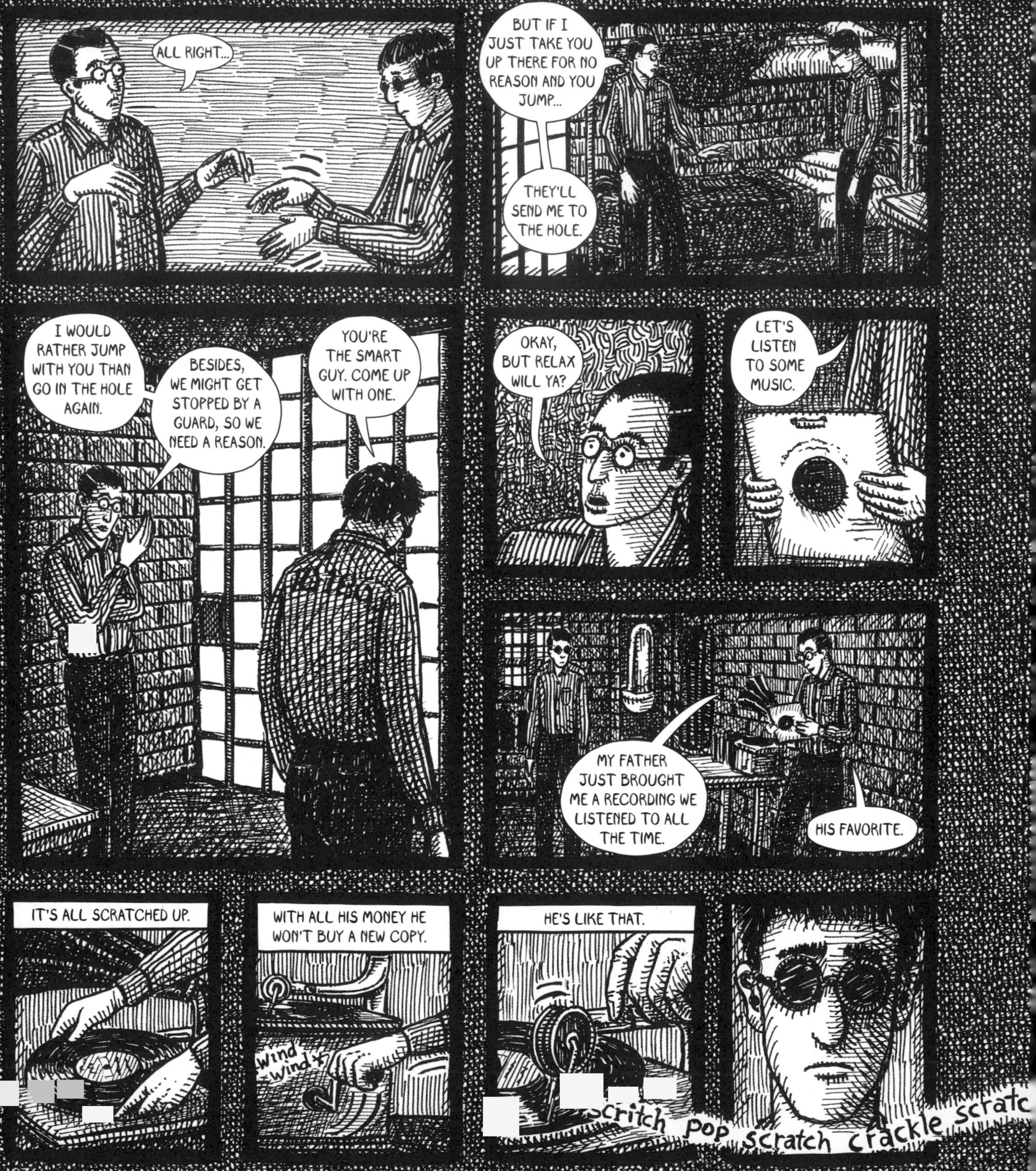
ALL RIGHT...
BUT IF I JUST TAKE YOU UP THERE FOR NO REASON AND YOU JUMP...
THEY'LL SEND ME TO THE HOLE.
I WOULD RATHER JUMP WITH YOU THAN GO IN THE HOLE AGAIN.
BESIDES, WE MIGHT GET STOPPED BY A GUARD, SO WE NEED A REASON.
YOU'RE THE SMART GUY. COME UP WITH ONE.
OKAY, BUT RELAX WILL YA?
LET'S LISTEN TO SOME MUSIC.
MY FATHER JUST BROUGHT ME A RECORDING WE LISTENED TO ALL THE TIME.
HIS FAVORITE.
IT'S ALL SCRATCHED UP.
WITH ALL HIS MONEY HE WON'T BUY A NEW COPY.
wind wind
HE'S LIKE THAT.
scritch pop scratch crackle scratc

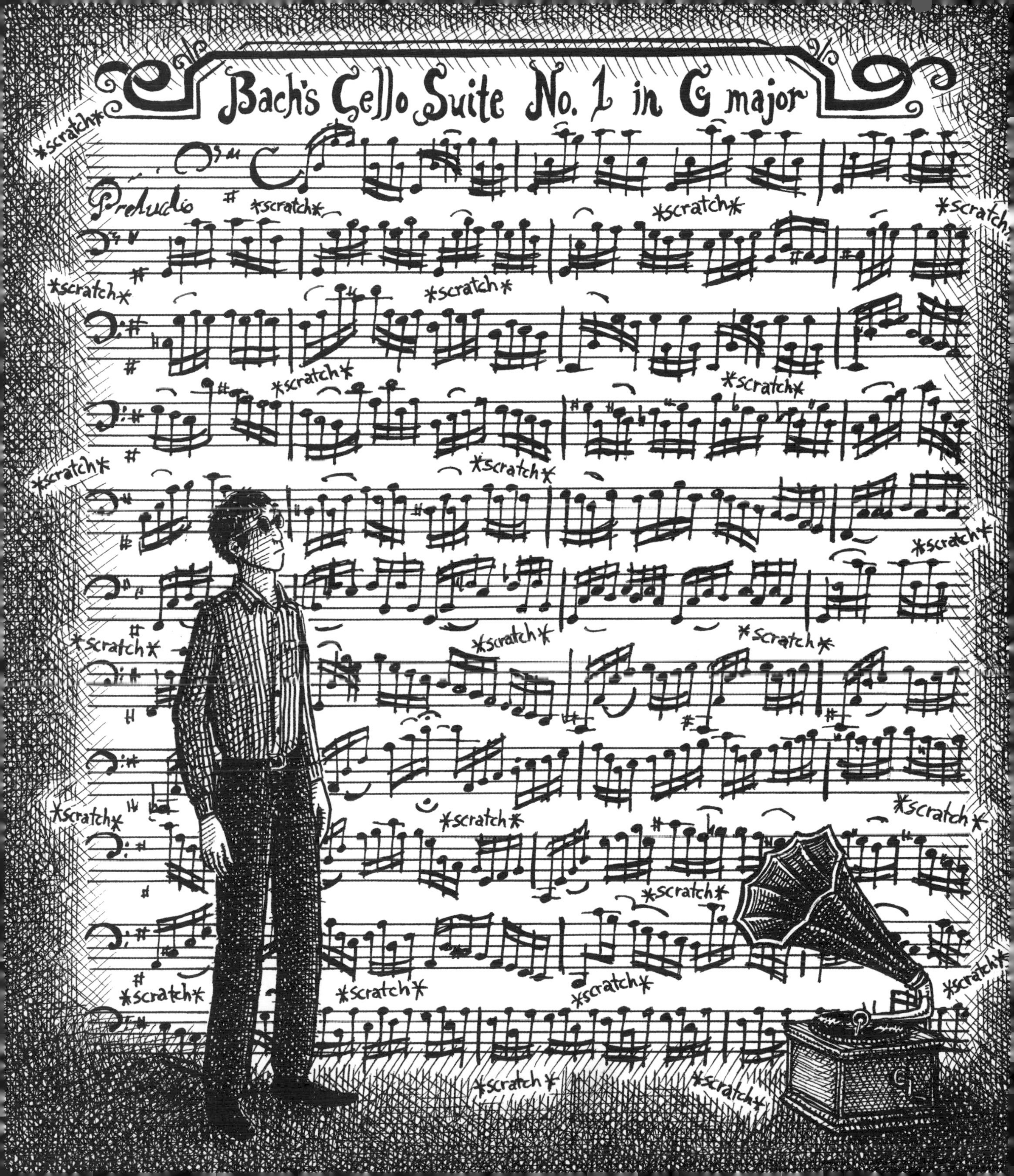
Bach's Cello Suite No. 1 in G major
Preludio
scratch

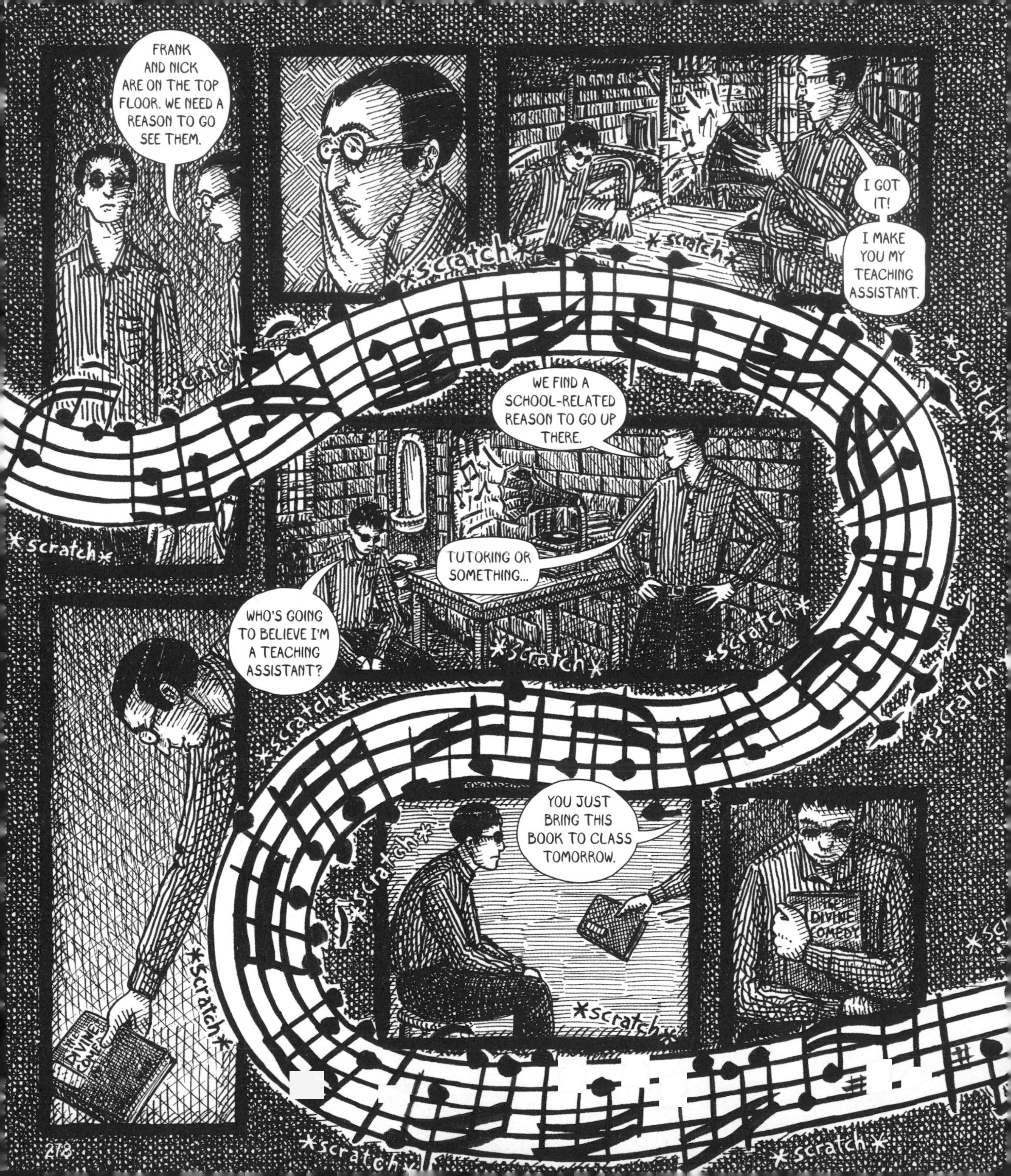

FRANK AND NICK ARE ON THE TOP FLOOR. WE NEED A REASON TO GO SEE THEM.
scratch
I GOT IT!
I MAKE YOU MY TEACHING ASSISTANT.
scratch
scratch
scratch
scratch
WE FIND A SCHOOL-RELATED REASON TO GO UP THERE.
TUTORING OR SOMETHING...
WHO'S GOING TO BELIEVE I'M A TEACHING ASSISTANT?
scratch
scratch
scratch
scratch
YOU JUST BRING THIS BOOK TO CLASS TOMORROW.
THE DIVINE COMEDY
scratch
scratch
scratch
scratch
scratch
scratch

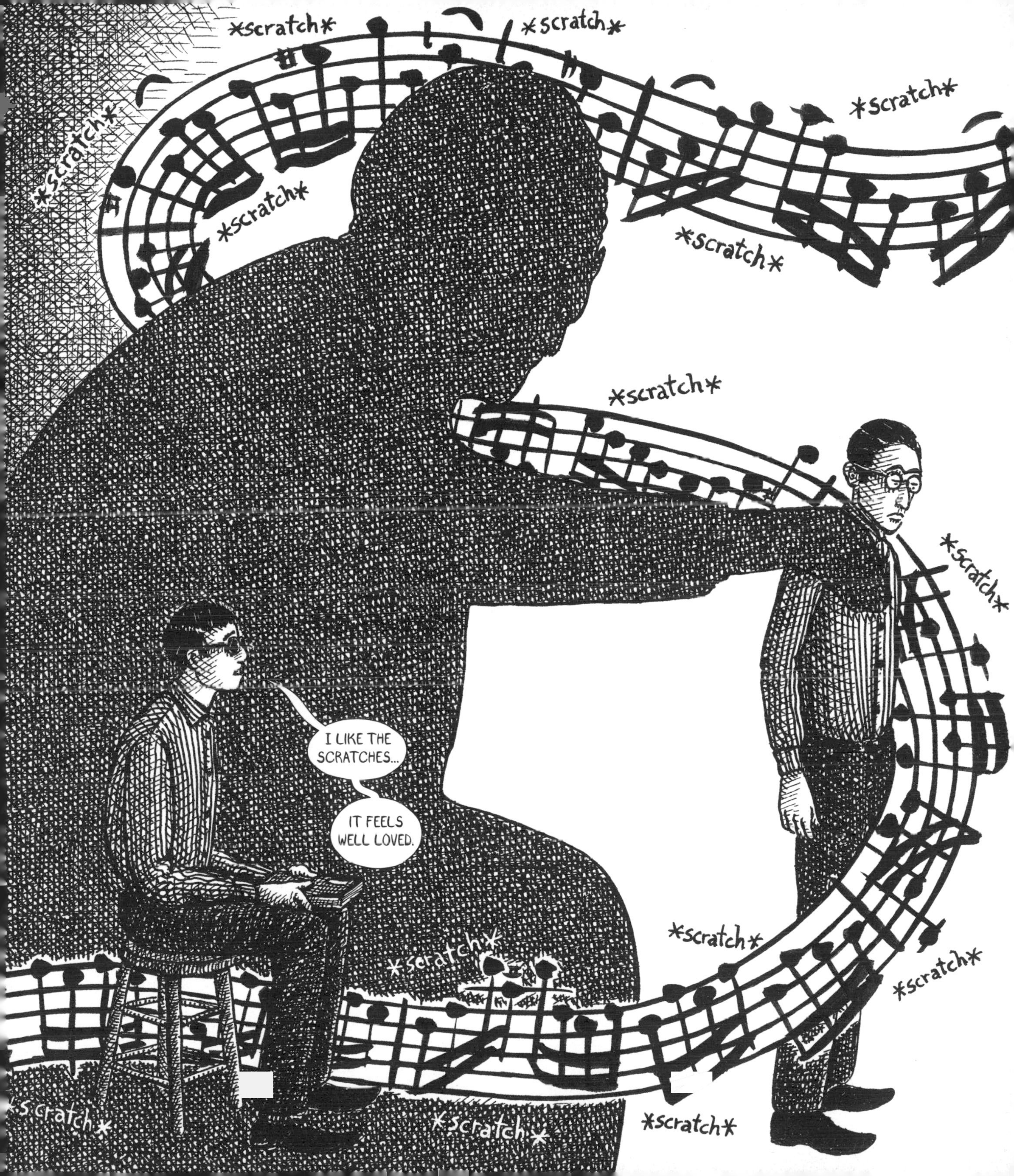
scratch
scratch
scratch
scratch
scratch
scratch
scratch
scratch
I LIKE THE SCRATCHES...
IT FEELS WELL LOVED.
scratch
scratch
scratch
scratch
scratch
scratch

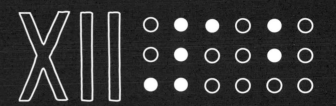

XII

THE WOODS OF THE SUICIDES

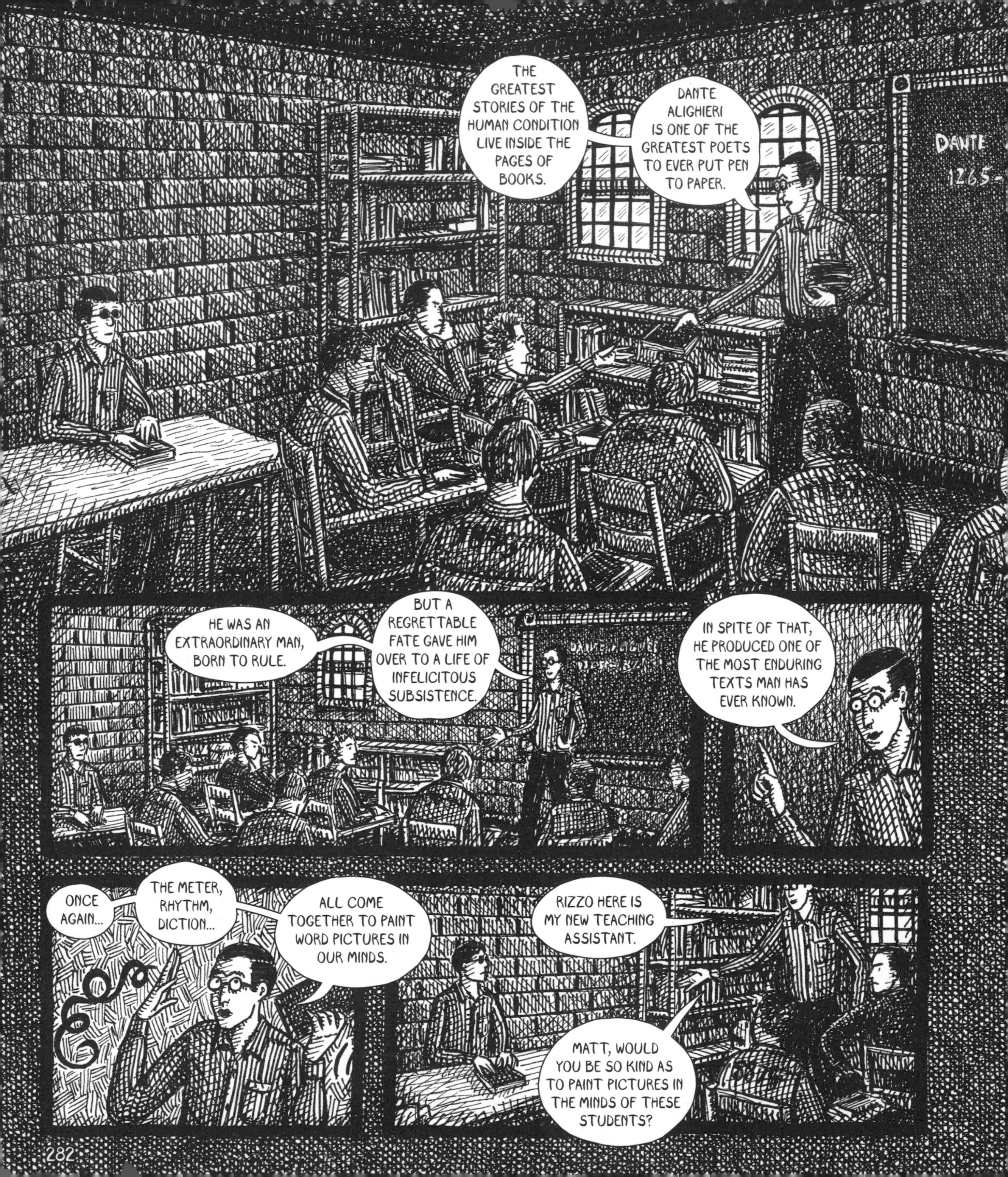
THE GREATEST STORIES OF THE HUMAN CONDITION LIVE INSIDE THE PAGES OF BOOKS.
DANTE ALIGHIERI IS ONE OF THE GREATEST POETS TO EVER PUT PEN TO PAPER.
DANTE
1265-
HE WAS AN EXTRAORDINARY MAN, BORN TO RULE.
BUT A REGRETTABLE FATE GAVE HIM OVER TO A LIFE OF INFELICITOUS SUBSISTENCE.
IN SPITE OF THAT, HE PRODUCED ONE OF THE MOST ENDURING TEXTS MAN HAS EVER KNOWN.
ONCE AGAIN...
THE METER, RHYTHM, DICTION...
ALL COME TOGETHER TO PAINT WORD PICTURES IN OUR MINDS.
RIZZO HERE IS MY NEW TEACHING ASSISTANT.
MATT, WOULD YOU BE SO KIND AS TO PAINT PICTURES IN THE MINDS OF THESE STUDENTS?

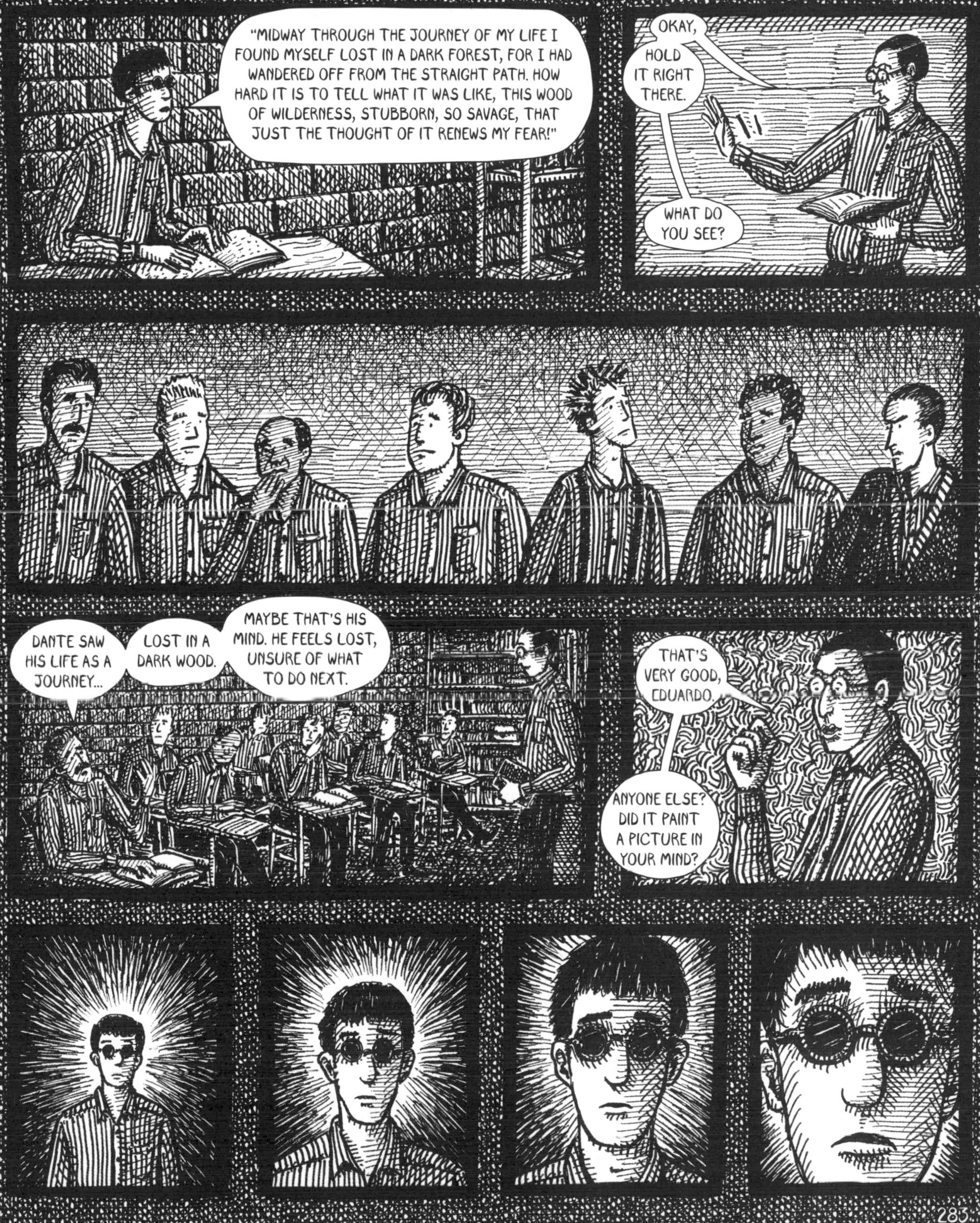

"MIDWAY THROUGH THE JOURNEY OF MY LIFE I FOUND MYSELF LOST IN A DARK FOREST, FOR I HAD WANDERED OFF FROM THE STRAIGHT PATH. HOW HARD IT IS TO TELL WHAT IT WAS LIKE, THIS WOOD OF WILDERNESS, STUBBORN, SO SAVAGE, THAT JUST THE THOUGHT OF IT RENEWS MY FEAR!"
OKAY,
HOLD IT RIGHT THERE.
WHAT DO YOU SEE?
DANTE SAW HIS LIFE AS A JOURNEY...
LOST IN A DARK WOOD.
MAYBE THAT'S HIS MIND. HE FEELS LOST, UNSURE OF WHAT TO DO NEXT.
THAT'S VERY GOOD, EDUARDO.
ANYONE ELSE? DID IT PAINT A PICTURE IN YOUR MIND?

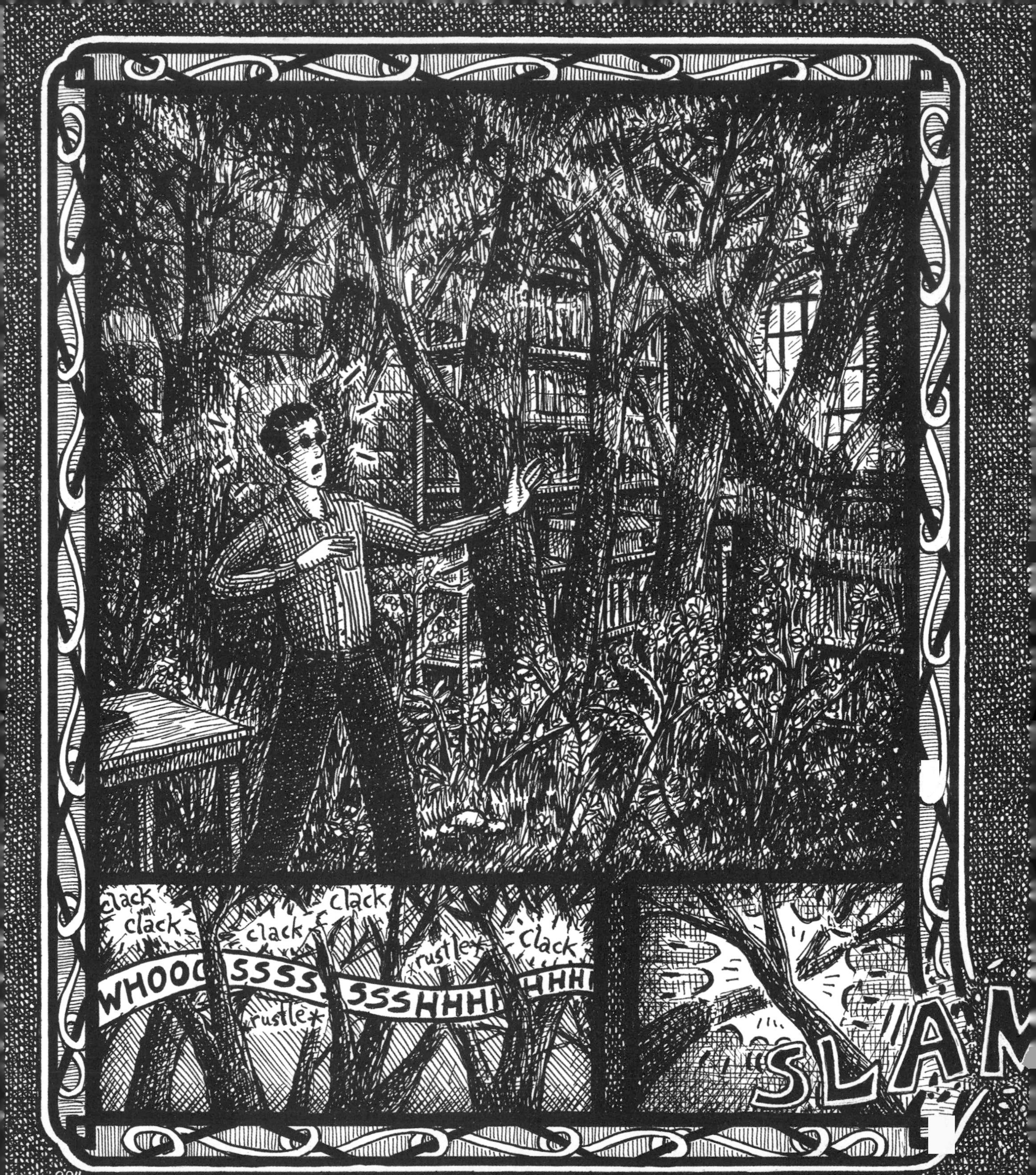
clack
clack
clack
clack
rustle
clack
WHOOOSSSSS SSSSHHHHHHHHH
rustle
SLAM

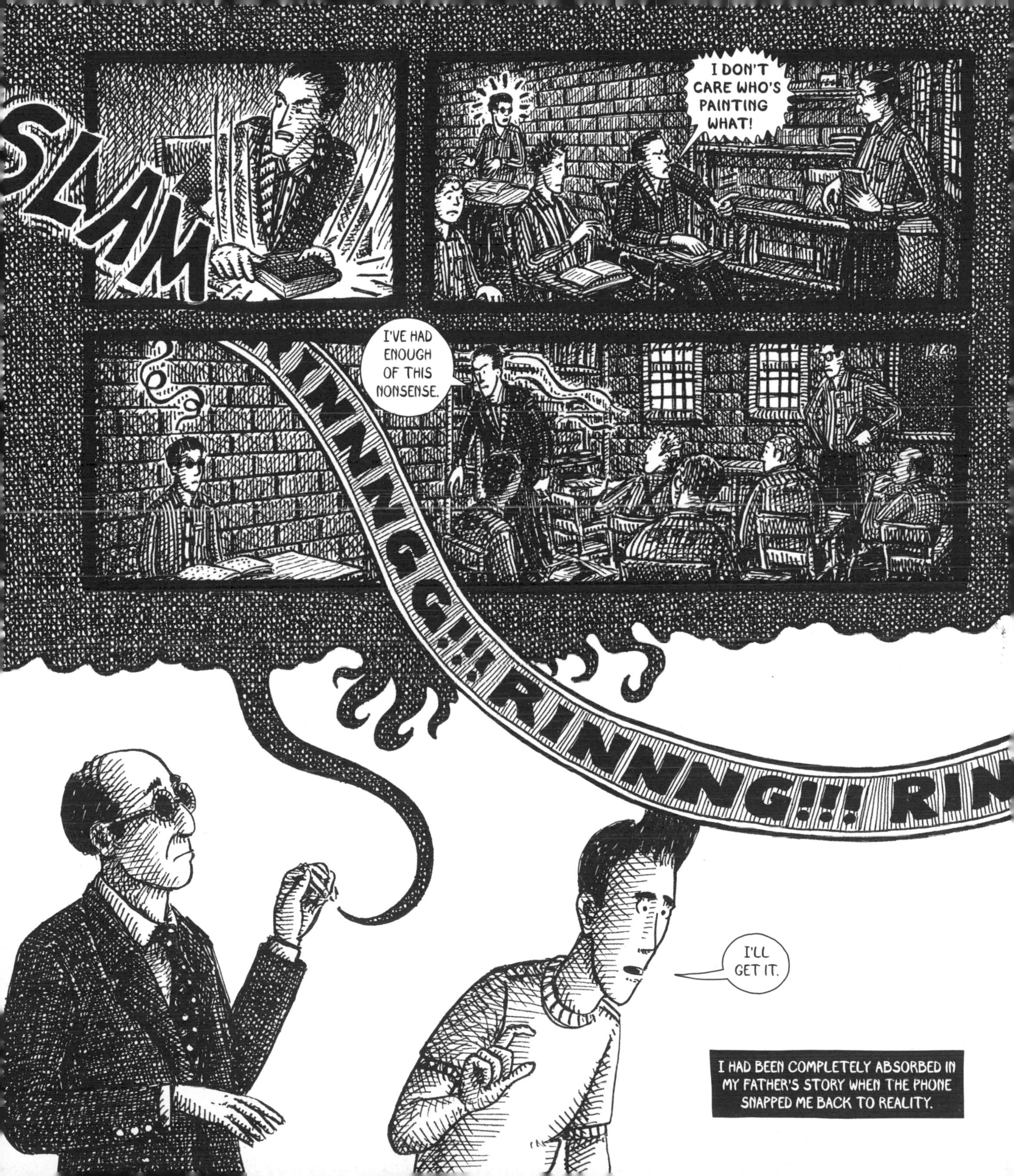
SLAM
I DON'T CARE WHO'S PAINTING WHAT!
I'VE HAD ENOUGH OF THIS NONSENSE.
RINNNG!!! RINNNG!!! RIN
I'LL GET IT.
I HAD BEEN COMPLETELY ABSORBED IN MY FATHER'S STORY WHEN THE PHONE SNAPPED ME BACK TO REALITY.

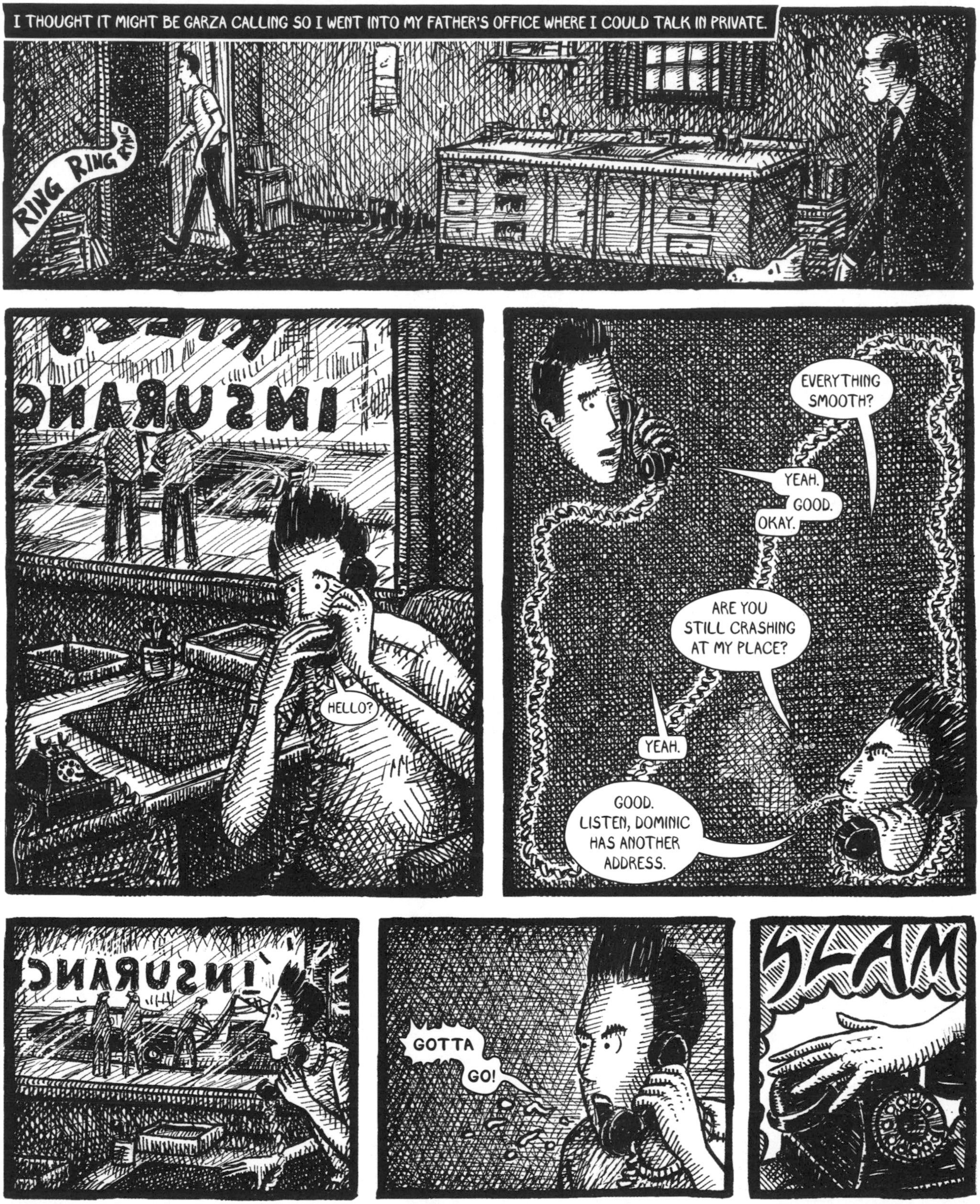
I THOUGHT IT MIGHT BE GARZA CALLING SO I WENT INTO MY FATHER'S OFFICE WHERE I COULD TALK IN PRIVATE.
RING RING RING
INSURANC
HELLO?
EVERYTHING SMOOTH?
YEAH.
GOOD.
OKAY.
ARE YOU STILL CRASHING AT MY PLACE?
YEAH.
GOOD. LISTEN, DOMINIC HAS ANOTHER ADDRESS.
INSURANC
GOTTA
GO!
SLAM

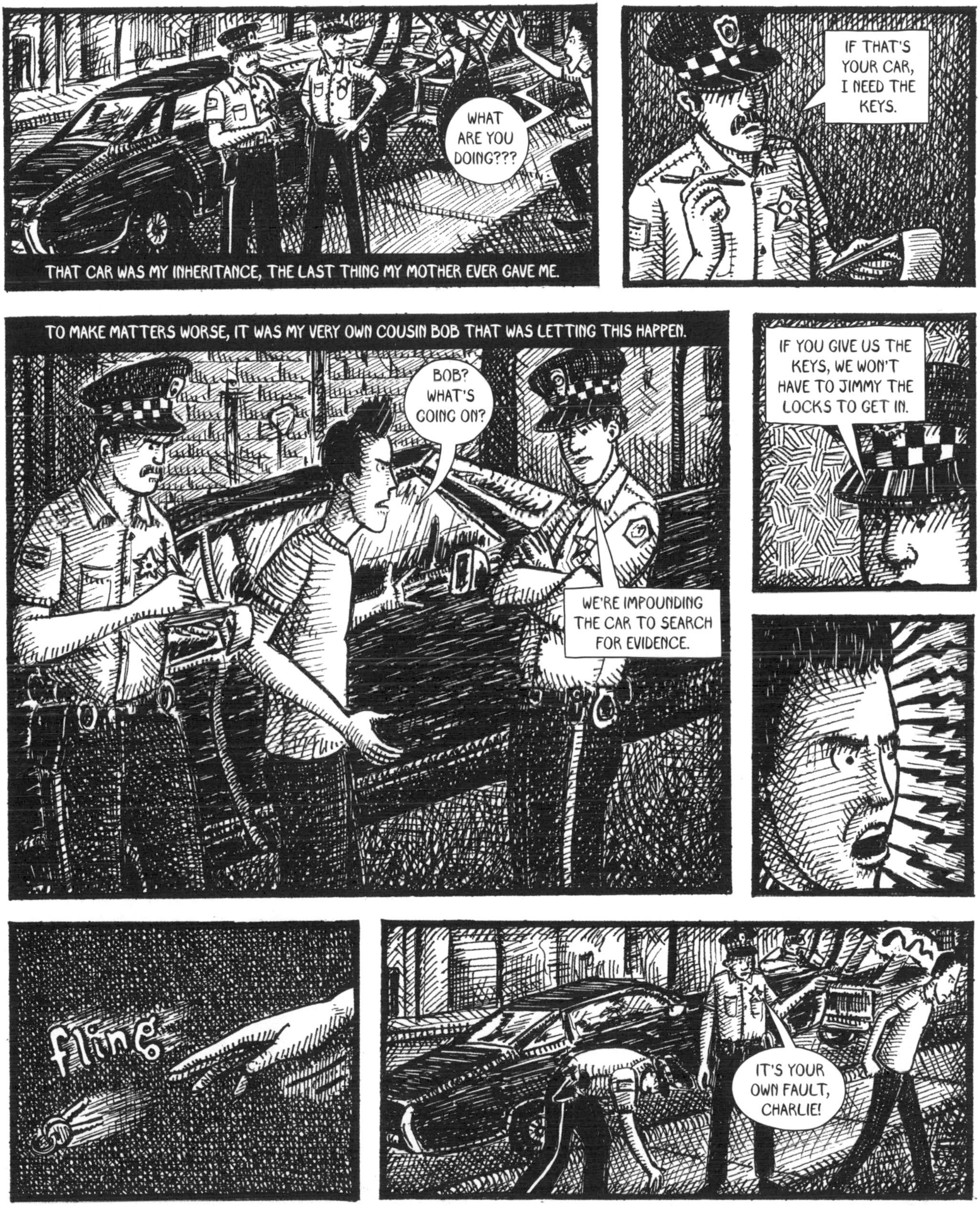
WHAT ARE YOU DOING???
THAT CAR WAS MY INHERITANCE, THE LAST THING MY MOTHER EVER GAVE ME.
IF THAT'S YOUR CAR, I NEED THE KEYS.
TO MAKE MATTERS WORSE, IT WAS MY VERY OWN COUSIN BOB THAT WAS LETTING THIS HAPPEN.
BOB? WHAT'S GOING ON?
WE'RE IMPOUNDING THE CAR TO SEARCH FOR EVIDENCE.
IF YOU GIVE US THE KEYS, WE WON'T HAVE TO JIMMY THE LOCKS TO GET IN.
fling
IT'S YOUR OWN FAULT, CHARLIE!

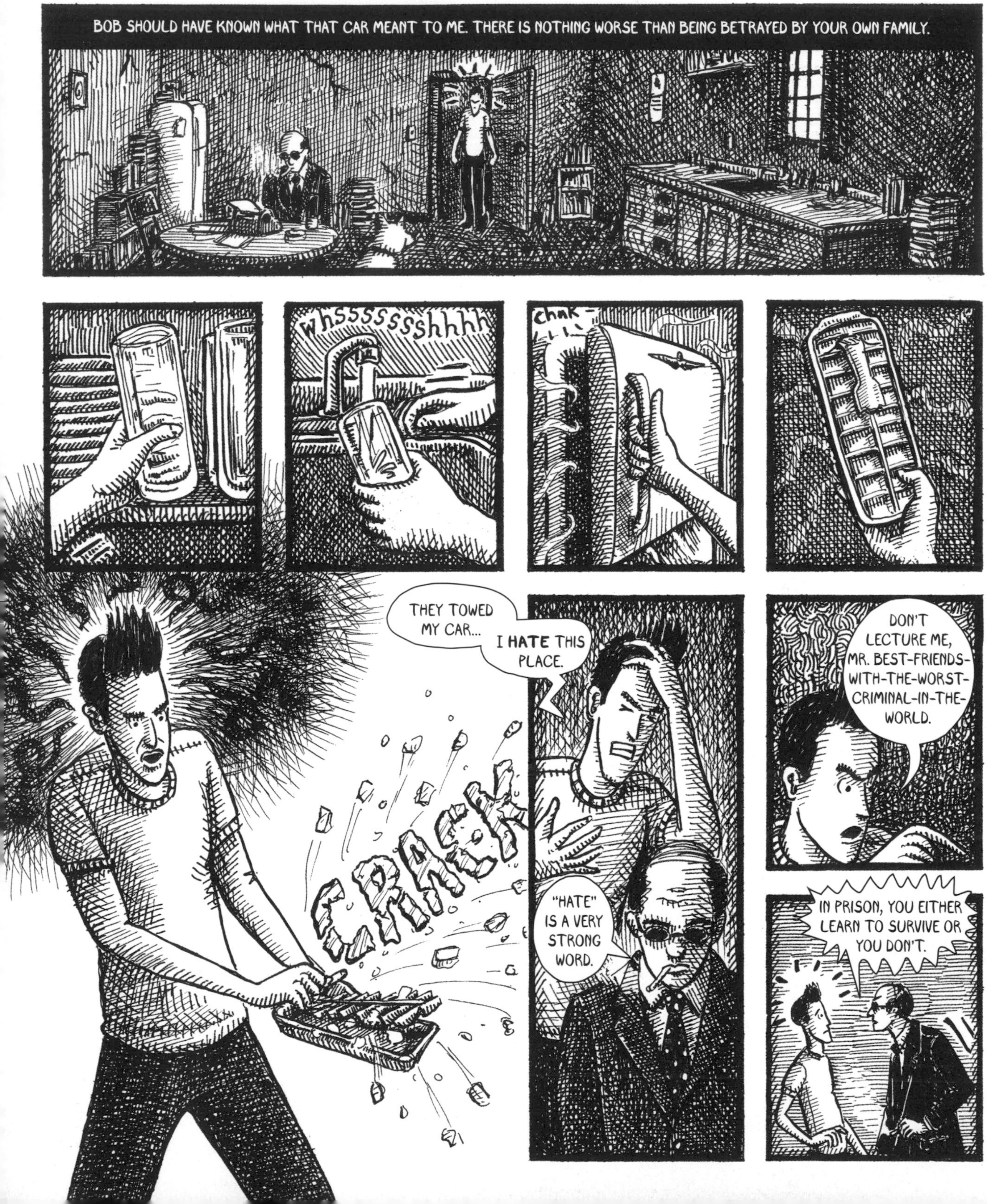
BOB SHOULD HAVE KNOWN WHAT THAT CAR MEANT TO ME. THERE IS NOTHING WORSE THAN BEING BETRAYED BY YOUR OWN FAMILY.
whsssssssshhhh
chak
CRACK
THEY TOWED MY CAR...
I **HATE** THIS PLACE.
"HATE" IS A VERY STRONG WORD.
DON'T LECTURE ME, MR. BEST-FRIENDS-WITH-THE-WORST-CRIMINAL-IN-THE-WORLD.
IN PRISON, YOU EITHER LEARN TO SURVIVE OR YOU DON'T.

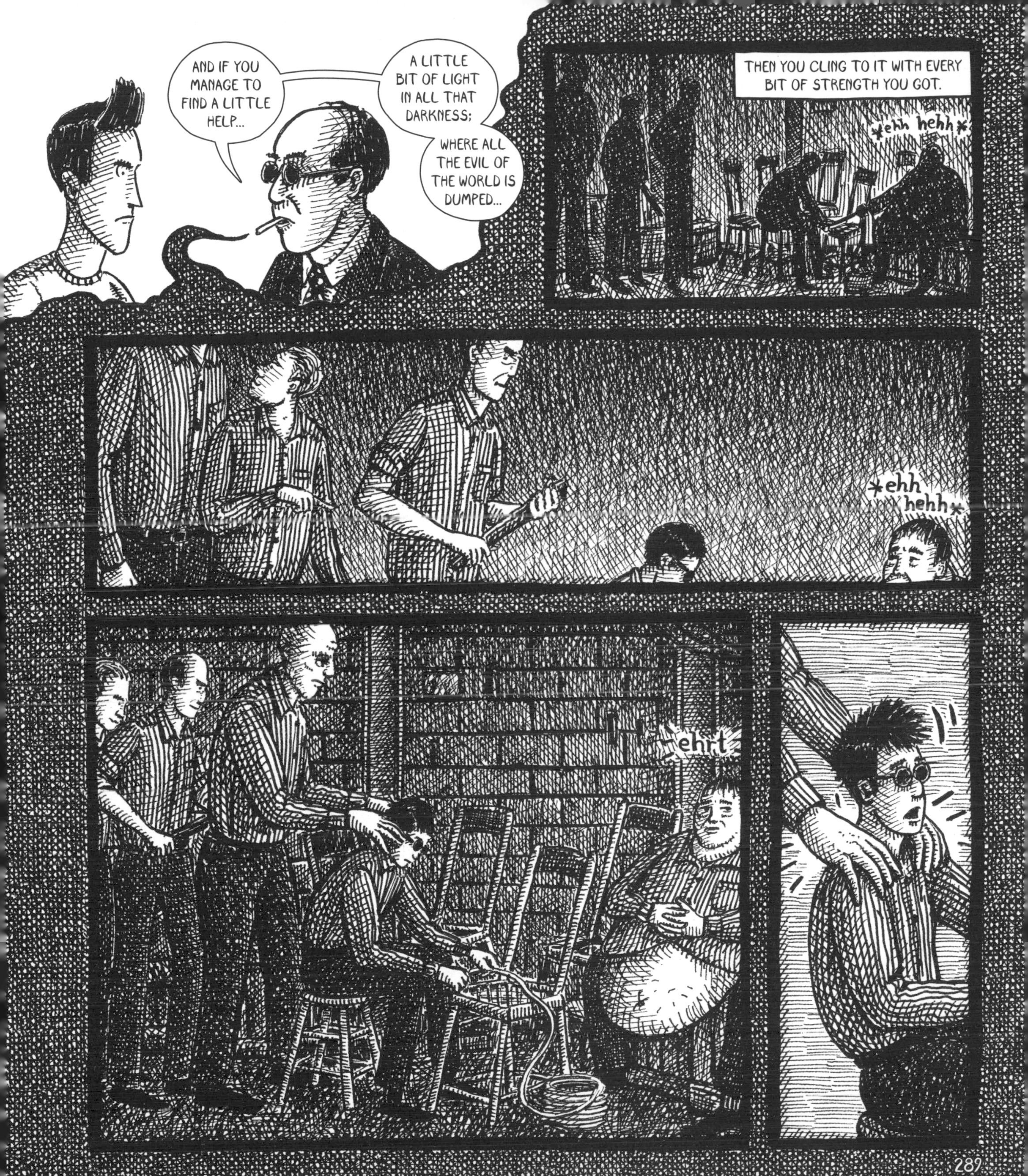
AND IF YOU MANAGE TO FIND A LITTLE HELP...
A LITTLE BIT OF LIGHT IN ALL THAT DARKNESS;
WHERE ALL THE EVIL OF THE WORLD IS DUMPED...
THEN YOU CLING TO IT WITH EVERY BIT OF STRENGTH YOU GOT.
ehh hehh
ehh hehh
ehrt
!

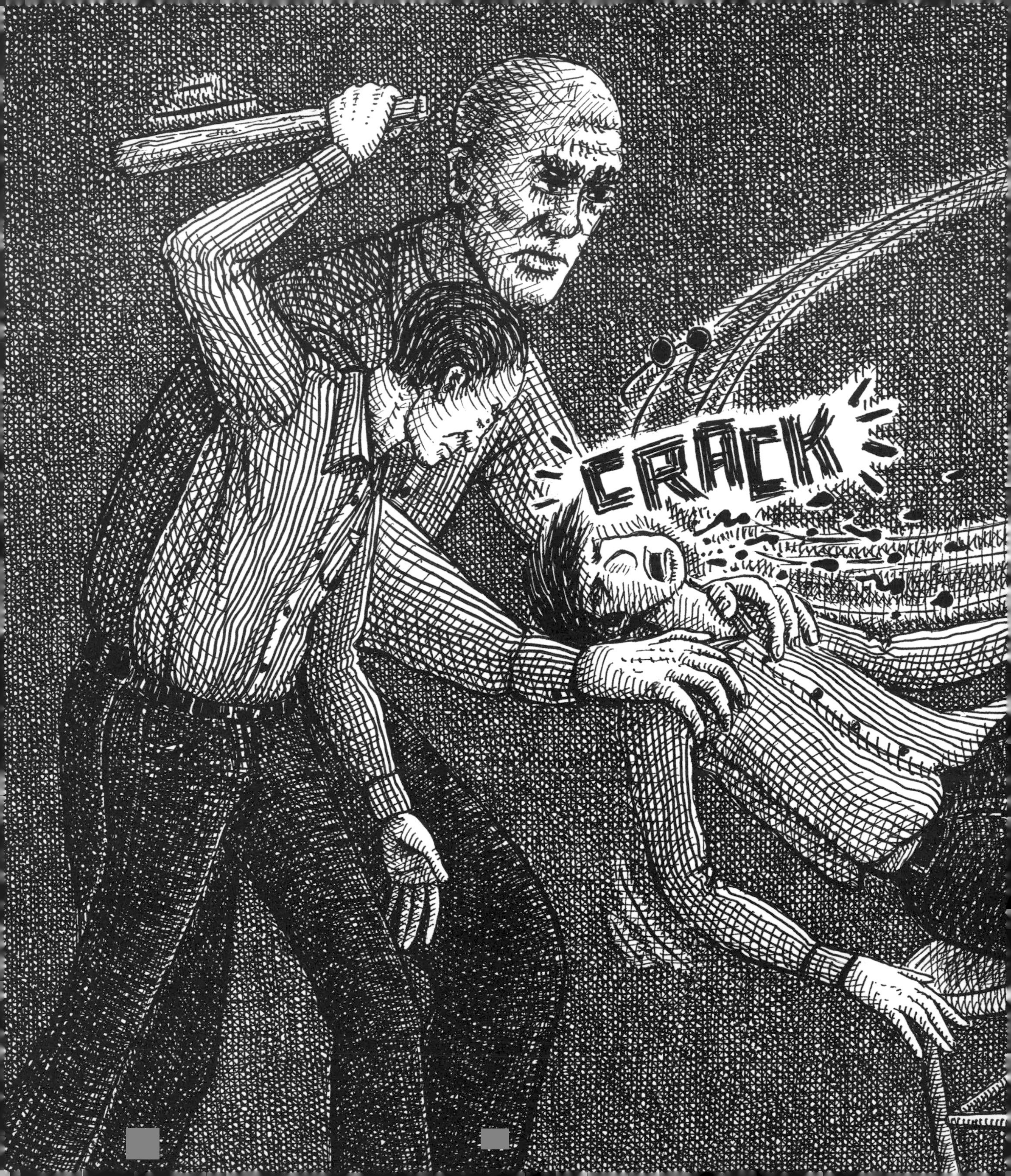
CRACK

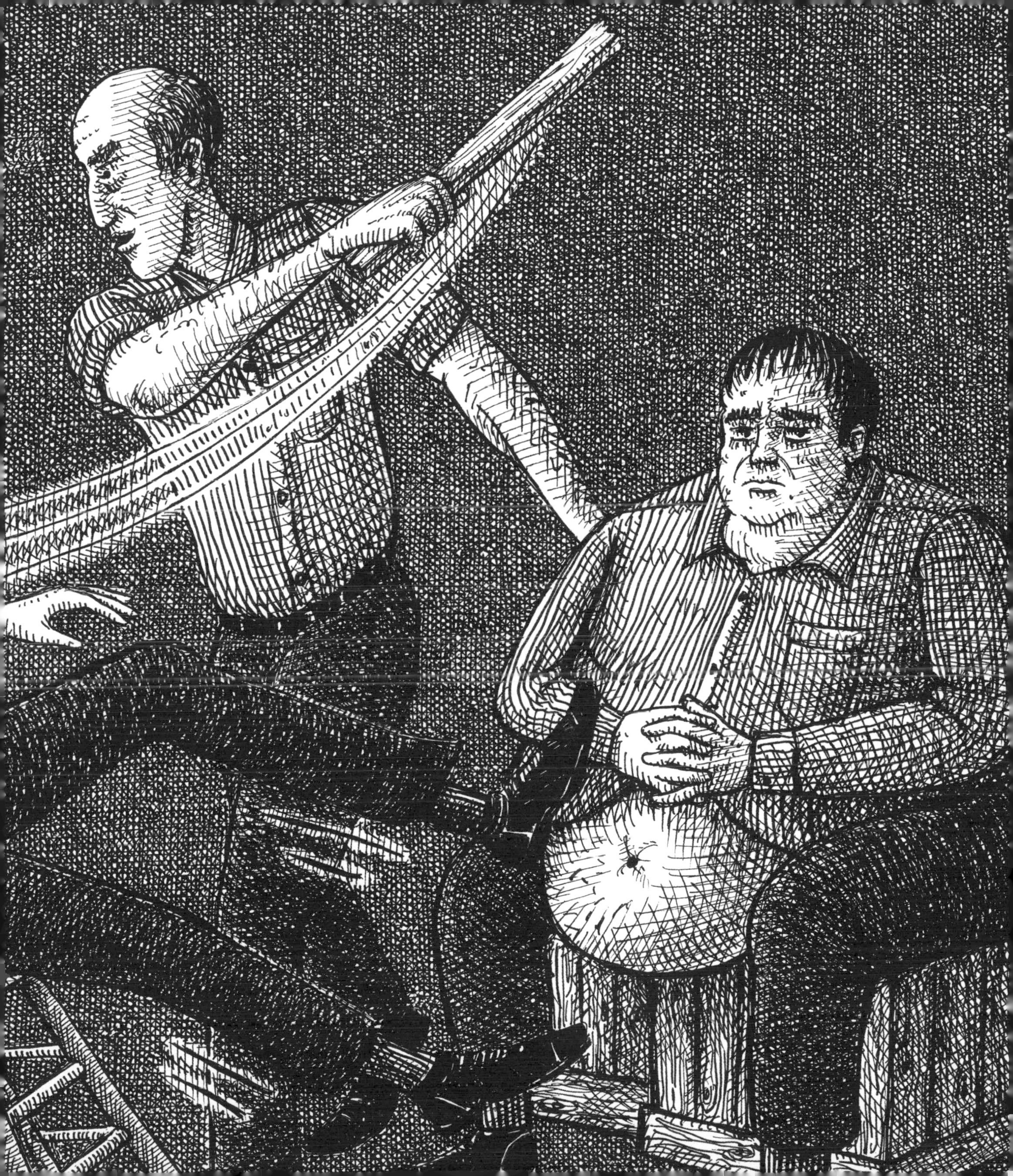

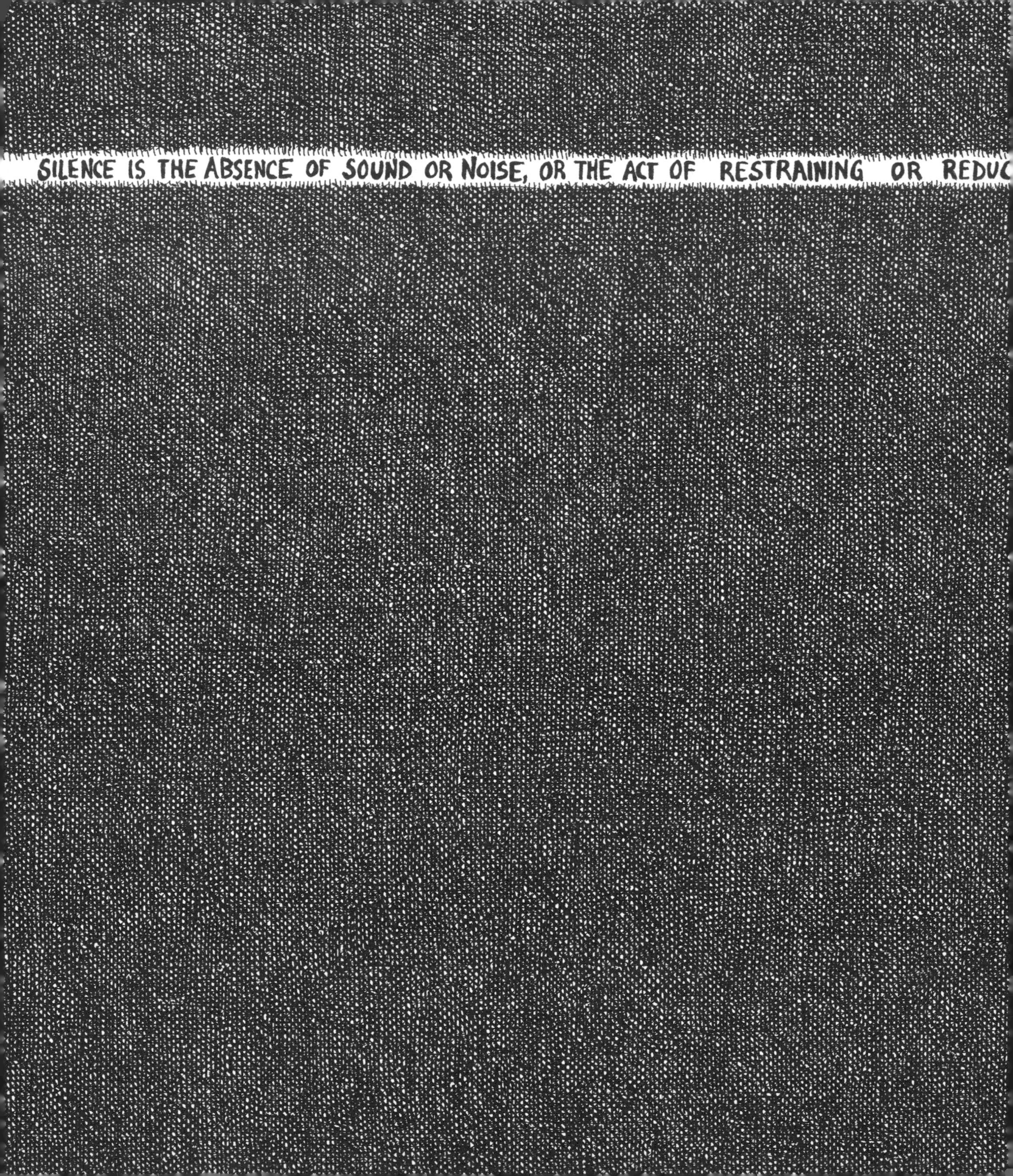
SILENCE IS THE ABSENCE OF SOUND OR NOISE, OR THE ACT OF RESTRAINING OR REDUC

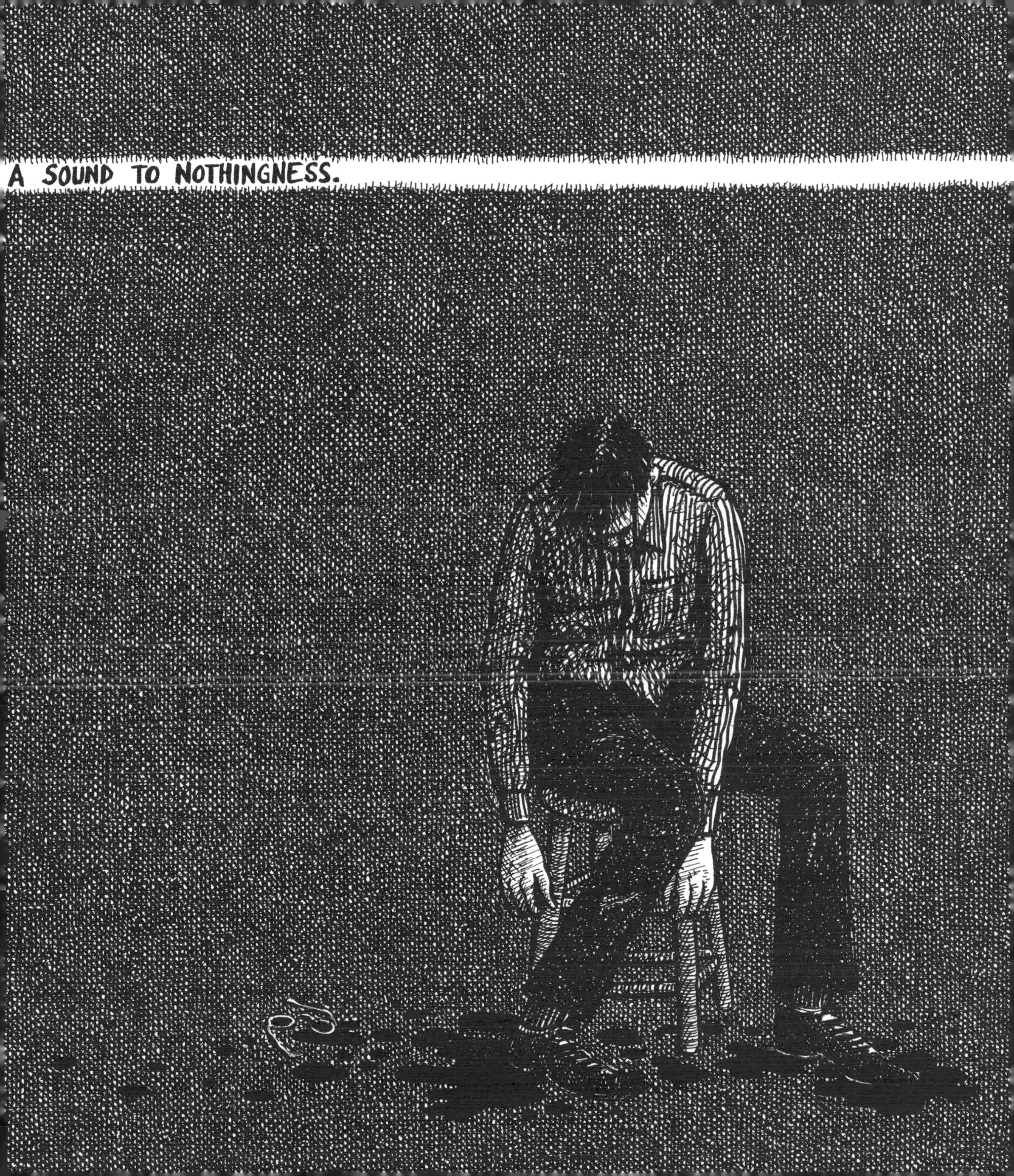
A SOUND TO NOTHINGNESS.

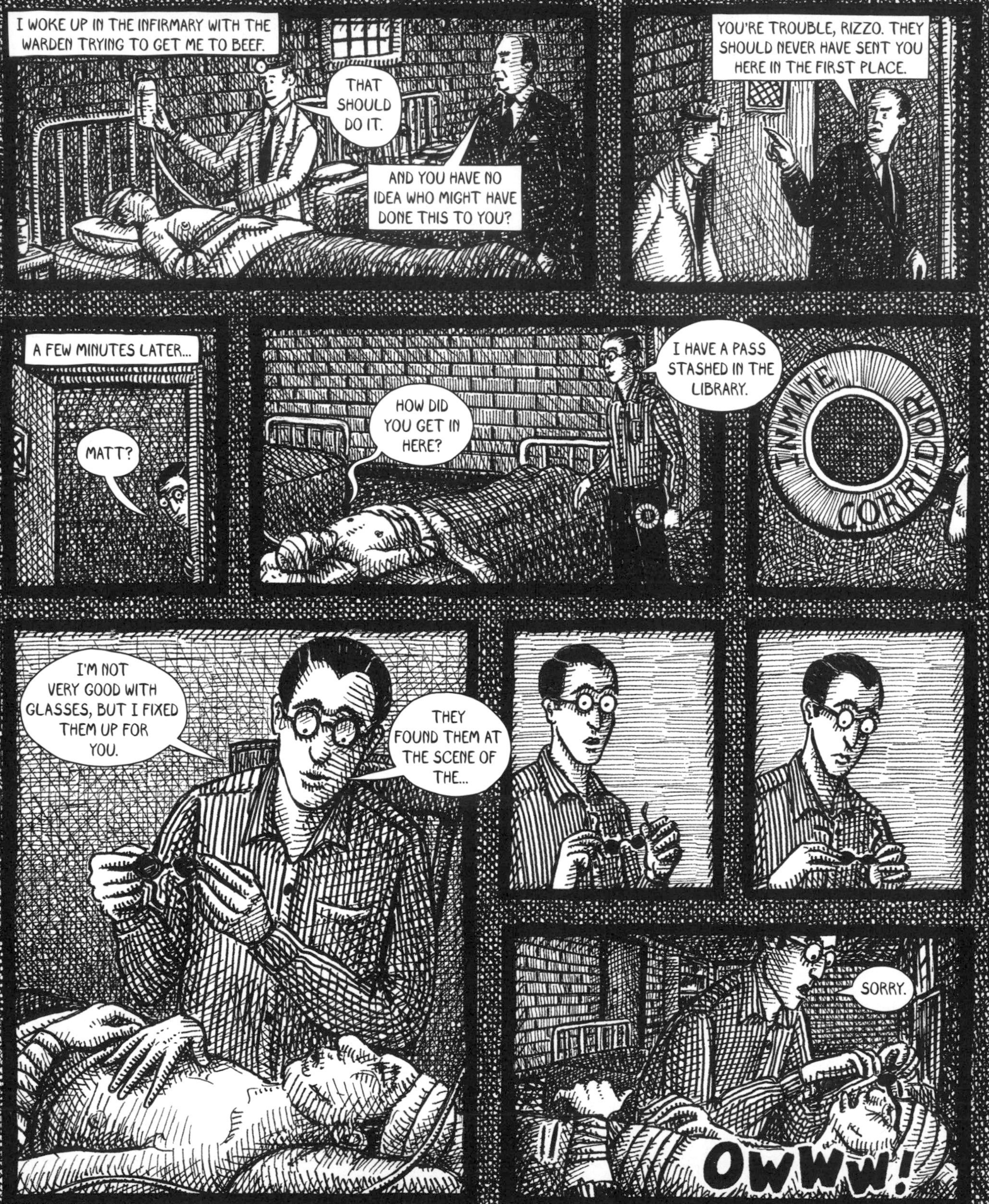
I WOKE UP IN THE INFIRMARY WITH THE WARDEN TRYING TO GET ME TO BEEF.
THAT SHOULD DO IT.
AND YOU HAVE NO IDEA WHO MIGHT HAVE DONE THIS TO YOU?
YOU'RE TROUBLE, RIZZO. THEY SHOULD NEVER HAVE SENT YOU HERE IN THE FIRST PLACE.
A FEW MINUTES LATER...
MATT?
HOW DID YOU GET IN HERE?
I HAVE A PASS STASHED IN THE LIBRARY.
INMATE CORRIDOR
I'M NOT VERY GOOD WITH GLASSES, BUT I FIXED THEM UP FOR YOU.
THEY FOUND THEM AT THE SCENE OF THE...
SORRY.
OWWW!

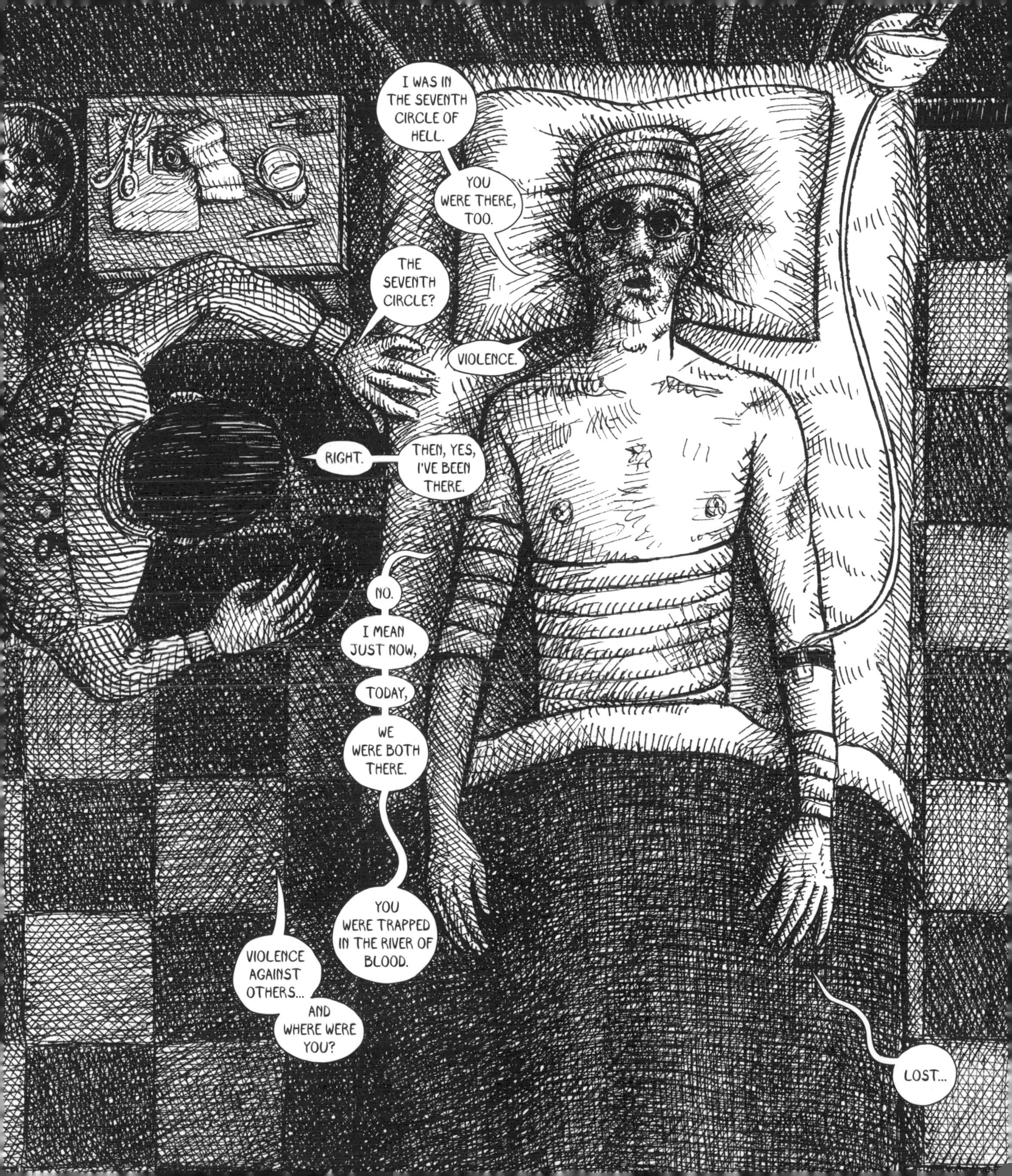
I WAS IN THE SEVENTH CIRCLE OF HELL.
YOU WERE THERE, TOO.
THE SEVENTH CIRCLE?
VIOLENCE.
RIGHT.
THEN, YES, I'VE BEEN THERE.
NO.
I MEAN JUST NOW,
TODAY,
WE WERE BOTH THERE.
YOU WERE TRAPPED IN THE RIVER OF BLOOD.
VIOLENCE AGAINST OTHERS...
AND WHERE WERE YOU?
LOST...

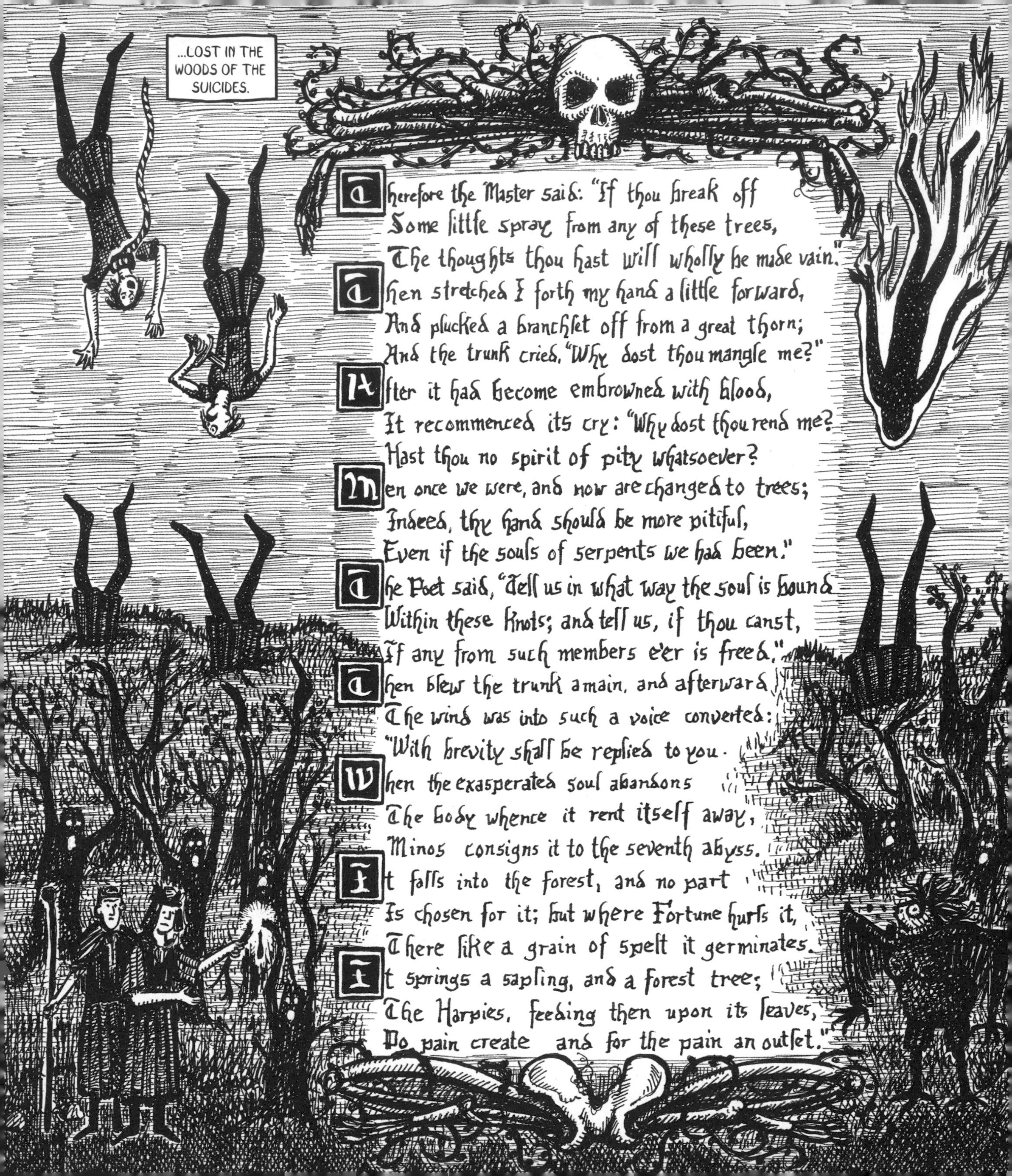
...LOST IN THE WOODS OF THE SUICIDES.
Therefore the Master said: "If thou break off
Some little spray from any of these trees,
The thoughts thou hast will wholly be made vain."
Then stretched I forth my hand a little forward,
And plucked a branchlet off from a great thorn;
And the trunk cried, "Why dost thou mangle me?"
After it had become embrowned with blood,
It recommenced its cry: "Why dost thou rend me?
Hast thou no spirit of pity whatsoever?
Men once we were, and now are changed to trees;
Indeed, thy hand should be more pitiful,
Even if the souls of serpents we had been."
The Poet said, "Tell us in what way the soul is bound
Within these knots; and tell us, if thou canst,
If any from such members e'er is freed."
Then blew the trunk amain, and afterward
The wind was into such a voice converted:
"With brevity shall be replied to you.
When the exasperated soul abandons
The body whence it rent itself away,
Minos consigns it to the seventh abyss.
It falls into the forest, and no part
Is chosen for it; but where Fortune hurls it,
There like a grain of spelt it germinates.
It springs a sapling, and a forest tree;
The Harpies, feeding then upon its leaves,
Do pain create and for the pain an outlet."

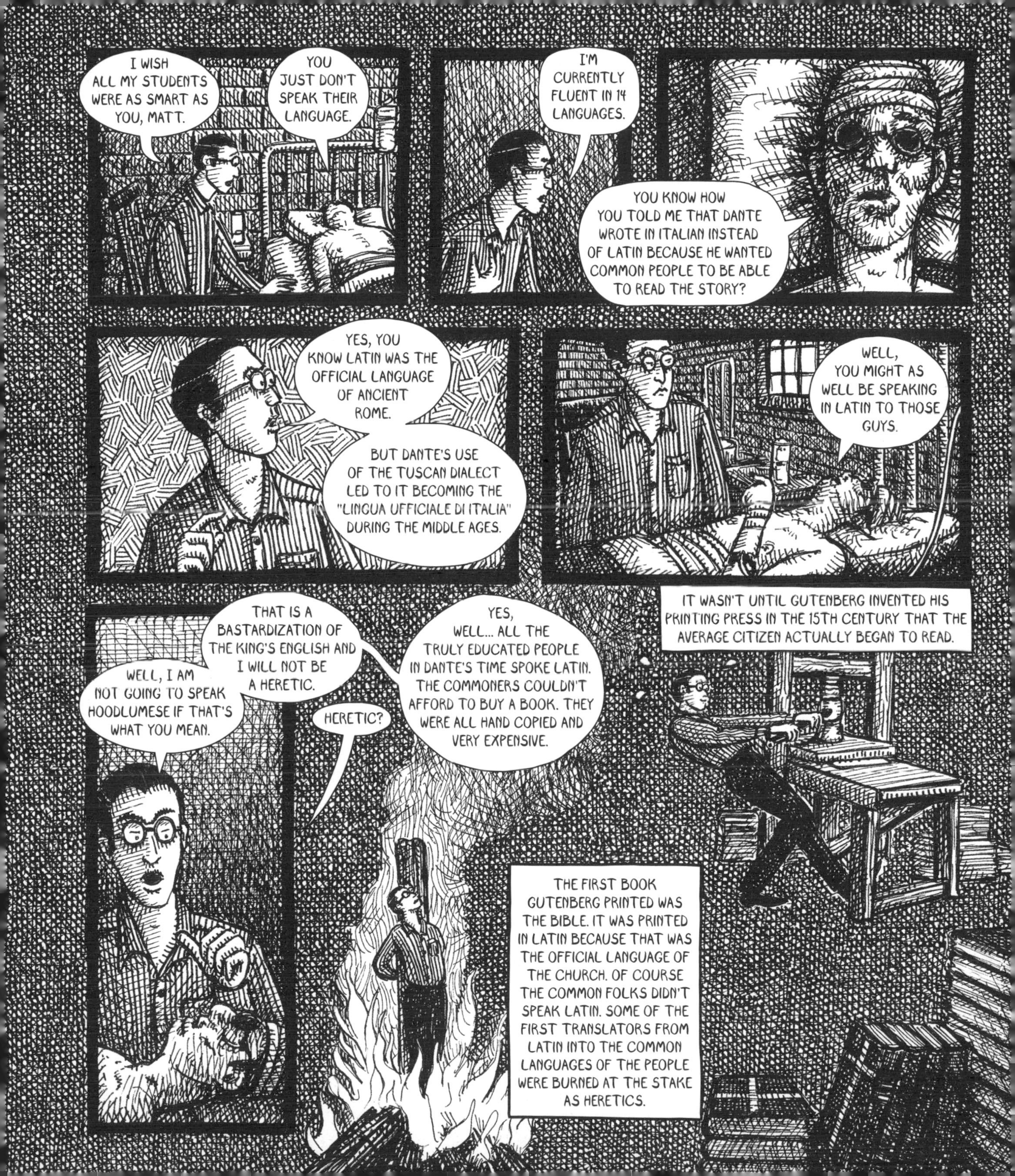
I WISH ALL MY STUDENTS WERE AS SMART AS YOU, MATT.
YOU JUST DON'T SPEAK THEIR LANGUAGE.
I'M CURRENTLY FLUENT IN 14 LANGUAGES.
YOU KNOW HOW YOU TOLD ME THAT DANTE WROTE IN ITALIAN INSTEAD OF LATIN BECAUSE HE WANTED COMMON PEOPLE TO BE ABLE TO READ THE STORY?
YES, YOU KNOW LATIN WAS THE OFFICIAL LANGUAGE OF ANCIENT ROME.
BUT DANTE'S USE OF THE TUSCAN DIALECT LED TO IT BECOMING THE "LINGUA UFFICIALE DI ITALIA" DURING THE MIDDLE AGES.
WELL, YOU MIGHT AS WELL BE SPEAKING IN LATIN TO THOSE GUYS.
WELL, I AM NOT GOING TO SPEAK HOODLUMESE IF THAT'S WHAT YOU MEAN.
THAT IS A BASTARDIZATION OF THE KING'S ENGLISH AND I WILL NOT BE A HERETIC.
HERETIC?
YES, WELL... ALL THE TRULY EDUCATED PEOPLE IN DANTE'S TIME SPOKE LATIN. THE COMMONERS COULDN'T AFFORD TO BUY A BOOK. THEY WERE ALL HAND COPIED AND VERY EXPENSIVE.
IT WASN'T UNTIL GUTENBERG INVENTED HIS PRINTING PRESS IN THE 15TH CENTURY THAT THE AVERAGE CITIZEN ACTUALLY BEGAN TO READ.
THE FIRST BOOK GUTENBERG PRINTED WAS THE BIBLE. IT WAS PRINTED IN LATIN BECAUSE THAT WAS THE OFFICIAL LANGUAGE OF THE CHURCH. OF COURSE THE COMMON FOLKS DIDN'T SPEAK LATIN. SOME OF THE FIRST TRANSLATORS FROM LATIN INTO THE COMMON LANGUAGES OF THE PEOPLE WERE BURNED AT THE STAKE AS HERETICS.

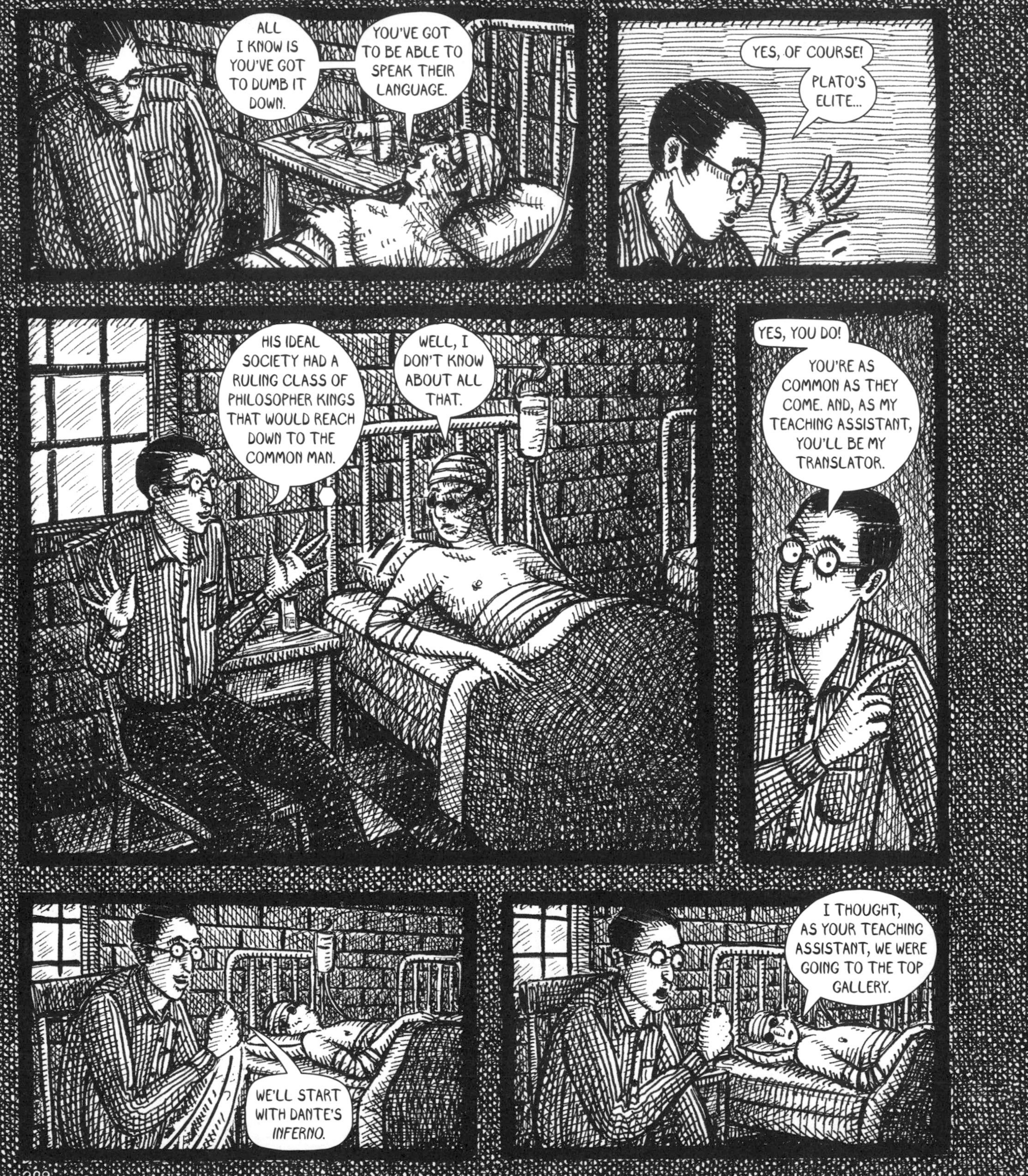
ALL I KNOW IS YOU'VE GOT TO DUMB IT DOWN.
YOU'VE GOT TO BE ABLE TO SPEAK THEIR LANGUAGE.
YES, OF COURSE!
PLATO'S ELITE...
HIS IDEAL SOCIETY HAD A RULING CLASS OF PHILOSOPHER KINGS THAT WOULD REACH DOWN TO THE COMMON MAN.
WELL, I DON'T KNOW ABOUT ALL THAT.
YES, YOU DO!
YOU'RE AS COMMON AS THEY COME. AND, AS MY TEACHING ASSISTANT, YOU'LL BE MY TRANSLATOR.
WE'LL START WITH DANTE'S *INFERNO*.
I THOUGHT, AS YOUR TEACHING ASSISTANT, WE WERE GOING TO THE TOP GALLERY.

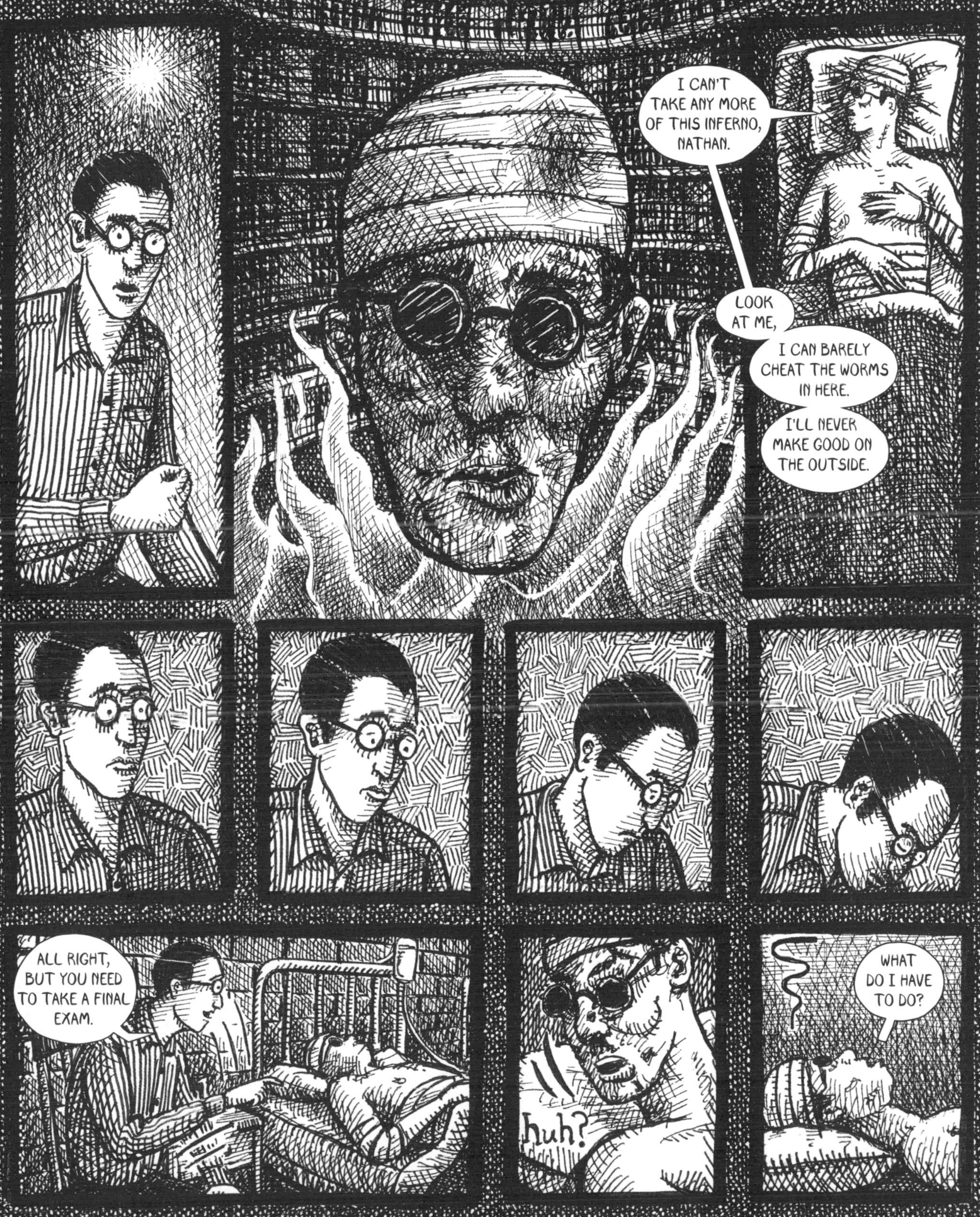
I CAN'T TAKE ANY MORE OF THIS INFERNO, NATHAN.
LOOK AT ME,
I CAN BARELY CHEAT THE WORMS IN HERE.
I'LL NEVER MAKE GOOD ON THE OUTSIDE.
ALL RIGHT, BUT YOU NEED TO TAKE A FINAL EXAM.
huh?
WHAT DO I HAVE TO DO?

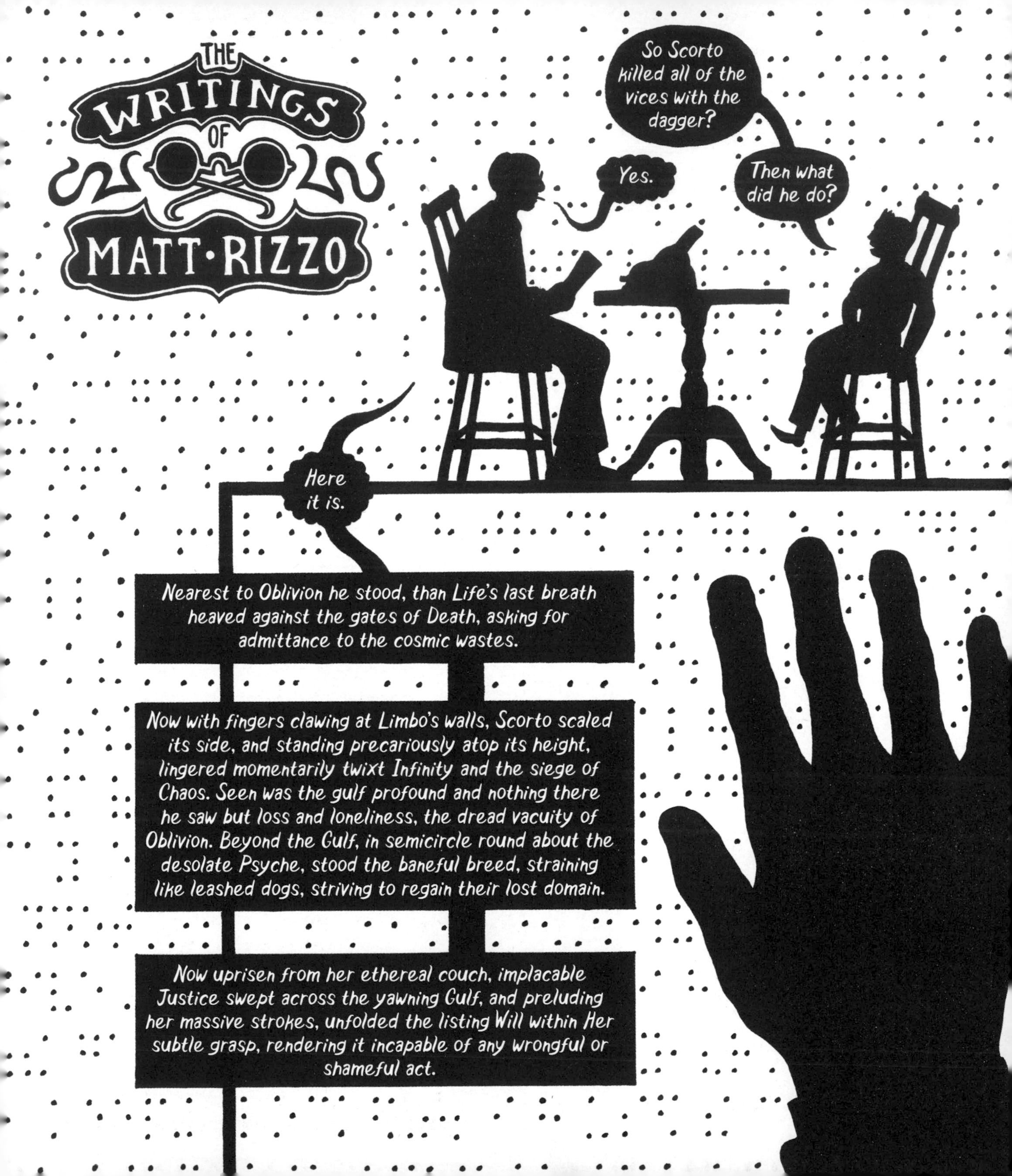
THE WRITINGS OF MATT·RIZZO
So Scorto killed all of the vices with the dagger?
Yes.
Then what did he do?
Here it is.
Nearest to Oblivion he stood, than Life's last breath heaved against the gates of Death, asking for admittance to the cosmic wastes.
Now with fingers clawing at Limbo's walls, Scorto scaled its side, and standing precariously atop its height, lingered momentarily twixt Infinity and the siege of Chaos. Seen was the gulf profound and nothing there he saw but loss and loneliness, the dread vacuity of Oblivion. Beyond the Gulf, in semicircle round about the desolate Psyche, stood the baneful breed, straining like leashed dogs, striving to regain their lost domain.
Now uprisen from her ethereal couch, implacable Justice swept across the yawning Gulf, and preluding her massive strokes, unfolded the listing Will within Her subtle grasp, rendering it incapable of any wrongful or shameful act.

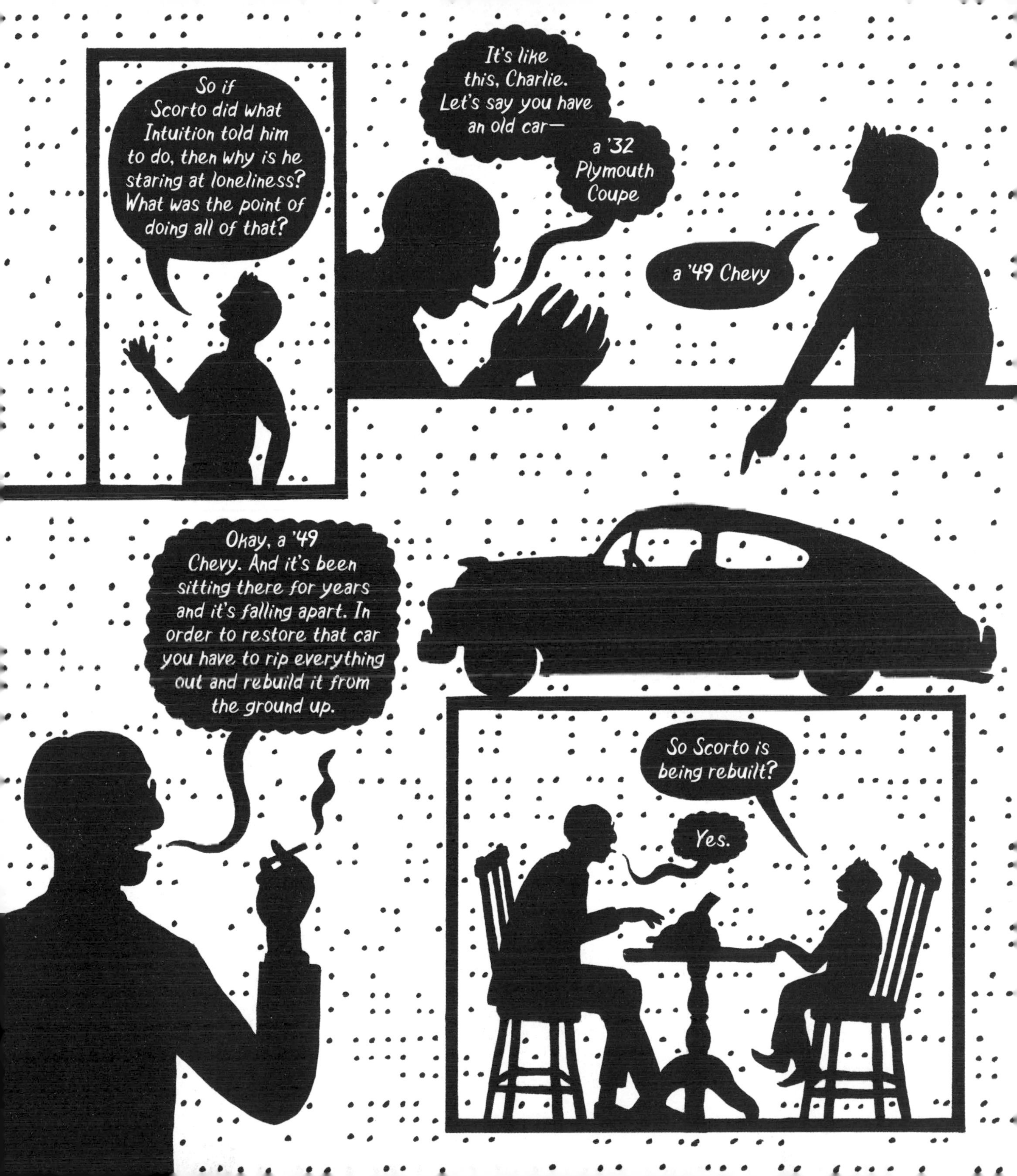
So if Scorto did what Intuition told him to do, then why is he staring at loneliness? What was the point of doing all of that?
It's like this, Charlie. Let's say you have an old car—
a '32 Plymouth Coupe
a '49 Chevy
Okay, a '49 Chevy. And it's been sitting there for years and it's falling apart. In order to restore that car you have to rip everything out and rebuild it from the ground up.
So Scorto is being rebuilt?
Yes.

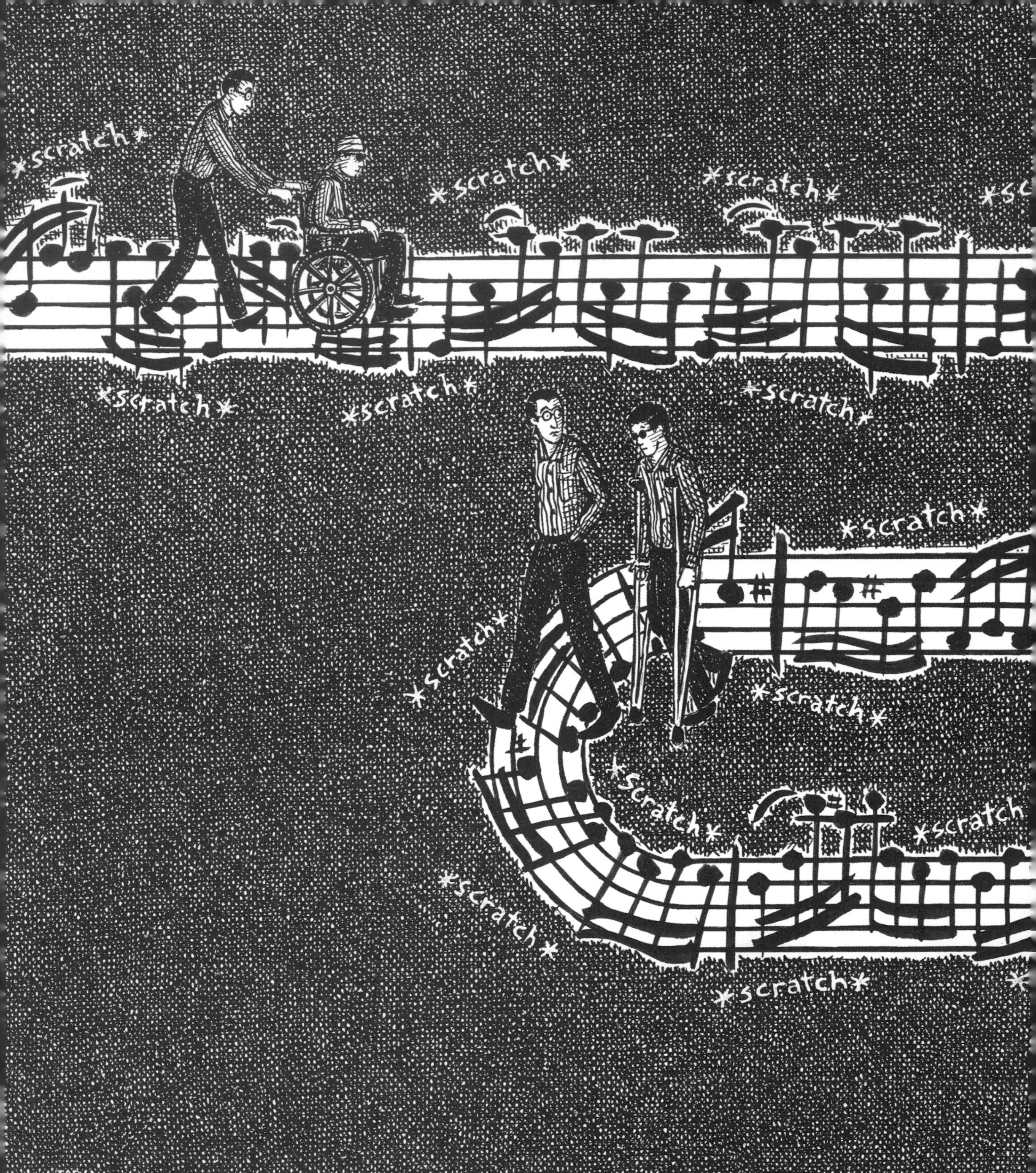
scratch
scratch
scratch
scratch
scratch
scratch
scratch
scratch
scratch
Scratch
*scratch
scratch
scratch

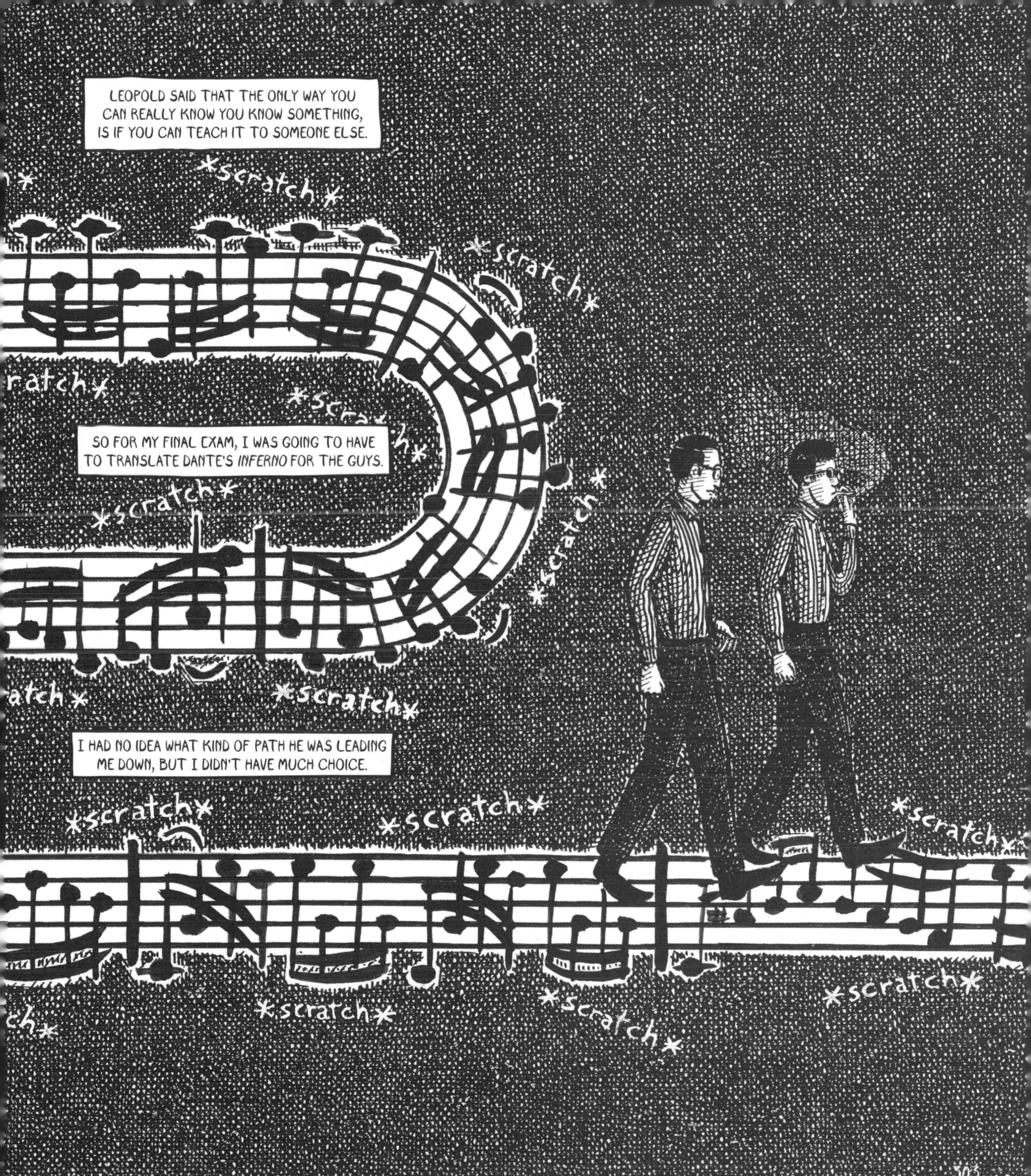
LEOPOLD SAID THAT THE ONLY WAY YOU CAN REALLY KNOW YOU KNOW SOMETHING, IS IF YOU CAN TEACH IT TO SOMEONE ELSE.
scratch
scratch
SO FOR MY FINAL EXAM, I WAS GOING TO HAVE TO TRANSLATE DANTE'S *INFERNO* FOR THE GUYS.
scratch
scratch
scratch
I HAD NO IDEA WHAT KIND OF PATH HE WAS LEADING ME DOWN, BUT I DIDN'T HAVE MUCH CHOICE.
scratch
scratch
scratch
scratch
scratch
scratch

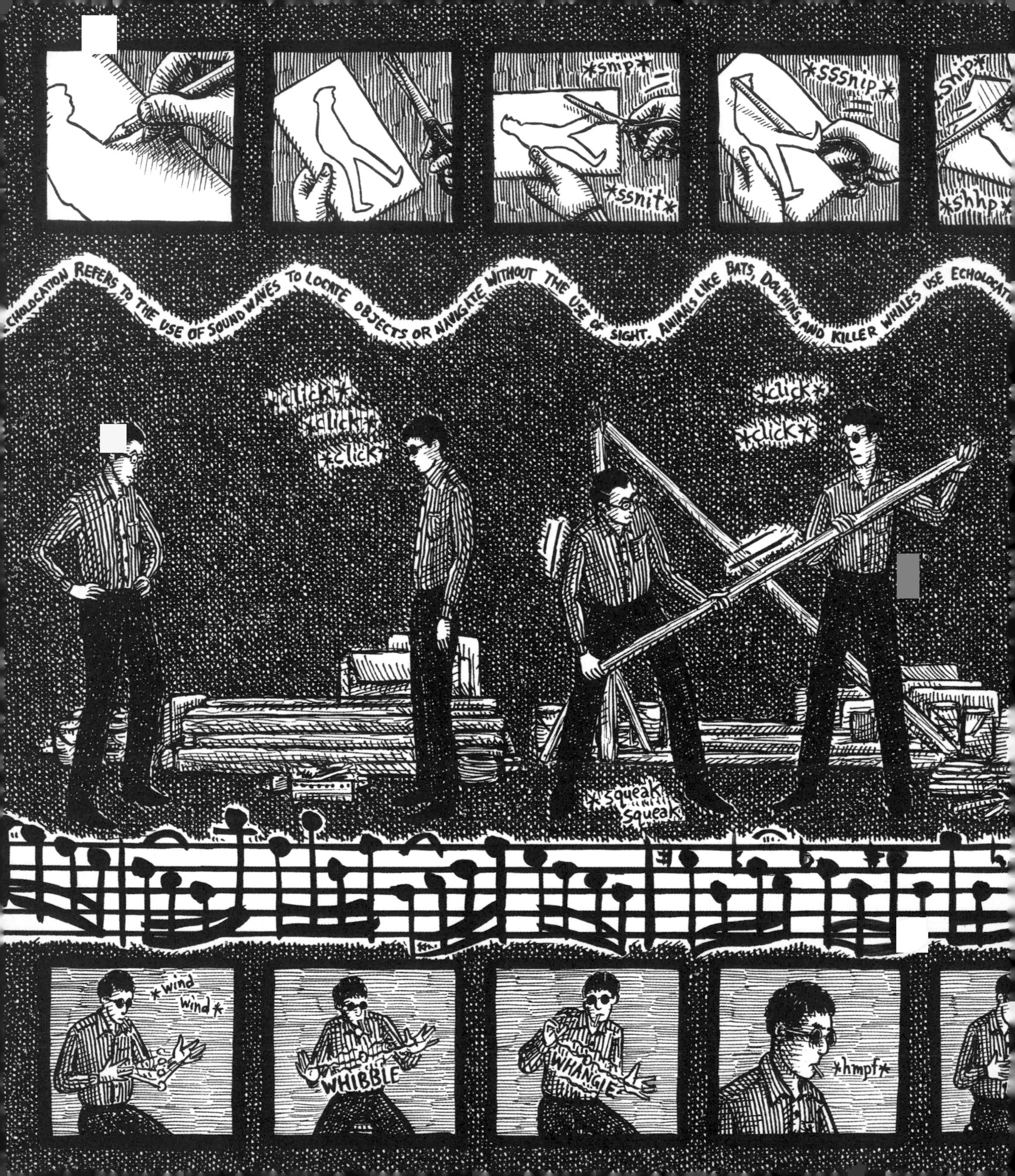
snip
ssnit
SSSnip
snip
shhp
ECHOLOCATION REFERS TO THE USE OF SOUNDWAVES TO LOCATE OBJECTS OR NAVIGATE WITHOUT THE USE OF SIGHT. ANIMALS LIKE BATS, DOLPHINS, AND KILLER WHALES USE ECHOLOCATION
click
click
click
click
click
squeak squeak
wind wind
WHIBBLE
WHANGLE
hmpf

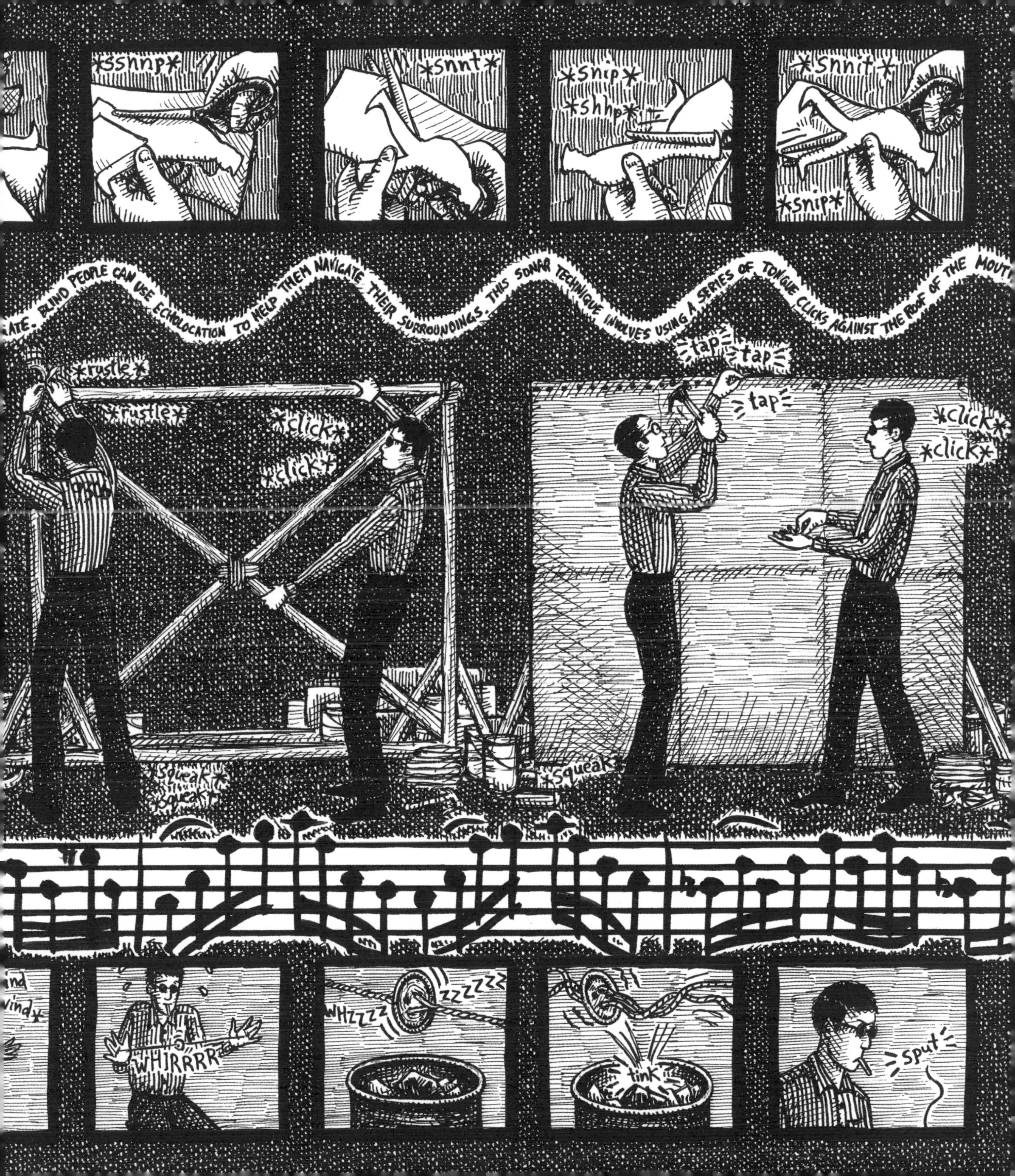
ssnnp
snnt
Snip
shhp
Snnit
snip
ATE. BLIND PEOPLE CAN USE ECHOLOCATION TO HELP THEM NAVIGATE THEIR SURROUNDINGS. THIS SONAR TECHNIQUE INVOLVES USING A SERIES OF TONGUE CLICKS AGAINST THE ROOF OF THE MOUT
rustle
rustle
click
click
tap
tap
tap
click
click
squeak
squeak
squeak
WHIRRRR
WHZZZZ
ZZZZZZ
tink
sput

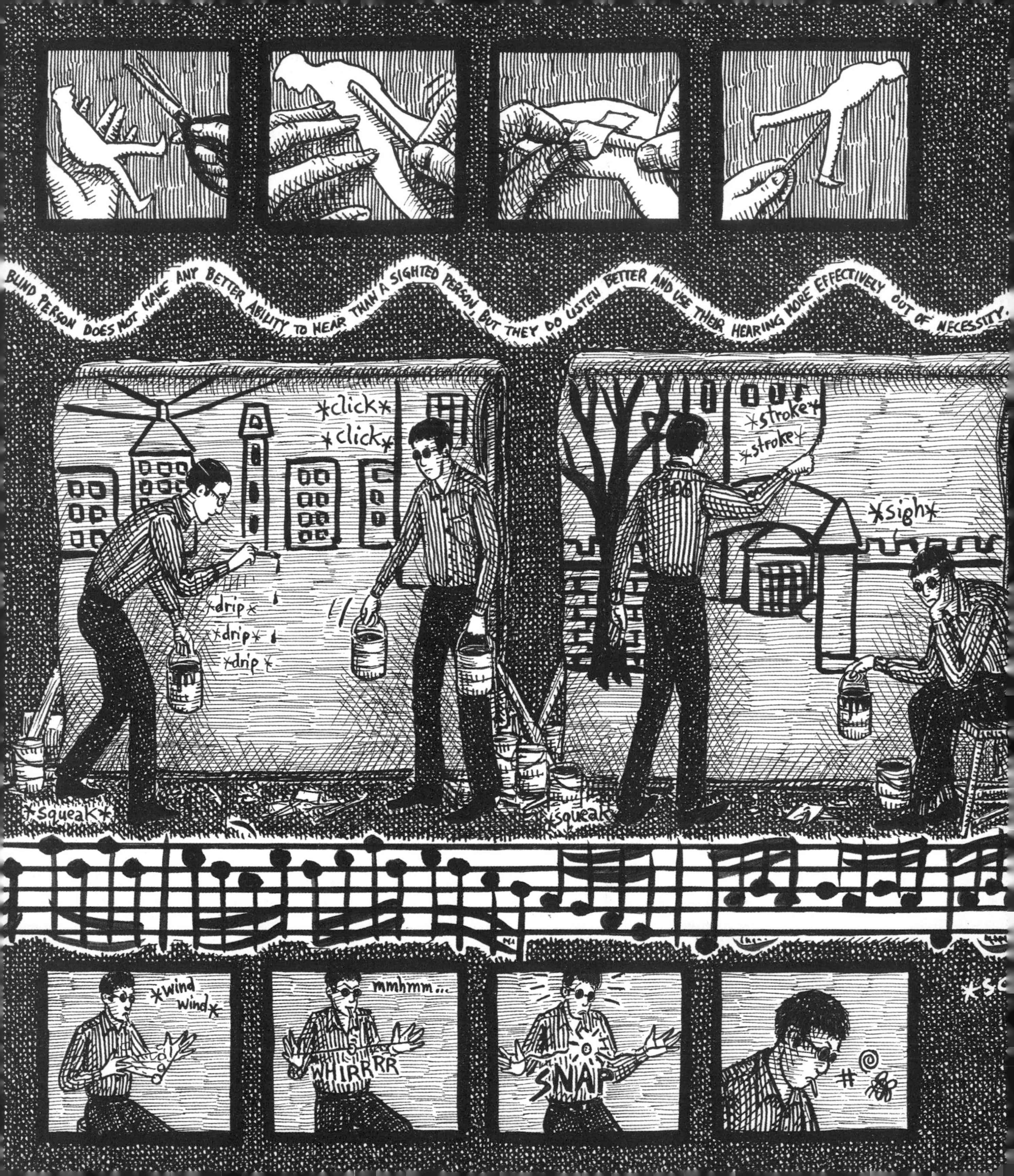
BLIND PERSON DOES NOT HAVE ANY BETTER ABILITY TO HEAR THAN A SIGHTED PERSON, BUT THEY DO LISTEN BETTER AND USE THEIR HEARING MORE EFFECTIVELY OUT OF NECESSITY.
click
click
drip
drip
drip
squeak
stroke
stroke
sigh
squeak
*wind
wind*
mmhmm...
WHIRRRR
SNAP

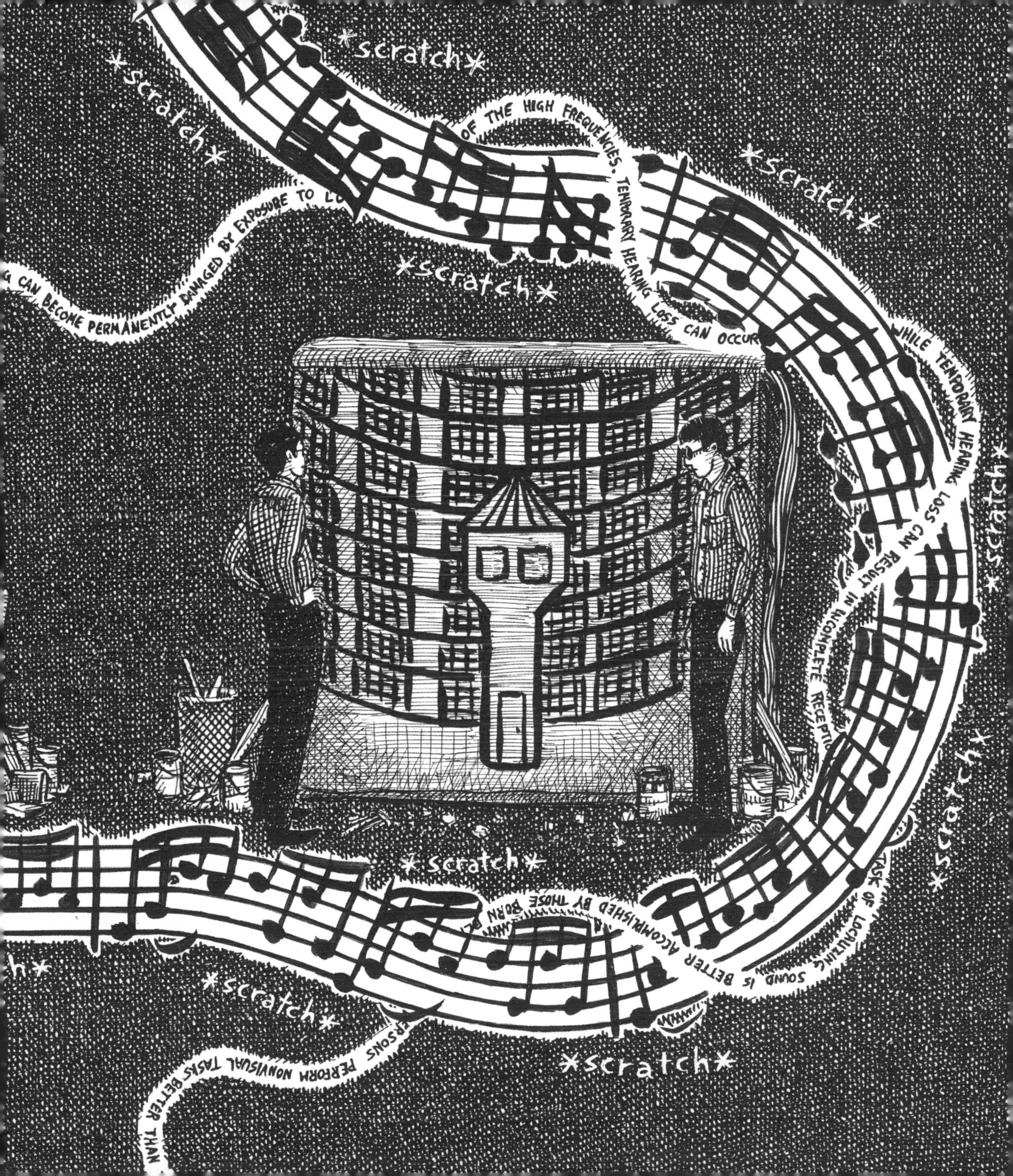
scratch
CAN BECOME PERMANENTLY DAMAGED BY EXPOSURE TO
OF THE HIGH FREQUENCIES. TEMPORARY HEARING LOSS CAN OCCUR
WHILE TEMPORARY HEARING LOSS CAN RESULT IN INCOMPLETE
TASK OF LOCALIZING SOUND IS BETTER ACCOMPLISHED BY THOSE BORN
PERFORM NONVISUAL TASKS BETTER THAN

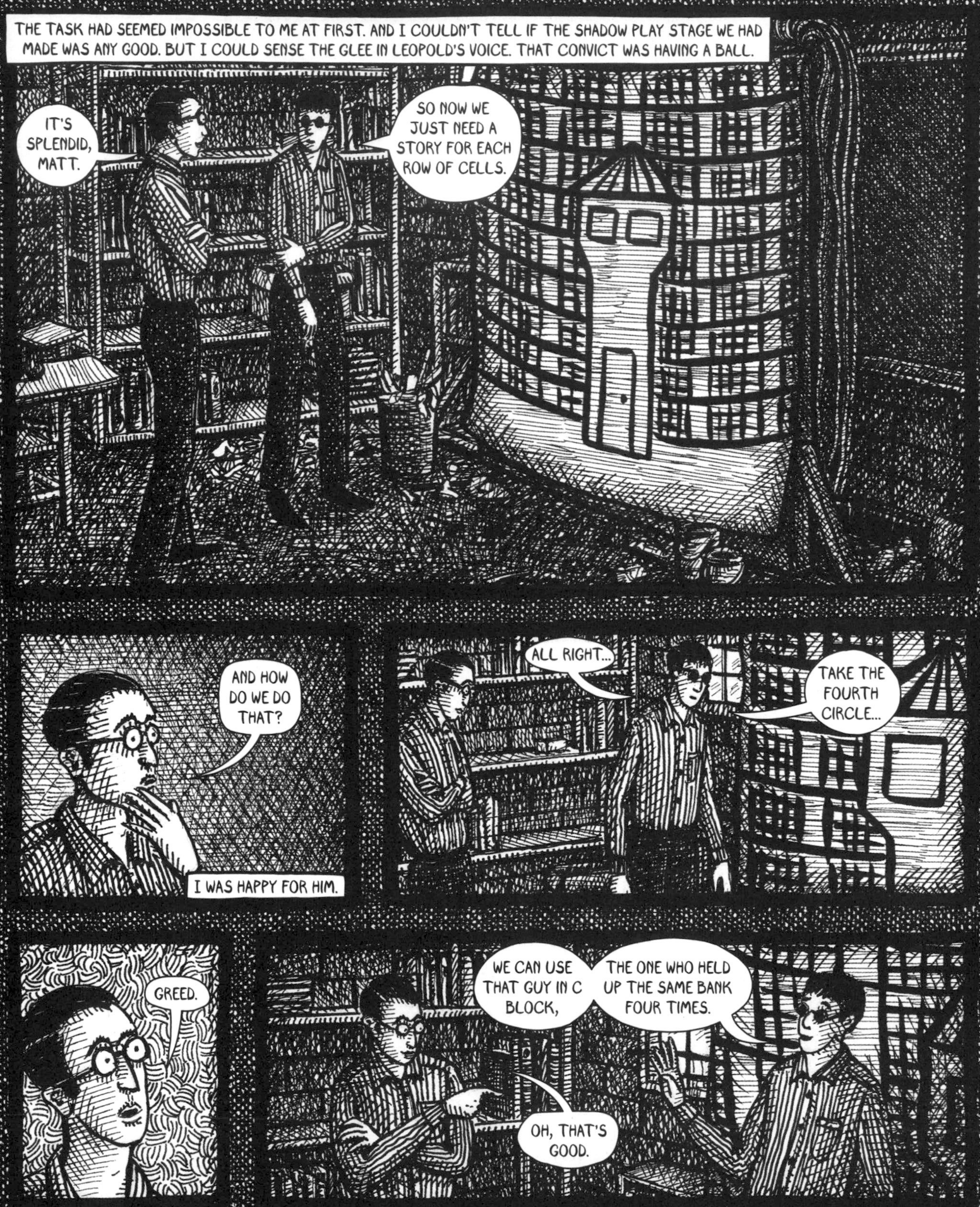
THE TASK HAD SEEMED IMPOSSIBLE TO ME AT FIRST. AND I COULDN'T TELL IF THE SHADOW PLAY STAGE WE HAD MADE WAS ANY GOOD. BUT I COULD SENSE THE GLEE IN LEOPOLD'S VOICE. THAT CONVICT WAS HAVING A BALL.
IT'S SPLENDID, MATT.
SO NOW WE JUST NEED A STORY FOR EACH ROW OF CELLS.
AND HOW DO WE DO THAT?
I WAS HAPPY FOR HIM.
ALL RIGHT...
TAKE THE FOURTH CIRCLE...
GREED.
WE CAN USE THAT GUY IN C BLOCK,
THE ONE WHO HELD UP THE SAME BANK FOUR TIMES.
OH, THAT'S GOOD.

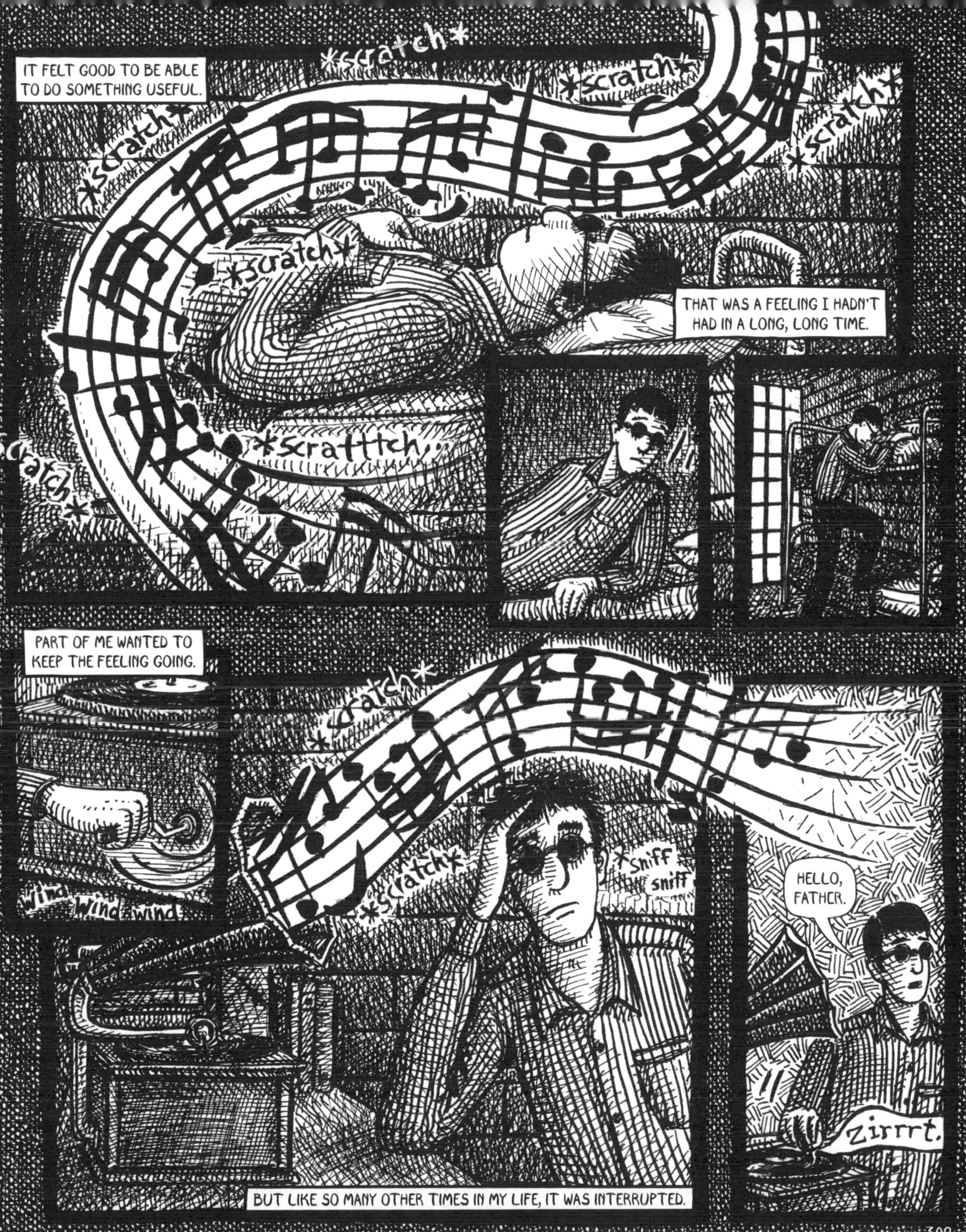
IT FELT GOOD TO BE ABLE TO DO SOMETHING USEFUL.
scratch
scratch
scratch
scratch
scratch
scratch
scratttch
scratch
THAT WAS A FEELING I HADN'T HAD IN A LONG, LONG TIME.
PART OF ME WANTED TO KEEP THE FEELING GOING.
wind wind wind
scratch
scratch
*sniff sniff
HELLO, FATHER.
!!
zirrrt.
BUT LIKE SO MANY OTHER TIMES IN MY LIFE, IT WAS INTERRUPTED.

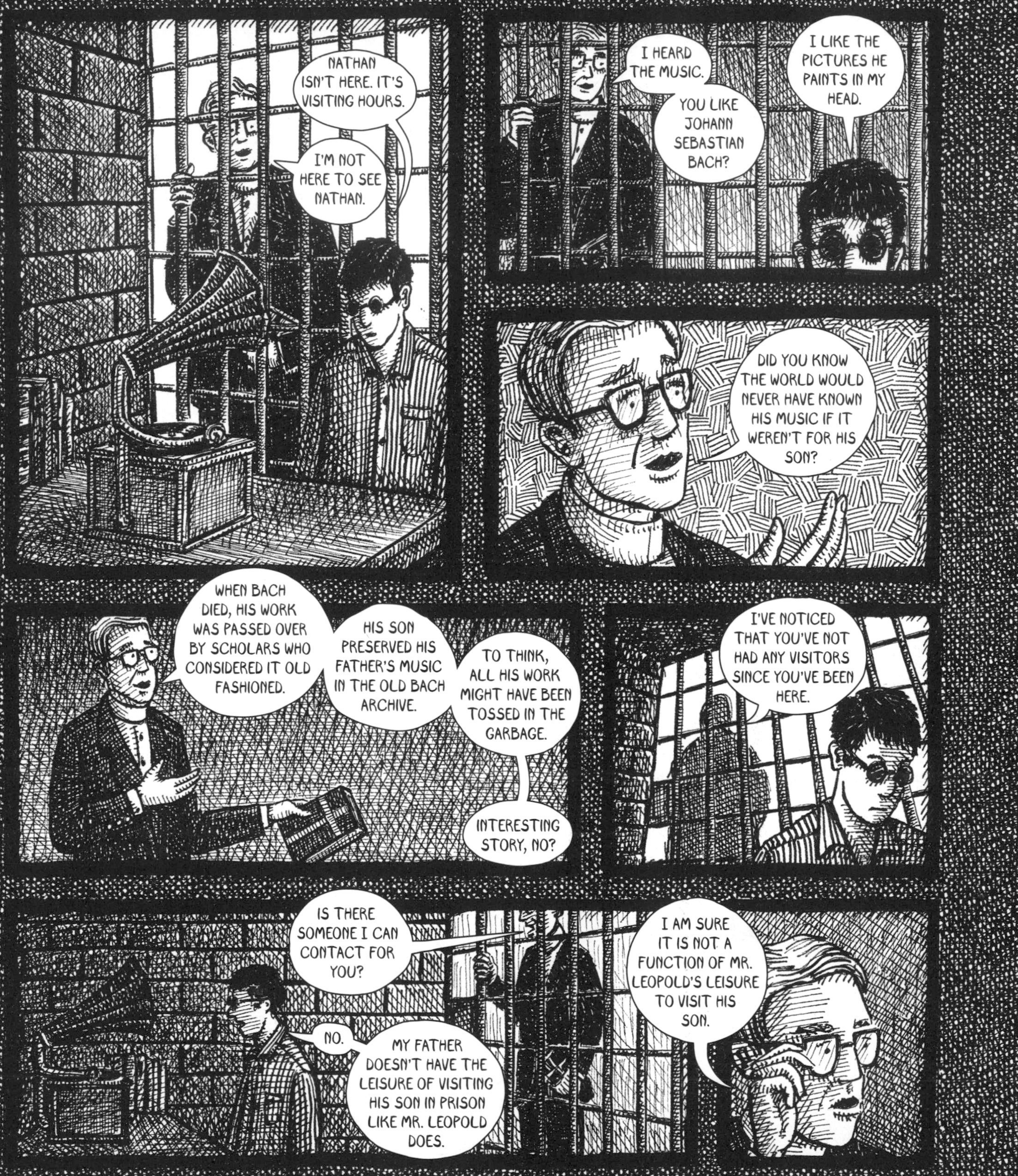
NATHAN ISN'T HERE. IT'S VISITING HOURS.
I'M NOT HERE TO SEE NATHAN.
I HEARD THE MUSIC.
YOU LIKE JOHANN SEBASTIAN BACH?
I LIKE THE PICTURES HE PAINTS IN MY HEAD.
DID YOU KNOW THE WORLD WOULD NEVER HAVE KNOWN HIS MUSIC IF IT WEREN'T FOR HIS SON?
WHEN BACH DIED, HIS WORK WAS PASSED OVER BY SCHOLARS WHO CONSIDERED IT OLD FASHIONED.
HIS SON PRESERVED HIS FATHER'S MUSIC IN THE OLD BACH ARCHIVE.
TO THINK, ALL HIS WORK MIGHT HAVE BEEN TOSSED IN THE GARBAGE.
INTERESTING STORY, NO?
I'VE NOTICED THAT YOU'VE NOT HAD ANY VISITORS SINCE YOU'VE BEEN HERE.
IS THERE SOMEONE I CAN CONTACT FOR YOU?
NO.
MY FATHER DOESN'T HAVE THE LEISURE OF VISITING HIS SON IN PRISON LIKE MR. LEOPOLD DOES.
I AM SURE IT IS NOT A FUNCTION OF MR. LEOPOLD'S LEISURE TO VISIT HIS SON.

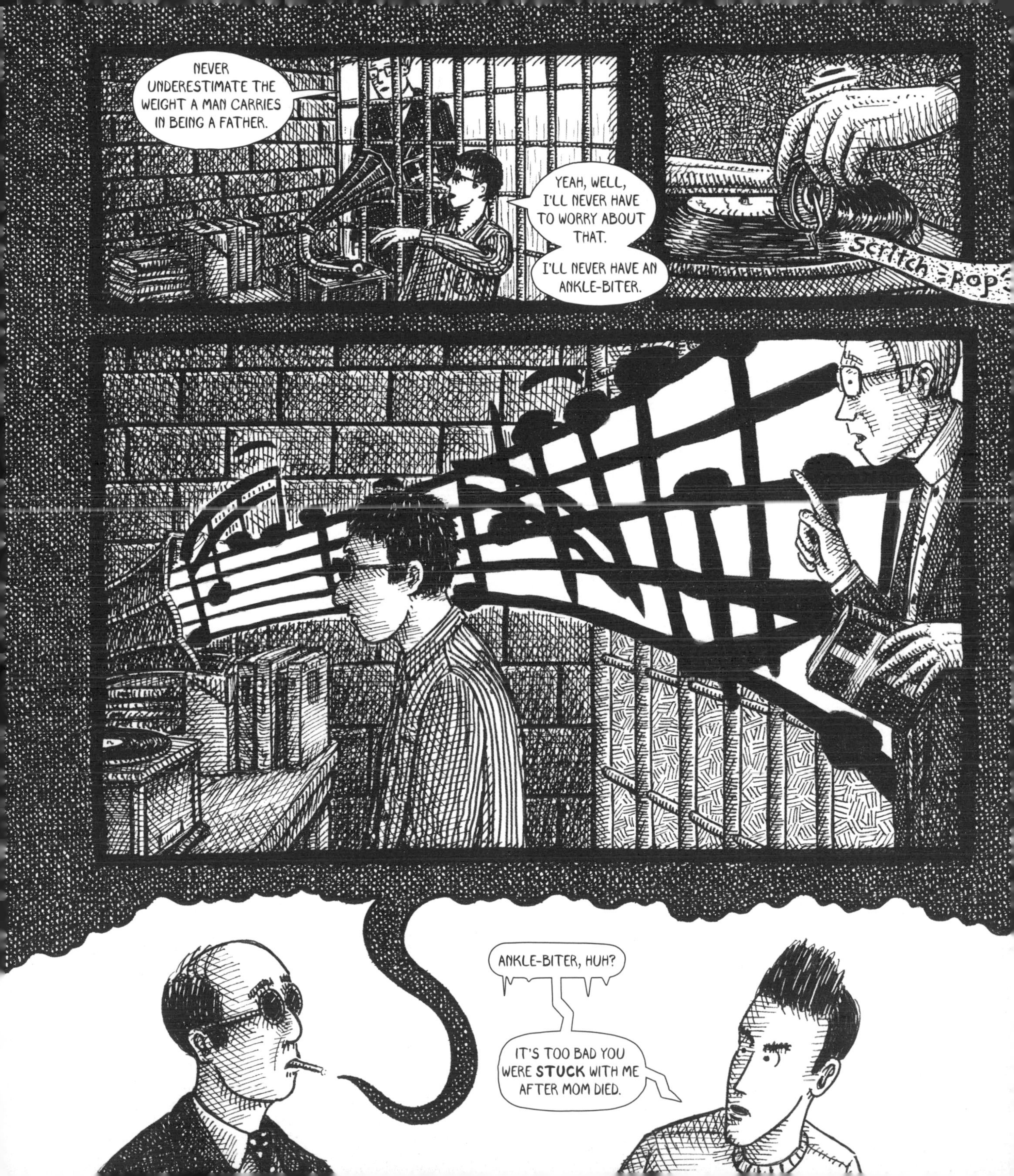
NEVER UNDERESTIMATE THE WEIGHT A MAN CARRIES IN BEING A FATHER.
YEAH, WELL, I'LL NEVER HAVE TO WORRY ABOUT THAT.
I'LL NEVER HAVE AN ANKLE-BITER.
SCRITCH
POP
ANKLE-BITER, HUH?
IT'S TOO BAD YOU WERE **STUCK** WITH ME AFTER MOM DIED.

CHARLIE, YOU ARE THE BEST THING THAT EVER HAPPENED TO ME.

BUT BACK THEN, I COULDN'T EVEN IMAGINE A FUTURE ON THE OUTSIDE.

EVERY SPARE MOMENT WAS SPENT WORKING ON THE SHOW. I DON'T KNOW WHAT IT COST LEOPOLD TO PULL TOGETHER EVERYTHING WE NEEDED TO PUT ON A SHADOW PLAY FOR THE CLASS, BUT I'M SURE IT WASN'T CHEAP. EVEN THE SCREWS WERE HELPING OUT.

O'DONNELL, GET THE LIGHTS.

CLICK

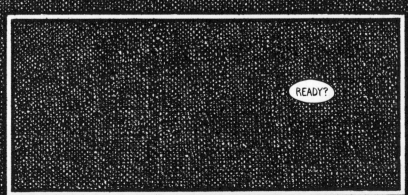

READY?

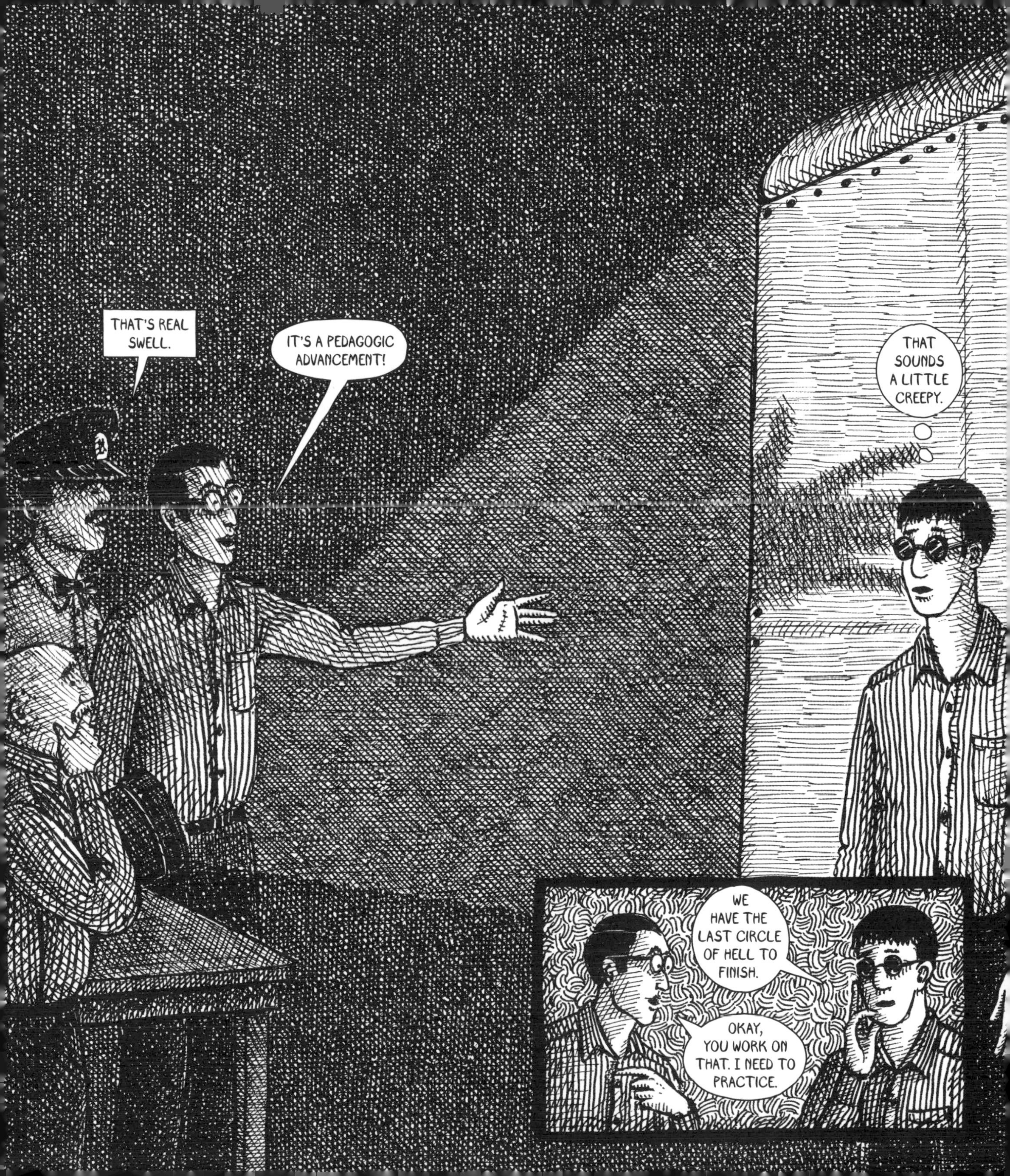

THAT'S REAL SWELL.
IT'S A PEDAGOGIC ADVANCEMENT!
THAT SOUNDS A LITTLE CREEPY.
WE HAVE THE LAST CIRCLE OF HELL TO FINISH.
OKAY, YOU WORK ON THAT. I NEED TO PRACTICE.

XIII ::::::
FINAL EXAM

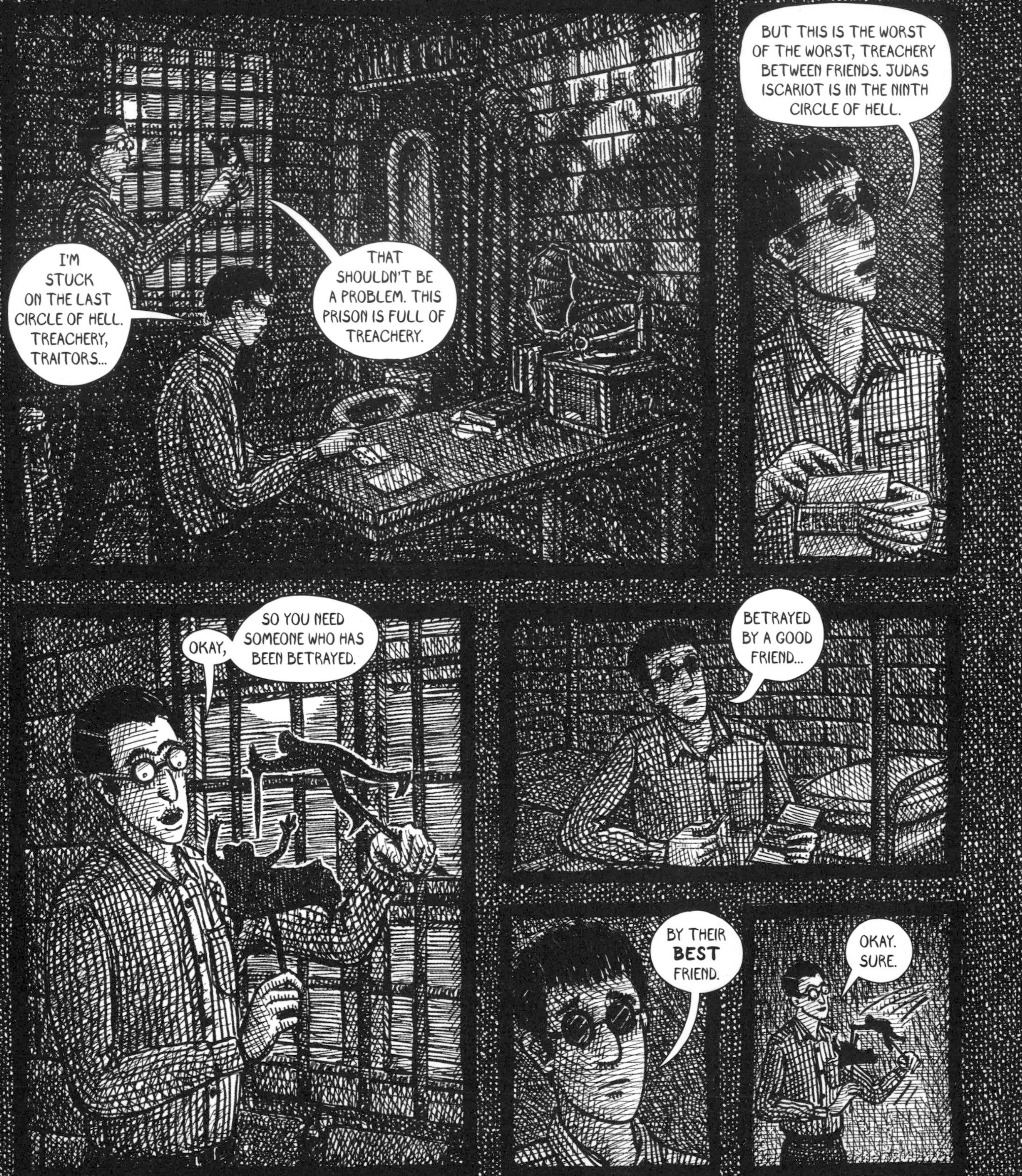

I'M STUCK ON THE LAST CIRCLE OF HELL. TREACHERY, TRAITORS...
THAT SHOULDN'T BE A PROBLEM. THIS PRISON IS FULL OF TREACHERY.
BUT THIS IS THE WORST OF THE WORST, TREACHERY BETWEEN FRIENDS. JUDAS ISCARIOT IS IN THE NINTH CIRCLE OF HELL.
OKAY,
SO YOU NEED SOMEONE WHO HAS BEEN BETRAYED.
BETRAYED BY A GOOD FRIEND...
BY THEIR **BEST** FRIEND.
OKAY. SURE.

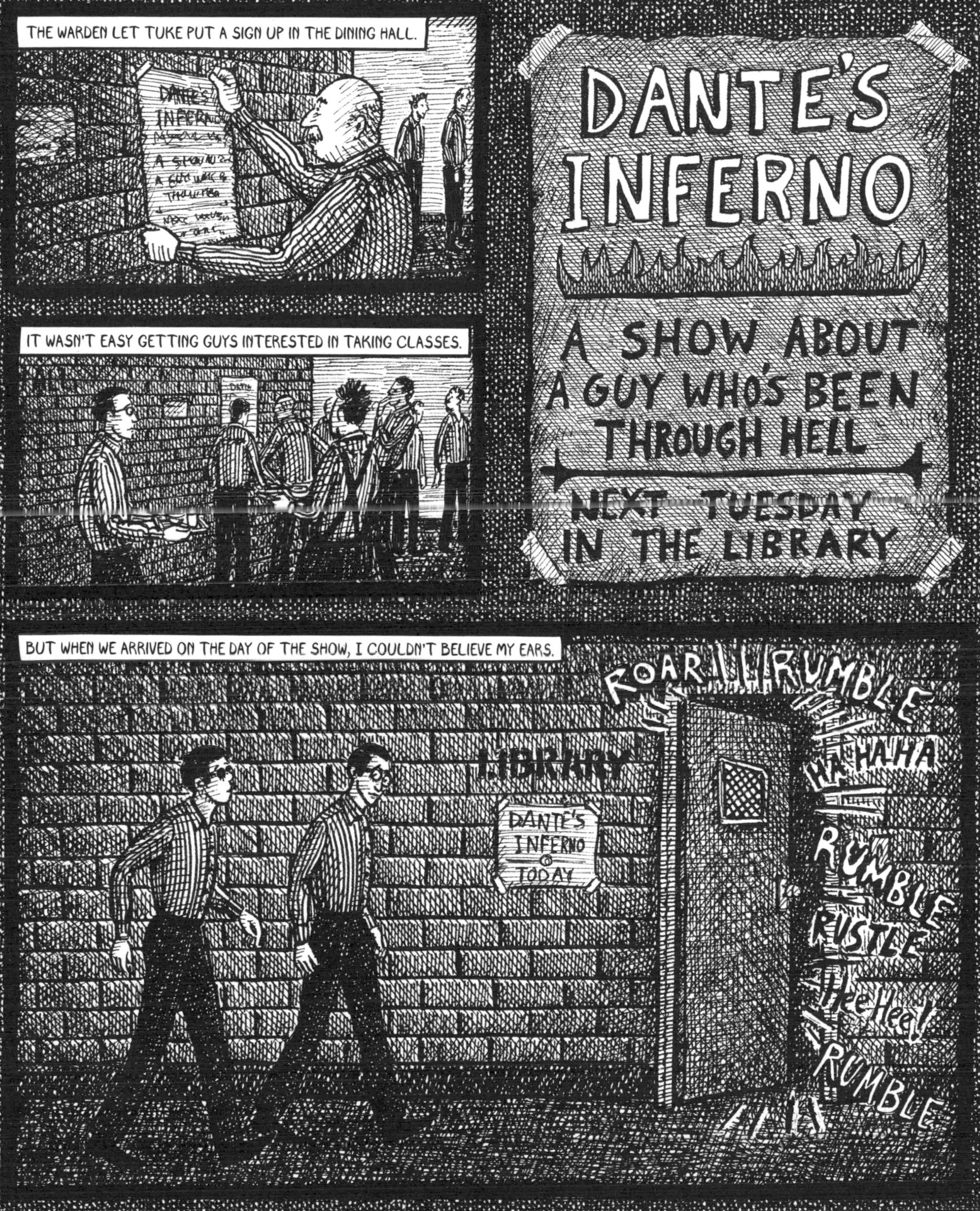
THE WARDEN LET TUKE PUT A SIGN UP IN THE DINING HALL.
DANTE'S INFERNO
A SHOW ABOUT A GUY WHO'S BEEN THROUGH HELL
NEXT TUESDAY IN THE LIBRARY
IT WASN'T EASY GETTING GUYS INTERESTED IN TAKING CLASSES.
BUT WHEN WE ARRIVED ON THE DAY OF THE SHOW, I COULDN'T BELIEVE MY EARS.
ROAR!
RUMBLE
HA HA HA
LIBRARY
DANTE'S INFERNO TODAY
RUMBLE
RUSTLE
Hee Hee!
RUMBLE

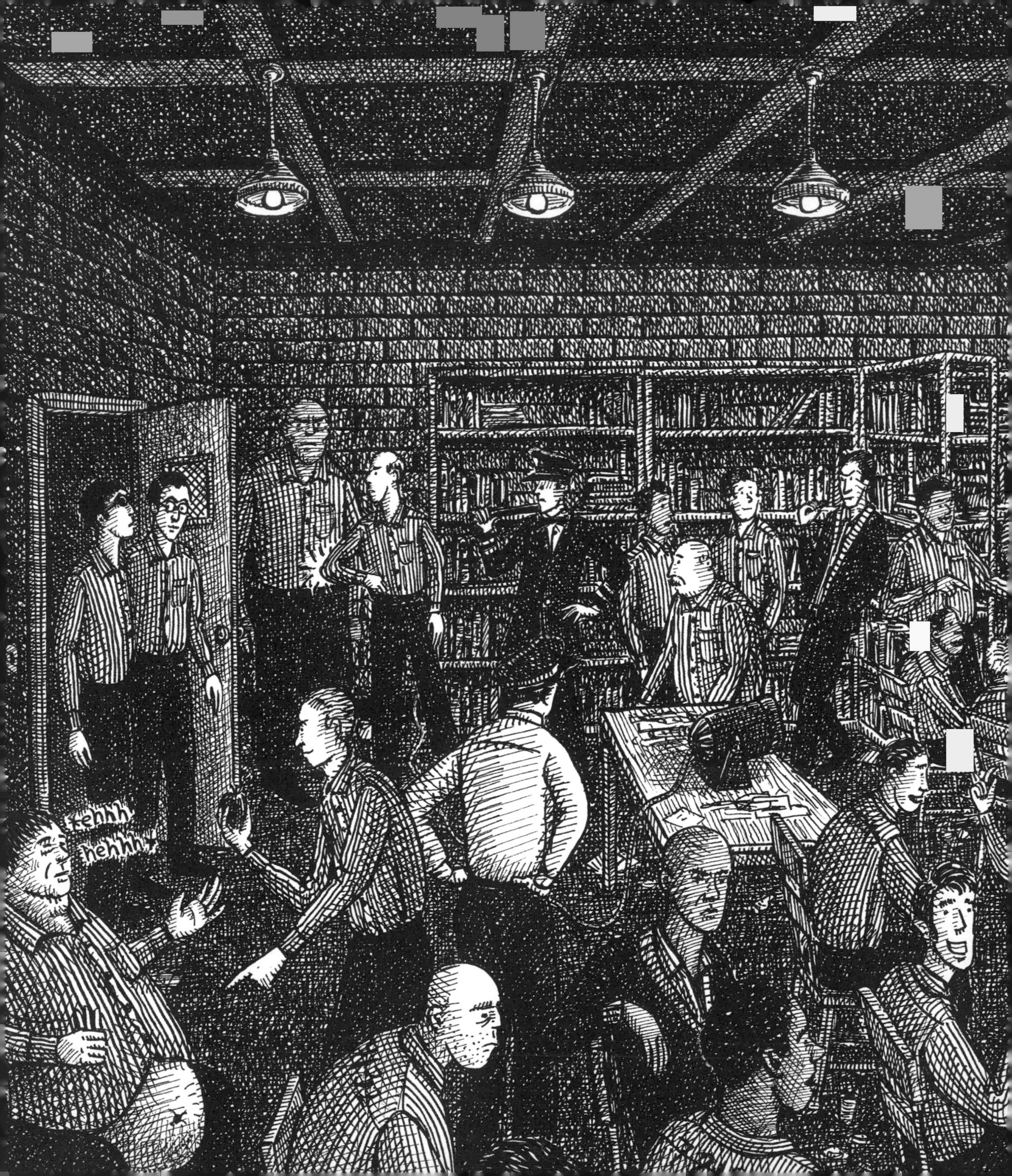
tehhh
hehhh

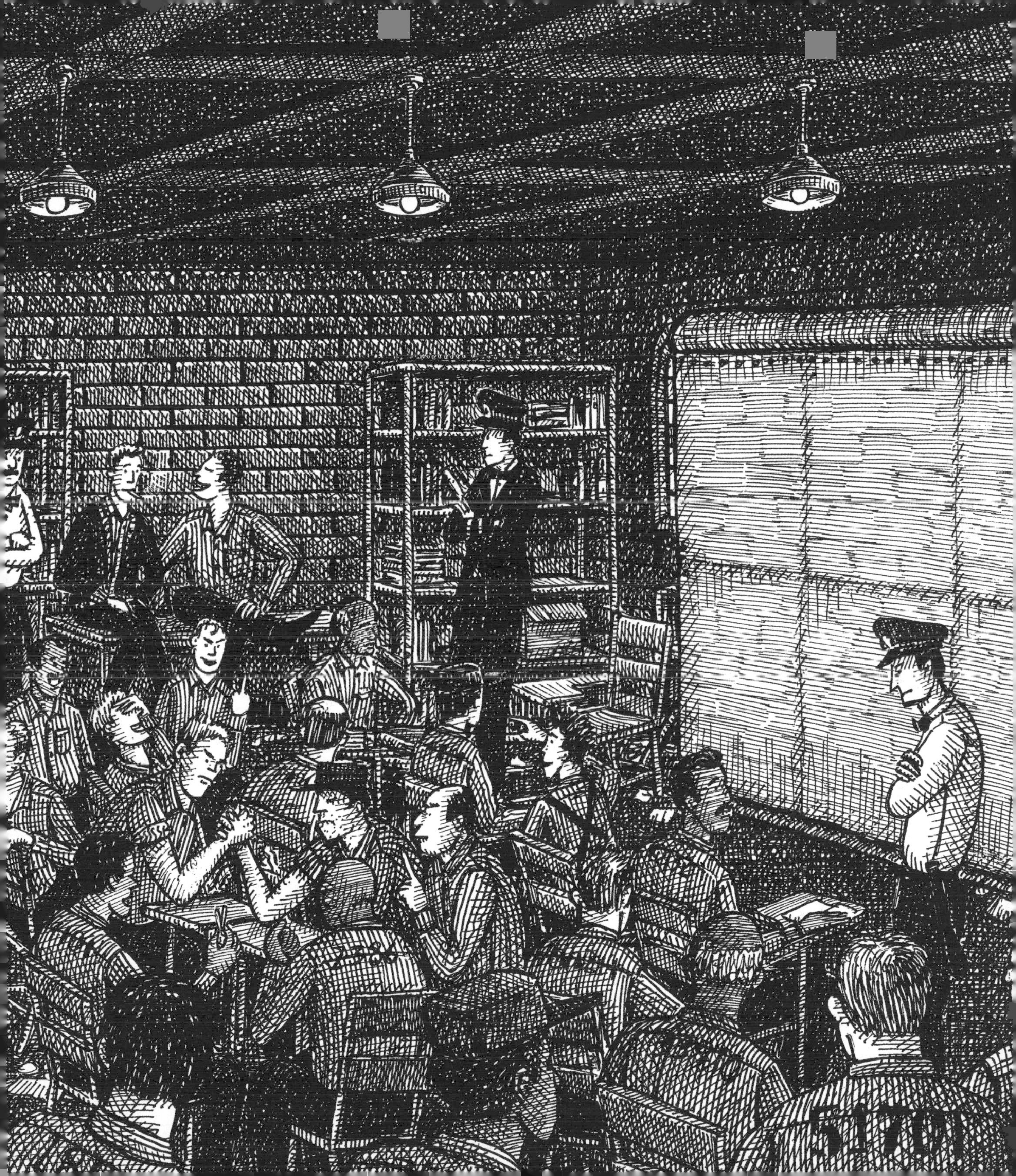

ENTERTAINMENT IS HARD TO COME BY IN PRISON AND WORD OF A SHOW IN THE LIBRARY SPREAD QUICKLY.

I HADN'T GIVEN MUCH THOUGHT TO IT, SO I WAS PRETTY NERVOUS AS I FUMBLED WITH MY BRAILLE SCRIPT.

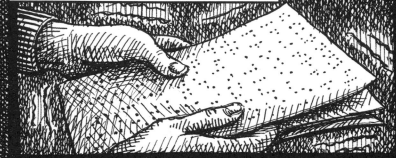

WE HAD WHAT YOU MIGHT CALL, A CAPTIVE AUDIENCE.

LIGHTS!

CLICK

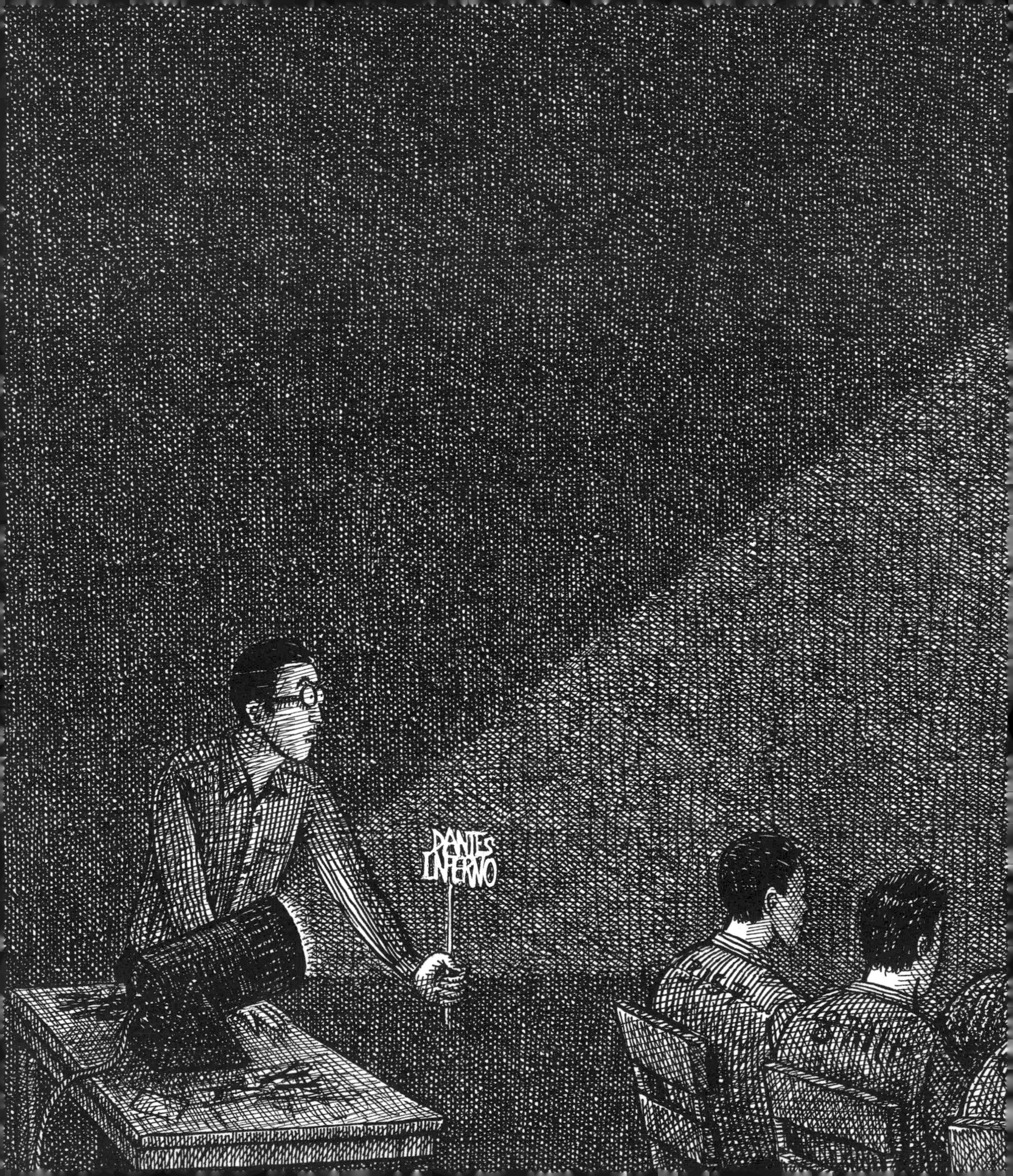
DANTE'S
INFERNO

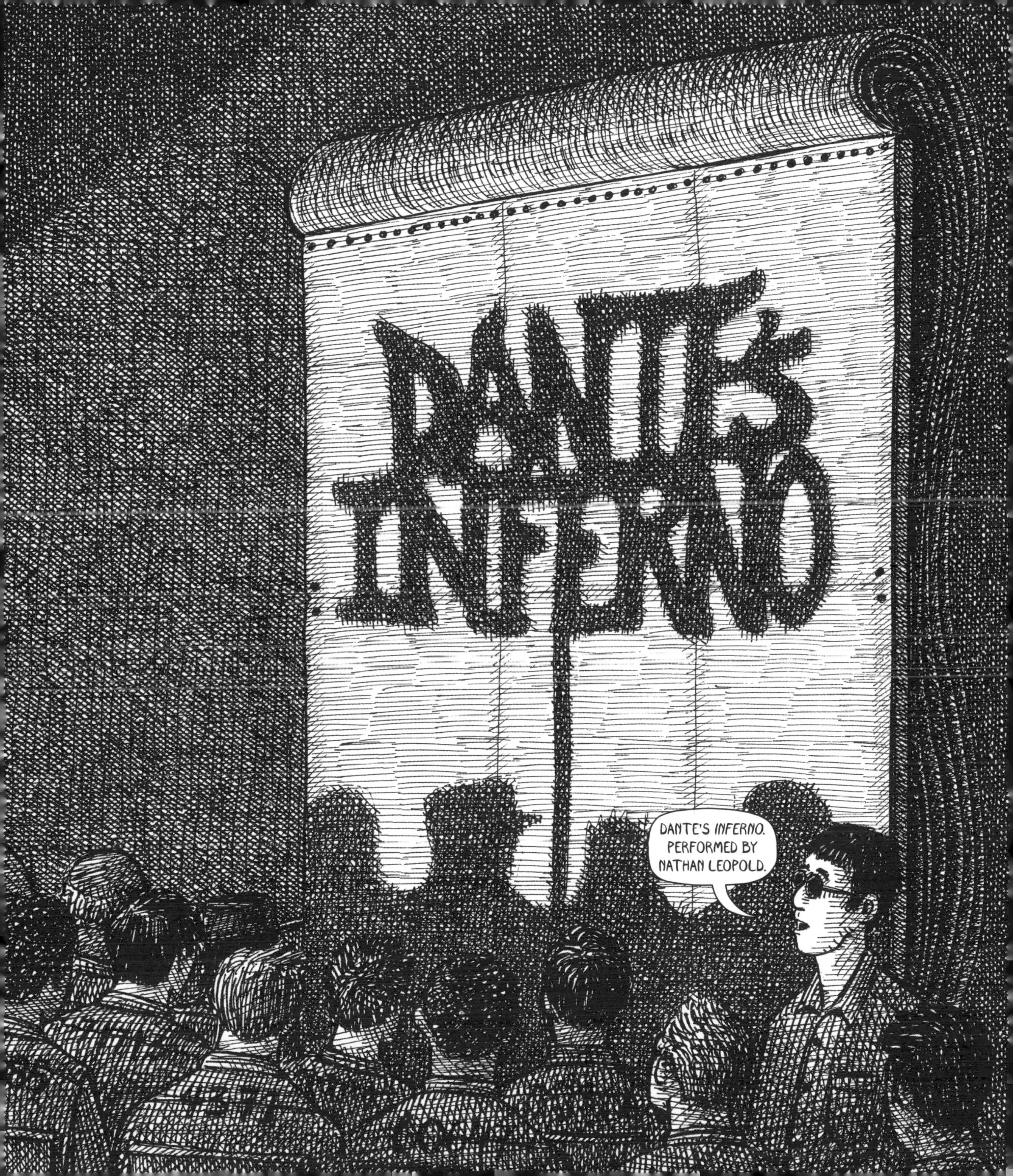
DANTE'S INFERNO
DANTE'S INFERNO. PERFORMED BY NATHAN LEOPOLD.

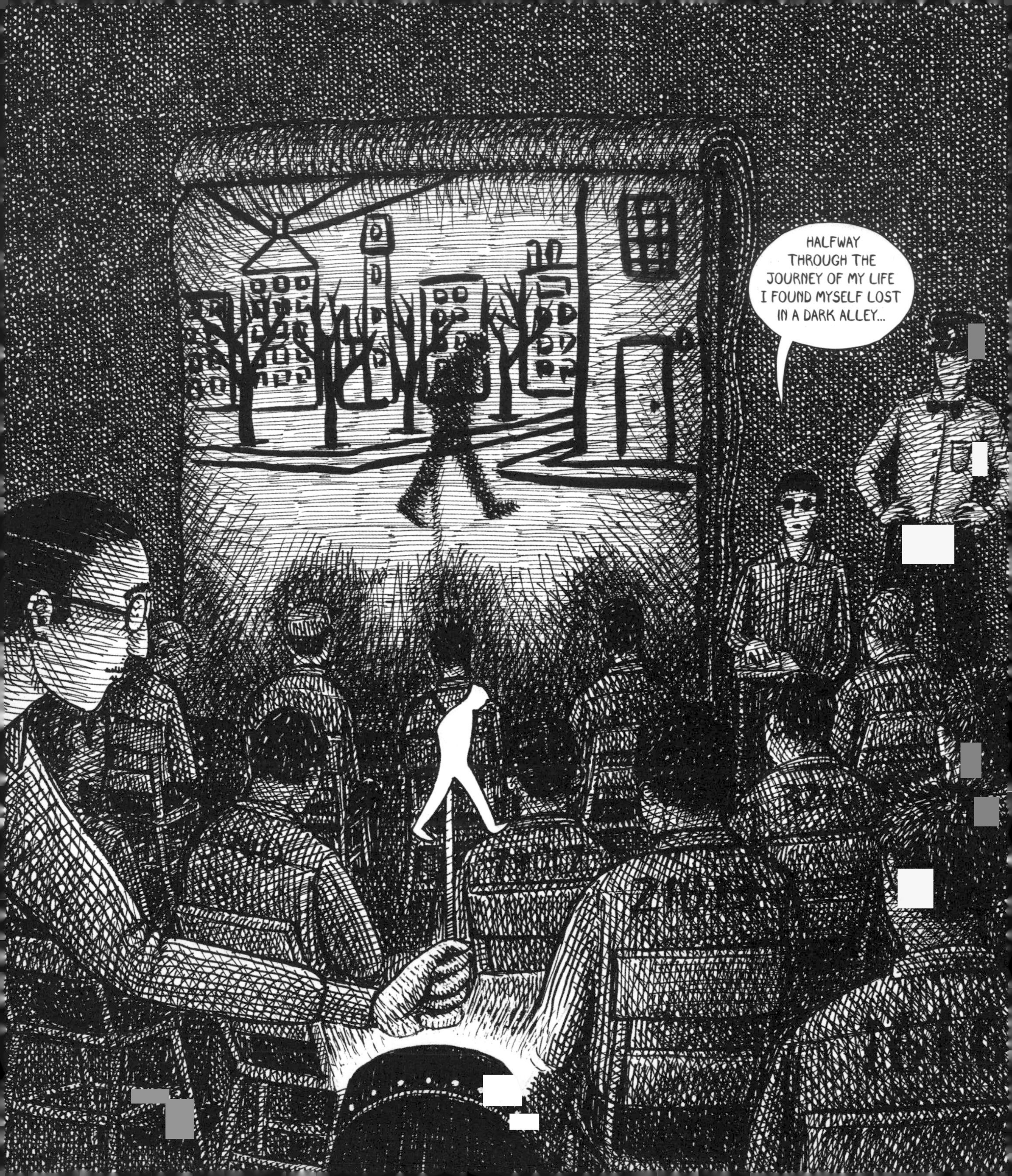
HALFWAY THROUGH THE JOURNEY OF MY LIFE I FOUND MYSELF LOST IN A DARK ALLEY...

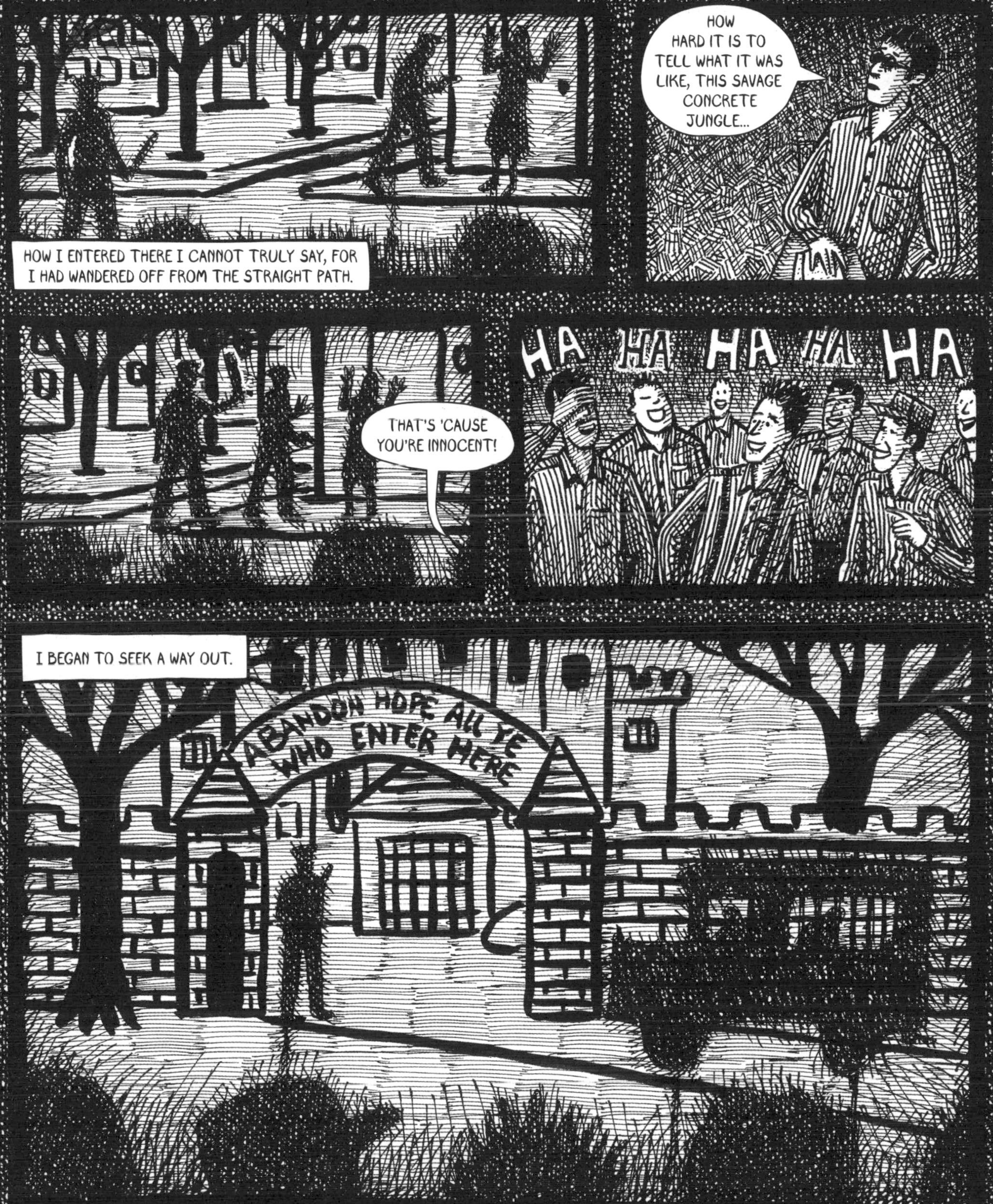
HOW I ENTERED THERE I CANNOT TRULY SAY, FOR I HAD WANDERED OFF FROM THE STRAIGHT PATH.
HOW HARD IT IS TO TELL WHAT IT WAS LIKE, THIS SAVAGE CONCRETE JUNGLE...
THAT'S 'CAUSE YOU'RE INNOCENT!
HA HA HA HA HA
I BEGAN TO SEEK A WAY OUT.
ABANDON HOPE ALL YE WHO ENTER HERE

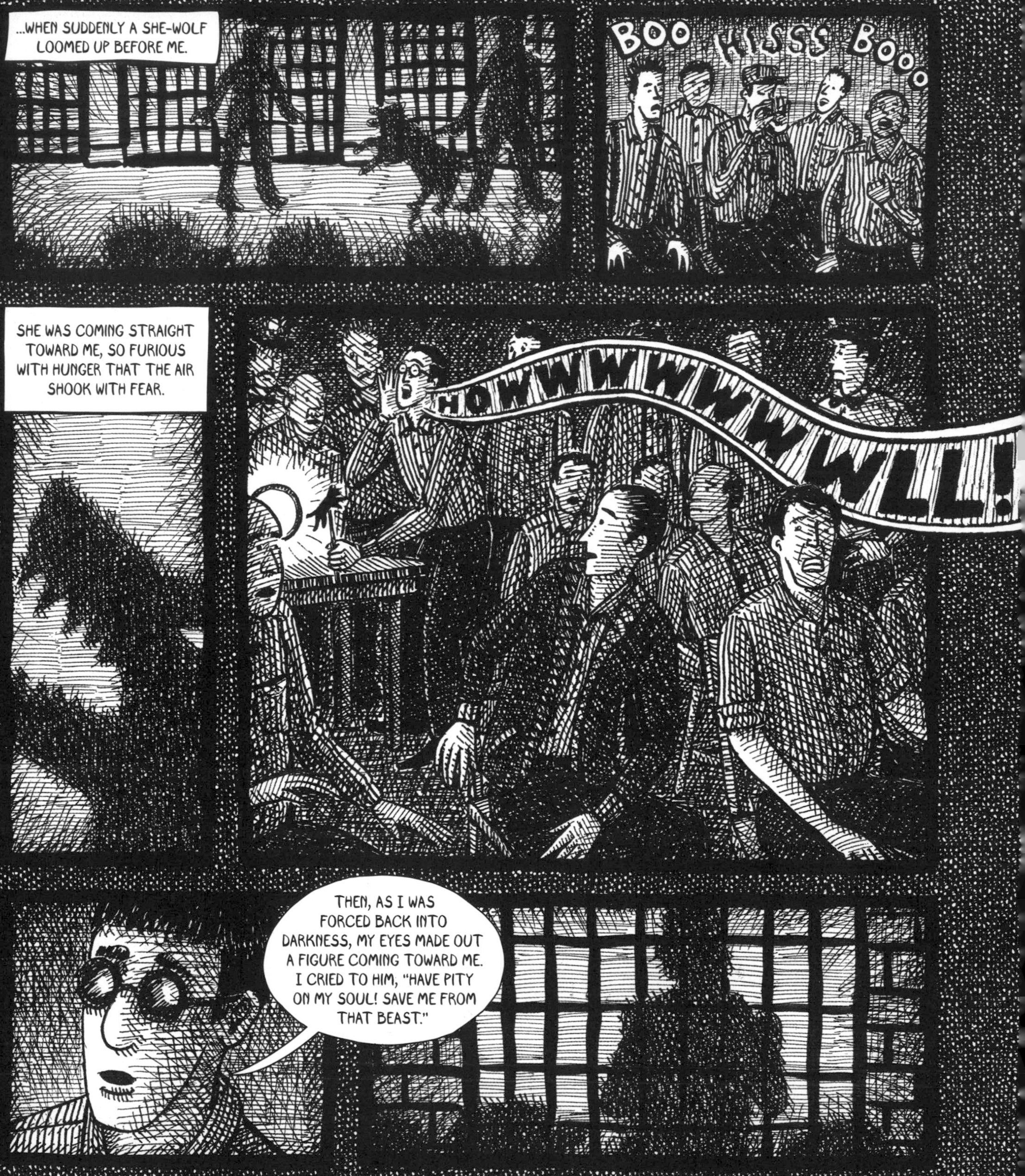
...WHEN SUDDENLY A SHE-WOLF LOOMED UP BEFORE ME.
BOO HISSS BOOO
SHE WAS COMING STRAIGHT TOWARD ME, SO FURIOUS WITH HUNGER THAT THE AIR SHOOK WITH FEAR.
HOWWWWWWWWLL!
THEN, AS I WAS FORCED BACK INTO DARKNESS, MY EYES MADE OUT A FIGURE COMING TOWARD ME. I CRIED TO HIM, "HAVE PITY ON MY SOUL! SAVE ME FROM THAT BEAST."

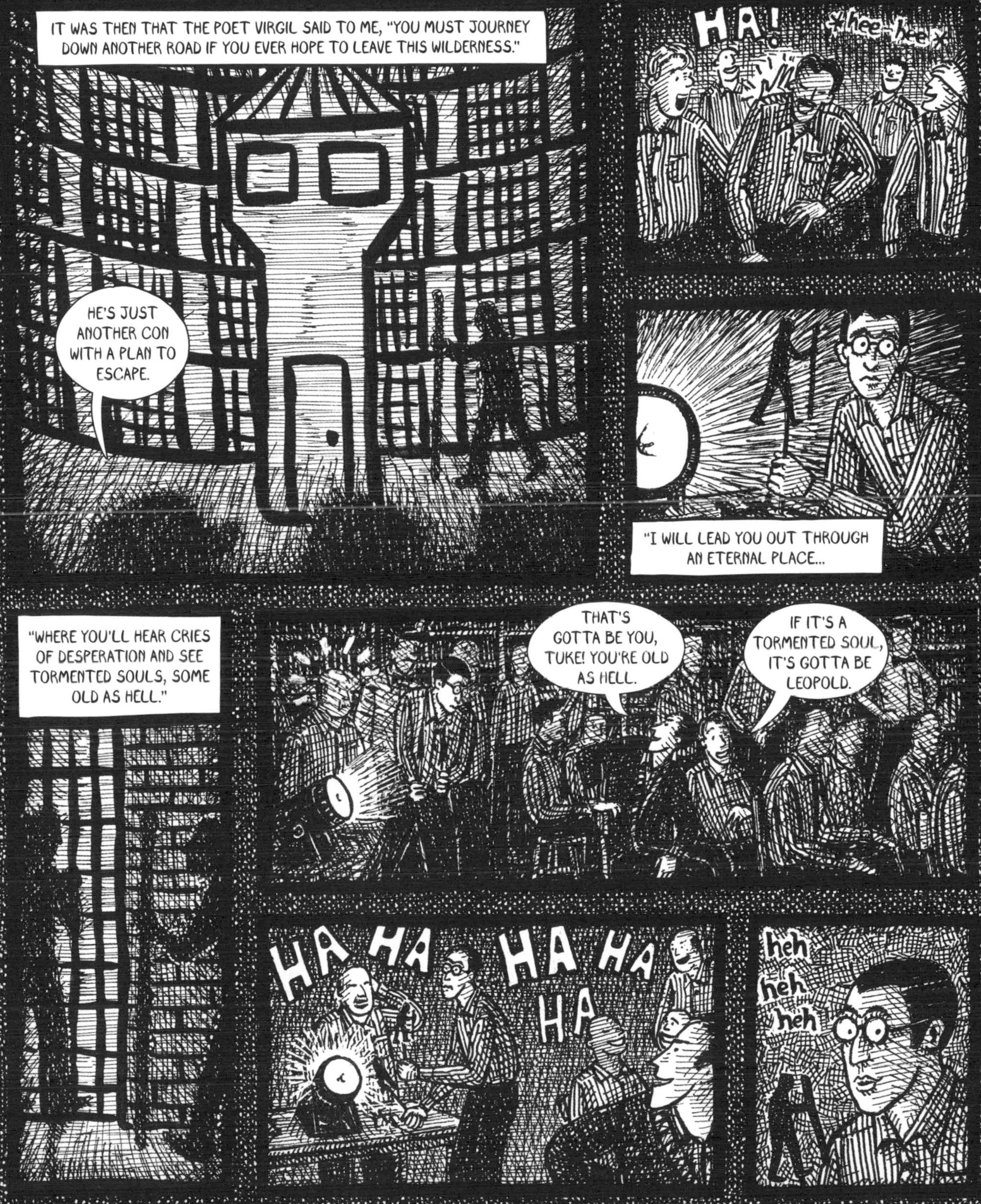

IT WAS THEN THAT THE POET VIRGIL SAID TO ME, "YOU MUST JOURNEY DOWN ANOTHER ROAD IF YOU EVER HOPE TO LEAVE THIS WILDERNESS."
HE'S JUST ANOTHER CON WITH A PLAN TO ESCAPE.
HA!
hee-hee
"I WILL LEAD YOU OUT THROUGH AN ETERNAL PLACE...
"WHERE YOU'LL HEAR CRIES OF DESPERATION AND SEE TORMENTED SOULS, SOME OLD AS HELL."
THAT'S GOTTA BE YOU, TUKE! YOU'RE OLD AS HELL.
IF IT'S A TORMENTED SOUL, IT'S GOTTA BE LEOPOLD.
HA HA HA HA HA HA
heh heh heh

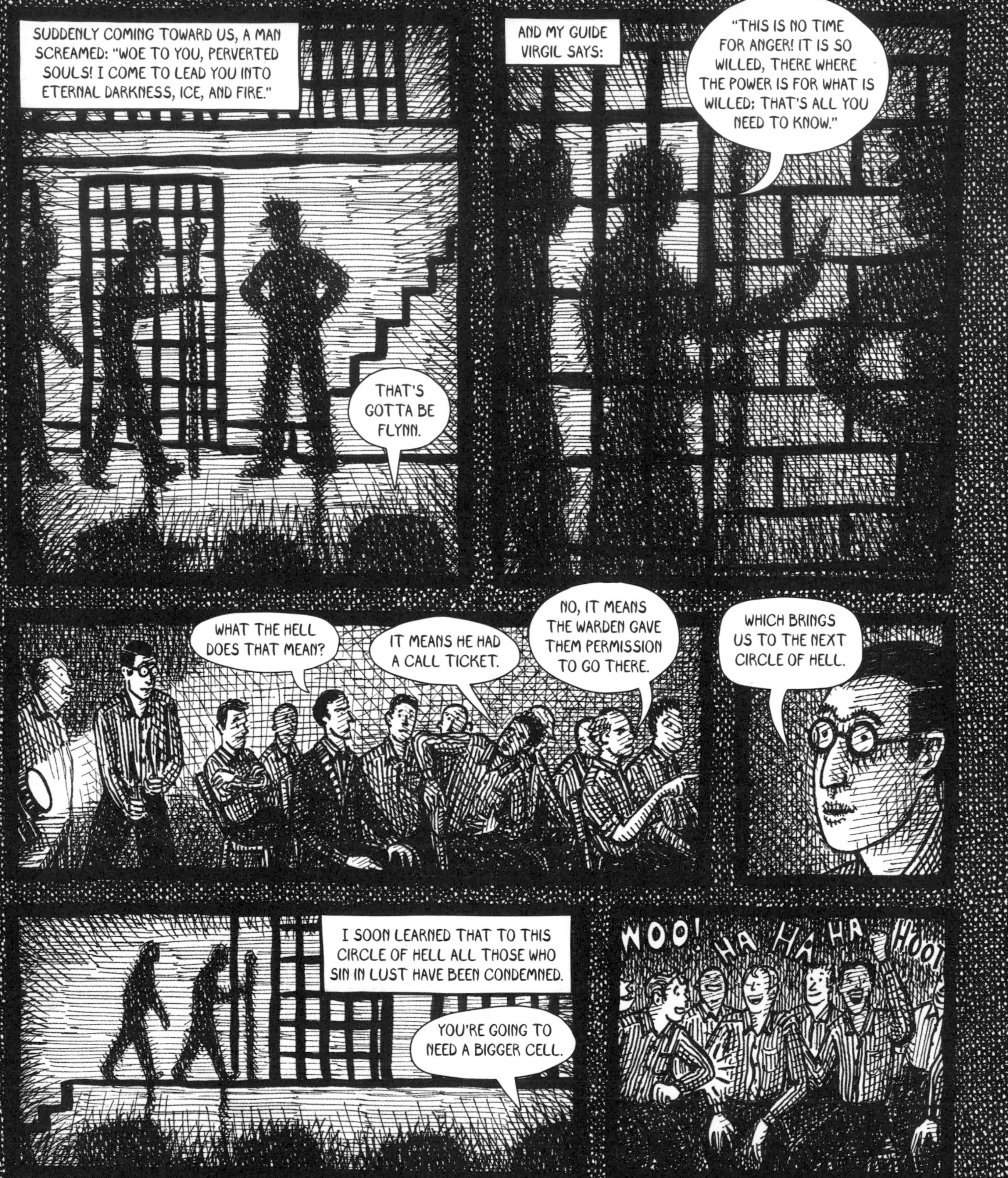

SUDDENLY COMING TOWARD US, A MAN SCREAMED: "WOE TO YOU, PERVERTED SOULS! I COME TO LEAD YOU INTO ETERNAL DARKNESS, ICE, AND FIRE."
THAT'S GOTTA BE FLYNN.
AND MY GUIDE VIRGIL SAYS:
"THIS IS NO TIME FOR ANGER! IT IS SO WILLED, THERE WHERE THE POWER IS FOR WHAT IS WILLED; THAT'S ALL YOU NEED TO KNOW."
WHAT THE HELL DOES THAT MEAN?
IT MEANS HE HAD A CALL TICKET.
NO, IT MEANS THE WARDEN GAVE THEM PERMISSION TO GO THERE.
WHICH BRINGS US TO THE NEXT CIRCLE OF HELL.
I SOON LEARNED THAT TO THIS CIRCLE OF HELL ALL THOSE WHO SIN IN LUST HAVE BEEN CONDEMNED.
YOU'RE GOING TO NEED A BIGGER CELL.
WOO! HA HA HA HOOT

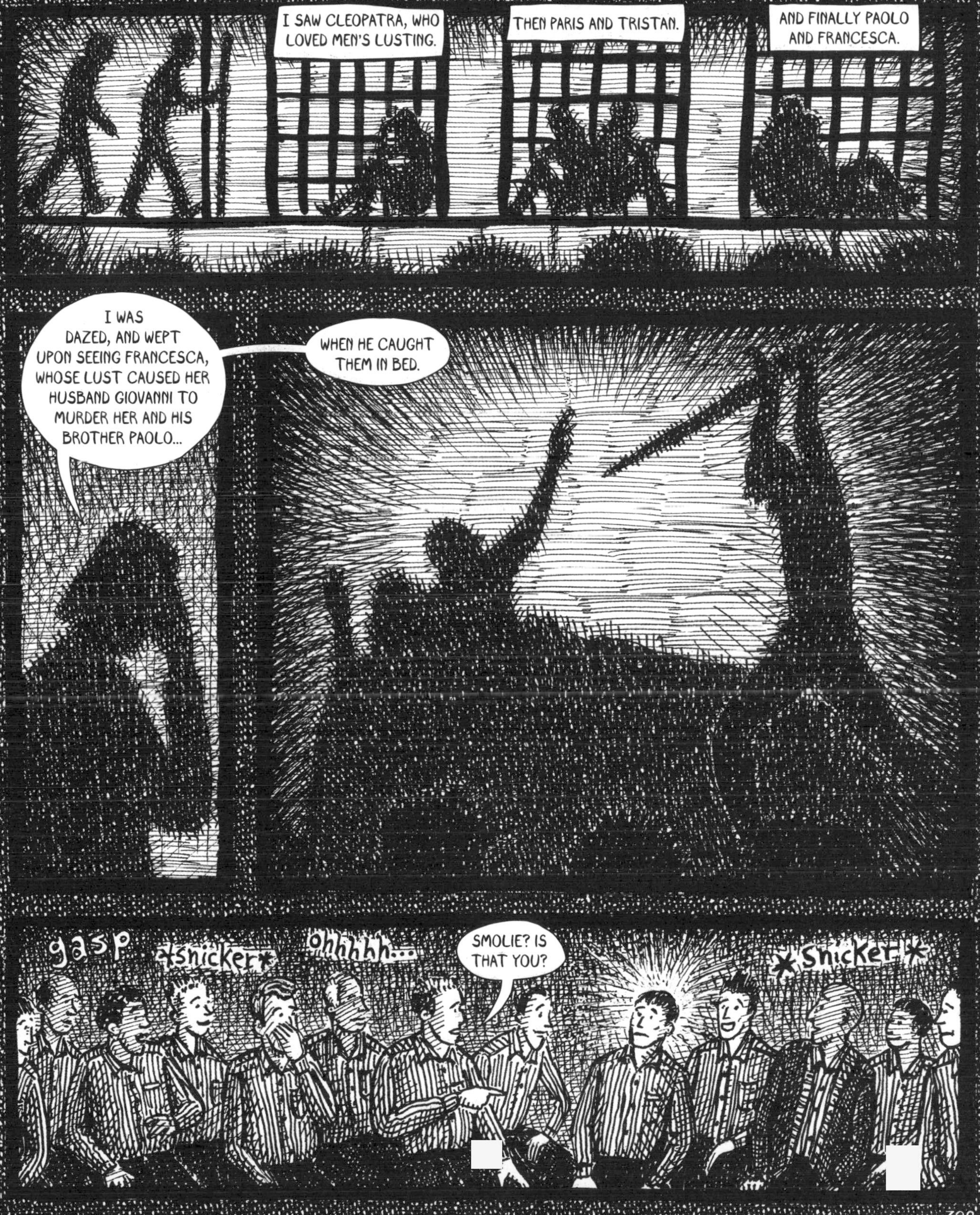
I SAW CLEOPATRA, WHO LOVED MEN'S LUSTING.
THEN PARIS AND TRISTAN.
AND FINALLY PAOLO AND FRANCESCA.
I WAS DAZED, AND WEPT UPON SEEING FRANCESCA, WHOSE LUST CAUSED HER HUSBAND GIOVANNI TO MURDER HER AND HIS BROTHER PAOLO...
WHEN HE CAUGHT THEM IN BED.
gasp
snicker
ohhhhh...
SMOLIE? IS THAT YOU?
Snicker

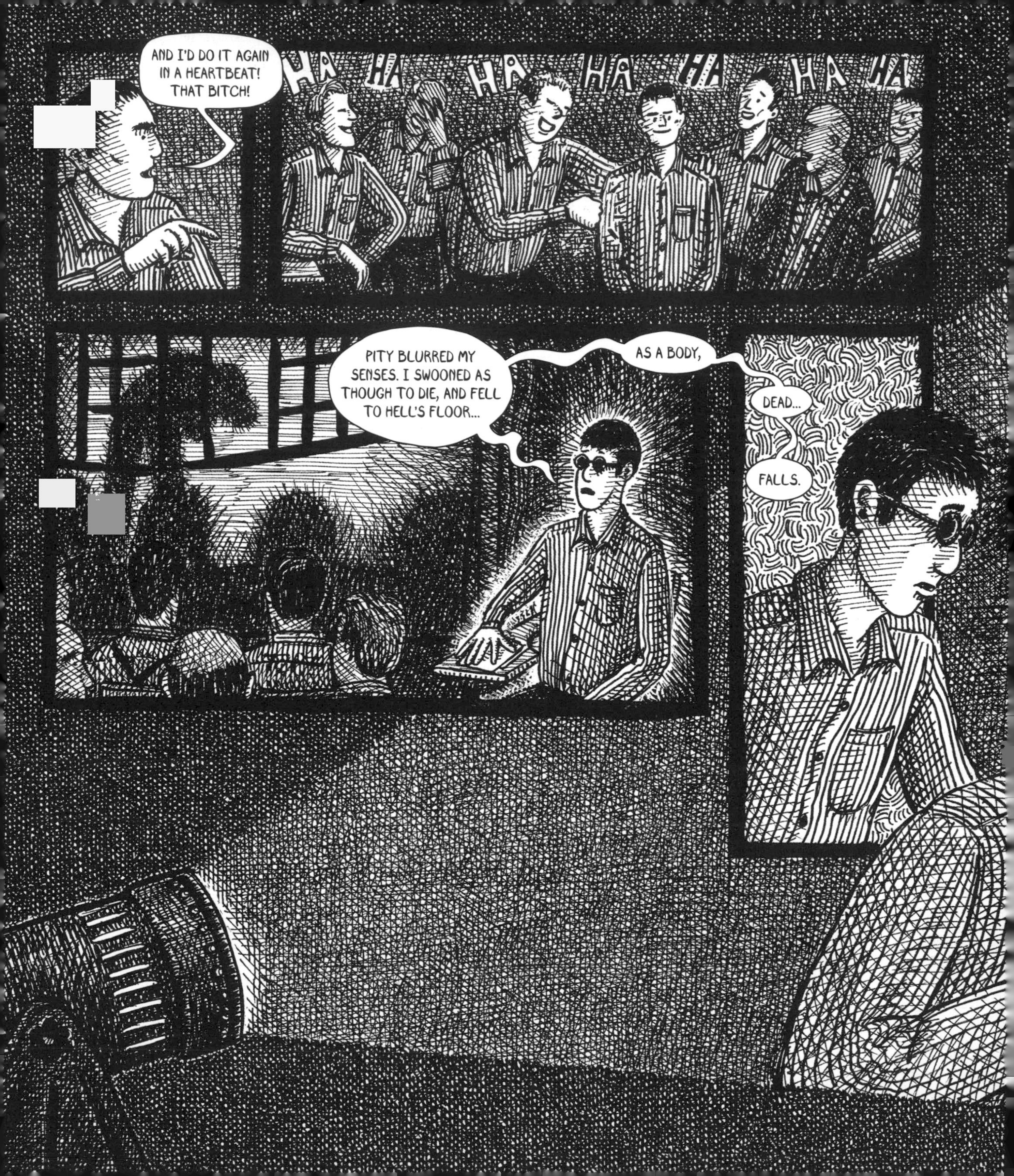
AND I'D DO IT AGAIN IN A HEARTBEAT! THAT BITCH!
HA HA HA HA HA HA HA
PITY BLURRED MY SENSES. I SWOONED AS THOUGH TO DIE, AND FELL TO HELL'S FLOOR...
AS A BODY,
DEAD...
FALLS.

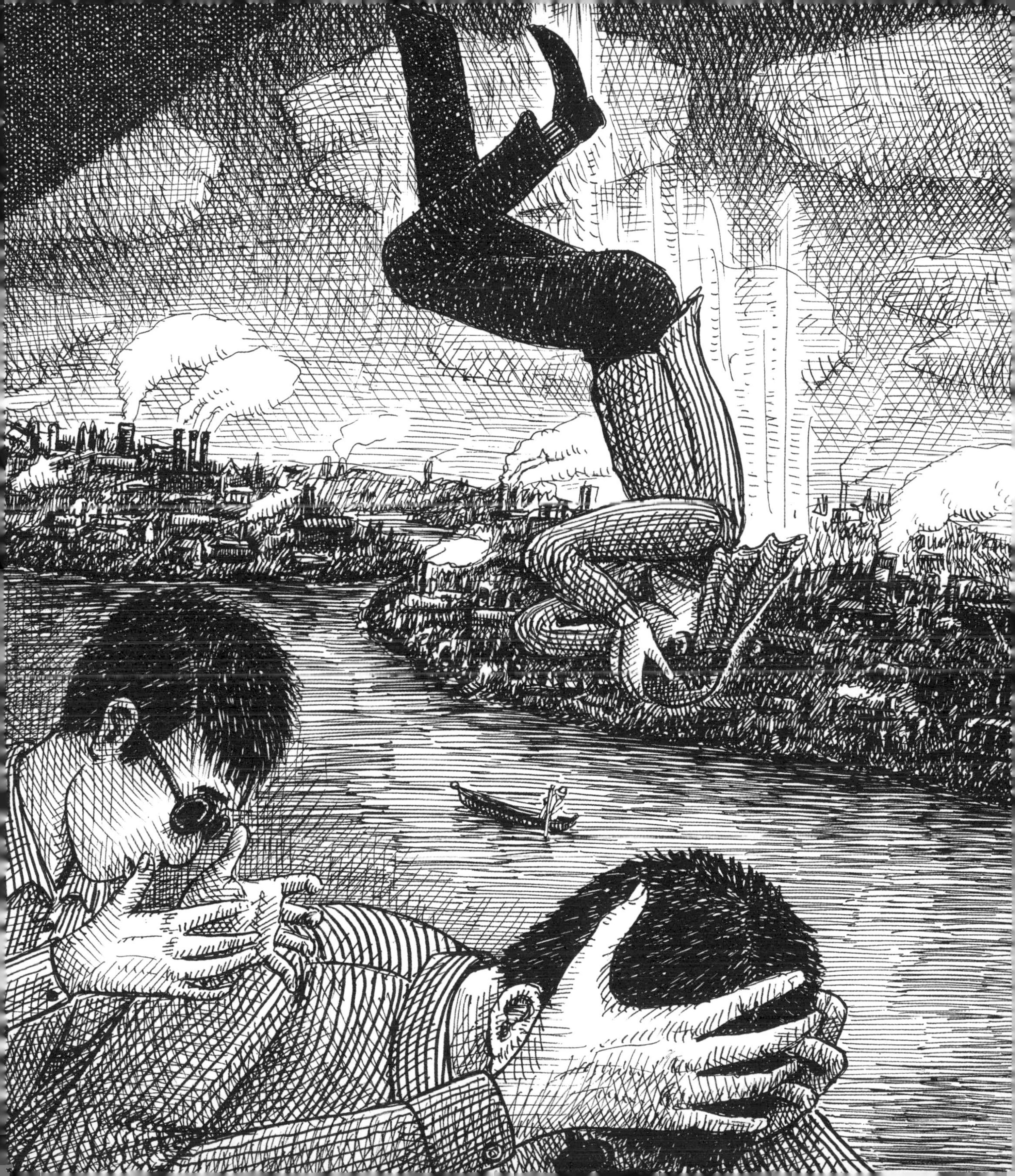

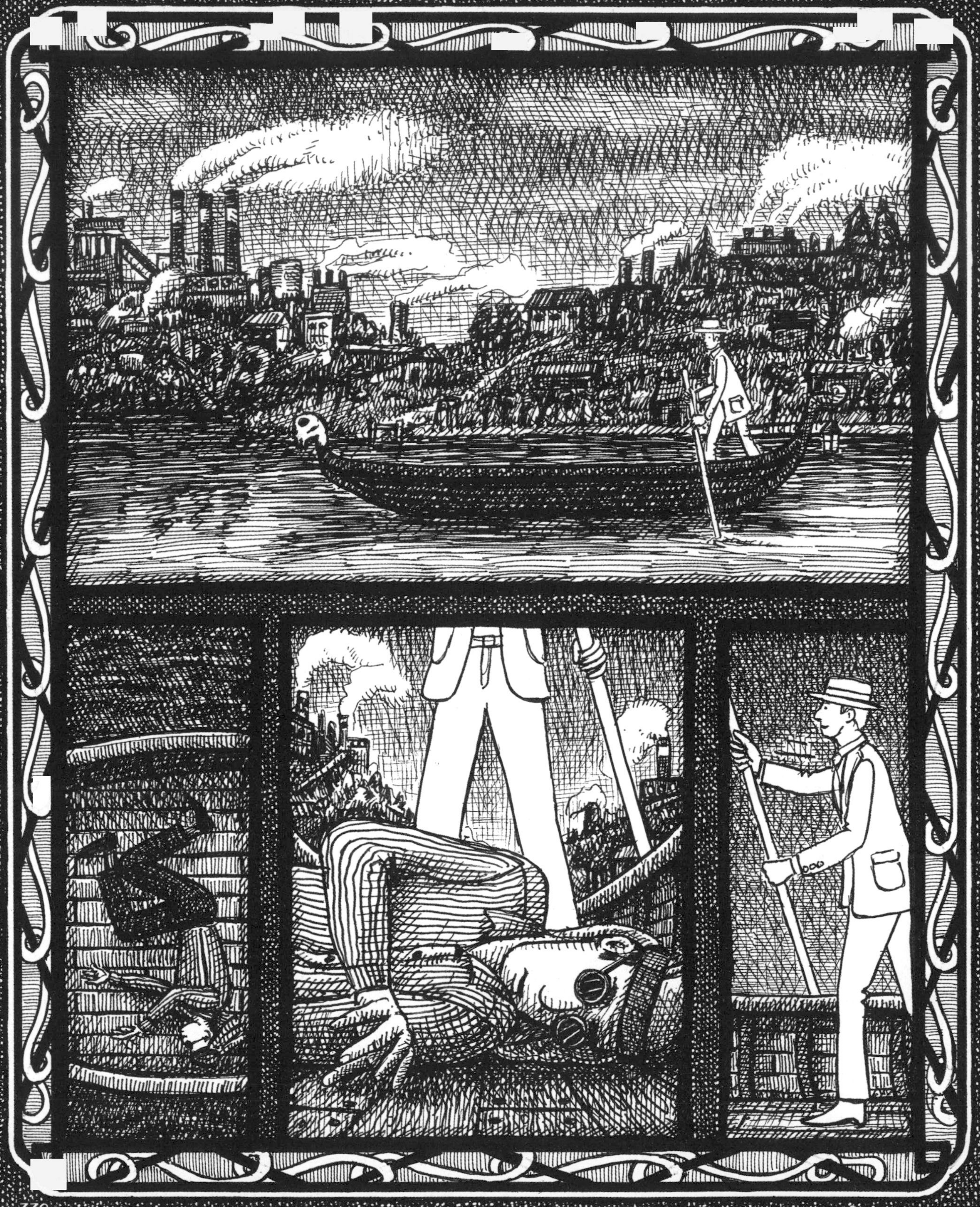

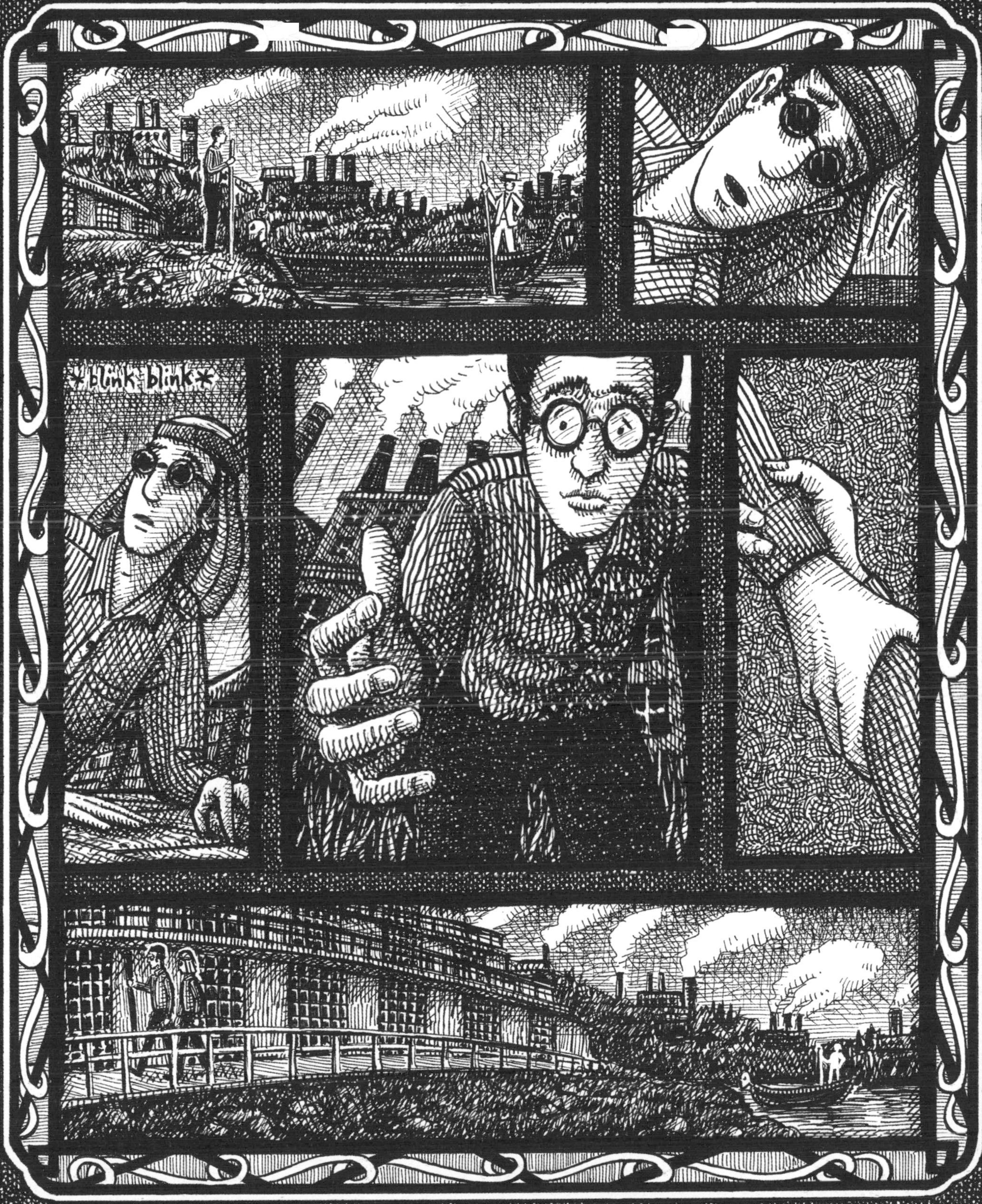
blink blink

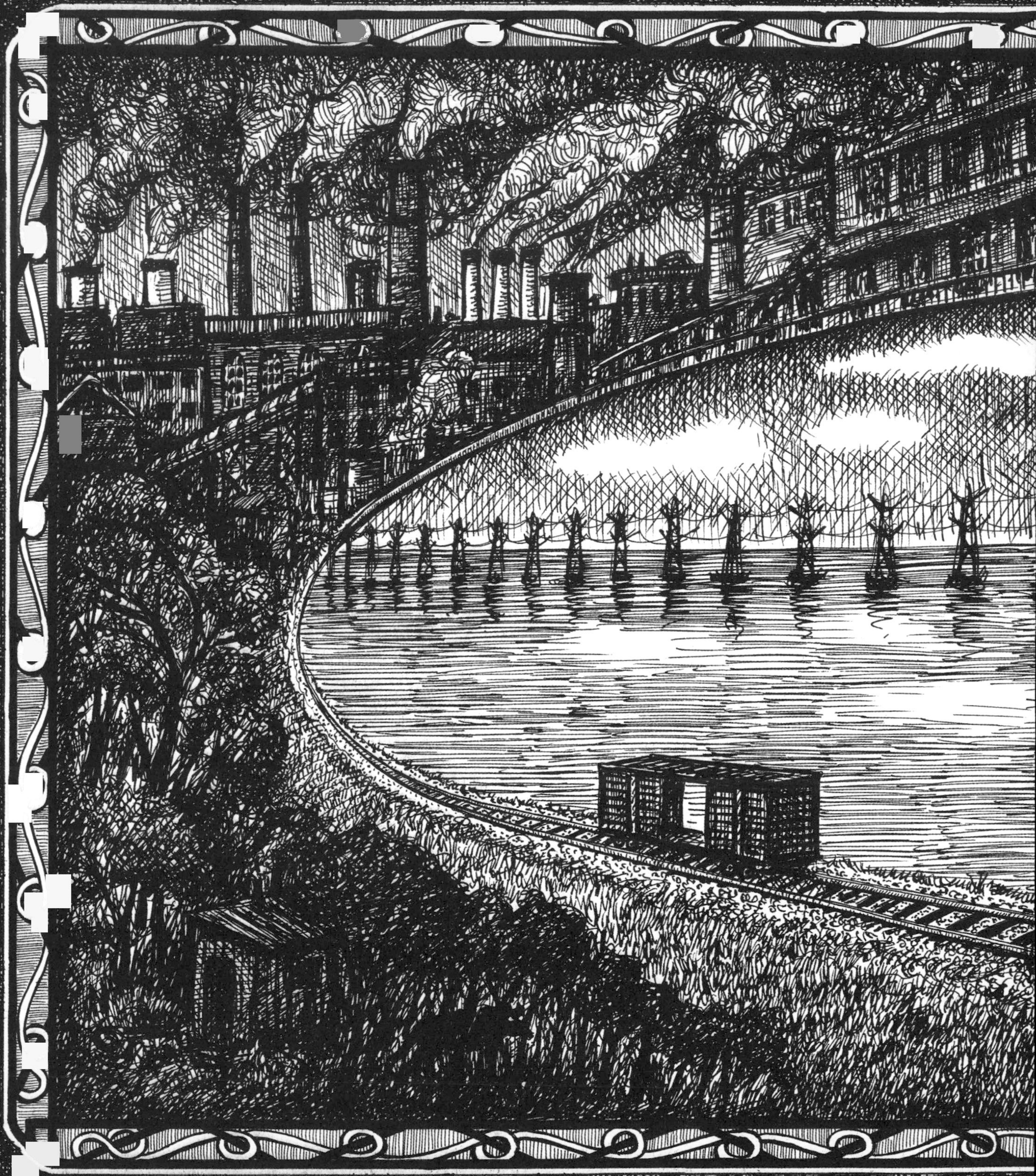

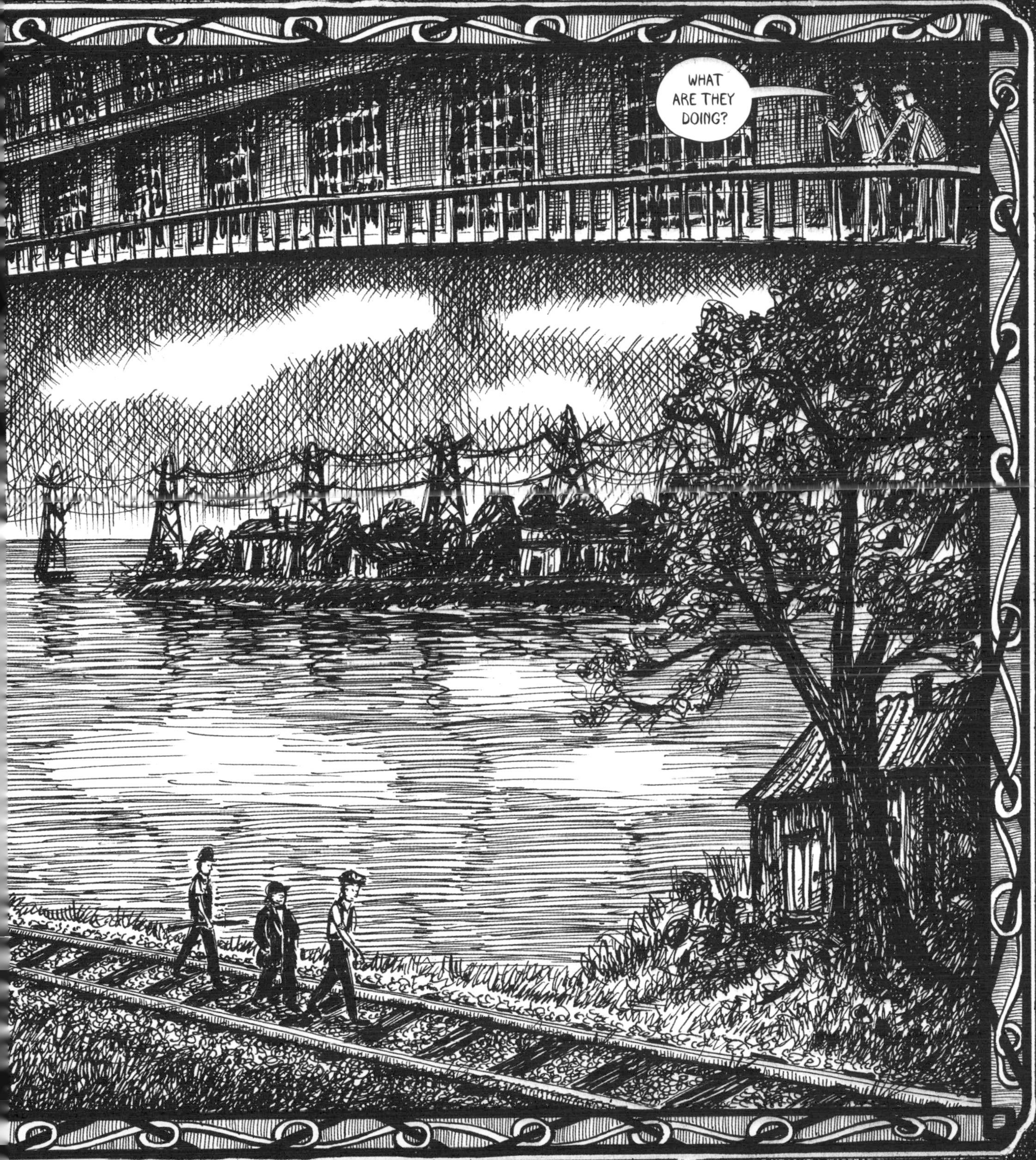
WHAT ARE THEY DOING?

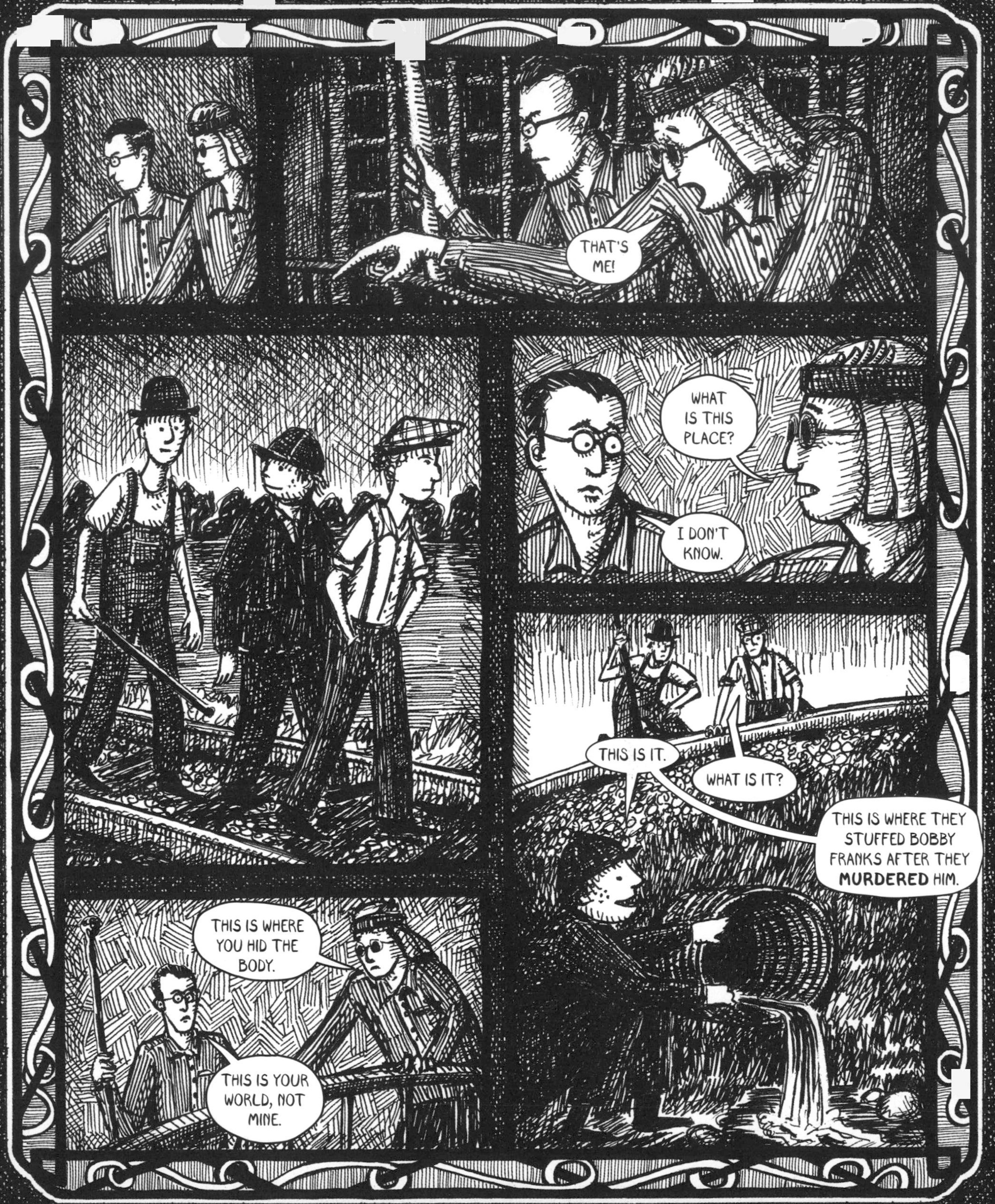
THAT'S ME!
WHAT IS THIS PLACE?
I DON'T KNOW.
THIS IS IT.
WHAT IS IT?
THIS IS WHERE THEY STUFFED BOBBY FRANKS AFTER THEY **MURDERED** HIM.
THIS IS WHERE YOU HID THE BODY.
THIS IS YOUR WORLD, NOT MINE.

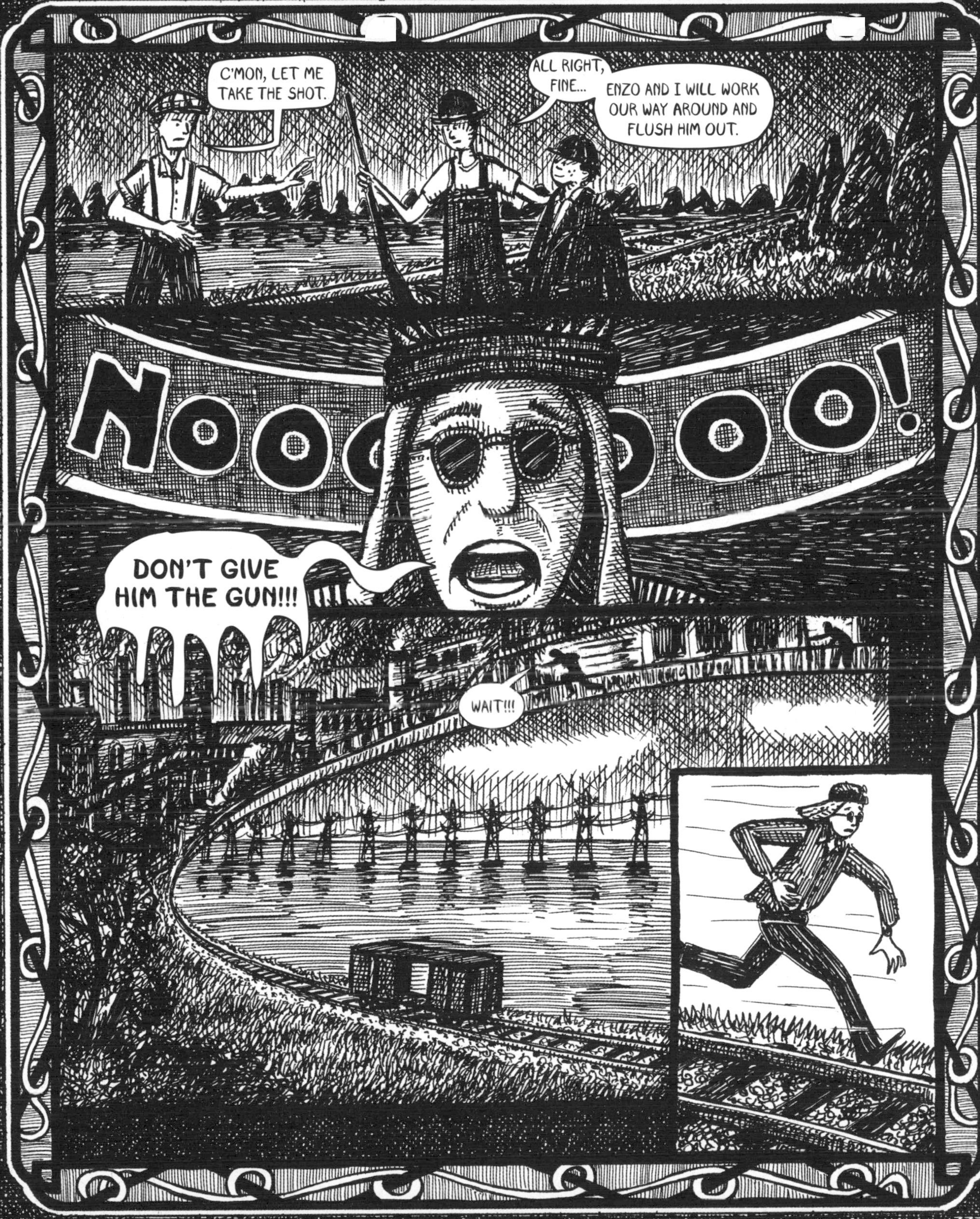
C'MON, LET ME TAKE THE SHOT.
ALL RIGHT, FINE...
ENZO AND I WILL WORK OUR WAY AROUND AND FLUSH HIM OUT.
NOOOOOOO!
DON'T GIVE HIM THE GUN!!!
WAIT!!!

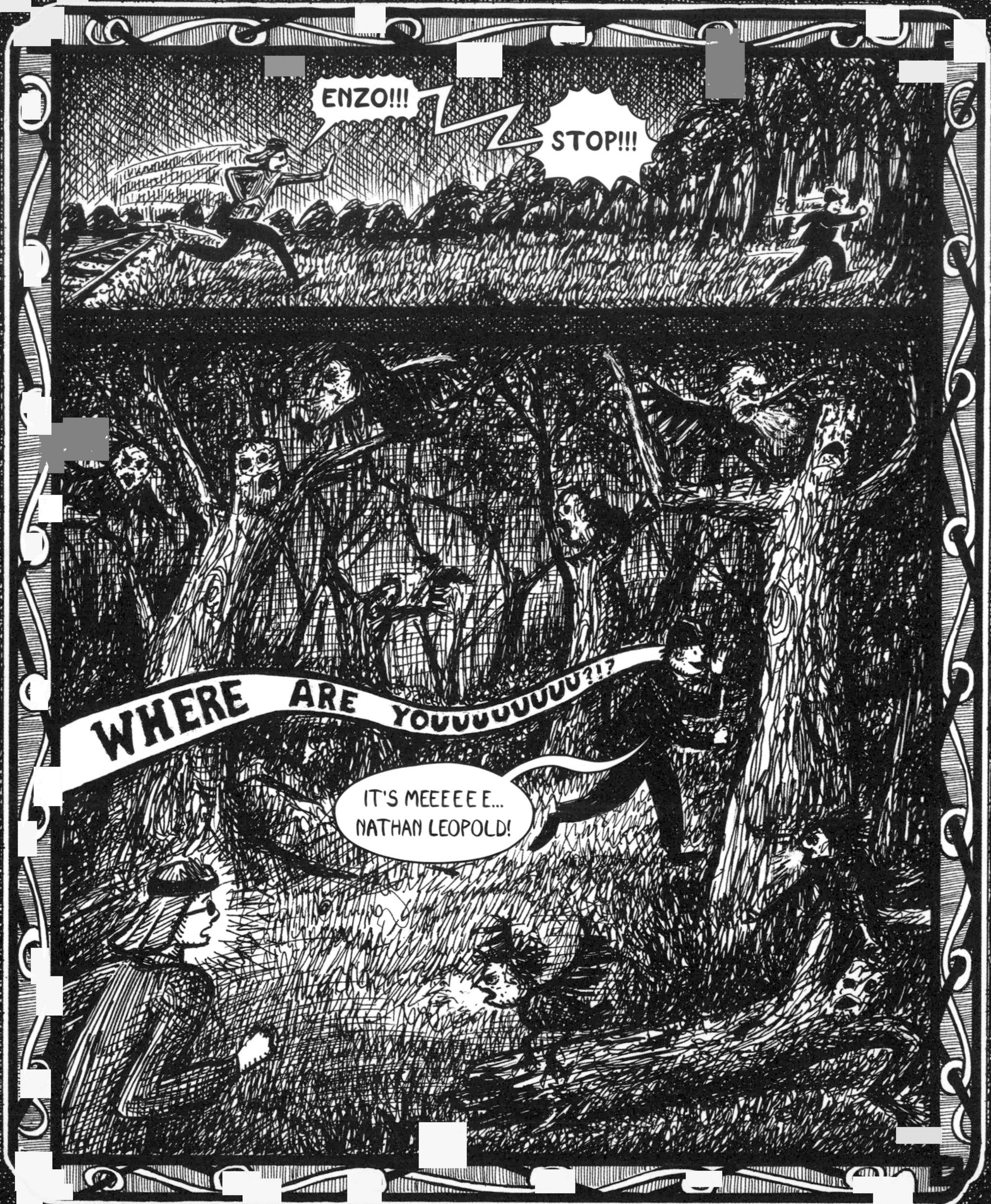
ENZO!!!
STOP!!!
WHERE ARE YOUUUUUUUU?!?
IT'S MEEEEEE...
NATHAN LEOPOLD!

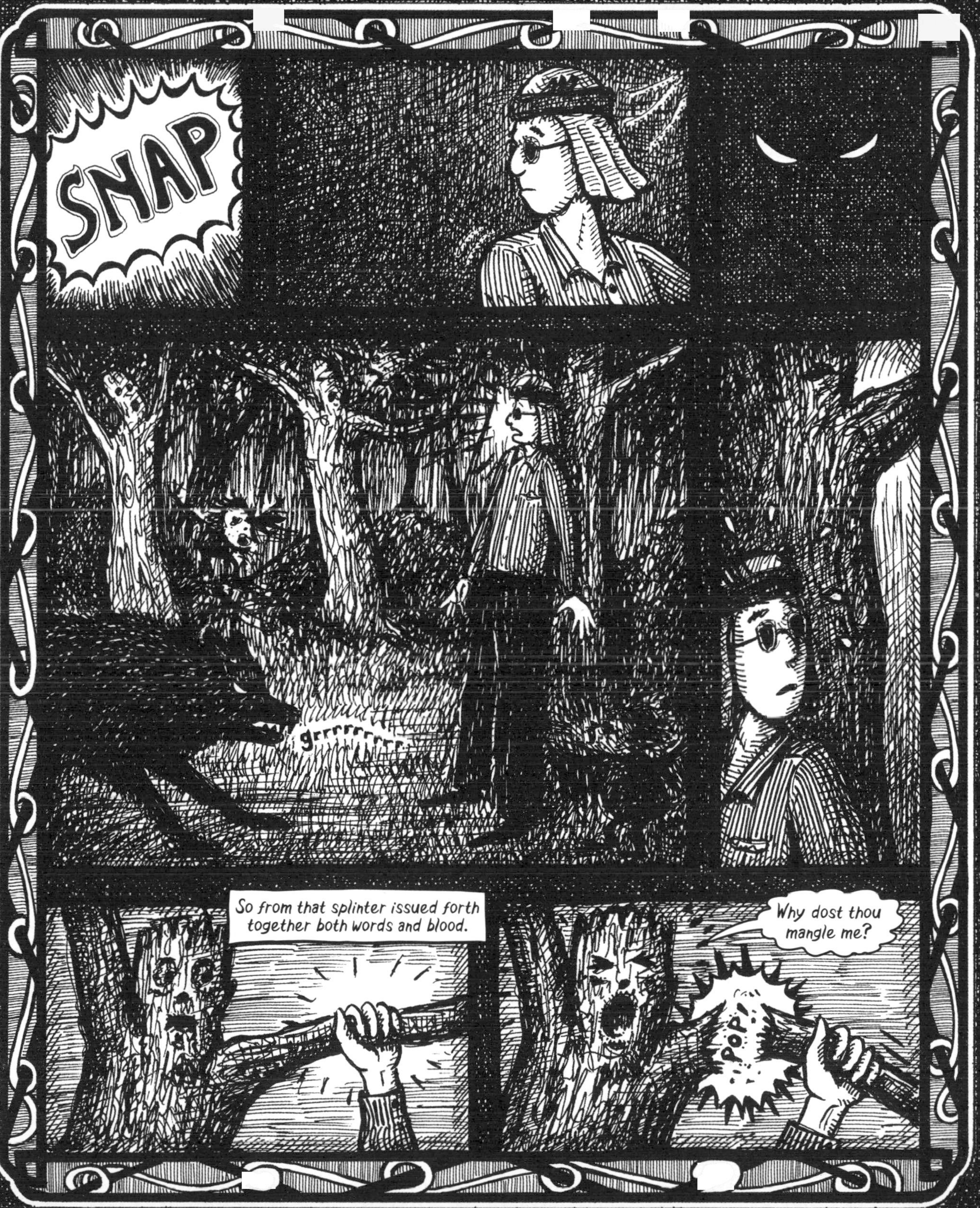
SNAP
grrrrrrrrr
So from that splinter issued forth together both words and blood.
Why dost thou mangle me?
POP!

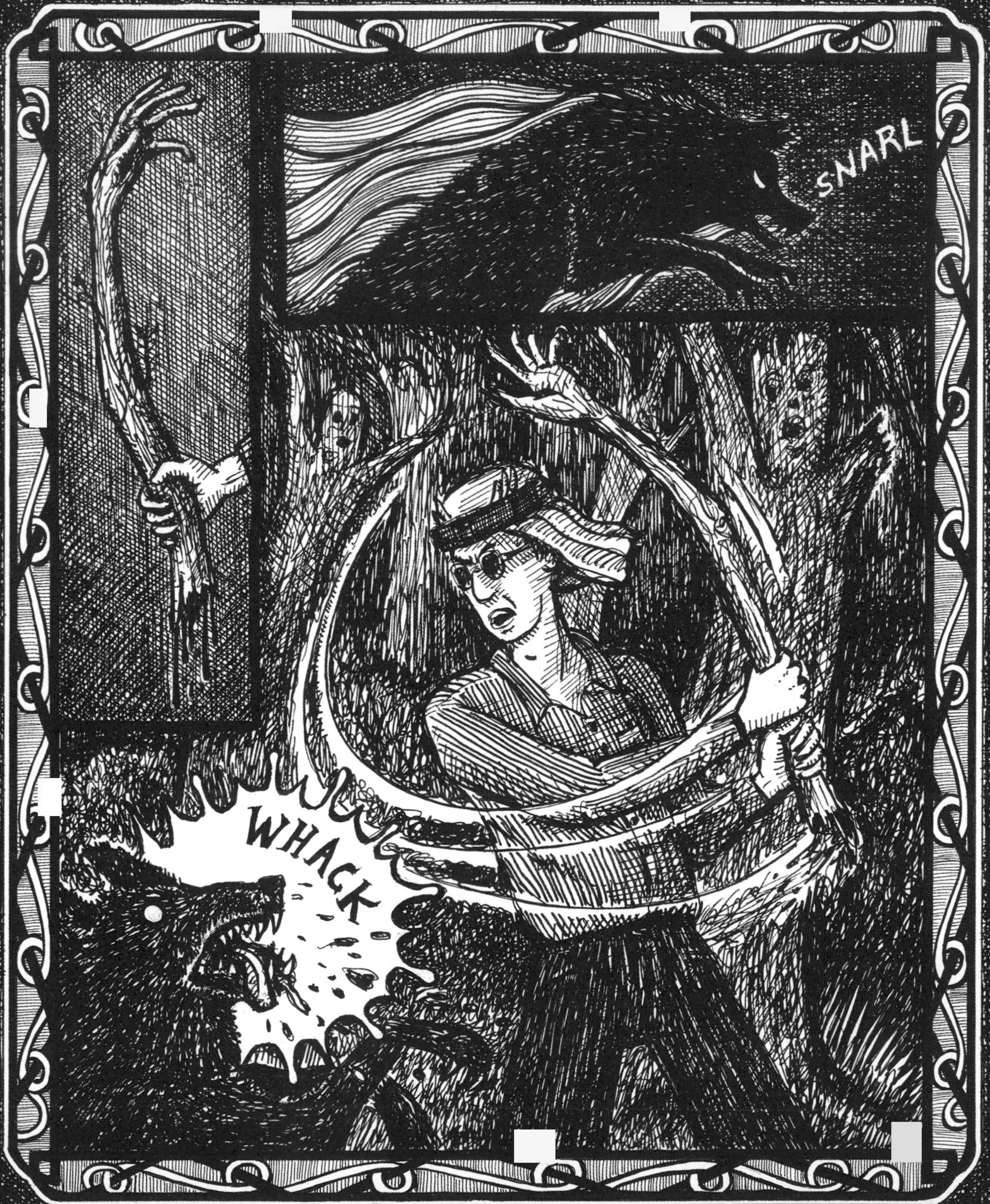
SNARL
WHACK

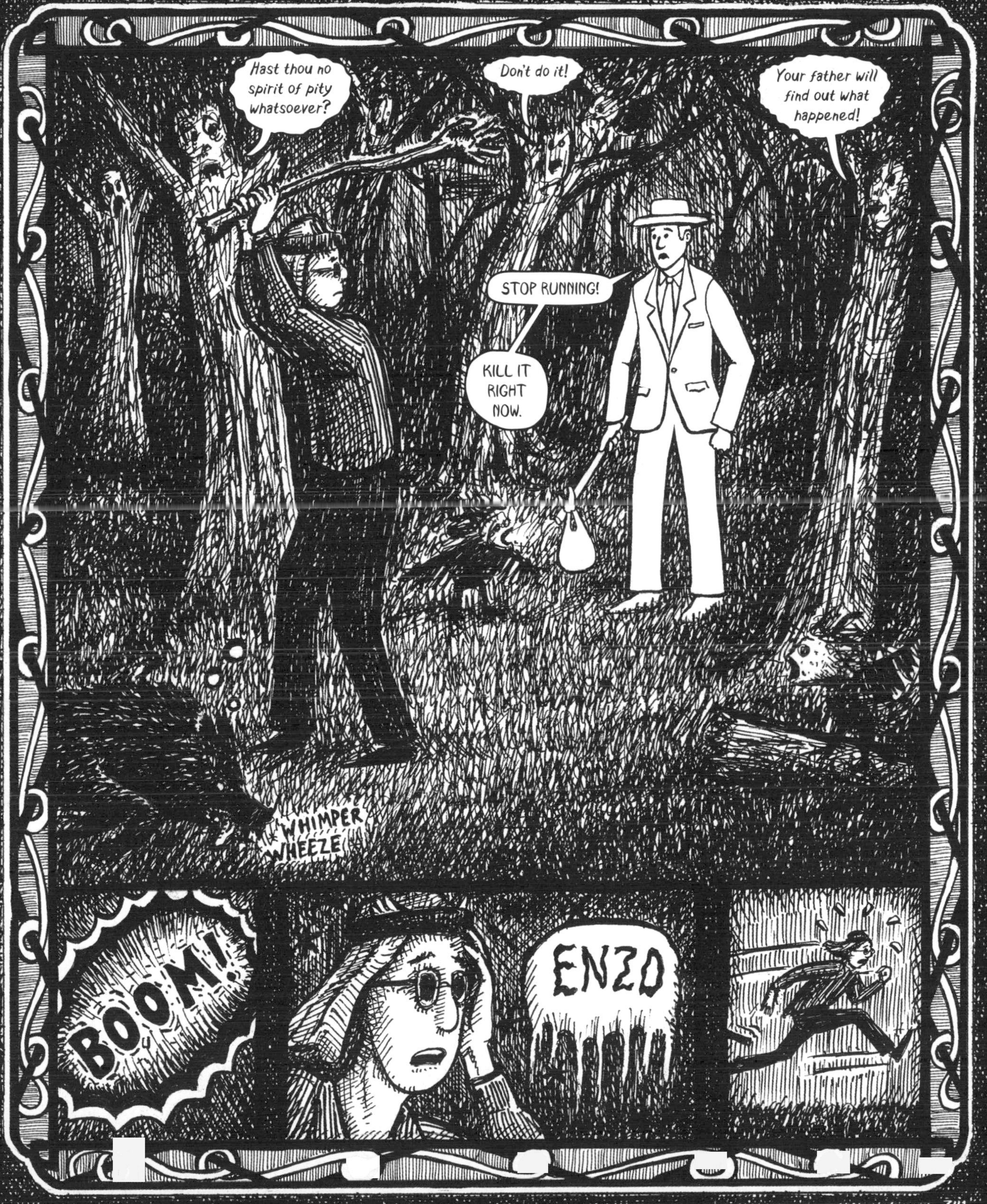
Hast thou no spirit of pity whatsoever?
Don't do it!
Your father will find out what happened!
STOP RUNNING!
KILL IT RIGHT NOW.
WHIMPER
WHEEZE
BOOM!
ENZO

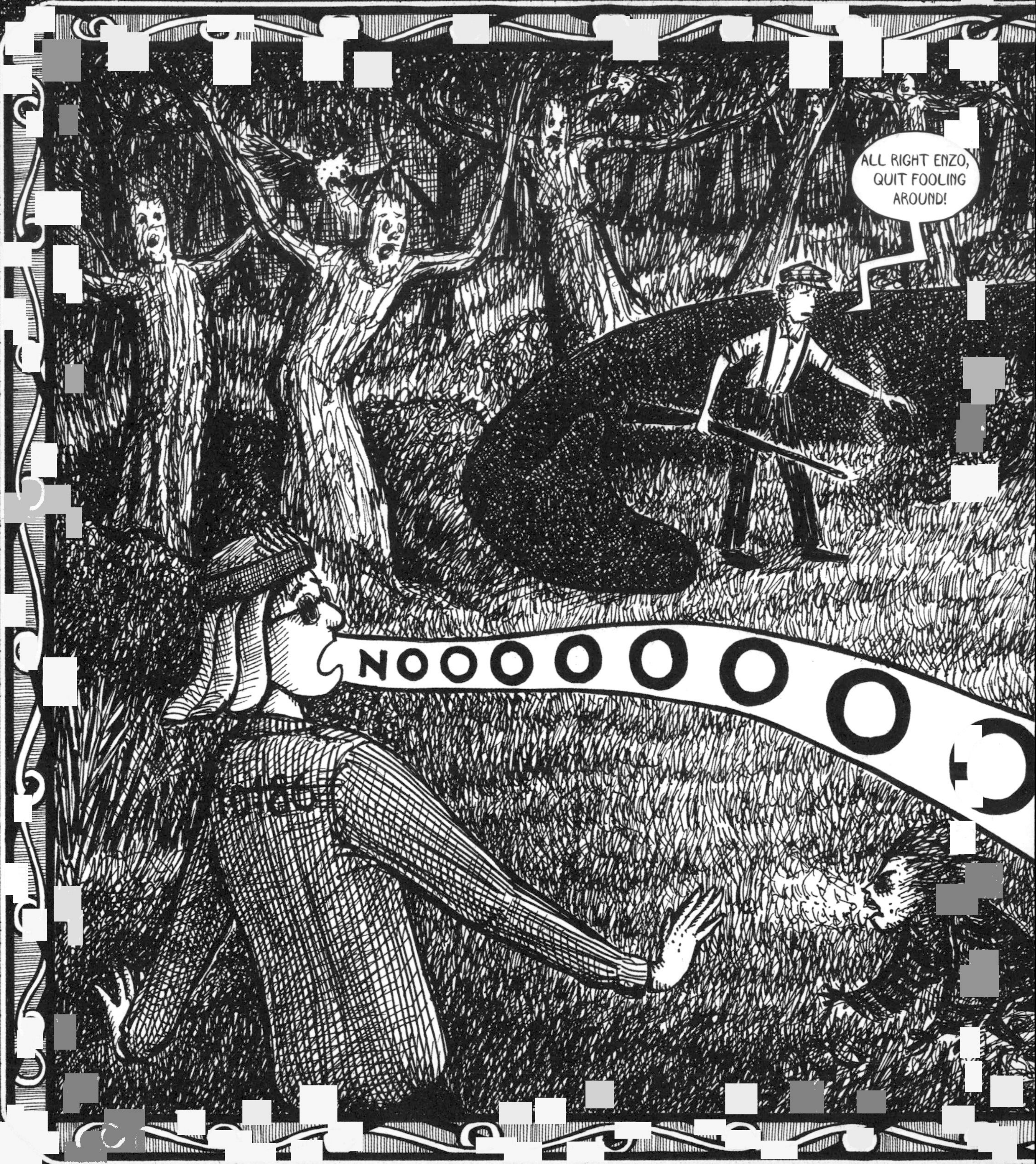
ALL RIGHT ENZO, QUIT FOOLING AROUND!
NOOOOOOOO

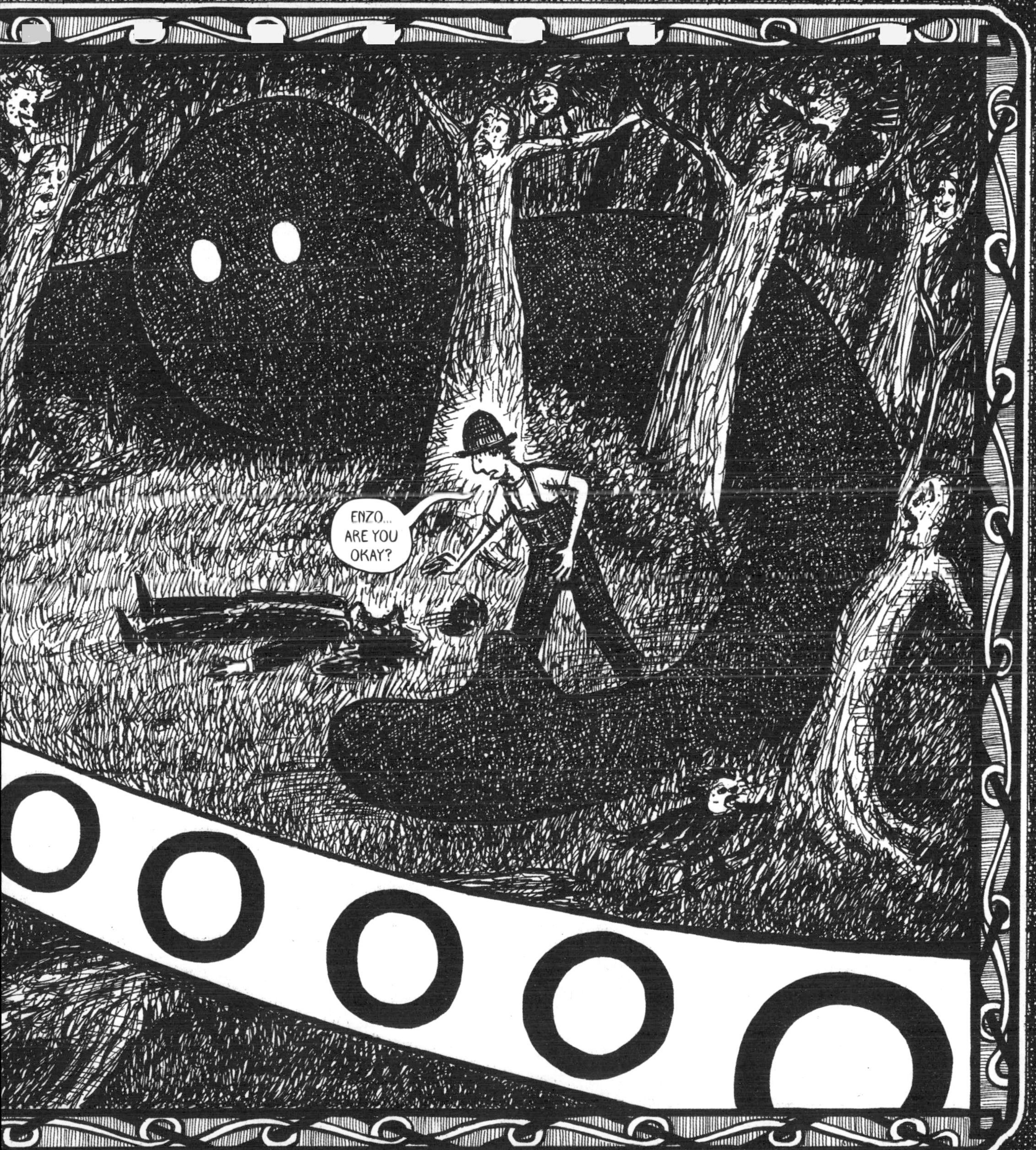
ENZO... ARE YOU OKAY?

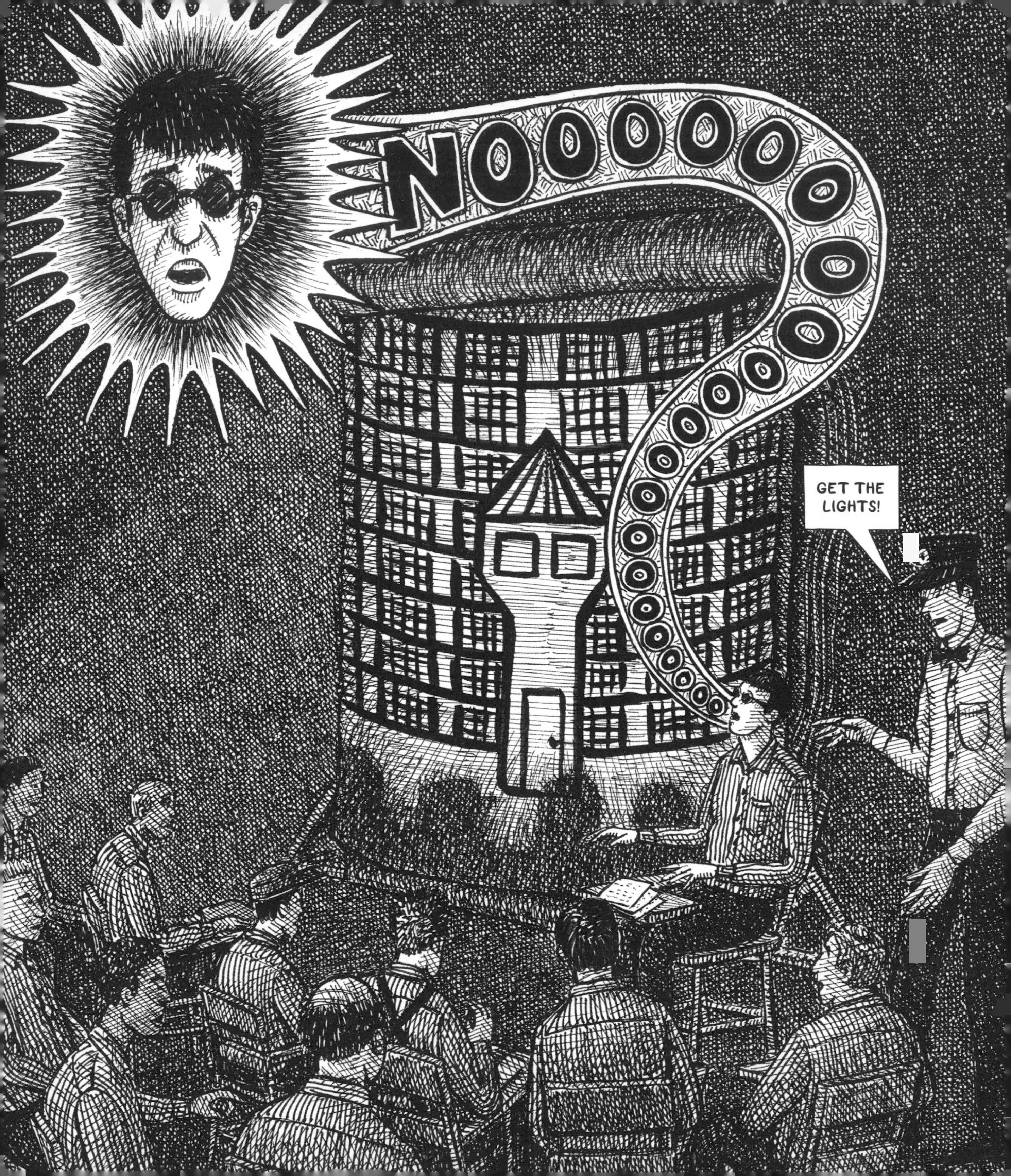
NOOOOOOOOOOOOOOOOOOOOOOOOOOOOO
GET THE LIGHTS!

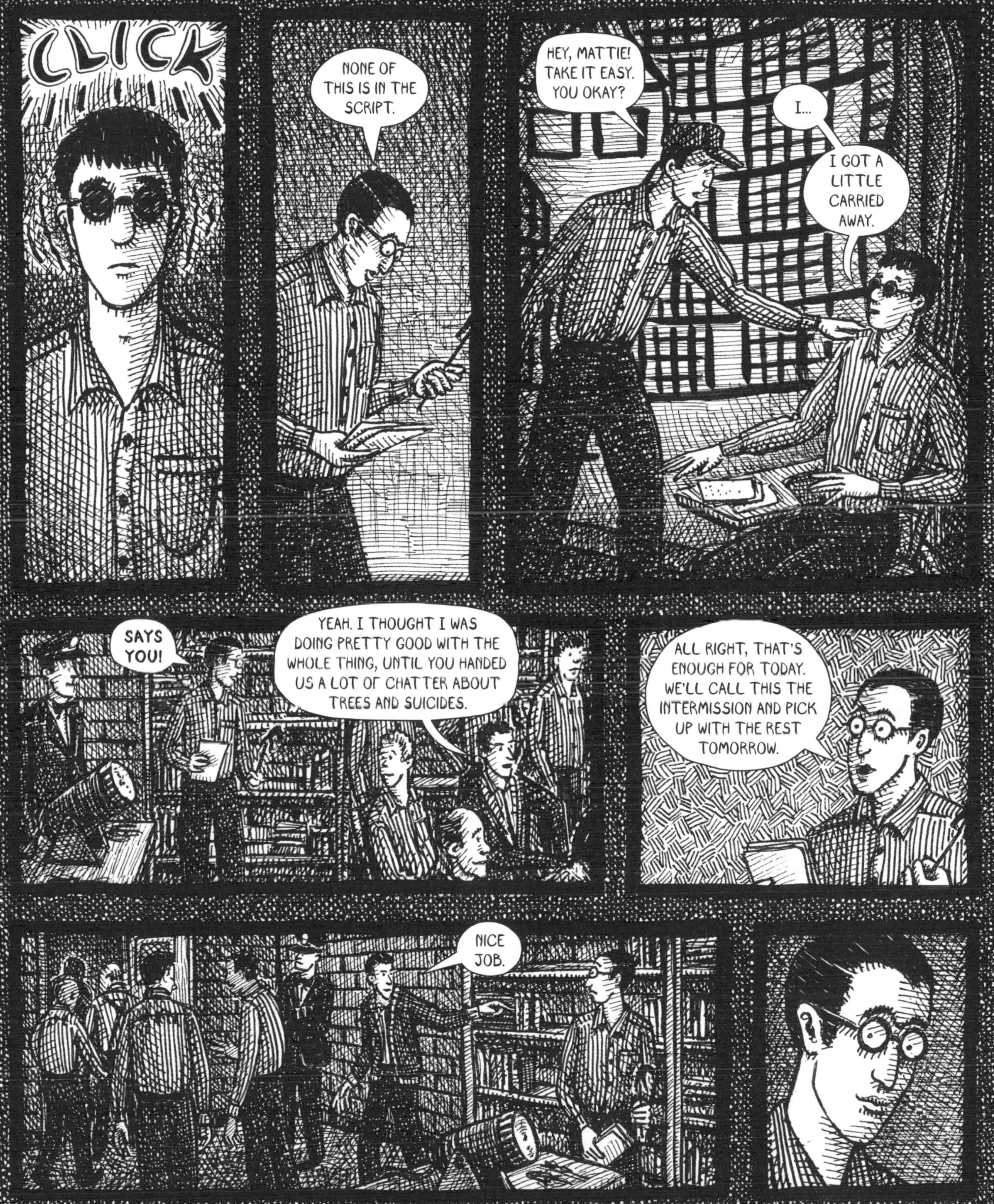
CLICK
NONE OF THIS IS IN THE SCRIPT.
HEY, MATTIE! TAKE IT EASY. YOU OKAY?
I...
I GOT A LITTLE CARRIED AWAY.
SAYS YOU!
YEAH. I THOUGHT I WAS DOING PRETTY GOOD WITH THE WHOLE THING, UNTIL YOU HANDED US A LOT OF CHATTER ABOUT TREES AND SUICIDES.
ALL RIGHT, THAT'S ENOUGH FOR TODAY. WE'LL CALL THIS THE INTERMISSION AND PICK UP WITH THE REST TOMORROW.
NICE JOB.

XIV

THE SINS OF
THE FATHERS

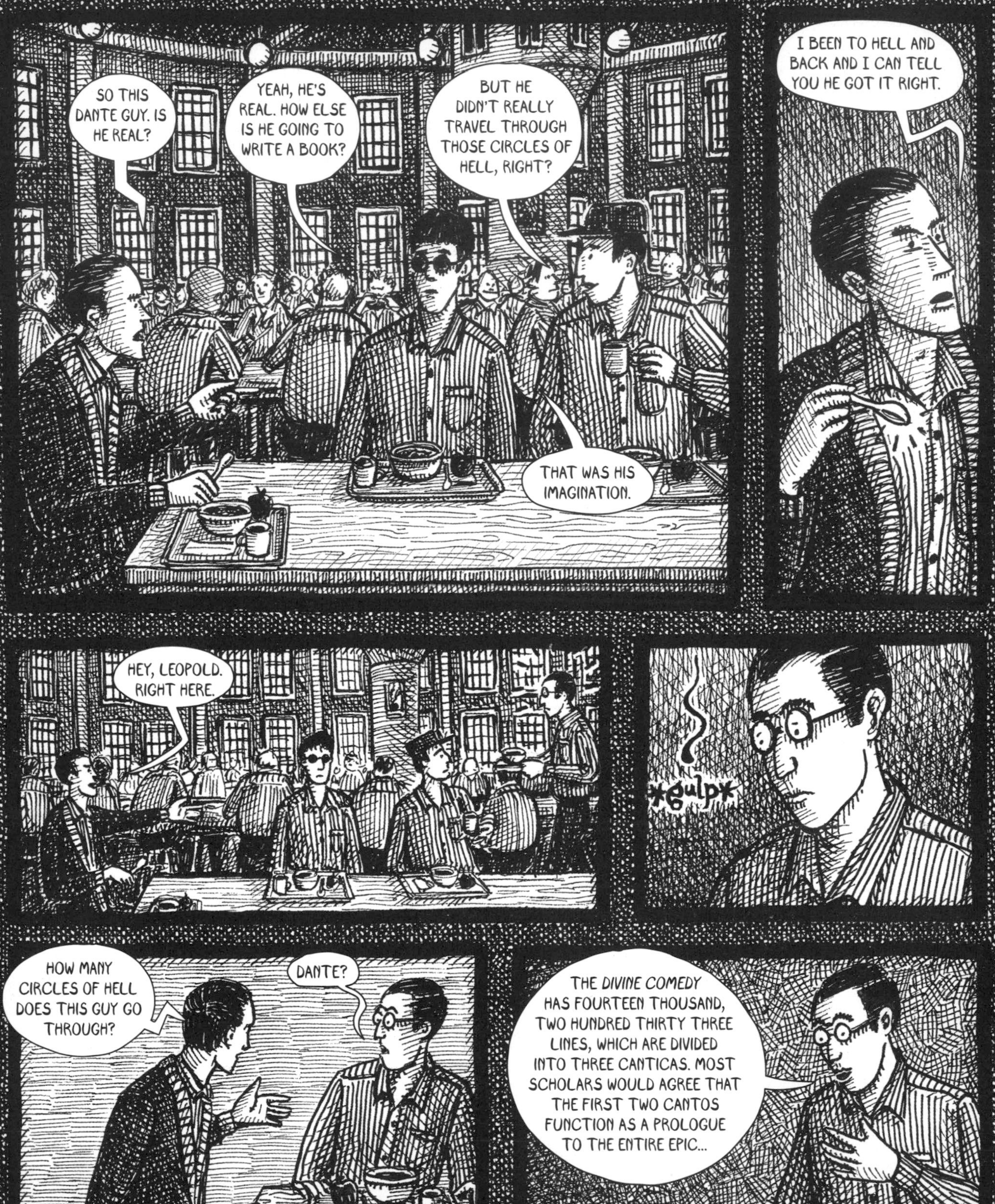
SO THIS DANTE GUY. IS HE REAL?
YEAH, HE'S REAL. HOW ELSE IS HE GOING TO WRITE A BOOK?
BUT HE DIDN'T REALLY TRAVEL THROUGH THOSE CIRCLES OF HELL, RIGHT?
THAT WAS HIS IMAGINATION.
I BEEN TO HELL AND BACK AND I CAN TELL YOU HE GOT IT RIGHT.
HEY, LEOPOLD. RIGHT HERE.
gulp
HOW MANY CIRCLES OF HELL DOES THIS GUY GO THROUGH?
DANTE?
THE *DIVINE COMEDY* HAS FOURTEEN THOUSAND, TWO HUNDRED THIRTY THREE LINES, WHICH ARE DIVIDED INTO THREE CANTICAS. MOST SCHOLARS WOULD AGREE THAT THE FIRST TWO CANTOS FUNCTION AS A PROLOGUE TO THE ENTIRE EPIC...

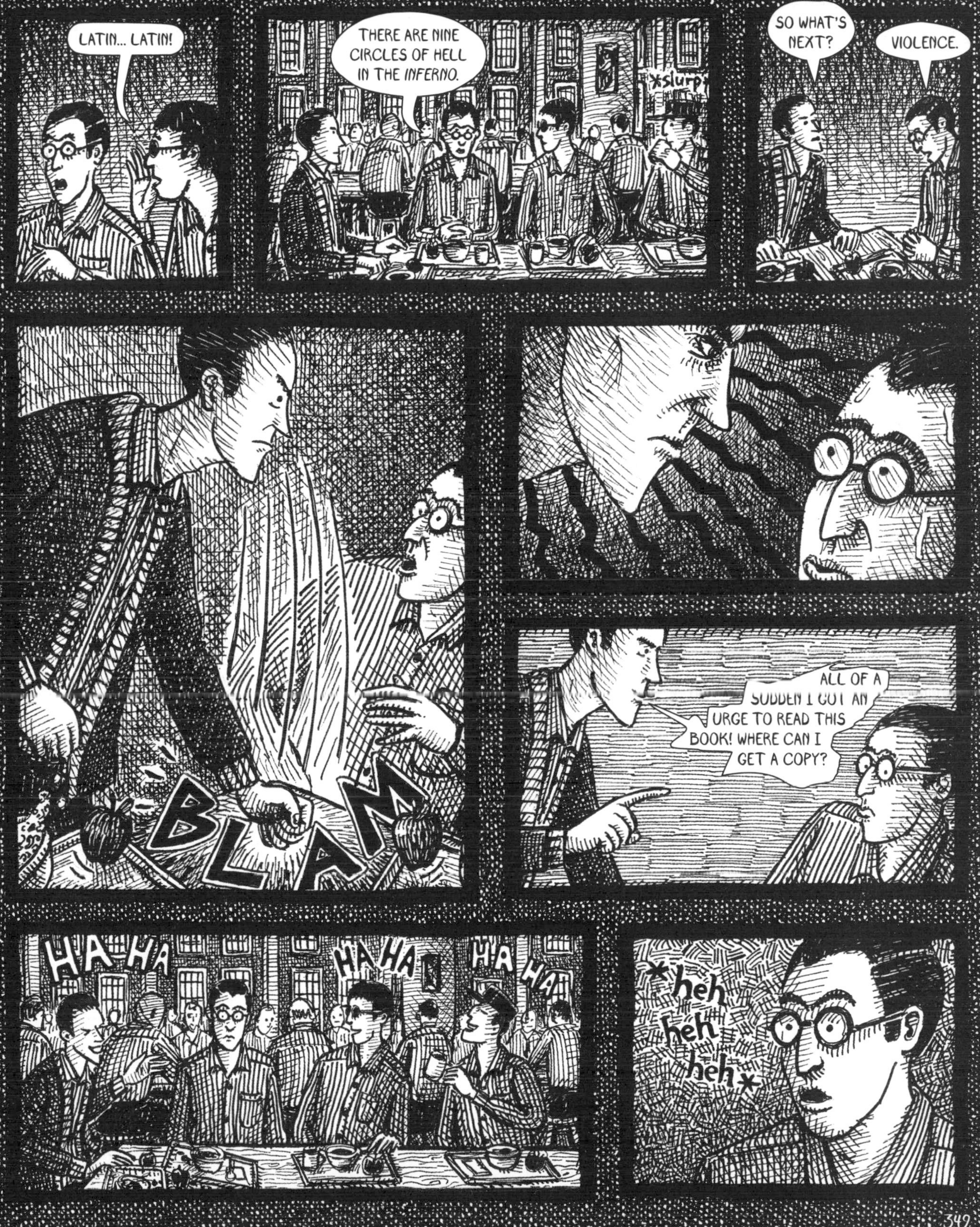
LATIN... LATIN!
THERE ARE NINE CIRCLES OF HELL IN THE INFERNO.
slurp
SO WHAT'S NEXT?
VIOLENCE.
BLAM
ALL OF A SUDDEN I GOT AN URGE TO READ THIS BOOK! WHERE CAN I GET A COPY?
HA HA
HA HA
HA HA
heh heh heh

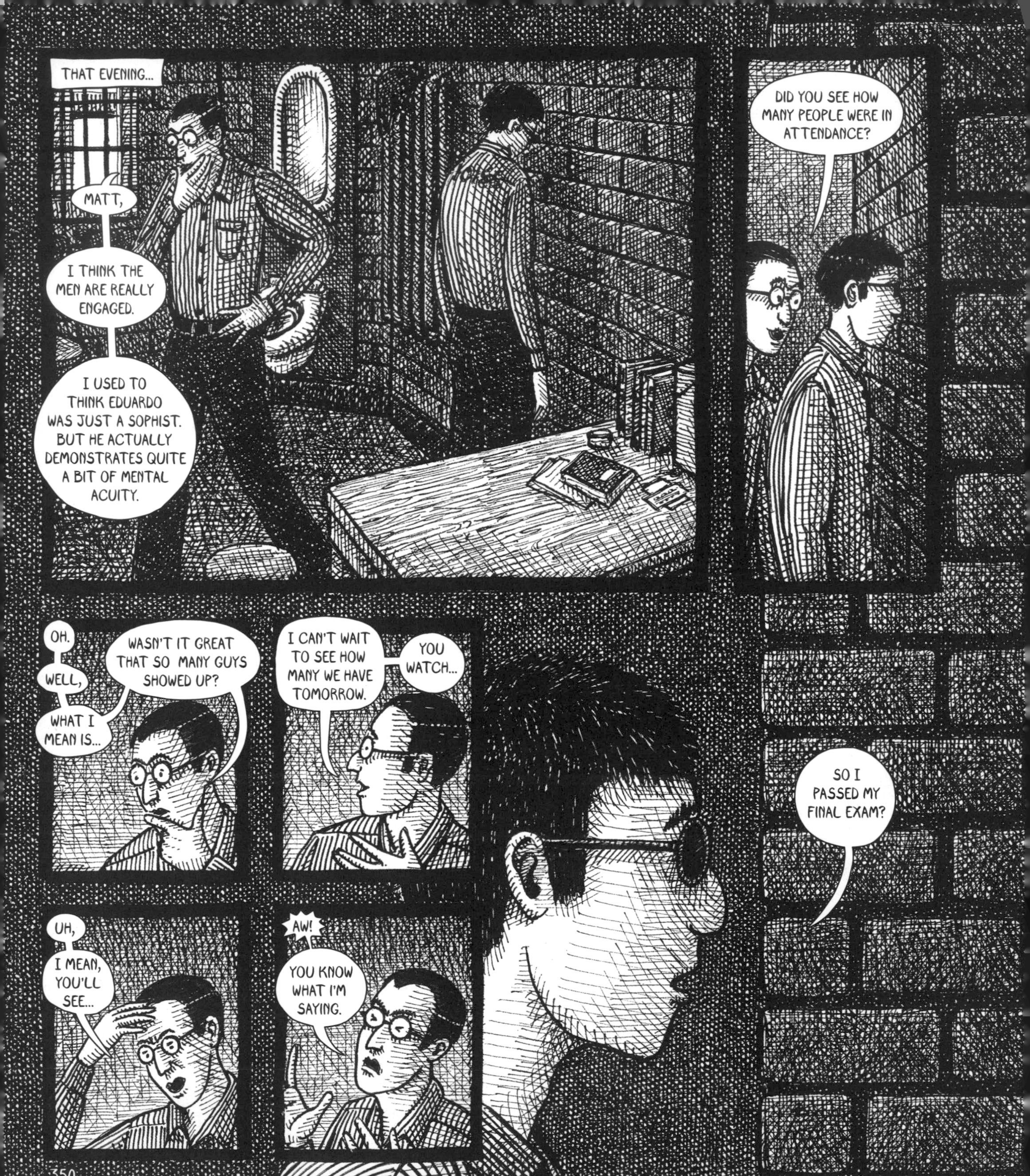

THAT EVENING...
MATT,
I THINK THE MEN ARE REALLY ENGAGED.
I USED TO THINK EDUARDO WAS JUST A SOPHIST. BUT HE ACTUALLY DEMONSTRATES QUITE A BIT OF MENTAL ACUITY.
DID YOU SEE HOW MANY PEOPLE WERE IN ATTENDANCE?
OH.
WELL,
WHAT I MEAN IS...
WASN'T IT GREAT THAT SO MANY GUYS SHOWED UP?
I CAN'T WAIT TO SEE HOW MANY WE HAVE TOMORROW.
YOU WATCH...
UH,
I MEAN, YOU'LL SEE...
AW!
YOU KNOW WHAT I'M SAYING.
SO I PASSED MY FINAL EXAM?

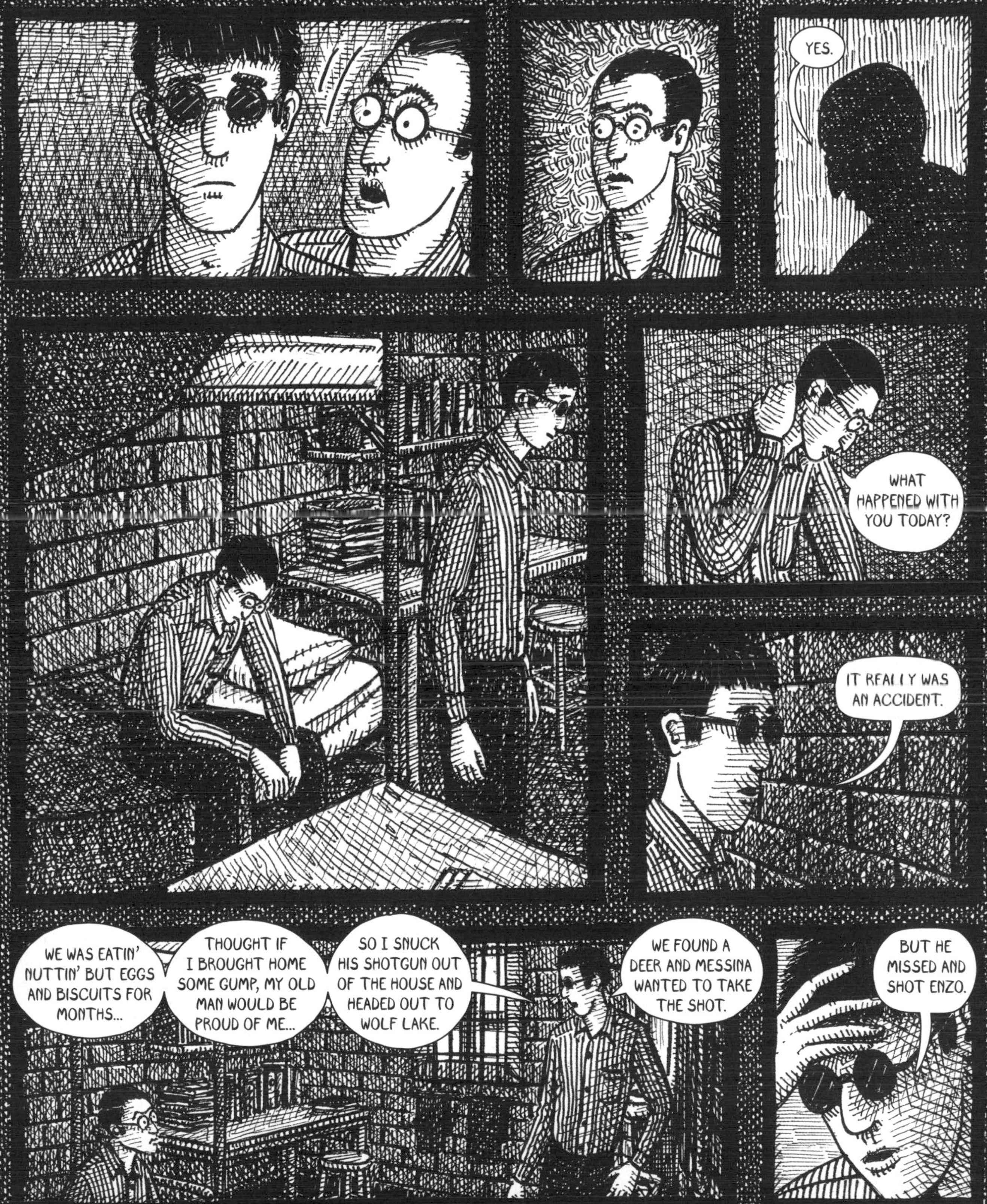
YES.
WHAT HAPPENED WITH YOU TODAY?
IT REALLY WAS AN ACCIDENT.
WE WAS EATIN' NUTTIN' BUT EGGS AND BISCUITS FOR MONTHS...
THOUGHT IF I BROUGHT HOME SOME GUMP, MY OLD MAN WOULD BE PROUD OF ME...
SO I SNUCK HIS SHOTGUN OUT OF THE HOUSE AND HEADED OUT TO WOLF LAKE.
WE FOUND A DEER AND MESSINA WANTED TO TAKE THE SHOT.
BUT HE MISSED AND SHOT ENZO.

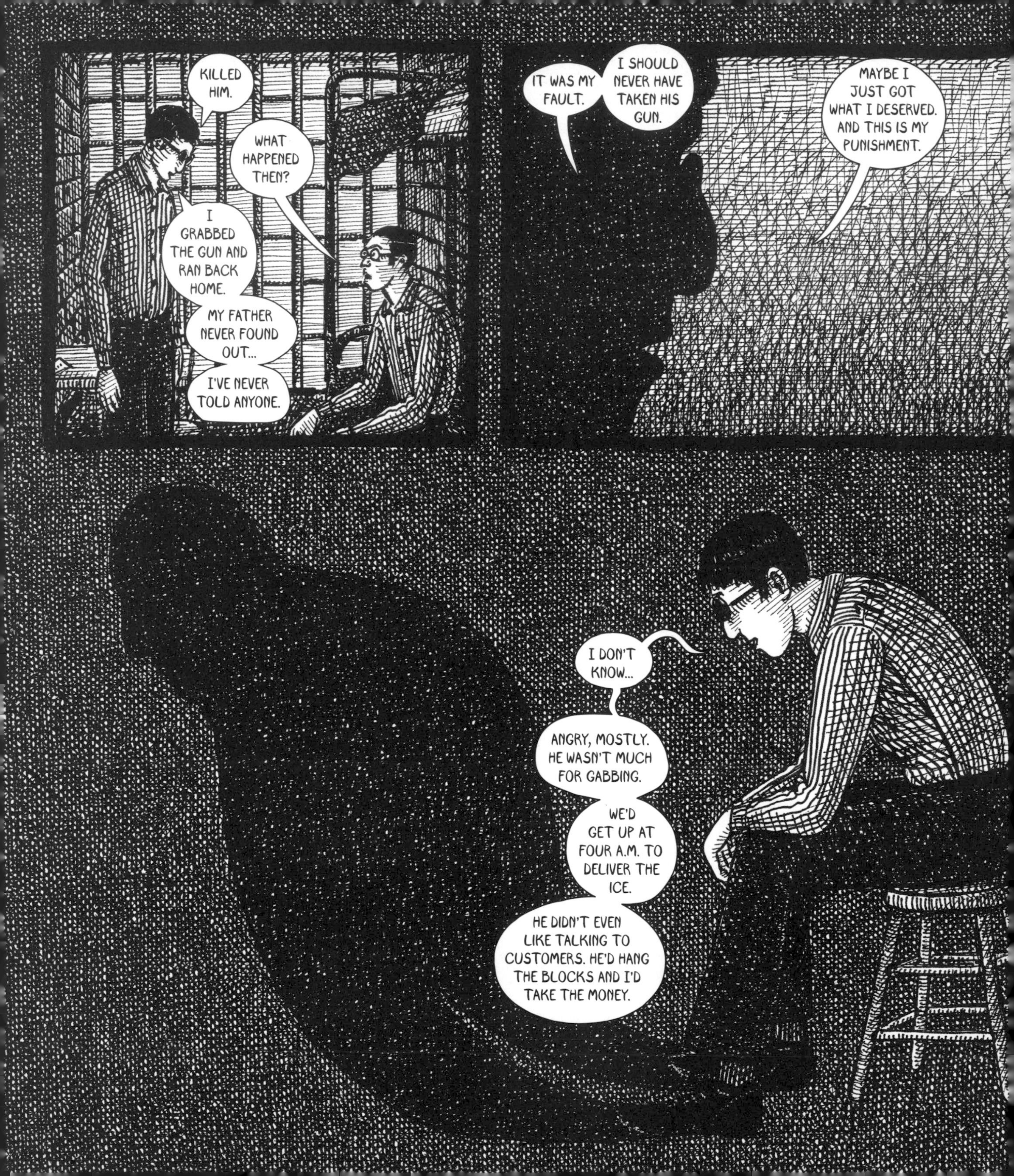
KILLED HIM.
WHAT HAPPENED THEN?
I GRABBED THE GUN AND RAN BACK HOME.
MY FATHER NEVER FOUND OUT...
I'VE NEVER TOLD ANYONE.
IT WAS MY FAULT.
I SHOULD NEVER HAVE TAKEN HIS GUN.
MAYBE I JUST GOT WHAT I DESERVED. AND THIS IS MY PUNISHMENT.
I DON'T KNOW...
ANGRY, MOSTLY. HE WASN'T MUCH FOR GABBING.
WE'D GET UP AT FOUR A.M. TO DELIVER THE ICE.
HE DIDN'T EVEN LIKE TALKING TO CUSTOMERS. HE'D HANG THE BLOCKS AND I'D TAKE THE MONEY.

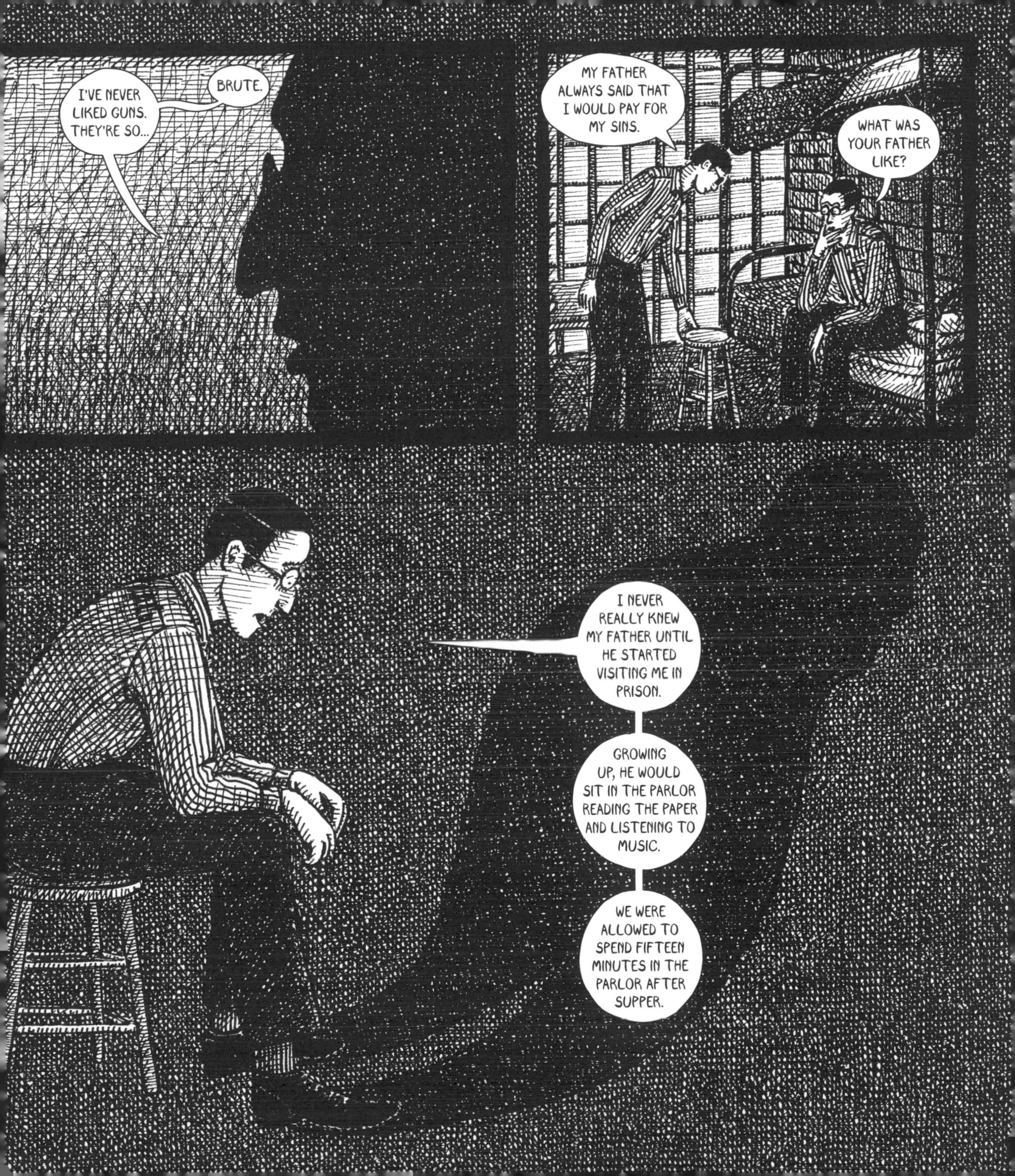
I'VE NEVER LIKED GUNS. THEY'RE SO...
BRUTE.
MY FATHER ALWAYS SAID THAT I WOULD PAY FOR MY SINS.
WHAT WAS YOUR FATHER LIKE?
I NEVER REALLY KNEW MY FATHER UNTIL HE STARTED VISITING ME IN PRISON.
GROWING UP, HE WOULD SIT IN THE PARLOR READING THE PAPER AND LISTENING TO MUSIC.
WE WERE ALLOWED TO SPEND FIFTEEN MINUTES IN THE PARLOR AFTER SUPPER.

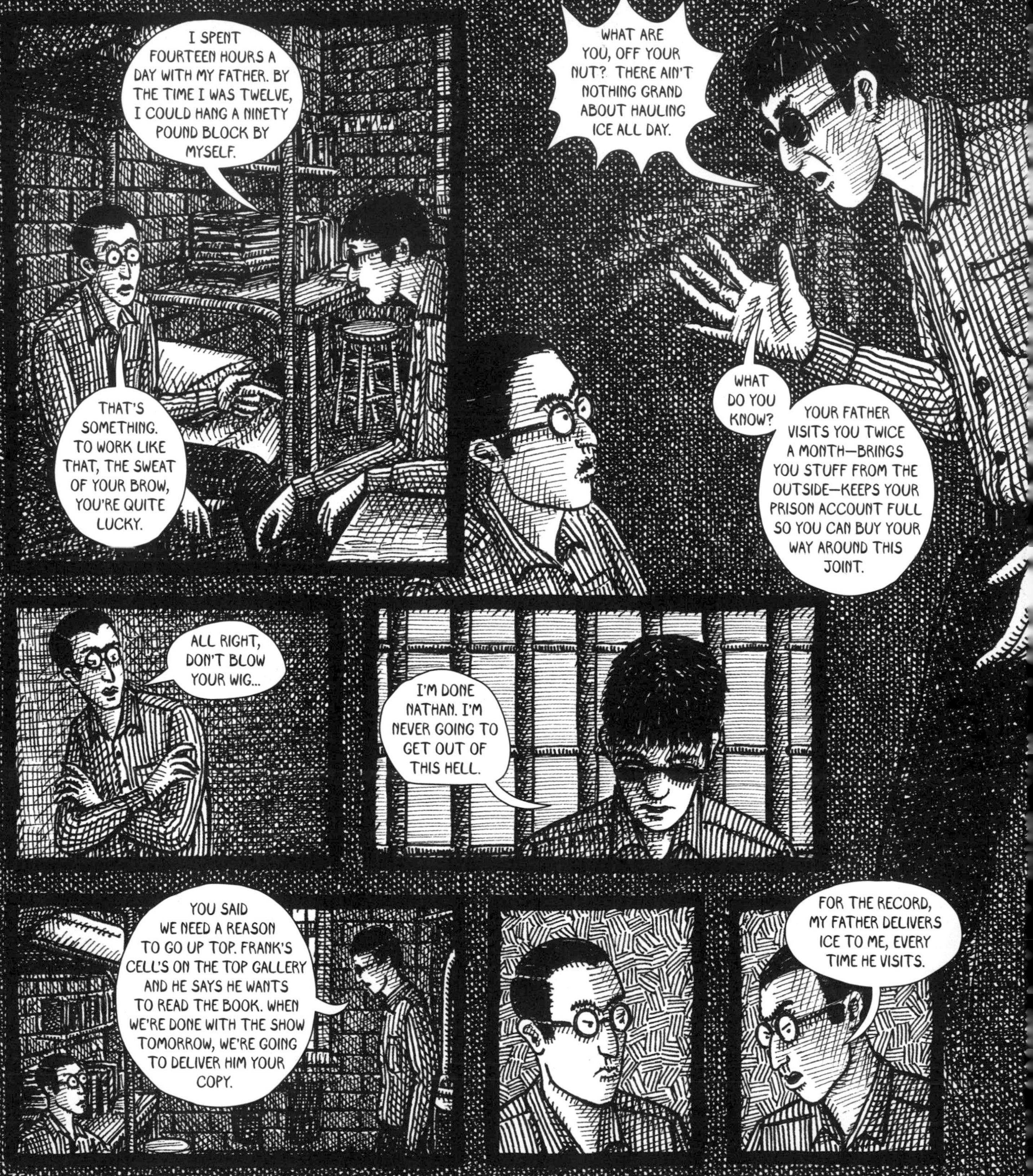
I SPENT FOURTEEN HOURS A DAY WITH MY FATHER. BY THE TIME I WAS TWELVE, I COULD HANG A NINETY POUND BLOCK BY MYSELF.
THAT'S SOMETHING. TO WORK LIKE THAT, THE SWEAT OF YOUR BROW, YOU'RE QUITE LUCKY.
WHAT ARE YOU, OFF YOUR NUT? THERE AIN'T NOTHING GRAND ABOUT HAULING ICE ALL DAY.
WHAT DO YOU KNOW?
YOUR FATHER VISITS YOU TWICE A MONTH—BRINGS YOU STUFF FROM THE OUTSIDE—KEEPS YOUR PRISON ACCOUNT FULL SO YOU CAN BUY YOUR WAY AROUND THIS JOINT.
ALL RIGHT, DON'T BLOW YOUR WIG...
I'M DONE NATHAN. I'M NEVER GOING TO GET OUT OF THIS HELL.
YOU SAID WE NEED A REASON TO GO UP TOP. FRANK'S CELL'S ON THE TOP GALLERY AND HE SAYS HE WANTS TO READ THE BOOK. WHEN WE'RE DONE WITH THE SHOW TOMORROW, WE'RE GOING TO DELIVER HIM YOUR COPY.
FOR THE RECORD, MY FATHER DELIVERS ICE TO ME, EVERY TIME HE VISITS.

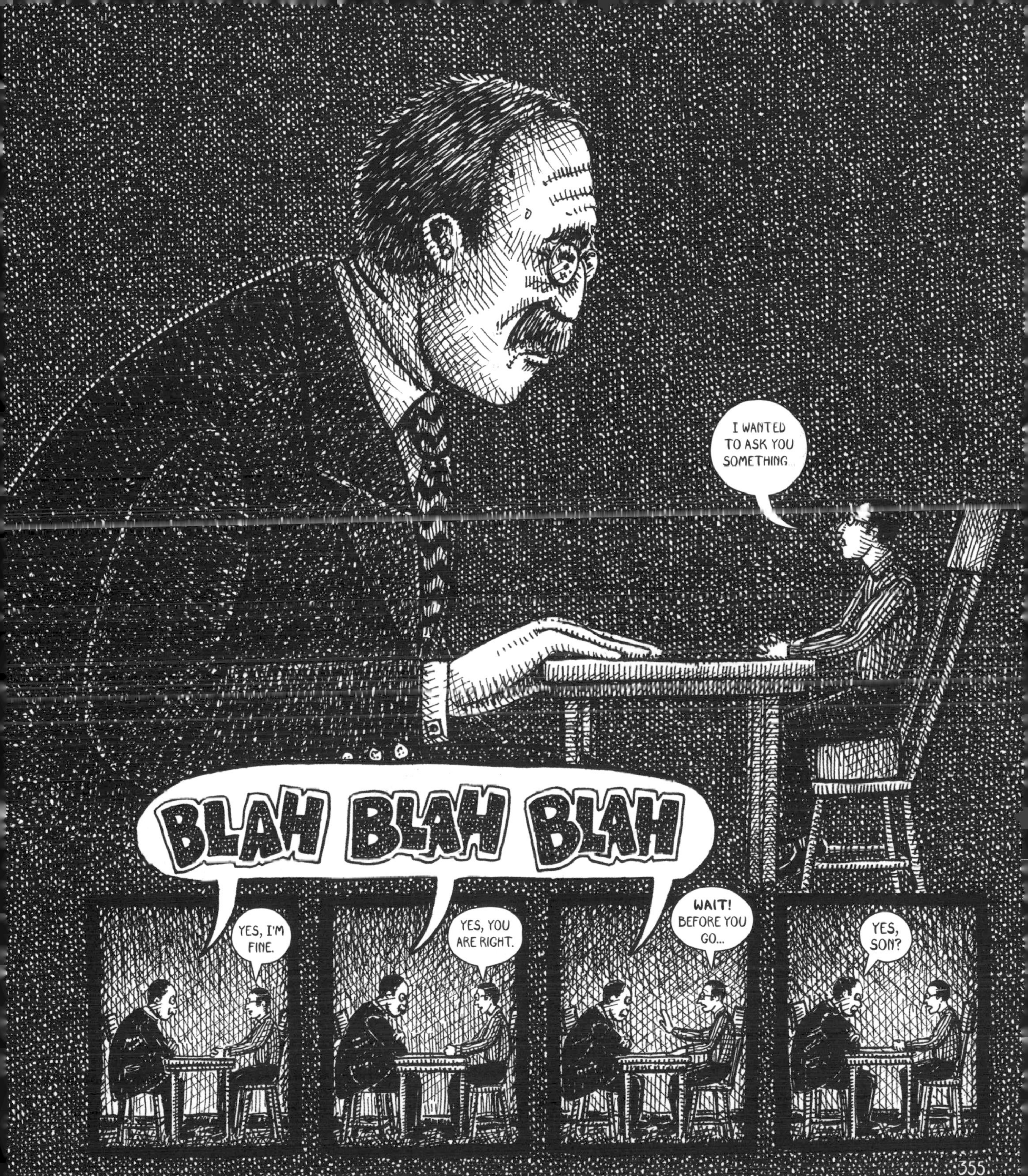
I WANTED TO ASK YOU SOMETHING...
BLAH BLAH BLAH
YES, I'M FINE.
YES, YOU ARE RIGHT.
WAIT! BEFORE YOU GO...
YES, SON?

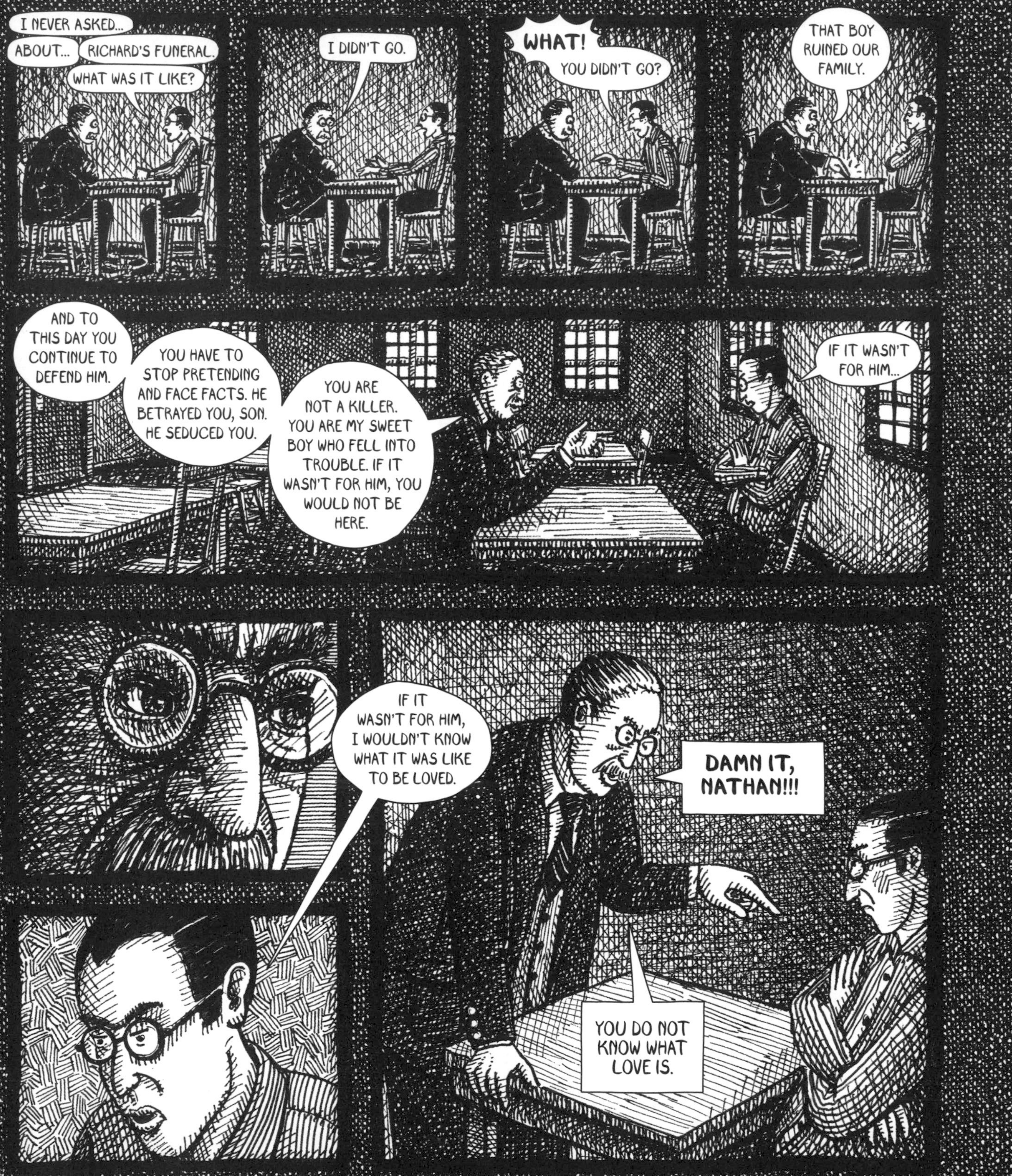
I NEVER ASKED...
ABOUT...
RICHARD'S FUNERAL.
WHAT WAS IT LIKE?
I DIDN'T GO.
WHAT!
YOU DIDN'T GO?
THAT BOY RUINED OUR FAMILY.
AND TO THIS DAY YOU CONTINUE TO DEFEND HIM.
YOU HAVE TO STOP PRETENDING AND FACE FACTS. HE BETRAYED YOU, SON. HE SEDUCED YOU.
YOU ARE NOT A KILLER. YOU ARE MY SWEET BOY WHO FELL INTO TROUBLE. IF IT WASN'T FOR HIM, YOU WOULD NOT BE HERE.
IF IT WASN'T FOR HIM...
IF IT WASN'T FOR HIM, I WOULDN'T KNOW WHAT IT WAS LIKE TO BE LOVED.
DAMN IT, NATHAN!!!
YOU DO NOT KNOW WHAT LOVE IS.

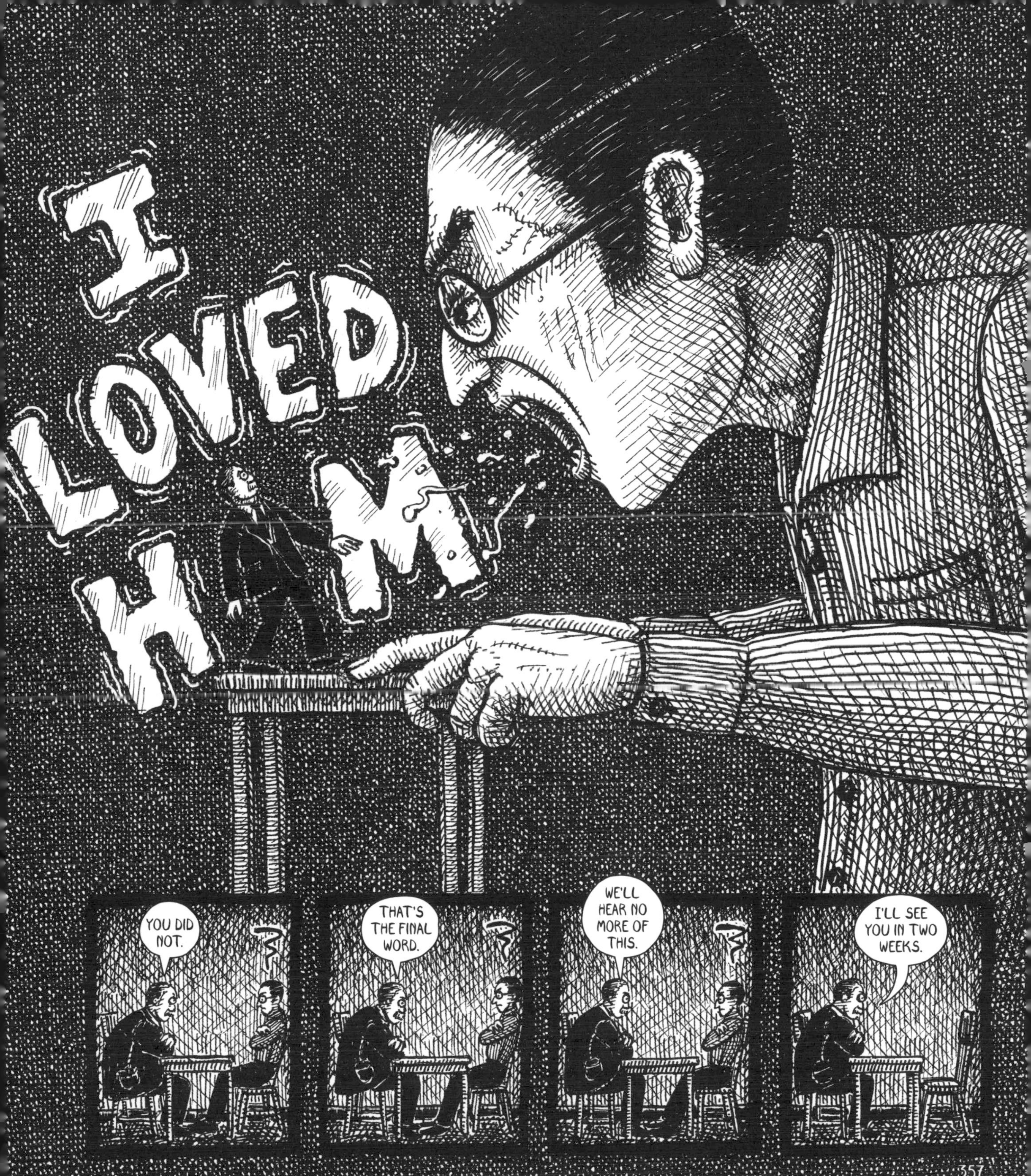
I LOVED HIM!
YOU DID NOT.
THAT'S THE FINAL WORD.
WE'LL HEAR NO MORE OF THIS.
I'LL SEE YOU IN TWO WEEKS.

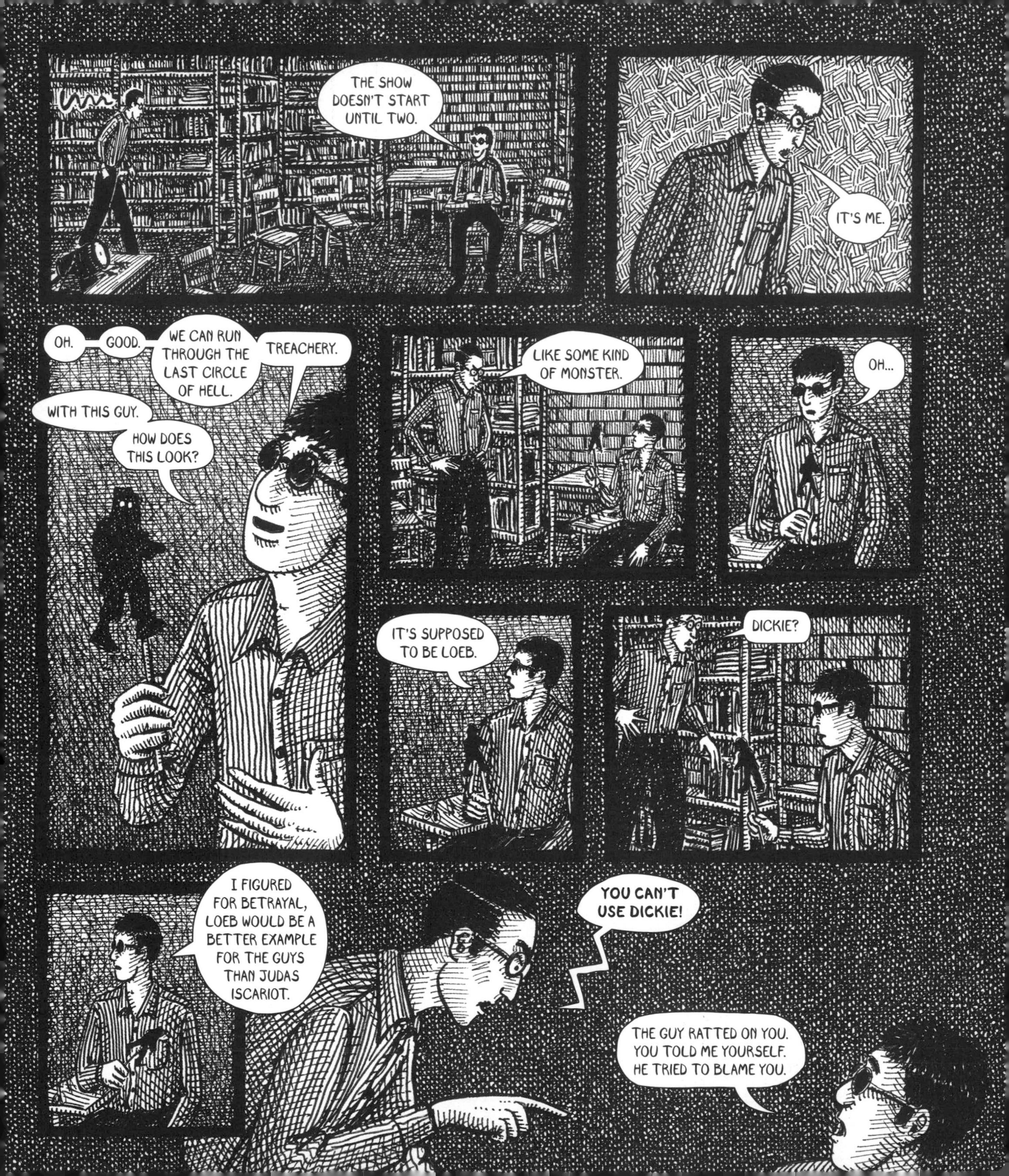
THE SHOW DOESN'T START UNTIL TWO.
IT'S ME.
OH.
GOOD.
WE CAN RUN THROUGH THE LAST CIRCLE OF HELL.
TREACHERY.
WITH THIS GUY.
HOW DOES THIS LOOK?
LIKE SOME KIND OF MONSTER.
OH...
IT'S SUPPOSED TO BE LOEB.
DICKIE?
I FIGURED FOR BETRAYAL, LOEB WOULD BE A BETTER EXAMPLE FOR THE GUYS THAN JUDAS ISCARIOT.
YOU CAN'T USE DICKIE!
THE GUY RATTED ON YOU. YOU TOLD ME YOURSELF. HE TRIED TO BLAME YOU.

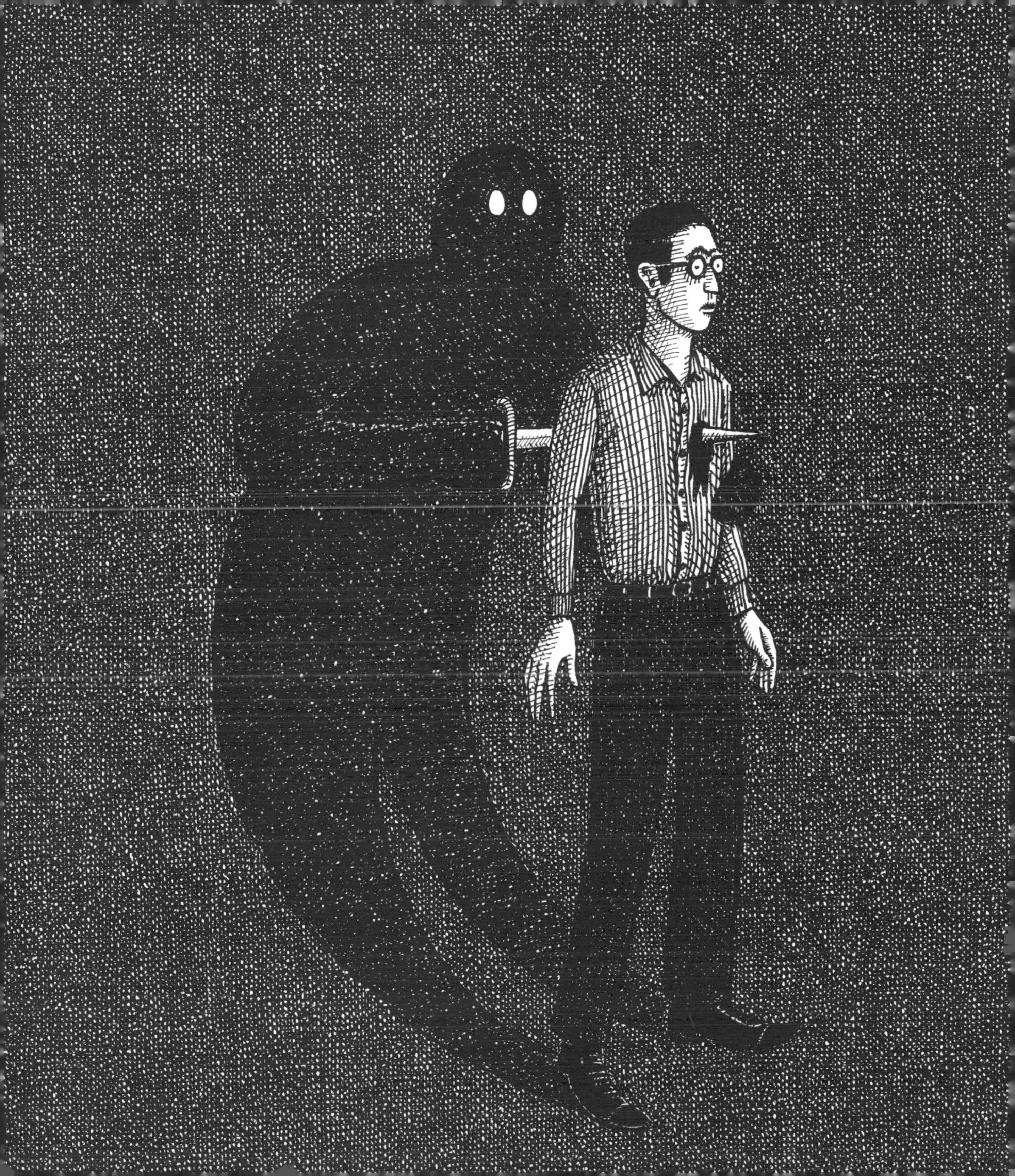

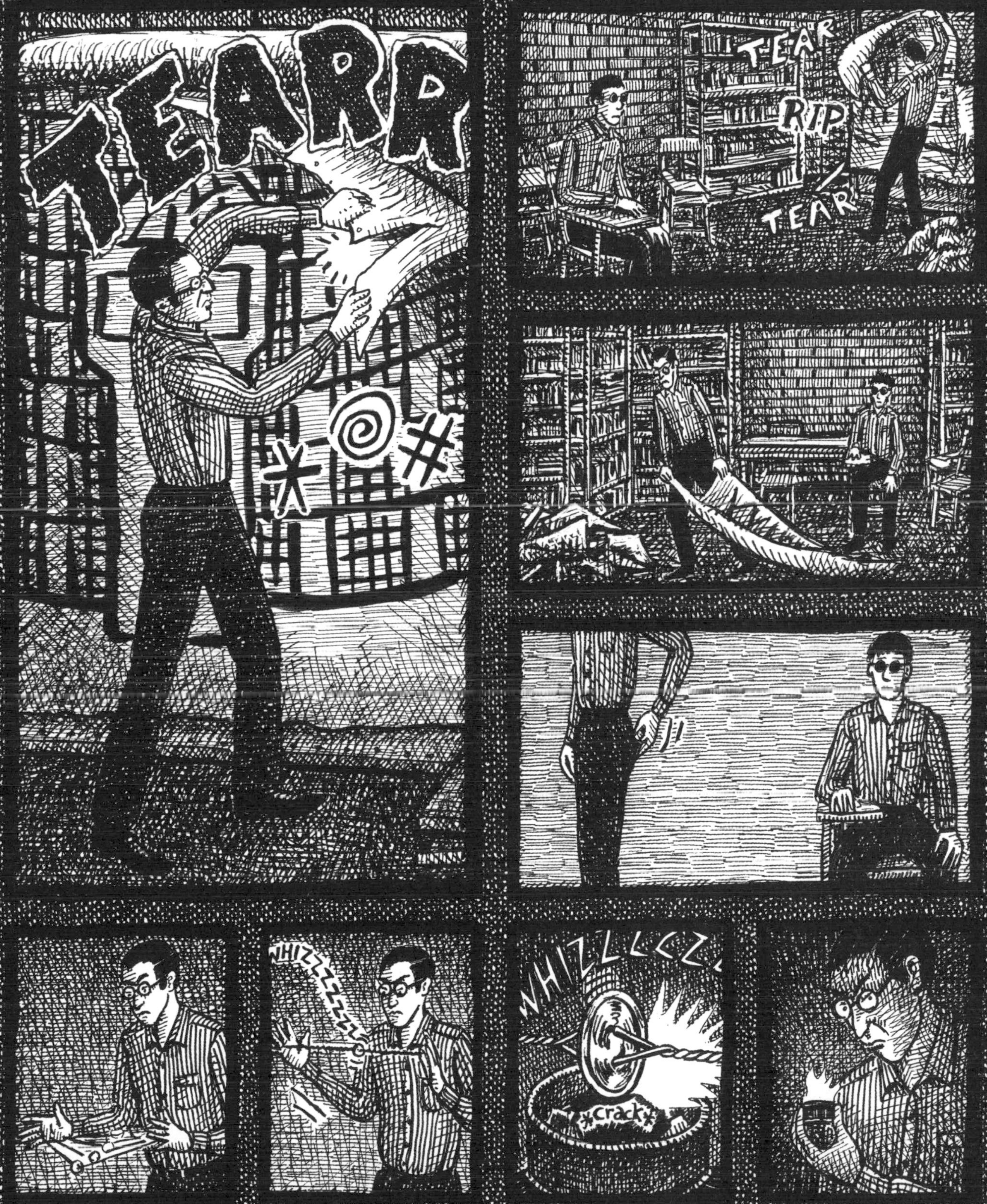
TEARR
TEAR
RIP
TEAR
WHIZZZZZZZ
WHIZZZZZZ
crack

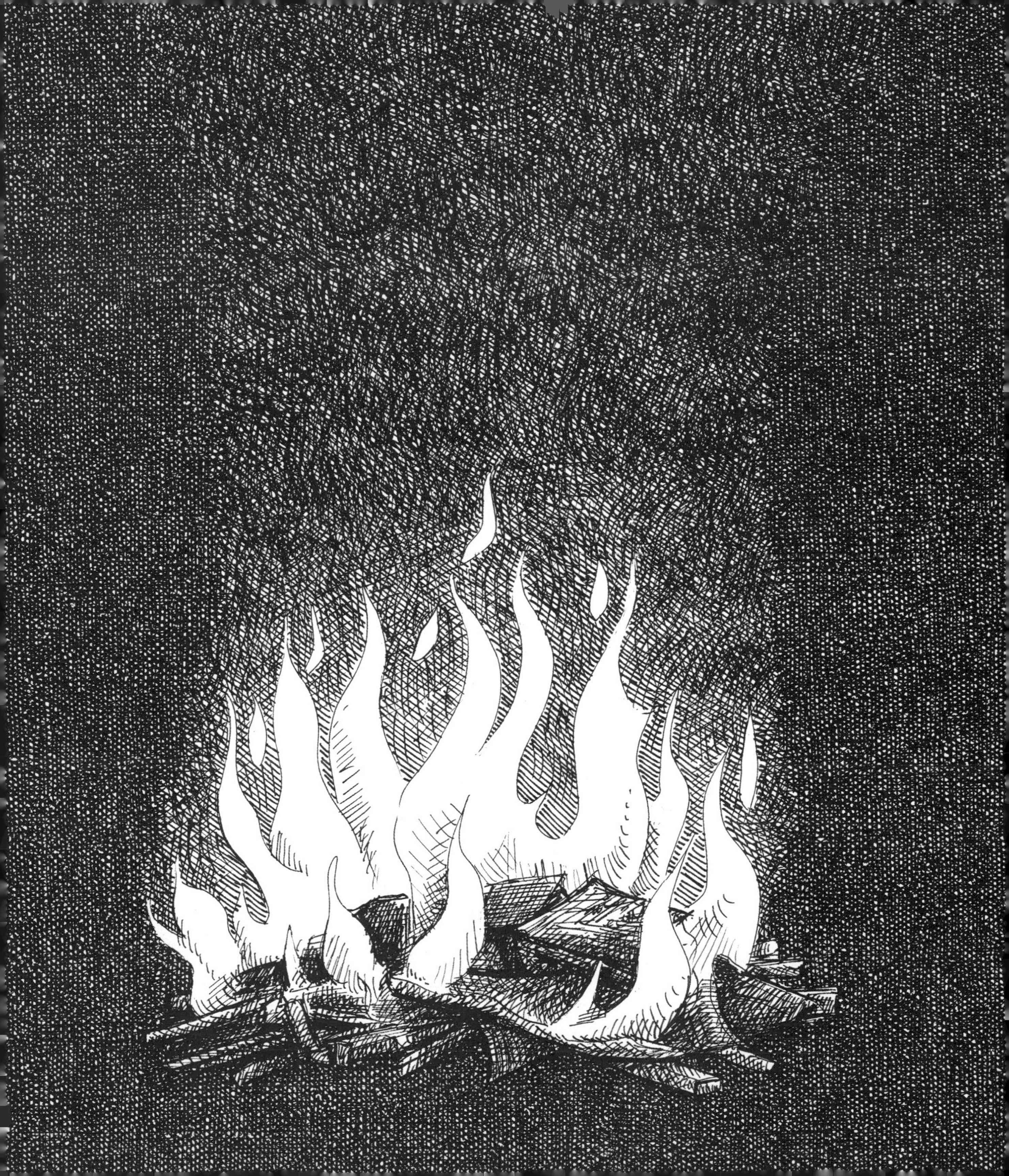

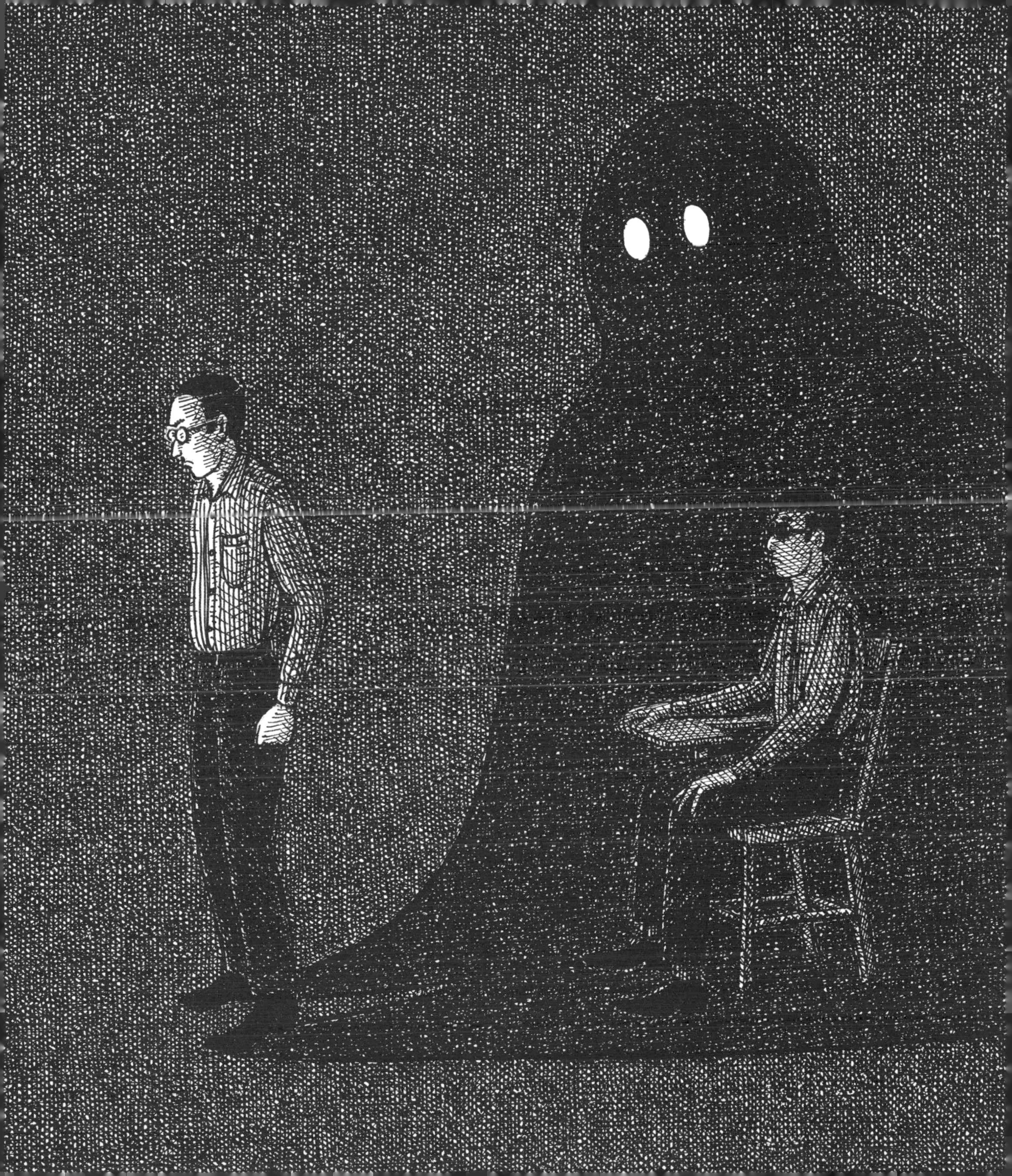

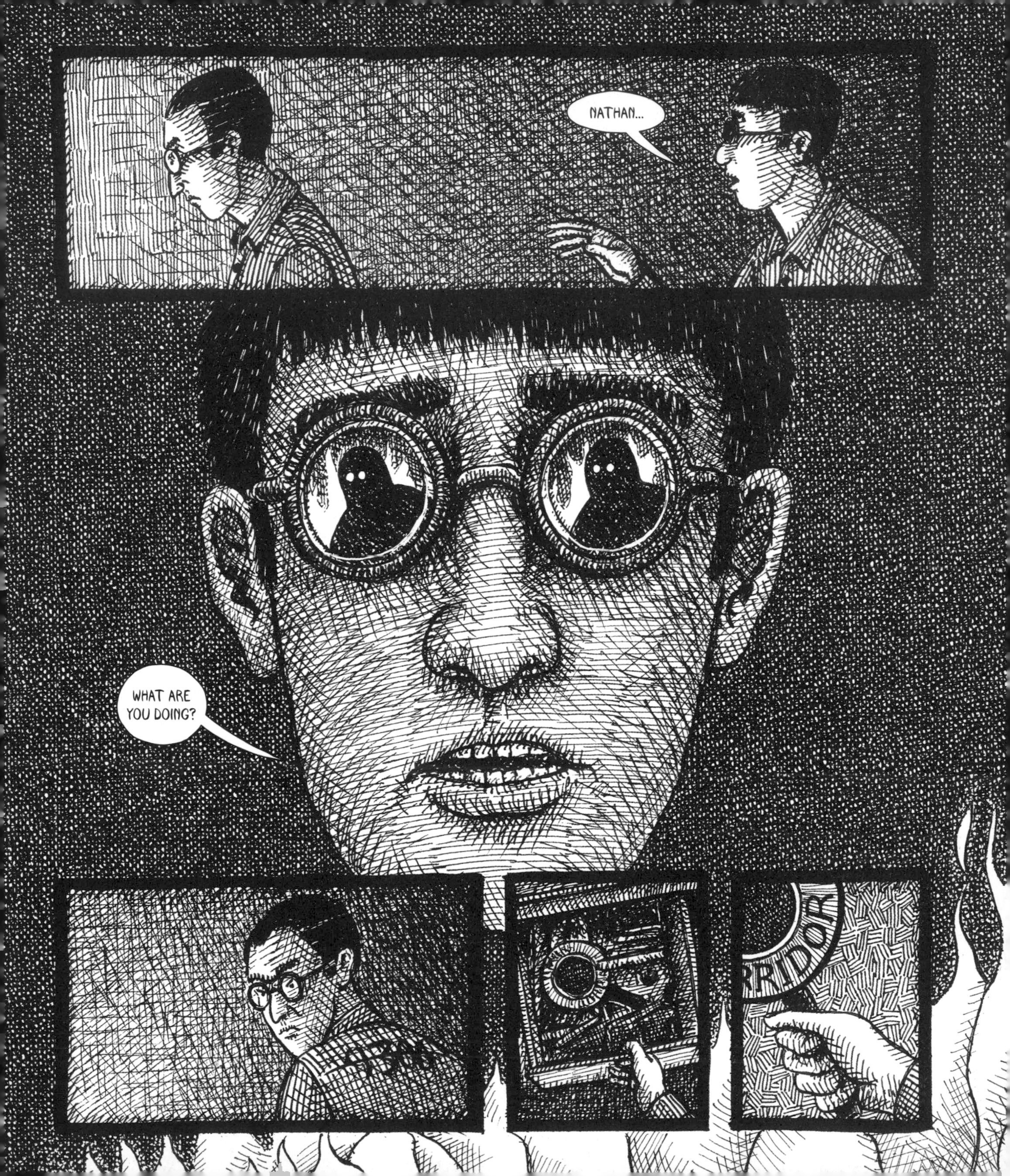
NATHAN...
WHAT ARE YOU DOING?
RRIDOR

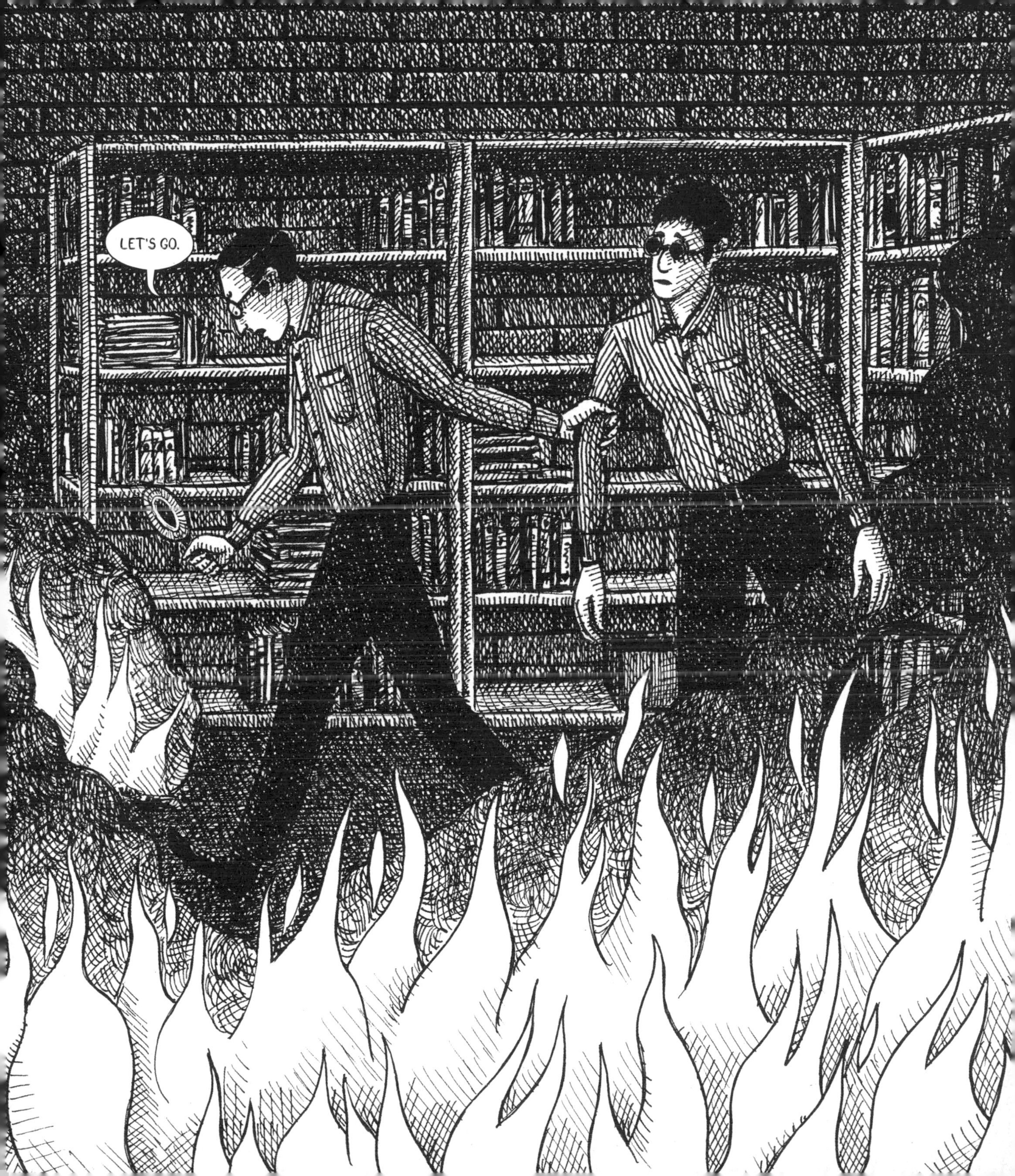
LET'S GO.

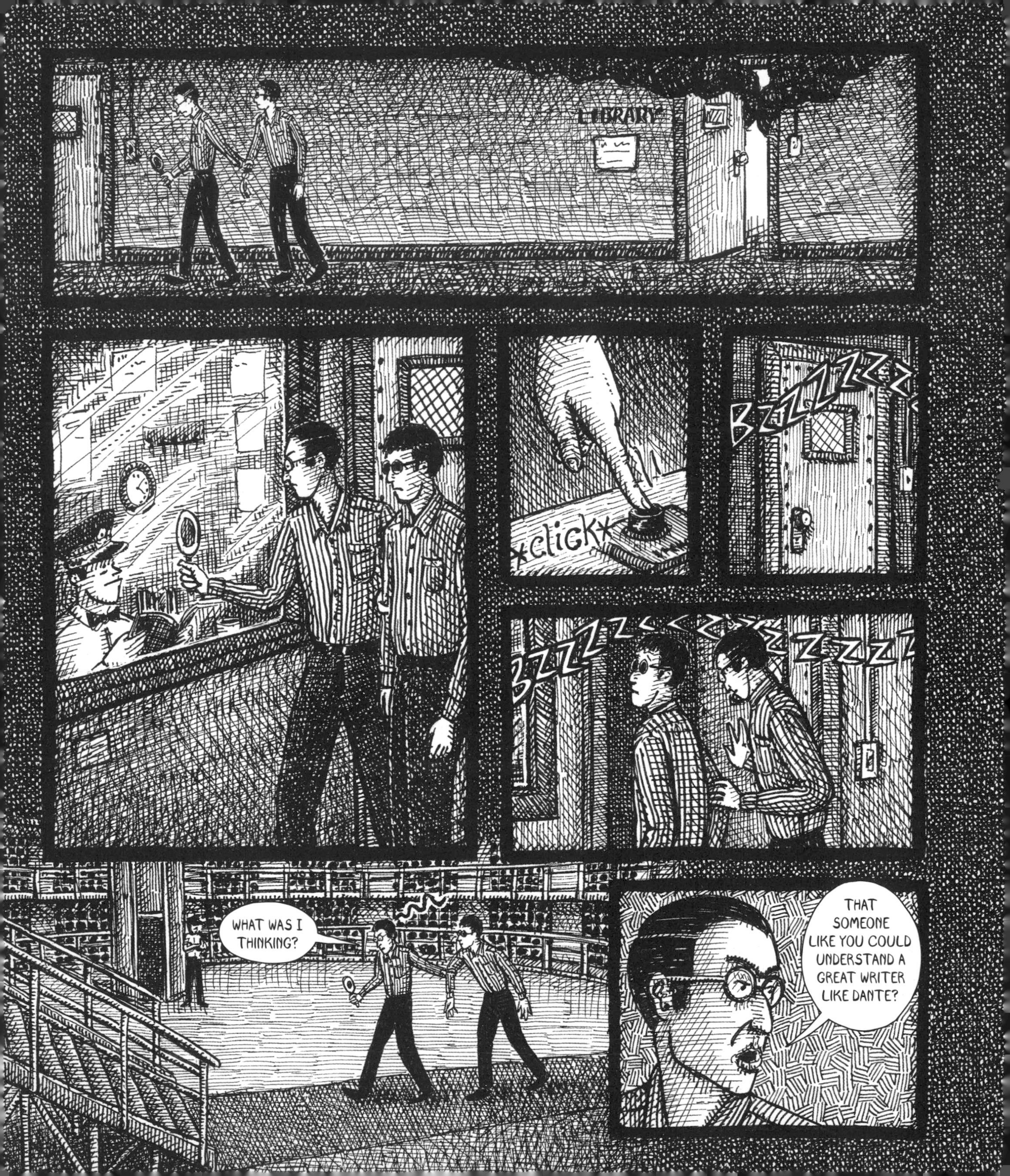
LIBRARY
CLICK
BZZZZZZZZ
BZZZZZZZZZZZZZZZ
WHAT WAS I THINKING?
THAT SOMEONE LIKE YOU COULD UNDERSTAND A GREAT WRITER LIKE DANTE?

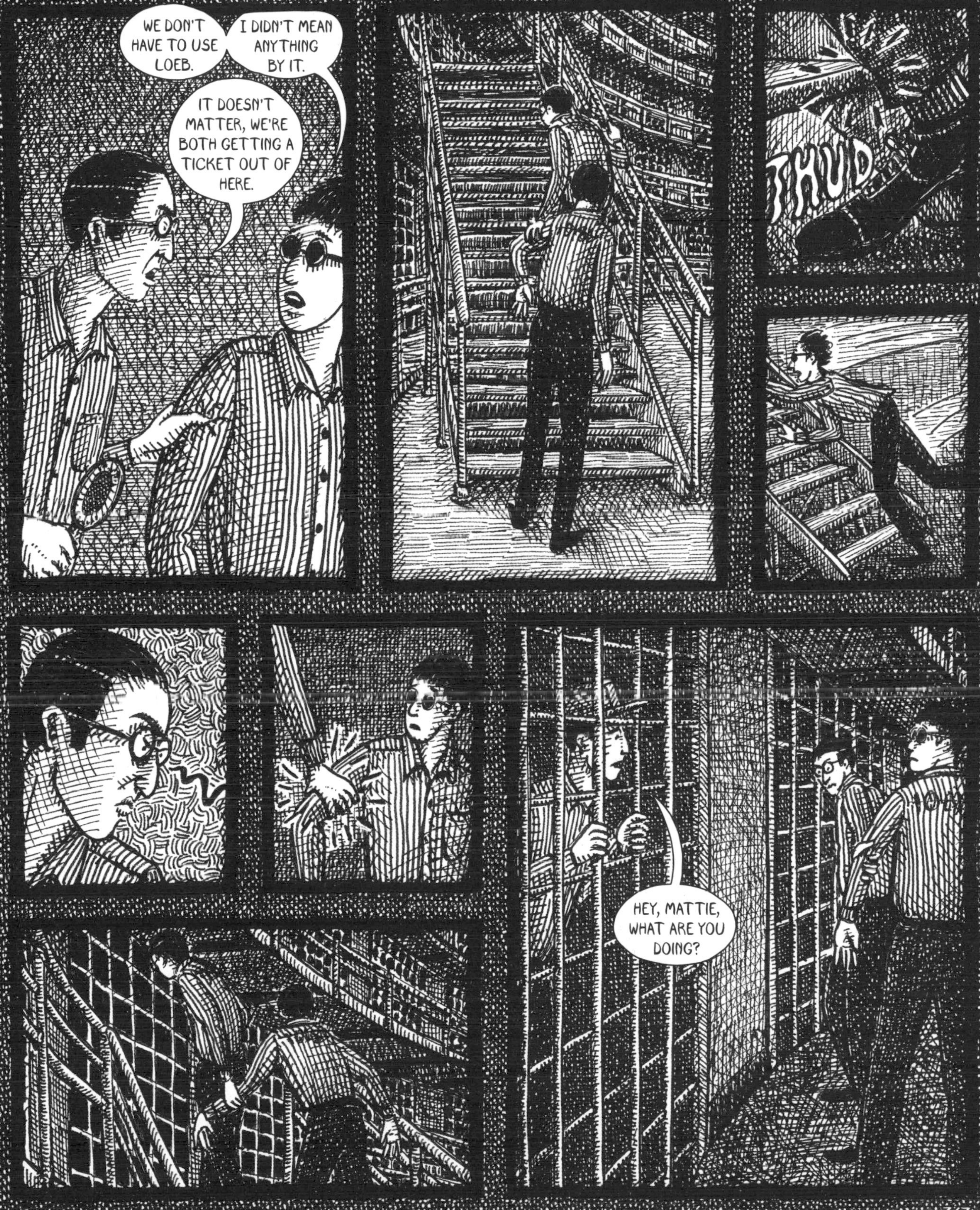
WE DON'T HAVE TO USE LOEB.
I DIDN'T MEAN ANYTHING BY IT.
IT DOESN'T MATTER, WE'RE BOTH GETTING A TICKET OUT OF HERE.
THUD
HEY, MATTIE, WHAT ARE YOU DOING?

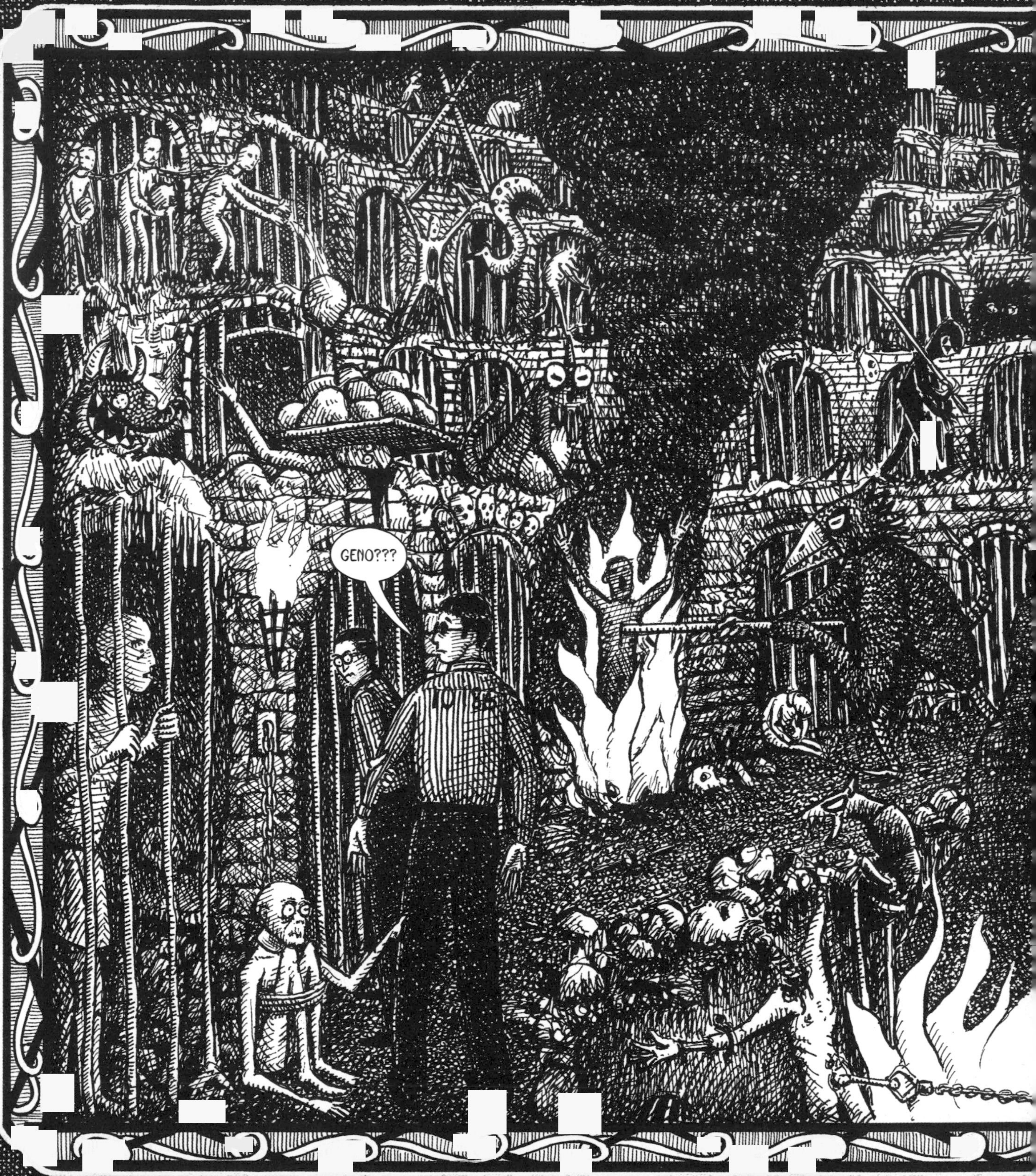
GENO???

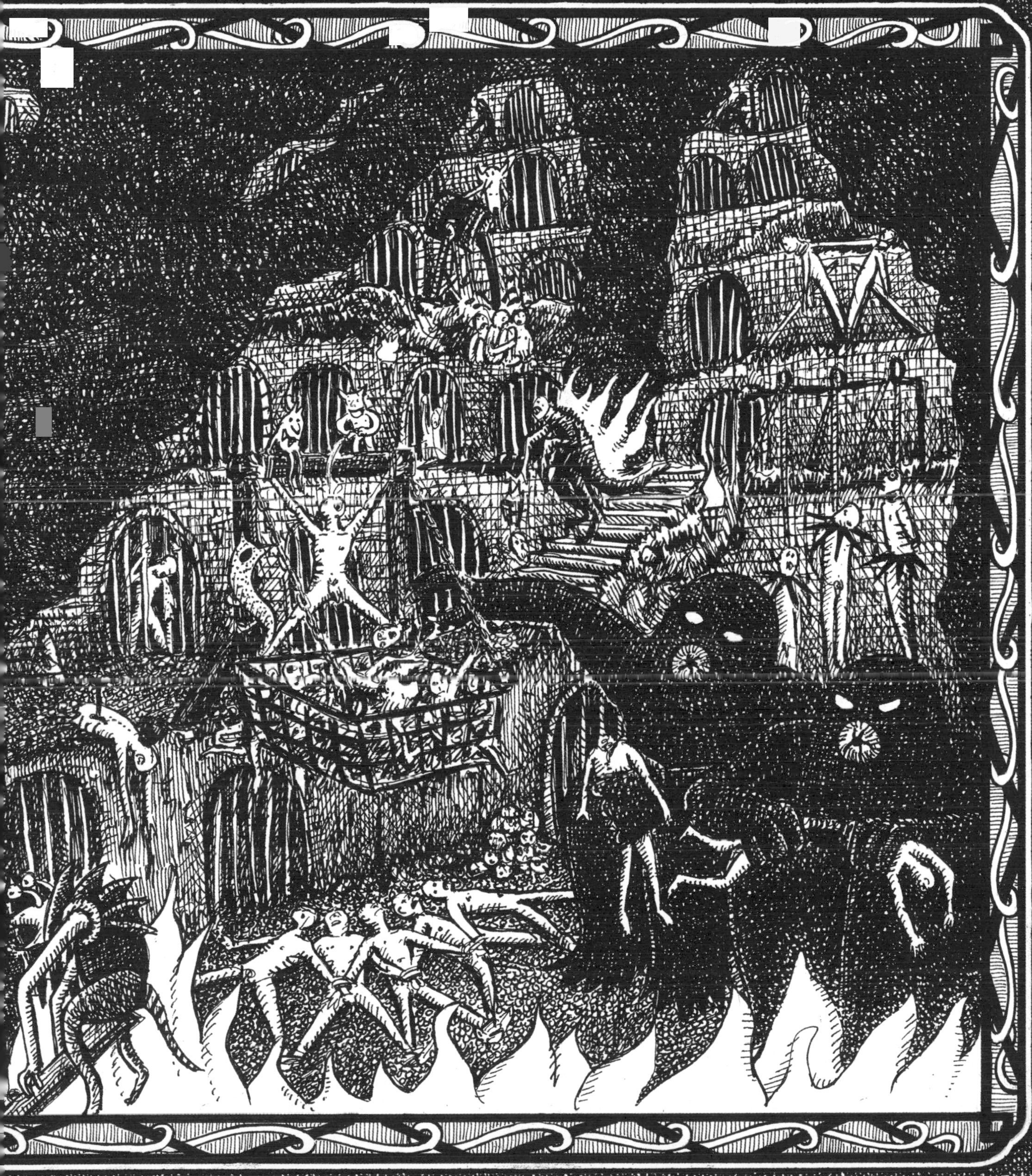

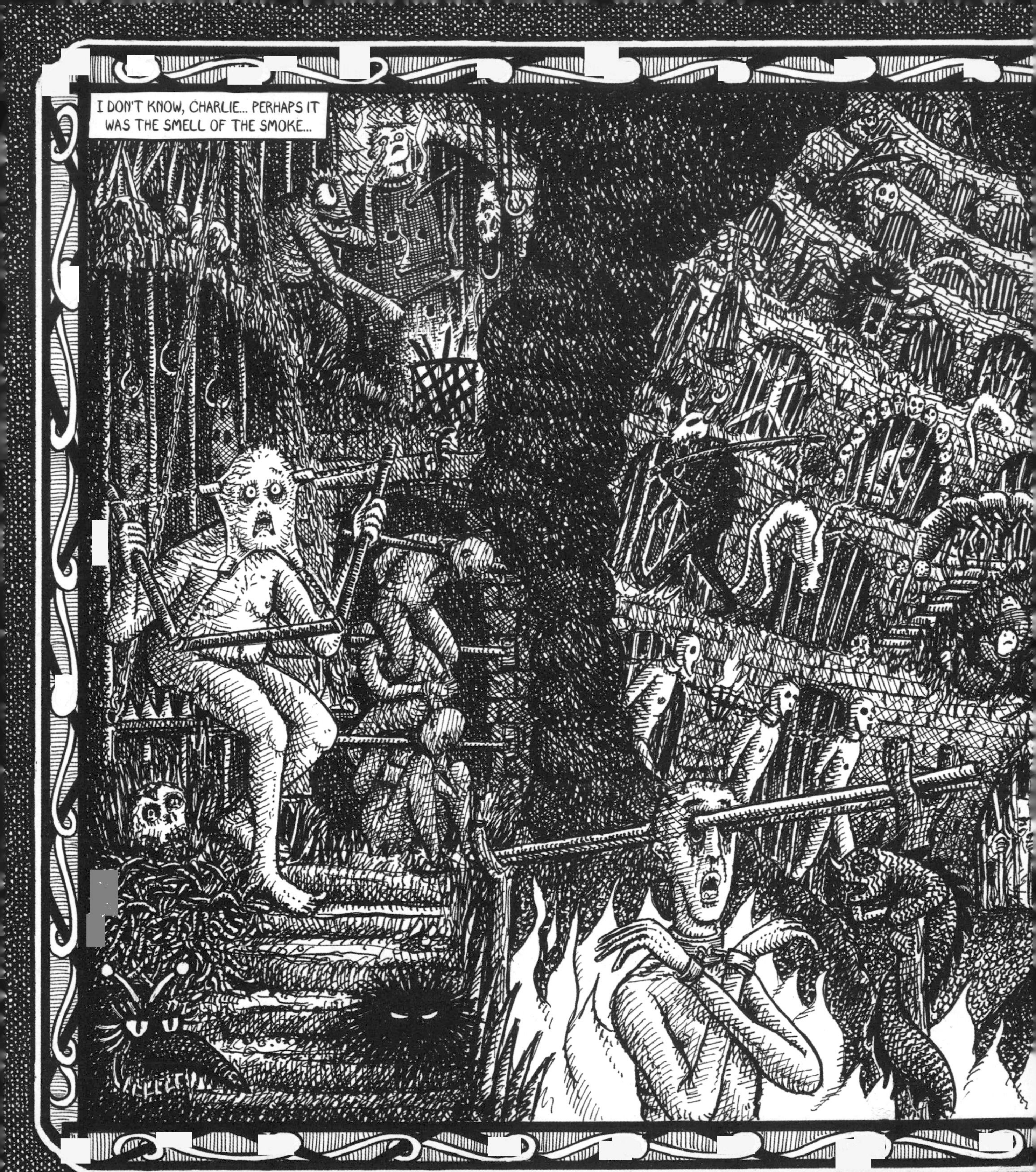
I DON'T KNOW, CHARLIE... PERHAPS IT WAS THE SMELL OF THE SMOKE...

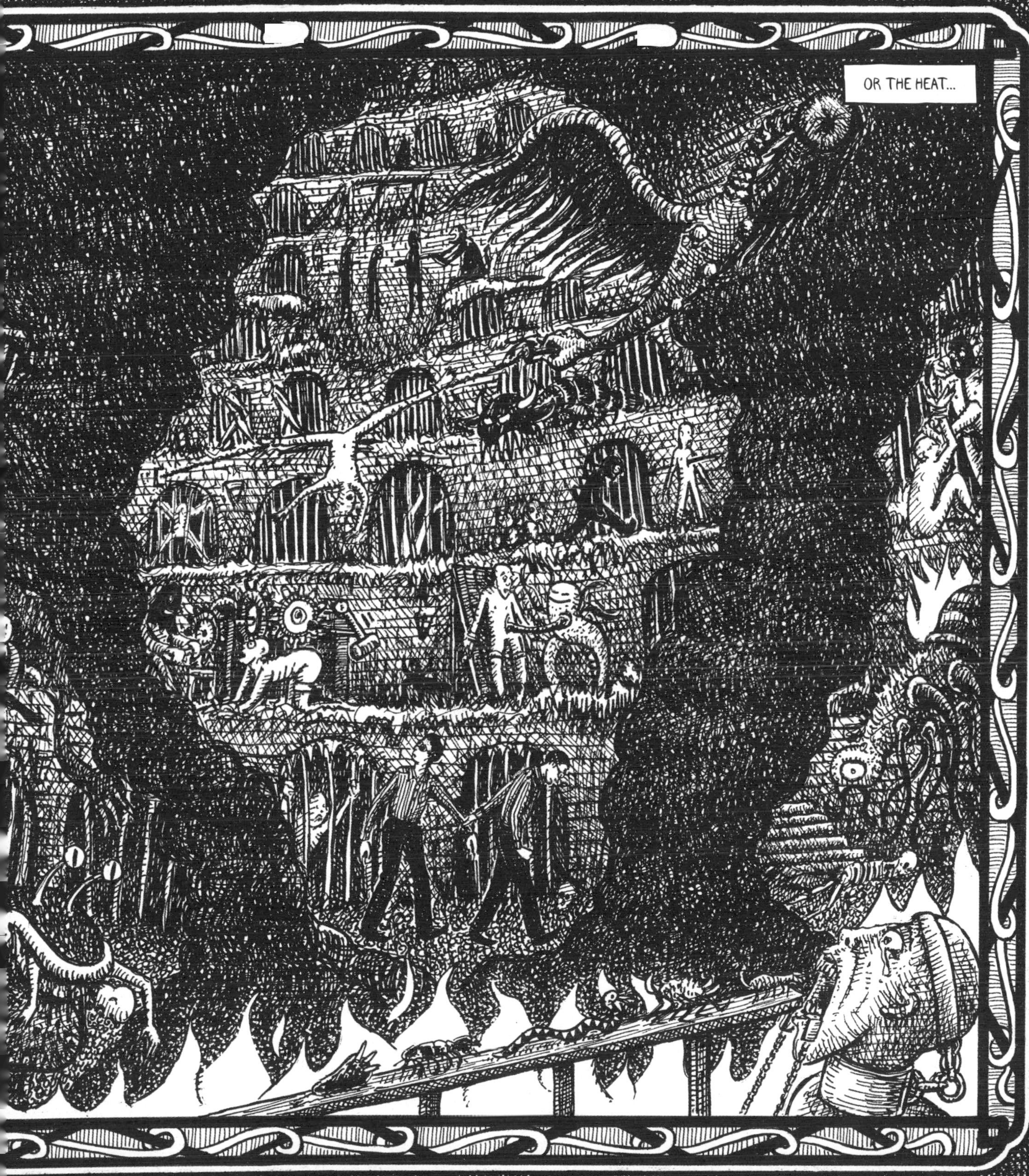
OR THE HEAT...

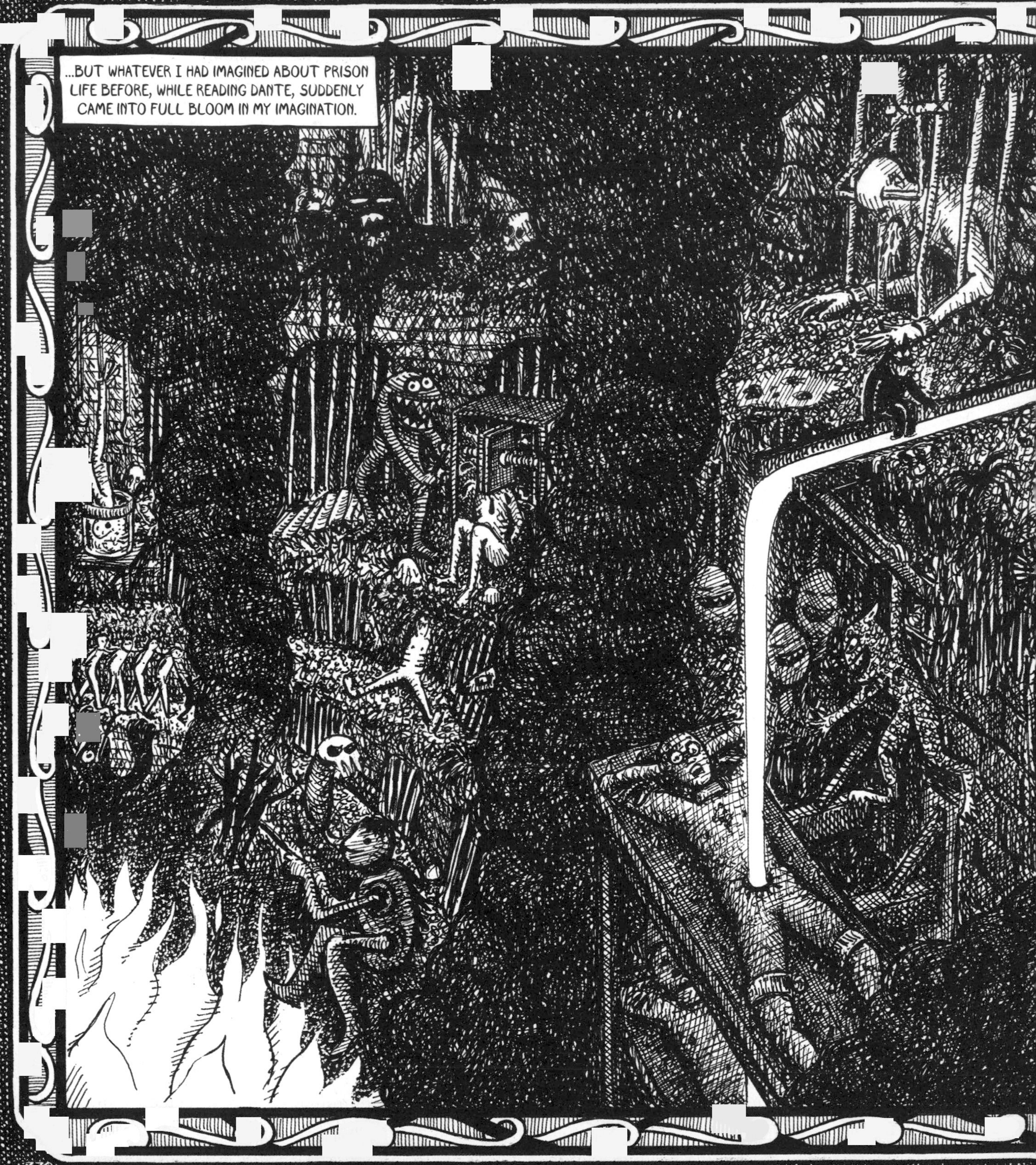
...BUT WHATEVER I HAD IMAGINED ABOUT PRISON LIFE BEFORE, WHILE READING DANTE, SUDDENLY CAME INTO FULL BLOOM IN MY IMAGINATION.

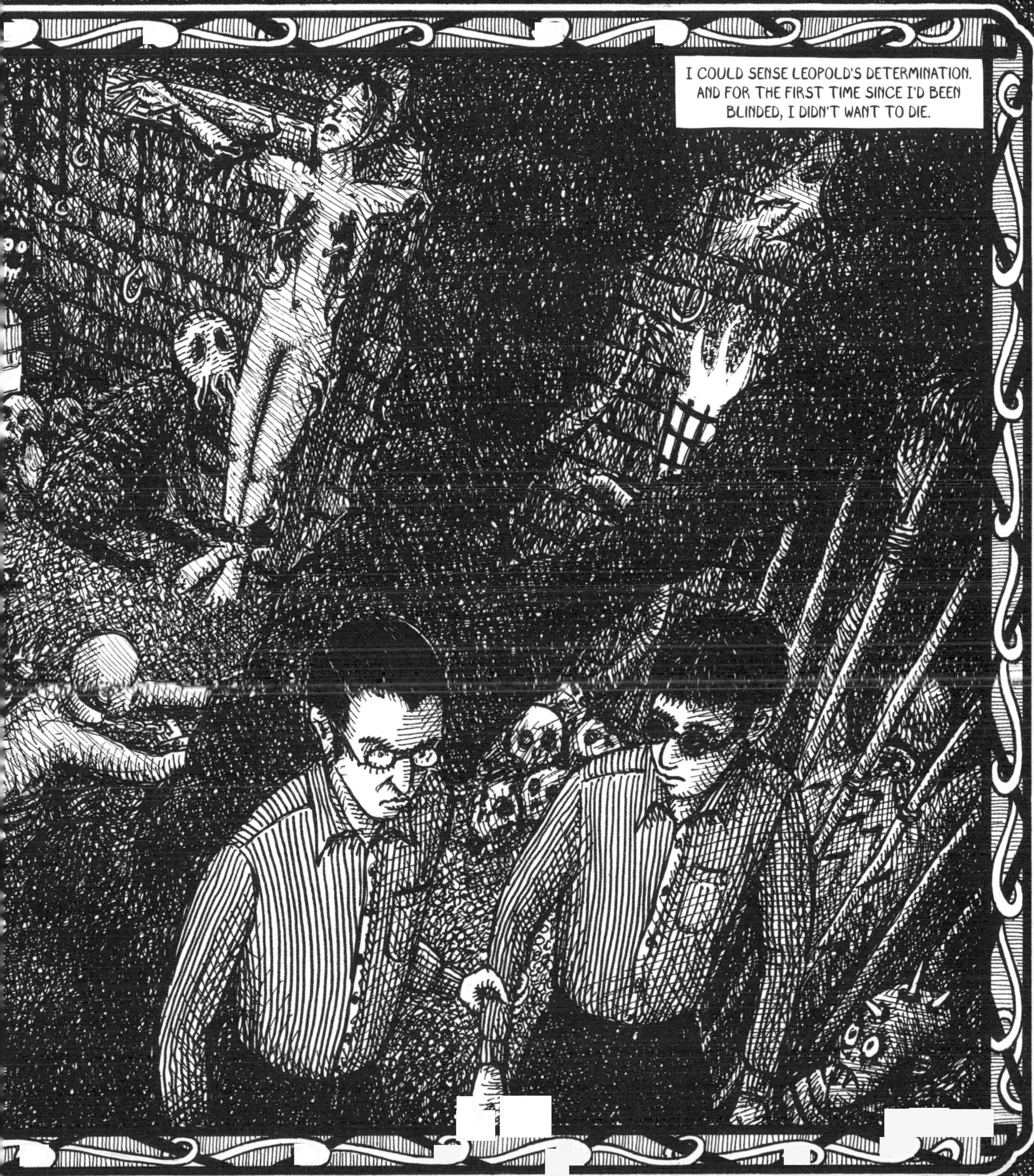
I COULD SENSE LEOPOLD'S DETERMINATION. AND FOR THE FIRST TIME SINCE I'D BEEN BLINDED, I DIDN'T WANT TO DIE.

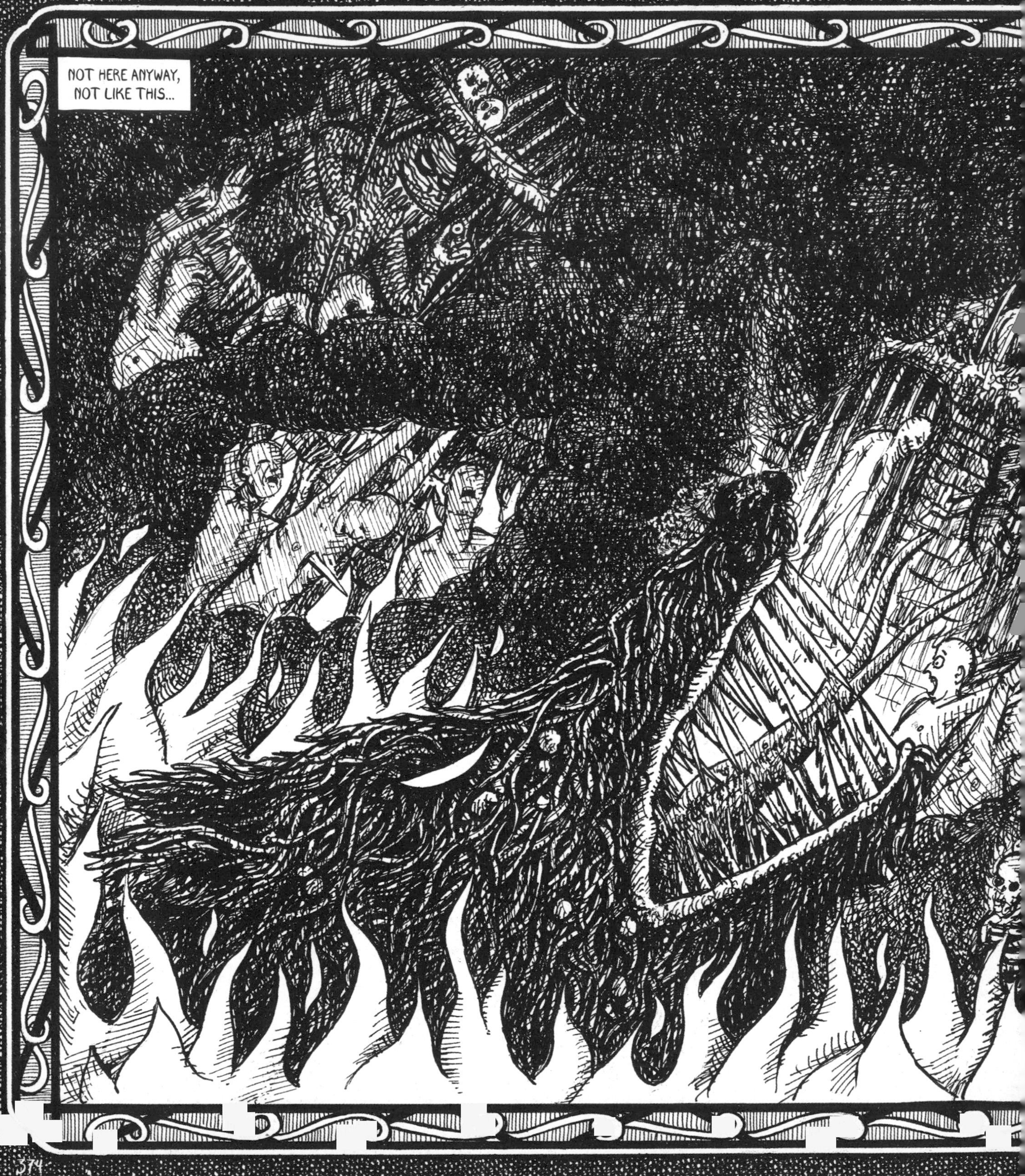
NOT HERE ANYWAY,
NOT LIKE THIS...

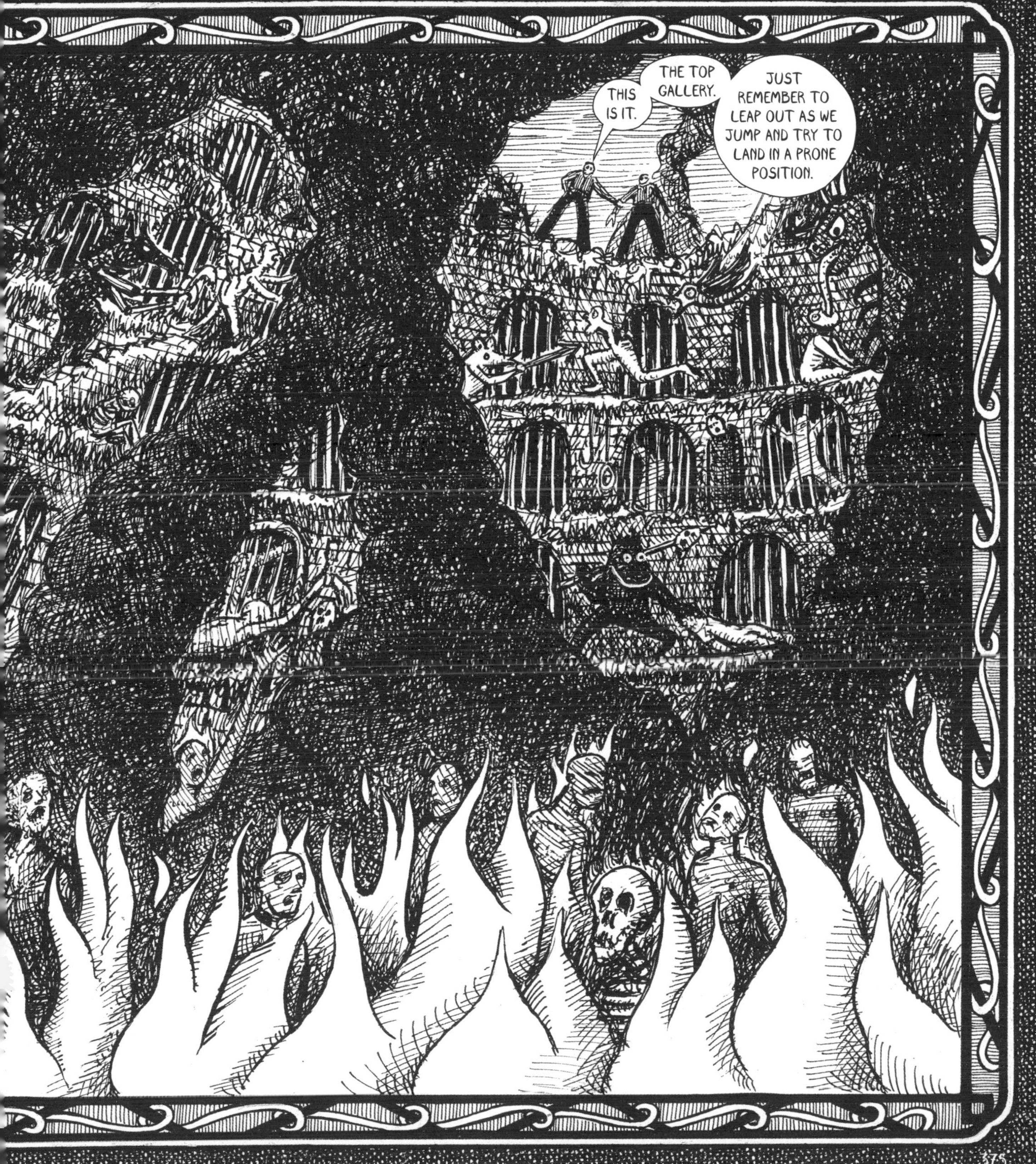
THIS IS IT.
THE TOP GALLERY.
JUST REMEMBER TO LEAP OUT AS WE JUMP AND TRY TO LAND IN A PRONE POSITION.

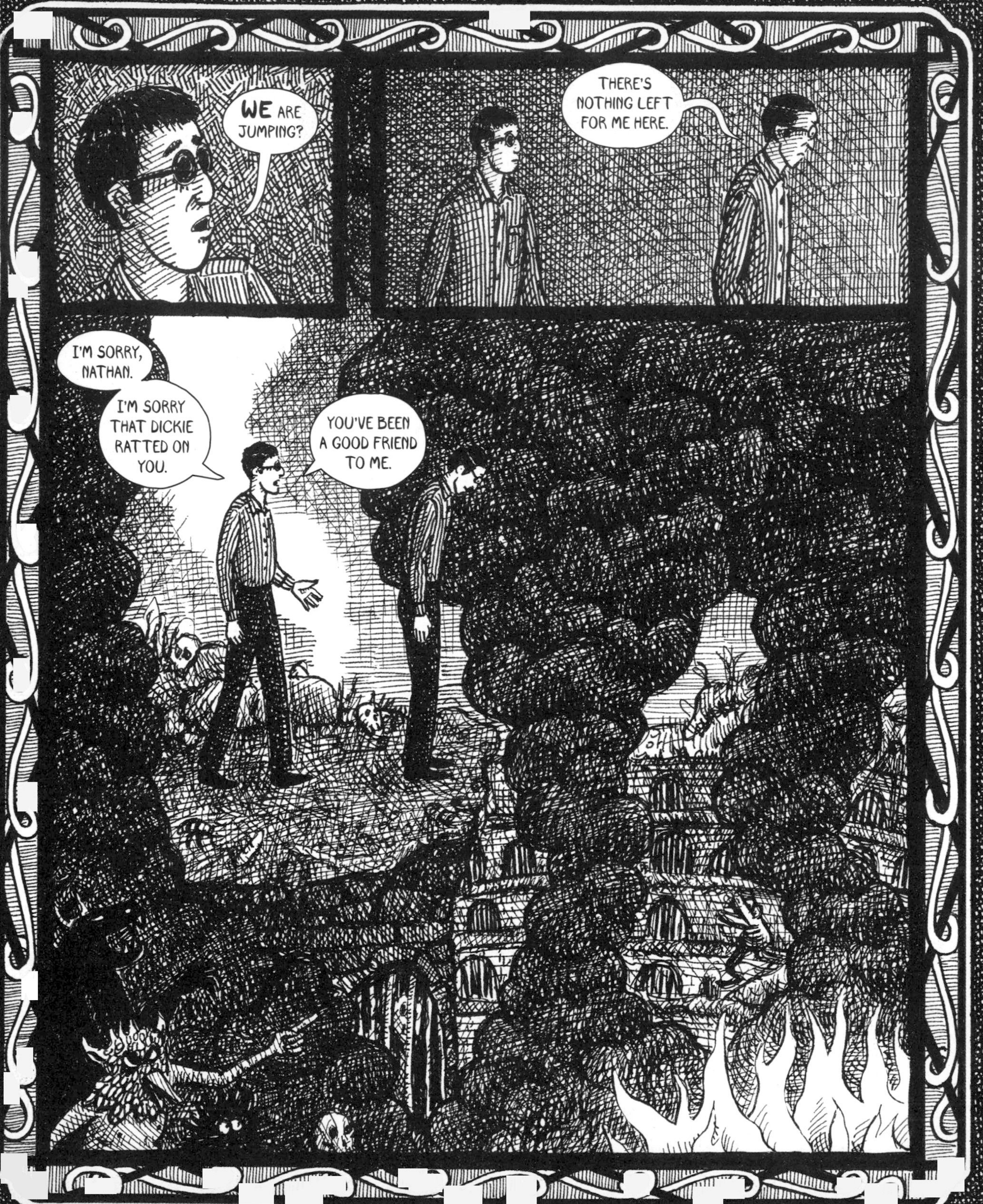
WE ARE JUMPING?
THERE'S NOTHING LEFT FOR ME HERE.
I'M SORRY, NATHAN.
I'M SORRY THAT DICKIE RATTED ON YOU.
YOU'VE BEEN A GOOD FRIEND TO ME.

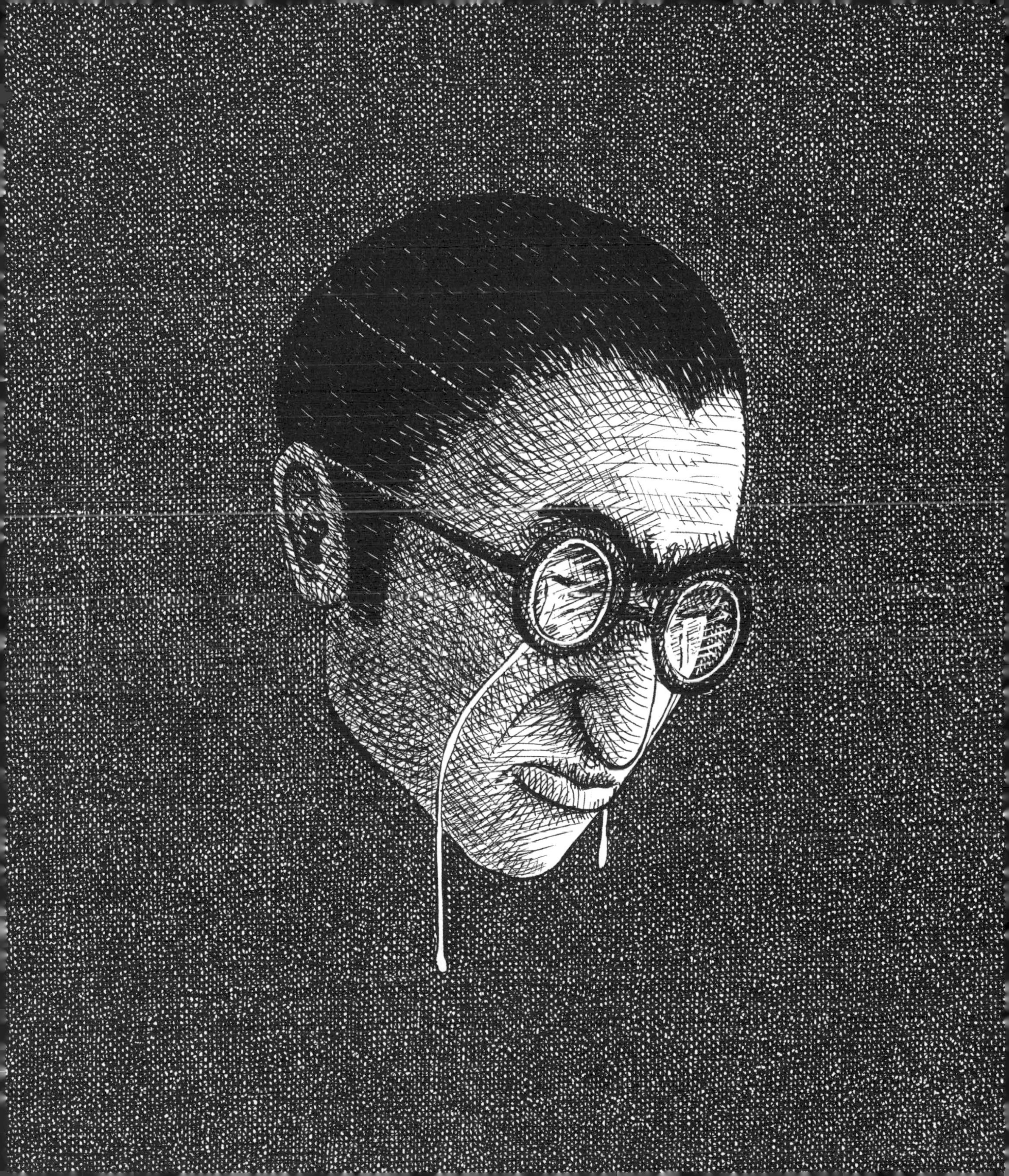

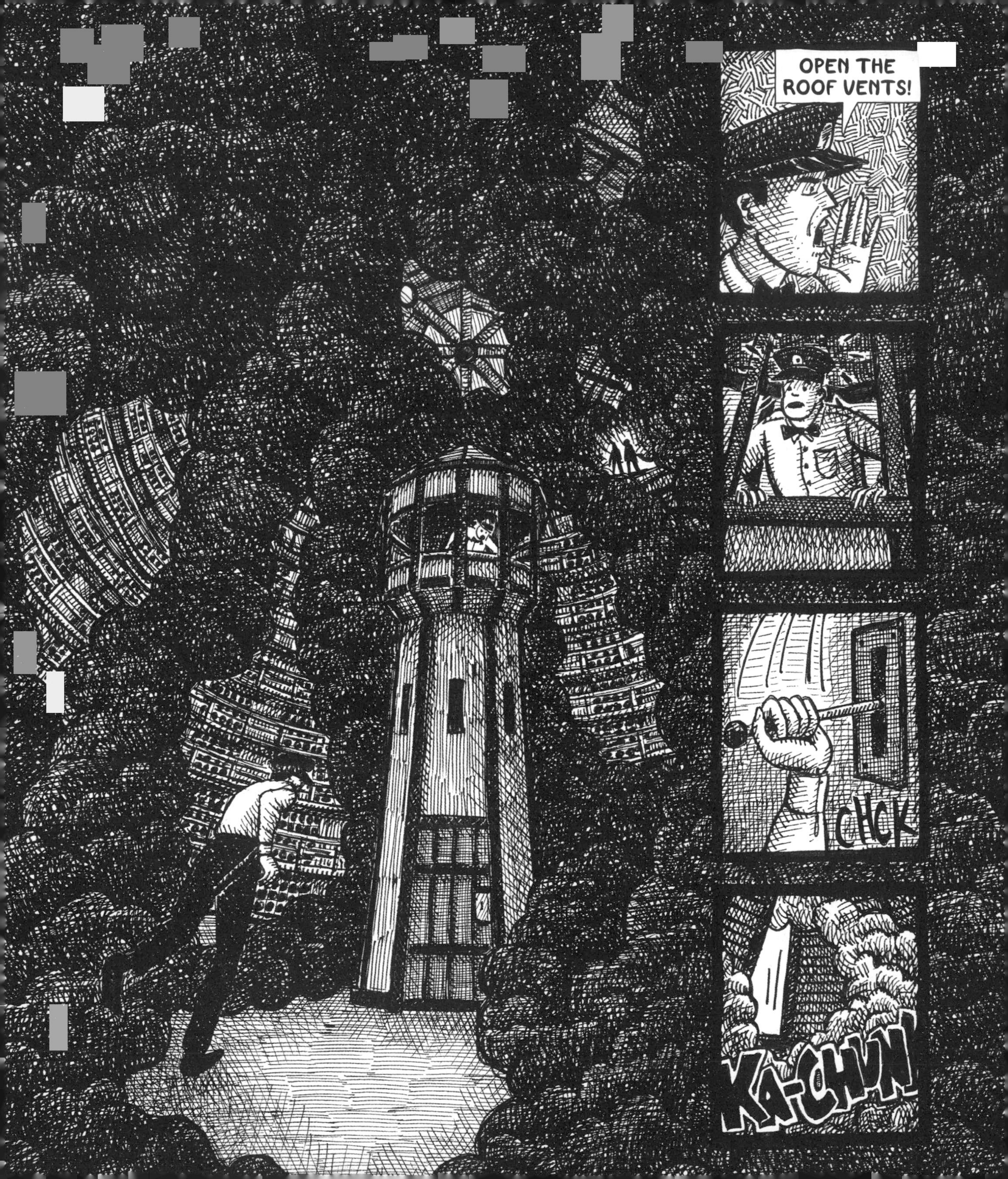
OPEN THE ROOF VENTS!
CHCK
KA-CHUN

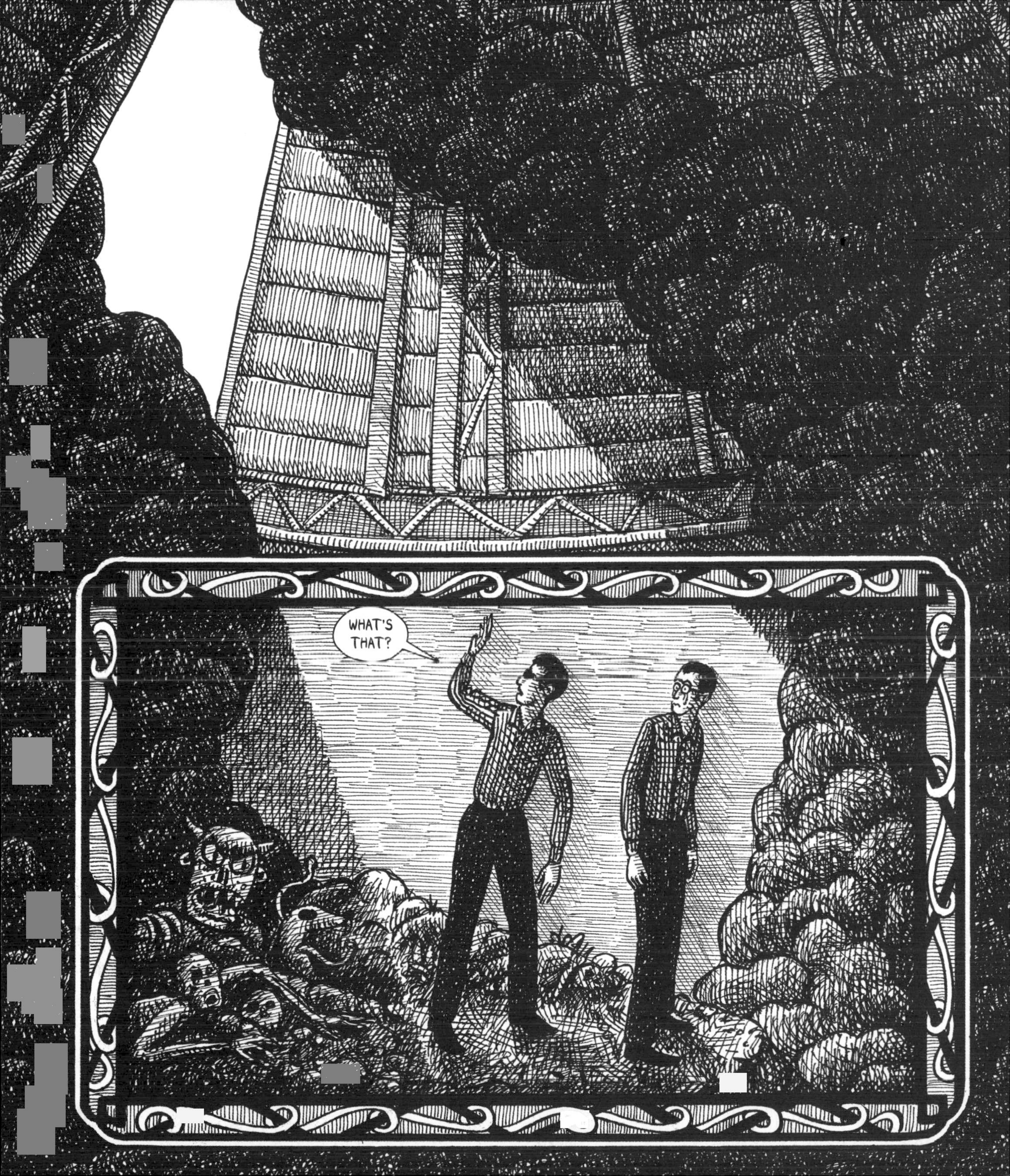
WHAT'S THAT?

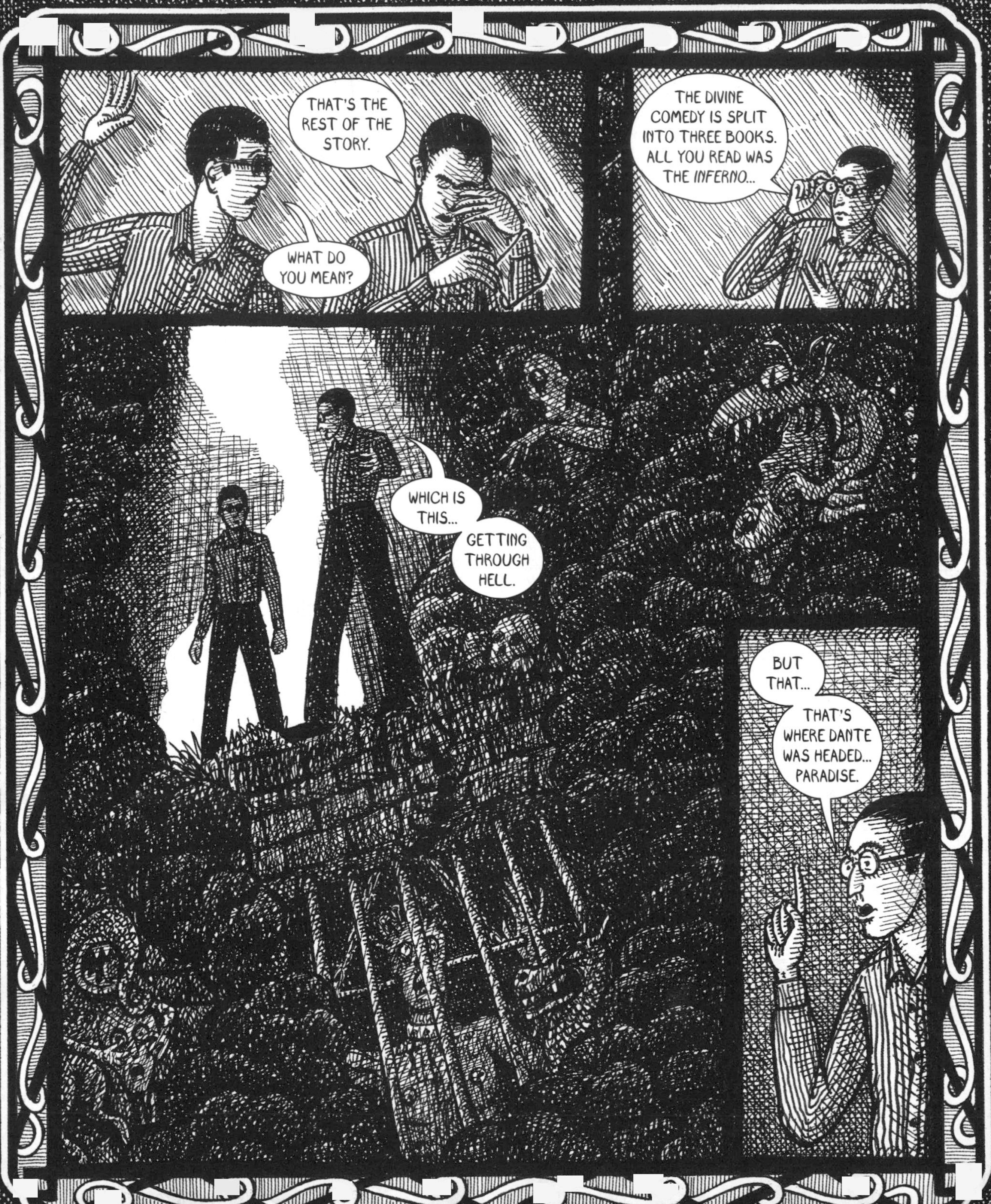
THAT'S THE REST OF THE STORY.
WHAT DO YOU MEAN?
THE DIVINE COMEDY IS SPLIT INTO THREE BOOKS. ALL YOU READ WAS THE *INFERNO*...
WHICH IS THIS...
GETTING THROUGH HELL.
BUT THAT...
THAT'S WHERE DANTE WAS HEADED... PARADISE.

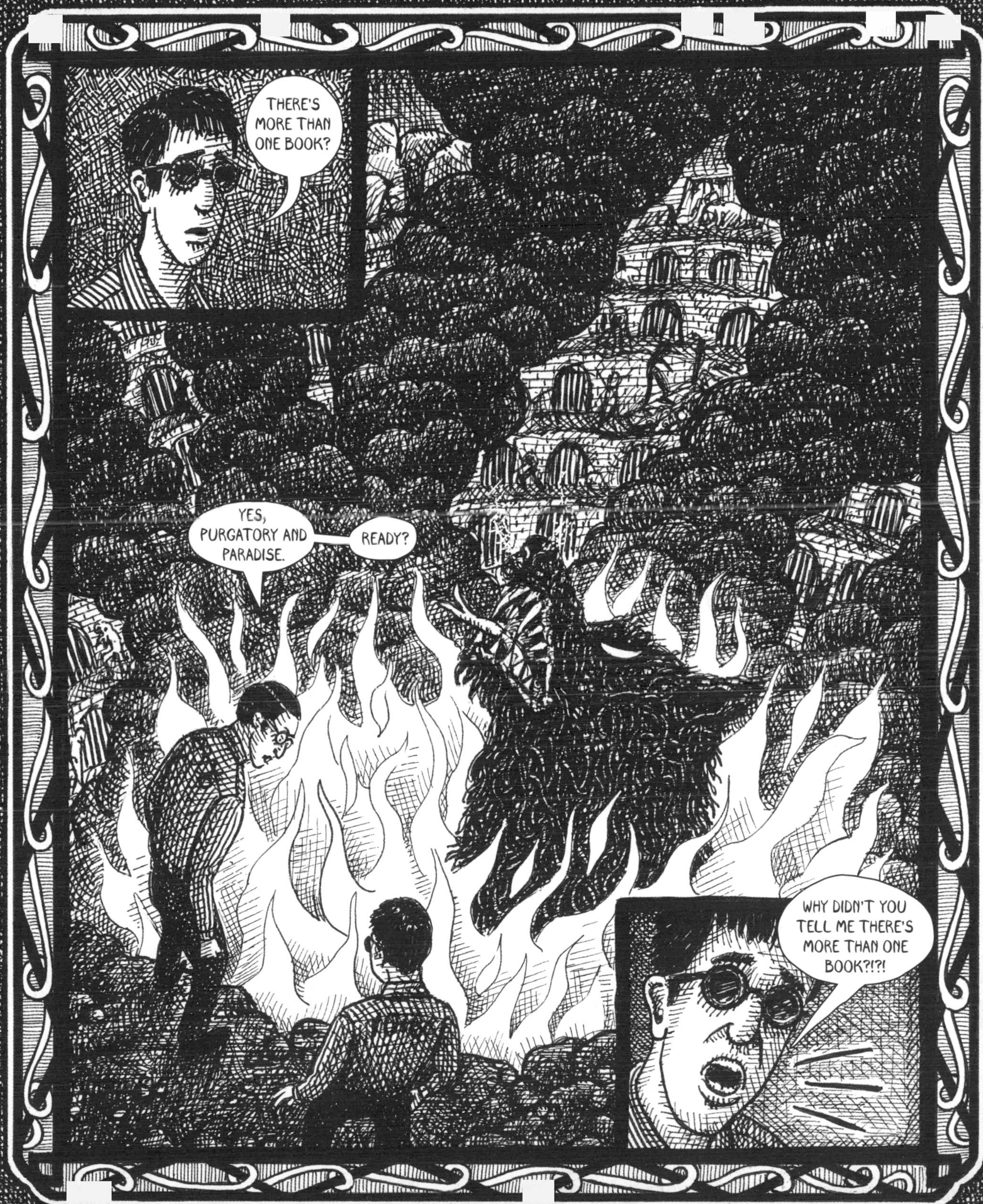
THERE'S MORE THAN ONE BOOK?
YES, PURGATORY AND PARADISE.
READY?
WHY DIDN'T YOU TELL ME THERE'S MORE THAN ONE BOOK?!?!

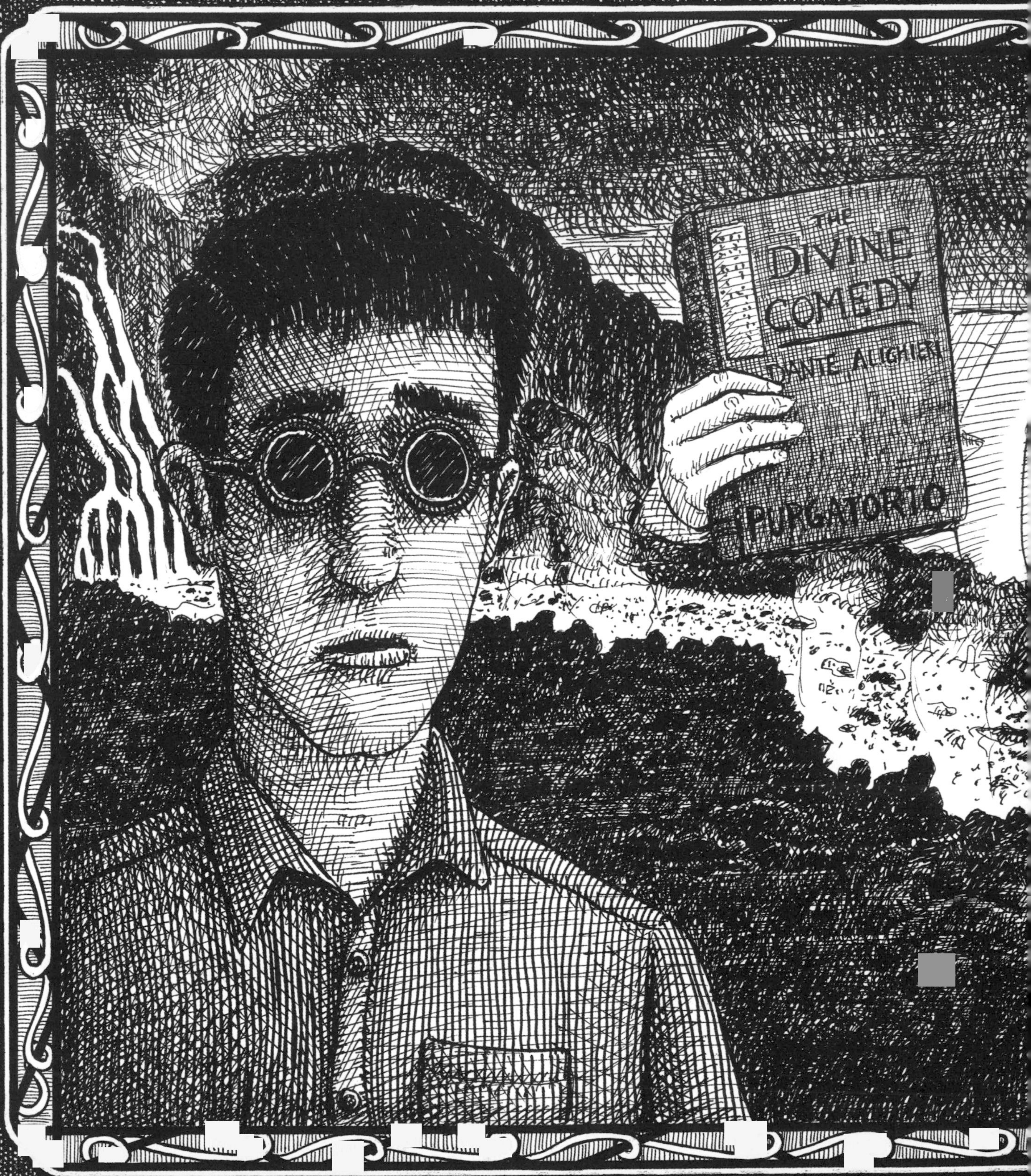
THE DIVINE COMEDY
DANTE ALIGHIERI
PURGATORIO

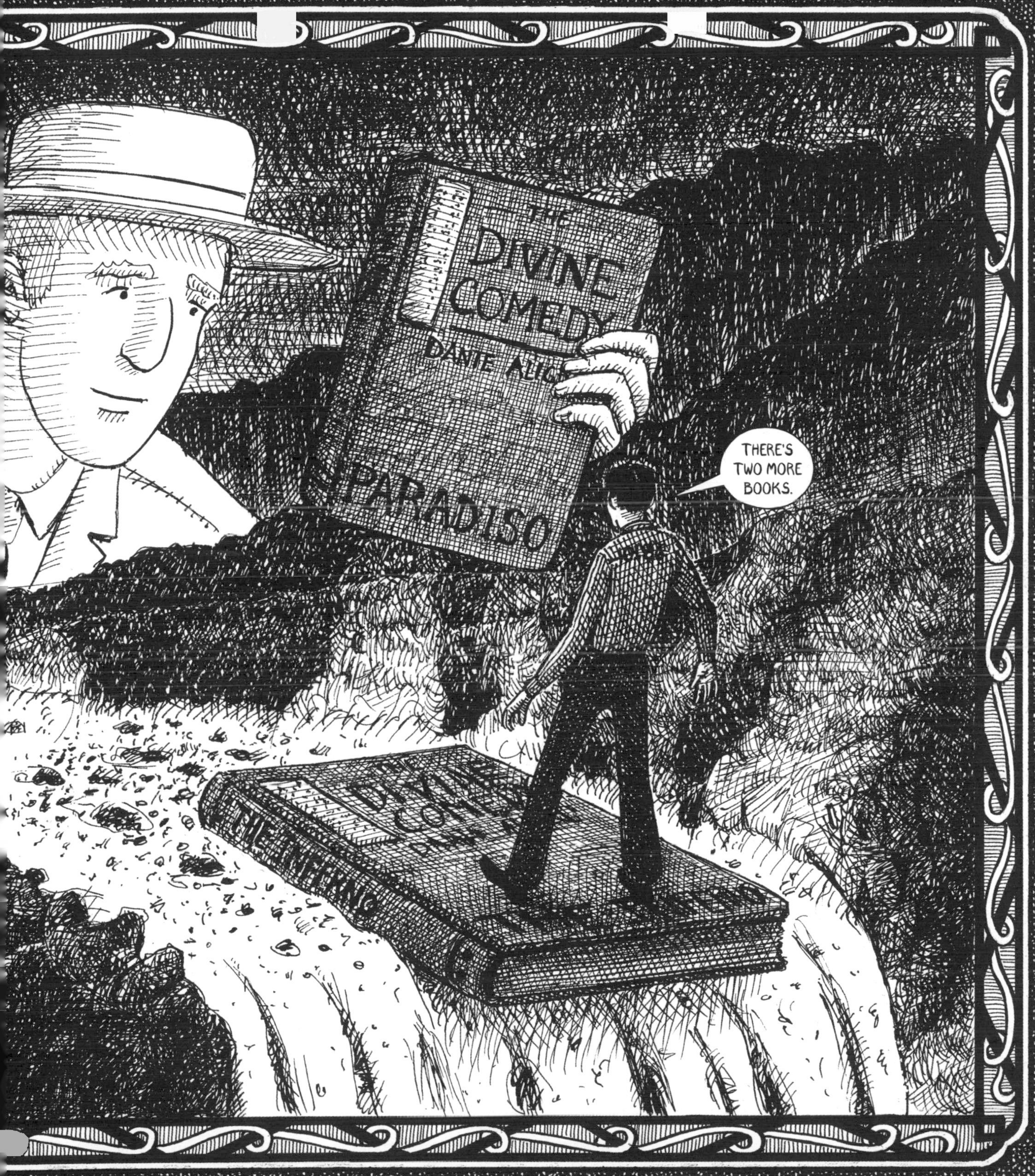
THE DIVINE COMEDY
PARADISO
THERE'S TWO MORE BOOKS.

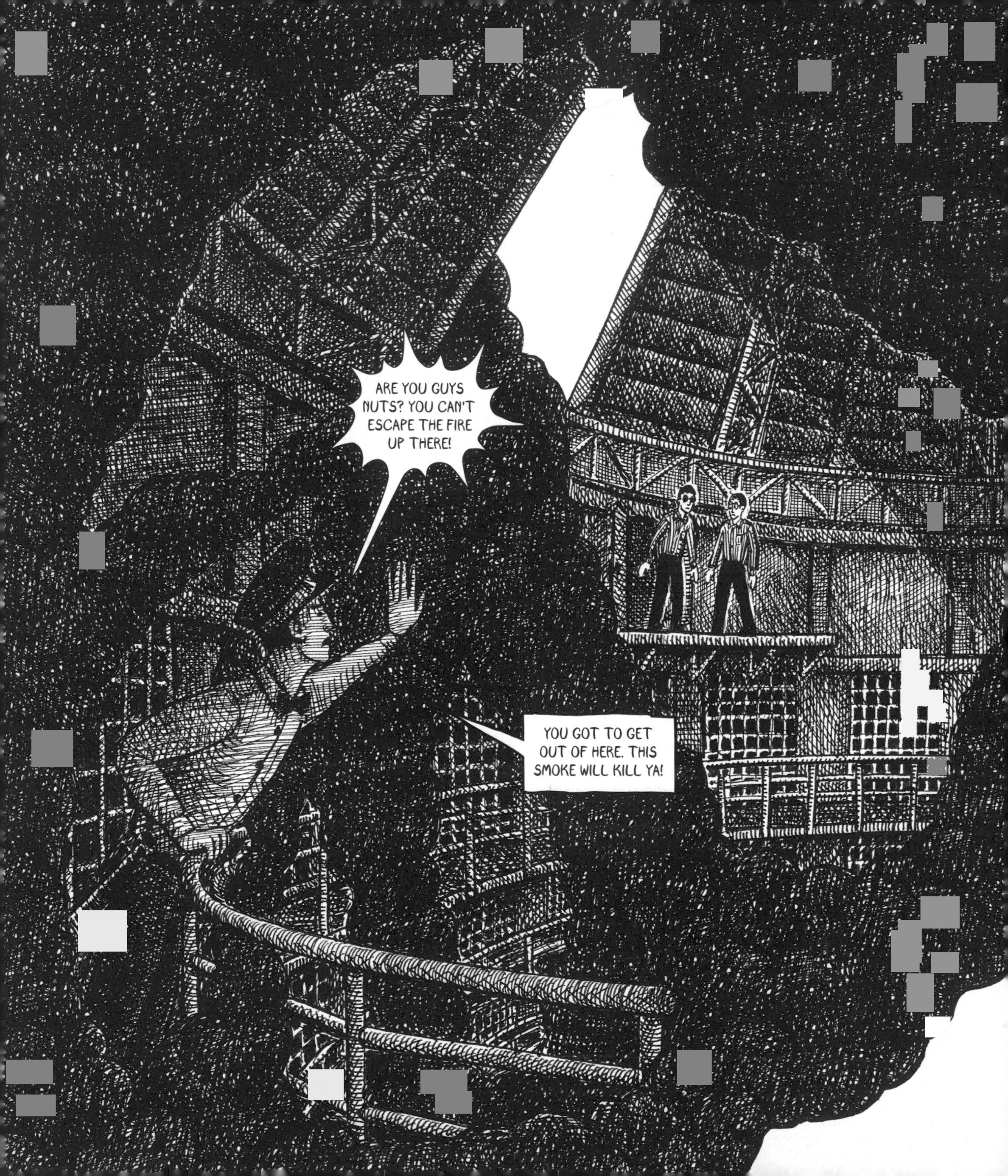
ARE YOU GUYS NUTS? YOU CAN'T ESCAPE THE FIRE UP THERE!
YOU GOT TO GET OUT OF HERE. THIS SMOKE WILL KILL YA!

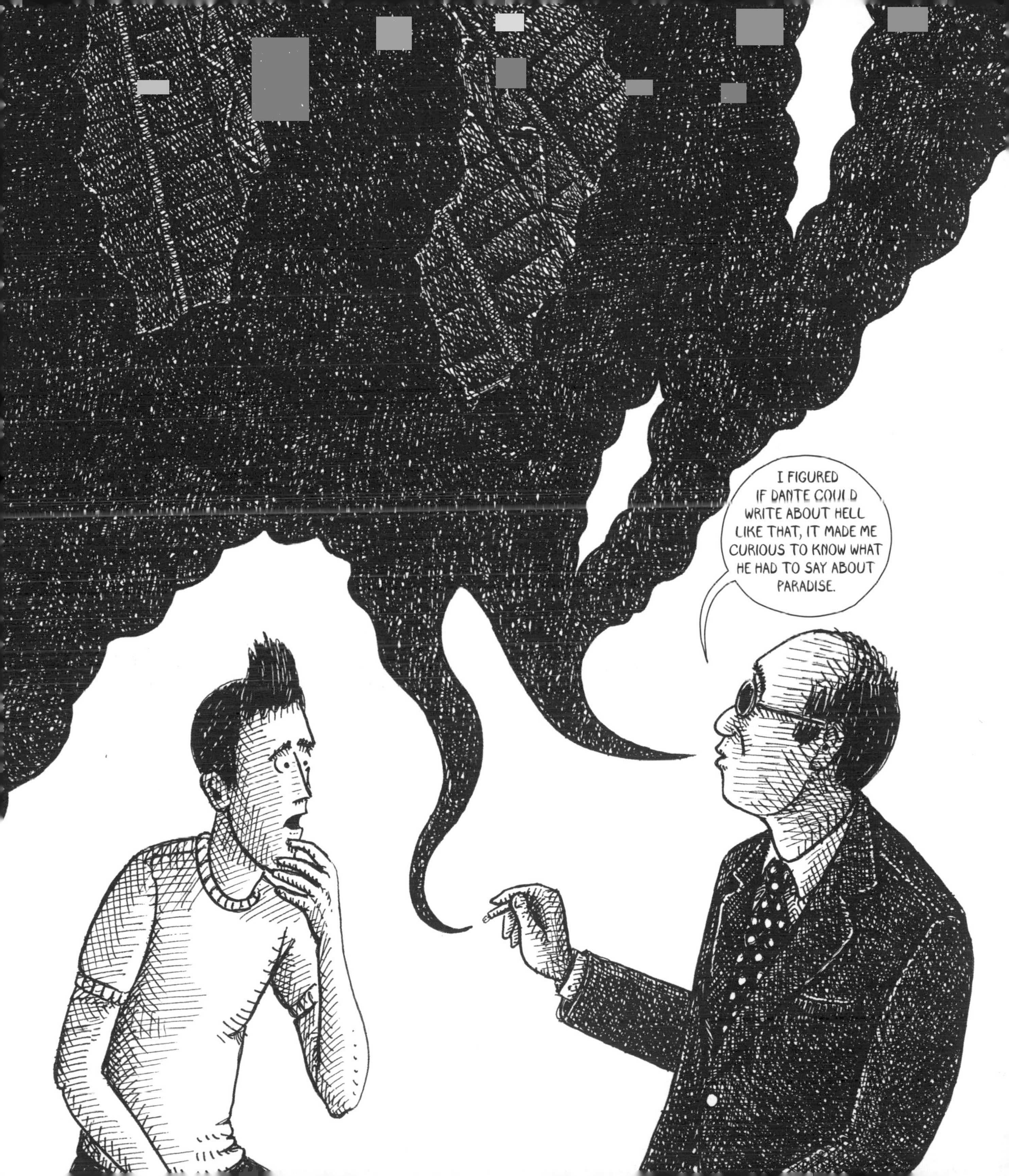
I FIGURED IF DANTE COULD WRITE ABOUT HELL LIKE THAT, IT MADE ME CURIOUS TO KNOW WHAT HE HAD TO SAY ABOUT PARADISE.

XV

THE GLIM BOX

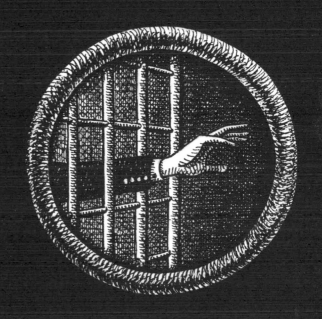

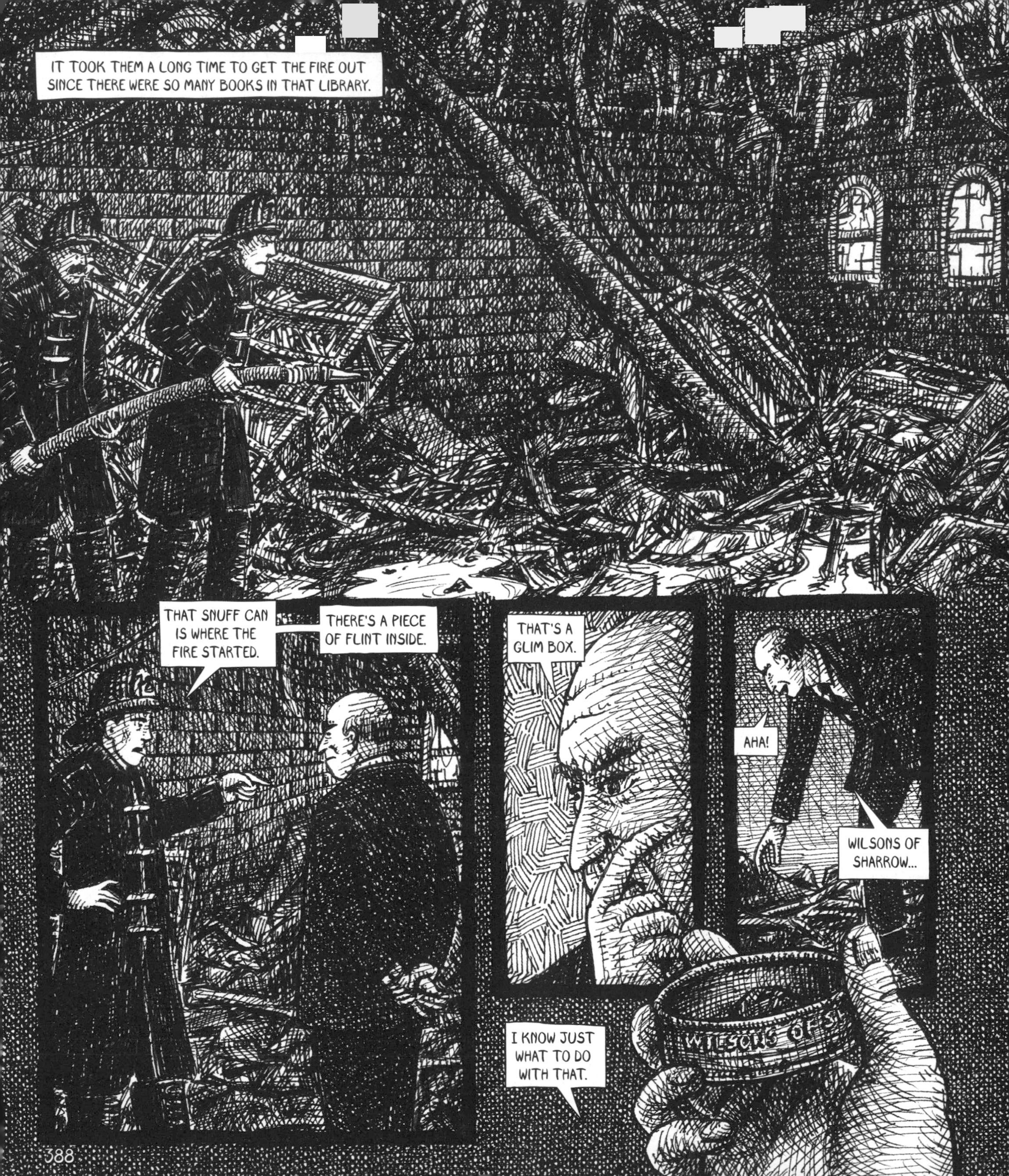
IT TOOK THEM A LONG TIME TO GET THE FIRE OUT SINCE THERE WERE SO MANY BOOKS IN THAT LIBRARY.
THAT SNUFF CAN IS WHERE THE FIRE STARTED.
THERE'S A PIECE OF FLINT INSIDE.
THAT'S A GLIM BOX.
AHA!
WILSONS OF SHARROW...
I KNOW JUST WHAT TO DO WITH THAT.
WILSONS OF

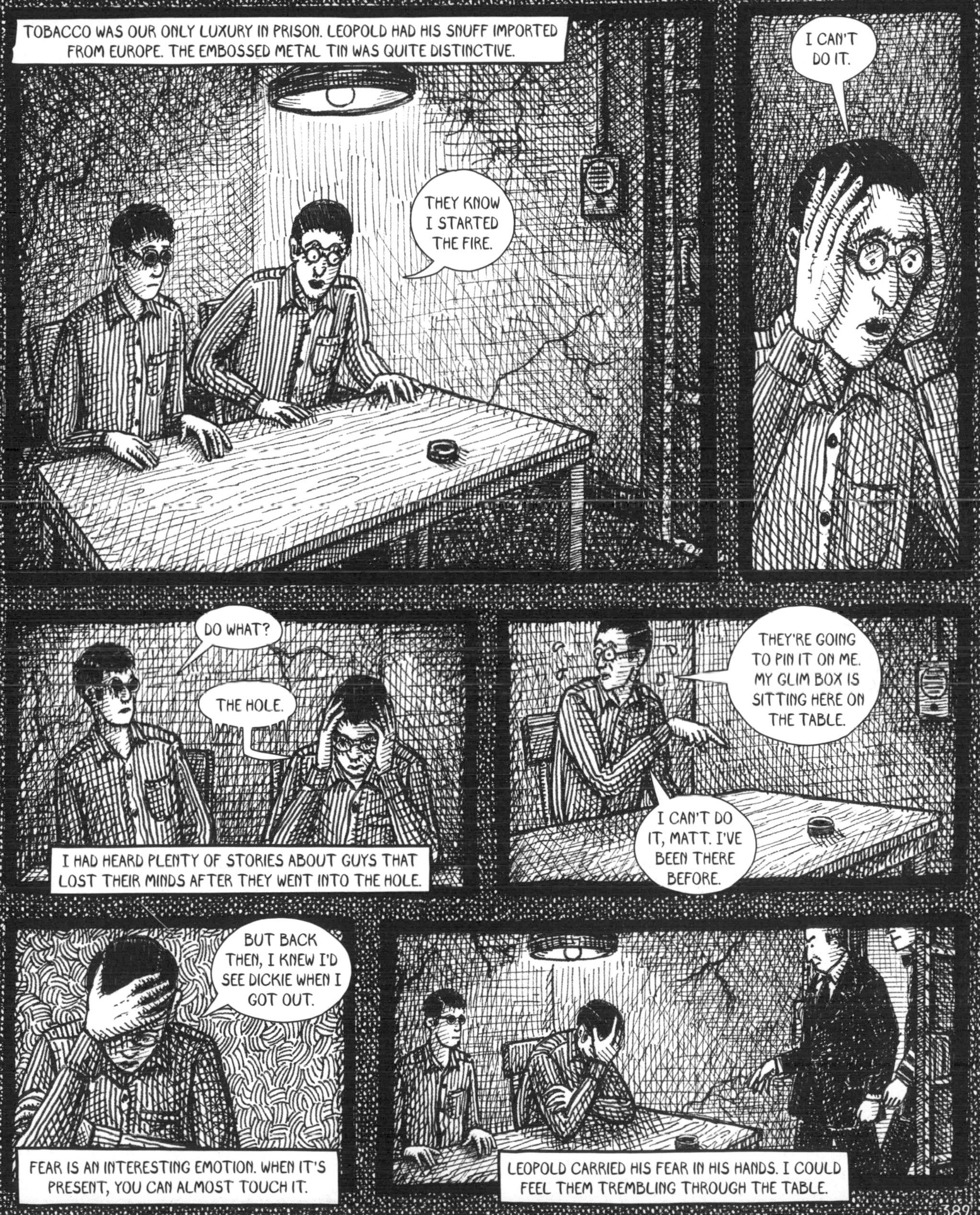
TOBACCO WAS OUR ONLY LUXURY IN PRISON. LEOPOLD HAD HIS SNUFF IMPORTED FROM EUROPE. THE EMBOSSED METAL TIN WAS QUITE DISTINCTIVE.
THEY KNOW I STARTED THE FIRE.
I CAN'T DO IT.
DO WHAT?
THE HOLE.
I HAD HEARD PLENTY OF STORIES ABOUT GUYS THAT LOST THEIR MINDS AFTER THEY WENT INTO THE HOLE.
THEY'RE GOING TO PIN IT ON ME. MY GLIM BOX IS SITTING HERE ON THE TABLE.
I CAN'T DO IT, MATT. I'VE BEEN THERE BEFORE.
BUT BACK THEN, I KNEW I'D SEE DICKIE WHEN I GOT OUT.
FEAR IS AN INTERESTING EMOTION. WHEN IT'S PRESENT, YOU CAN ALMOST TOUCH IT.
LEOPOLD CARRIED HIS FEAR IN HIS HANDS. I COULD FEEL THEM TREMBLING THROUGH THE TABLE.

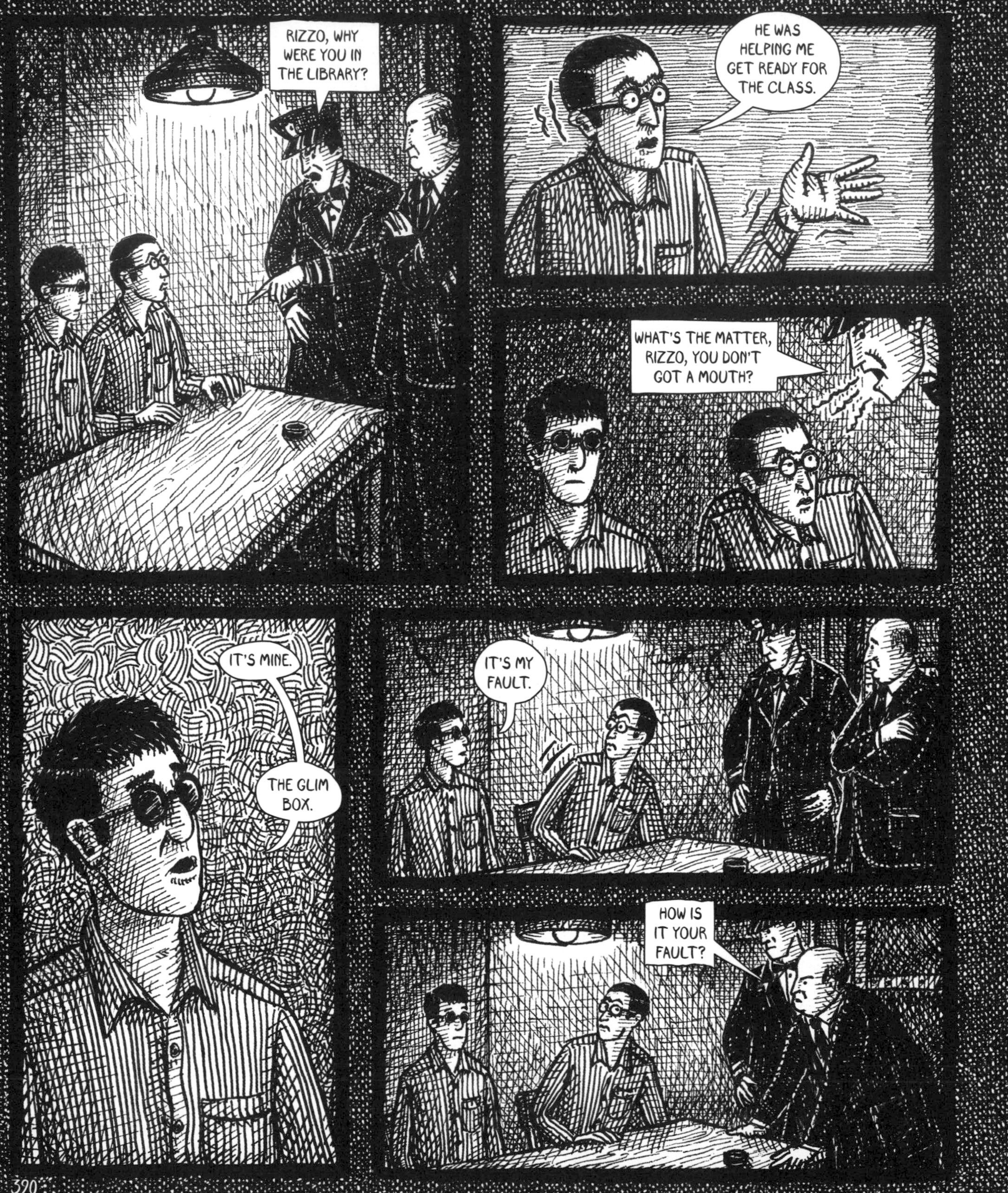

RIZZO, WHY WERE YOU IN THE LIBRARY?
HE WAS HELPING ME GET READY FOR THE CLASS.
WHAT'S THE MATTER, RIZZO, YOU DON'T GOT A MOUTH?
IT'S MINE.
THE GLIM BOX.
IT'S MY FAULT.
HOW IS IT YOUR FAULT?

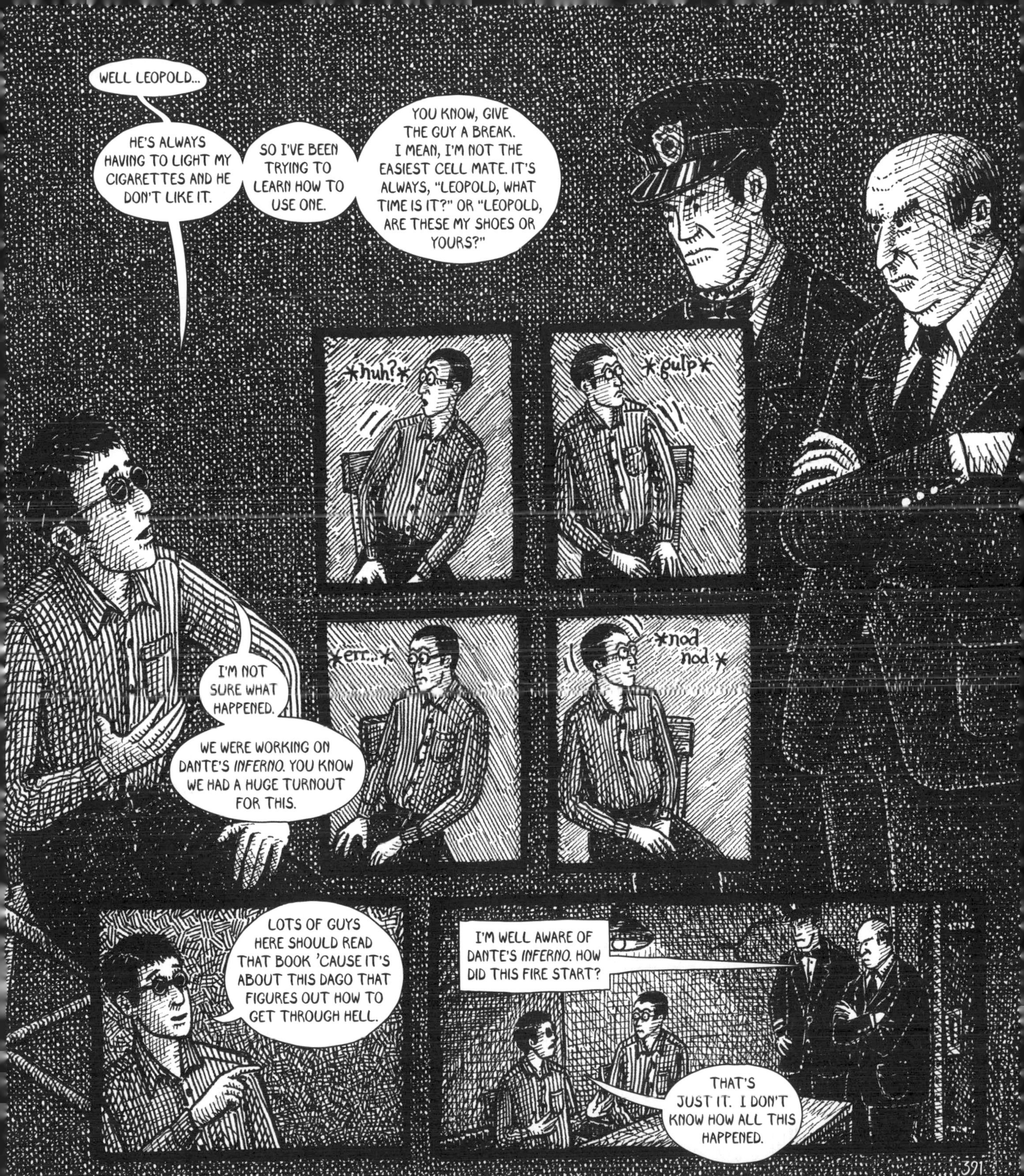
WELL LEOPOLD...
HE'S ALWAYS HAVING TO LIGHT MY CIGARETTES AND HE DON'T LIKE IT.
SO I'VE BEEN TRYING TO LEARN HOW TO USE ONE.
YOU KNOW, GIVE THE GUY A BREAK. I MEAN, I'M NOT THE EASIEST CELL MATE. IT'S ALWAYS, "LEOPOLD, WHAT TIME IS IT?" OR "LEOPOLD, ARE THESE MY SHOES OR YOURS?"
huh?
gulp
I'M NOT SURE WHAT HAPPENED.
WE WERE WORKING ON DANTE'S *INFERNO*. YOU KNOW WE HAD A HUGE TURNOUT FOR THIS.
err...
nod nod
LOTS OF GUYS HERE SHOULD READ THAT BOOK 'CAUSE IT'S ABOUT THIS DAGO THAT FIGURES OUT HOW TO GET THROUGH HELL.
I'M WELL AWARE OF DANTE'S *INFERNO*. HOW DID THIS FIRE START?
THAT'S JUST IT. I DON'T KNOW HOW ALL THIS HAPPENED.

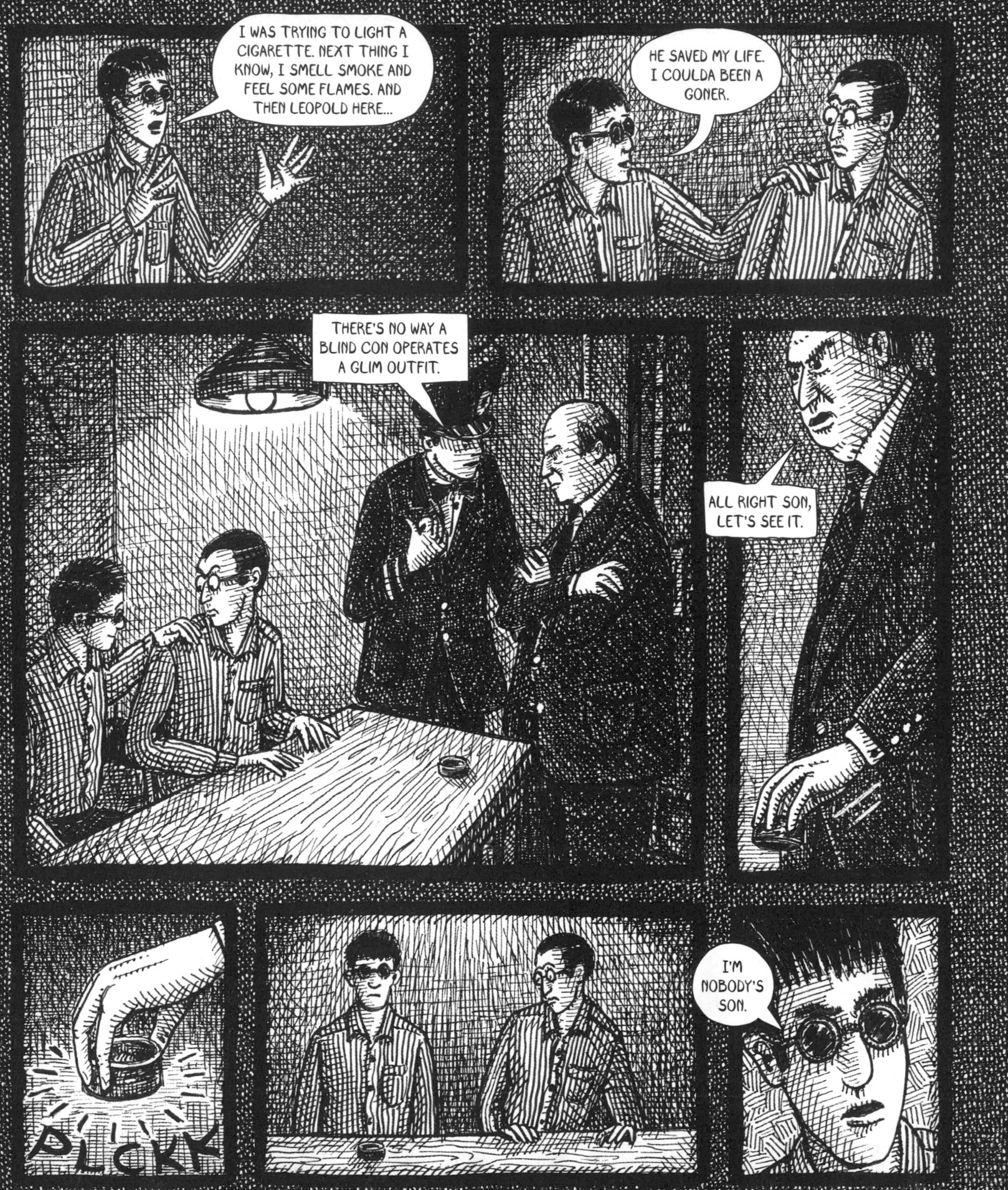
I WAS TRYING TO LIGHT A CIGARETTE. NEXT THING I KNOW, I SMELL SMOKE AND FEEL SOME FLAMES. AND THEN LEOPOLD HERE...
HE SAVED MY LIFE. I COULDA BEEN A GONER.
THERE'S NO WAY A BLIND CON OPERATES A GLIM OUTFIT.
ALL RIGHT SON, LET'S SEE IT.
PLCKK
I'M NOBODY'S SON.

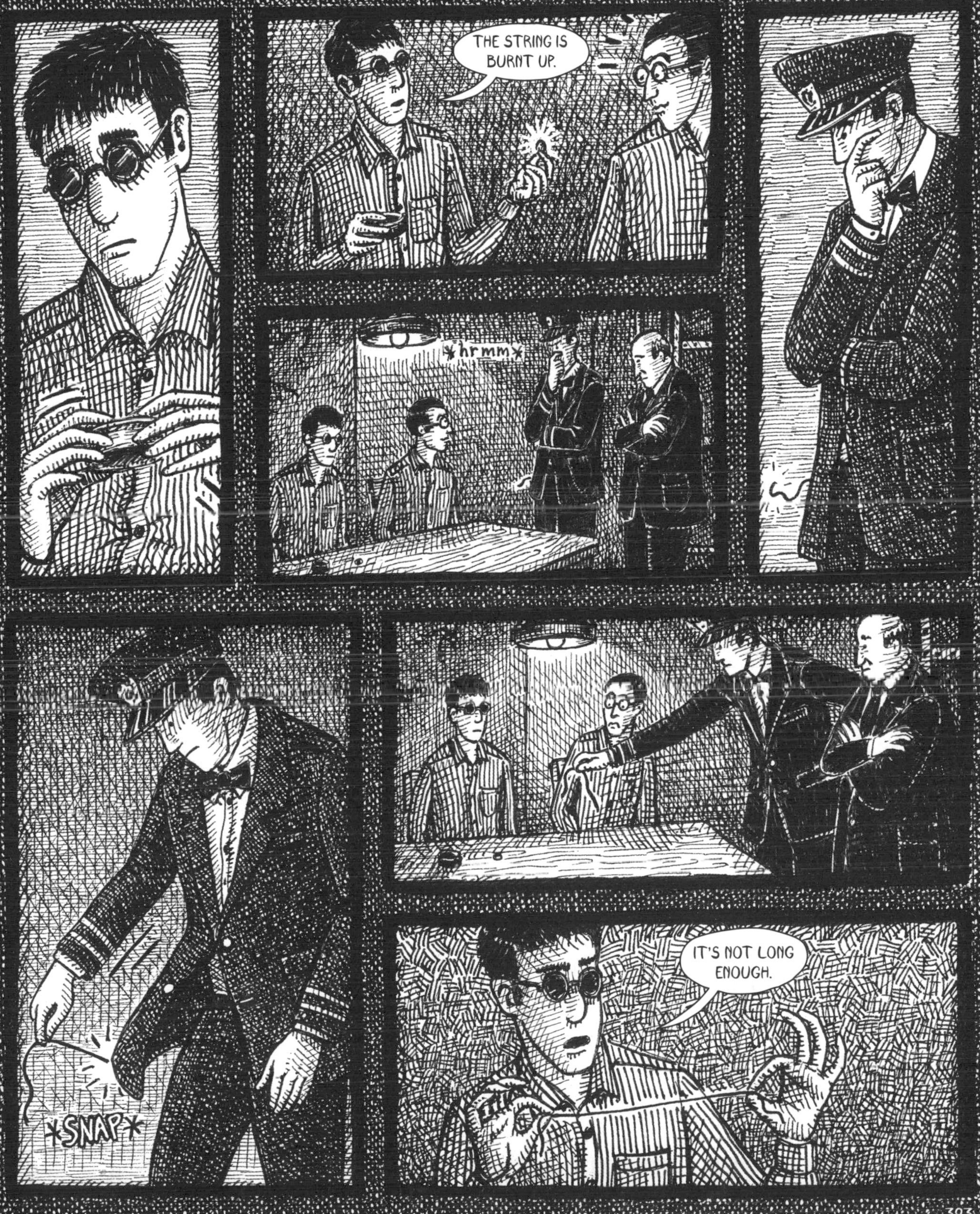
THE STRING IS BURNT UP.
hrmm
SNAP
IT'S NOT LONG ENOUGH.

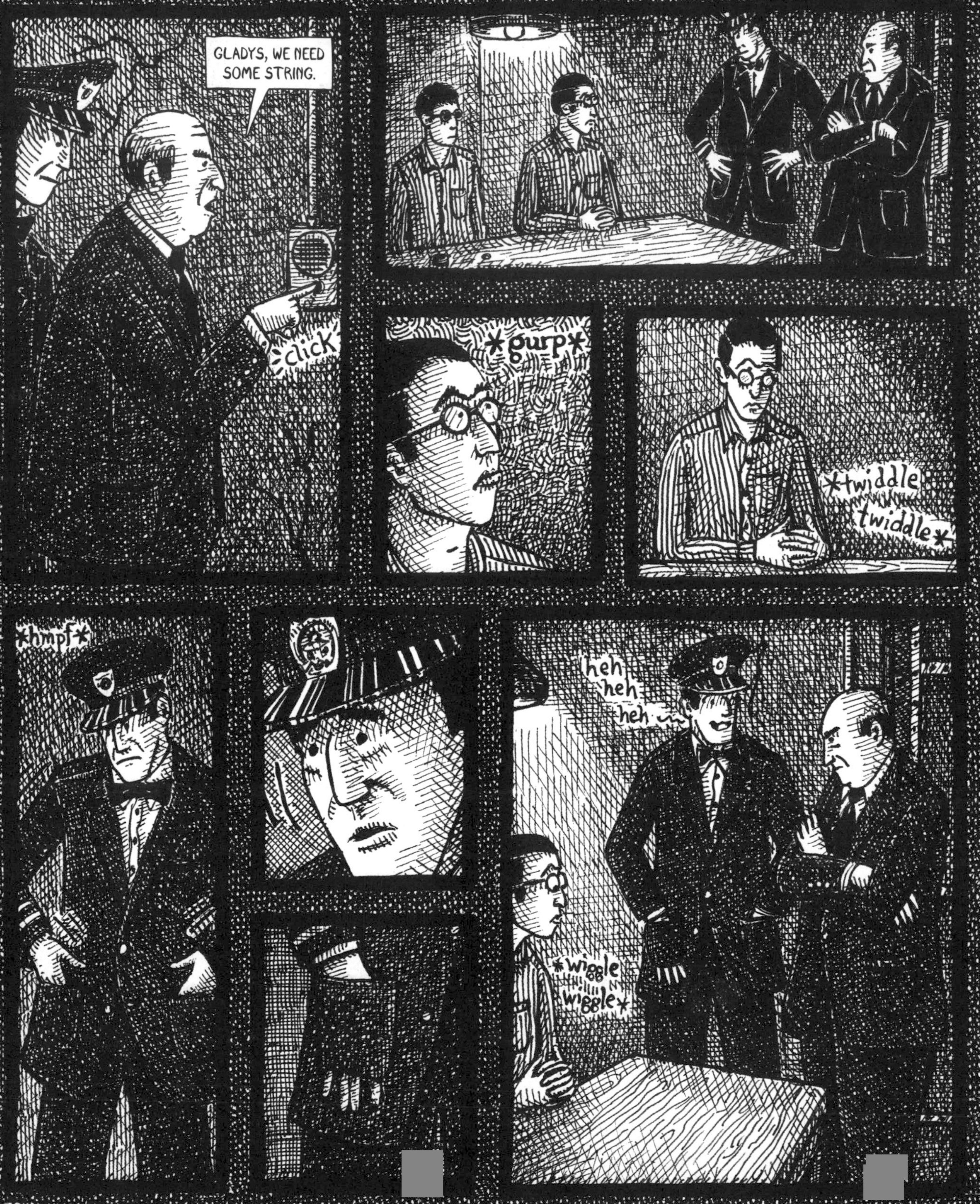
GLADYS, WE NEED SOME STRING.
click
gurp
twiddle twiddle
hmpf
heh heh heh
wiggle wiggle

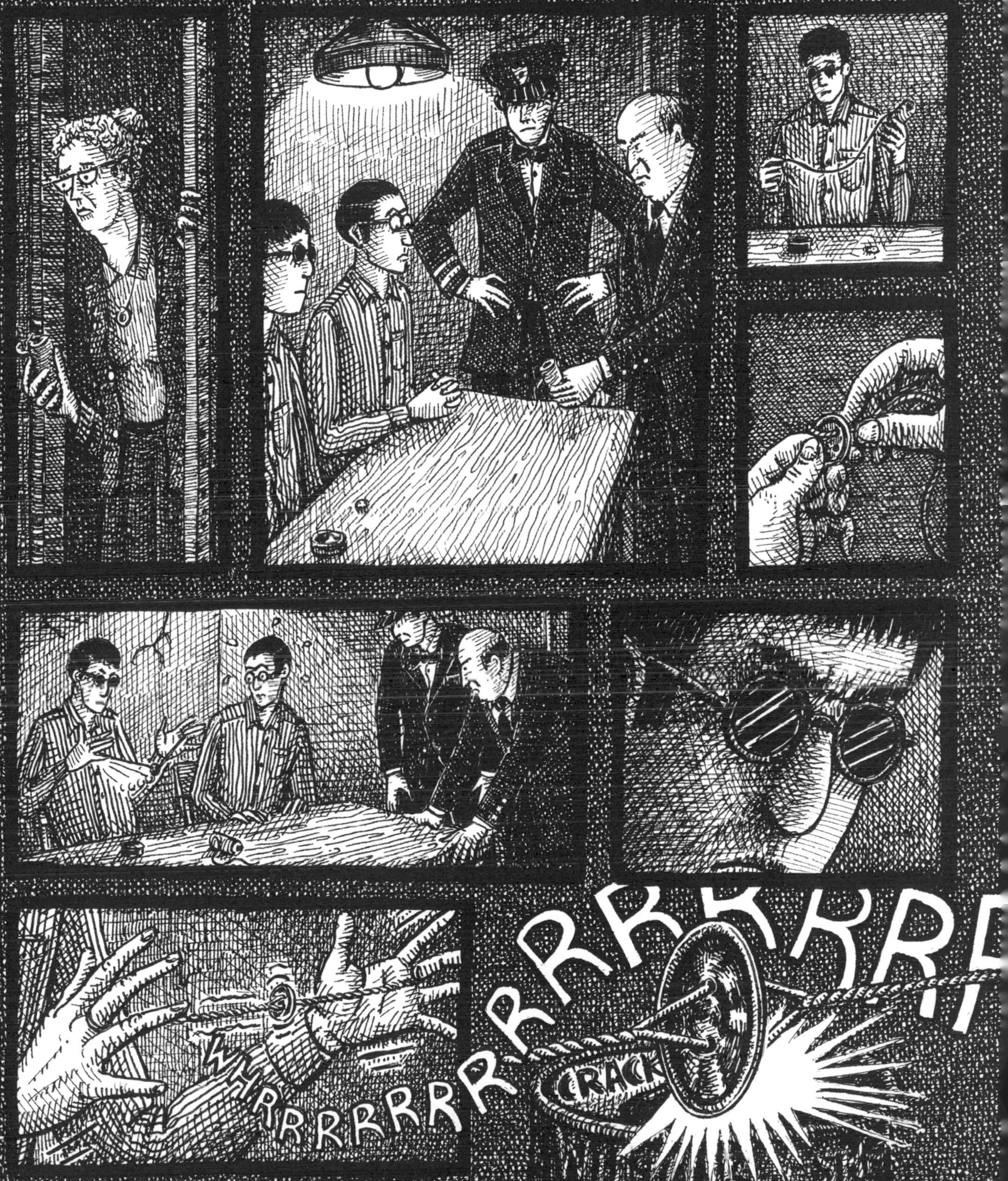
WHRRRRRRRRRRRRRRRRRRR
CRACK

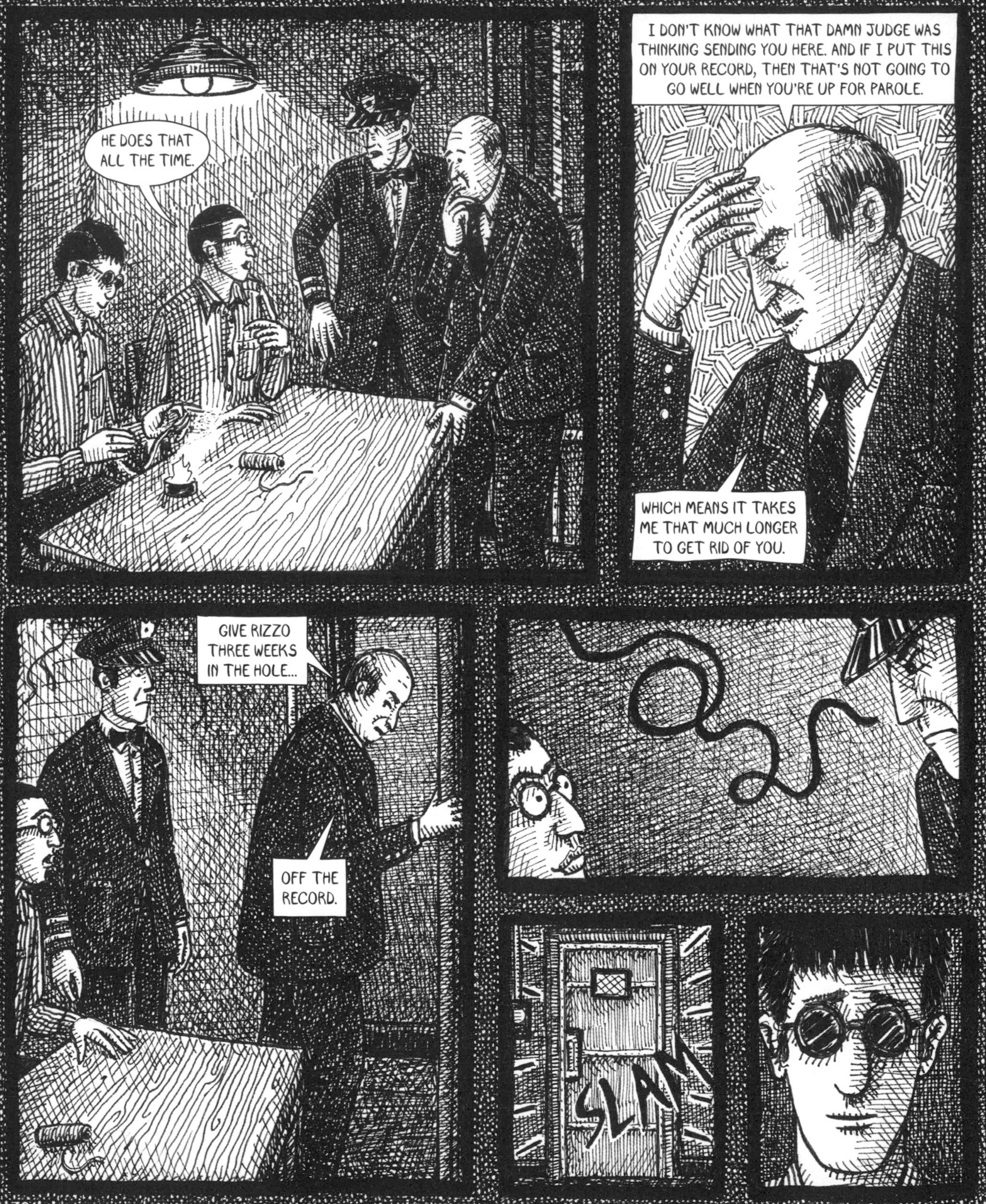
HE DOES THAT ALL THE TIME.
I DON'T KNOW WHAT THAT DAMN JUDGE WAS THINKING SENDING YOU HERE. AND IF I PUT THIS ON YOUR RECORD, THEN THAT'S NOT GOING TO GO WELL WHEN YOU'RE UP FOR PAROLE.
WHICH MEANS IT TAKES ME THAT MUCH LONGER TO GET RID OF YOU.
GIVE RIZZO THREE WEEKS IN THE HOLE...
OFF THE RECORD.
SLAM

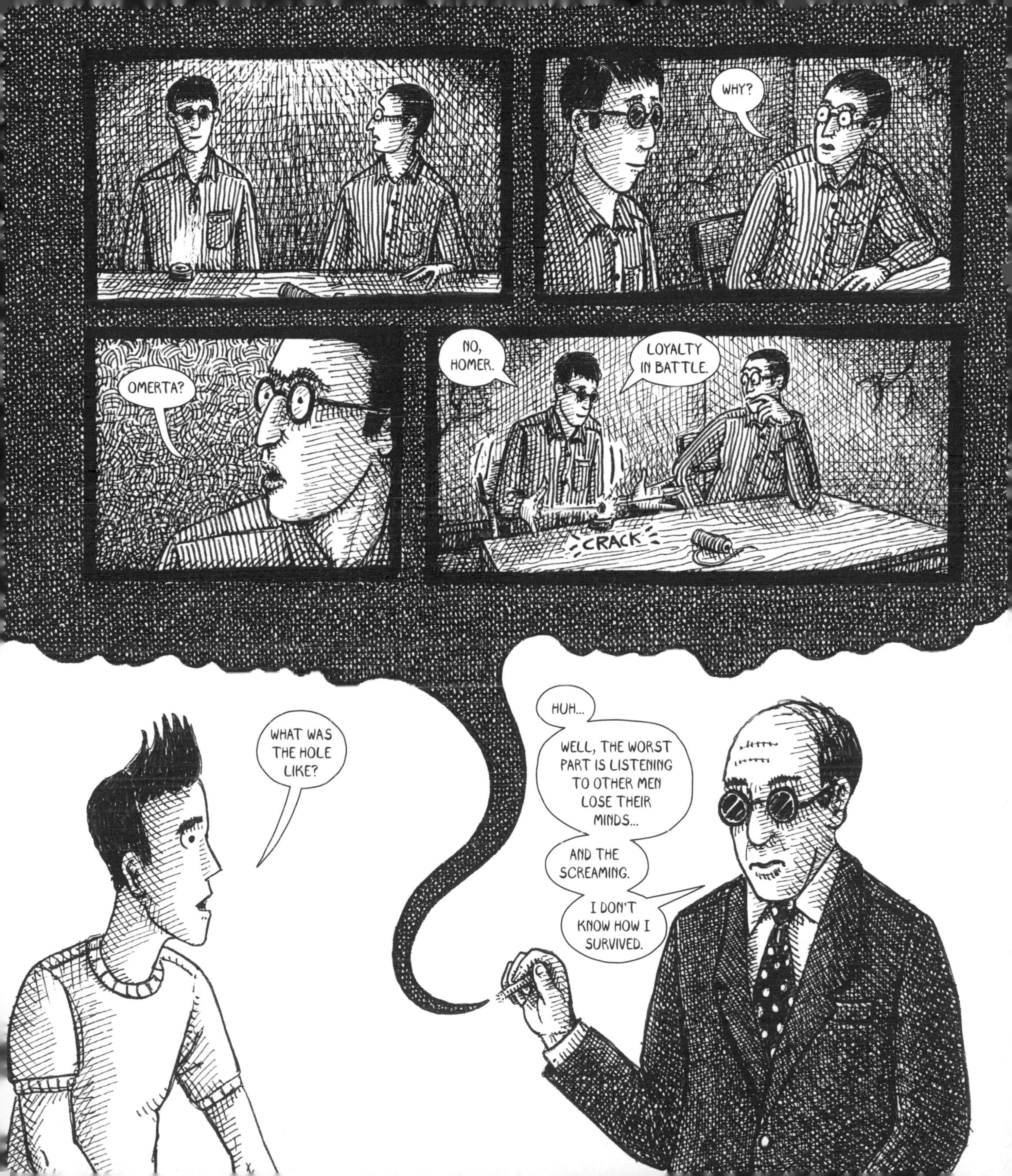
WHY?
OMERTA?
NO, HOMER.
LOYALTY IN BATTLE.
CRACK
WHAT WAS THE HOLE LIKE?
HUH...
WELL, THE WORST PART IS LISTENING TO OTHER MEN LOSE THEIR MINDS...
AND THE SCREAMING.
I DON'T KNOW HOW I SURVIVED.

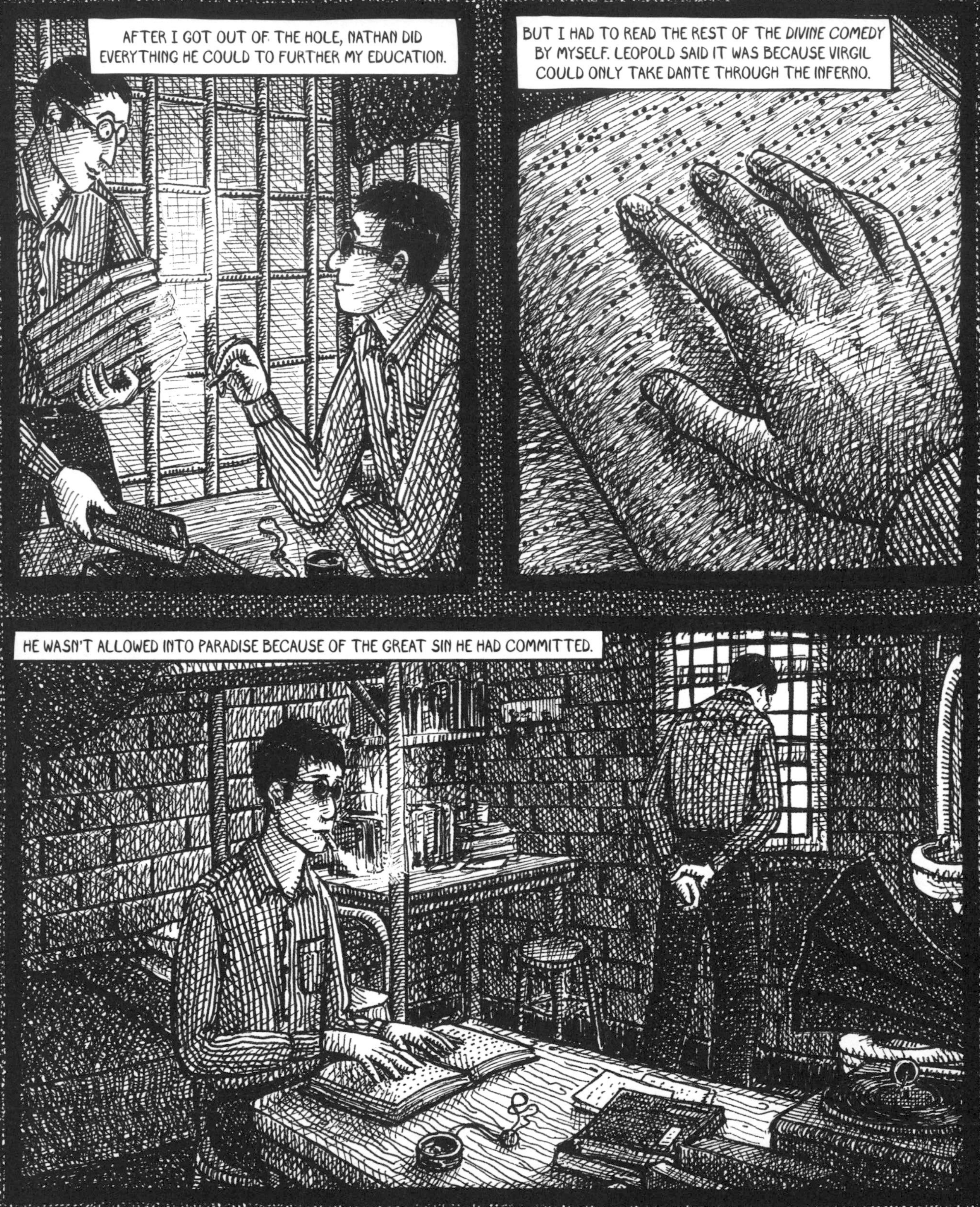
AFTER I GOT OUT OF THE HOLE, NATHAN DID EVERYTHING HE COULD TO FURTHER MY EDUCATION.
BUT I HAD TO READ THE REST OF THE *DIVINE COMEDY* BY MYSELF. LEOPOLD SAID IT WAS BECAUSE VIRGIL COULD ONLY TAKE DANTE THROUGH THE INFERNO.
HE WASN'T ALLOWED INTO PARADISE BECAUSE OF THE GREAT SIN HE HAD COMMITTED.

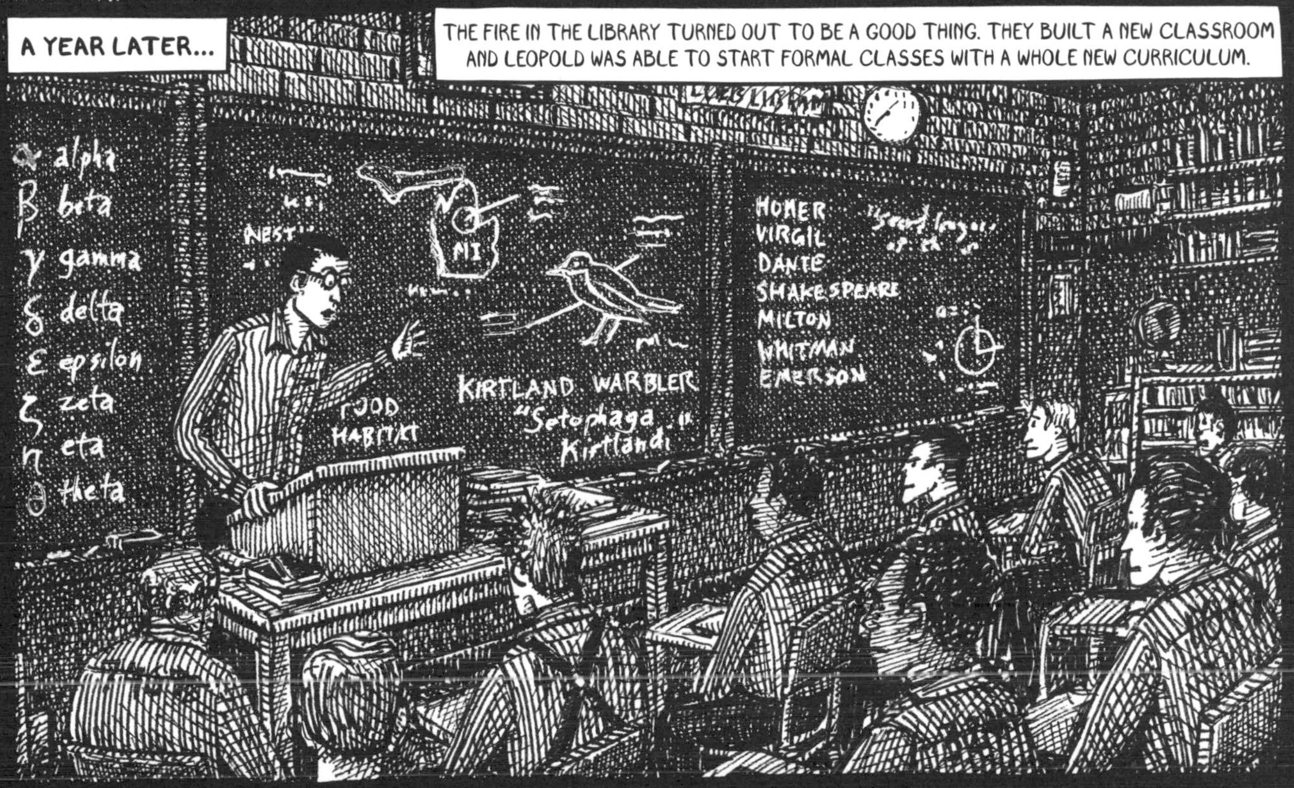
A YEAR LATER...
THE FIRE IN THE LIBRARY TURNED OUT TO BE A GOOD THING. THEY BUILT A NEW CLASSROOM AND LEOPOLD WAS ABLE TO START FORMAL CLASSES WITH A WHOLE NEW CURRICULUM.
alpha
beta
gamma
delta
epsilon
zeta
eta
theta
NEST
MI
KIRTLAND WARBLER
"Setophaga Kirtlandi"
HABITAT
HOMER
VIRGIL
DANTE
SHAKESPEARE
MILTON
WHITMAN
EMERSON

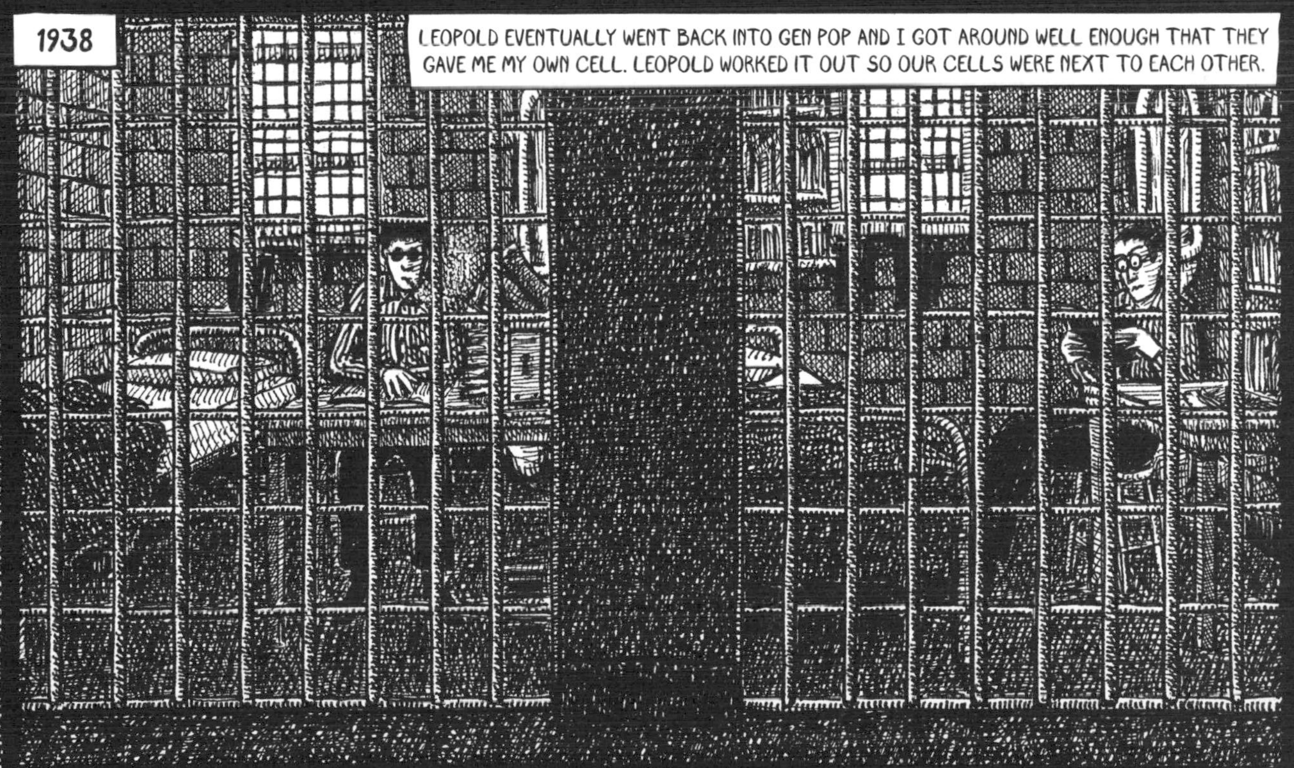
1938
LEOPOLD EVENTUALLY WENT BACK INTO GEN POP AND I GOT AROUND WELL ENOUGH THAT THEY GAVE ME MY OWN CELL. LEOPOLD WORKED IT OUT SO OUR CELLS WERE NEXT TO EACH OTHER.

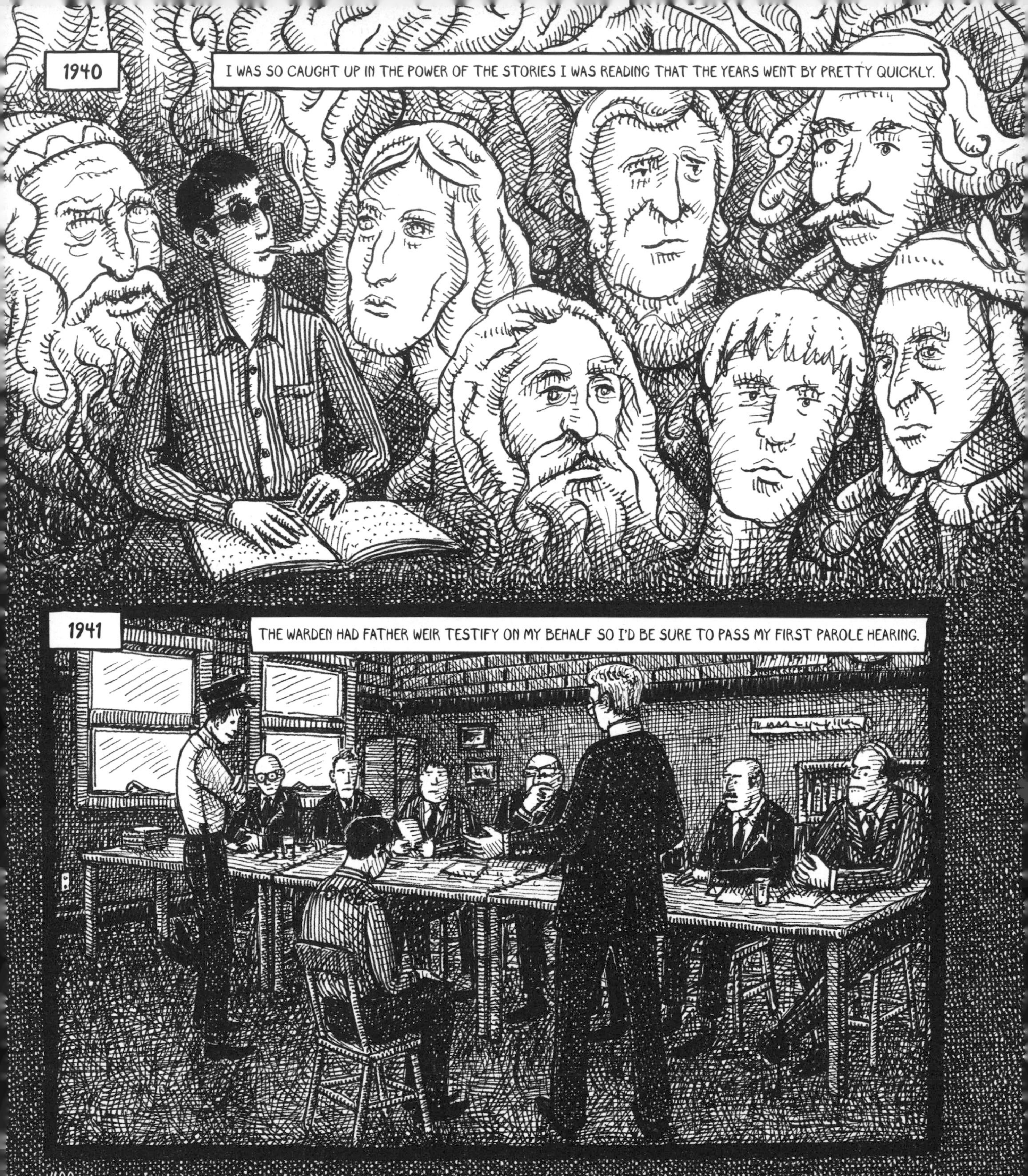
1940
I WAS SO CAUGHT UP IN THE POWER OF THE STORIES I WAS READING THAT THE YEARS WENT BY PRETTY QUICKLY.
1941
THE WARDEN HAD FATHER WEIR TESTIFY ON MY BEHALF SO I'D BE SURE TO PASS MY FIRST PAROLE HEARING.

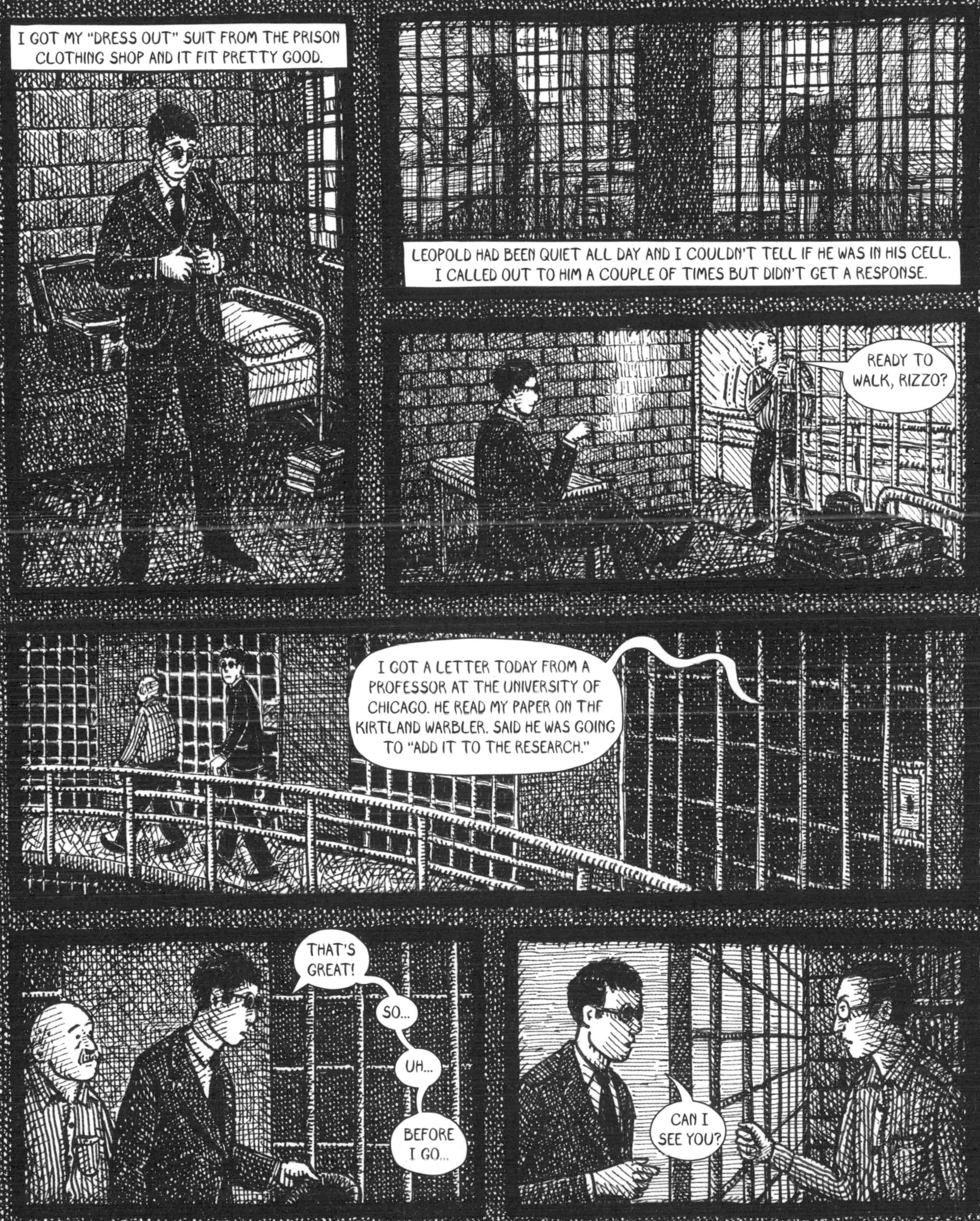
I GOT MY "DRESS OUT" SUIT FROM THE PRISON CLOTHING SHOP AND IT FIT PRETTY GOOD.
LEOPOLD HAD BEEN QUIET ALL DAY AND I COULDN'T TELL IF HE WAS IN HIS CELL. I CALLED OUT TO HIM A COUPLE OF TIMES BUT DIDN'T GET A RESPONSE.
READY TO WALK, RIZZO?
I GOT A LETTER TODAY FROM A PROFESSOR AT THE UNIVERSITY OF CHICAGO. HE READ MY PAPER ON THE KIRTLAND WARBLER. SAID HE WAS GOING TO "ADD IT TO THE RESEARCH."
THAT'S GREAT!
SO...
UH...
BEFORE I GO...
CAN I SEE YOU?

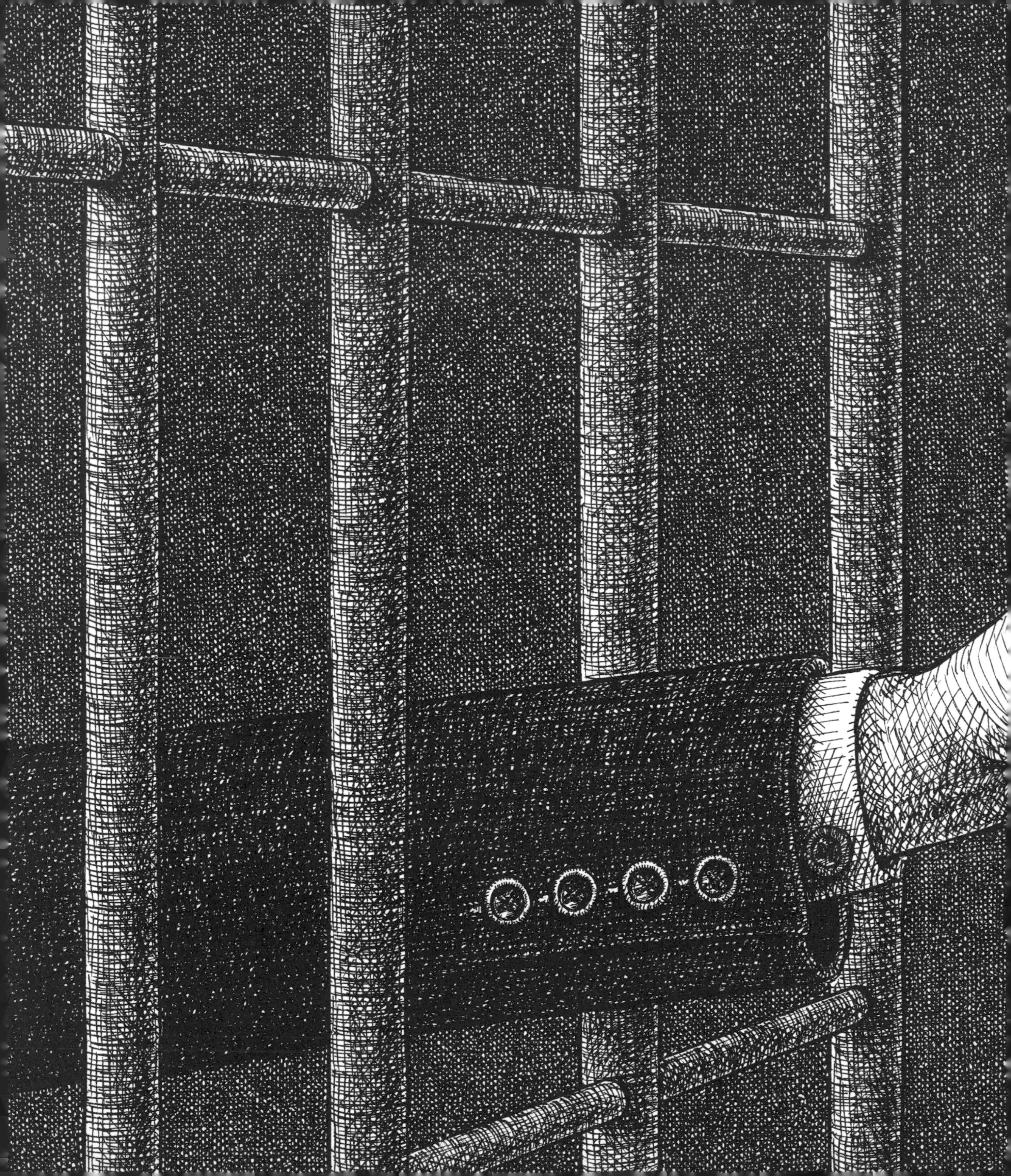

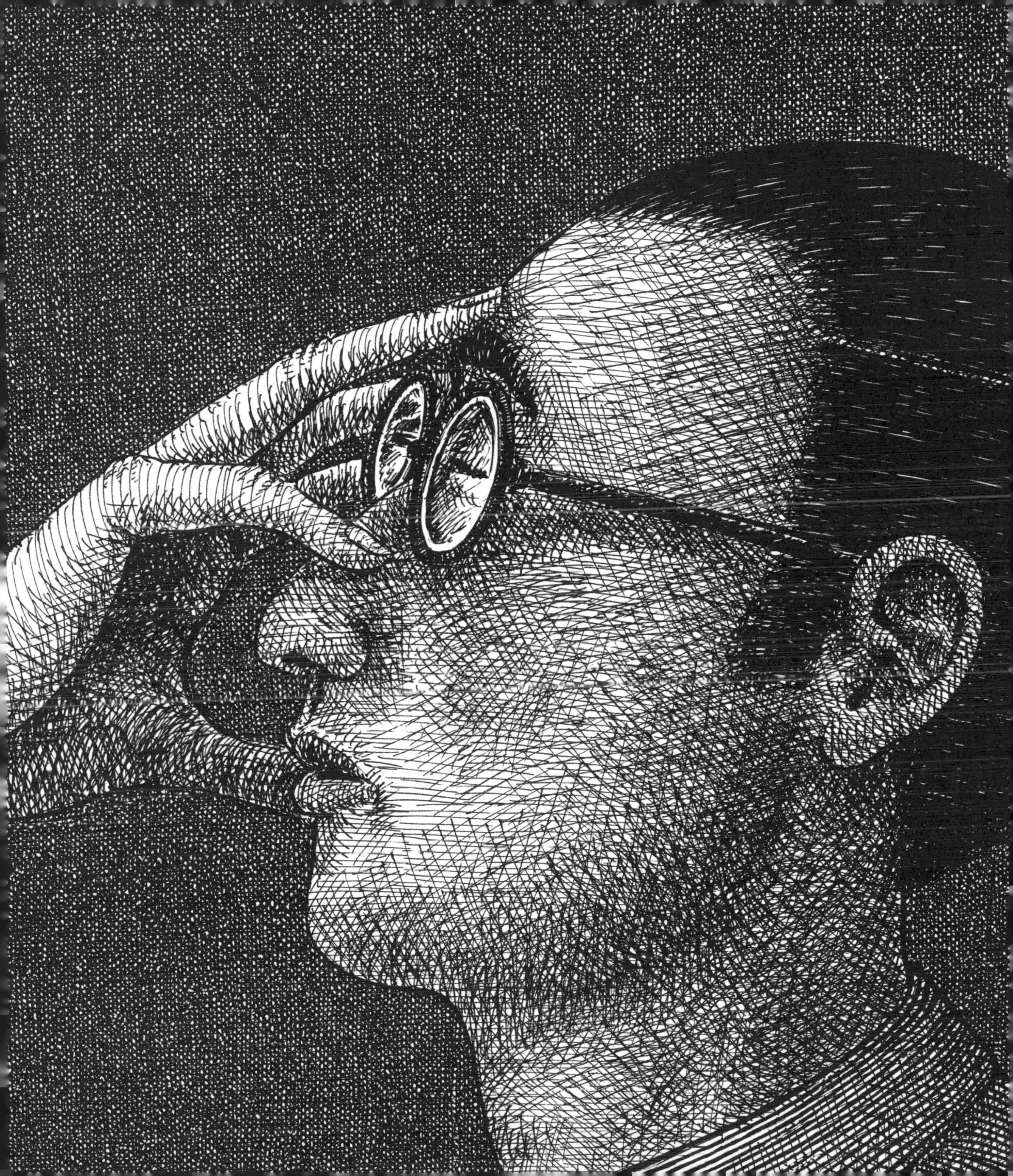

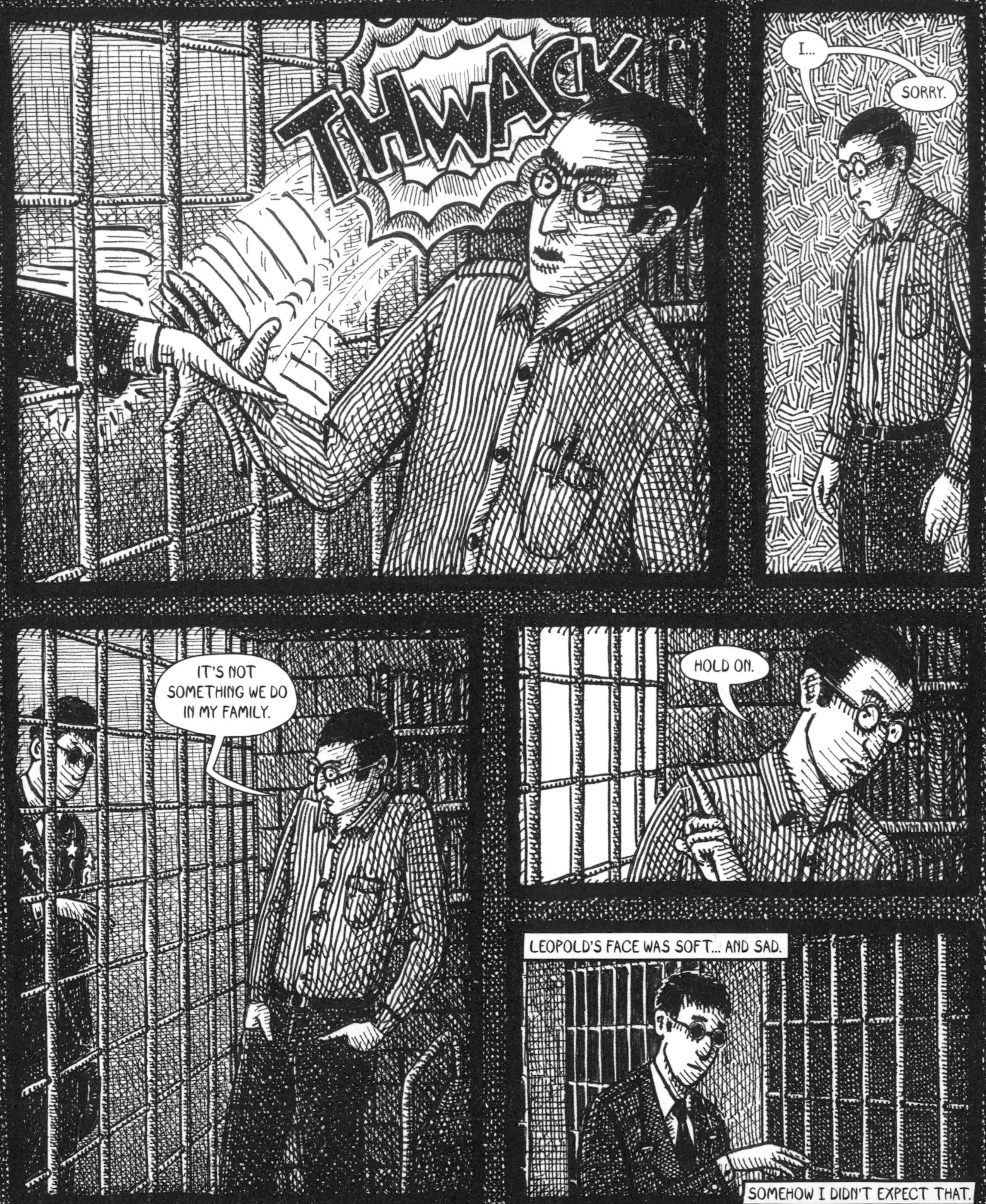
THWACK!
I...
SORRY.
IT'S NOT SOMETHING WE DO IN MY FAMILY.
HOLD ON.
LEOPOLD'S FACE WAS SOFT... AND SAD.
SOMEHOW I DIDN'T EXPECT THAT.

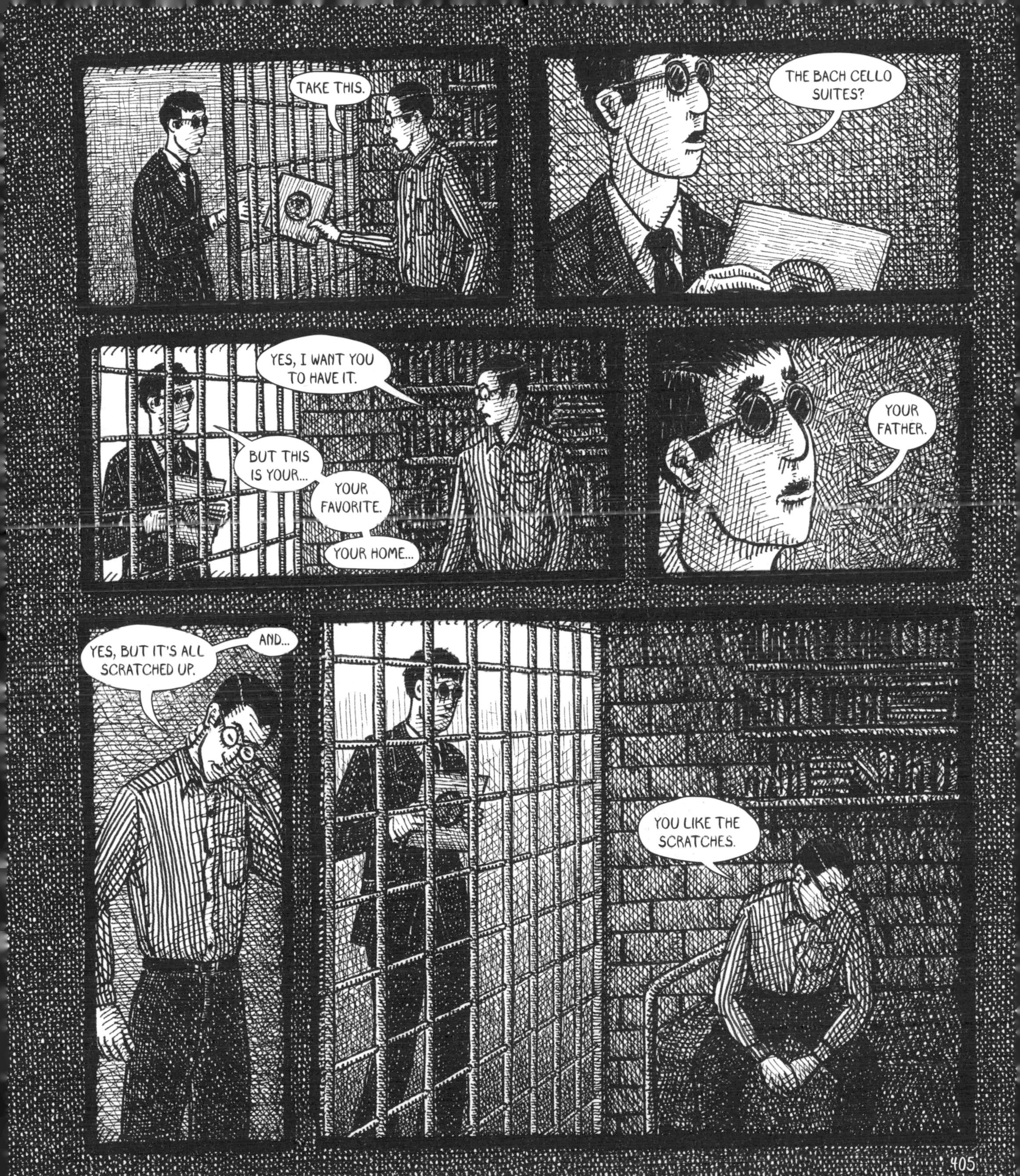
TAKE THIS.
THE BACH CELLO SUITES?
YES, I WANT YOU TO HAVE IT.
BUT THIS IS YOUR...
YOUR FAVORITE.
YOUR HOME...
YOUR FATHER.
YES, BUT IT'S ALL SCRATCHED UP.
AND...
YOU LIKE THE SCRATCHES.

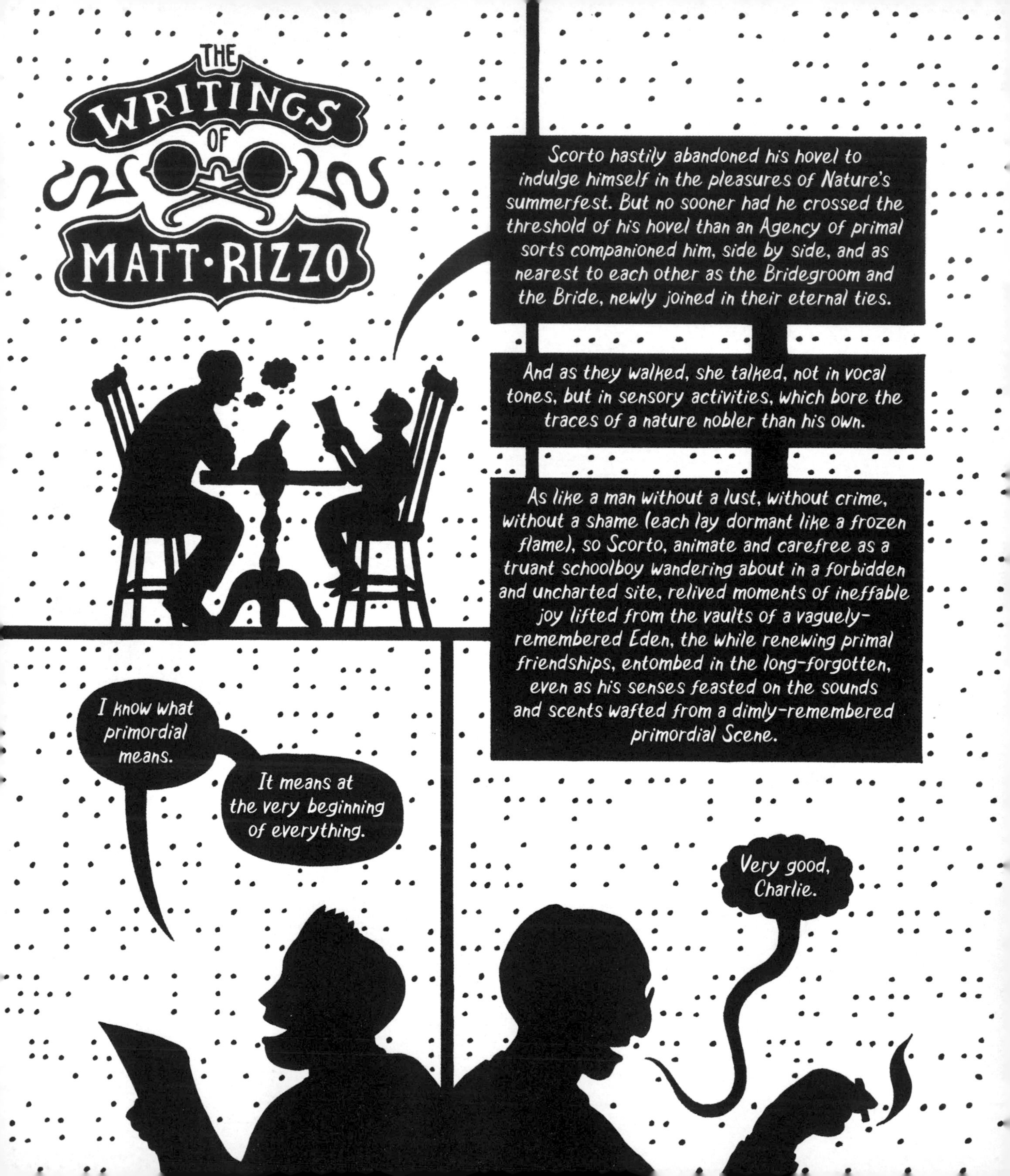
THE WRITINGS OF MATT·RIZZO
Scorto hastily abandoned his hovel to indulge himself in the pleasures of Nature's summerfest. But no sooner had he crossed the threshold of his hovel than an Agency of primal sorts companioned him, side by side, and as nearest to each other as the Bridegroom and the Bride, newly joined in their eternal ties.
And as they walked, she talked, not in vocal tones, but in sensory activities, which bore the traces of a nature nobler than his own.
As like a man without a lust, without crime, without a shame (each lay dormant like a frozen flame), so Scorto, animate and carefree as a truant schoolboy wandering about in a forbidden and uncharted site, relived moments of ineffable joy lifted from the vaults of a vaguely-remembered Eden, the while renewing primal friendships, entombed in the long-forgotten, even as his senses feasted on the sounds and scents wafted from a dimly-remembered primordial Scene.
I know what primordial means.
It means at the very beginning of everything.
Very good, Charlie.

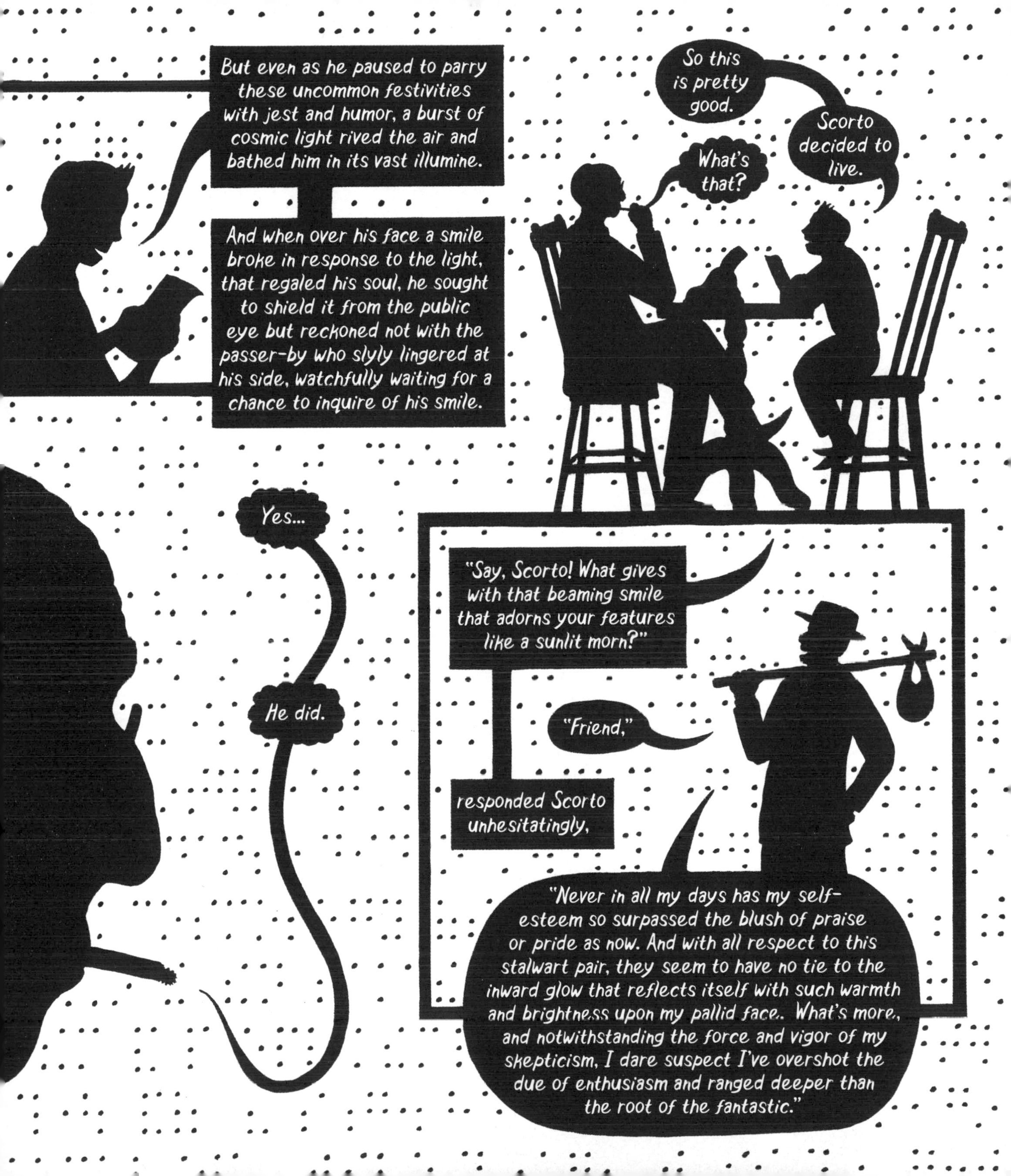

But even as he paused to parry these uncommon festivities with jest and humor, a burst of cosmic light rived the air and bathed him in its vast illumine.
And when over his face a smile broke in response to the light, that regaled his soul, he sought to shield it from the public eye but reckoned not with the passer-by who slyly lingered at his side, watchfully waiting for a chance to inquire of his smile.
So this is pretty good.
What's that?
Scorto decided to live.
Yes...
He did.
"Say, Scorto! What gives with that beaming smile that adorns your features like a sunlit morn?"
"Friend,"
responded Scorto unhesitatingly,
"Never in all my days has my self-esteem so surpassed the blush of praise or pride as now. And with all respect to this stalwart pair, they seem to have no tie to the inward glow that reflects itself with such warmth and brightness upon my pallid face. What's more, and notwithstanding the force and vigor of my skepticism, I dare suspect I've overshot the due of enthusiasm and ranged deeper than the root of the fantastic."

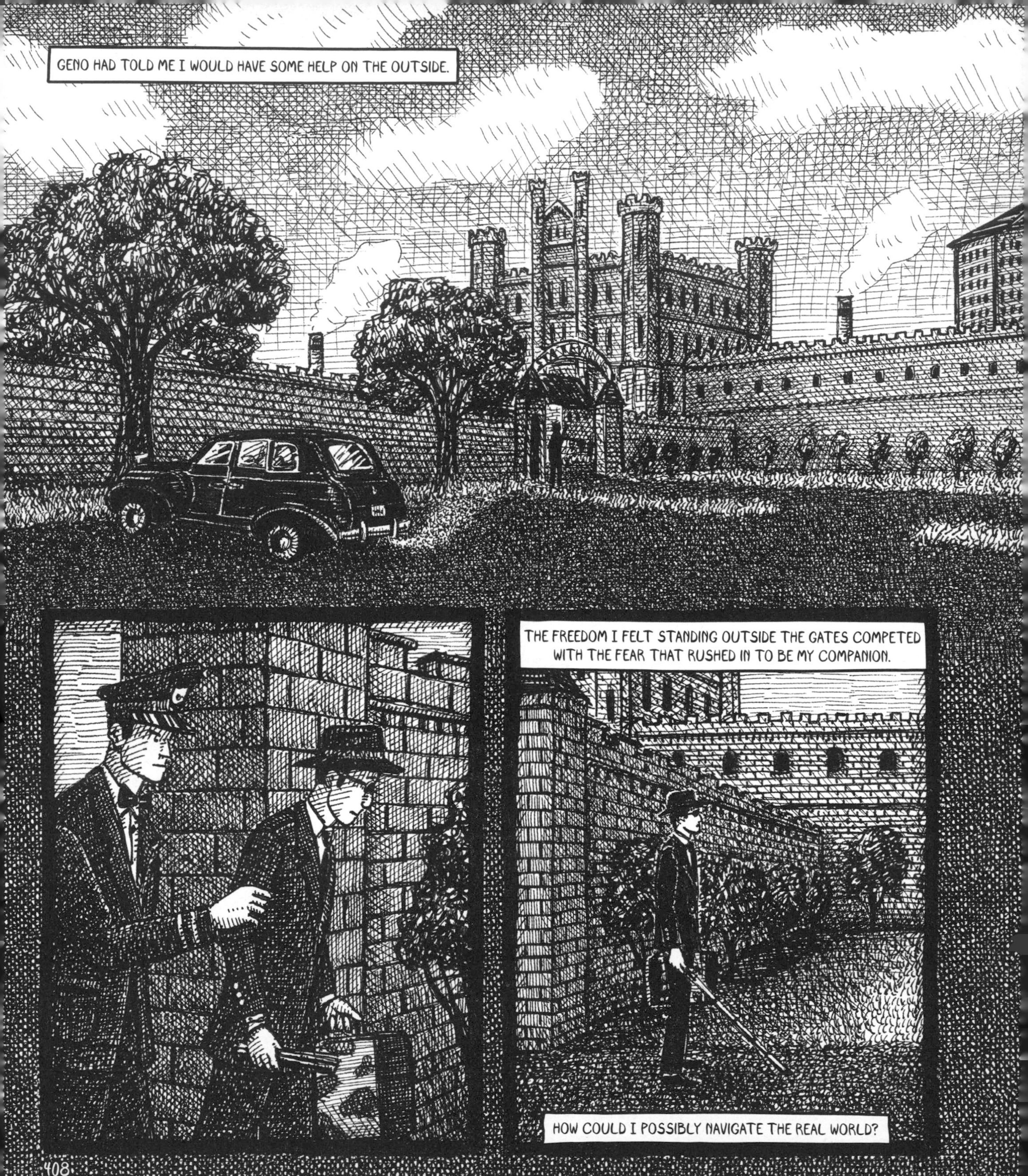
GENO HAD TOLD ME I WOULD HAVE SOME HELP ON THE OUTSIDE.
THE FREEDOM I FELT STANDING OUTSIDE THE GATES COMPETED WITH THE FEAR THAT RUSHED IN TO BE MY COMPANION.
HOW COULD I POSSIBLY NAVIGATE THE REAL WORLD?

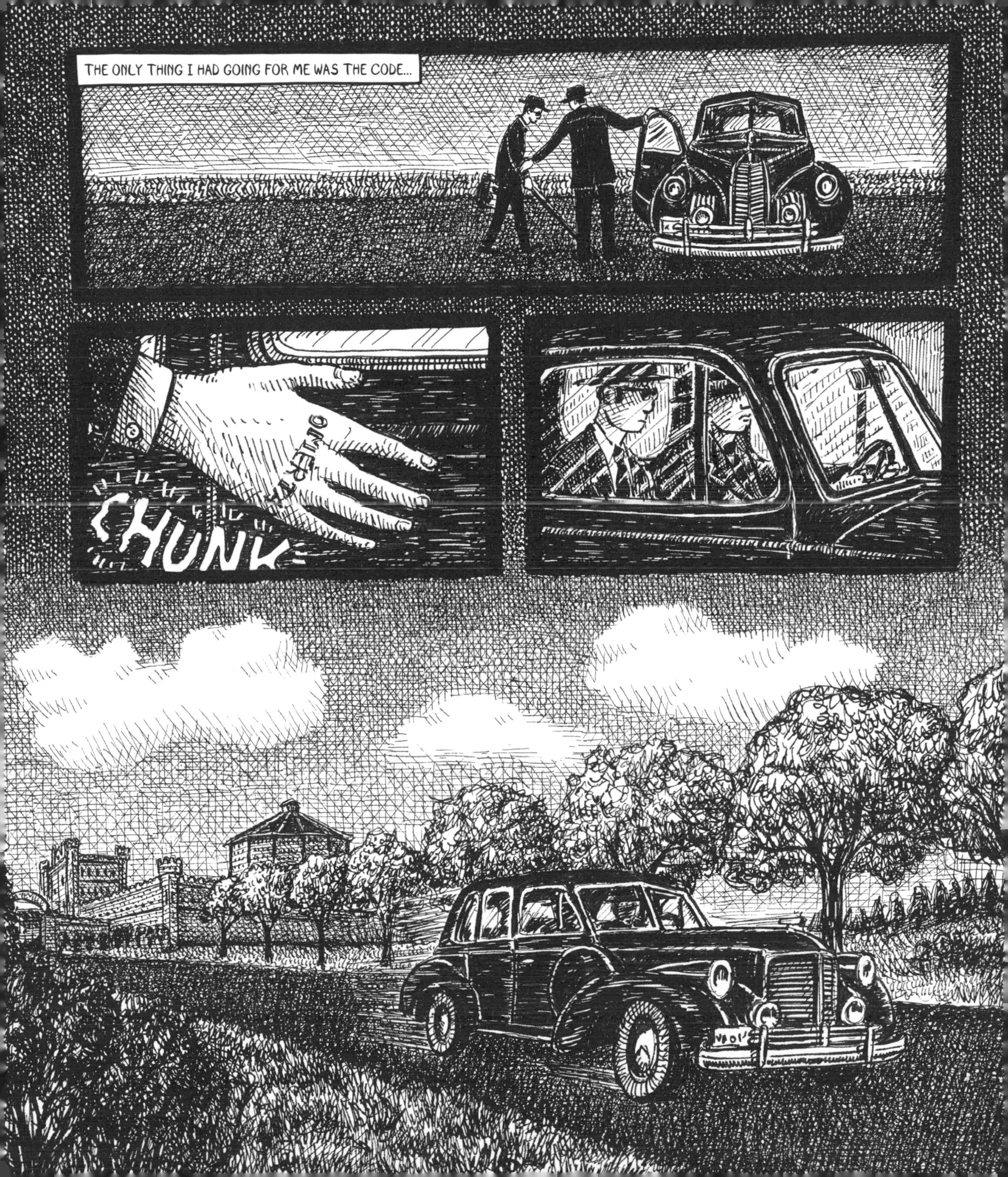
THE ONLY THING I HAD GOING FOR ME WAS THE CODE...
CHUNK

XVI
THE LETTER

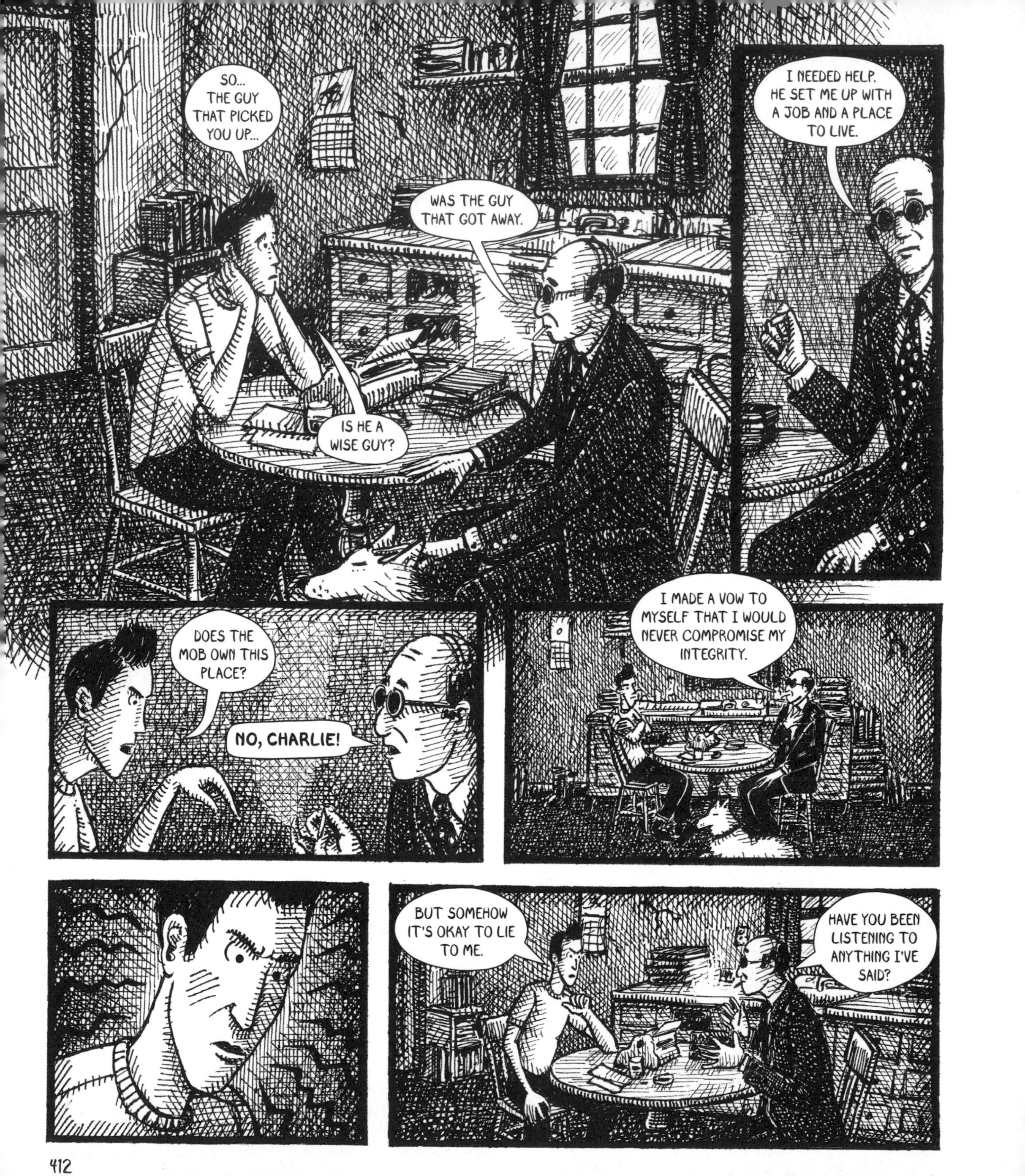

SO... THE GUY THAT PICKED YOU UP...
WAS THE GUY THAT GOT AWAY.
IS HE A WISE GUY?
I NEEDED HELP. HE SET ME UP WITH A JOB AND A PLACE TO LIVE.
DOES THE MOB OWN THIS PLACE?
NO, CHARLIE!
I MADE A VOW TO MYSELF THAT I WOULD NEVER COMPROMISE MY INTEGRITY.
BUT SOMEHOW IT'S OKAY TO LIE TO ME.
HAVE YOU BEEN LISTENING TO ANYTHING I'VE SAID?

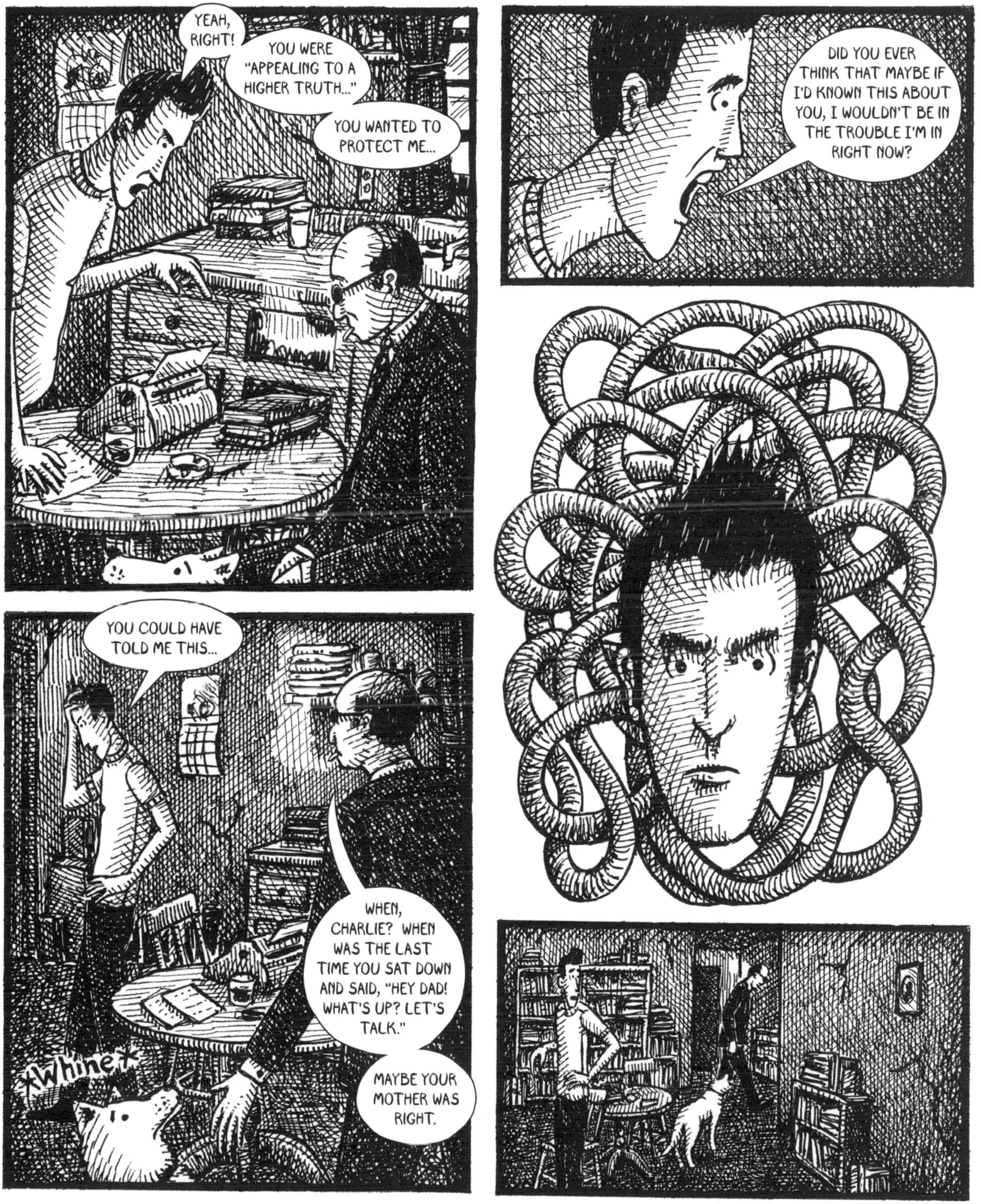
YEAH, RIGHT!
YOU WERE "APPEALING TO A HIGHER TRUTH..."
YOU WANTED TO PROTECT ME...
DID YOU EVER THINK THAT MAYBE IF I'D KNOWN THIS ABOUT YOU, I WOULDN'T BE IN THE TROUBLE I'M IN RIGHT NOW?
YOU COULD HAVE TOLD ME THIS...
WHEN, CHARLIE? WHEN WAS THE LAST TIME YOU SAT DOWN AND SAID, "HEY DAD! WHAT'S UP? LET'S TALK."
MAYBE YOUR MOTHER WAS RIGHT.
WHINE

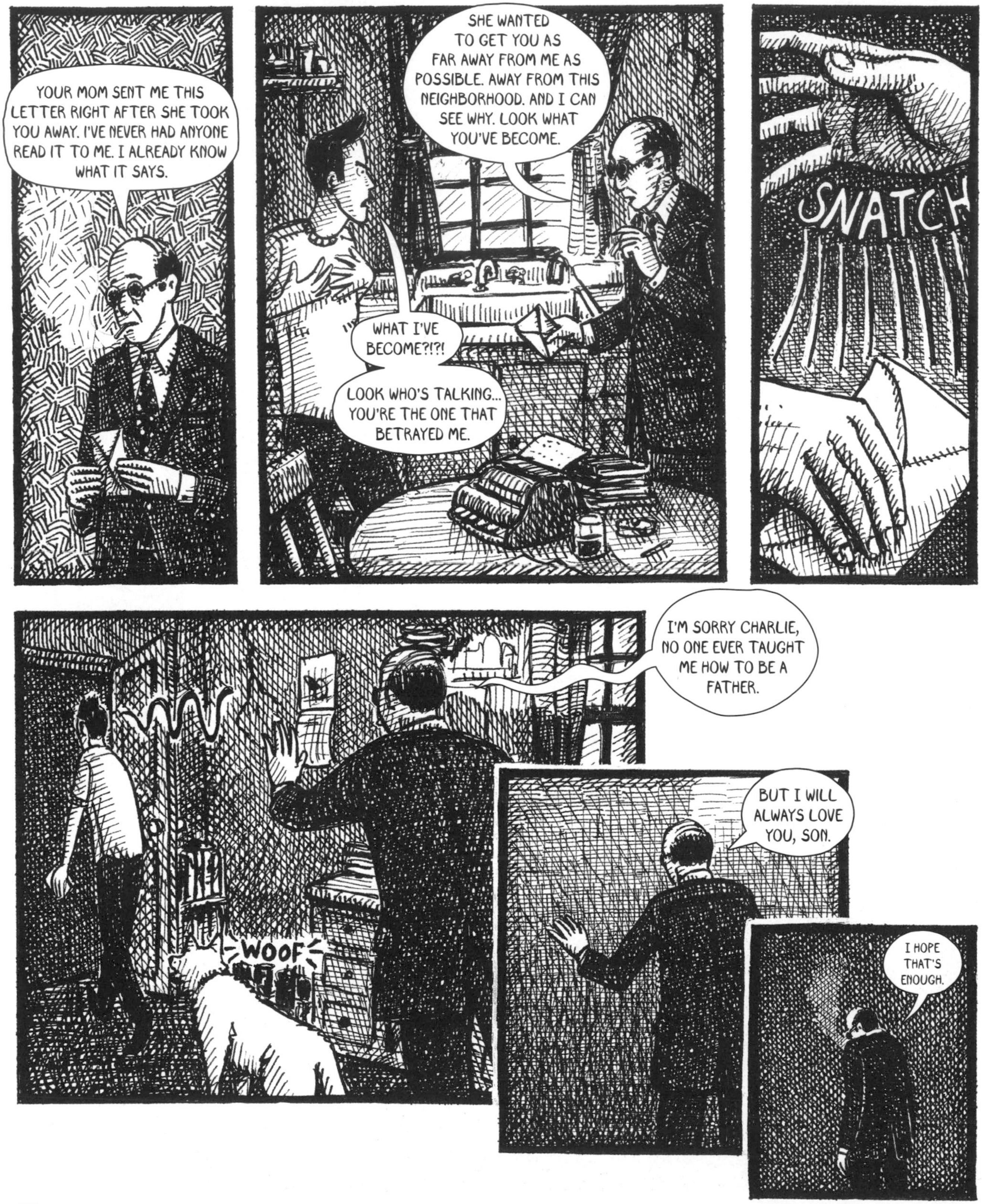
YOUR MOM SENT ME THIS LETTER RIGHT AFTER SHE TOOK YOU AWAY. I'VE NEVER HAD ANYONE READ IT TO ME. I ALREADY KNOW WHAT IT SAYS.
SHE WANTED TO GET YOU AS FAR AWAY FROM ME AS POSSIBLE. AWAY FROM THIS NEIGHBORHOOD. AND I CAN SEE WHY. LOOK WHAT YOU'VE BECOME.
WHAT I'VE BECOME?!?!
LOOK WHO'S TALKING... YOU'RE THE ONE THAT BETRAYED ME.
SNATCH
I'M SORRY CHARLIE, NO ONE EVER TAUGHT ME HOW TO BE A FATHER.
WOOF
BUT I WILL ALWAYS LOVE YOU, SON.
I HOPE THAT'S ENOUGH.

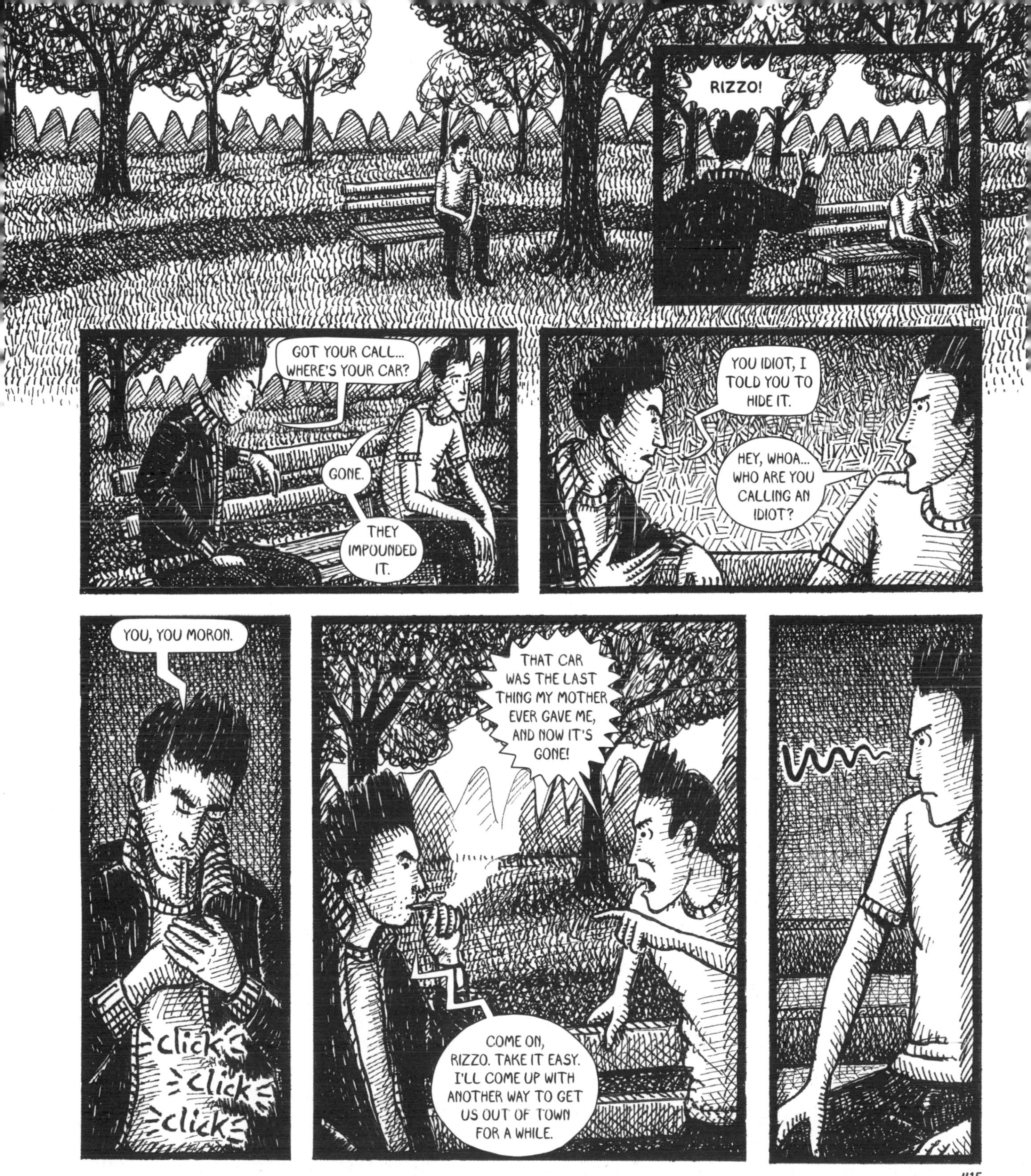
RIZZO!
GOT YOUR CALL... WHERE'S YOUR CAR?
GONE.
THEY IMPOUNDED IT.
YOU IDIOT, I TOLD YOU TO HIDE IT.
HEY, WHOA... WHO ARE YOU CALLING AN IDIOT?
YOU, YOU MORON.
click
click
click
THAT CAR WAS THE LAST THING MY MOTHER EVER GAVE ME, AND NOW IT'S GONE!
COME ON, RIZZO. TAKE IT EASY. I'LL COME UP WITH ANOTHER WAY TO GET US OUT OF TOWN FOR A WHILE.

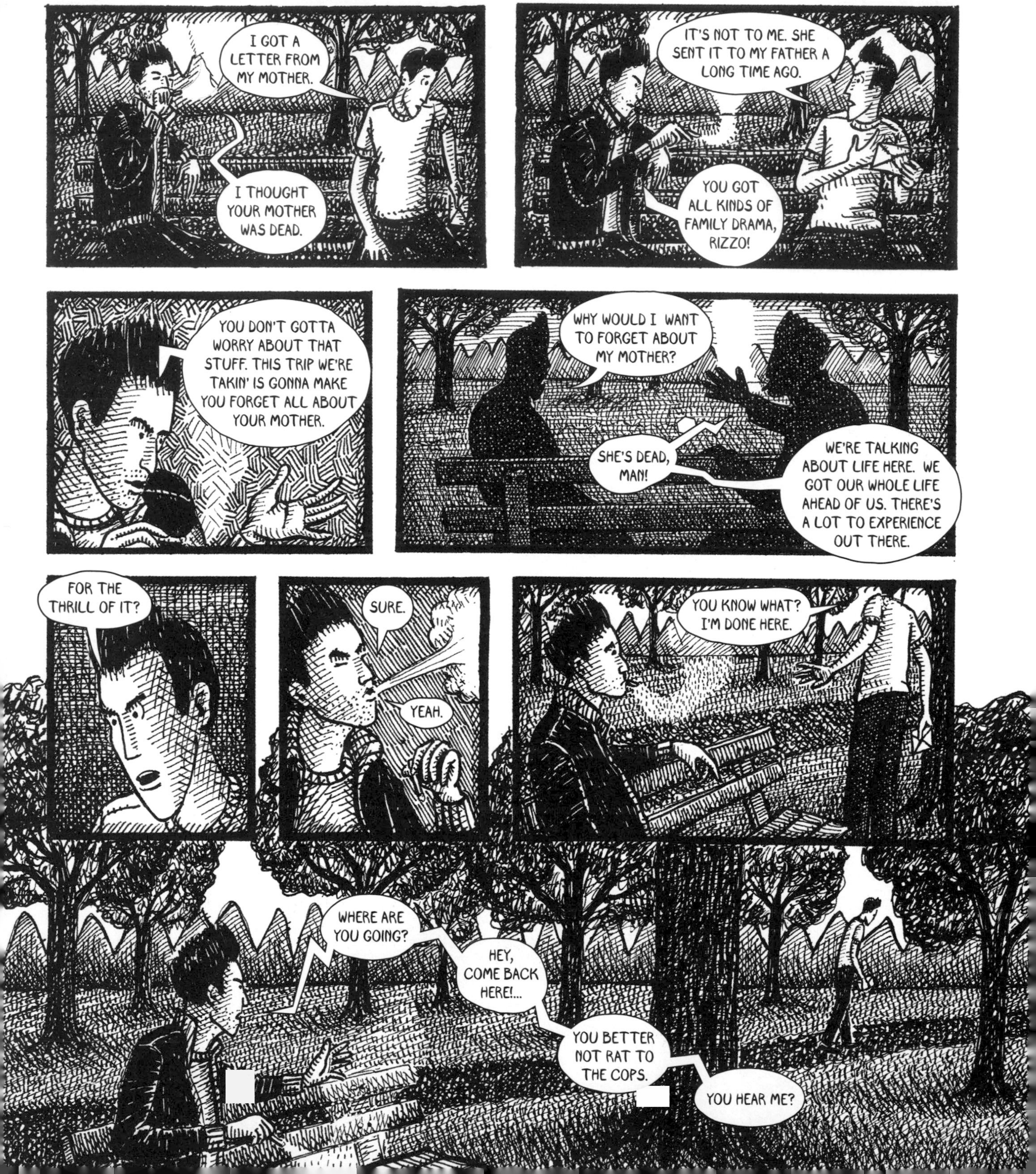
I GOT A LETTER FROM MY MOTHER.
I THOUGHT YOUR MOTHER WAS DEAD.
IT'S NOT TO ME. SHE SENT IT TO MY FATHER A LONG TIME AGO.
YOU GOT ALL KINDS OF FAMILY DRAMA, RIZZO!
YOU DON'T GOTTA WORRY ABOUT THAT STUFF. THIS TRIP WE'RE TAKIN' IS GONNA MAKE YOU FORGET ALL ABOUT YOUR MOTHER.
WHY WOULD I WANT TO FORGET ABOUT MY MOTHER?
SHE'S DEAD, MAN!
WE'RE TALKING ABOUT LIFE HERE. WE GOT OUR WHOLE LIFE AHEAD OF US. THERE'S A LOT TO EXPERIENCE OUT THERE.
FOR THE THRILL OF IT?
SURE.
YEAH.
YOU KNOW WHAT? I'M DONE HERE.
WHERE ARE YOU GOING?
HEY, COME BACK HERE!...
YOU BETTER NOT RAT TO THE COPS.
YOU HEAR ME?

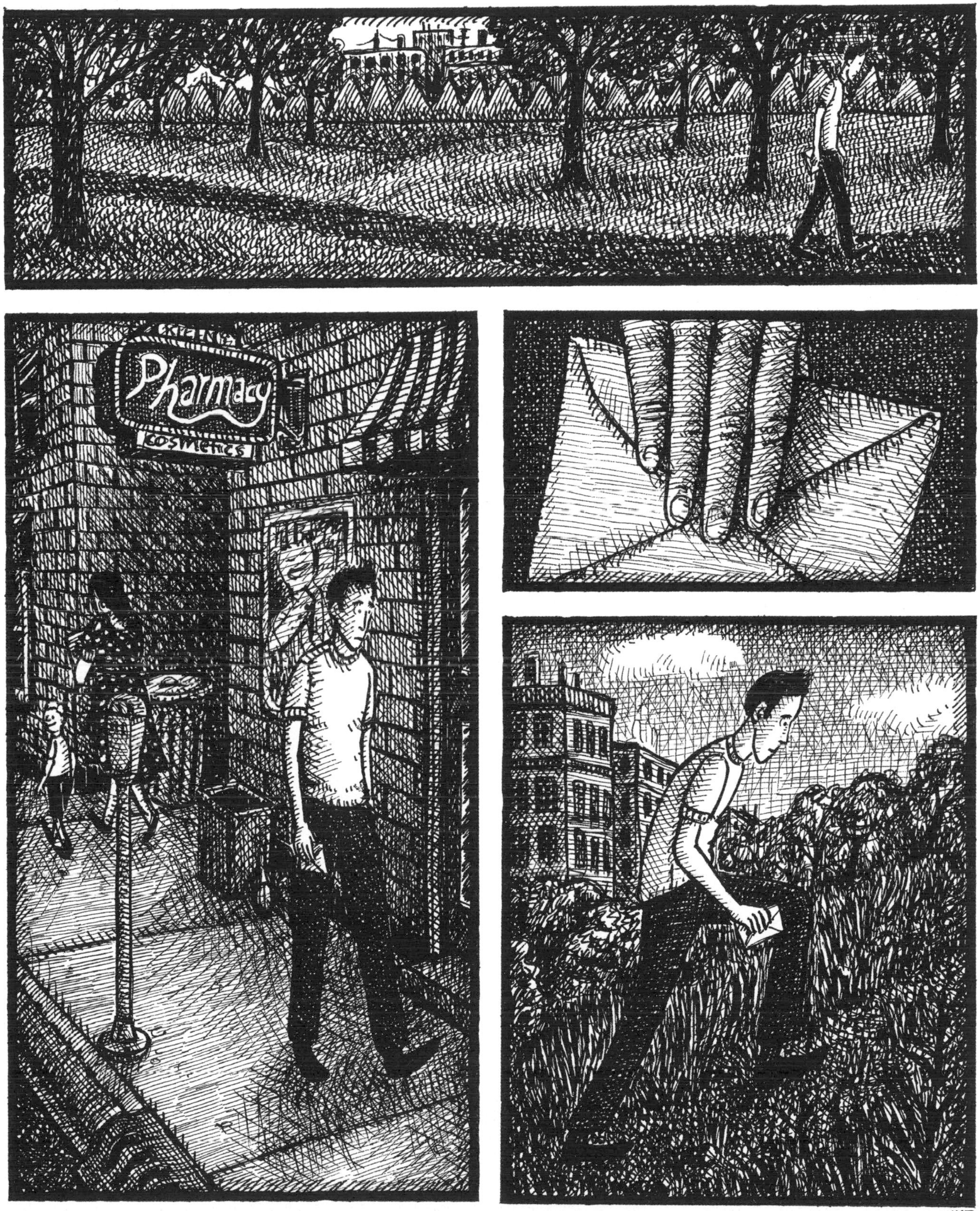
Pharmacy
cosmetics

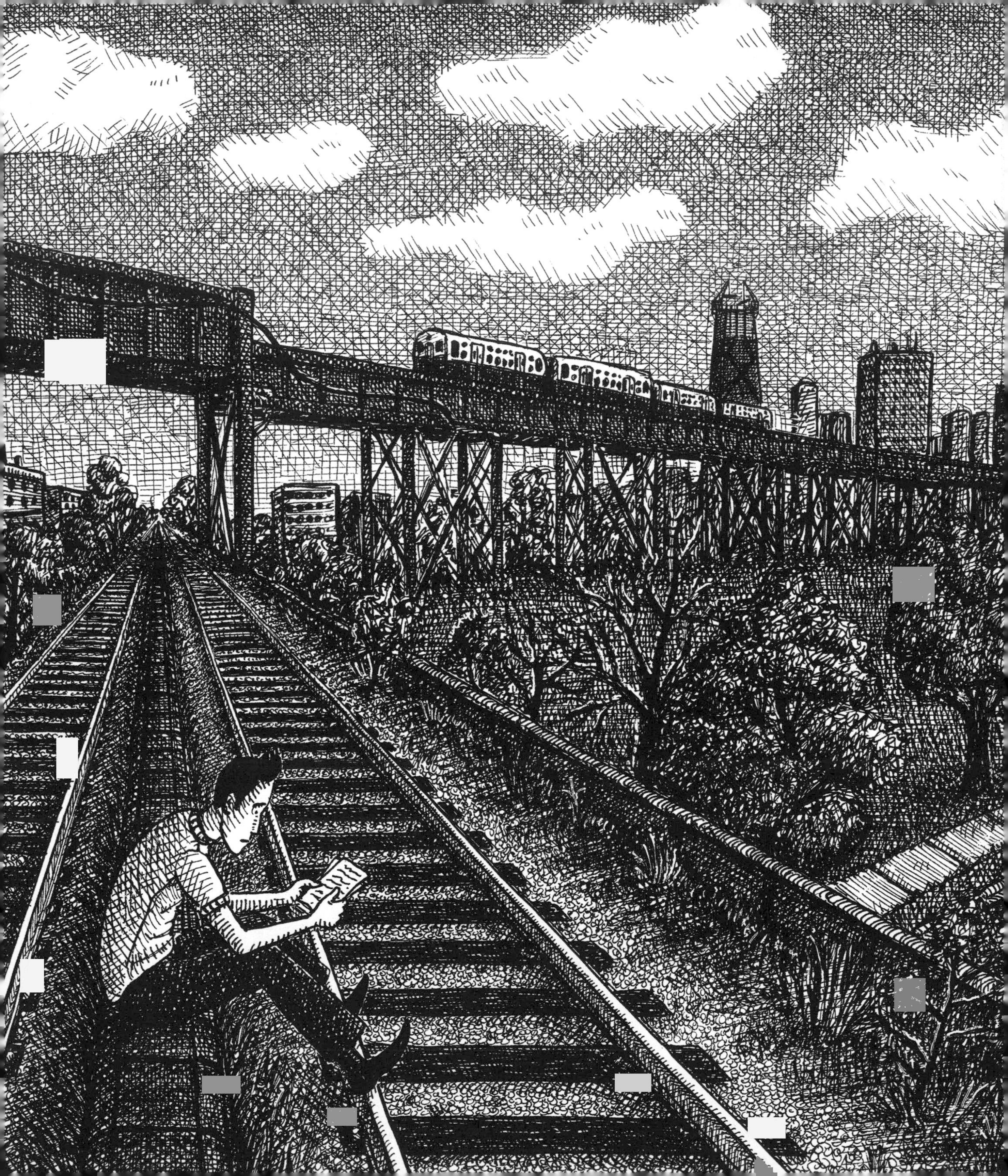

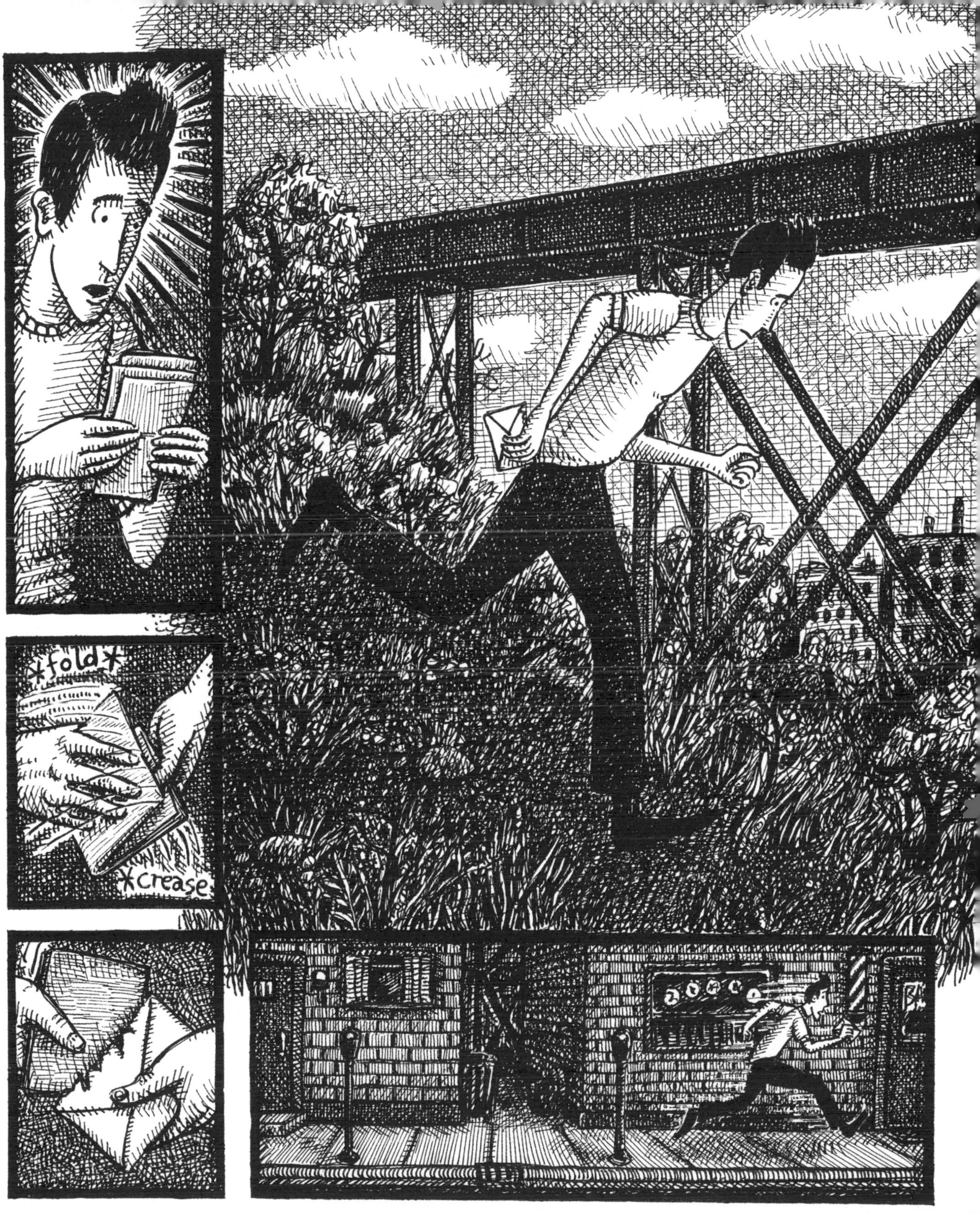
fold
*crease

DAD! LISTEN TO THIS!

RIGHT HERE IN THE LETTER, YOU NEED TO HEAR...

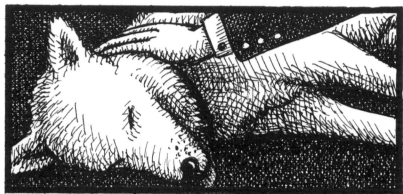

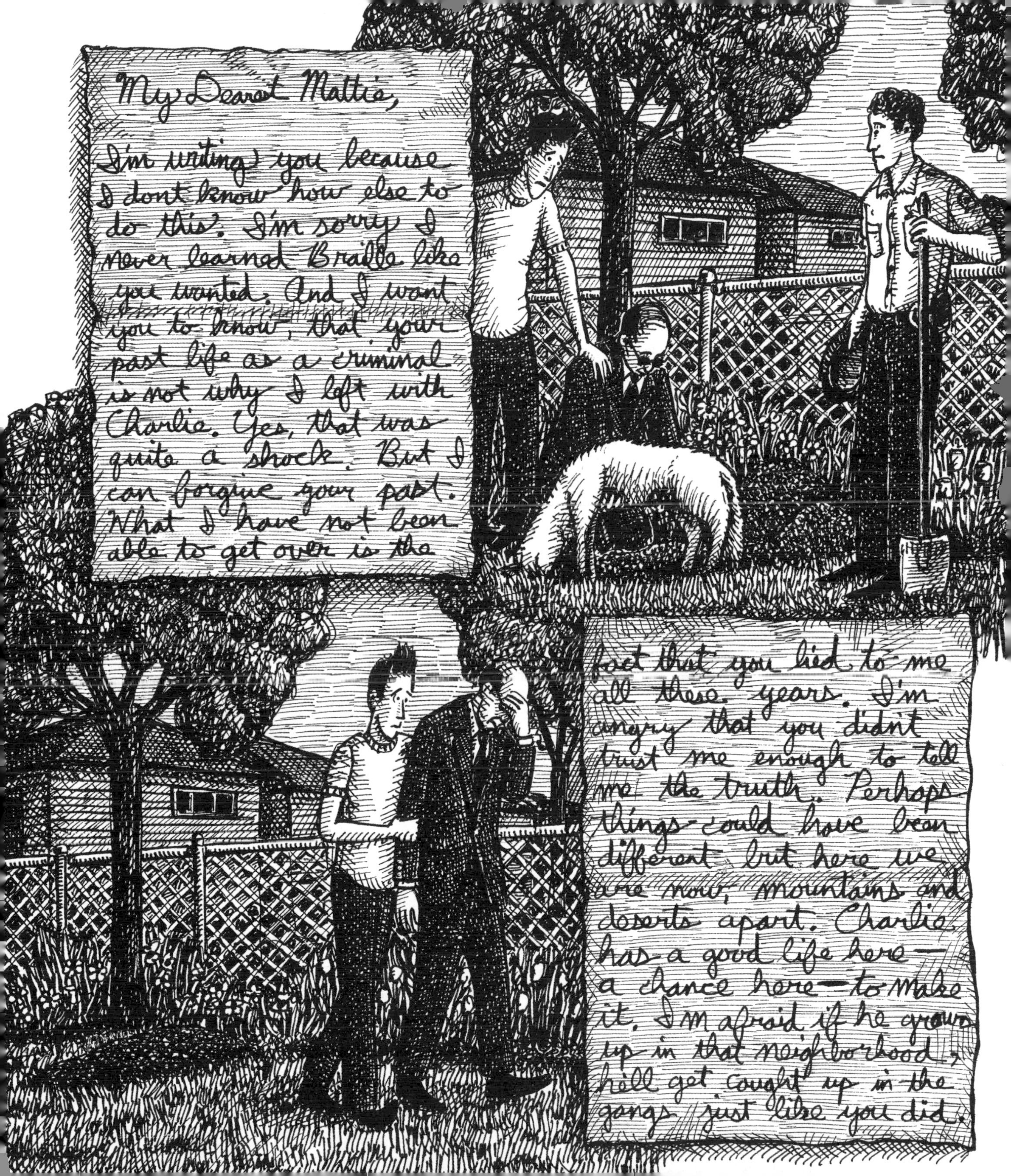
My Dearest Mattie,
I'm writing you because I dont know how else to do this. I'm sorry I never learned Braille like you wanted. And I want you to know, that your past life as a criminal is not why I left with Charlie. Yes, that was quite a shock. But I can forgive your past. What I have not been able to get over is the
fact that you lied to me all these years. I'm angry that you didn't trust me enough to tell me the truth. Perhaps things could have been different but here we are now, mountains and deserts apart. Charlie has a good life here — a chance here — to make it. I'm afraid if he grows up in that neighborhood, he'll get caught up in the gangs just like you did.

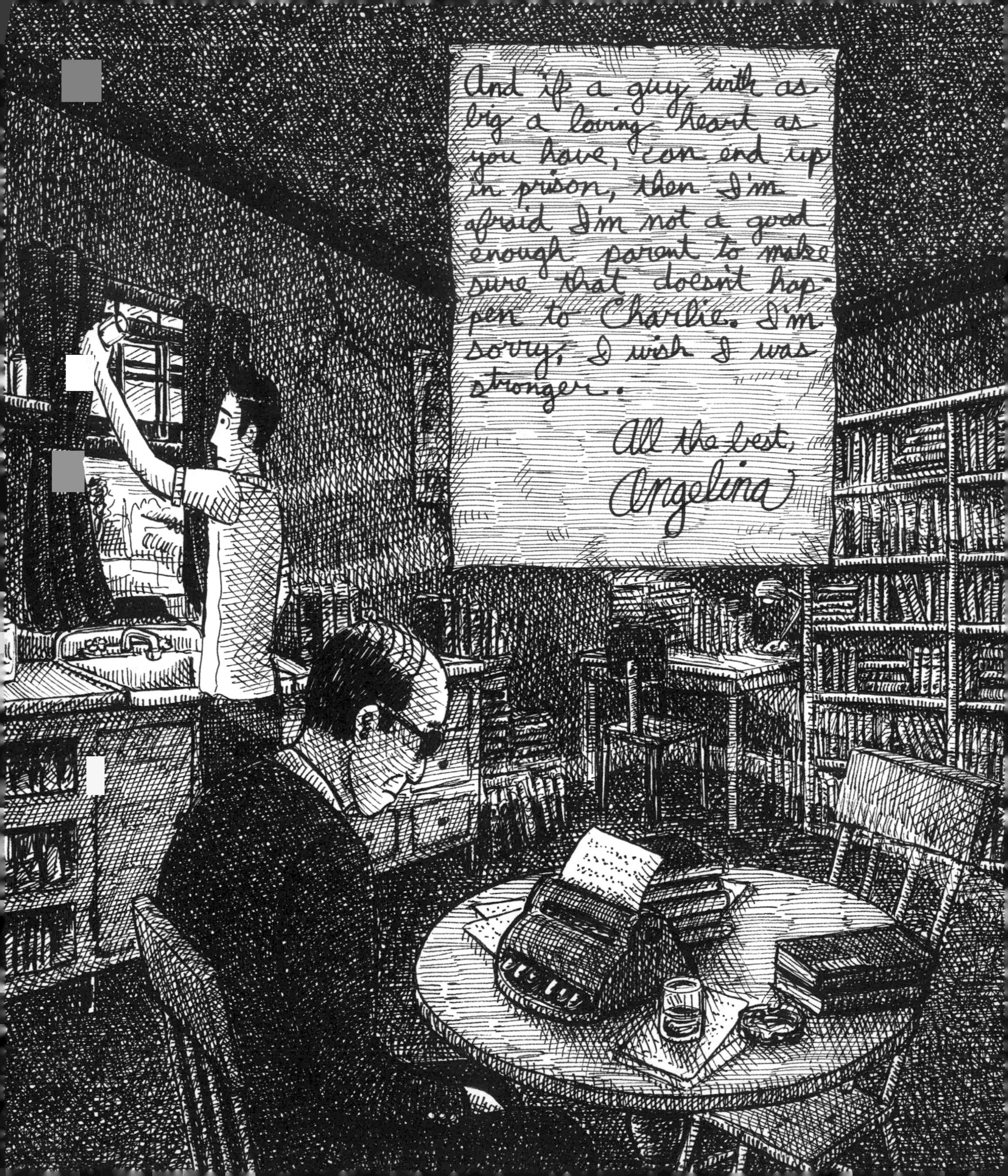
And if a guy with as big a loving heart as you have, can end up in prison, then I'm afraid I'm not a good enough parent to make sure that doesn't happen to Charlie. I'm sorry, I wish I was stronger.
All the best,
Angelina

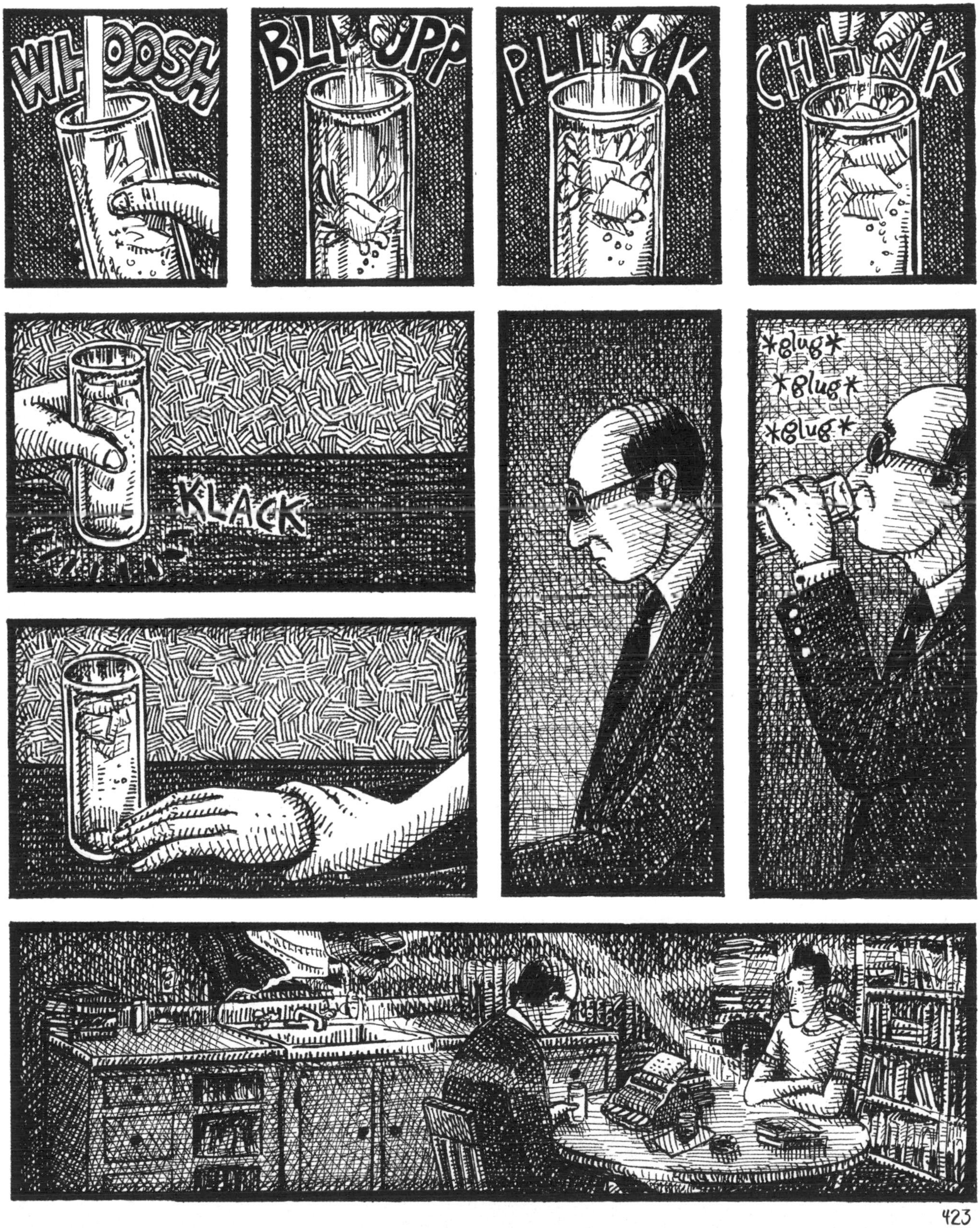
WHOOSH
BLLUPP
PLINK
CHHNK
KLACK
glug
glug
glug

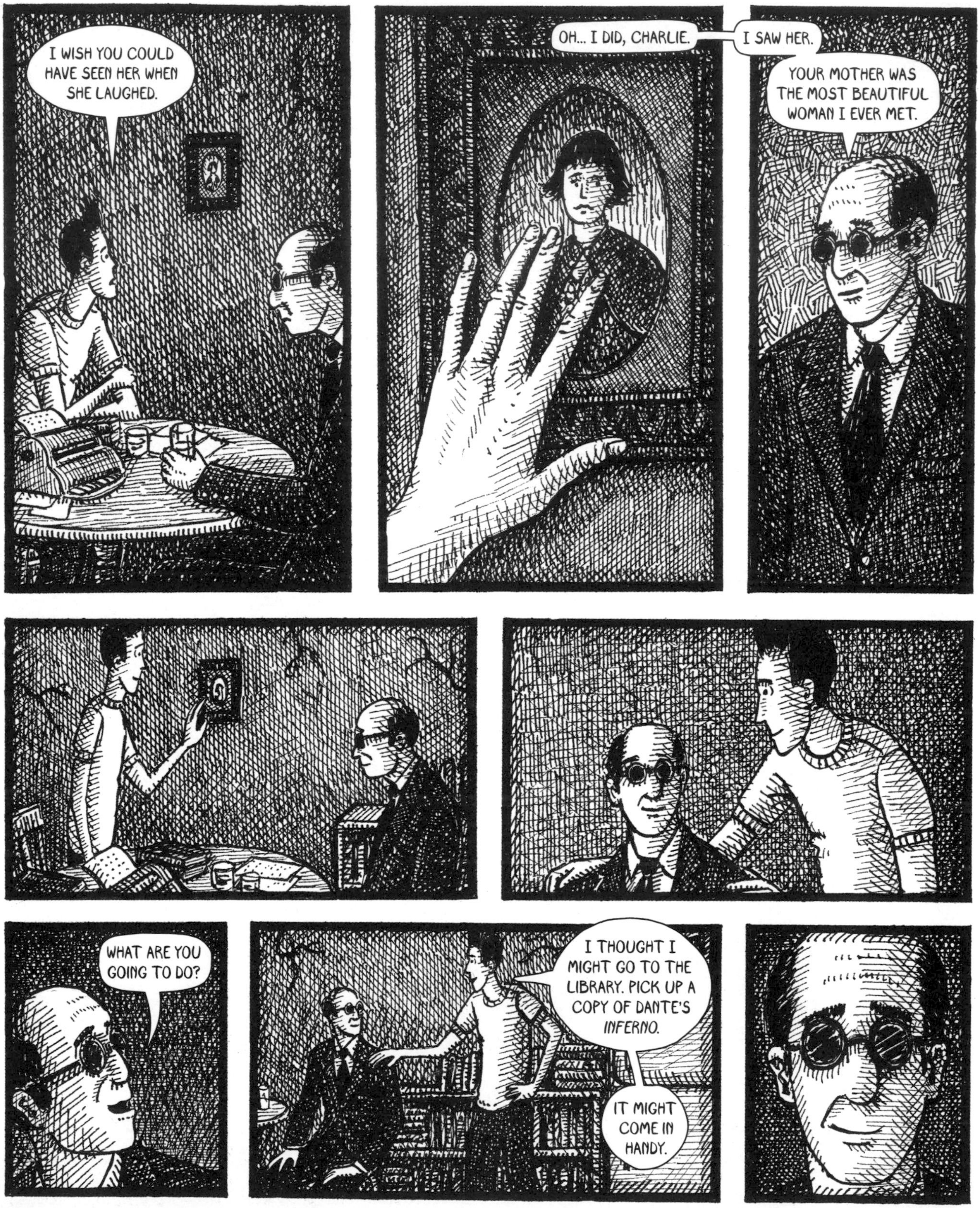
I WISH YOU COULD HAVE SEEN HER WHEN SHE LAUGHED.
OH... I DID, CHARLIE.
I SAW HER.
YOUR MOTHER WAS THE MOST BEAUTIFUL WOMAN I EVER MET.
WHAT ARE YOU GOING TO DO?
I THOUGHT I MIGHT GO TO THE LIBRARY. PICK UP A COPY OF DANTE'S *INFERNO*.
IT MIGHT COME IN HANDY.

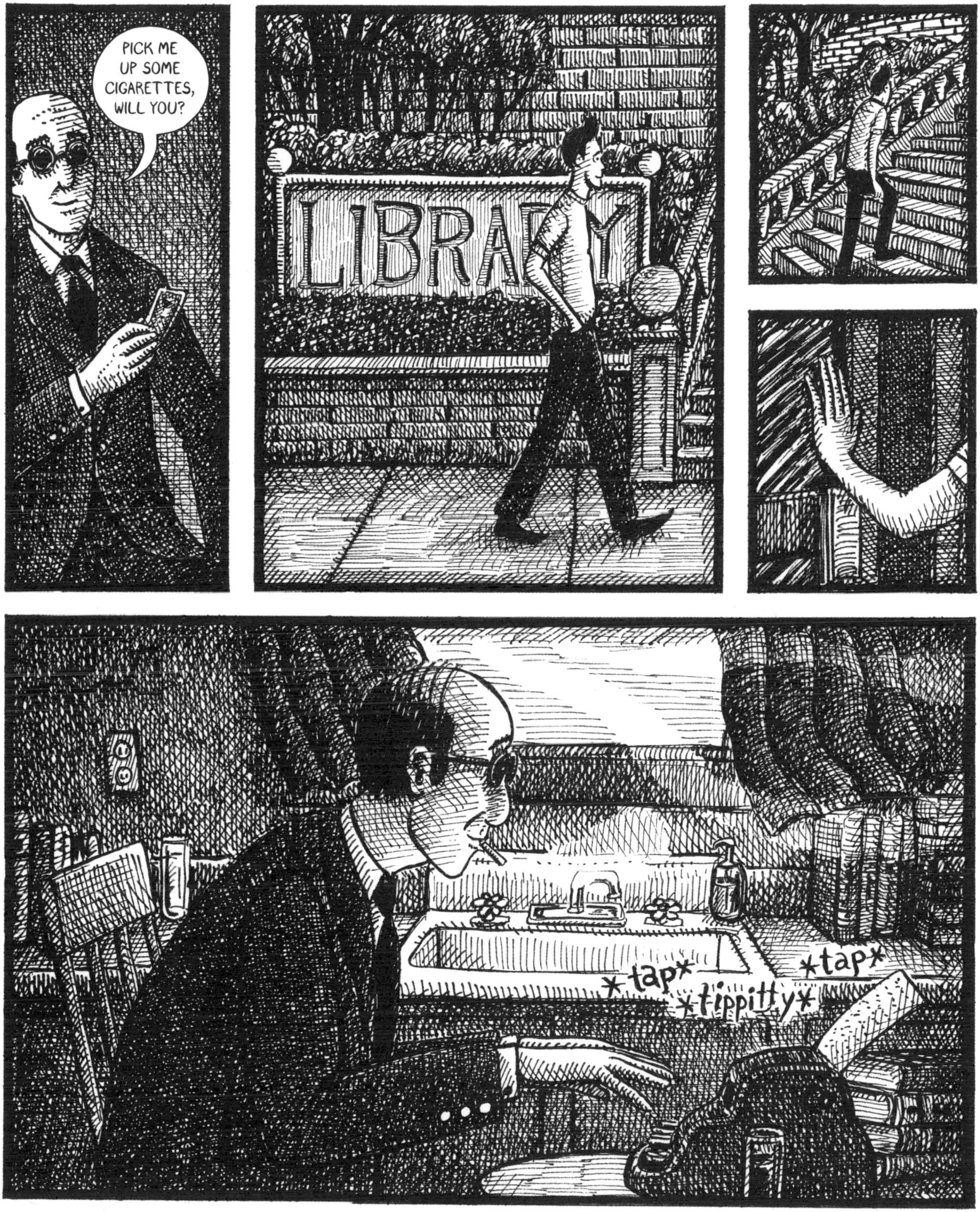
PICK ME UP SOME CIGARETTES, WILL YOU?
LIBRARY
tap
tippitty
tap

XVII

PURGATORIO

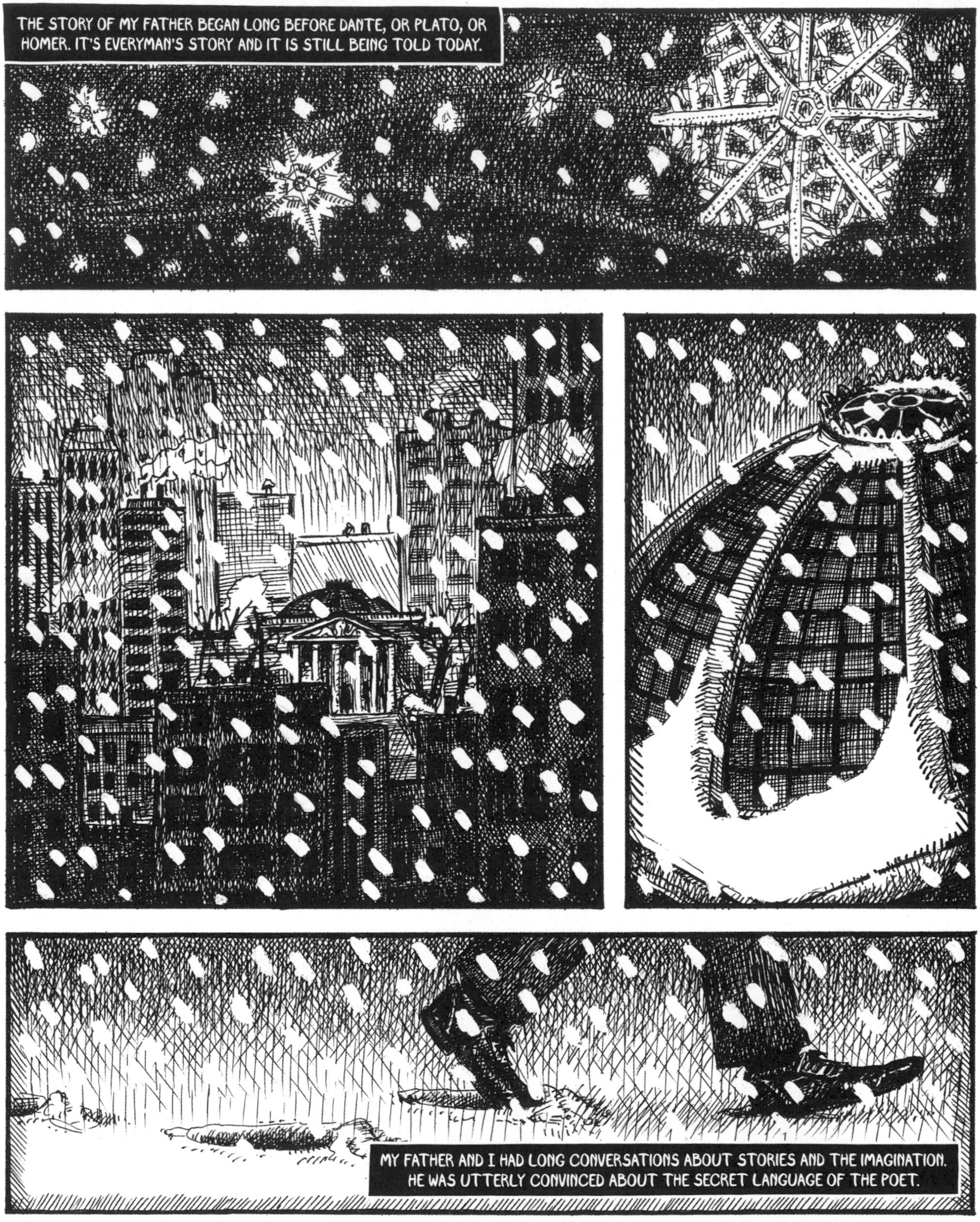
THE STORY OF MY FATHER BEGAN LONG BEFORE DANTE, OR PLATO, OR HOMER. IT'S EVERYMAN'S STORY AND IT IS STILL BEING TOLD TODAY.
MY FATHER AND I HAD LONG CONVERSATIONS ABOUT STORIES AND THE IMAGINATION. HE WAS UTTERLY CONVINCED ABOUT THE SECRET LANGUAGE OF THE POET.

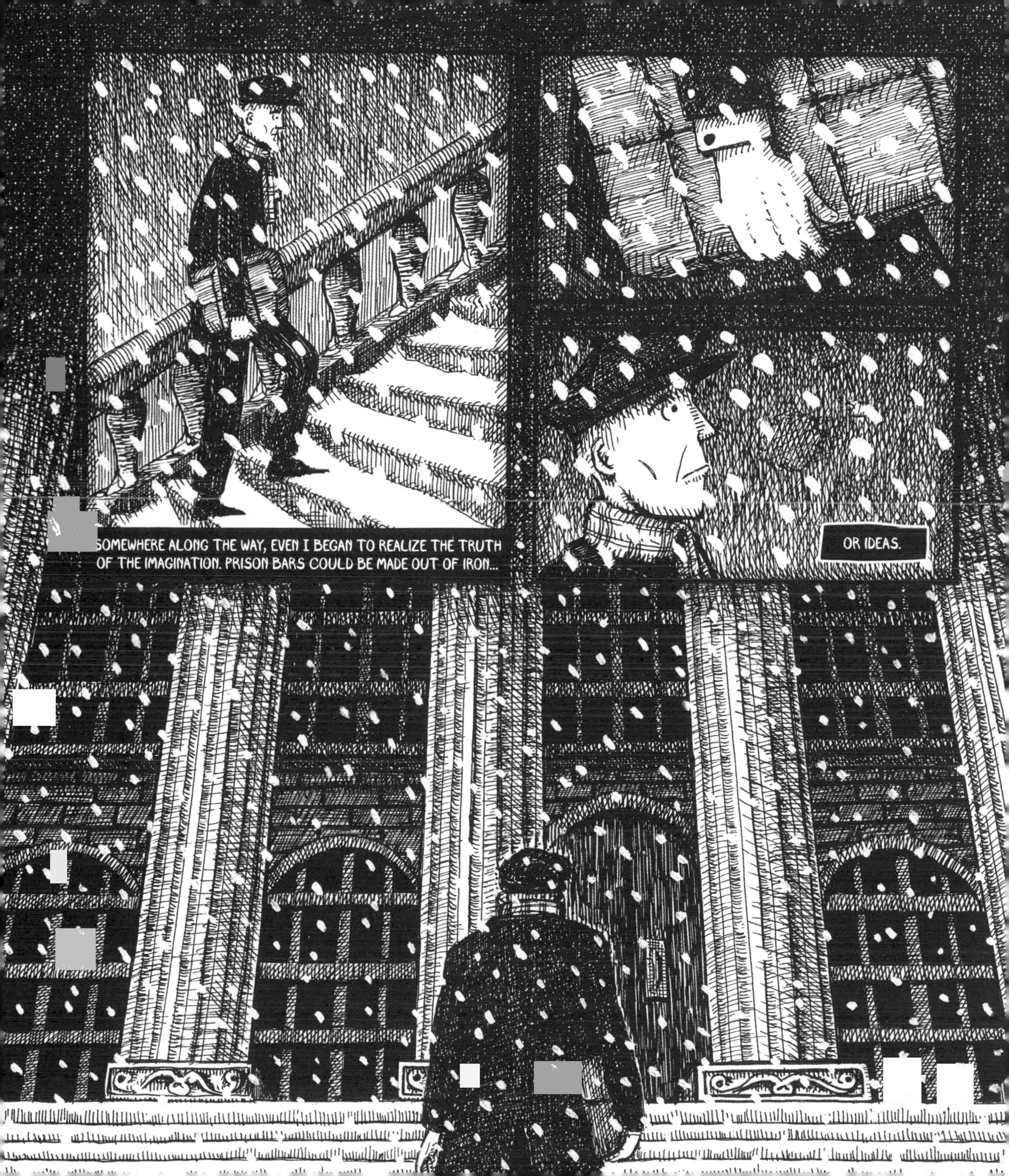
SOMEWHERE ALONG THE WAY, EVEN I BEGAN TO REALIZE THE TRUTH OF THE IMAGINATION. PRISON BARS COULD BE MADE OUT OF IRON...
OR IDEAS.

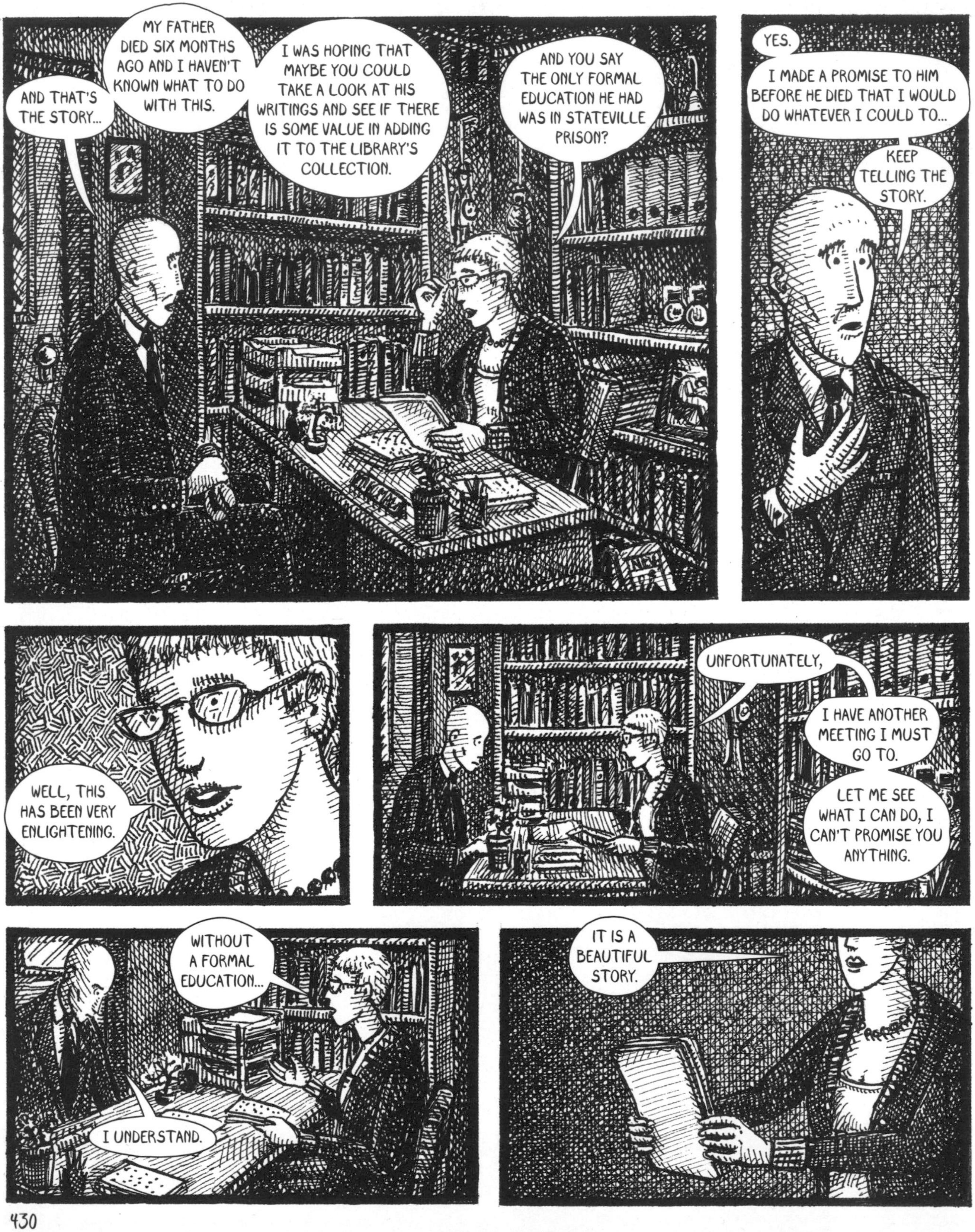
AND THAT'S THE STORY...
MY FATHER DIED SIX MONTHS AGO AND I HAVEN'T KNOWN WHAT TO DO WITH THIS.
I WAS HOPING THAT MAYBE YOU COULD TAKE A LOOK AT HIS WRITINGS AND SEE IF THERE IS SOME VALUE IN ADDING IT TO THE LIBRARY'S COLLECTION.
AND YOU SAY THE ONLY FORMAL EDUCATION HE HAD WAS IN STATEVILLE PRISON?
YES.
I MADE A PROMISE TO HIM BEFORE HE DIED THAT I WOULD DO WHATEVER I COULD TO...
KEEP TELLING THE STORY.
WELL, THIS HAS BEEN VERY ENLIGHTENING.
UNFORTUNATELY,
I HAVE ANOTHER MEETING I MUST GO TO.
LET ME SEE WHAT I CAN DO, I CAN'T PROMISE YOU ANYTHING.
WITHOUT A FORMAL EDUCATION...
I UNDERSTAND.
IT IS A BEAUTIFUL STORY.

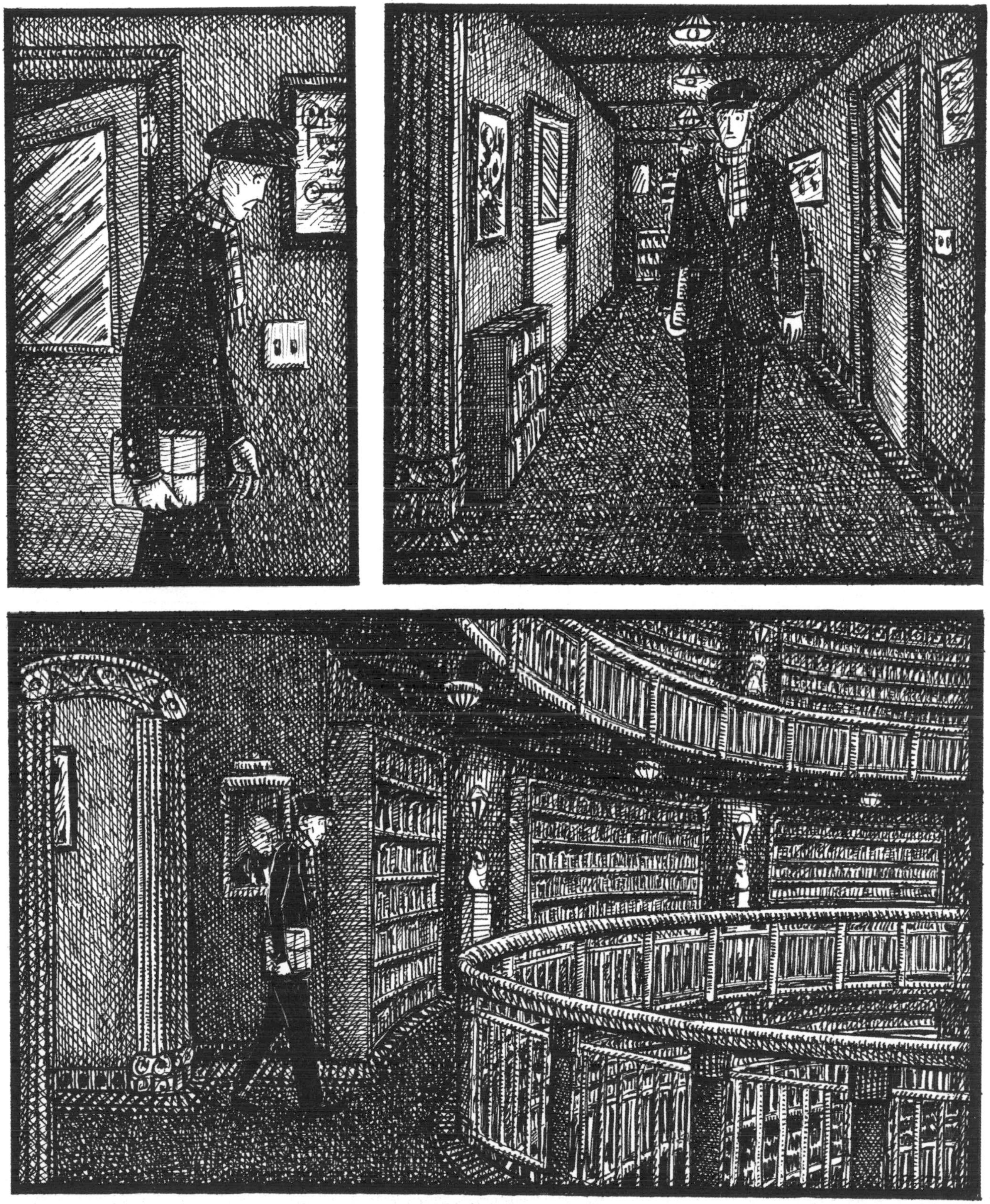

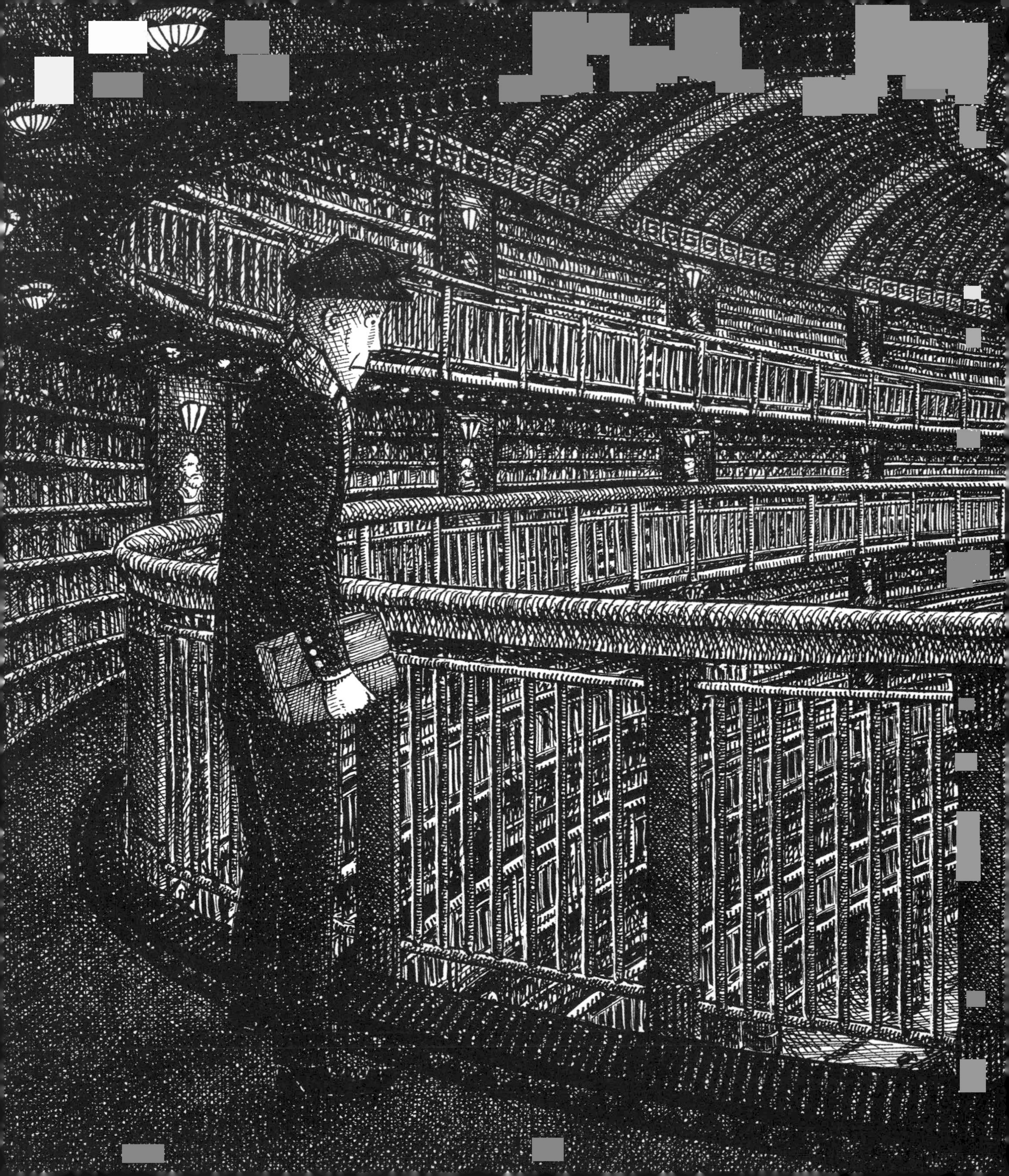

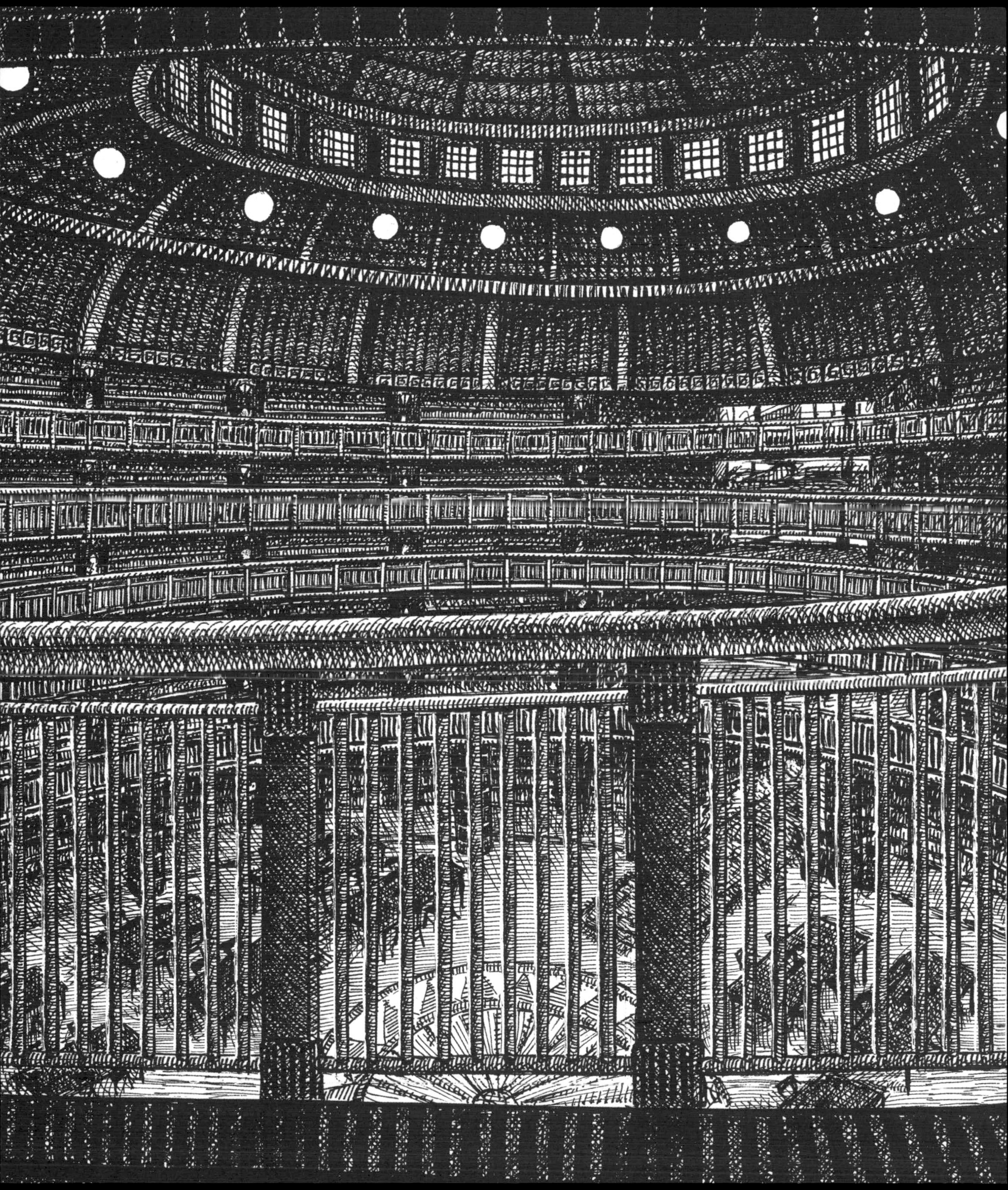

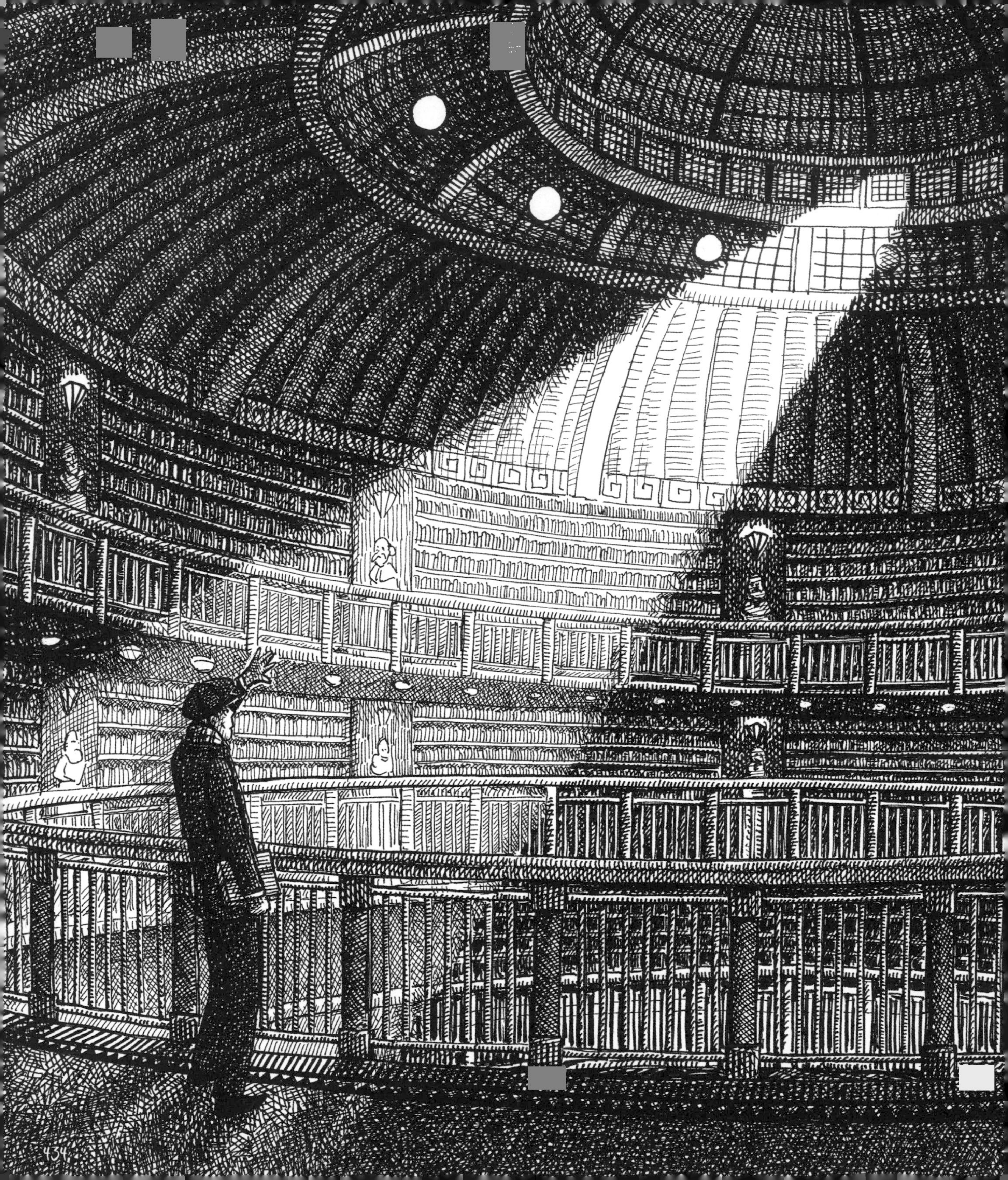

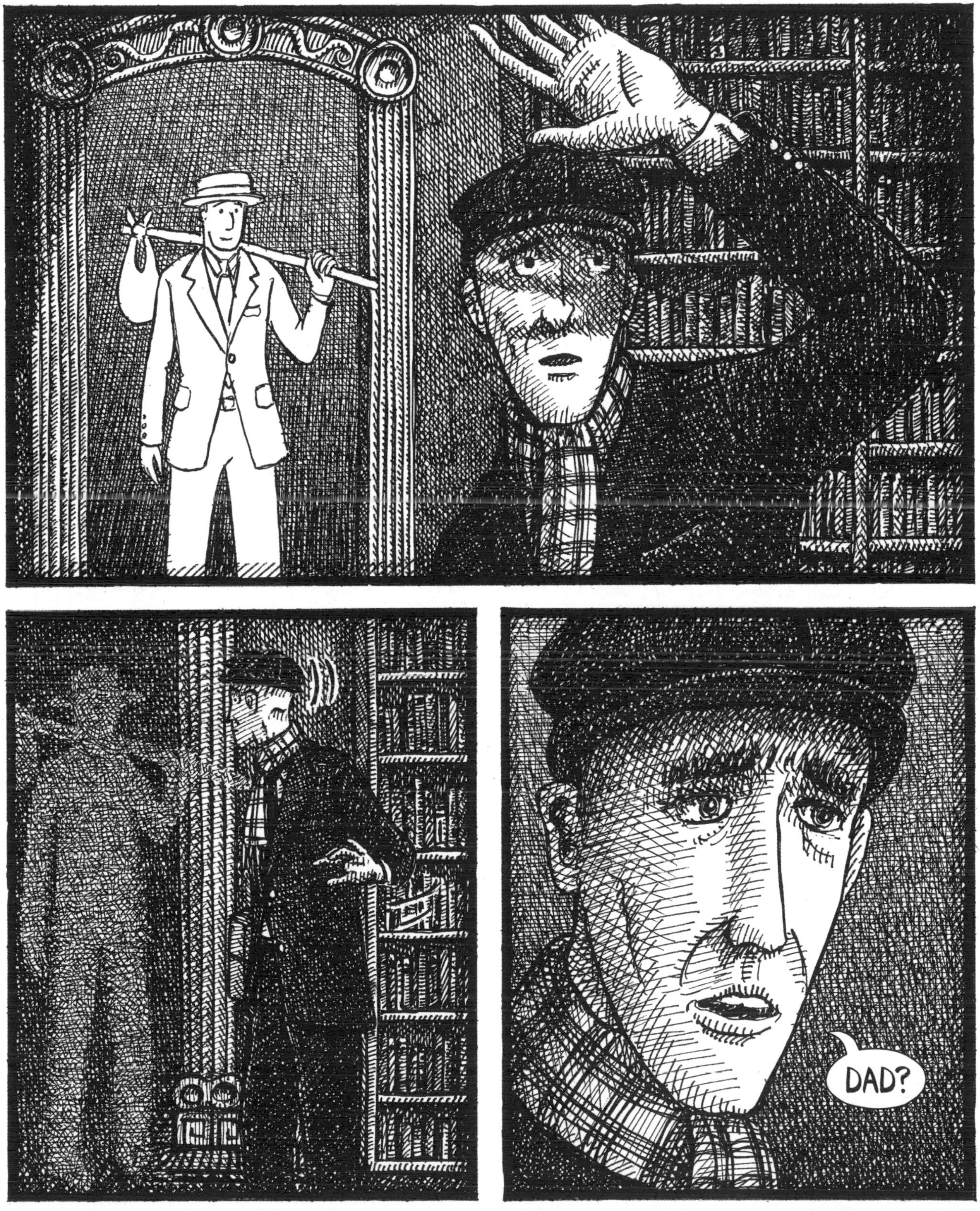
DAD?

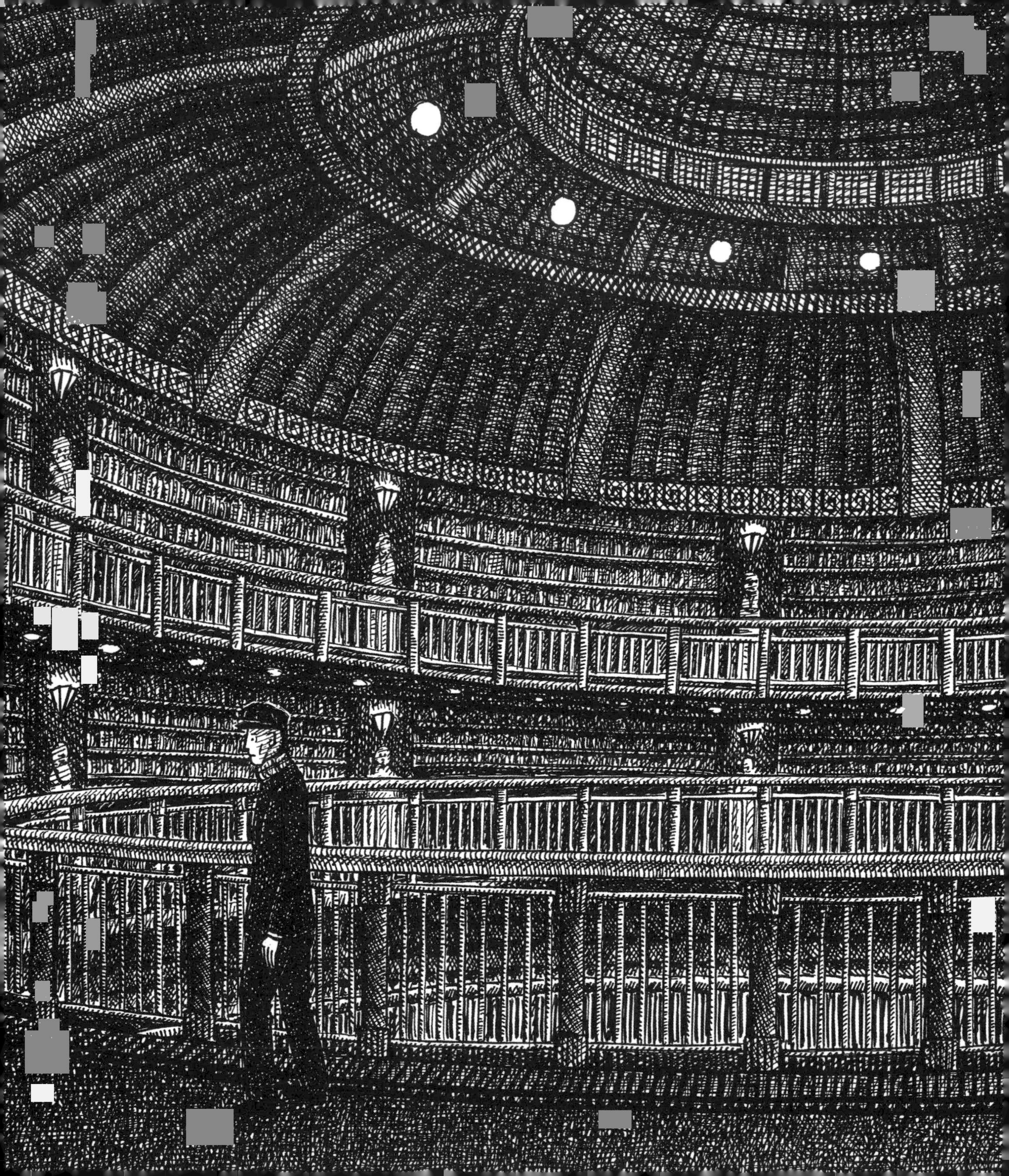

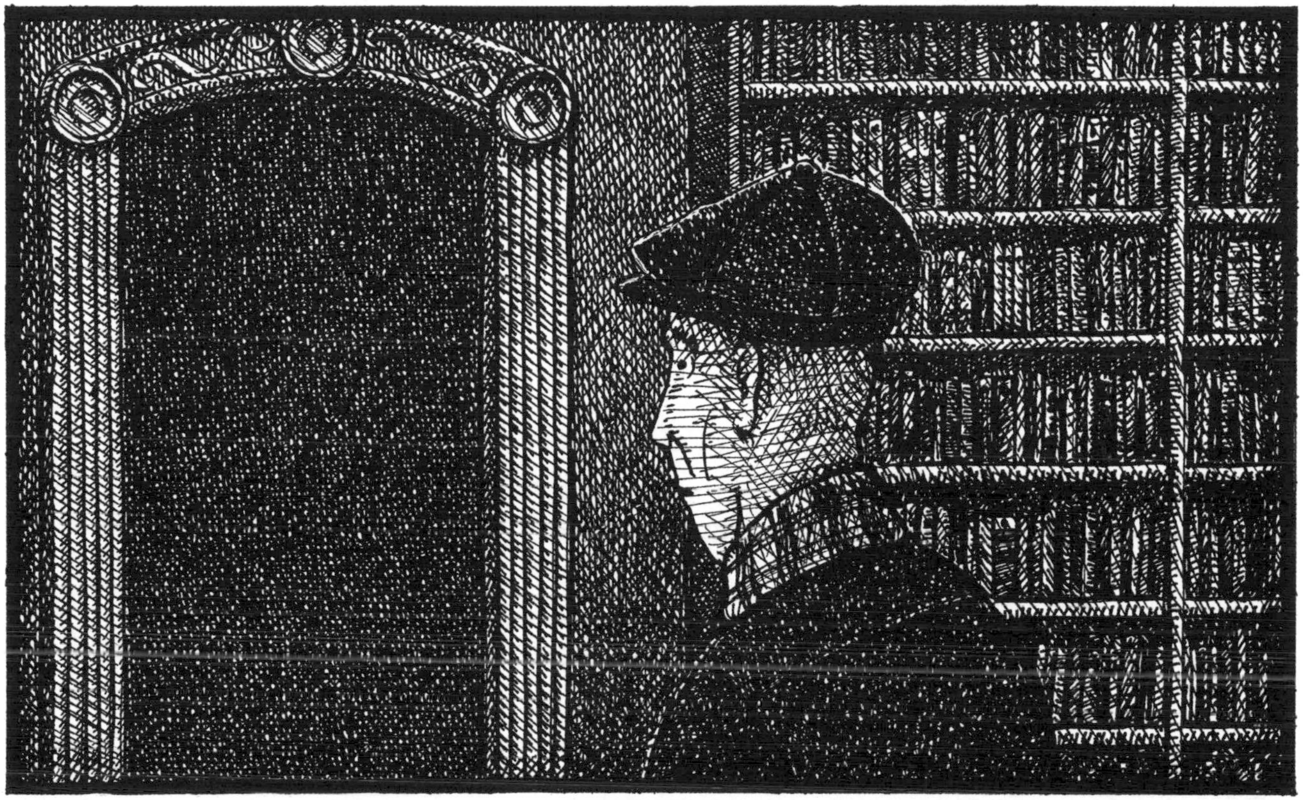

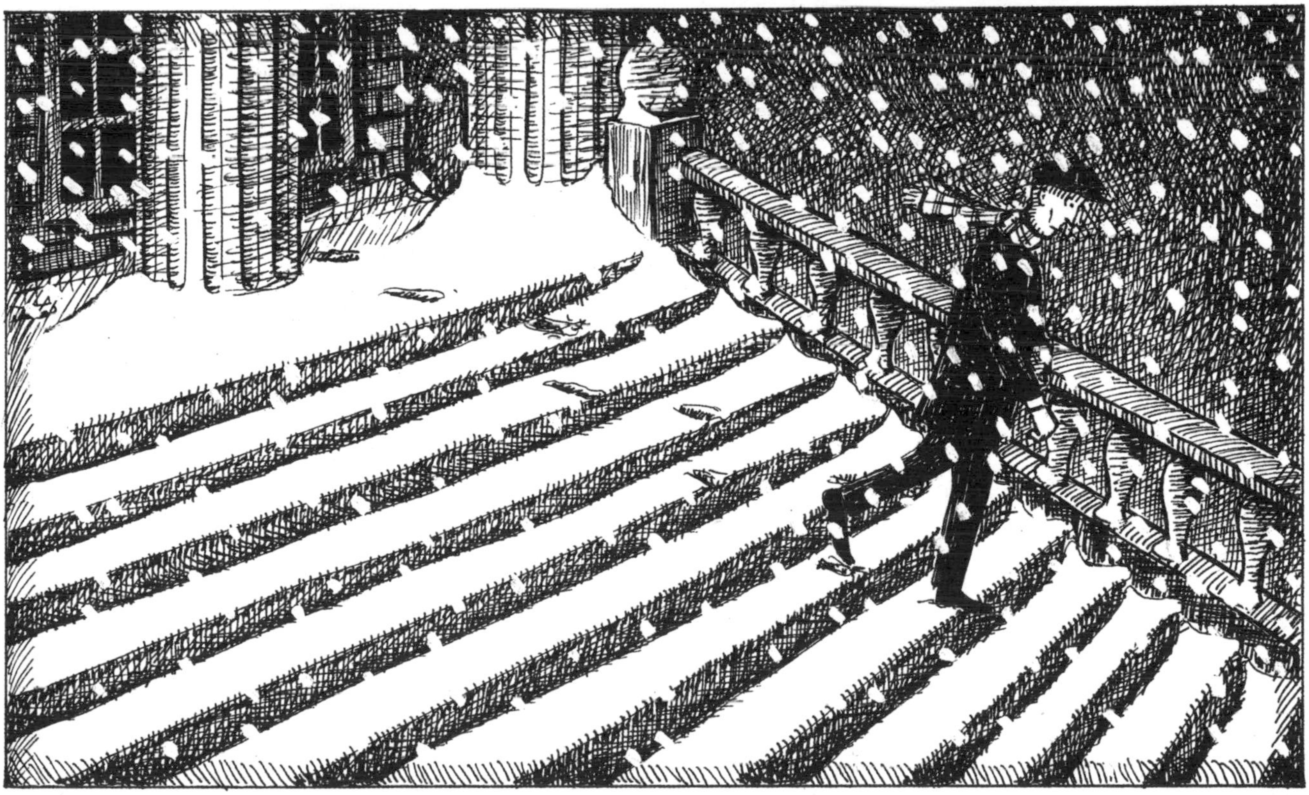

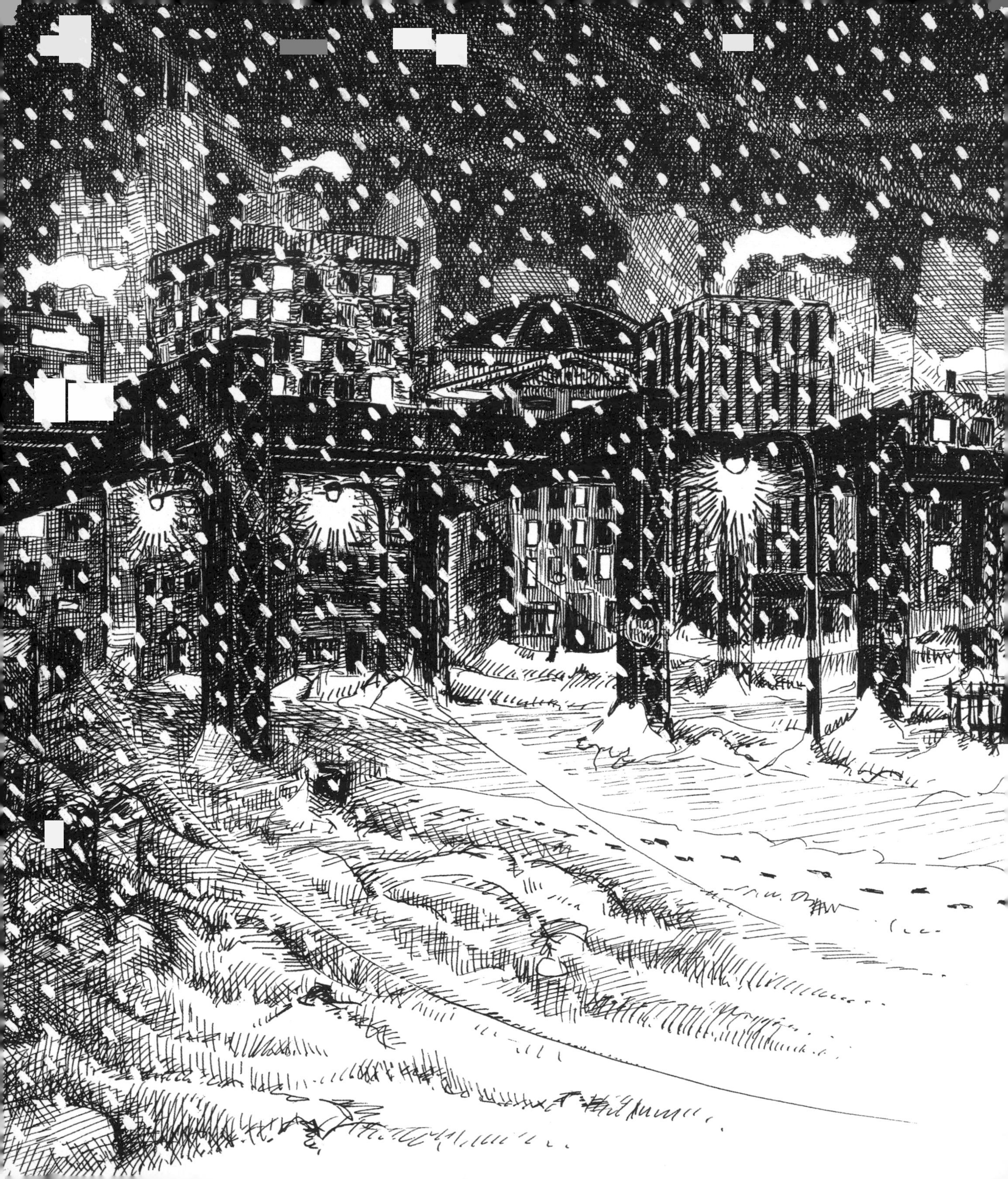

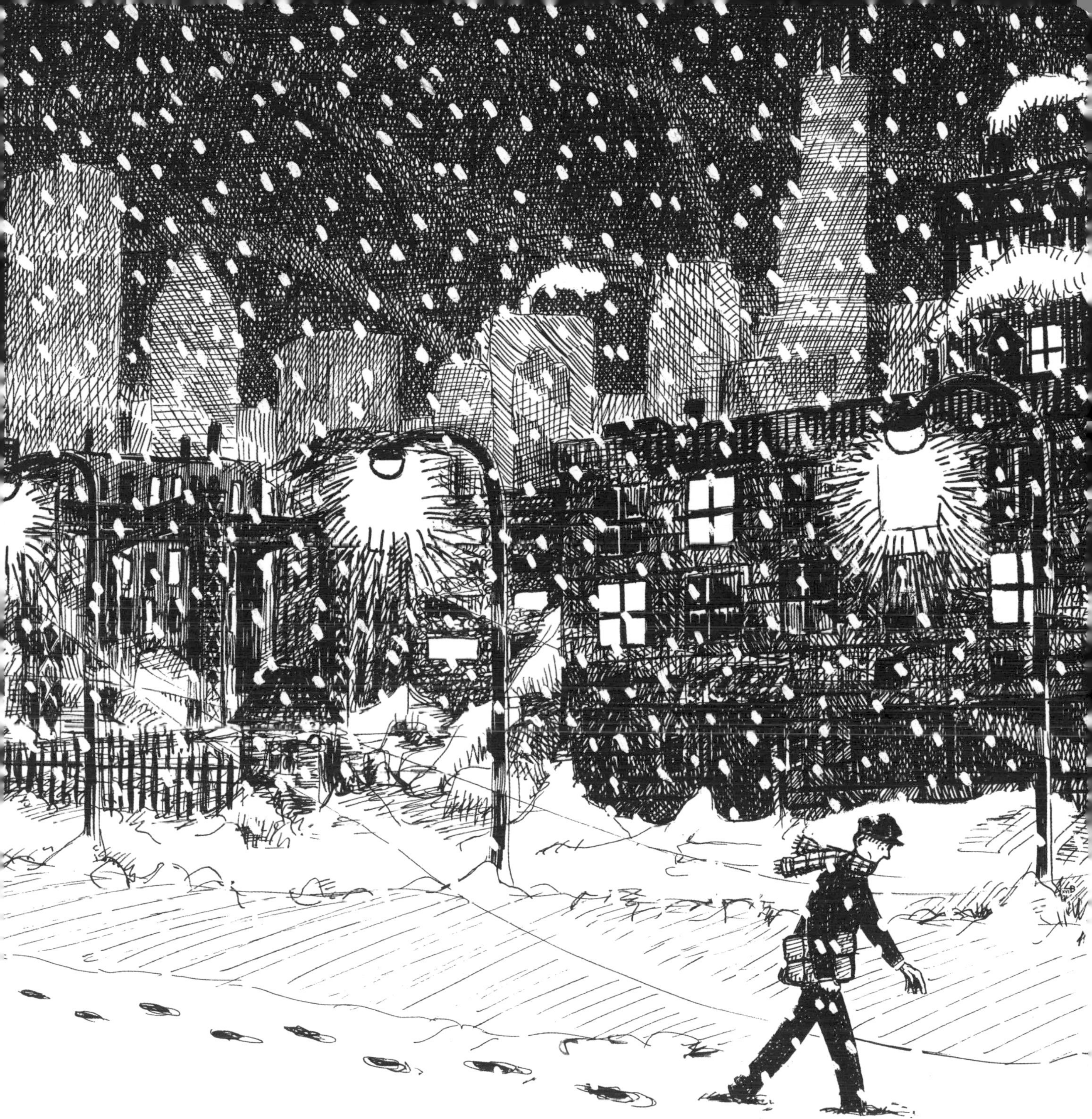

XVIII ⠿

PARADISO

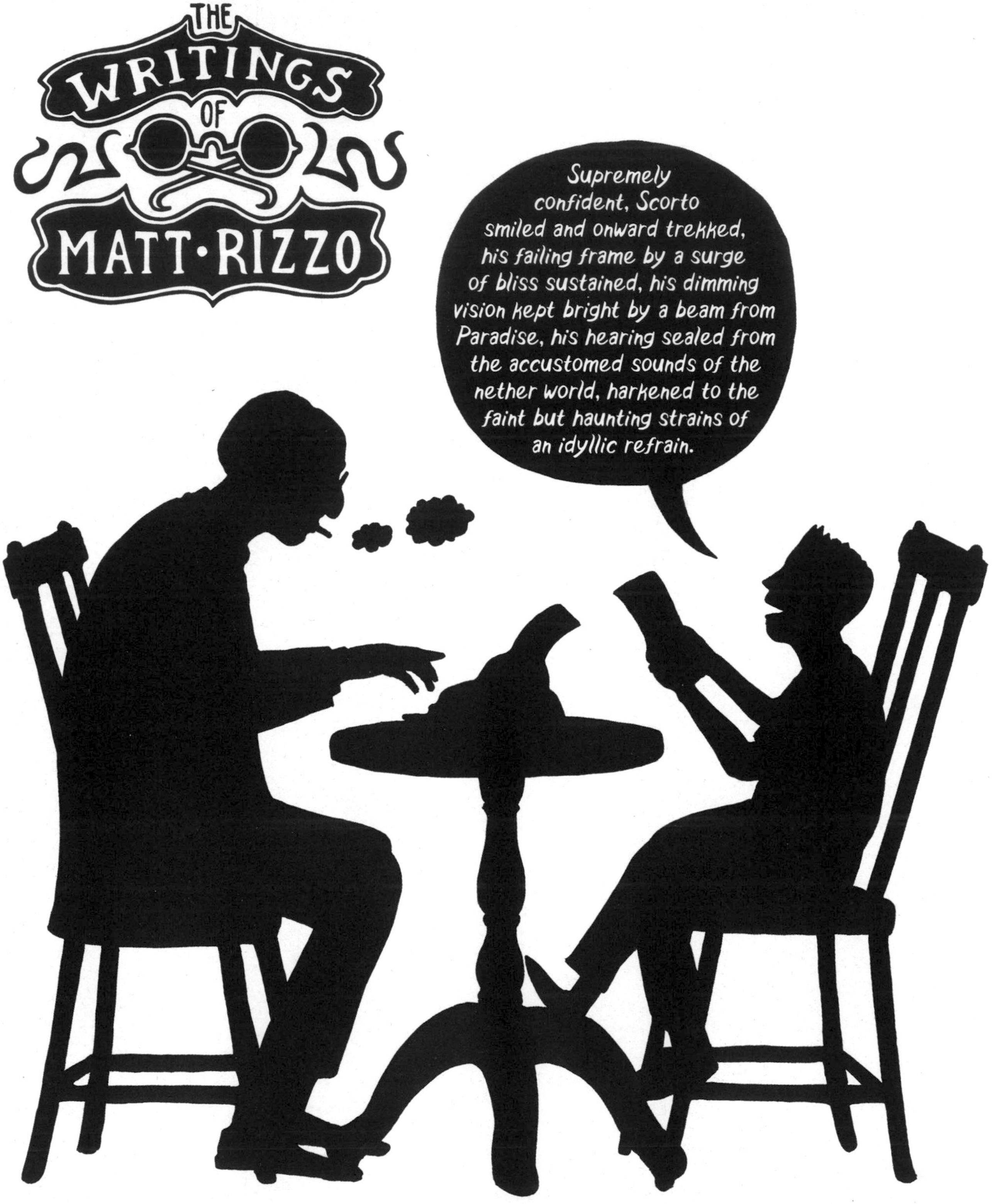
THE WRITINGS OF MATT·RIZZO
Supremely confident, Scorto smiled and onward trekked, his failing frame by a surge of bliss sustained, his dimming vision kept bright by a beam from Paradise, his hearing sealed from the accustomed sounds of the nether world, harkened to the faint but haunting strains of an idyllic refrain.

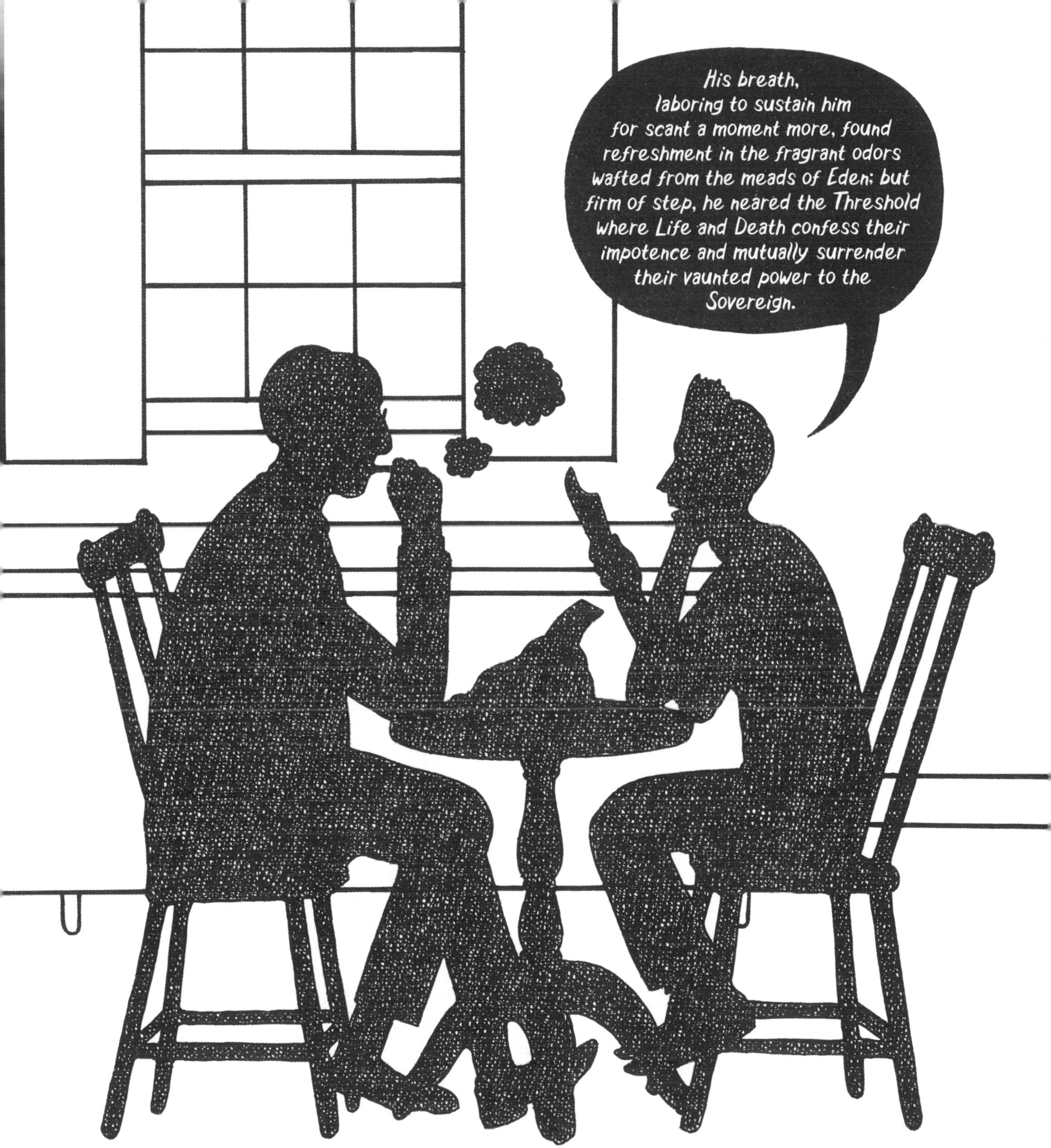
His breath, laboring to sustain him for scant a moment more, found refreshment in the fragrant odors wafted from the meads of Eden; but firm of step, he neared the Threshold where Life and Death confess their impotence and mutually surrender their vaunted power to the Sovereign.

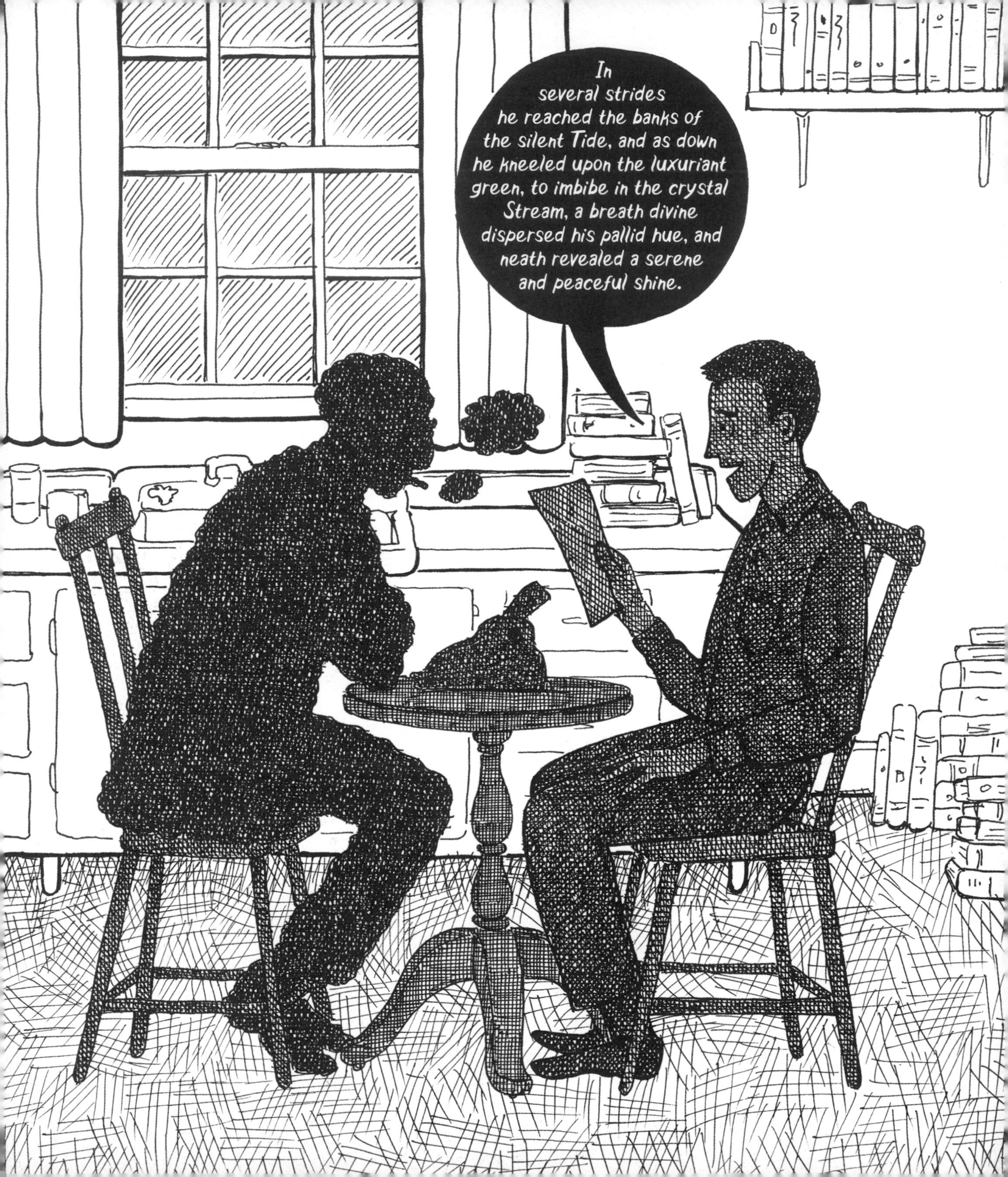
In several strides he reached the banks of the silent Tide, and as down he kneeled upon the luxuriant green, to imbibe in the crystal Stream, a breath divine dispersed his pallid hue, and neath revealed a serene and peaceful shine.

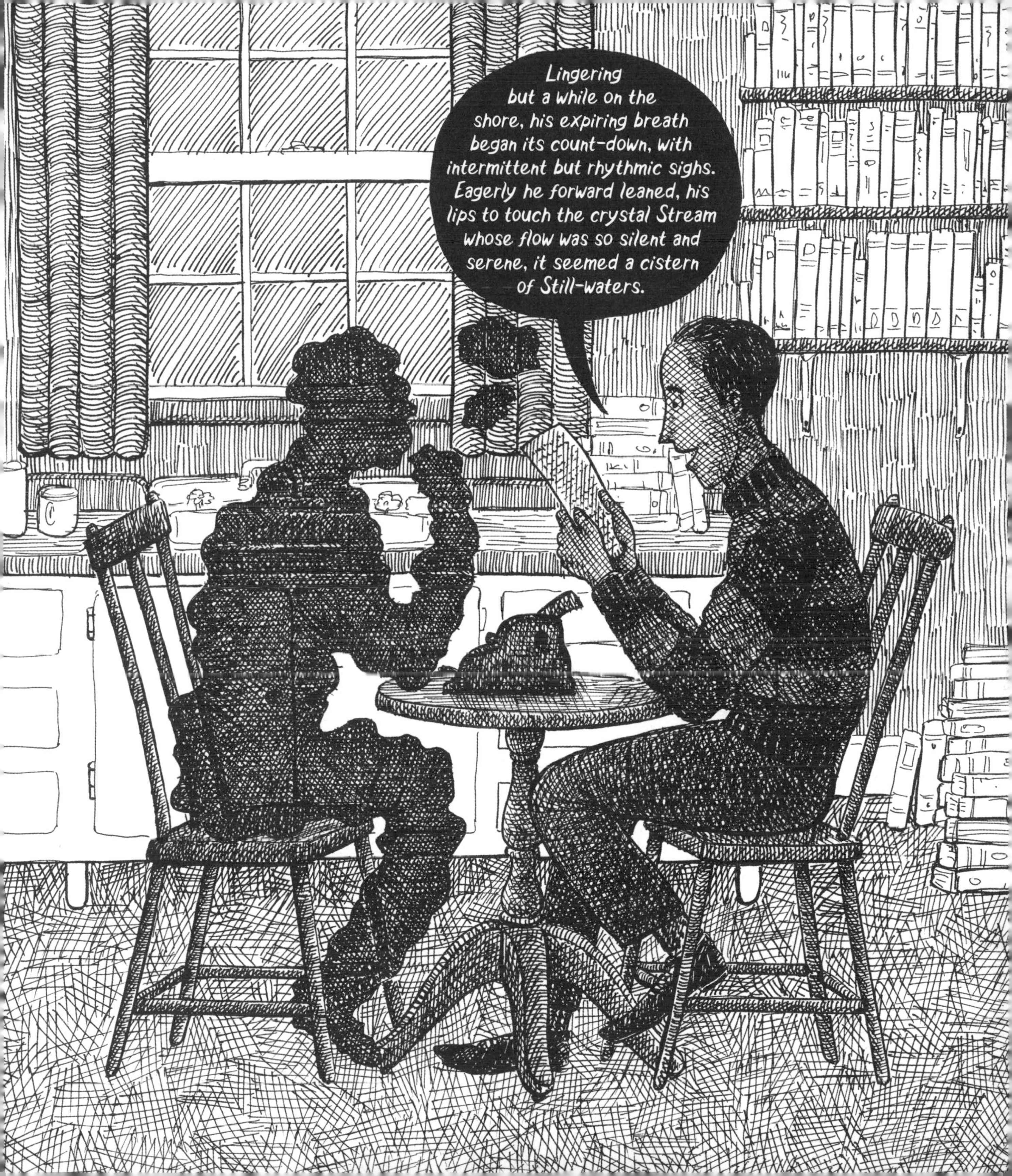
Lingering but a while on the shore, his expiring breath began its count-down, with intermittent but rhythmic sighs. Eagerly he forward leaned, his lips to touch the crystal Stream whose flow was so silent and serene, it seemed a cistern of Still-waters.

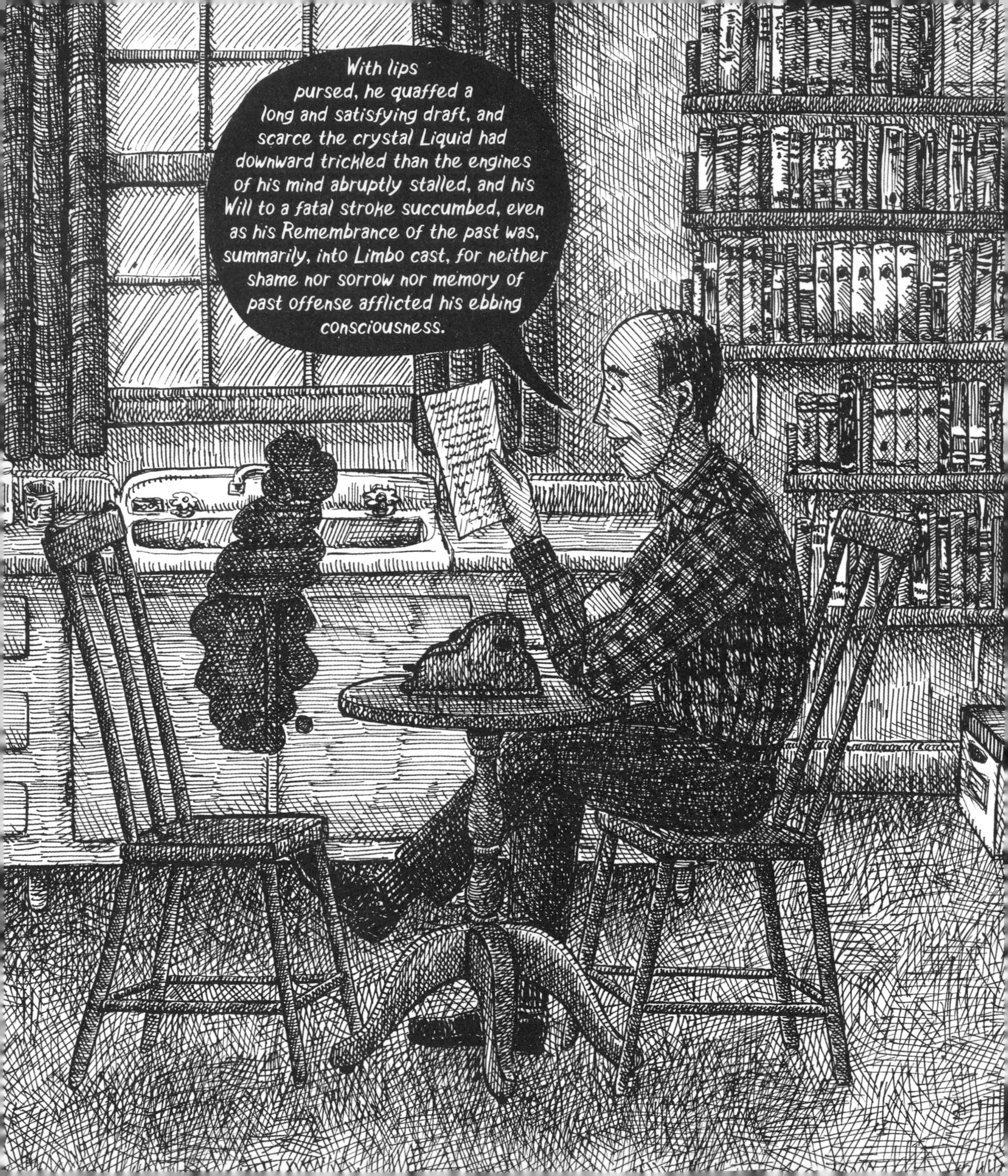
With lips pursed, he quaffed a long and satisfying draft, and scarce the crystal Liquid had downward trickled than the engines of his mind abruptly stalled, and his Will to a fatal stroke succumbed, even as his Remembrance of the past was, summarily, into Limbo cast, for neither shame nor sorrow nor memory of past offense afflicted his ebbing consciousness.

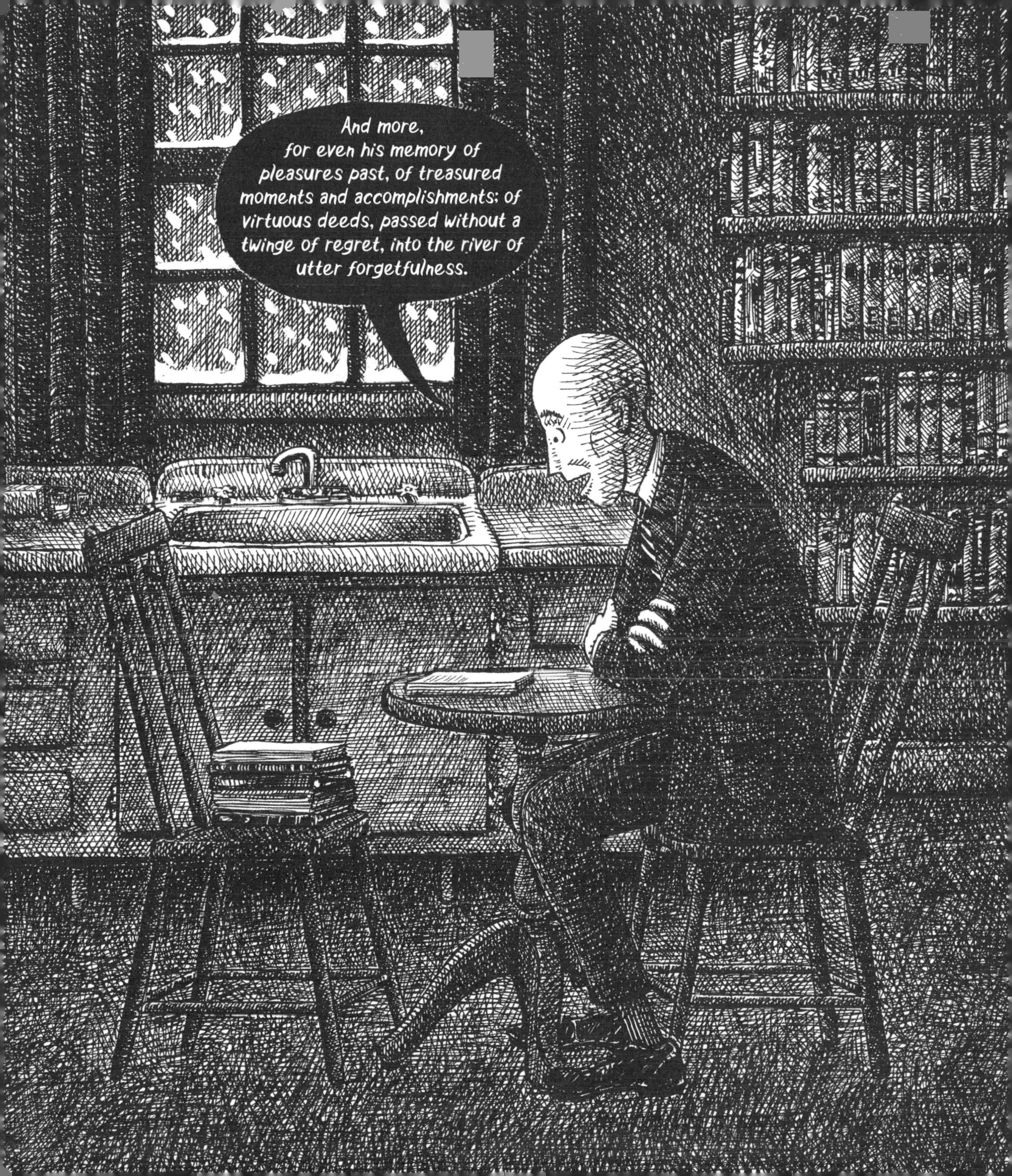
And more, for even his memory of pleasures past, of treasured moments and accomplishments; of virtuous deeds, passed without a twinge of regret, into the river of utter forgetfulness.

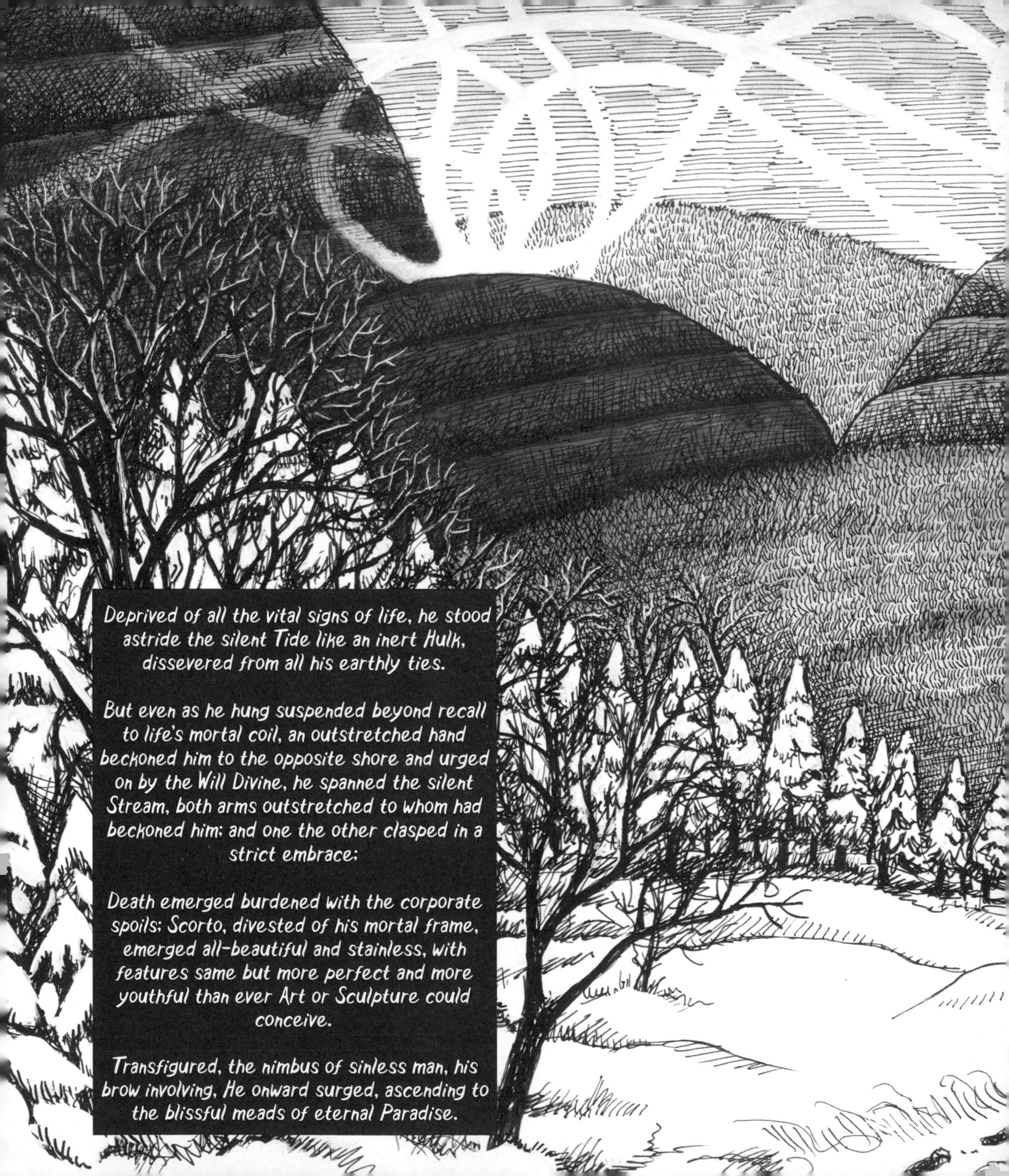
Deprived of all the vital signs of life, he stood astride the silent Tide like an inert Hulk, dissevered from all his earthly ties.
But even as he hung suspended beyond recall to life's mortal coil, an outstretched hand beckoned him to the opposite shore and urged on by the Will Divine, he spanned the silent Stream, both arms outstretched to whom had beckoned him; and one the other clasped in a strict embrace;
Death emerged burdened with the corporate spoils; Scorto, divested of his mortal frame, emerged all-beautiful and stainless, with features same but more perfect and more youthful than ever Art or Sculpture could conceive.
Transfigured, the nimbus of sinless man, his brow involving, He onward surged, ascending to the blissful meads of eternal Paradise.

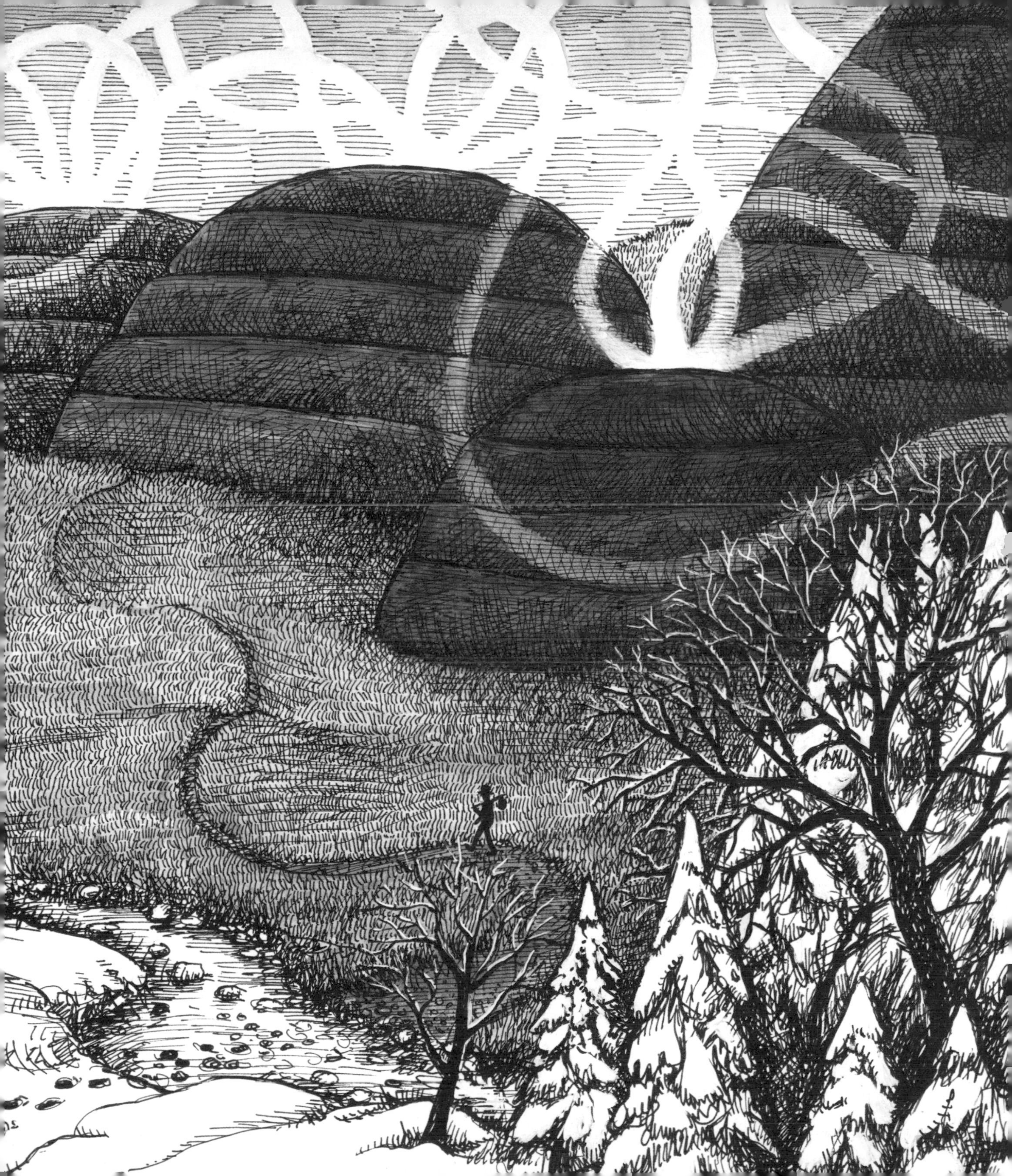

CHARLIE RIZZO RECEIVED THREE YEARS' PROBATION FOR HIS CRIME.

STEVE GARZA CONTINUED HIS LIFE OF CRIME. THREE YEARS LATER, HE MADE THE MISTAKE OF STEALING JEWELS FROM LEVINSON'S JEWELERS. HIS BODY WAS FOUND STUFFED IN THE TRUNK OF A CAR. HIS PENIS HAD BEEN CUT OFF AND PLACED IN HIS MOUTH.

NATHAN LEOPOLD JR. WAS PAROLED IN 1958 AFTER 33 YEARS IN PRISON. CARL SANDBURG TESTIFIED AT THE PAROLE HEARING AND TOLD THE STORY OF LEOPOLD AND RIZZO.

JESSE OWENS WON FOUR GOLD MEDALS AT THE 1936 OLYMPICS IN GERMANY. THREE YEARS LATER, HITLER STARTED WORLD WAR II.

AFTER LEAVING VIRGIL IN PURGATORY, DANTE ALIGHIERI FINALLY MADE IT TO PARADISE WITH THE HELP OF HIS BELOVED BEATRICE.

MATT RIZZO'S COLLECTED WORKS NOW RESIDE IN THE ARCHIVES OF THE NEWBERRY LIBRARY IN CHICAGO. FOR THE COMPLETE TEXT OF *THE CRUCIAL HINT*, THE STORY EXCERPTED IN "THE WRITINGS OF MATT RIZZO," VISIT THECRUCIALHINT.COM.

ILLINOIS STATE PENITENTIARY

Name *Matt Rizzo* Reg. No. 10186

Alias Color White

Crime *Robbery armed* Sentence *1 - Life* County Cook Co.

Received JAN 7 - 1936 Race

Remarks

Age *21 in 1935*

Apparent Age

Nationality *Italian*

Birthplace *Ills.*

Occupation *Packer*

Education *2 yrs H.S.*

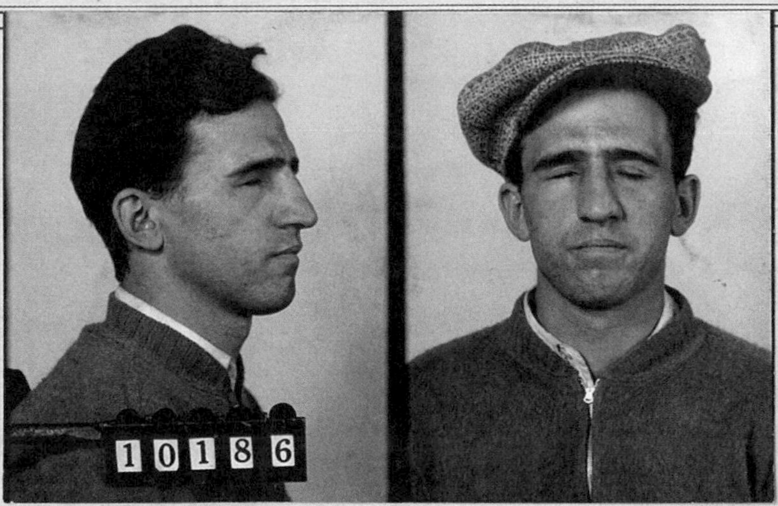

10186

Height *5* Ft. *7+* In.

Weight *126*

Build *Slender*

Complexion *Med Dk*

Hair *Black*

Color of Eyes *(Blind)*

Scars, Marks, etc. *II Vert cut sc 1 1/4 x 1/8 center of outer forearm. III r*

Criminal History *1 Term I.S.R. Pontiac #1359 S.N. P&V.*

2933-19489

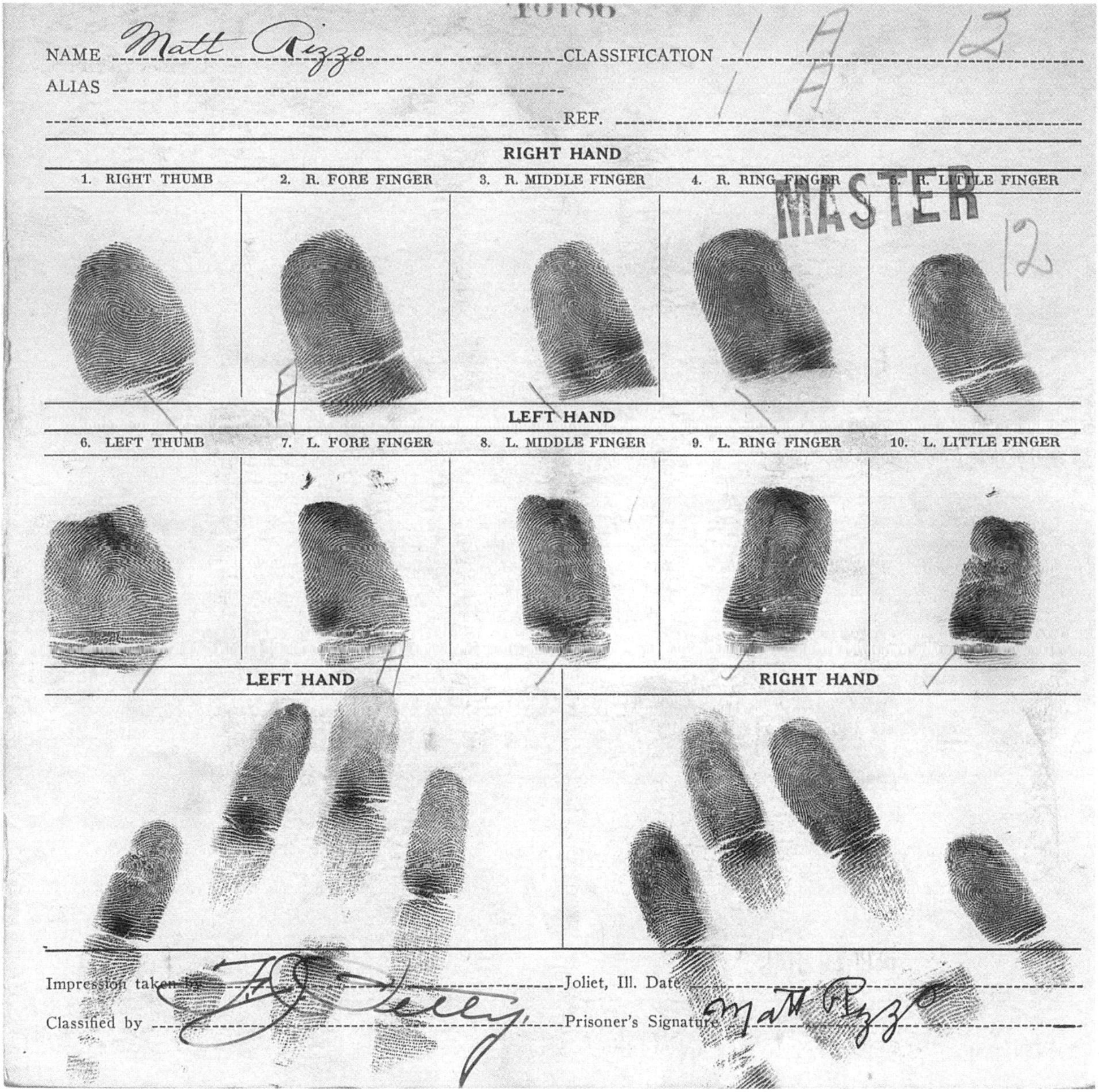
10186

NAME Matt Rizzo CLASSIFICATION 1 A 12
1 A

ALIAS

REF.

RIGHT HAND

1. RIGHT THUMB	2. R. FORE FINGER	3. R. MIDDLE FINGER	4. R. RING FINGER	5. R. LITTLE FINGER

MASTER

12

LEFT HAND

6. LEFT THUMB	7. L. FORE FINGER	8. L. MIDDLE FINGER	9. L. RING FINGER	10. L. LITTLE FINGER

LEFT HAND	RIGHT HAND

Impression taken by Joliet, Ill. Date

Classified by Prisoner's Signature Matt Rizzo

AFTERWORD

We were sitting at breakfast in a little diner when my friend Charlie started telling me about his father, Matt Rizzo. My eggs grew cold on the plate as I listened to him tell his father's tale of blindness, prison, the Crime of the Century, and somehow, the great poets of Western Civilization. In Chicago, Leopold and Loeb are still the legendary thrill-killers that committed their heinous crime in 1924. And the Chicago mob continues to make headlines today. I wanted to know more.

Charlie and I spent about six months going over the details of Matt's life. I read Matt's writings and Leopold's autobiography. I listened to audio recordings of Matt that Charlie had kept. I spent many hours at the Chicago History Museum and the archives at the Northwestern University Library in Evanston, Illinois. The Leopold and Loeb story is one of the most documented murders in history.

The further I got into the material, the harder it became to think about how to tell this story. There were so many fascinating ways to dig into the material. I had the good fortune to spend time with an amazing story guru, Bobette Buster, who helped me work through the structure of the complicated real-life relationships. In the end, certain scenes and dialogs had to be imagined, based on the best available information. And while those parts of the story are a product of the imagination, I would argue as the poet John Keats did for the "truth of imagination."

Ever since the Enlightenment, the western world has increasingly relied on ratiocination as the best (and perhaps only) way to navigate the world we live in. Arts and music are the first things cut in education budgets. Efficiency is King. And yet the imagination is as authentic as any fact we can describe. This story is an effort to revive the magic and wonder of the human experience, if only for a few hundred pages.

—David L. Carlson

DAVID L. CARLSON

Writer

DAVID L. CARLSON HAS BEEN
A FILMMAKER, MUSICIAN,
CAR SALESMAN, EXPERIENCE
DESIGNER, AND IS THE
COFOUNDER OF OPERA-MATIC,
A NONPROFIT STREET OPERA
COMPANY IN CHICAGO. THIS IS
HIS FIRST BOOK.

LANDIS BLAIR

Illustrator

LANDIS BLAIR IS A PEN AND INK
ILLUSTRATOR, KNOWN IN THE
INDEPENDENT COMIC SCENE
FOR HIS CROSS HATCHED
DRAWINGS AND DELIGHTFULLY
MORBID PICTURE BOOKS.
HE IS CURRENTLY BASED OUT
OF CHICAGO, ILLINOIS,
WHERE HE IS ILLUSTRATING
A FORTHCOMING BOOK ON
DEATH AS WELL AS SEVERAL
STORIES OF HIS OWN.

First Second

Published by First Second
First Second is an imprint of Roaring Brook Press, a division of
Holtzbrinck Publishing Holdings Limited Partnership
175 Fifth Avenue, New York, New York 10010
All rights reserved

Library of Congress Control number: 2016961544

ISBN: 978-1-62672-676-5

Our books may be purchased in bulk for promotional, educational, or business use.
Please contact your local bookseller or the Macmillan Corporate and Premium Sales Department
at (800) 221-7945 ext. 5442 or by e-mail at MacmillanSpecialMarkets@macmillan.com.

First edition 2017
Book design by Andrew Arnold
Printed in China

"The Writings of Matt Rizzo" is an excerpt of "The Crucial Hint" by Matt Rizzo.
The complete story can be found at thecrucialhint.com.
Matt Rizzo's collected works are archived at the Newbery Library in Chicago.

Penciled with light blue erasable Prismacolor pencils. Inked with Lamy Safari fountain pens (broad,
medium, and extra fine nibs) using Noodler's Bulletproof Black ink. Text bubbles added digitally
and lettered using a font based on Landis Blair's handwriting.

1   3   5   7   9   10   8   6   4   2